THE TAMING OF THE SHREW

Shakespeare Criticism
Philip C. Kolin, *General Editor*

THE TAMING
OF THE SHREW
CRITICAL ESSAYS

EDITED BY DANA E. ASPINALL

ROUTLEDGE
NEW YORK AND LONDON

Published in 2002 by
Routledge
29 West 35th Street
New York, NY 10001

Published in Great Britain by
Routledge
11 New Fetter Lane
London EC4P 4EE

Routledge is an imprint of Taylor & Francis Group.

10 9 8 7 6 5 4 3 2 1

Library of Congress Cataloging-in-Publication Data

The taming of the shrew: critical essays / edited by Dana E. Aspinall.
    p. cm.—
    Includes bibliographical references.
    ISBN 0–8153–3515–6 (alk. paper)
    1. Shakespeare, William, 1564–1616. Taming of the shrew. I. Aspinall, Dana, E.,
1961– .
  PR2832 .A87 2000
    822.3'3—dc21   00–047063

Printed on acid-free, 250-year-life paper.
Manufactured in the United States of America.

#45064831

FOR AMY

My bounty is as boundless as the sea,
My love as deep; the more I give to thee
The more I have, for both are infinite.
—Shakespeare, *Romeo and Juliet*

A WITTIE

AND PLEASANT

COMEDIE

Called

The Taming of the Shrew.

As it was acted by his Maiesties
Seruants at the Blacke Friers
and the Globe.

Written by VVill. Shakespeare.

LONDON,
Printed by *W. S.* for *Iohn Smethwicke*, and are to be
sold at his Shop in Sain Dunstones Church-
yard vnder the Diall.
1631.

Title page from "A Wittie and Pleasant Comedie Called *The Taming of the Shrew*" (Q4), 1631. Used with the permission of the Folger Shakespeare Library.

Contents

PART III. The *Taming of the Shrew* on Stage, in Film, and on Television

General Editor's Introduction

The continuing goal of the Shakespeare Criticism series is to provide the most significant and original contemporary interpretations of Shakespeare's works. Each volume in the series is devoted to a Shakespeare play or poem (e.g., the sonnets, *Venus and Adonis*, *Othello*) and contains eighteen to twenty-five new essays exploring the text from a variety of critical persepectives.

A major feature of each volume in the series is the editor's introduction. Each volume editor provides a substantial essay identifying the main critical issues and problems the play (or poem) has raised, charting the critical trends in looking at the work over the centuries, and assessing the critical discourse that has linked the play or poem to various ideological concerns. In addition to examining the critical commentary in light of important historical and theatrical events, each introduction functions as a discursive bibliographic essay citing and evaluating significant critical works—books, journal articles, theater documents, reviews, and interviews—giving readers a guide to the vast amounts of research on a particular play or poem.

Each volume showcases the work of leading Shakespeare scholars who participate in and extend the critical discourse on the text. Reflecting the most recent approaches in Shakespeare studies, these essays approach the play from a host of criticial positions, including but not limited to feminist, Marxist, new historical, semiotic, mythic, performance/staging, cultural, and/or a combination of these and other methodologies. Some volumes in the series include bibliographic analyses of a Shakespeare text to shed light on its critical history and interpretation. Interviews with directors and/or actors are also part of some volumes in the series.

At least one, sometimes as many as tow or three, of the essays in each volume is devoted to a play in performance, beginning with the earliest adn most significant productions and proceeding to the most recent. These essays, which ultimatley provide a theater history of the play, should not be regarded as different from or rigidly isolated from the critical work on the script. Over the last thirty years or so Shakespeare criticism has understandably been labeled the "Age of Performance." Readers will find information in these essays on non-English speaking production of Shakespeare's plays as well as landmark performances in English. Editors and contributors also include photographs from productions across the world to help readers see and further appreciate the ways a Shakespeare play has taken shape in the theater.

Ultimately, each volume in the Shakespeare Criticism Series strives to give readers a balanced, representative collection of the most engaging and thoroughly researched criticism on the given Shakespeare text. In essence, each volume provides a careful survey of essential materials in the history of the criticism for a Shakespeare play or poem as well as cutting-edge essays that extend and enliven our understanding of the work in its critical context. In offering readers innovatively and fulfilling new essays, volume editors have made invaluable contributions to the literary and theatrical criticism of Shakespeare's greatest legacy, his work.

Philip C. Kolin
University of Southern Mississippi

Acknowledgments

I am grateful to Philip C. Kolin for allowing me to undertake this worthy project, as well as to Angela Kao, editorial assistant at Routledge, for her guidance throughout its final stages. I also would like to thank the journals, presses, newspapers, and authors who generously granted me permission to reprint these articles and reviews. Thank you as well to the registrar, librarians, and photographers at the Folger Shakespeare Library in Washington, DC, for their assistance and guidance during the project's many stages.

Assumption College has been more than generous, providing me with time and financial assistance. Special thanks to Provost Charles Flynn, Jr., for all his help; the excellent library reference staff at Assumption College—Carol Maksian, Larry Spongberg, Kimberly West, and Liz McDermott—for all the time spent with me; and Ron Bishop and Lynn Cooke of Computer Services for timely assistance and guidance. Assumption's Faculty Development Committee and the English Department both deserve my gratitude as well, as do two very fine students, Abbey Dick and Molly Taylor.

Finally, to my lovely wife, Amy, thank you for your patience and assistance throughout this past year; without you, I would not be where I am now, nor would I have a reason for being here.

Illustrations

PART I.
A Critical History
of *The Taming of the Shrew*

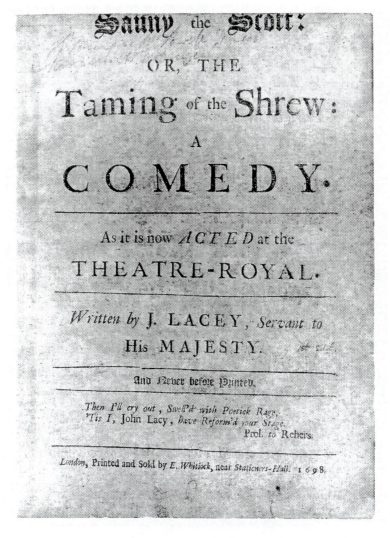

Figure 1. Title page from John Lacey's *Sauny the Scot: Or, The Taming of the Shrew*, 1698. Used with the permission of the Folger Shakespeare Library.

Figure 2. Petruchio holding Kate's arm, saying, "But for my bonny Kate, she must with me" (3.2.216). Painted by Francis Wheatley, engraved by H. Partout. Used with the permission of the Folger Shakespeare Library.

The Play and the Critics

DANA E. ASPINALL

As with nearly every Shakespeare play, culturally and politically informed scholarship on *The Taming of the Shrew* has flourished over the past forty years. Arising from this scholarship and virtually unique to *Shrew*, however, are two matters of great interest (and some consternation as well) for the play's readers and audiences. First, even the most cursory of research into *Shrew* criticism reveals that much discussion of the play assumes a cultural or political bent from the start. The reason behind this is obvious: Katherine's final speech, where she urges the "foul contending rebel" wives—both those on stage and in the audience or reading the text—to "seek for rule, supremacy, and sway" from their "honest" husbands. Since its first appearance some time between 1588 and 1594, *Shrew* has elicited a panoply of heartily supportive, ethically uneasy, or altogether disgusted responses to its rough-and-tumble treatment of the "taming" of the "curst shrew" Katherine, and obviously, of all potentially unruly wives.

Second, and closely related to the first matter, a great deal of the more recent scholarship generally confines itself to a rather narrow range of issues beyond those implicit in Kate's final lines—the longest speech, incidentally, of the entire play. In Lena Cowen Orlin's estimation, only two primary issues outside Kate's capitulation (or ironic enactment of one, depending upon one's reading of the scene) concern us: "the relation of *The Shrew* to *The Taming of a Shrew* [and] the role of the induction" (167). Quite possibly, the debate concerning whether or not Katherine submits herself to Petruchio at the end of *Shrew* (and what this means to each succeeding reader or auditor) continues so heatedly that the other two issues are raised, as often as not, only as aids in determining a satisfactory interpretation of what transpires in act 5, including of course Petruchio's hearty response to it: "Why there's a wench! Come on, and kiss me, Kate." Whatever the case may be, I believe Orlin correct in her observation and in further identifying each of these three issues as "vexed" (167).

In this volume of scholarship on *Shrew*, I attempt to map out, first in this introduction and then through my selection of the essays themselves, a chronological overview of the stipulations and qualities inherent in these three issues which so preoccupy and vex us. I include here scholars' continually evolving arguments involving gender relations and women's cultural and domestic roles, male fantasies of domination and control, female autonomy, genre, language and speech, privacy, and wealth, among other related issues. Much of *Shrew*'s early publication and theater history also will be outlined, as well as a summary of some of the theories concerning the Induction's relationship to the main play. The introduction, I hope, will serve as a forum for those earlier critics whose comments either helped to shape the twentieth century's thoughts on these matters or have provoked some often strongly contradictory reactions to them. I also try to acknowledge and give voice to some of the many essays and commentaries not included in this volume, situating their arguments among those of the early critics and of the authors included. In short, I aim to provide a solid general foundation from which the essays in this volume will explore in much fuller detail as many treatments of the three issues as possible. Because Jan MacDonald's, Margaret Loftus Ranald's, Ann Christensen's, and Barbara Hodgdon's admirably thorough overviews of the stage, film, and screen productions of *Shrew* are included in the volume, I end the introduction's stage history with the advent of the twentieth century.

In all, I have selected for inclusion in this volume nineteen essays and reviews, each of which represents a major focus or change of thought concerning *Shrew*. In keeping with the speculation concerning offered above, I allow most space for the wide range of viewpoints inspired by the scene involving her final speech. It is here, I believe, that the play becomes most resonant in our own culture as we enter a new century of critical inquiry. This scene also seems to bring to the fore the most vexing issue of the three, for the arguments surrounding a wife's duties and behavior seem to shape not only the tones and strategies of the play's (and in some instances, perhaps more accurately, Petruchio's) supporters and detractors, but also are at least partially responsible for confining other examinations of the play to the two other issues mentioned above. Regardless of the particular issue at hand, moreover, the attention that *Shrew* perpetually garners with each generation of readers and theater-goers confirms most forcefully Annabel Patterson's claim that Shakespeare's "plays and poems seem to suggest, at some deeper level than we yet have a terminology for, that male/female relations in his environment were somehow imbricated with the sociopolitical relations supervised or represented by government and the law" (1994, 305).

Wherever I quote from *The Shrew* in the introduction, I have used David Bevington's edition of *The Complete Works of Shakespeare*, 4th edition (Harper Collins, 1992), and where I quote from *A Shrew*, I have used the Malone Society facsimilie edition (Oxford, 1998). I also have relied heavily on, and owe much gratitude to, past editors of *Shrew* and Shakespeare for many of the facts, dates, and conjectures included in my introduction: Bevington, Bond, Capell, Dolan, Evans, Hanmer, Johnson, Malone, Morris, Oliver, Pope, Quiller-Couch and Wilson, Rowe, Theobald, Thompson, Warburton, and Wright, among others. I also have included a bibliography of other essays pertaining to *Shrew* for further reading.

EARLY PUBLICATION HISTORY OF *SHREW*

The dates surrounding *Shrew*'s early textual and stage history create more questions than they answer, simply because we do not know whether we are piecing together the facts concerning one, two, or possibly even three different plays. Furthermore, we can only guess at the relationships between any one of these *Shrew* plays and the others. The plays in question, in order of their appearance to scholars devoting time to studies of them, consist of the following: (1) *A Pleasant Conceited Historie, called The taming of a Shrew*, which first appeared in quarto in 1594; (2) *The Taming of the Shrew*, which was included in the 1623 First Folio, and (3) a lost play that may or may not have existed and that may or may not be a source for one or both the 1594 and 1623 *Shrews*. Theories surrounding these plays are varied and, in Richard Hosley's words, "can be explained equally well by the one theory as by the other" (1964; 291). From this morass of conjecture emerge, however, three generally accepted postulates: the 1594 text (hereafter referred to as *A Shrew*) is a source for the 1623 text (hereafter *The Shrew*); *A Shrew* is a "bad" quarto—either a memorial reconstruction or an "imitation" (Wells and Taylor 1987, 351)—of *The Shrew*; or *A Shrew* is a bad quarto of the lost *Shrew* text, which also is the source for *The Shrew*. Currently, most scholars reject the first postulate (that *A Shrew* is a source of *The Shrew*) and lean toward the second (that *A Shrew* is a bad quarto of *The Shrew*). However, none of the theories presented above is accepted with any certainty. In fact, new—or at least newly reconfigured—theories abound, including Leah Marcus's recent argument that *A Shrew* ought to be accepted as a viable alternative to *The Shrew*, because, among other equally compelling arguments, some "of the most profoundly patriarchal language of *The Shrew* is not present in *A Shrew*" (1992; 185).

As Orlin has noted and the above summary of *Shrew*'s several manifestations attest, issues surrounding the play vex us with both possibility and doubt. Let us now, for a moment, leave behind the uncertainty and turn to the facts we have. The first documented appearance, both on stage and in print, of *Shrew* was 1594. On May 2, to the publisher Peter Short, was entered in the Stationer's Register, "a booke intituled A plesant Conceyted historie called the Tayminge of a Shrowe" (Chambers 1930, 1:322). This text was produced again by Short in 1596, to be sold by the bookseller Cuthbert Burby at his shop in the Royal Exchange. On January 22, 1607, the rights to *A Shrew* were transferred by Burby to Nicholas Linge (Short had died in 1603, and the facts behind Burby's ownership of the rights are uncertain); during that same year, a third quarto of *A Shrew* was printed by Valentine Simmes for Linge. And on November 19, 1607, the rights were transferred again, this time to John "Smythick" (Smethwick). As far as we know, Smethwick did not publish *A Shrew* between the year of his acquisition of *A Shrew* and 1623, when a considerably different version appeared in the First Folio (Oliver 13–15).

This different version, of course, is *The Taming of the Shrew*, which shares the same three plotlines and most of the various intersections between its main plot and subplots: Kate's shrewishness and subsequent unmarriageability, the several rivals' wooing of Kate's sister—*A Shrew* provides Kate with two sisters, Emelia and Philema, and the "Induction," so-named by Alexander Pope. Yet, *The Shrew* differs from *A Shrew* in several respects. These variances include the many name changes (except for Sly's and Kate's, all characters' names are different), length (*A Shrew* is only sixty percent as long as *The Shrew* and does not have the characters corresponding to Gremio or Tranio from *The Shrew*), and setting (*A Shrew* takes place in Athens, not Padua).

More importantly, the drunken tinker Christopher Sly (spelled "Slie" in *A Shrew*), who opens both versions of the play (although in slightly different apparitions), "disappears" from *The Shrew* at the end of act 1 scene 1 and is not heard from again. In *A Shrew*, Slie remains an intrusive presence throughout the play, even coming on at the play's end to announce, after watching Ferando's (*The Shrew*'s Petruchio) complete subordination of Kate unto him:

> I know now how to tame a shrew,
> I dreamt vpon it all this night till now,
> And thou hast wakt me out of the best dreame
> That euer I had in my life, but Ile to my
> Wife presently and tame her too
> And if she anger me. (52, ll. 1619–24)

Slie's presence and his more frequent interruptions of the main plot throughout *A Shrew* provide this play with a completely closed frame; with such total closure, Thelma Nelson Greenfield (1954) and Alan C. Dessen (1997) have argued, *A Shrew* provides through Slie's final speech a "moral" that can—and, perhaps, will—be initiated on both the play's other wives and the actual wives watching in the audience or reading the text. Furthermore, if *A Shrew* is a source for, or a bad quarto of, *The Shrew*, then this moral may apply equally (or, perhaps, more stridently) to the 1623 printed version. The moral, of course, insists on the proposition that wives are bound in obedience and duty to their husbands' wills, and promises harsh mistreatment if wives break the bond.

SHREW'S POSSIBLE SOURCES AND ANALOGUES

Let us consider for a moment a possible consequence that the presence of this moral may obtain for the play's auditors and readers. First, in combination with *A Shrew*'s altered lines in Kate's final speech—

> The King of Kings the glorious God of heauen,
> Who in six daies did frame his heauenly worke,
> And made all things to stand in perfit course.
> Then to his image he did make a man.
> Olde *Adam* and from his side asleepe,
> A rib was taken, of which the Lord did make,
> The woe of man so termd by *Adam* then,
> Woman for that, by her came sinne to vs,
> And for her sin was *Adam* doomd to die— (50, ll. 1559–67)

Slie's moral echoes uncannily the myriad other shrew-taming tales and ballads circulating throughout this period of, to borrow David Underdown's (1985) phrase, "strained gender relations" (136). To state this point another way, the "shorter and simpler" (Dessen 1997, 42) *A Shrew* leaves little doubt concerning its close relation to and agreement with the complex of folk tales that W. B. Thorne (1968) argues "provided Shakespeare not only a useful pattern of symbols but also the key to a structural method" in *The Shrew* (482).

Quoting from Aarne and Thompson's *The Types of Folk-Tale* (1928), Jan Harold Brunvand (1966) summarizes these folk sources as loosely fitting the following paradigm: "The youngest of three sisters is a shrew. For their disobedience the husband shoots his dog and his horse. Brings his wife to submission. Wager: whose wife is the most obedient" (345). Although not exact, the pattern obviously closely parallels both *A Shrew* and *The Shrew*. This pattern also hints at and advocates the methods of "correction" wrought upon shrewish wives that appear in both the numerous folk publications and *A Shrew* itself. Although many examples of these folk sources exist, including the anonymous *The Wife Wrapt in a Wether's Skin* and *The Cucking of a Scold* (ca. 1615–ca. 1630), I would like to focus momentarily upon the plot of *A Merry Jest of a Shrewd and Curst Wife Lapped in Morel's Skin, for Her Good Behavior* (ca. 1550), which contains probably the most thorough description of—and illustrates the extremes of—violence exacted upon women in these tracts.

A Merry Jest (Dolan 1996) opens with a father, who, "true and just withall" (l. 54), has two daughters: one, the younger of the two and her father's favorite, is pursued by several suitors, while the elder, Joan, is shrewish and "cause[s] her father's heart to bleed" (l. 44). Unlike either *A Shrew* or *The*

Shrew, this family unit includes a mother, who, "To play the master she would not lain [feign, hide] / And make her husband bow" (ll. 19–20). She encourages the elder daughter to seek and preserve dominance in all her relationships. When a suitor for the daughter bursts on the scene, the father warns him of Joan's flaws; nevertheless, after intense negotiations with both mother and daughter, the young man agrees to marry her. Their marriage agreement stipulates, however, that Joan must, "by God, now and then, . . . bear the bell [win; come out ahead]" in their diurnal relations (ll. 241–44). Despite some fearful reservations (the father expresses some further misgivings as well), the young man confidently proceeds with the wedding ceremony. They marry, celebrate, and later take to their marriage bed. On the following morning, however, the young man beats Joan and warns her, "In all sports to abide my will" (l. 516). The beating does little good, however, as the young wife continues her shrewish ways, offering "lewd words" (l. 608) to the servants, continually cursing her husband, and refusing to perform many of the wifely duties at which her mother brags she is adept. After she threatens violence on the husband, he leaves and contemplates his situation:

> For there was ne'er man, iwis,
> So hampered with one wife as I am now,
> Wherefore I think, withouten miss,
> She shall repent it, I make God a vow [. . .]
> . . . .
> That I shall her coil [beat] both back and bone,
> And make her blue and also black,
> That she shall groan again for woe. (ll. 761–64, 768–70)

The young husband decides to return home, kill his loyal but old horse "Morel" and skin its carcass, and then beat his wife and wrap her "white corse" (l. 872) in Morel's salted hide. Upon returning home, the husband finds Joan in the same state of unruliness; he brings her to the cellar and whips her until "on the ground the blood was seen" (l. 977). When he wraps her in the hide, Joan then begs him to stop, promising

> Your commandments I will, both far and near,
> Fulfill in every degree. (ll. 1022–1023)

Having done himself "great good, / And her also" (ll. 1032–33), the husband then invites both Joan's parents and his neighbors to a feast, where they can marvel at his remarkable accomplishment.

As witnessed in *A Merry Jest*, these folk sources saw little or no moral conflict in physically resolving any problems arising from unmannerly women. In fact, *A Merry Jest* succinctly reinforces Valerie Wayne's (1985) contention that the insubordinate woman was "the prime agent of discord in her world" (164) and provides an environment where the scold's bridles and cucking stools described by Lynda Boose and others reify themselves with a chilling concreteness.

A Shrew's other possible sources, including those not necessarily from the oral and folk traditions, further substantiate contemporary fears surrounding women's unruliness. They often incorporate and/or advocate brutal violence against outspoken or uncontrollable women as well. We can place here the many tracts and pamphlets admonishing witchcraft (influenced by, incidentally, James VI of Scotland's *Newes from Scotland* [1591] and *Daemonologie* [1597]). We also must note the several continental sources, including Ariosto's *I Suppositi*, the most obvious of Shakespeare's sources for the Bianca-Lucentio subplot which George Gascoigne drew upon for his *Supposes* (1566, pub. 1573), as well as *Supposes* itself. And although not classified as actual sources, attention must be paid as well, momentarily, to the disturbingly prevalent anti-feminist tracts and books circulating throughout this period, in which both *A Shrew* and *The Shrew* may also situate themselves. As is common with this particular type of literature, both texts betray a peculiar tendency to identify a woman's tongue as the main source of her unruliness.

Linda Woodbridge (1984) notes that female aggressiveness frequently found "more verbal than physical" expression and argues that contemporary discussions of a woman's speech focused on her "volubility" (207–8). Gail Kern Paster (1993) adds that early modern discourse on women's prolixity equated their ramblings with incontinence, with a lack of self-control (55). Although broadening her exploration to include early modern men as well, Carla Mazzio (1997) also recognizes a rampant cultural dis-ease underlying the tongue's "ambivalent" nature: "Early modern fantasies about the tongue often suggest a nervousness about its apparent agency" (54–55). Wayne identifies this nervousness in both religious and social contexts: a woman's unruly behavior "was unregenerate from a religious point of view because she made excessive and sinful use of her speech. It was inordinate from a social point of view because she challenged her husband's position as head of the marital hierarchy" (161). Moreover, as Boose comments, early modern culture's nervousness frequently found expression in "suppressing women's speech" (184), often through the same violence as that exemplified in *Merry Jest*.

These scholars draw their conclusions from myriad contemporary taxonomies of the tongue and the many concurrent denunciations of its wayward character. By its very nature, according to some, the tongue possessed a unique ability to occupy two places at once, to travel as if outside the body into distant locales, and to affect, sometimes adversely, even perfect strangers. Its dual—and potentially malignant—nature finds its source in its construction, for, as John Banister writes in his *Historie of Man* (1578),

> [I]t seemeth (if so it must be described) ii. muscles, the toung hauing in the
> middle a white lyne, to distinguish the right from the left part, under which
> is a *Ligament* in children (oft tymes) requiring to be cut, because it is an
> impediment . . . at first to sucking. (From 4th Book)

As these taxonomies grew in number, so too did the denunciations of the
tongue. In addition, the denunciations often revealed an acute awareness of,
and in fact often exaggerated, the tongue's close associations to woman.
Oliver Jacques's *A Discourse of Women, shewing Their Imperfections Alphabetically* (1662) illustrates this connection:

> Women have such a propensity to talk, that the greatest punishment they can
> suffer, is hindring them from babling . . . I find out the secret of this imper-
> fection in Genesis; for God forming the woman of a Rib, hard and crackling,
> and man of earth, importing his indisposition to noise, it was a kind of fore-
> judging, that man by nature should be silent and reserved, and the woman
> talkative and babling. (54–55)

Moreover, just as Kate alludes in *A Shrew* and Jacques hints above, a woman's
clamorous tongue often was linked with Satan and the Fall of Adam. William
Averell, in his *A meruailous combat of Contrarieties* (1588), claims that the
tongue not only "stirreth up treasons, and provoketh traitours," among a host
of other rebellious impulses, but, "though [the tongue] bee as simple as doues
[does], yet [she] be as wise as the serpent Aspis" (C2$_v$–C3). Averell and his
contemporaries draw their equations from James's Epistle, which states,

> So the tongue is a little member and boasts of great things. How great a for-
> est is set ablaze by a small fire!
>   And the tongue is a fire. The tongue is an unrighteous world among our
> members, staining the whole body, setting on fire the cycle of nature, and set
> on fire by hell. For every kind of beast and bird, of reptile and sea creature,
> can be tamed and has been tamed by humankind, but no human being can
> tame the tongue—a restless evil, full of deadly poison. With it we bless the
> Lord and Father, and with it we curse men, who are made in the likeness of
> God. (3: 5–9)

In other words, the "unrighteous" and protean (in its unique ability of movement both inside and outside of the body) tongue is capable of debilitating
both its own and others' heretofore sound and healthy bodies. With such a dual
and untamable nature, according to Jacques, "it is no marvel if very often [the
tongue] be injurious" (80).

However, all these sources and contemporary documents that help to
approximate *Shrew* with the sixteenth century's prevailing antifeminism can

be used just as effectively to illustrate how anomalous the play is to that sentiment. For example, Kate's final speech in *The Shrew*, according to Peter Berek (1988), abandons "the muddled redaction of Genesis" (95) and its negative implications for women and instead employs a more secular, political conceit:

> Thy husband is thy lord, thy life, thy keeper,
> Thy head, thy sovereign; one that cares for thee,
> And for thy maintenance commits his body
> To painful labor both by sea and land,
> To watch the night in storms, the day in cold,
> Whilst thou liest warm at home, secure and safe;
> And craves no other tribute at thy hands
> But love, fair looks, and true obedience—
> Too little payment for so great a debt. (5.2.150–158)

Michael West's (1974) study of folk sources similarly urges readers to consider how Shakespeare employs dance rituals, dialogue ballads, and folk fertility festivals and dramas, as well as the animal imagery all three share, to create a play where "a spirited young creature's sexual initiation [is brought about] by a handsomely qualified male animal" (70) and Kate's "willing capitulation thus fulfills a rhythm fundamental to much comic drama" (71; see Joan Hartwig [1982] and Jeanne Addison Roberts for divergent conclusions regarding Shakespeare's use of animal imagery in the play). Germaine Greer (1970) concurs, stating that *Shrew* "is the cunning adaptation of a folk-motif to show the forging of a partnership between equals" (111).

Even when not considering its ties to possible sources and analogues, many critics read Shakespeare's *The Shrew* as a vast improvement in terms of early modern attitudes toward women over its possible sources or *A Shrew*. These critics often attribute much of this improvement to the play's placement into a particular literary genre: E. K. Chambers (1925), Mark Van Doren (1939), Robert B. Heilman, Peter Saccio (1984), and Thomas Moisan (1995), among others, all measure in varying degrees the amount of farce Shakespeare infuses into the play. Interestingly, those who see the most farce in *Shrew* also seem least inclined to disparage or condemn Shakespeare for any perceptible ideological alignment with either his folk or continental sources or his era's pervasive antifeminist sentiments. Like many students of the play, Chambers recognizes and acknowledges the brutality that permeates *Shrew*, yet attributes its presence to the "tradition of farce" (1925; 45). This "tradition" of farce also precludes, in its "genially diffusive guise" (Moisan 1995, 110), any humanized "characterizing" (Van Doren 1939, 38) whereby we may sympathize with Kate's situation or ironize her final speech. Read as a farce, Heilman posits, *Shrew* provides characters who "succumb to the habits of generic form" (154).

Moving in a slightly different direction, Jeanne Addison Roberts, Barbara Roche Rico (1985), and Barry Weller (1992) believe the play to contain certain Ovidean motifs, devices which point to a transformation of sorts for some of the characters involved—namely, Sly and Kate (see Marjorie B. Garber's [1974] discussion of *Shrew* for a different interpretation of the transformative process occurring in the play). Roberts also identifies "important elements of romance" (159) in her reading of the text, while John C. Bean (1980) and David Daniell view *The Shrew* as a romantic comedy. Daniell, in fact, insists that *The Shrew* is "a play unusually about marriages as well as courtships, and the quality of the marriage of Katharine and Petruchio might be expected to depend [upon is] a special quality of mutuality" (28).

Daniell is not alone in citing this element of mutuality that invigorates Katherine's and Petruchio's relationship. Studying the prevailing marriage rituals circulating among early modern England's more affluent citizens, George R. Hibbard (1964) cites an evolving bifurcation occurring at this time. Based largely upon the greed in parents's eyes as they arranged the marriages of their children between themselves, these rituals begin to give way, first, to newer, more romantically informed experiments advocated by both "divines and clerics" (18) who abhorred the greed, and then to the notions of readers and translators of continental romance who began to view romantic love as an absolute—an end in itself. Hibbard sees Shakespeare's *Shrew* as both a continuation of many of the newer texts advocating a more companionable marriage arrangement and an improvement on their premises: although arranged marriages remain susceptible to parents's voracity, purely romantic obsession often leads to situations much like the one Lucentio finds himself stuck in with the shrewish and unregenerate Bianca at the end of the play. Alternatively, Hibbard argues, Shakespeare plots a course where Kate and Petruchio develop—out of the more "durable" (21) arranged marriage contract—a mutual "knowledge of, and . . . trust in, each other" (27).

Margaret Lael Mikesell, Robert S. Miola and others comb many of the same sources as Hibbard, including Gascoigne's *Supposes* and its constituent sources, and expand and redirect their studies in search of further confirmations of mutuality between Kate and Petruchio. Miola conducts a comparative examination of both *A Shrew* and New Comedy's *Eunuchus* and *Captivi*, discovering the same monetary preoccupations in New Comedy as Hibbard saw in the marriage rituals enacted by England's propertied classes. Miola (1997) declares, however, and only in partial agreement with Hibbard, that "Shakespeare places love at the center of the action, depicting it as the powerful and irrational raison d'etre for comedic intrigue" (29). And although substantiating Hibbard's assertions with a thorough scouring of the several Protestant conduct books and domestic tracts that urge parents to retain authority in their children's marriage negotiations, Mikesell also parts from Hibbard somewhat in claiming that love "is the linchpin of the companionate marriage" (142).

According to Mikesell, Shakespeare proposes a paradoxical "coexistence of dominance and mutuality" (143), where Kate must practice obedience and Petruchio must express loving care—abstaining, of course, from the violence advocated in the folk and continental sources.

Building largely on Hibbard's conjectures, Mikesell and others read the many tracts, pamphlets, and books dealing with early modern courtship and marriage as Shakespeare's possible inspiration for instilling the Kate-Petruchio relationship with mutuality, companionship, and, perhaps, even romantic affection. What these manuals attempted, in Bean's words, was reconcilement of "the notion of matrimonial friendship, which tended to make husband and wife equals, with the notion of hierarchy, which asserted the husband's supremacy" (70). Shakespeare illustrates these two theories of marriage by paralleling Hortensio's, Lucentio's and Gremio's attempts to train Bianca in the arts of music and language with Petruchio's much more unorthodox—and successful—education of Kate in the rules of humanist companionate marriage. By the end of the play, Kate has proven herself a much more willing and able student than Bianca, who still insists on haughtily expressing her will: "Am I your bird? I mean to shift my bush" (5.2.46).

Miola also sees an educative process stemming from *The Shrew*'s incorporation of mutuality into the marriage contract, a process that "transforms rather than articulates the old dichotomy" (32) between wife (or obedient servant) and husband (or domineering master). By the end of the play Kate has learned "that the acceptance of social role and its limitations need not be demeaning or incapacitating; played correctly, such acceptance can bring freedom, fulfillment, and power" (29–30). Again drawing from the marriage tracts, Shakespeare proposes through Petruchio's outrageous actions an education whereby Kate is to employ her tongue "properly" and redirect her "linguistic willfulness" (see Newman, 90) toward a behavior denoting a more harmonious compatibility with her husband and her culture. And although differing in several respects from the transformations Roberts and others identify through their explorations of Ovid, Kate's humanist education nevertheless similarly seems to open the door to a more positive integration into her society.

Many who have considered Petruchio at any length arrive at similar conclusions regarding his value as educator. M. C. Bradbrook (1958) admires Petruchio's unique ability to "pierce below the surface of Kate's angry, thwarted, provocative abuse to the desire to be mastered and cherished which her conduct unconsciously betrays" (142). E. M. W. Tillyard (1964) locates Katherine's improved state in Petruchio's enactment of a "more kindly and educative method" (113). Alexander Legatt (1974) attributes Kate's "transformation of character" (41) to Petruchio's teaching her an "inner order" (49) and a sense of "conventional decent behavior" (53). Wayne believes Petruchio tames Katherine "for her own good" (171), and Camille Wells Slights (1989) argues that Shakespeare "is less interested in suggesting the proper distribution of power between men and women than in exploring the comedy inherent in the human desire for both individual freedom and fulfillment as a social being" (169). Ignoring for the moment the possibility that Petruchio's treatment parallels in some ways the brutal corrective measures of *Shrew*'s possible sources, as well as the concomitant possibilities that some of these critics either emulate on some level this fantasy of male dominance and desire (as Barbara Hodgdon and Ann C. Christensen discuss in their overviews of stage, film, and television productions) or that they struggle with some culturally informed reluctance in themselves to sully Shakespeare's reputation as an "enlightened" man, Petruchio does seem to lead Kate to a better life. Some critics argue that Petruchio's enhancement of not only Kate's social position but also her demeanor and, possibly, her ability to become, in Laurie Maguire's words, "a synecdoche for 'woman'" (130) lies in his unconventional application of contemporary humanist thought and marital reform circulating around him.

Tita French Baumlin (1989) attributes Kate's education at least partially to Petruchio's mastery of "rhetorical arts," through which he can "create for his bride a new reality grounded in play, self-respect and love" (237). Similarly, Wayne believes that Petruchio teaches Katherine to "mimic" the role of obedient wife and thus "transcend the roles and hierarchies that govern their world" (173). Many critics, in fact, note the prominence either of charisma (Burt 1984, 298) or of rhetoric and mimicry in bringing about a harmonious relationship between Katherine and Petruchio. Much discussion acknowledges Petruchio's aping of Kate, both in word and deed, as well as the one exception to his mimicry: Petruchio stops short of any physical violence, instead warning her that, "I swear I'll cuff you if you strike again" (2.1.216).

THE INDUCTION AND *A SHREW*'S POSSIBLE RELATIONSHIPS TO *THE SHREW*

Before moving on, we should note that many discussions concerning Petruchio's mimicry or rhetorical capacities—his "rope tricks," to borrow Wayne A. Rebhorn's (1995) phrase—focus on Petruchio's shortcomings—and, in some eyes, even failure—as rhetor; Rebhorn argues that Petruchio's success in controlling Kate comes more from his "co-opting her will" (307) than from any masterful application of persuasive oratory. Joel Fineman (1985) notes the play's success in taking Kate's own "discourse of subversion" and through it actually "resecur[ing] the very order" which her language seems to oppose (138), yet limits Petruchio's part in this phenomenon to "mimicking her language—throwing it back at her" (142). Viewing from a feminist-psychoanalytic aperture the couple's continuous struggle for mastery through linguistic dexterity, Karen Newman argues that Kate actually eclipses Petruchio in language, using to her advantage a specific form of mimesis: "Kate's self-consciousness about the power of discourse, her punning and irony, and her techniques of linguistic masquerade, are strategies of italics. . . . Instead of figuring a gender-marked woman's speech, they deform language by subverting it, that is, by turning it inside out so that metaphors, puns and other forms of wordplay manifest their veiled equivalences" (99).

Such contrasting views on how one should read *Shrew* often find substantial fodder in the Induction, that sequence of two scenes where Christopher Sly first is degraded publicly for his inability to pay his tavern bill and then subjected to a transformation of his own by a Lord whose various theatrical manipulations lead Sly to believe he is a nobleman awaking from a long and diseased sleep. Read one way, the Induction parallels Kate's own degradation and subsequent rebuilding and reintegration along any of the lines that Miola, Mikesell, Roberts, Daniell, Garber, and others variously suggest. Maynard Mack (1968) sums up the gist of many of these arguments by stating, "What the Lord and his servants do in thrusting a temporary identity on Sly is echoed in what Petruchio does for Kate at a deeper level of psychic change" (279–80).

Read another way, Sly becomes a sort of prototype Petruchio. Duped by the Lord into thinking he is more than he is—he already reveals a fantasy of elevated social status in his familial boast that "we came in with Richard Conqueror" (Induction 1.4), Sly never realizes the extent to which he becomes a joke both to the Lord and the play's readers and auditors. Similarly, the joke on him may foreshadow Petruchio's own delusion in thinking either that he has tamed Kate or that he fully controls any sphere of her being. If we read Sly's Induction experience in this light, two possibilities arise. First, by rendering Petruchio "fooled by a role [Kate] has assumed" (Kahn 1975, 90), the reader may be invited to witness Kate delivering her last speech in a flourish of irony. She can pretend to acquiesce, yet all the time maintain much of her dignity, autonomy, and self-will; in the modern theater, this ironic reading often is accompanied by a subtle wink from Katherine, a practice made famous by Mary Pickford in the 1929 Columbia Pictures *Taming of the Shrew*, also starring Douglas Fairbanks, Jr. The other possibility invokes once again various motifs of transformation, although this time insisting upon a more equal sharing of credit for the characters's improved lots. According to Burns, "the ending of the play gives the jokes some point; Kate's mock elevation of Petruchio results in a genuine elevation, a release from the limitations of his earlier role (fortune-teller, bully, etc.), reflecting her release from her role" (54).

Read yet another way, the Induction scene performs exactly the opposite task: if Sly indeed is so completely indoctrinated into a false perception of his reality—his sense of self totally obliterated by the Lord's machinations, then perhaps Petruchio's conquest of Katherine represents at least an equal demolition of her psyche. Michael Shapiro sees many of Petruchio's actions as "superimposing the image of gentlewoman upon his gentle wife" (159). Orlin regards the "gender issue" as "mooted in the Induction"; through "Sly we get our first glimpse in *The Shrew* of a power relationship that constructs male authority as key to social order" (185). Emily A. Detmer (1997) suggests a more viciously thorough obliteration of Katherine's autonomous being by comparing Kate's experience to that of a Stockholm Syndrome victim.

In nearly every reading of *Shrew*'s Induction presented above, there emerges at least a tacit acknowledgement of a "metatheatrical awareness" (I borrow Shapiro's term) implicit in the Induction's action and its connection to the Kate-Petruchio and Bianca-Lucentio plots. In Juliet Dusinberre's estimation, *Shrew*'s audience is "required to react to two competing dramas: a stage representation of a traditional courtship and taming drama; and a more covert drama which constantly interrupts and comments on the taming drama" (67). Graham Holderness (1987) points out the "standard Elizabethan stage practice" of dressing boys as women characters. In *Shrew*, however, the practice "has its mechanisms exposed, its devices laid bare" when the Lord directs his servant Barthol'mew (or Boy, depending on whether one reads or watches *The Shrew* or *A Shrew*) to play the part of Sly's wife. In Holderness's view this directive enables the reader or audience to "acquire a self-conscious, metadramatic awareness of the illusion" (9) enacted upon both Sly and itself.

The term also focuses our attention, in Moisan's words, on those moments in *Shrew*'s text that "give dramatic life to contemporary anxieties" (105). Obviously, as our discussion of the three possible readings of the Induction suggest, these "moments" include scenes depicting anxieties about "pervasive transgressions of the social hierarchy that would elide prescribed distinctions between commoner and lord, servant and master, and disrupt the proper relations between fathers and sons, and sons-in-law and newly begotten fathers-in-law" (Moisan 105–6).

As with most issues concerning *Shrew*, however, discussions of the play's metatheatricality are dominated by those investigating relationships of "husband and wife" (Moisan 105), particularly Kate's relationship to Petruchio and its implications for all married couples. According to Shapiro, the female roles taken by Pembroke's Men's male actors (or those in any of the other possible companies acting the play) "either idealized married gentlewomen or their unruly antitypes." These female characters "appeared not only as theatrical constructions but also as female stereotypes as outlined in conduct books and marriage manuals" (144). As such, "the two scenes of the Induction provide several opportunities for reflexive contrasts in levels and styles of female impersonation" (150). In other words, the audience or reader is invited to place Kate, once she enters the play, as well as themselves, into a desired social and marital frame. Newman views the play's metatheatrical treatment of Kate and Petruchio another way and argues, "in the Induction, . . . relationships of power and gender, which in Elizabethan treatises, sermons and homilies, and behavioral handbooks and the like were figured as natural and divinely ordained, are subverted by the metatheatrical foregrounding of such roles and relations as culturally constructed" (88). Therefore, although Kate seemingly submits to Petruchio in all respects at the play's final moment, nevertheless her "having the last word contradicts the very sentiments she speaks" (99).

Our reflections on the various "levels and styles of female impersonation" and the possibly "subverted" nature of them in *The Shrew* certainly are altered by both the existence of *A Shrew* and of Slie's and his moral's reappearance at the end of the 1594 quarto. Much time is devoted, in fact, to determining satisfactorily the relationship between *A Shrew* and *The Shrew* and the implications of this relationship. For example, does reading *A Shrew* as a source of *The Shrew* necessarily mean that *The Shrew* is any more—or less—ideologically impacted than *A Shrew* may be? Does one's reading of *The Shrew* as an independent offshoot of a lost source for both plays make it any more or less antifeminist? Does the placement of Christopher Sly into scenes occurring throughout the play—including his sporadic interruptions of the main plot—entail a different significance for him? Are one, both, or all three *Shrew*s Shakespeare's? Why do editors prefer Sly's presence in the Induction only, while stage and film producers and directors increasingly invoke the authority of *A Shrew* by casting him in any number of scenes? Perhaps these questions are approached most effectively by turning to *Shrew*'s print history after the *Shrew*'s first appearance in 1623 and exploring the several different treatments of Sly's scenes.

Up until 1623 the reading public had only one *Shrew*—the 1594 *A Shrew*—for its consideration. And as witnessed earlier in our discussion, this *Shrew* closes its frame with Slie's reappearance and presentation of his moral. Despite this radically different ending, no existing evidence suggests that the two texts ever were distinguished one from the other until well into the eighteenth century. When John Smethwick, who obtained the rights to *A Shrew* in 1607, published in quarto in 1631 "A Wittie and Pleasant Comedie Called The Taming of the Shrew," he presented to the public a text much closer to the Folio's *The Shrew* than to his own *A Shrew*—an indication, according to Ann Thompson (1984), that he "did not discriminate between the plays" (2). Alexander Pope (1723), too, evidently saw Shakespeare's hand in both texts, for he included *A Shrew*'s Slie ending as an appended part of his *Shrew* text and remarked in his preface that in many of the plays collected in the Folio, "a number of beautiful passages which are extant in the first singal editions, are omitted . . . as it seems, without any other reason, than their willingness to shorten some scenes . . . to make [Shakespeare] just fit for their stage" (xvii).

In much the same manner as did Pope, subsequent editors continued to view *A Shrew* and *The Shrew* as interchangeable texts. Marcus observes that the editors Theobald (1733), Hanmer (1744–1746), Warburton (1747),

Johnson (1765), and Capell (1767–1768) all chose to incorporate "some or all of the Sly materials" (179–80) into their *Shrew*s. In 1790, however, all this changed with Edmund Malone's *Shakespeare's Plays and Poems*. Malone argued that *A Shrew* was a source for *The Shrew* and omitted all Sly's appearances except for the two scenes of the Induction and his brief lines at the end of act 1 scene 1.

Malone's theory flourished, finding adherents in W. C. Hazlitt (1964), R. Warwick Bond (1904), and Geoffrey Bullough (1957–1975) (he reprints the entire text of *A Shrew* in his *Narrative and Dramatic Sources*), among others. Dominating the nineteenth and much of the twentieth centuries, Malone's *Shrew* text (the text, incidentally, with which modern readers are most familiar) and theory really were not challenged until Peter Alexander proposed in the *Times Literary Supplement* of September 16, 1926 that, "If the quarto, in spite of the entry in the Stationers' Register, could be shown to be no more than a pirate's version of the play as given in the folio, Henslowe's entry would then have to be taken as a reference to Shakespeare's comedy" (614). Alexander's "bad" quarto theory grew rapidly in acceptance (see, for example, Hosley 1961 and 1964), especially after John Dover Wilson supported it in his 1928 Cambridge edition. Alexander's theory now shares prominence alongside H. J. Oliver's conjecture (which also originates, partially, in Wilson's edition of *Shrew* and in G. I. Duthie's arguments [1943]) that there may be a third *Shrew*, a source for both *A Shrew* and *The Shrew*. Oliver (1984) observes that *A Shrew* stands as an "abnormal" type of bad quarto: its construction involves "a good deal more conscious originality on the part of its author or authors than is usually to be observed in bad-quarto texts" (23). Simultaneously, he notes that *The Shrew* also "reveals signs of change of mind and is indeed self-contradictory" (23; see Wells and Taylor [1987] for additional coverage of the play's self-contradictions).

Interestingly, all three theories hesitate, by varying degrees, in associating *A Shrew* with Shakespeare's hand. Malone's camp sees the play completely as someone else's, while Alexander's and Oliver's parties distance it from Shakespeare by assigning hack writers and/or "editors" (Oliver's and, later, Marcus's term) for *A Shrew*'s several anomalous constituents. For many readers, it seems, *A Shrew* is too amateurish and/or antifeminist to be considered even an early product of Shakespeare's pen. Its outlandish hodgepodge of undeveloped characters and ill-delineated scenes and actions—Marcus alludes to previous critics's condemnations of it as "a heap of shards thrown together" (183)—do not seem to fit properly, somehow, Shakespeare's "vision."

Yet, for all its more carefully drawn characters and more logically articulated plot, according to Marcus, *The Shrew* over the years since Malone has become in many ways "a convenient mechanism by which the forcible suppression of female insurgency is naturalized as reality and truth" (182). Holderness (1989) observes that confinement of Sly's presence to the Induction alone elides much of the play's farcical quality. Where Sly's presence throughout *A Shrew* qualifies Kate's final lines as merely the final stage in the tinker's befuddlement, without him the play becomes "a naturalistic comedy (with varying degrees of farce) in which issues of marriage and sexual politics are dramatised (with more or less seriousness) by actors presenting themselves as real characters within a convincingly realistic social and dramatic setting" (7). In other words, *The Shrew*, despite the many discomforts its treatment of Katherine provokes, provides a paradigm where women's suppression may be accepted tacitly, perhaps even advocated. Although he never actually strikes Kate, Petruchio's handling of her after their marriage includes deprivation and often borders on torture. Marcus, Rebhorn, Fineman, Newman, Boose, and Detmer, among other, never lose sight either of what Maureen Quilligan (1993) calls the early modern theater's staging of "female obedience for the visual pleasure of its male auditors" (209) or what Katherine A. Sirluck (1991) terms "the total defeat" (418) of Kate.

EARLY STAGE HISTORY OF *SHREW*

Perhaps these self-sustaining mechanisms of suppression, gleaned from *Shrew*'s strong links to the oftentimes severely misogynist oral and folk tales, antifeminist publications, and continental sources—or, on the other hand, the play's impulse to interrogate and redefine early modern English marriage rites and rituals—are at least partially what spurred *Shrew*'s early stage popularity. The publications of the 1596 and 1607 quartos attest to an eager acceptance, and render anomalous Henslowe's notation that on June 13, 1594 at Newington Butts, "the tamynge of A Shrowe" earned the company only nine shillings—"a very poor day's takings" (Oliver 1984, 32 n. 1). The appearance of John Fletcher's *The Woman's Prize, or The Tamer Tamed* (ca. 1619) also suggests a sustained popularity both for *Shrew* and for plays focusing on negotiations of gender.

A countermand of sorts to Shakespeare's roughshod handling of women, *The Woman's Prize* picks up several years after *Shrew*'s closing scene: now widowed, Petruchio marries a chaste but shrewish Maria and is in turn subjected to abuses tantamount to those he enacted during his marriage to Kate. An early Prologue appended to the play both suggests the pervasiveness of the period's gender strife and echoes the play's evident support of women in the struggles they must endure during marriage:

> Ladies to you, in whose defence and right,
> Fletcher's brave Muse prepar'd her self to fight
> A battel without blood, 'twas well fought too,

(The victory's yours, though got with much ado.)
(Fletcher 1910, ll. 1–4, p. 2)

Shrew also may have been requested at court some time in 1594; the 1631 quarto states that the play was acted at the Globe and Blackfriars, further indicating a sustained popularity.

Although Henslowe writes in his *Diary* that *Shrew* was performed by "my Lord Admeralle men & my Lorde chamberlen men" on June 13, 1594 (1.17), the 1594 quarto tells us that *A Shrew* was "sundry times acted by the Right honorable the Earle of Pembrook his servants" (arguments exist for the Queen's Men as well; see Morris 1981, 51–52, and Thompson 1984, 2–3). According to Haring-Smith (1985) and others, *Shrew* probably was acted by Pembroke's Men in the provinces and then, falling on hard times, the company disbanded and sold the text to the Chamberlain's Men (7). Many other theories concerning both the acting companies who may have performed *Shrew* exist, as well as discussions concerning the possible versions of *Shrew* these companies performed. All we know with any certainty is by 1633, the play was in the hands of the King's Men, who performed it on November 26 "before the King and Queene." Master of the Revels Sir Henry Herbert reports the play was "likt" (Adams, 1964, p. 53; Bentley [1968] notes that Fletcher's *Woman's Prize* followed this production on November 28 [97]).

From this point on, both *A Shrew* and *The Shrew* slip into almost complete obscurity for the next 250 years. Although transferred on August 24, and again on September 14, 1642, according to the Stationers's Register, we have no record of the play being printed or performed from 1633 until England's civil wars. And after Parliament's forces took power and then relinquished it in 1660, we have only two other notices of *Shrew* appearing over the remainder of the seventeenth century. Galmini Salgádo (1975) cites a strange possible reference to *Shrew* in a 1659 speech to the Commons by Lord Henry Cromwell:

> The players have a play, where they bring in a tinker, and make him believe himself a lord, and when they have satisfied their humour, they made him a plain tinker again; gentlemen, but that this was a great while ago, I should have thought this play had been made of me: for if ever two cases were alike, 'tis the tinker's and mine. (48)

Herbert also notes a November 3, 1663, "Revived Play Taminge the Shrew" (138) occurring in London.

The eighteenth and nineteenth centuries show signs of an even further descent into obscurity for *Shrew*. Samuel Johnson rails at readers's ignorance of Shakespeare upon reading an account of shrew-taming in provincial England that appeared in *The Tatler*, September 30, 1710:

The youngest of four daughters of a gentleman in Lincolnshire is a shrew. A young man, despite the girl's well known character, decides to marry her. After living some time at her father's house, the husband goes off to prepare for her homecoming, and then returns to fetch his wife. He arrives riding a nag, accompanied by a dog and with a case of pistols before him; he makes his wife mount behind him and they ride off. The dog does not obey his command to open a gate and is shot; the horse stumbles twice and is killed with a sword. The wife is forced to carry the saddle home. Later all of the daughters and their husbands visit the father-in-law. The husbands plan a test of their wives while the wives are apart playing cards. Each is called, and the first three will not come until their gamer is finished. The reformed shrew throws down her cards and comes at once. Her husband takes her in his arms and assures her that he will be kind henceforth. (A summary by Brunvand 1966; 356)

What Johnson laments most is England's readers' inability to discern an almost point-for-point lifting of Shakespeare's play:

It cannot but seem strange that Shakespeare should be so little known to the author of *The Tatler* that he should suffer this story to be obtruded upon him; or so little known to the publick, that he could hope to make it pass upon his readers as a real narrative of a transaction in Lincolnshire; yet it is apparent, that he knew not himself whence the story was taken, or hoped that he might rob so obscure a writer without detection. (Quoted in Brunvand 1966; 356)

Although probably wrong in attributing the tale to Shakespeare (Brunvand 1966; 357), Johnson nevertheless points out the extent to which Shakespeare's play had been forgotten by readers and auditors.

Both Cromwell's and Herbert's somewhat cloudy citations point to what actually happens with *Shrew* from the Restoration until the late nineteenth century, for they hint at radical alterations of the play's text, which subsumed the *Shrew* of Shakespeare's stage. These alterations included a radical splitting apart of the three plotlines and a subsequent forming of them into their own entities. Starting a trend that edited texts of *Shrew* soon would follow, stage writers often removed entirely the Christopher Sly sequence of scenes from the two romantic plots. On April 9, 1667 Thomas Killigrew's King's Company staged *Sauny the Scot: or, the Taming of the Shrew* (pub. 1698), written by their leading comic actor John Lacey (d. 1681; he also played Sauny in its first run at the Theatre Royal). A rougher and more violent play than *Shrew* (although not without a certain charm), *Sauny the Scot* strips the plot bare, leaving only the courtship and marriage of Margaret/Peg (*Shrew*'s Katherine) and Petruchio. Lacey's play also paints a much more shrewish picture of Peg and presents an increasingly greedy and emotionless Petruchio.

Arriving in London with his Scottish servant Sauny, Petruchio explains his presence to his friend Geraldo (Hortensio):

> PET.: Hether I come to try my Fortunes, to see if good luck and my Friends
>   will help me to a Wife; will you wish me to one?
> GER.: What Quallifications do you look for?
> PET.: Why Money, a good Portion.
> GER.: Is that all?
> PET.: All man? all other things are in my making. (Lacey 1698, 5)

Petruchio and Geraldo agree to the same mutual aid of each other's cause as found in *Shrew*: Petruchio will introduce the disguised Geraldo to Beaufoy (Baptista) as a music teacher.

Upon Petruchio's and Peg's first meeting and Petruchio's subsequent revelation to her that he will marry her, Peg responds, "You shall be bak'd first, you shall; within there, ha!" Betraying neither fear nor shock, Petruchio responds,

> Hold, get me a stick there *Sauny*; by this hand, deny to Promise before your
> Father, I'll not Leave you a whole rib, I'll make you do't and be glad on't.
> (12)

Petruchio continues the threat when Peg's father approaches, stating, "Here comes your Father, never make denial, if you do, you know what follows" (12). Momentarily obedient to his will, but nevertheless eager for a challenge, Peg states in an aside, "The Devil's in this fellow, he has beat me at my own Weapon, *I* have a good mind to marry him to try if he can *Tame* me" (12).

From here the plot loosely follows that of *Shrew*. The major alterations include the scenes following their wedding, where Petruchio adds to his taming repertoire his threat to have Sauny undress her for bed and his forcing of Peg to drink beer and smoke tobacco—all the while, of course, withholding from her sleep, food, and water. At the beginning of act 5, we get a glimpse of the "progress" of Petruchio's treatment when Peg speaks to her sister Biancha:

> Had I serv'd him as had *Eve* did *Adam*, he could not have us'd me worse; but
> I am resolv'd now I'm got home again I'll be revenged, I'll muster up the
> Spight off all the Curs'd Women since *Noahs* Flood to do him mischief, and
> add new Vigour to my Tongue; I have not par'd my Nails this fortnight, they
> are long enough to do him some Execution, that's my Comfort. (39)

Good to her promise, Peg viciously insults Petruchio in front of Winlove (Lucentio); she then declares she will not speak to him for two months. Petruchio counters by asking her why she is so melancholy and proposes a toothache may be upsetting her. He sends Sauny for a barber, but when Sauny returns with the barber, Petruchio proclaims Peg is dead. He orders Sauny to strap Peg to a cart and to bury her. Finally, Peg speaks:

> Hold, hold my dear Petruchio, you have overcome me, and I beg your Pardon, henceforth I will not dare to think a thought shall cross your Pleasure, set me at Liberty, and on my knees I'll make my Recantation. (45)

The play ends with the same wager we see in *Shrew*; Peg, however, does not deliver any speech of submission.

Sauny the Scot sustained an immense popularity for over half a century; the play ran throughout the Restoration until its final performance on November 18, 1736. Although Samuel Pepys, who saw two productions of it (on April 9 and November 1, 1667), scorned it as a "mean" and "silly" play, he did praise "some very good pieces in it" (*London Stage* 1960–1968, vol. 1.106, 122). And despite plot devices and characterizations that Genest described as "of the lowest kind" (quoted by Haring-Smith 1985, 11), the play's success spurred James Worsdale's *A Cure for a Scold* (pub. 1735). Premiering at Drury Lane on February 25, 1735, *Cure for a Scold* borrows heavily from Lacey's plot, but "Englishes" and diminishes Archer (*Scold*'s Sauny), pushes the arranged marriage between Manley (Petruchio) and Peg (Kate) to a mere one hour after Sir William Worthy's (Baptista's) and Manley's successful negotiation, and eliminates the final scenes involving Petruchio's threat of tooth-pulling and burial. Instead, Worsdale (1735) embellishes the play's carnivalesque grotesquery, and has the Doctor recommend shaving Peg's head, applying blisters, and drawing blood from "some of the Veins under her Tongue" (55) when she refuses to speak to Manley. The farce also romanticizes slightly more the subplot between Gainlove (Lucentio) and Flora (Bianca) and features several "airs," which certain characters break into at moments of crisis. Many of the songs supplement and advocate the brutal measures with which Manley threatens Margaret:

> Of all the methods most in Vogue
>   For Keeping Women quiet,
> 'Tis best to let their Sleep be short,
>   And stint them in their Diet:
> For Fasting keeps their Bodies fine,
>   And makes their Spirits small,
> By Hunger wives, like Hawks, are taught
>   To know their Keeper's Call. (Worsdale 1735, 38)

Contrary to the Peg in Lacey's *Sauny*, Worsdale's Peg does offer at the end a short speech of repentance, where she states, "You have taught me what 'tis to be a Wife, and I shall make it my Study to be obliging and obedient" (57). The play enjoyed only a limited popularity.

In stark contrast to *The Shrew*, Sly's disappearance from these two alterations creates neither a more realistic nor a more marriage-focused environment. Situating themselves exclusively in the tradition of farce, neither play elicits sympathy for Peg, nor does either one inspire admiration for Petruchio-Manley's educative endeavors or indignation at his brutality. Instead, the plays emphasize brutish stereotypes of both shrew and shrew-tamer for purely comic effect—at the expense, of course, of women. In both plays as well (especially *Sauny*), the grossly exaggerated tandem of Peg and Petruchio is decentered somewhat by the presence of Sauny-Archer, a vulgar buffoon whose pleasure is "scratten and scrubben" (Lacey 1698, 4). Originating in the character of Grumio (actually, "Sauny" is a derivation of "Sander," the Grumio figure from *A Shrew*), Sauny-Archer's prominent personality also replaces much of Sly's function as well: like Sly he becomes the butt of many slapstick jokes and acts as the play's local-color idiot.

But Sauny-Archer's penchant for satisfying the Restoration stage's "appetite" for "outlandish behavior" (Haring-Smith 1985, 11) does not signal the end of Christopher Sly. Instead, Sly becomes the protagonist in several other farcical pieces. On January 22, 1662, Jacques Thierry and Will Schellinks saw *The New Made Nobleman* at the Red Bull. Although no conclusive evidence survives, Ethel Seaton (1935) believes that this may have been a droll made from the Christopher Sly Induction of *Shrew*. In 1716, Sly also appears in *The Cobler of Preston*, a farce written in two different versions by Charles Johnson and Christopher Bullock, respectively (both pub. 1716). Johnson's version, a two-act farce closely tied to political unrest in 1715, premiered at Drury Lane on February 3, 1716. The play was not popular. Bullock (1716), writing in his preface to the printed version of *Cobler* that he hopes to "be allow'd (without Offence) to take Shakespeare's *Tinker of Burton-heath*, and make him the *Cobler of Preston*" (vi-vii), produced a much more well received piece. (He also claimed to have written the play in two days and staged it in three, knowing that Johnson's version was in preparation at Drury Lane.) Bullock expands the characters of Toby Guzzle's (Sly's) wife Dorcas and the Hostess and creates a completely different set of adventures for his hero, including a sound beating by both his wife and the Hostess and a reunifying drinking bout between them. Bullock's piece premiered at Lincoln's Inn Fields on January 24, 1716. It later was altered slightly (fewer political allusions and a newly contrived love story) and presented as a musical farce at Drury Lane in 1817.

None of these alterations, however, enjoyed the popularity of David Garrick's three-act farcical afterpiece *Catharine and Petruchio*, which premiered on March 18, 1754 (pub. 1756). Starting with Henry Woodward as the first Petruchio and Mrs. Pritchard acting as Catharine, the play rapidly became "the sole version of Shakespeare's *Shrew* on the English and American stages from 1754 to 1844" (Haring-Smith 1985, 15), appearing 234 times between 1754 and 1800 alone. Although preserving more of *Shrew* than Lacey or Worsdale did, Garrick reduces the plot of *Shrew* to that involving Catharine and Petruchio only; he cuts the play extensively in other areas as well, opening the action with Petruchio's and Baptista's marriage negotiation, having Hortensio and Bianca already married before the play commences, and reducing the roles and lines of Grumio and other minor characters.

The result of such heavy cutting is the same as with Garrick's predecessors's alterations: character development is sacrificed in favor of rapidly moving visual and physical humor. However, glimpses of character peak out of Garrick's afterpiece from time to time, especially in the figures of Catharine and Petruchio. When Petruchio negotiates the marriage with Catharine's father Baptista, the father betrays a coldness toward Catharine that invites some sympathy for her—despite the fact she has not come on stage yet:

> And if with scurril taunt and squeamish pride
> She make a mouth and will not taste her fortune,
> I'll turn her forth to seek it in the world;
> Nor henceforth shall she know her father's doors. (Garrick 1981, 1.65–68)

When she does approach her father (after having smashed the lute over the Music-Master's head), her first words perhaps instill a deeper awareness of her hopeless situation:

> How? Turn'd adrift, nor know my father's house?
> Reduc'd to this, or more? The maid's last prayer?
> Sent to be woo'd, like bear unto the stake?
> Trim wooing like to be!—and he the bear. (1.135–38)

And when Baptista returns to ask how their first meeting has progressed, Catharine asks him, "Call you me daughter?" to which he responds, "Better this jack than starve; and that's your portion" (1.227). Yet Catharine soon reveals herself to be as malignant as the Pegs from *Sauny* and *Cure for a Scold*, and equally in need of correction.

Her "taming," however, fraught as it is with the by now expected withholding of food and other necessities, assumes a slightly different effect than in previous *Shrew*s. Once Catharine laments her stark situation in act 1, she steps back for most of the remainder of the play and allows Petruchio to establish himself as a respectable, at times even thoughtful, young man. The marriage negotiation contains almost no discussion of money, nor is the retelling of the wedding scene subsumed in his outrageousness. Instead, we see a Petruchio whom Garrick wants us to admire—with much the same conviction

Catharine feels when she thanks him for her taming: "So good a master cannot choose but mend me" (3.209).

Marcus argues that much of the difference between *A Shrew* and *The
Shrew* lies in *The Shrew*'s "more compelling aura of reality" (190). Implicit
in *The Shrew*'s more realistic portrayal of male-female relationships is the loss
of women's "power and autonomy, since there is nothing [in *The Shrew*] to
qualify the 'truth' of female subordination" realized at the play's end (190).
In other words, the fact remains that the mainstay of the play—from its roots
in medieval folk tales to *Sauny the Scot* and *Catharine and Petruchio*—is its
violent and unwaveringly strident dominance over women. Otherwise educated and often poignant arguments such as Heilman's, which view farce as
offering "a spectacle that resembles daily actuality but lets us participate without feeling the responsibilities and liabilities that the situation would normally
evoke" (152), often forget or ignore this reality.

John Philip Kemble's acting edition of Garrick's play (pub. 1810) illustrates the point. Kemble first began playing Garrick's Petruchio in 1786 and
around 1788 started carrying a whip—now a commonplace for many actors
of Petruchio. And despite having cut from his own performances many of
Petruchio's more violent scenes (possibly because of his several limitations
as an actor), Kemble nevertheless created in his edition a more verbally dex-
terous and much more physical Petruchio. For example, Kemble reintroduces
some of Shakespeare's lines from *The Shrew*, including "Thus have I, poli-
tickly, begun my reign" (4.1.157–80 in *The Shrew*; act 2 in Kemble 1810), and
adds more squabbling between Katharine (he changes the spelling of her back
to its original) and her husband—most of which merely adds to Katherine's
shrewish persona. (Later, Kemble's brother Charles increased the violence by
adding the throwing of dishes to the meat scene.) Kemble's changes expand
somewhat Garrick's slight attempts at characterization and bring Petruchio
closer into the fold of practical and expedient young eighteenth-century men.
(His whip obviously adds another, albeit silent, agent of his expediency.)

Beginning with Garrick's play in the mid-eighteenth century, then, Petruchio's actions are dredged from the more purely farcical *Sauny the Scot* and
Cure for a Scold and placed into realistically rehearsed representations of
male-dominated marriage and relationship. Somewhat paradoxically, however, Petruchio's actions remain—in spite of the whips and language—free
from ethical consideration, mostly because of his gentlemanly status. In this
context, Petruchio invites increasing admiration from readers and auditors for
these actions. And as the eighteenth century demands a greater realism and
with it a more "authentic" Shakespeare, both on stage and in print, this new-
found admiration for Petruchio accumulates rapidly.

Praise for Petruchio began, of course, much earlier than the eighteenth
century, as witnessed in Sir John Harington's (1596) wistful comments on the
efficacy of Petruchio's shrew-taming prowess:

> For the shrewd wife, reade the booke of taming a shrew, which hath made a
> number of us so perfect, that now every one can rule a shrew in our coun-
> trey, save he that hath her. But indeed there are but two good rules. One is,
> let them never have their willes; the other differs but a letter, let them ever
> have their willes, the first is the wiser, but the second is more in request, and
> therefore I make choice of it. (153–154)

But it really flourished with Garrick's and Kemble's creations of a more "dignified" Petruchio—a phenomenon which coincided, incidentally, with another
manifestation of the desire for "real" Shakespeare: the advent of affordable,
complete printed editions of Shakespeare and the introductory comments
appended to them. These editions and studies all heaped praise upon Petruchio as well. Nicholas Rowe, for example, who published in 1709 his *Works
of Mr. William Shakespear*, declared Petruchio "an uncommon Piece of
Humour" (xix), and Johnson (1765) commended as well the Kate-Petruchio
plot's many "eminently spritely and diverting" qualities (351). William Hazlitt
(1964) also confessed a fondness for Petruchio, proclaiming him "a character
which most husbands ought to study, unless perhaps the very audacity of
Petruchio's attempt might alarm them more than his success would encourage them" (342).

Although Garrick's *Catharine and Petruchio* did not relinquish fully its
place on the stage until the early twentieth century, the mid- and late nineteenth century's increased demand for more textually accurate Shakespeare
finally initiated, in George C. Odell's words, an opportunity for *Shrew*, "like
Ariel [to be] released from the magic of the evil spirits [of] the adapters"
(1920, 191). A brief run (four performances) of Frederic Reynolds's operatic
Shrew, complete with elaborate sets and musical accompaniment—including
an overture by Rossini, at Drury Lane in 1828 marks the first attempted departure from Garrick's text (O'Dell, 144). Then, on March 16, 1844, *The Taming
of the Shrew*, "from the original text," premiered at London's Haymarket Theatre. Produced by the Haymarket's manager Benjamin Webster at the request
of antiquarian James Robinson Planché and to commemorate the return to the
stage of Louisa Nisbett, this *Shrew* starred Webster as "Petrucio" (his
spelling), Nisbett as Kate, and Robert Strickland as Sly—who, according to
many accounts, stole the show. Anticipating in many ways William Poel's productions of *Shrew* in the spring of 1913 (see MacDonald's essay), the performance stands as probably the first since the early seventeenth century to
approximate on stage the 1623 folio's text and the early modern theater's set.
Although including the complete Sly Induction, Planché did not believe that
Shrew ever had an epilogue; yet, he keeps Sly on the stage throughout the play
but does not allow him any lines after the Induction scenes (during act divisions, actors bring Sly food and drinks). Planché ends the play with the Lord
reappearing, paying the remaining stage actors, and then leaving the stage;

once they leave, the principal actors finish their lines and remove the sleeping Sly from the stage.

The Webster-Planché production was notable also for its lack of elaborate scenery and adoption of Elizabethan stage costumes (including making up the Induction's actors to look like Shakespeare, Ben Jonson, and Richard Tarleton), two more attempts at theatrical realism that now accompanied the aforementioned recastings of Petruchio. The play featured as well changeable placards that indicated a shift in scene or of location. Webster had reduced the scene changes to two: that of a "little ale-house on a heath" (Planché, quoted by Wells 1997, 85) where Sly passes out, and the Lord's bedchamber, where the actors nail up tapestries (of early modern London, including scenes of the Globe) as a backdrop and then play out the Kate-Petruchio and Bianca-Lucentio subplots. Although the reviews were mixed and the performances (especially Petruchio's) did not arouse acclaim, the play was successful and was revived two years later.

The revival belongs to Samuel Phelps, who produced the play on November 15, 1856, at Sadler's Wells. Henry Marston played Petruchio and Phelps acted as Sly. Phelps strayed more frequently than did Webster-Planché from Shakespeare's text but his production was believed to be more "faithful to the flavor" (Haring-Smith 1985, 49) of *Shrew* than his predecessors', whose play seemed to both critics and spectators at times stiff. He achieved this sense of authenticity, interestingly, by removing most of the Induction's and the minor characters' bawdy allusions and slightly refining Katherine (she does not tie her sister's hands, for example), but still preserving Petruchio's "frantic" nature (he did remove, however, some of Petruchio's more distasteful lines and his demand that Katherine step on her cap in the final scene). A contemporary review of Phelps's production attests to the audience's eager acceptance of what they felt was a more realistic presentation: "the audience ... would not have lost a word. They come with the antique feeling to this theatre, throw themselves into the story, and having, by close attention and an intelligent sympathy, made personal acquaintance with the characters, they desire to know the history and the end of every one of them" (quoted by Odell 1920, 268). Another reviewer speaks of Petruchio's particular qualities as "manly, hearty, humorous, but, withal, the gentleman." William Winter (1915) notes that this type of Petruchio "is not portrayed as he is drawn by Shakespeare" (504); nevertheless, Phelps's production proved successful.

A "totally contrasting production" (MacDonald 1971; 169) took place when Augustin Daly premiered *Shrew* on May 29, 1888 at the Gaiety Theatre. Having met immense success already with his production of *Shrew* in New York (120 performances in 1887; much as in England, *Catharine and Petruchio* had dominated America's stage since 1766), Daly reinstituted elaborate stage settings (some of them obtained from an Italian palace) and eliminated the scene placards Planché and Webster attempted in 1844. Daly also condensed the scenes involving Hortensio and Tranio and even further curtailed much of Petruchio's brutish behavior, simultaneously speeding up the action and softening the scenes involving him and Kate. Kate in particular, played by Miss Ada Rehan, caught the attention of both critics and audiences alike for her "magnificent" (Odell 439) and "brilliant" (Winter 505) performances. The result, according to Haring-Smith (1985), was much more romantic comedy than farce (62–63).

EPILOGUE: THE TWENTIETH CENTURY

Daly refined Petruchio to fit even more closely the respectable and practical young gentleman of his age—including improved wedding attire and conspiratorial winks toward the audience, and found an actress (Rehan) who could play the part of Katherine "with the revelations of the woman's true heart" (Winter 524) and thus be tamed without loss of dignity. His efforts were rewarded not only with critical and financial success, but continued to be supported by an increased scholarly investigation of the text. R. Warwick Bond claimed in his 1904 edition of *Shrew* that Kate's behavior "contradicts natural law and the facts of life.... [H]ad the shrew married a husband she could bend, she would have been cheated of happiness by the discovery that she could not love him." As for Petruchio, Bond believed he "has on his side not merely physical strength . . . but also a better-grounded view of life" (lvi). Bond's comments, of course, anticipate Quiller-Couch's (1928) more notorious ones regarding "all the Petruchio-Katharina business" (xv) from the introduction to his 1928 Cambridge edition, including his disclosure that "one cannot help thinking a little wistfully that the Petruchian discipline had something to say for itself" (xxvi).

Despite Daly's creation of "perhaps the most polite taming of a shrew ever staged" (Haring-Smith 1985, 61), the equally successful productions of Oscar Asche (1904) and Poel (see MacDonald 1971), and the more diligent scholarly attention on both Shakespeare and *Shrew*, the twentieth century commences with a nascent sense of discomfort provoked by the play's total defeat of Katherine. Writing about Daly's production in a letter to the *Pall Mall Gazette* in 1888, George Bernard Shaw (who assumes in the letter a guise of "an Englishwoman, just come up . . . from Devonshire to enjoy a few weeks of the season in London") notes that however hard Petruchio tries "to persuade the audience that he is not in earnest, and that the whole play is a farce," he nevertheless "cannot make the spectacle of a man cracking a heavy whip at a starving woman other than disgusting and unmanly" (Wilson, 186–87).

Coming at a time only fifty or so years after the last recorded use of the bridles and branks Boose and Newman describe—a time "within the memory of persons still alive," according to Winter (494), Daly's and others's intensified attention to realistic detail—either in respect to the by now pervasive insistence on staging Shakespeare's "authentic" texts only or in terms of portraying Petruchio as a contemporary bourgeois Everyman—began to erode too effectively the facade of farce. In short, Kate's taming was no longer as funny as it once had been for some readers and spectators; her domination became, in Shaw's words, "altogether disgusting to modern sensibility" (Wilson, 188). And in this atmosphere of rapidly changing attitudes, both Petruchio's braggadocio taming and Kate's complete capitulation required yet another recasting.

In contrast to previous eras, however, the twentieth century distinguishes itself by offering several possible transformations of *Shrew* at once. This becomes especially true during the latter half of the century, when the textual *Shrew* begins to incite tremendous controversy concerning what should be the "correct" response to Petruchio's explanation of his marriage intentions ("I come to wive it wealthily in Padua; / If wealthily, then happily in Padua" [1.2.70–71]), his "taming" techniques ("This is a way to kill a wife with kindness" [4.1.177]), and Kate's apparent capitulation to him at the end ("Thy husband is thy lord, thy life, thy keeper" [5.2.150]). Kate's final speech, for example, undergoes several experimental interpretations, including ones steeped in irony, such as Columbia Pictures 1929 *Taming of the Shrew* where Kate winks as she advocates a woman's submission to her husband. Or, the entire play's farcical elements are reintegrated, as in the many productions that feature Petruchio as a wild-west cowboy or those that rely upon Sly's scenes now relegated to *A Shrew*.

Or, the play undergoes any one of several modern alterations, many of which seek to redefine the postwar American woman's role by placing her securely in a suburban home and providing her with an education "in her new role as a consumer of household cates"—a trend Natasha Korda claims began with the emergence of Shakespeare's *The Shrew* (112). While some of these alterations, most notably Cole Porter's 1948 *Kiss Me, Kate* (adapted for the screen by George Sidney in 1953), emphasize the universality of sexual desire, few of them, according to Barbara Hodgdon, "tolerate [any] ruptures within male dominance" (20). Included among these alterations are Paul Nickell's 1950 Westinghouse Theater One television production, Franco Zeffirelli's 1966 *The Taming of the Shrew* which starred Elizabeth Taylor and Richard Burton, and ABC television's 1986 episode of *Moonlighting*. Finally, *Shrew* occasionally presents itself "straight" and thereby tests the audience's capacity for disgust, sympathy, or even desire; although appearing less frequently than the ironic or farcical productions, these straight performances strip the play of much of its pretense to companionate marriage, benevolent male guidance, or even—as in the case of Charles Marowitz's 1974 production—comic or festive mood. Much of the performance interpretation and criticism produced in the twentieth century, in other words, contributes to our feelings of vexation regarding *Shrew*. The essays I have included in the *"The Taming of the Shrew* on Stage, in Film, and on Television" section treat these matters thoroughly, as well as others.

WORKS CITED

Adams, Joseph Quincy, ed. 1964. *The Dramatic Records of Sir Henry Herbert*. New York: Benjamin Blom.

Alexander, Peter. 1926. *"The Taming of a Shrew." Times Literary Supplement*, September 16, 614.

———. 1969 . "The Original Ending of *The Taming of the Shrew." Shakespeare Quarterly* 20, no. 2 (Summer), 111–16.

Averell, William. 1588. *A meruailous combat of contrarieties. Malignantlie striuing in the members of a mans bodies, allegoricallie representing vnto us the enuied state of our florishing common wealth: wherein dialogue-wise by the way, are touched the extreame vices of this present time.* London.

Banister, John. 1578. *The Historie of Man, Sucked from the Sappe of the Most Approved Anathomistes, in the Present Age.* London.

Barker, Francis, Peter Hulme, and Margaret Iverson, eds. 1991. *Uses of History: Marxism, Postmodernism, and the Renaissance.* Manchester and New York: Manchester University Press.

Baumlin, Tita French. 1989. "Petruchio the Sophist and Language as Creation in *The Taming of the Shrew." Studies in English Literature* 29, no. 2 (Spring): 237–57.

Bean, John C. 1980. "Comic Structure and the Humanizing of Kate in *The Taming of the Shrew."* In *The Woman's Part: Feminist Criticism of Shakespeare.* Edited by Carolyn Ruth Swift Lenz, Gayle Green, and Carol Thomas Neely. Urbana: University of Illinois Press.

Bentley, G.E. 1968. *The Jacobean and Caroline Stage.* 7 vols. Oxford: Clarendon Press.

Berek, Peter. 1988. "Text, Gender, and Genre in *The Taming of the Shrew."* In *'Bad' Shakespeare: Revaluations of the Shakespeare Canon.* Edited by Maurice Charney. Rutherford: Fairleigh Dickinson University Press; London and Toronto: Associated University Presses.

Bevington, David, ed. 1992. *The Complete Works of Shakespeare.* 4th ed. New York: Harper Collins.

Blake, Ann. 1981. *"The Taming of the Shrew* and *Much Ado about Nothing*: A Comparative Study." *Southern Review: Literary and Interdisciplinary Essays* 14, no. 1 (March): 52–63.

Bloom, Edward A., ed. 1964. *Shakespeare 1564–1964: A Collection of Modern Essays by Various Hands.* Providence: Brown University Press.

Bond, R. Warwick, ed. 1904. *The Taming of the Shrew.* The Works of Shakespeare. Indianapolis: Bobbs-Merrill.

Boose, Lynda E. 1994. *"The Taming of the Shrew*, Good Husbandry, and Enclosure." In *Shakespeare Reread: The Texts in New Contexts.* Edited by Russ McDonald. Ithaca and London: Cornell University Press.

Bradbrook, M. C. 1958. "Dramatic Role as Social Image: A Study of *The Taming of the Shrew." Shakespeare-Jarbuch* 94: 132–50.

Brown, Carolyn E. 1995. "Katherine of *The Taming of the Shrew*: A Second Grisel.'" *Texas Studies in Literature and Language* 37, no. 3 (Fall): 285–313.

Brunvand, Jan Harold. 1991. *The Taming of the Shrew: A Comparative Study of Oral and Literary Versions*. New York: Garland.

———. 1966. "The Folktale Origin of *The Taming of the Shrew*." *Shakespeare Quarterly* 7: 345–59.

Bullock, Christopher. 1716. *The Cobler of Preston. A Farce*. London.

Bullough, ed. *Narrative and Dramatics Sources at Shakespeare*. London: Routledge and Paul; New York: Columbia University Press, 1957–75.

Burt, Richard A. 1984. "Charisma, Coercion, and Comic Form in *The Taming of the Shrew*." *Criticism* 26, no. 4 (Fall): 295–311.

Capell, Edward ed. 1767–1768. *Mr. William Shakespeare: His Comedies, Histories, and Tragedies*. 10 vols. London: J. and R. Thonson. Reprinted New York: AMS Press, 1972.

Cerasano, S. P. and Marion Wynne-Davies, eds. 1992. *Gloriana's Face: Women, Public and Private, in the English Renaissance*. Detroit: Wayne State University Press.

Chambers, E. K. n.d. *Shakespeare: A Survey*. Reprint of 1925 edition. New York: Hill and Wang.

———. 1930. *William Shakespeare: A Study of Facts and Problems*. 2 vols. Oxford: Clarendon Press.

Charney, Maurice, ed. 1988. *'Bad' Shakespeare: Revaluations of the Shakespeare Canon*. Rutherford: Fairleigh Dickinson University Press; London and Toronto: Associated University Presses.

Collins, Michael J. ed. 1997. *Shakespeare's Sweet Thunder: Essays on the Early Comedies*. Newark: University of Delaware Press; London: Associated University Presses.

Croft, P. J. 1982. "The 'Friar of the Order Gray' and the Nun." *Review of English Studies* 13, no. 1 (January): 3–20.

Danson, Lawrence. 1986. "Continuity and Character in Shakespeare and Marlowe." *Studies in English Literature, 1500–1900* 26, no. 2 (Spring): 217–34.

Deats, Sara Munson, and Lagretta Tallent Lenker, eds. 1991. *The Aching Hearth: Family Violence in Life and Literature*. New York and London: Plenum Press.

Dessen, Alan C. 1993. "Taming the Script: *Henry VI*, *Shrew*, and *All's Well* in Ashland and Stratford." *Shakespeare Bulletin* 11, no. 2 (Spring): 34–37.

———. 1997. "The Tamings of the Shrews." In *Shakespeare's Sweet Thunder: Essays on the Early Comedies*. Edited by Michael J. Collins. Newark: University of Delaware Press; London: Associated University Press, 1997, pp. 35–49.

Detmer, Emily A. 1997. "Civilizing Subordination: Domestic Violation and *The Taming of the Shrew*. *Shakespeare Quarterly* 48, no. 3 (Fall): 273–94.

Dolan, Frances E., ed. 1996. *The Taming of the Shrew: Texts and Contexts*. Boston and New York: Bedford Books.

Duthie, George Ian. 1943. "*The Taming of a Shrew* and *The Taming of the Shrew*." *Review of English Studies* 19: 337–56.

———. 1951. *Shakespeare*. London: Hutchinson's University Library.

Evans, G. Blakemore, ed. 1974. *The Riverside Shakespeare*. Boston: Houghton Mifflin.

Evett, David. 1990. "'Surprising Confrontations': Ideologies of Service in Shakespeare's England." *Renaissance Papers*, 67–78.

Fineman, Joel. 1985. "The Turn of the Shrew." In *Shakespeare and the Question of
Theory*. Edited by Patricia Barker and Geoffrey Hartman. London: Methuen,
138–59.

Fletcher, John. 1910. *The Woman's Prize, or The Tamer Tam'd. The Works of Francis
Beaumont and John Fletcher*. Edited by A. R. Waller. Vol. 8. Cambridge: Cambridge University Press.

Garber, Marjorie. 1974. *Dream in Shakespeare: From Metaphor to Metamorphosis*.
New Haven and London: Yale University Press.

Garrick, David. 1981. *Catharine and Petruchio*. In *The Plays of David Garrick*. Edited
by Harry William Pedicord and Frederick Louis Bergmann. Vol. 3. Carbondale &
Evansville: Southern Illinois University Press.

Greenfield, Thelma Nelson. 1954, "The Transformation of Christopher Sly." *Philological Quarterly* 33: 34–42.

Greer, Germaine. 1970. *The Female Eunuch*. London: MacGibbon and Kee Ltd.

Greg, W. W. ed. 1939. *A Bibliography of the English Printed Drama to the Restoration*. 4 vols. London.

Hanmer, Thomas, ed. 1744–1746. *Shakespeare's Works*. 6 vols. Oxford: Oxford University Press.

Haring-Smith, Tori. 1985. *From Farce to Metadrama: A Stage History of "The Taming of the Shrew," 1594–1983*. Contributions in Drama and Theatre Studies, no.
16. Westport, CT: Greenwood Press.

Harington, Sir John. 1962. *A new discourse of a stale subject, called The Metamorphosis of Ajax* (1596). Edited by Elizabeth Story Donno. New York: Columbia
University Press.

Hartwig, Joan. 1982. "Horses and Women in *The Taming of the Shrew*." *Huntington
Library Quarterly* 45, no. 4 (Autumn): 285–94.

Hazlitt, William. 1964. *The Round Table & Characters of Shakespear's Plays*. London: Dent; New York: Dutton (Everyman's Library).

Henslowe, Philip. 1904. *Diary. Part I: Text* . Edited by W. W. Greg. London: A.H.
Bullen.

Hibbard, George R. 1964. "*The Taming of the Shrew*: A Social Comody." In *Shakespearian Essays*. Edited by Alwin Thaler and Norman Sanders. Knoxville: University of Tennessee Press.

Highfill, Philip H., Jr., ed. 1982. *Shakespeare's Craft: Eight Lectures*. Carbondale and
Edwardsville: Southern Illinois University Press for The George Washington University.

Holderness, Graham. 1989. *Shakespeare in Performance: 'The Taming of the Shrew'*.
Manchester and New York: Manchester University Press.

Hosley, Richard. 1961. "Was there a 'Dramatic Epilogue' to *The Taming of the Shrew*?"
Studies in English Literature, 1500–1900 1, no. 2: 17–34.

———. 1964. "Sources and Analogues of *The Taming of the Shrew*." *Huntington
Library Quarterly* 27, no. 3: 289–308.

Howard, Jean E. 1986. "The Difficulties of Closure: An Approach to the Problematic
in Shakespearian Comedy." *Comedy from Shakespeare to Sheridan: Change and*

Continuity in the English and European Dramatic Tradition. Edited by A. R. Braunmuller, J. C. Bulman, and Maynard Mack. Newark and London: University of Delaware Press.

Howard-Hill, T. H. 1970. *'The Taming of the Shrew': A Concordance to the Text of the First Folio.* Oxford, Clarendon Press.

Jacques, Oliver. 1662. *A Discourse of Women, Shewing Their Imperfections Alphabetically.* London.

James VI of Scotland. 1591. *Newes from Scotland.* London.

————. 1597. *Daemonologie, in forme of a Dialogue.* Edinburgh.

Jayne, Sears. 1966. "The Dreaming of *The Shrew.*" *Shakespeare Quarterly* 17, no. 1 (Winter): 41–56.

Charles, Johnson. 1716. *The Cobler of Preston.* London.

Johnson, Samuel, ed. 1765. *Shakespeare's Plays.* 8 vols. London: J. and R. Tonson, 1765.

————. 1968. *The Yale Edition of the Works of Samuel Johnson.* Edited by Arthur Sherbo. 16 vols. New Haven and London: Yale University Press.

Jones-Davies, Margaret. 1980–1981. "The Disfiguring Power of Figures in *The Taming of the Shrew.*" *Studia Germanica Gandensia* 21: 223–31.

Kahn, Coppélia. 1975. "*The Taming of the Shrew*: Shakespeare's Mirror of Marriage. *Modern Language Studies* 5, no. 1: 88–102.

Kay, Carol McGinnis, and Henry E. Jacobs, eds. 1978. *Shakespeare's Romances Reconsidered.* Lincoln: University of Nebraska Press.

Kehler, Dorothea. 1986. "Echoes of the Induction in *The Taming of the Shrew.*" *Renaissance Papers*, 31–42.

Kemble, John Philip. 1810. *Shakespeare's Katherine and Petruchio, A Comedy; taken by David Garrick from The Taming of A Shrew: Revised by J.P. Kemble.* London.

Kishi, Tetsuo, Roger Pringle, and Stanley Wells, eds. 1994. *Shakespeare and Cultural Traditions. The Selected Proceedings of the International Shakespeare Association World Congress, Tokyo, 1991.* Newark: University of Delaware Press; London and Toronto: Associated University Presses.

Lacey, John. 1698. *Sauny the Scot: or, the Taming of the Shrew: A Comedy As it is now Acted at the Theatre-Royal.* London.

Lee, Hyung Shik. 1989. "Two Worlds in Shakespeare's Comedies." *The Journal of English Language and Literature* 35, no. 4 (Winter): 735–45.

Leggatt, Alexander. 1974. *Shakespeare's Comedy of Love.* London: Methuen and Co.

Lenz, Carolyn Ruth Swift, Gayle Greene, and Carol Thomas Neely, eds. 1980. *The Woman's Part: Feminist Criticism of Shakespeare.* Urbana: University of Illinois Press.

Levin, Richard. 1971. "Grumio's 'Rope-Tricks's and the Nurse's 'Ropery'." *Shakespeare Quarterly* 22: 82–86.

————. 1979. *New Readings vs. Old Plays.* Chicago: University of Chicago Press.

London Stage, The. 1960–1968. Carbondale: Southern Illinois University Press.

MacDonald, Jan. 1971. "*The Taming of the Shrew* at the Haymarket Theatre, 1844 and 1847." In *Essays on Nineteenth Century British Theatre: The Proceedings of a Symposium Sponsored by the Manchester University Department of Drama.* Edited by Kenneth Richards and Peter Thomson. London: Methuen and Co.

Mack, Maynard. 1962. "Engagement and Detachment in Shakespeare's Plays," in *Essays . . . in Honor of Hardin Craig*, ed. Richard Hosley. Columbia: University of Missouri Press, 1962.

Maguire, Laurie E. 1992. "'Household Kates': Chez Petruchio, Percy, and Platagenet." In *Gloriana's Face: Women, Public and Private, in the English Renaissance*. Edited by S.P. Cerasano and Marion Wynne-Davies. Detroit: Wayne State University Press.

Malone, Edmund, ed. 1790. *Shakespeare's Plays and Poems*. 10 vols. London: J. Rivington and Son.

Marcus, Leah. 1992. "The Shakespearian Editor as Shrew-Tamer." *English Literary Renaissance* 22, no. 2 (Spring): 177–200. Revised and reprinted as "The Editor as Tamer" in *Unediting the Renaissance*. London and New York: Routledge, 1996.

Mazzio, Carla. 1997. "Sins of the Tongue." In *The Body in Parts: Fantasies of Corporeality in Early Modern Europe*. Edited by David Hillman and Carla Mazzio. New York and London: Routledge.

McLuskie, Kathleen. 1977. "Feminist Deconstruction: The Example of Shakespeare's *Taming of the Shrew*." *Red Letters* 12: 33–40.

McMillin, Scott. 1972. "Casting for Pembroke's Men: The *Henry VI* Quartos and *The Taming of the Shrew*." *Shakespeare Quarterly* 23: 141–59.

Miola, Robert S. 1997. "The Influence of New Comedy on *The Comedy of Errors* and *The Taming of the Shrew*." In *Shakespeare's Sweet Thunder: Essays on the Early Comedies*. Edited by Michael J. Collins. Newark: University of Delaware Press; London: Associated University Press.

Moisan, Thomas. 1995. "Interlinear Trysting and 'household stuff': The Latin Lesson and the Domestication of Learning in *The Taming of the Shrew*." *Shakespeare Studies* 23: 100–19.

———. 1991. "'Knock Me Here Soundly': Comic Misprision and Class Consciousness in Shakespeare." *Shakespeare Quarterly* 42, no. 3 (Fall): 276–90.

Montrose, Louis. 1983. "'Shaping Fantasies': Gender and Power in Elizabethan Culture." *Representations* 1: 61–94.

Moore, William H. 1964. "An Allusion in 1593 to *The Taming of the Shrew*?" *Shakespeare Quarterly* 15, no. 1: 55–60.

Morris, Brian, ed. 1981. *The Taming of the Shrew*. The Arden Shakespeare. London and New York: Methuen.

Newman, Karen. 1986. "Renaissance Family Politics and Shakespeare's *The Taming of the Shrew*." *English Literary Renaissance* 16, no. 1 (Winter): 86–100. Reprinted in Newman's book, *Refashioning Femininity and the English Renaissance Drama* (Chicago: University of Chicago Press, 1991), 33–50.

Novy, Marianne L. 1979. "Patriarchy and Play in *The Taming of the Shrew*." *English Literary Renaissance* 9: 264–80.

Odell, George C. D. 1920. *Shakespeare from Betterton to Irving*. 2 vols. New York: Charles Scribner's Sons. Reprinted New York: Dover, 1966.

Oliver, H. J., ed. 1984. *The Taming of the Shrew*. The Oxford Shakespeare. Oxford and New York: Oxford University Press.

Orgel, Stephen. 1988. "Prospero's Wife." In *Representing the English Renaissance*. Edited by Stephen Greenblatt. Berkeley: University of California Press.

Parker, Patricia, and Geoffrey Hartman, eds. 1985. *Shakespeare and the Question of Theory*. New York and London: Methuen.

Paster, Gail Kern. 1993. *The Body Embarrassed: Drama and the Disciplines of Shame in Early Modern England*. Ithaca: Cornell University Press.

Patterson, Annabel. 1994. "Framing *The Taming*." In *Shakespeare and Cultural Traditions. The Selected Proceedings of the International Shakespeare Association World Congress, Tokyo, 1991*. Edited by Tetsuo Kishi, Roger Pringle, and Stanley Wells. Newark: University of Delaware Press; London and Toronto: Associated University Presses.

Perret, Marion D. 1983. "Petruchio: The Model Wife." *Studies in English Literature* 23.2 (Spring 1983): 223–35.

———. 1982. "Of Sex and the Shrew." *Ariel* 13, no. 1 (January): 3–20.

Pope, Alexander. 1723. *The Works of Shakespear. Volume the First. Consisting of Comedies*. London: Printed for Jacob Tonson. Reprinted New York: AMS Press, 1969.

Price, Joseph G., and Helen D. Willard, eds. 1975. *The Triple Bond: Plays, Mainly Shakespearean, in Performance*. Altoona, PA: Pennsylvania State University Press.

Priest, Dale G. 1994. "Catherina's Conversion in *The Taming of the Shrew*: A Theological Heuristic." *Renascence* 47, no. 1 (Fall): 31–40.

Pursell, Michael. 1980. "Zeffirelli's Shakespeare: The Visual Realization of Tone and Theme." *Literature Film Quarterly* 8: 210–18.

Quiller-Couch, Sir Arthur, and John Dover Wilson, eds. 1962. *The Taming of the Shrew*. Reprint of 1928 edition. Cambridge: Cambridge University Press.

Quilligan, Maureen. 1993. "Staging Gender: William Shakespeare and Elizabeth Cary." In *Sexuality and Gender in Early Modern Europe: Institutions, Texts, Images*. Edited by James Grantham Turner. Cambridge: Cambridge University Press.

Quint, David, Margaret W. Ferguson, G. W. Pigman III, and Wayne Rebhorn, eds. 1992. *Creative Imagination: New Essays on Renaissance Literature in Honor of Thomas M. Greene*. Binghamton, N.Y.: Medieval and Renaissance Texts and Studies.

Ranald, Margaret Loftus. 1979. "'As Marriage Binds, and Blood Breaks': English Marriage and Shakespeare." *Shakespeare Quarterly* 30: 68–81.

———. "The Manning of the Haggard; or, The Taming of the Shrew." *Essays in Literature* 1: 149–65.

Rebhorn, Wayne A. 1995. "Petruchio's 'Rope Tricks': *The Taming of the Shrew* and the Renaissance Discourse of Rhetoric." *Modern Philology* 92, no. 3 (February): 294–327.

Richards, Kenneth, and Peter Thomson, eds. 1971. *Essays on Nineteenth-Century British Theatre: The Proceedings of a Symposium Sponsored by the Manchester University Department of Drama*. London: Methuen.

Rico, Barbara Roche. 1985. "From 'Speechless Dialect' to 'Prosperous Art': Shakespeare's Recasting of the Pygmalion Image." *Huntington Library Quarterly* 48, no. 3 (Summer): 285–95.

Rowe, Nicholas. 1709. *The Works of Mr. William Shakespear; in Six Volumes*. London: Printed for Jacob Tonson. Reprinted London: Pickering and Chatto.

Saccio, Peter. 1984. "Shrewd and Kindly Farce." *Shakespeare Survey* 37: 33–40.

Salgádo, Gamini. 1975. *Eyewitnesses of Shakespeare: First Hand Accounts of Performances, 1590–1890*. London: Printed for Sussex University Press.

Sams, Eric. 1985. "The Timing of the *Shrews*." *Notes and Queries* 32, no. 1 (March): 33–45.

Schulz, Max F., William D. Templeman, and Charles R. Metzger, eds. 1968. *Essays in American and English Literature Presented to Bruce Robert McElderry, Jr.* Athens: Ohio University Press.

Seaton, Ethel. 1935. *Literary Relations of England and Scandinavia*. Oxford: Clarendon Press.

Seronsy, Cecil C. 1963. "*Supposes* as the Unifying Theme in *The Taming of the Shrew*." *Shakespeare Quarterly* 14: 15–30.

Sirluck, Katherine A. 1991. "Patriarchy, Pedagogy, and the Divided Self in *The Taming of the Shrew*." *University of Toronto Quarterly* 60, no. 4 (Summer): 417–34.

Wells Slights, Camille. 1989. "The Raw and the Cooked in *The Taming of the Shrew*." *Journal of English and Germanic Philology* 88, no. 2 (April): 168–89.

Smith, Molly Easo. 1995. "John Fletcher's Response to the Gender Debate: *The Woman's Prize* and *The Taming of the Shrew*." *Papers on Language and Literature* 31, no. 1 (Winter): 38–60.

Sokol, B. J. 1985. "A Spenserian Idea in *The Taming of the Shrew*." *English Studies* 66, no. 4 (August): 310–16.

Taming of a Shrew, The. 1594. Malone Society Reprints, vol. 160. Oxford: Oxford University Press.

Theobald, Lewis, ed. 1733. *Shakespeare's Works*. 7 vols. London: Bettesworth and C. Hitch, J. Tonson.

Thorne, W. B. 1968. "Folk Elements in *The Taming of the Shrew*." *Queen's Quarterly* 75: 482–96.

Thompson, Ann, ed. 1984. *The Taming of the Shrew*. The New Cambridge Shakespeare. Cambridge: Cambridge University Press.

Tillyard, E. M. W., 1964. "The Fairy-Tale Element in *The Taming of the Shrew*." In *Shakespeare: 1564–1964, A Collection of Modern Essays by Various Hands*. Edited by Edward A. Bloom. Providence: Brown University Press, 1964.

Turner, James Grantham, ed. 1993. *Sexuality and Gender in Early Modern Europe: Institutions, Texts, Images*. Cambridge: Cambridge University Press.

Underdown, David. 1985. "The Taming of the Scold: The Enforcement of Patriarchal Authority in Early Modern England." In *Order and Disorder in Early Modern England*. Edited by Anthony Fletcher and John Stevenson. Cambridge: Cambridge University Press.

Van Doren, Mark. 1939. *Shakespeare*. New York: Henry Holt and Co.

Warburton, William, ed. 1747. *Shakespeare's Works*. 8 vols. London: J. and P. Knapton, 1747.

Wayne, Valerie. 1985. "Refashioning the Shrew." *Shakespeare Studies* 17: 159–87.

Weller, Barry. 1992. "Induction and Influence: Theater, Transformation, and the Construction of Identity in *The Taming of the Shrew*." In *Creative Imitation: New*

Essays on Renaissance Literature In Honor of Thomas M. Greene. Edited by David Quint, Margaret W. Ferguson, G.W. Pigman III, and Wayne A. Rebhorn. Binghamton: Medieval and Renaissance Texts and Studies.

Wells, Stanley. 1980. "*The Taming of the Shrew* and *King Lear*: A Structural Comparison." *Shakespeare Survey* 33: 55–66.

———, ed. 1997. *Shakespeare in the Theatre: An Anthology of Criticism*. Oxford: Clarendon Press.

——— and Gary Taylor. 1987, "No Shrew, A Shrew, and The Shrew: Internal Revision in *The Taming of the Shrew*." In *Shakespeare: Text, Language, Criticism. Essays in Honour of Marvin Spevack*. Edited by Bernhard Fabian and Kurt Tetzeli von Rosador. Hildesheim, Zurich, and New York: Olms-Weidman.

Wentersdorf, Karl P. 1978. "The Original Ending of *The Taming of the Shrew*: A Reconsideration." *Studies in English Literature, 1500–1900* 18: 201–15.

West, Michael. 1974. "The Folk Background of Petruchio's Wooing Dance: Male Supremacy in *The Taming of the Shrew*." *Shakespeare Studies* 7: 65–73.

Williams, George Walton. 1991. "Kate and Petruchio: Strength and Love." *English Language Notes* 29, no. 1 (September): 18–24.

Wilson, Edwin, ed. 1971. *Shaw on Shakespeare: An Anthology of Bernard Shaw's Writings on the Plays and Production of Shakespeare*. Freeport, N.Y.: Books for Libraries Press.

Winter, William. 1915. *Shakespeare on the Stage*, second series. New York: Moffat, Yard and Co.

Woodbridge, Linda. 1984. *Women and the English Renaissance: Literature and the Nature of Womankind, 1540–1620*. Urbana: University of Illinois Press.

Worsdale, James. 1735. *A Cure for a Scold. A Ballad Farce of Two Acts*. London.

Wright, Louis B., gen. ed. 1963. *The Taming of the Shrew*. New York: Pocket Books (Washington Square Press).

Yachnin, Paul. 1996. "Personations: *The Taming of the Shrew* and the Limits of Theoretical Criticism." *Early Modern Literary Studies* 2, no. 1 (April): 1–31.

PART II.
The Taming of the Shrew:
Critical Appraisals

Figure 3. David Garrick with arm around bust of Shakespeare. Used with the permission of the Folger Shakespeare Library.

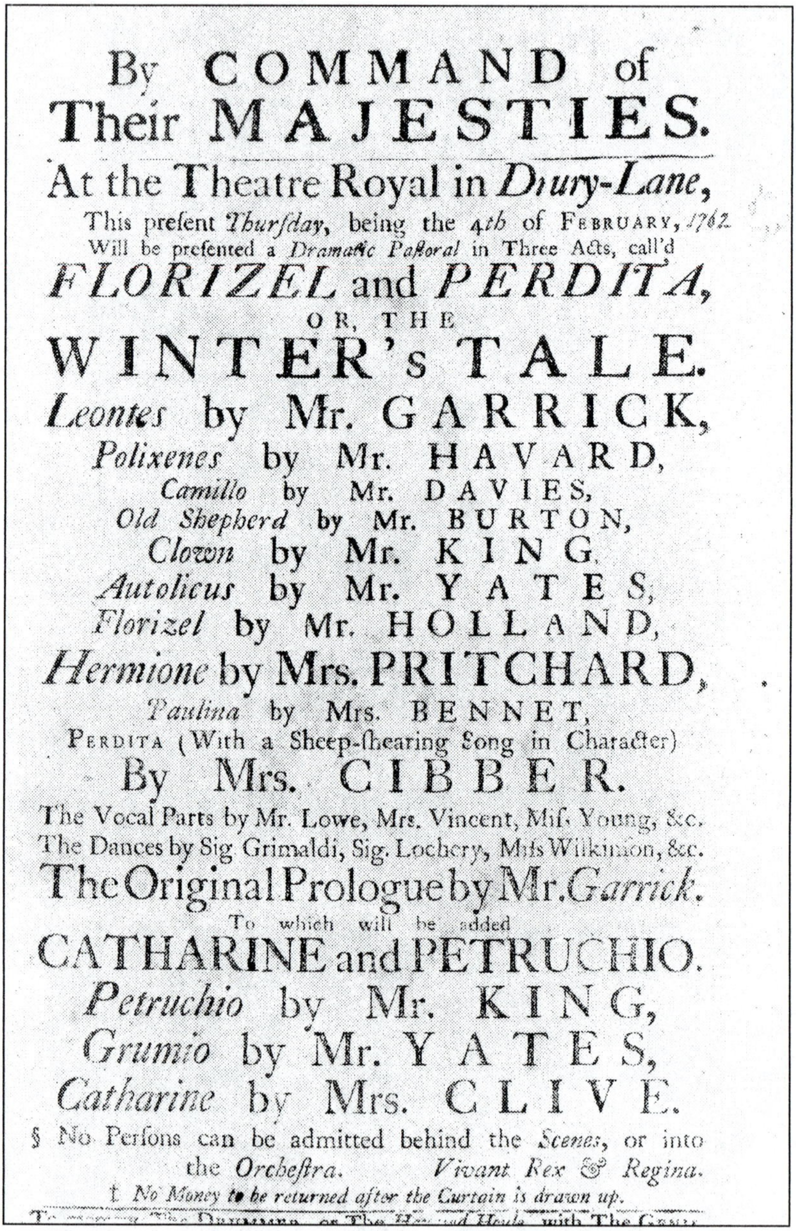

By COMMAND of
Their MAJESTIES.

At the Theatre Royal in *Drury-Lane*,
This present *Thurſday*, being the 4*th* of FEBRUARY, 1762
Will be preſented a *Dramatic Paſtoral* in Three Acts, call'd
FLORIZEL and *PERDITA*,
OR, THE
WINTER's TALE.
Leontes by Mr. GARRICK,
Polixenes by Mr. HAVARD,
Camillo by Mr. DAVIES,
Old Shepherd by Mr. BURTON,
Clown by Mr. KING,
Autolicus by Mr. YATES,
Florizel by Mr. HOLLAND,
Hermione by Mrs. PRITCHARD,
Paulina by Mrs. BENNET,
PERDITA (With a Sheep-ſhearing Song in Character)
By Mrs. CIBBER.
The Vocal Parts by Mr. Lowe, Mrs. Vincent, Miſs Young, &c.
The Dances by Sig. Grimaldi, Sig. Lochery, Miſs Wilkinſon, &c.
The Original Prologue by Mr. *Garrick*.
To which will be added
CATHARINE and PETRUCHIO.
Petruchio by Mr. KING,
Grumio by Mr. YATES,
Catharine by Mrs. CLIVE.
§ No Perſons can be admitted behind the *Scenes*, or into the *Orcheſtra*. *Vivant Rex & Regina.*
‡ *No Money to be returned after the Curtain is drawn up.*

Figure 4. Playbill for *Winter's Tale* and *Catherine and Petruchio,* Theatre Royal, February 4, 1762. Used with the permission of the Folger Shakespeare Library.

From His Introduction to
The Taming of the Shrew (1928)

SIR ARTHUR QUILLER-COUCH

So we turn back from the intrigue of Ariosto to the real stuff of our play; the Induction and all the Petruchio-Katharina business. The "sources" or "derivation" of both of these can be dismissed by sensible men at once; the Induction theme—of the drunken sleeper awakened—being at least as old as the poem to the tale of Abu Hassan in *The Arabian Nights*, the shrew-taming scenes as old as the hills. Who ever possessed a grandfather that could not be roused from the chimney corner as by the sound of a trumpet to cap either of them with an analogous local tradition? The affair of the wives' wager at the end, too, is pure folk-lore. Shrews in especial, and stories of them, stick in the memories of old men who can "mind" when there were such things as ducking-stools. And this kind of robust story imposed upon jejune Italian intrigue undoubtedly gives *The Shrew* something racy, English and highly Elizabethan. *I Suppositi* has its polite revenge in civilising much of *A Shrew* which is in places coarse, and unforgivably coarse when it puts some of its grossest words into the mouth of Katharina. Indeed we may own not only of *A Shrew* but of *The Shrew* that they have not outworn the centuries comparably with the mass of Shakespeare's better plays. They are of primitive, somewhat brutal, stuff. We may not in this age have harked back to the chivalry of the Courts of Love or idealising of womanhood which the worship of Mary carried as a noble fashion into Court and tourney: we may understand as we read Chaucer the concomitance in his day of *Troilus* or *The Knight's Tale* with the lewder stories of his pilgrims, and even fit their meanings together intelligently in the *Prologue* and *Tale* of the *Wyfe of Bath*. But we do not and cannot, whether for better or worse, easily think of woman and her wedlock vow to obey quite in terms of—

> A spaniel, a wife and a walnut tree,—
> The more you whip 'em, the better they be.

Let us put it that to any modern civilised man, reading *A Shrew* or *The Shrew* in his library, the whole Petruchio business (in *A Shrew* he is called Ferrando) may seem, with its noise of whip- cracking, scoldings, its throwing about of cooked food, and its general playing of "the Devil amongst the Tailors," tiresome—and to any modern woman, not an antiquary, offensive as well. It is of its nature rough, *criard*: part of the fun of those fairs at which honest rustics won prizes by grinning through horse-collars.

To call *The Shrew* a masterpiece is not only to bend criticism into sycophancy and a fawning upon Shakespeare's name. It does worse. Accepted, it sinks our standard of judgment, levels it, and by levelling forbids our understanding of how a great genius operates; how consummate it can be at its best, how flagrantly bad at its worst.

We hold that no one walking on any such safe respectable level between heaven and hell can ever grasp the range of a Shakespeare to whom, in the writing of Comedy, *The Shrew* came in the day's work with (let us say) *Twelfth Night* or *The Tempest*. To pretend that *The Shrew*, with its 'prentice grasp on poetry, can compare for a moment with *A Midsummer Night's Dream* or with *Twelfth Night* is an affectation, as foolish as most other human folly; as to assert *The Shrew*'s underplot (the whole Ariosto intrigue) as master-work. Any careful, candid examination will expose it as patchwork, and patched none too cleverly.

But the trouble about *The Shrew* is that, although it reads rather ill in the library, it goes very well on the stage, in spite of the choice of managers and adapters to present it without the Induction—the one block of it which indelibly stamps it as Shakespeare's. Samuel Pepys on April 7, 1667, went to the King's house and

> there saw *The Taming of a Shrew* which hath some very good pieces in it, but generally is but a mean play; and the best part, "Sawny" done by Tracy [*sic*]; and hath not half its life, by reason of the words, I suppose, not being understood at least by me.

Being a play which invites rant and in places even demands it, *The Shrew* as naturally tempts the impersonator of Petruchio to unintelligible shouting and mouthing. Yet there is a delicacy in the man underlying his boisterousness throughout, which should be made to appear, and, allowed to appear, is certain to please. He has to tame this termagant bride of his, and he does it in action with a very harsh severity. But while he storms and raves among servants and tailors, showing off for her benefit, to her his speech remains courteous and restrained—well restrained and, with its ironical excess, elaborately courteous. It is observable that through all the trials he imposes on her, he never says the sort of misprising word that hurts a high-mettled woman more than any rough deed and is seldom if ever by any true woman forgotten or quite forgiven. This underlying delicacy observed by the actor presenting Petruchio, the play can never fail to "act well," or—as Pope and Johnson put it—to divert.

As for Katharina, only a very dull reader can miss recognising her, under her froward mask, as one of Shakespeare's women, marriageable and willing to mate; a Beatrice opposing a more repellent barrier, yet behind it willing, even seeking, to surrender. Her true quarrel with her sister Bianca (who has something in her of the pampered cat, with claws) slips out in the words which *A Shrew* gives to her—

> But yet I will consent and marry him;
> For I, methinks, have been too long a maid,
> And match him to [too], or else his manhood's good;*

and in her outburst upon her father in *The Shrew*—

> *She* is your treasure, *she* must have a husband.
>   (2.1.32; emphasis Quiller-Couch's)

And there are truly few prettier conclusions in Shakespeare than her final submission—

> Nay, I will give thee a kiss, now pray thee, love, stay. (5.1.140)

There have been shrews since Xantippe's time and since Solomon found that a scolding woman was a scourge shaken to and fro: and it is not discreet perhaps for an editor to discuss, save historically, the effective ways of dealing with them. Petruchio's was undoubtedly drastic and has gone out of fashion. But avoiding the present times and recalling Dickens, most fertile of inventors since Shakespeare, with Dickens's long gallery of middle-aged wives who make household life intolerable by various and odious methods, one cannot help thinking a little wistfully that the Petruchian discipline had something to say for itself. It may be that these curses on the hearth are an inheritance of our middle-class, exacerbating wives by deserting them, most of the day, for desks and professional routine; that the high feudal lord would have none of it, and as little would the rough serf or labourer with an unrestrained hand. Let it suffice to say that *The Taming of the Shrew* belongs to a period, and is not ungallant, even so. The works of our author do not enforce set lessons in morals. If we require moral instruction of them we must take them in the large and let the instruction almost imperceptibly sink in and permeate. He teaches no express doctrine anywhere, unless it be the value of charity as interpreting law. He is nowhere an expositor of creed or dogma, but simply always an exhorter, by quiet, catholic influence, to valiancy and noble conduct of life. Indeed it were no paradox to use even of this rough play the saying of St. Jerome concerning the Son of Sirach, that we read Shakespeare not for establishment of doctrine but for improvement of manners.

NOTES

Originally published as part of Professor Quiller-Couch's introduction to *Taming of the Shrew* (Cambridge University Press, 1923; reprinted 1953 and 1962). Reprinted with permission of Cambridge University Press.

*Quiller-Couch quotes from *A Shrew* as found in "Shakespeare's Library" (Hazlitt's ed., Part II, vol. 2, scene 5, pp. 70–72). For Quiller-Couch's quotations of *The Shrew*, I refer the reader to *The Complete Works of Shakespeare*, ed. David Bevington, 4th ed. (1992).

The *Taming* Untamed, or, The Return of the Shrew

ROBERT B. HEILMAN

For some three hundred years Shakespeare's *Taming of the Shrew* was generally accepted as being about the taming of a shrew. Kate was a shrew, Petruchio was a tamer, and he tamed Kate. In the theater the taming developed a long tradition of boisterousness and rowdiness: Petruchio did a good deal of roaring about and cracking a whip. Indeed, for three centuries audiences so relished Petruchio's gaining his mastery that they rarely saw the full Shakespeare in the theater but were content in its stead with a series of raucous shorter plays, one by Garrick himself, that offered much coarser and less adult transactions between the tamer and the shrew.[1] No one seems to have been distressed by this or moved to deny that Kate was at first an insufferable woman and that Petruchio dealt with her in sound fashion. As late as 1904 R. Warwick Bond could say that Kate's early style "contradicts natural law and the facts of life," that Petruchio "demonstrates [to her] the misery of life without self-discipline," and that Kate acknowledges "the justice of the lesson"; and his concluding statement is that "it will be many a day ... ere men cease to need, or women to admire, the example of Petruchio."[2] In 1928 Sir Arthur Quiller-Couch could remark, rather touchingly, "one cannot help thinking a little wistfully that the Petruchian discipline had something to say for itself."[3] A decade later H. B. Charlton could treat the play as strictly antiromantic, Petruchio as a "madcap ruffian," and Kate as simply a shrew; in fact, Charlton is so convinced of her exclusive shrewishness that he sees only inconsistency in those passages in which she complains, laments her fate, speaks of tears, and actually sheds them.[4] When modern editors insist, as many of them feel compelled to do, that Petruchio should not brandish a whip on the stage, they are not denying his role as a tamer, but pointing out that such methods are not called for by the text.

Yet at the same time they are consistent with a certain modern revisionism in the interpretation of the play, primarily of the relations between Petruchio and Kate. Perhaps in reaction against the rowdy Petruchio of the popular plays based on Shakespeare, critics have tended, for at least sixty years, to insist that Petruchio is a much subtler tamer than he had once seemed, that he is not a slam-bang wife-beating type, but a generous and affectionate fellow whose basic method is to bring out the best in his fiancée and wife by holding up before her an image both of what she is and of what she can become. But historically this moderating of the boisterous Petruchio is less than a tremendous revisionary leap that occurred after World War II. Of this leap, there were actually a few intimations long ago. Even Bond, who thought Petruchio an example for us all, feared that Petruchio's order to Kate "to throw off her cap and tread on it" was a "needless affront to her feelings" (lviii). Before Bond, however, there had been a still stronger outbreak of modern sensibility. As early as 1890 George Bernard Shaw, without questioning the basic relationship of tamer and shrew, had nevertheless declared that a modern gentleman, if he attended the play with a woman companion, was bound to be embarrassed by Kate's long speech of submission near the end of act 5, scene 2. The scene, he said, is "altogether disgusting to modern sensibility."[5]

The first step in revision, then, is to back off from the play as it stands and to find Shakespeare out of line with modern feeling: women do not and should not submit. Sir Arthur Quiller-Couch acknowledged, though reluctantly, that Shakespeare is in some respects passé, that "Petruchio's [method] was undoubtedly drastic and has gone out of fashion" (xxvi). Yet this is a mild demurrer compared with the second step, the leap as I have called it, that began about fifteen years ago: the real and more astonishing revisionism, far from declaring Shakespeare out of line with modern sentiment, is to declare him actually consistent with it but in ways appreciated only now in mid-twentieth century. In brief, he has really presented Kate, not as a shrew, but as a modern girl. This new being has only "developed the defensive technique of shrewishness" against her "horrible family"—that is, a father ready to "sell" her to "the highest bidder," and "her sly little sister." This is from Nevill Coghill in 1950. According to Coghill, Kate triumphs not only over that family, but likewise over Petruchio himself, though, "like most of those wives that are the natural superiors of their husbands, she allows Petruchio the mastery in public."[6] This remarkable view found confirmation and elaboration a year later in the work of the late Harold Goddard. To him, Kate's "shrewishness," a term he declared applicable only "in the most superficial sense," is "the inevitable result of her father's gross partiality"; Kate is no more than "a cross child who is starved for love." Baptista is a "family tyrant," and it is Bianca who is more nearly the shrew.

> And the play ends with the prospect that Kate is going to be more nearly the tamer than the tamed, Petruchio more nearly the tamed than the tamer, though his wife naturally will keep the true situation under cover. So taken,

the play is an early version of *What Every Woman Knows*—what every woman knows being, of course, that the woman can lord it over the man so long as she allows him to think he is lording it over her.[7]

The modern Petruchio is now simply the man who is fooled. In 1958 Margaret Webster—whose great-grandfather Ben Webster in 1844 had restored the original Shakespeare *Taming* to the stage as a rival to Garrick's shorter and simpler version—carried on from Coghill and Goddard. To her, Kate is "a 'modern' woman, of intellect, courage, and enormous energy of mind and body, shut up in a society where women were supposed only to look decorative." It is as if Shakespeare's script had been rewritten by Ibsen. This Kate, unlike Goddard's, does not want to get married; she thinks the local boys "beneath contempt"; she "despises her father . . . and her silly, pretty, popular, horrid little sister. She takes exasperated refuge in terrifying everybody in sight."[8]

So much for the unusual development of Kate, for the complete turn of the shrew. Let us look for a moment at her final speech of submission, which Shaw was the first to find distasteful. It has been variously read. Mark Van Doren was the first recent critic (1939) to help establish the modern trend. This long speech, he says, "would be painful to us were she a person as Portia and Imogen are persons."[9] That is, she is less a human being than a mechanical figure in farce. On the other hand Donald Stauffer, even while making a rather modern reading of the play ten years after Van Doren, reminds the reader, "No less than Milton, Shakespeare accepts the natural subordination of woman to man in the state of marriage."[10] In the next year (1950) Nevill Coghill, who as we have seen starts Kate's career as a clever modern girl, acknowledges that the concept of wifely obedience is "generously and charmingly asserted by Katerina at the end."[11] A year later George I. Duthie felt constrained to issue a warning that the play is "liable to be seriously misunderstood by the modern reader" and to insist, "Katharine's last speech in the play is an enunciation of the doctrine of order as applied to the domestic milieu. . . . An insubordinate wife corresponds to a rebellious subject."[12] But in that same year (1951) Goddard exclaims violently over the submission speech, "How intolerable it would be if she and Shakespeare really meant it (as if Shakespeare could ever have meant it!)."[13] And seven years later, in 1958, Margaret Webster treats the speech outright as an ironic jest by Kate; it expresses her "delicious realization . . . that to 'serve, love and obey' in all outward seeming is the surest road to victory."[14] So judicious a critic as Francis Fergusson suggests that the speech might be used "to return us to the sadder and wiser human world," but his key phrase about the speech is "ironic as it is."[15] The ironic follow-up to this is Peter Alexander's remark three years later in 1961. Kate, he says, "shows a strength and independence that make us wish that Shakespeare could have contrived in the end to show more clearly that she stoops to conquer."[16]

There is something almost shocking about Alexander's restraint. While others boldly modernize Kate, Alexander merely wishes that Shakespeare had modernized her.

After three centuries of relative stability, then, Petruchio has developed rather quickly, first from an animal tamer to a gentleman-lover who simply brings out the best in Kate, and then at last to a laughable victim of the superior spouse who dupes him. Kate, at the same time, develops from a shrew to a mistreated and lovelorn daughter to a fighting young feminist who defeats both family and husband. Not only have we tamed the tamer; we have been taming *The Taming* itself. We have been hacking away at its bounding and boisterous freedom, and, with inclinations that would doubtless be called liberal, imprisoned the play in a post-Ibsen world modified by the Wilde of *The Importance of Being Earnest* and the Shaw of *Man and Superman*. We have domesticated a free-swinging farce and made it into a brittlely ironic closet drama, the voice of a woman's world in which apron strings, while proclaiming themselves the gentle badge of duty, snap like an overseer's lash. We have, as I shall try to show, got too far away from the text, or at least from some of it. We have done so, in the main, because, perhaps out of some unrecognized aesthetic snobbery, we have gradually become less willing to recognize *The Taming* as a farce. It is true that most critics of the play have continued to use the term *farce*,[17] and relatively few have made an issue of wanting to qualify or do away with the term.[18] But even when the term itself is used, there is an underground tendency to move away from the concepts normally implied by it. Further, the flight from farce, if we may call it that, reflects a rather hazy idea about the nature of farce, and this haziness has naturally not increased the clarity of discussions of *The Taming*.[19] We tend to take farce simply as hurly-burly theater, with much slapstick, roughhouse (Petruchio with a whip, as in the older productions), pratfalls, general confusion, trickery, uproars, gags, practical jokes, and so on. Yet such characteristics, which often do appear in farce, are surface manifestations. What we need to identify is the "spirit of farce" which lies behind them. We should then be able to look more discerningly at *The Taming*—to see in what sense it is a farce, and what it does with the genre of farce.

II

A genre is a conventionalized way of dealing with actuality, and different genres represent different habits of the human mind, or minister to the human capacity for finding pleasure in different styles of artistic representation. "Romance," for instance, is the genre which conceives of obstacles, dangers, and threats, especially those of an unusual or spectacular kind, as yielding to human ingenuity, spirit, or just good luck. On the other hand "naturalism," as a literary mode, conceives of man as overcome by the pressure of outer forces, especially those of a dull, grinding persistence. The essential procedure of farce is to deal with people as if they lack, largely or totally, the physical, emotional, intellectual, and moral sensitivity that we think of as "normal." The undying popularity of farce for several thousand years indicates that, though "farce" is often a term of disparagement, a great many people, no doubt all of us at times, take pleasure in seeing human beings acting as if they were very limited human beings. Farce offers a spectacle that resembles daily actuality but lets us participate without feeling the responsibilities and liabilities that the situation would normally evoke. Perhaps we feel superior to the diminished men and women in the plot; perhaps we harmlessly work off aggressions (since verbal and physical assaults are frequent in farce). Participation in farce is easy on us; in it we escape the full complexity of our own natures and cut up without physical or moral penalties. Farce is the realm without pain or conscience. Farce offers a holiday from vulnerability, consequences, costs. It is the opposite of all the dramas of disaster in which a man's fate is too much for him. It carries out our persistent if unconscious desire to simplify life by a selective anaesthetizing of the whole person; in farce, man retains all his energy yet never gets really hurt. The give-and-take of life becomes a brisk skirmishing in which one needs neither health insurance nor liability insurance; when one is on the receiving end and has to take it, he bounces back up resiliently, and when he dishes it out, his pleasure in conquest is never undercut by the guilt of inflicting injury.

In farce, the human personality is without depth. Hence action is not slowed down by thought or by the friction of competing motives. Everything goes at high speed, with dash, variety, never a pause for stocktaking, and ever an athlete's quick glance ahead at the action coming up next. No sooner do the Players come in than the Lord plans a show to help bamboozle Sly. As soon as Baptista appears with his daughters and announces the marriage priority, other lovers plan to find a man for Kate, Lucentio falls in love with Bianca and hits on an approach in disguise, Petruchio plans to go for Kate, Bianca's lovers promise him support, Petruchio begins his suit and introduces Hortensio into the scramble of disguised lovers. Petruchio rushes through the preliminary business with Baptista and the main business with Kate, and we have a marriage. The reader is hurried over the rivalries of Bianca's lovers, making their bids to Baptista and appealing directly to the girl herself, back to Kate's wedding-day scandals and out into the country for the postmarital welter of disturbances; then we shift back and forth regularly from rapid action in the Kate plot to almost equally rapid action in the Bianca plot. And so on. The driving pace made possible, and indeed necessitated, by the absence of depth is brilliantly managed.

In the absence of depth one is not bothered by distractions; in fact, what are logically distractions are not felt as such if they fit into the pattern of carefree farcical hammer and tongs, cut and thrust. At Petruchio's first appearance the "knocking at the gate" confusion is there for fun, not function (1.2.1–45). The first hundred lines between Grumio and Curtis (4.1) are a lively rattle, full of the verbal and physical blows of farce, but practically without bearing on the action. Kate is virtually forgotten for sixty lines (4.3) as Petruchio and Grumio fall into their virtuoso game of abusing the tailor. Furthermore, action without depth has a mechanical, automatic quality: when two Vincentios appear (5.1), people do not reason about the duplication, but, frustrated by confusion and bluffing, quickly have recourse to blows and insults, accusations of madness and chicanery, and threats of arrest—standard procedures in farce from Plautus on. Vincentio's "Thus strangers may be haled and abused" is not a bad description of the manners of farce, in which incapacity to sort things out is basic. Mechanical action, in turn, often tends to symmetrical effects (shown most clearly in *The Comedy of Errors*, in which Shakespeare has two pairs of identical twins): the lovers of Kate and Bianca first bargain with Baptista, then approach the girls; Hortensio and Tranio (as Lucentio) resign their claims to Bianca in almost choral fashion; Bianca and the Widow (Hortensio's new spouse) respond identically to the requests of their husbands. In this final scene we have striking evidence of the manipulation of personality in the interest of symmetrical effect. Shakespeare unmistakably wants a double reversal of role at the end, a symmetry of converse movements. The new Kate has developed out of a shrew, so the old Bianca must develop into a shrew. The earlier treatment of her hardly justifies her sudden transformation, immediately after marriage, into a cool, offhand, recalcitrant, even challenging wife. Like many another character in farce, she succumbs to the habits of the generic form. Yet some modern critics treat her as harshly as if from the start she were a particularly obnoxious female.

All these effects come from a certain arbitrarily limited sense of personality. Those who have this personality are not really hurt, do not think much, are not much troubled by scruples. Farce often turns on practical jokes, in which the sadistic impulse is not restrained by any sense of injury to the victim. It would never occur to anyone that Sly might be pained or humiliated by acting as a Lord and then being let down. No one hesitates to make rough jokes about Kate (even calling her "fiend of hell") in her hearing. No one putting on a disguise to dupe others has any ethical inhibitions; the end always justifies the means. When Kate "breaks the lute to" Hortensio, farce requires that he act terrified; but it does not permit him to be injured or really resentful or grieved by the loss of the lute, as a man in a nonfarcical world might well be. Verbal abuse is almost an art form; it does not hurt, as it would in ordinary life. No one supposes that the victims of Petruchio's manhandling and tantrums—the priest and sexton at the wedding, the servants and tradesmen at his home—really feel the outrageous treatment that they get. When Petruchio and Hortensio call "To her" to Kate and the Widow, it is like starting a dogfight or cockfight. Petruchio's order to Kate to bring out the other wives is like having a trained dog retrieve a stick. The scene is possible because one husband and three wives are not endowed with full human personalities; if they were, they simply could not function as trainer, retriever, and sticks.

In identifying the farcical elements in *The Shrew*, we have gradually shifted from the insensitivity that the characters must have to the mechanicalness of their responses. These people rarely think, hesitate, deliberate, or choose; they act just as quickly and unambiguously as if someone had pressed a control button. Farce simplifies life by making it not only painless but also automatic; indeed, the two qualities come together in the concept of man as machine. (The true opposite of farce is Capek's *R.U.R.*, in which manlike robots actually begin to feel.) There is a sense in which we might legitimately call the age of computers a farcical one, for it lets us feel that basic choices are made without mental struggle or will or anxiety, and as speedily and inevitably as a series of human ninepins falling down one after another on the stage when each is bumped by the one next to it. "Belike you mean," says Kate to Petruchio, "to make a puppet of me" (4.3.103). It is what farce does to all characters.

Now the least obvious and at the same time most fundamental illustration of the farcical view of life lies not in some of the peripheral goings on that we have been observing, but in the title action itself: the taming of the shrew. Essentially—we will come shortly to the necessary qualifications—Kate is conceived of as responding automatically to a certain kind of calculated treatment, as automatically as an animal to the devices of a skilled trainer. Petruchio not only uses the word *tame* more than once, but openly compares his method to that used in training falcons (4.1.191 ff.). There is no reason whatever to suppose that this was not meant quite literally. Petruchio is not making a great jest or developing a paradoxical figure but is describing a process taken at face value. He tells exactly what he has done and is doing—withholding food and sleep until the absolute need of them brings assent. (We hardly note that up to a point the assumptions are those of the "third degree" and of the more rigorous "cures" of bad habits: making it more unprofitable to assert one's will or one's bad habits than to act differently.) Before he sees Kate, he explicitly announces his method: he will assert, as true, the opposite of whatever she says and does and is, that is to say, he will frustrate the manifestations of her will and establish the dominance of his own. Without naming them, he takes other steps that we know to be important in animal training. From the beginning he shows that he will stop at nothing to achieve his end, that he will not hesitate for a second to do anything necessary—to discard all dignity or carry out any indecorous act or any outrageousness that will serve. He creates an image of utter invincibility, of having no weakness through which he can be appealed to. He does not use a literal whip, such as stage Petruchios habitually used, but he unmistakably uses a symbolic whip. Like a good trainer, however, he uses the carrot as well as the whip—not only marriage, but a new life, a happier personality for Kate. Above all, he offers love; in the end, the trainer succeeds best who makes the trainee feel the presence of something warmer than technique, rigor, and invincibility. Not that Petruchio fakes love, but that love has its part, ironically, in a process that is farcically conceived and that never wholly loses the markings of farce.

Only in farce could we conceive of the occurrence, almost in a flash, of that transformation of personality which, as we know only too well in modern experience, normally requires a long, gradual, painstaking application of psychotherapy. True, conversion is believable and does happen, but even as a secular experience it requires a prior development of readiness, or an extraordinary revelatory shock, or both. (In the romantic form of this psychic event, an old hag, upon marriage to the knight, suddenly turns into a beautiful maiden.) Kate is presented initially as a very troubled woman; aggressiveness and tantrums are her way of feeling a sense of power. Though modern, the argument that we see in her the result of paternal unkindness is not impressive. For one thing, some recent research on infants—if we may risk applying heavy science to light farce—suggests that basic personality traits precede, and perhaps influence, parental attitudes to children. More important, the text simply does not present Baptista as the overbearing and tyrannical father that he is sometimes said to be. Kate has made him almost as unhappy as she is, and driven him toward Bianca; nevertheless, when he heavily handicaps Bianca in the matrimonial sweepstakes, he is trying to even things up for the daughter who he naturally thinks is a poor runner. Nor is he willing to marry her off to Petruchio simply to get rid of her; "her love," he says, "is all in all." On her wedding day he says, kindly enough, "I cannot blame thee now to weep," and at the risk of losing husbands for both daughters he rebukes Petruchio (3.2.99 ff.). (The Baptista that some modern commentators think they see would surely have said, "What do you expect, you bitch?") We cannot blacken Baptista to save Kate. Shakespeare presents her binding and beating Bianca (2.1.1 ff.) to show that he is really committed to a shrew; such episodes make it hard to defend the view that she is an innocent victim or is posing as a shrew out of general disgust.

To sum up: in real life her disposition would be difficult to alter permanently, but farce secures its pleasurable effect by assuming a ready and total change in response to the stimuli applied by Petruchio as if he were going through an established and proved training routine. On the other hand, only farce makes it possible for Petruchio to be so skillful a tamer, that is, so unerring, so undeviating, so mechanical, so uninhibited an enforcer of the rules for training in falconry. If Petruchio were by nature the disciplinarian that he acts for a while, he would hardly change after receiving compliance; and if he were, in real life, the charming and affectionate gentleman that he becomes in the play, he would find it impossible so rigorously to play the falcon-tamer, to outbully the bully, especially when the bully lies bleeding on the ground, for this role would simply run afoul of too much of his personality. The point here is not that the play is "unrealistic" (this would be a wholly irrelevant criticism), but that we can understand how a given genre works by testing it against the best sense of reality that we can bring to bear. It is the farcical view of life that makes possible the treatment of both Kate and Petruchio.

III

But this picture, of course, is incomplete; for the sake of clarity we have been stressing the purely generic in *The Shrew* and gliding over the specific variations. Like any genre, farce is a convention, not a strait jacket; it is a fashion, capable of many variations. Genre provides a perspective, which in the individual work can be used narrowly or inclusively: comedy of manners, for instance, can move toward the character studies of James's novels or toward the superficial entertainments of Terence Rattigan. Shakespeare hardly ever uses a genre constrictively. In both *The Comedy of Errors* and *The Taming of the Shrew*, the resemblances between which are well known, Shakespeare freely alters the limited conception of personality that we find in "basic farce" such as that of Plautus, who influences both these plays. True, he protects both main characters in *The Shrew* against the expectable liabilities that would make one a less perfect reformer, and the other less than a model reformee, but he is unwilling to leave them automatons, textbook types of reformer and reformee. So he equips both with a good deal of intelligence and feeling that they would not have in elementary farce. Take sex, for instance. In basic farce, sex is purely a mechanical response, with no more overtones of feeling than ordinary hunger and thirst; the normal "love affair" is an intrigue with a courtesan. Like virtually all Renaissance lovers, Petruchio tells Kate candidly that he proposes to keep warm "in thy bed" (2.1.269). But there is no doubt that Petruchio, in addition to wanting a good financial bargain and enjoying the challenge of the shrew, develops real warmth of feeling for Kate as an individual—a warmth that makes him strive to bring out the best in her, keep the training in a tone of jesting, well-meant fantasy, provide Kate with face-saving devices (she is "curst . . . for policy" and only "in company" [2.1.294, 307]), praise her for her virtues (whether she has them or not) rather than blame her for her vices, never fall into boorishness, repeatedly protest his affection for her, and, by asking a kiss at a time she thinks unsuitable, show that he really wants it. Here farce expands toward comedy of character by using a fuller range of personality.

Likewise with Kate. The fact that she is truly a shrew does not mean that she cannot have hurt feelings, as it would in a plainer farce; indeed, a shrew may be defined—once she develops beyond a mere stereotype—as a person who has an excess of hurt feelings and is taking revenge on the world for them. Although we dislike the revenge, we do not deny the painful feelings that may lie behind. Shakespeare has chosen to show some of those feelings, not making Kate an insentient virago on the one hand, or a pathetic victim on the other. She plainly is jealous of Bianca and her lovers; she accuses Baptista of favoritism (in my opinion, without justification); on her wedding day she suffers real anguish rather than simply an automatic, conventionally furious resolve for retaliation. The painful emotions take her way beyond the limitations of the essentially painfree personality of basic farce. Further, she is witty, though, truth to tell, the first verbal battle between her and Petruchio, like various other such scenes, hardly goes beyond verbal farce, in which words are mechanical jokes or blows rather than an artistic game that delights by its quality, and in which all the speed of the short lines hardly conceals the heavy labors of the dutiful but uninspired punster (the best jokes are the bawdy ones). Kate has imagination. It shows first in a new human sympathy when she defends the servants against Petruchio (4.1.159, 172). Then it develops into a gay, inspired gamesomeness that rivals Petruchio's own. When he insists, "It shall be what o'clock I say it is" (4.3.197) and "[The sun] shall be moon or star or what I list" (4.5.7), he is at one level saying again that he will stop at nothing, at no irrationality, as tamer; but here he moves the power-game into a realm of fancy in which his apparent willfulness becomes the acting of the creative imagination. He is a poet, and he asks her, in effect, less to kiss the rod than to join in the game of playfully transforming ordinary reality. It is the final step in transforming herself. The point here is that, instead of not catching on or simply sulking, Kate has the dash and verve to join in the fun, and to do it with skill and some real touches of originality.

This episode on the road to Padua (4.5.149), when Petruchio and Kate first transform old Vincentio into a "Young budding virgin, fair and fresh and sweet," and then back into himself again, is the high point of the play. From here on, it tends to move back closer to the boundaries of ordinary farce. When Petruchio asks a kiss, we do have human beings with feelings, not robots; but the key line, which is sometimes missed, is Petruchio's "Why, then let's home again. Come, sirrah, let's away" (5.1.152). Here Petruchio is again making the same threat that he made at 4.5.8–9, that is, not playing an imaginative game but hinting the symbolic whip, even though the end is a compliance that she is inwardly glad to give. The whole wager scene falls essentially within the realm of farce: the responses are largely mechanical, as is their symmetry. Kate's final long speech on the obligations and fitting style of wives (5.2.136–179) we can think of as a more or less automatic statement—that is, the kind appropriate to farce—of a generally held doctrine. The easiest way to deal with it is to say that we no longer believe in it, just as we no longer believe in the divine right of kings that is an important dramatic element in many Shakespeare plays.

But to some interpreters Kate has become such a charming heroine that they cannot stand her being anything less than a modern feminist. Hence the claim that in the submission speech she is speaking ironically. There are two arguments against this interpretation. One is that a careful reading of the lines will show that most of them have to be taken literally; only the last seven or eight lines can be read with ironic overtones, but this means, at most, a return to the imaginative gamesomeness of 4.5 rather than a denial of the doctrine that she is formally asserting. The second is that some forty lines of straight irony would be too much to be borne; it would be inconsistent with the straightforwardness of most of the play, and it would really turn Kate back into a hidden shrew whose new technique was sarcastic indirection, side-mouthing at the audience while her not very intelligent husband, bamboozled, cheered her on. It would be a poor triumph. If one has to modernize the speech of the obedient wife, a better way to do it is to develop a hint of Goddard's: that behind a passé doctrine lies a continuing truth—that there are real differences between the sexes, and that they are to be kept in mind. Such a view at least does not strain the spirit of Kate's speech.

The Katolatry which has developed in recent years reveals the romantic tendency to create heroes and heroines by denying the existence of flaws in them and by imputing all sorts of flaws to their families and other associates. We have already seen how the effort to save Kate has resulted in an untenable effort to make Baptista into a villainous, punitive father and Bianca into a calculating little devil whose inner shrewishness slowly comes out. But it is hard to see why, if we are to admire Kate's spirit of open defiance at the beginning, and her alleged ironic defiance at the end, we should not likewise admire the spirit of Bianca and Hortensio's widow at the end. It is equally hard to see why we should admire Kate's quiet, ironic, what-every-woman-knows victory, as some would have it, over an attractive man at the end, but should not admire Petruchio's open victory over a very unattractive woman earlier. In fact, it is a little difficult to know just what Kate's supposed victory consists in. The play gives no evidence that from now on she will be twisting her husband around her finger. The evidence is rather that she will win peace and quiet and contentment by giving in to his wishes, and that her willingness will entirely eliminate unreasonable and autocratic wishes in him. But after all, the unreasonable and the autocratic are his strategy, not his nature; he gives up an assumed vice, while Kate gives up a real one. The truth is that, with Petruchio's help, Kate's great victory is over herself; she has come to accept herself as having enough merit so that she can be content without having the last word and scaring everybody off. To see this means to acknowledge that she was originally a shrew, whatever virtues may also have been latent in her personality.

What Shakespeare has done is to take an old, popular farcical situation and turn it into a well-organized, somewhat complex, fast-moving farce of his own. He has worked with the basic conceptions of farce—mainly that of a somewhat limited personality that acts and responds in a mechanical way and hence moves toward a given end with perfection not likely if all the elements in human nature were really at work. So the tamer never fails in his technique, and the shrew responds just as she should. Now this situation might have tempted the dramatist to let his main characters be flat automatons—he a dull and rough whip-wielder, and she a stubborn intransigent until beaten into insensibility (as in the ballad which was perhaps a Shakespearean source). Shakespeare, however, makes a gentleman and lady of his central pair. As tamer, Petruchio is a gay and witty and precocious artist and, beyond that, an affectionate man; and hence, a remarkable therapist. In Kate, Shakespeare has imagined not merely a harridan who is incurable or a moral stepchild driven into a misconduct by mistreatment, but a difficult woman—a shrew, indeed— who combines willfulness with feelings that elicit sympathy, with imagination, and with a latent cooperativeness that can bring this war of the sexes to an honorable settlement. To have started with farce, to have stuck to the main lines of farce, and yet to have got so much of the suprafarcical into farce— this is the achievement of *The Taming of the Shrew*, and the source of the pleasure that it has always given.

If we can see *The Taming* in this way, we can have it untamed, freed from the artifices of a critical falconry that endeavors to domesticate it within the confines of recent sensibility; and we can have a return of the shrew without turning Kate into only a shrew.

NOTES

Originally published in *Modern Language Quarterly* 27, no. 1 (January 1966): 147–61. Copyright © 1966, University of Washington. All rights reserved. Reprinted by permission of Duke University Press.
  1.   See Harold Child, "The Stage-History of *The Taming of the Shrew*" *The Taming of the Shrew*, ed. by Sir Arthur Quiller-Couch and John Dover Wilson (Cambridge, Eng., 1928; repr. 1953), 181–86.
  2.   R. Warwick Bond, *The Taming of the Shrew*, Arden edition (London, 1904), lvii, lix.
  3.   Sir Arthur Quiller-Couch, Introduction, Cambridge edition, xxvi.
  4.   H. B. Charlton, *Shakespearian Comedy* (London, 1938), 97.
  5.   Edwin Wilson, ed., *Shaw on Shakespeare* (New York, 1961), 188.
  6.   Neville Coghill, "The Basis of Shakespearian Comedy," in *Shakespeare Criticism, 1935–60*, ed. Anne Ridler, Oxford World's Classics (London, 1963), 207–9.
  7.   Harold Goddard, *The Meaning of Shakespeare* (Chicago, 1951), I: 69, 68.
  8.   Margaret Webster, "Director's Comments," in *The Taming of the Shrew*, Laurel edition, gen.ed. Francis Fergusson (New York, 1958), 21–22. (Hereafter Laurel edition.)
  9.   Mark Van Doren, *Shakespeare* (New York, 1939), 52.
 10.   Donald Stauffer, *Shakespeare's World of Images* (New York, 1949), 44.
 11.   Coghill, 207.
 12.   George I. Duthie, *Shakespeare* (London, 1951), 57, 58–59.

13. Goddard, 1:71.

14. Laurel edition, 23.

15. Laurel edition, 13.

16. Peter Alexander, *Shakespeare's Life and Art* (New York, 1961), 67. Richard Hosley, though more under the influence of modern revisionism, is also restrained: "Kate's speech ... was probably, without denial of the basic validity of its doctrine, as susceptible to an ironic interpretation in Shakespeare's day as in our own." Introduction to the Pelican edition of *The Taming of the Shrew* (Baltimore, 1964), 16.

17. Namely, Stauffer, Fergusson, Webster, and Van Doren. Charlton employs the concept although not the word.

18. Namely, Hardin Craig, *An Interpretation of Shakespeare* (Columbia, Mo., 1948), 90–91. Goddard refers to scenes "where farce and comedy get mixed" (I: 70).

19. The one critic of *The Taming* who makes an implicit definition that goes beyond the external phenomena and essays to grasp its spirit is Van Doren (*Shakespeare*, 48–52).

Horses and Hermaphrodites

Metamorphoses in *The Taming of the Shrew*

JEANNE ADDISON ROBERTS

The relationship between the world of nature and the world of human beings is always of special interest in Shakespeare's plays; and in discussing the "romantic" comedies critics since Northrop Frye have routinely noted the alternation in settings between the "normal world" and the "green world of romance."[1] Just as routinely they have excluded *The Taming of the Shrew* from discussions of "romantic" comedy on the grounds of its "realism" and its farcical qualities.[2] I should like to suggest that important elements of romance do in fact lie under the surface of this play and that an appreciation of these elements helps to illuminate its picture of the interaction of natural and human worlds. Some of the links between the worlds are supplied by Ovid.

I

It is a truth universally acknowledged that Shakespeare was well-versed in Ovid and that Ovidian literature shaped and permeated his writing. In the playwright's early works Ovid's influence is manifest especially in *Venus and Adonis* and *Titus Andronicus*. *The Taming of the Shrew* virtually advertises its Ovidian connections, with two Latin lines from Penelope's letter to Odysseus in *Heroides* actually quoted in Cambio's first Latin lesson with Bianca (2.1.28–29). There is a reference to *The Art to Love* (the *Ars Amatoria*) in the second Latin lesson (4.2.7).[3] There are allusions in the play to the outcast Ovid and to Adonis and Cytherea, Daphne and Apollo, Io, Leda's daughter, Europa, Dido, Hercules, and the Cumaean sybil, all of whom Shakespeare could have learned about in the *Metamorphoses*. Even two dogs have Ovidian names: Echo and Troilus. And most suggestively for my purposes, there is, at the crucial moment of the play, a submerged but significant reminder of the myth of Salmacis and Hermaphroditus.

Superficially it might seem that the mythical and supernatural world of

58

Ovid, with its obvious affinity for the gory surrealism of *Titus* and the rowdy eroticism of *Venus and Adonis*, would be antithetical to the realism and farce of *The Taming of the Shrew*. But I will argue that an appreciation of Ovidian overtones can move our perception of the comedy in the direction of romance, thereby enhancing our pleasure in the complexity of a play that is often thought to be lacking in subtlety.

Metamorphoses ought to be useful in comedy—a form committed by its very nature to the belief that people can change. Muriel Bradbrook has illustrated the use of metamorphoses in early Elizabethan dramas such as *The Old Wives' Tale*, *Love's Metamorphoses*, and *The Maid's Metamorphosis*. She observes, however, that the influence of such Ovidian transformations rapidly faded, and that Shakespeare never employed the device at all, since his comedies are concerned with the subtler forms of change involved in growing up.[4] I think that Bradbrook is essentially right. Although there are hints of Ovidian metamorphoses in the transformations of Bottom and Falstaff, these metamorphoses pose a basic threat to comedy since the changes are nearly always for the worse.

Ovid's metamorphoses are, in fact, not true changes at all but terminal revelations of stasis.[5] People turn into animals, trees, or stones because they cannot grow. Shakespeare's changes are more likely to be genuine. They are signaled by mini-metamorphoses such as metaphors, pretenses, disguises, or stage images. They are distinctive in that they may be temporary or reversible, and they are often progressive rather than static or regressive.

Whereas in Ovid people turn into animals, a primary motif of *The Taming of the Shrew* is the elevation of animals into people—and not only into people but into suitable spouses, a rather more difficult feat. In the Induction Sly is transformed from a monstrous swine-like beast (Ind. 1.34) into a happy husband and a lord. And Kate and Petruchio move through a whole zoo of animal metaphors before they achieve the dignity of a human marriage. Each tries insistently and repeatedly to demote the other to bestial status. And while their refusal to respect the gap between animal and human in the Chain of Being is the stuff of low comedy, it is also a violation of humane interrelation. For Kate and Petruchio an important progressive image is that of the horse, and I shall pay particular attention to its uses throughout the play.

II

For the purposes of my discussion it will be helpful to abandon, at least for the moment, the received view of this play as a realistic farce controlled by the masterful Petruchio. It is true that the title invites this view and that folktales and analogues support it, but it is worthwhile to entertain the possibility of a subtext which runs counter to this traditional interpretation—a subtext resonant of romance and fairy-tales in its depiction of two flawed lovers in

quest of an ideal union. This approach flies in the face of long critical practice
and requires a considerable suspension of disbelief, but it will, I believe, prove
fruitful.

First, consider the "Induction." Why is it there? Why is it open-ended?
Why does it linger repeatedly and, it seems, needlessly on details of sport and
hunting? Why the persistent talk of dreams? Why the theme of deferred sexual consummation? And finally why is Sly taken for his metamorphosis to the
Lord's "fairest chamber" hung round with "wanton pictures," presumably
those described later by the servants as representations of the metamorphoses
of Adonis, Io, and Daphne?

The use of the induction or frame is, of course, a standard device of distancing, of signaling a movement from the "real" world to a domain of
instincts, romance, and supernatural possibility. The classic instances are *The
Thousand and One Nights* and *The Decameron*, but there are many other
examples. The frame is not, however, a favorite Shakespearean device. The
closest approaches to it in his other plays are the Theseus-Hippolyta plot in *A
Midsummer Night's Dream* and the use of Gower in *Pericles*. In both cases the
frame encloses a fluid romantic world within the fixed perimeters of known
history. The repeated references to dreams in the Induction of *Shrew* and Sly's
resolve at the end to "Let the world slip" can be seen as creating a similar
effect. The chief difference is that the frame in *The Taming of the Shrew* is
open-ended.

Metaphors of the hunt and the use of hunting scenes serve regularly in
Shakespeare as transitions between the worlds of history and romance, especially between the city and the forest.[6] On one level this is predictable and
obvious. Hunting is a sport that takes civilized man into the woods. But in
myth and fairy-tale the journey into the forest world is commonly an exploration of the instinctual and especially of the sexual. In *Shrew* the Lord moves
from his offer to Sly of a "couch / Softer and sweeter than the lustful bed" of
Semiramis (Ind. 2.37–39) by natural progression to his offer of gorgeously
trimmed horses, soaring hawks, and baying hounds. The servants switch easily back to images of lust—Venus', Jupiter's, and Apollo's. These metaphors
alert us to the important themes of animality and sexual pursuit in the play
proper, and they ought also to sensitize us to the play's mythological overtones.

The fair chamber hung round with wanton pictures prepares, of course,
for sexual themes. But even more important, it is a landmark on the road to
romance. Frye points out that what he calls romances of descent frequently
begin with scenes of passing through a mirror—as in the case of Lewis Car-
roll's Alice—or of sleep in a room with such modulations of mirrors as tapestries or pictures. Such sleep, says Frye, is typically followed by dreams of
metamorphoses.[7] In the case of Sly, as in the case of the chief protagonists in
Shrew proper, the metamorphoses we behold represent improvement,

progress. Although Sly's transformation is superficial and externally imposed, we are not allowed to witness his regression. And the play convinces us that Kate and Petruchio are permanently altered. Only the merest trace of true Ovidian metamorphosis—the revelation of stasis—remains buried in the play. I hope to demonstrate this, as well as to show that the deferral of sexual consummation (made bearable for Sly by the diversion of the players) also energizes the courtship of Kate and Petruchio (premarital and postmarital)—not consummated, I suggest, until the latter's final invitation, "Come, Kate, we'll to bed."[8]

III

As we turn from the Induction to the play itself, the most obvious romance convention is that of the paired heroines. It is never safe, of course, to ignore the possible influence of available actors when one analyzes Shakespeare's practice in characterization; one remembers perforce the dark and blonde pairs of *A Midsummer Night's Dream*, and the double female roles of *The Comedy of Errors*, *Love's Labor's Lost* (redoubled), *The Merchant of Venice*, *The Merry Wives of Windsor*, *Much Ado About Nothing*, *As You Like It*, and *Twelfth Night*. But, although available actors may have facilitated its realization, the theme of the multiplication of lovers seems to have been central to Shakespeare's romantic comedy. Often such multiplication serves to emphasize the urgency and irrationality of sexual instincts. In *Shrew* it suggests rather the two sides of one psyche.[9] One cannot make too much of the fact that Bianca and Katherina are sisters: the plot demands it. However, the dark, sometimes demonic older sister and the fair, milder younger sister *are* recurrent figures of romance (Frye cites the example of *Arcadia*), and frequently one sister is killed off or sacrificed in the renewal of the other's life. The argument for linking Bianca and Katherina can be made quite directly: the elder sister complains that she is being made a "stale" (one meaning of the word is "decoy," i.e., double) for the younger sister (1.1.58); Bianca's suitors hope to "set her free" by finding a husband for her sister (1.1.138); and the younger sister appears literally bound and enslaved to the elder at the start of Act 2. When Katherina is carried away from her own marriage feast, her father placidly proposes to "let Bianca take her sister's room" (3.2.250).

Early in the play Katherina has been identified by everyone as an animal—not only seen as a shrew but also assaulted with an extraordinary thesaurus of bestial and diabolical terms. She is called devil, devil's dam, fiend, curst, foul, rough, wild cat, wasp, and hawk, to offer only a selection of epithets and adjectives. Bianca, by contrast, appears sweet, gentle, and compliant until two wry but tell-tale metaphors surface toward the end from the disappointed lovers, Tranio and Hortensio. The former remarks her "beastly" courting of Lucentio; the latter calls her a "proud disdainful haggard" (4.2.39).

At the very moment that Kate is graduating to full human and marital status at the play's end, Bianca reveals her own animality with references to heads and butts, and heads and horns. Her words imply acceptance of animal status: "Am I your bird? I mean to change my bush" (5.2.46). At this point she says that, though "awaken'd," she means to "sleep again" (5.2.42–43); and she virtually vanishes, reappearing only as a shrewish echo in two final rebellious lines. The two figures have merged into one—one more fully human than either of the parts. This is the technique of folk tales rather than of realistic drama.

IV

The relationship of the two girls to their father is also of considerable interest. According to Bruno Bettelheim, children in fairy-tales are turned into animals by parental anger.[10] Baptista's favoritism toward his younger daughter is abundantly clear in the first scene: he assures her of his love; he praises her delight in music and poetry; and he singles her out for private conversation. Later (2.1.26) he angrily chides Kate as a "hilding of a devilish spirit" ("hilding" is a word applied to a horse in its earliest appearance in the *OED* [Oxford English Dictionary] in 1589); and, when a potential suitor for her appears, Baptista actually tries to discourage him. In fairy-tales children transformed into animals are regularly turned back to humans by love, especially in marriage; but in addition they must establish harmonious relationships with the offending parent. It is significant, I think, that both Bianca and Kate are married in the presence of "false" fathers. Baptista never acknowledges a loving relationship with Kate until her transformation is revealed at the very end of the play; then he finally offers "Another dowry to another daughter, / For she is chang'd, as she had never been" (5.2.114–15). Bianca is married with the blessing of her own father (on the wrong man) and that of the Pedant, Lucentio's substitute father. The potential merging of these fathers into one true father is signaled on the road to Padua after the turning point between Kate and Petruchio when Kate says to Vincentio, Lucentio's true father, "Now I perceive thou art a reverend father." And Petruchio goes even further when he discovers the old man's identity, insisting "now by law as well as reverend age, / I may entitle thee my loving father" (2.5.48, 60–61). As daughters merge into one, so do fathers. In the last scene "jarring notes" are said finally to "agree," and Bianca and Lucentio welcome each other's true fathers (5.2.1–5). Lucentio has aptly summed up the situation with his declaration, "Love wrought these miracles" (5.1.124).

The forces working to metamorphose humans into animals are not merely parental, however. Katherina is associated with more animal metaphors than any other female character in Shakespeare. The images come from every direction, but especially from Petruchio. A great deal of the humor of the first meeting between Kate and her suitor (2.1.181–278), for example, depends on the determination of each to reduce the other to subhuman status. She connects him successively with a join'd-stool, a jade, a buzzard, a cock, and a crabapple. He responds by associating her with a turtledove, a wasp, and a hen—and of course his resolution to tame her implies the sustained hawking analogy underlying most of his behavior.[11] In their first encounter each wishes to reduce the other to a laboring animal. Kate starts with "Asses are made to bear, and so are you," and the double (or perhaps triple) entendre of Petruchio's riposte, "Women are made to bear, and so are you," helps to activate a second animalistic analogy which underlies the play—the fallacious picture of beast and rider as a suitable emblem for harmonious marriage.[12]

V

There can be no doubt that the equation of women with horses was operative in Elizabethan culture. Perhaps the most relevant example is that of one of the possible sources of Shakespeare's play, the long poem called "A Merry Jeste of a shrewde and curst Wyfe, Lapped in Morrelles Skin for Her Good behavyour" (London, 1580). The poem is of special interest because it too features two sisters (rather than the three sisters of the old play *The Taming of a Shrew* or the one sister of the source of the subplot, Gascoigne's *Supposes*),[13] the younger and more docile of whom is cherished by the father and disappears early in the tale. In this poem the groom (the double meaning of this word invites equine elaboration) quarrels with his wife and in his anger mounts his old horse Morrell, a blind, lame nag unable to draw and given to falling in the mire; as he rides away, the groom conceives the idea of killing the horse, flaying it, and wrapping his wife in Morrell's skin "for her good behavior." There is no need to recount the brutal details of how he carries out his plan. The point is clear: he wants his wife to be a horse and, in effect, succeeds in turning her into one.

The association of women and horses surfaces also in other Shakespearean plays—notably in Cleopatra's envy of Antony's horse (1.2.21) and in Hermione's reference to women being ridden by their husbands (*The Winter's Tale*, 1.2.94–96). In *The Taming of the Shrew* Gremio swears that he would give Kate's bridegroom "the best horse in Padua" and declares that in Petruchio's search for money he would wed "an old trot with ne'er a tooth in her head though she have as many diseases as two and fifty horses." This grim marital metaphor materializes in the description of Petruchio's arrival at his wedding mounted on exactly such a horse; meanwhile, Petruchio himself has visibly deteriorated to match the horse. The play does not accept the emblem of horse and rider as a proper model for marriage. On the contrary, the Petruchio of this scene is, like his specifically characterized lackey, "a monster, a very monster in apparel, and not like a Christian [. . .]" (3.2.69–70). Biondello says that it is not Petruchio who comes, but "his horse . . . with him on his back." Baptista's remonstrance that "That's all one" and Biondello's enigmatic and apparently gratuitous "A horse and a man / Is more than one / And yet not many" (3.2.84–86) might even be taken as a mock description of marriage—in which man and horse are one flesh. Petruchio has come, not like a proper bridegroom, but like a parody of the centaur at the wedding feast. However, he has none of the virility of the mythical centaur arrived to rape the bride. He looks readier for "The Battle of the Centaurs to be sung by an Athenian eunuch to the harp" than for sexual consummation.[14] And though Shakespeare's play has nothing comparable to those lines in *A Shrew* that overtly reveal the bride's readiness for marriage,[15] most stage productions supply some sign of her awakened interest in her suitor. Her disappointment in Petruchio's tardy and tawdry appearance reflects more than a concern about his breach of etiquette.

And yet the aura of the centaur is not altogether lacking. Petruchio does commit a sort of rape in carrying off his bride against her will. Nor is his comparison of Kate to Lucrece and Grissel unapt; he proceeds to treat her like each of these women in turn. There have been some overtones of the monster in Petruchio right from the start. Critics have often been conditioned by interpretations of the play that depict Petruchio as the wise teacher experienced in animal psychology,[16] and by productions which encourage a blind enjoyment of his macho self-confidence. And yet the text does not necessarily support such responses. From the start Petruchio displays an irrational irascibility that leads his servant to call him mad and drives his friend Hortensio to rebuke him for the treatment he accords his "ancient, trusty, pleasant servant Grumio" (1.2.47). When the violent hero speaks of his coming to Padua as a way of thrusting himself "into this maze" (1.2.55) in order to wive, there may be some doubt as to whether he should be linked with Theseus or with the minotaur. As understandable as the expectation of a good dowry was to an Elizabethan audience, Petruchio's single-minded insistence that wealth is the burden of his wooing dance, and his willingness to accept a Xanthippe or worse if she is rich enough, seems the extreme of folly even to his friends. He compares himself and Kate to two raging fires which will consume "the thing that feeds their fury" (2.1.132–33). His thoughts of wooing are formulated with hunting analogies: "Have I not . . . heard lions roar? / Have I not heard the sea . . . / Rage like an angry boar chafed with sweat?" (1.2.200–2). And his courtship repeatedly reminds us of the hawking metaphor in which he sees himself as the hunter. Hunters in mythology, however, are often themselves in danger of metamorphosis, and from the moment of his venereal triumph Petruchio is transformed into a beast. Granted that his transformation is in part assumed, it nonetheless seems excessive and shocking. He is, says Baptista, "An eyesore at our solemn festival" (2.2.101), and his gross behavior in the church is carefully removed from view on stage. He is a "grumbling groom," "a devil, a devil, a very fiend" (3.2.155), and indeed Kate's journey with him to his country house is for her a descent into hell. The fairy-tale of the two sisters is now eclipsed by shades of Pluto and Proserpina, or of Beauty and the Beast.

VI

The quester one finds in a fairy-tale or romance is frequently accompanied by a dwarf or an animal. It is therefore both amusing and fitting to discover that Grumio, the first to speak in the new hellish setting of Petruchio's house, is a sort of dwarf, "a little pot" (4.1.5) and a "three-inch fool" (4.1.23), and that one of Petruchio's first acts is to call for his spaniel Troilus. Dogs, one recalls, are regularly resident in the lower world. Rather more significant is the description of the newlyweds' journey. In addition to the association of horses with women, it is a Renaissance commonplace that horses represent the passions, which must be reined in by the rational rider for a harmonious and moderate life. The skilled equestrian or the chariot driver is a model for well-governed individual existence. The marital goal of Kate and Petruchio will be, not to ride each other but to ride side by side, in control of their horses, back to Padua. It is a goal constantly frustrated. The curious account of their problems with their horses en route to Petruchio's country estate has no parallel in *The Taming of a Shrew*. The idea might have been suggested by Morrell's tendency to fall in the mire or by a passage in Gascoigne's *Supposes*, where Paquetto speaks of the "foule waye that we had since wee came from this *Padua*" and expresses his fear that the mule "would have lien fast in the mire.[17] In Shakespeare the reported incidents (3.2.55–84) serve as fitting prologue to the scenes at Petruchio's house. Both Kate and her husband, it seems, have lost control of their passions (i.e., they have been thrown from their horses) as they came down a "foul hill." Kate's horse has actually fallen on her, and she has waded through dirt, "bemoiled" and disoriented. The suggestion that her former identity has been destroyed is supported by the discussion among the servants about whether or not she has a face of her own (3.2.99–104), and later by the report that she "knows not which way to stand, to look, to speak, / And sits as one new risen from a dream" (4.1.185–86). Unlike Proserpina, she is eager to eat in this frigid underworld but instead is starved (literally and figuratively), denied proper apparel (cf. Grissel), and assaulted with "sermons of continency" (4.1.182–83).

VII

Throughout Act 4 Petruchio continues to speak of his wife as an animal, explicitly as a falcon (4.1.190–96), and to treat her accordingly. I have never found these scenes very funny. For me, they reinforce Curtis' observation that by now "he is more shrew than she" (4.1.85–86). Kate justly complains that

her husband wants to make a puppet of her (4.3.103). The promised journey
to her father's house is aborted by their quarrel over the time, and the horses
to be ridden to Padua remain unmounted at Long-lane End (4.3.185). In 4.5 it
appears likely that travel plans will be canceled again as the two start out for
Padua a second time and momentarily disagree. But this disagreement leads
to the turning point of their relationship. Kate learns to play Petruchio's game
and acquiesces in his apparently whimsical identification of the sun as the
moon.

It is at this moment that one encounters the submerged evocation of Ovid
to which I referred earlier. Petruchio continues his game by addressing Vincentio as "gentle mistress." Hortensio protests that it "will make the man mad,
to make the woman of him." But now the "game" turns suddenly into a kind
of shared vision. Following Petruchio's lead, Kate greets Vincentio as "young
budding virgin," and then goes on to say,

> Happy the parents of so fair a child,
> Happier the man whom favorable stars
> Allots thee for his lovely bedfellow. (4.5.39–41)

Editors have noted[18] that this speech echoes Salmacis' words in Golding's
translation of the *Metamorphoses*:

> . . . right happy is (I say)
> Thy mother and thy sister too (if any be:) . . .
> But far above all other, far more blisse than these is she
> Whom thou for thy wife and bedfellow vouchsafest for to bee.[19]

What has not been analyzed is the logic and significance of the connection. In
Ovid Salmacis is addressing Hermaphroditus, the young man who subsequently fuses with her to become a hermaphrodite.

The language takes on obvious relevance in *The Taming of the Shrew*,
where the speakers are transforming a man metaphorically into a woman. The
word "bedfellow" evokes the idea of sexual consummation; and the hermaphrodite was a popular Elizabethan emblem for the miracle of marriage,
which joined male and female.[20] One emblem features, above the figure of the
hermaphrodite, the sun and moon (on male and female sides respectively),
reinforcing the idea of the union of these qualities in marriage and adding resonance to Shakespeare's scene, where the two heavenly bodies have become
interchangeable. The alchemical Rebis features a similar image of the hermaphrodite flanked by sun and moon, symbolizing the first stage of the
"chemical marriage" which produces pure gold.[21] Another emblem shows the
male and female being joined under a burst of light from heaven, comparable
to the light that has "bedazzled" Kate's eyes. At this moment the hell of

estrangement is lifted. Kate explains her vision as the result of "eyes, / That have been so bedazzled with the sun / That everything I look on seemeth green" (4.5.45–47). As a couple she and Petruchio have emerged from the underworld of lost and mistaken identities to the green world presided over by the true father (cf. *A Midsummer Night's Dream* and *As You Like It*). It is this moment that makes consummation possible. The same moment leads Hortensio to resolve to marry his widow and presumably coincides with the nuptial ceremony of Bianca and Lucentio. And following this moment, Kate and Petruchio mount their respective horses and ride to Padua.

Beryl Rowland suggests that the Latin word *equus* is related to the word for equal—because horses drawing a chariot needed to be well-matched.[22] It is pleasant to suppose that some sense of this meaning inheres in Shakespeare's image, even though it is obvious that the idea cannot be pushed too far. There can be no question that the view of the dominant male and the submissive female survives to the end of the play. It would be absurd to argue otherwise. And yet the substitution of the vision of the hermaphrodite with its two human components for the earlier images of horse and rider or falcon and falconer is progress. And in independence of mind and liveliness of spirit the two riders do seem well matched.

VII

In the final scene of the play bestial metaphors and figures of the hunt reappear—but with a difference. They are no longer in the mouths of Kate and Petruchio except when Kate rebukes the other women as "unable worms" (5.2.169). The widow's reference to the shrew is dismissed by Kate as a "very mean meaning" (5.2.31). Bianca speaks of head and butt, and head and horn, and "becomes" a bird to be hunted and shot at (5.2.46–51). Petruchio denigrates Tranio's greyhound imagery as "something currish" (5.2.54) and insists on the distinction between his wife and his hawk and hound (5.2.72–73). The transformation of the protagonists bodes "peace . . . and love, and quiet life." In this context the trial of Kate (a trial is a recurring feature of the final stage of romance) culminates in the revelation of her true identity and prepares the way for the long-deferred consummation.

The end of this play is not the social celebration characteristic of festive comedy. It shows, rather, the kind of individual salvation typical of romance. As Petruchio says, "We three are married, but you two are sped." The figurative transformation of Bianca into a bird is a true Ovidian metamorphosis— the revelation of terminal stasis. The lonely lovers create a private sanctuary for themselves, but the surrounding world continues to be paralyzed by its illusions.[23]

The benign green world of *The Taming of the Shrew* is explicitly manifest only in the brief shared epiphany of the main protagonists. The violence, both psychic and physical, and the bestial metaphors belong to another kind of natural world—a world of nightmares and unrestrained instincts. The bestial metaphors are not merely weapons in the war of attempted manipulation of others; they are also passing pictures in a fluid scene where transformations are still possible. The very assertion of false images facilitates their confrontation and rejection. In the end it is possible to believe that Petruchio has given up his view of Kate as goods and chattels or as his horse or his falcon, even as Kate has relinquished her headstrong humor. It is, after all, the "sped" Hortensio and Lucentio who persist in the assertion that Petruchio has succeeded in "taming" "a curst shrew." Petruchio himself is equally "tamed."

I am willing to concede that this is not the most obvious reading of the play. Still, if the romantic subtext I have attempted to trace is actually operative, it should not be totally ignored; and a stage production might effectively emphasize it. It demonstrates an oblique, probably unconscious, use of source materials which is, I believe, typical of Shakespeare. It also reveals the poet's uncanny ability to modify a standard tale of male supremacy with a humane vision which helps to account for the survival of his most sexist comedy as a play acceptable to and even pleasurable to modern audiences—truly a miraculous metamorphosis.

NOTES

Originally published in *Shakespeare Quarterly* 34, no. 2 (Summer 1983): 159–71. Reprinted by permission of Jeanne Addison Roberts and *Shakespeare Quarterly*.

1. *Anatomy of Criticism* (Princeton: Princeton University Press, 1957), 182.
2. H.B. Charlton, *The Taming of the Shrew* (Manchester: Manchester University Press, 1932), 6. Charlton is typical in his contention that no Englishman would find the play romantic. He concedes germinal romanticism to the Bianca plot but finds none in the main plot.
3. References to *The Taming of the Shrew* and other Shakespearean plays are drawn from *The Riverside Shakespeare*, ed. G. Blakemore Evans (Boston: Houghton Mifflin, 1974).
4. *The Growth and Structure of Elizabethan Comedy* (London: Chatto and Windus; repr. Baltimore: Penguin, 1963), 88. "Growing up" involves, of course, the development of potentialities already present. Metamorphosis in Ovid involves the denial of potentialities.
5. See Irving Massey, *The Gaping Pig: Literature and Metamorphosis* (Berkeley: University of California Press, 1976). Shakespeare's use of Ovidian metamorphoses is discussed in my "Animals as Agents of Revelation: The Horizontalizing of the Chain of Being in Shakespeare's Comedies," in *Shakespearean Comedy*, ed. Maurice Charney, special edition of *New York Literary Forum* (1980): 79–96.
6. Note that 2.2 in *Titus Andronicus* marks a transition from town to forest; 4.1 and 2 in *Love's Labor's Lost* precede the scenes of male capitulation, 4.1.103–39 in

A Midsummer Night's Dream marks the end of the "dream," and 2.1 and 4.2 in *As You Like It*, with their hunting references, punctuate the green world of Arden.

7. Northrop Frye, *The Secular Scripture* (Cambridge, Mass.: Harvard University Press, 1976), 108–9. For other pertinent passages on romance conventions, see 142–43, 105, 115, and 139.

8. It is noteworthy that Shakespeare again uses the strategy of play as foreplay in delayed consummation in *A Midsummer Night's Dream* and *The Tempest*.

9. The same approach might be used in the case of other such paired siblings as those of *The Comedy of Errors* and *Twelfth Night*.

10. Bruno Bettelhenim, *The Uses of Enchantment* (New York: Alfred A. Knopf, 1976; repr. Vintage, 1977), 70. Bettelheim cites hedgehogs and porcupines. Shrews belong to the same biological family and share the reputation of being unpleasant to deal with. For a discussion of the relation of shrews as animals to shrews as women, see the New Arden edition of *The Taming of the Shrew*, ed. Brian Morris. (London: Methuen, 1981), 121–24.

11. For an analysis of the methods of hawk-taming and their use in the play, see George Hibbard, "*The Taming of the Shrew*: A Social Comedy," in *Shakespearean Essays*, ed. Alwin Thaler and Norman Sanders, Special No. 2, *Tennessee Studies in Literature* (1964): 15–28; and Margaret Loftus Ranald, "The Manning of the Haggard or *The Taming of the Shrew*," *Essays in Literature* 1 (1974): 149–65.

12. This idea is touched on by Marianne Novy, "Patriarchy and Play in *The Taming of the Shrew*," *English Literary Renaissance* 9 (1979): 264–80. Since I wrote this essay I have also heard a good development of the use of the horse and rider emblem in a paper by Joan Hartwig, "Horses and Women in *The Taming of the Shrew*," delivered at the Southeastern Renaissance Conference, Chapel Hill, North Carolina, March 27, 1982 (forthcoming in *Huntington Library Quarterly*). Although asses can be ridden, they are more likely to be beasts of burden, which is the primary analogy implied by Kate. As Petruchio picks up the image, however, it suggests (1) that women must bear burdens, (2) that women must bear children, (3) that women must bear males in the sex act, and even perhaps (4) that women as representative of passion must be "ridden" by rational male "riders."

13. *A Pleasant Conceited Historie, called The Taming of a Shrew* (London, 1594). Whether this play is a source, an analogue, or a bad quarto of Shakespeare's play is still debated, but opinion seems to be moving toward the idea of bad quarto. *Supposes* was printed in *The Posies of George Gascoigne* (London, 1575).

14. Shakespeare's association of Centaurs with the story of how the Centaurs invited to the wedding feast of Theseus' friend Pirithous tried to carry off the bride, Hippodamia (note the horse allusion in "Hippo"), and thus precipitated a bloody battle, is apparent in *A Midsummer Night's Dream*, 5.1.44–45, and *Titus Andronicus*, 5.2.203.

15. In *A Shrew*, sig. B3, Kate says in an aside, "But yet I will consent and marry him, For I Methinkes have livde too long a maid" (sig. B3).

16. See, for example, Robert B. Heilman, "The *Taming* Untamed, or The Return of the Shrew," *Modern Language Quarterly* 27 (1966): 147–61.

17. *Gascoigne*, 18.

18. See, for example, the Arden edition, ed. R. Warwick Bond (London: Methuen, 1904; rev. and repr. 1929), 132.

19. Quoted in Geoffrey Bullough, *Narrative and Dramatic Sources of Shakespeare*
     (London: Routledge and Kegan Paul, 1957), I: 169–73, as a source of *Venus and
     Adonis*. As in Petruchio's speech earlier (4.5.30), Ovid's passage also contains
     reference to white and red (apples and Ivorie) in the face of the object of obser-
     vation. A few lines further on the passage reads,

> And even as *Phebus* beames
> Against a myrour pure and clere rebound
> With broken gleames;
> Even so his eyes did sparcle fire.

The lines are comparable to Kate's:

> Pardon ... my mistaking eyes,
> That have been so bedazzled with the sun. ...

Ovid's original may be even closer to Shakespeare than Golding's translation.
It reads:

> flagrant guoque lumina nymphae,
> non aliter quam cum puro nitidissimus orbe
> opposita speculi referitur imagine Phoebus. ...

See Ovid's *Metamorphoses* in the Loeb Classical Library, with translation by
Frank Justus Miller (Cambridge, Mass.: Harvard University Press, 1977), 202, ll.
347–49. The word "nitidissimus" suggests "bedazzled." The same passage,
echoed in *Troilus and Cressida* (2.3.241) in a speech by Ulysses to Diomed, is
even closer to the Latin. Ovid himself echoes Odysseus' speech to Nausicaa
(6.149–59) in Homer's *Odyssey*. Although it does not prove Shakespeare's knowledge of Greek, the original is followed by an intriguingly apposite elaboration:
"And for yourself, may the gods grant you all that your heart desires; a husband
and a home ... and oneness of heart. ... For nothing is greater or better than this,
when a man and wife dwell in a home in one accord, a great grief to their foes
and a joy to their friends" (6.180–85). The translation is by G. Karl Galinsky,
Ovid's "Metamorphoses": An Introduction to the Basic Aspects (Berkeley: University of California Press, 1975), 188.

20. For a discussion of hermaphrodites in poetry, see William Keach's *Elizabethan
     Erotic Narratives* (New Brunswick: Rutgers University Press, 1977), chapter 8.

21. I am indebted to Robert Kimbrough for directing my attention to the Hermetic
     androgyne.

22. Beryl Rowland, *Animals with Human Faces* (Knoxville: University of Tennessee
     Press, 1973), 107.

23. This idea is elaborated in Novy, 277.

The Good Marriage
of Katherine and Petruchio

DAVID DANIELL

Nowadays, *The Taming of the Shrew* is taken in its entirety, without mutilation, crude business with whips (imported by Kemble) or announcements of the embarrassing incompetence of the prentice Shakespeare. It is winning increasing praise, for the structure of its interlocking parts among other things, and is becoming understood as a fast-moving play about various kinds of romance and fulfillment in marriage.[1]

Problems remain, of course, particularly with Katherine's final speech: modern solutions making it a statement of contemporary doctrine, or of male fantasy, or of almost unbelievably sustained irony, do not any of them seem to suggest that there is much for Katherine and Petruchio to look forward to in marriage. The speech is a disappointment after the tender moment of "Nay, I will give thee a kiss" (5.1.133) which suggested that something was coming with a lot of good feeling in it, an impression later supported by her having the wit to win Petruchio's wager for him. Moreover, submission, as it is first, and strongly, presented in the play, in the Induction, scene 1, is denigration, a game played by pretended attendants; and *wifely* submission, shown even more strongly in the following scene, is sport by a page dressed as the sham wife of a ridiculously deceived "husband." It is all a pastime, and false.

Sly, however, disappears for good, and this is surely right in view of the serious point about marriage which can be seen to be made at the end of the play by Katherine. I want to suggest that it is a truly Shakespearian marriage-play, and as such takes marriage seriously and makes as high a claim for the state of matrimony as, from experience of him elsewhere, we should expect Shakespeare to do. The way into this, I suggest, is through the play's special sense of theatricality, linked with an understanding that it is wrong to think of such a marriage-play having a firmly closed ending.

That *The Taming of the Shrew* is imbued with a fresh excitement about the potentials of theatre now needs little elaboration. The most modern commentators take that as understood, and indeed enlarge on the matter with some precision. G. R. Hibbard in the New Penguin edition (see note 2) refers to

> bravura pieces, conscious displays of the rhetorical arts of grotesque description, farcical narrative, and inventive vituperation. Language is being deliberately exploited for effect; and what, in another context, might well appear cruel, outrageous, or offensive is transformed into comic exuberance by a linguistic virtuosity that delights in the exercise of its own powers.

Brian Morris in his Arden edition notes among much else a contrast of "physical violence with the eloquence of persuasions and the rituals of debate." H. J. Oliver sums up a major part of the introduction to his Oxford Shakespeare edition with the words "Shakespeare certainly plays with the subject of theatrical illusion, and through the Induction and elsewhere seems to warn his audience of the ambiguity of 'belief'."[2] Theatricality is everywhere. The Bianca plot works because people dress up as other people and assume roles. Petruchio, as is now frequently said, plays a part like an actor until he has subdued Katherine. It is universally agreed that the Induction spells out clearly that theatrical illusion can have powerful effect, and that this is important for the rest of the play. In the Lord's two long speeches which so dominate the play's first 136 lines he shows himself to be obsessed with the notion of acting, particularly with the careful creation of an illusion of a rich world for Sly to come to life in. This is even more developed in the following scene as his servants get the hang of the idea and fantasize freely about what sensual delights are in their power to offer. By the time Lucentio and Tranio enter to start the specially mounted play some quite large areas of the capability of theatre to create illusion have been coloured in.

Two things should reinforce the importance of this stress on theatricality itself for the rest of the play. The first is that the opening two scenes are not, in Folio, quite as detached as they are often assumed to be. The labels "Induction, scene 1" and "Induction, scene 2" used in virtually all modern editions, though in some senses technically correct (if un-Shakespearian) only go back as far as Pope.[3] The Folio text begins firmly "*Actus primus. Scoena Prima.*" (and then forgets all about divisions until "*Actus Tertia*"). Though the non-appearance of Sly in the Folio after the end of the first scene of the Bianca plot causes worry to some critics, the Folio arrangement of the scenes might prevent a general tendency to detach him too far. As I shall show, it is not true to say that Sly's concerns are later absorbed into the main action—that Katherine's arrival in a new world created for her has, as it were, consummated Sly's action. But the relentless insistence on the creation of controlled illusion from "*Actus primus. Scoena Prima.*" does, as we shall see, have an important effect on the main actions, and particularly on the relation between Petruchio and Kate.

Secondly, it is difficult to miss the point about theatrical illusion when two early moments of transition in the first scene are so odd. It is peculiar that the hunting Lord's first thought on seeing the "monstrous beast" (having apostrophized death in one line) should be to play such an elaborate trick. That is hardly an expected response. Then, to cap that, he hears a trumpet, and confidently expects "some noble gentleman that means, / Travelling some journey, to repose him here." But it is no such thing. It is "players / That offer service to your lordship." Their arrival, in view of the game of "supposes" that he has in hand, is altogether too apt.

The two opening scenes bring together three of the play's chief concerns: hunting, acting, and the creation of an illusion of a powerfully rich world. As the second play-within-the-play begins (the first is "Sly as lord") Lucentio and Tranio are caught up in a business which carries all three things forward. Lucentio has no doubt of the richness of Bianca: "I saw sweet beauty in her face . . . I saw her coral lips to move, / And with her breath she did perfume the air" (1.1.162, 169–70). With Tranio, he is going to hunt her down: "I burn, I pine, I perish, Tranio, / If I achieve not this young modest girl" (ll. 150–51). And he is soon involved in a situation which makes play-acting both essential and exciting. The direct wooing of Bianca is forbidden by her father, and there are rivals. Indeed, disguise and part-playing are positively invited, as Baptista encourages the rivals to produce "schoolmasters" who will be kept "within my house." The theatrical game spins merrily, with Tranio playing Lucentio, Lucentio playing "Cambio," Hortensio playing "Licio"—and Bianca playing the adorable young girl. Presently a Pedant plays Vincentio. At the end of the play all the disguises have come off. Lucentio is himself and successfully wedded to Bianca who, married, is not quite as she appeared to be when wooed. Tranio is himself, and seems to have been forgiven, as he comports himself boldly. The Pedant and the real Vincentio have, in a good deal of wonderfully rapid business, faced each other out and the truth has triumphed.

All this, however, is more a matter of simple change of name. The Pedant does not even need a disguise. Lucentio is disguised, and Tranio puts on Lucentio's finery (*"Enter Tranio brave,"* 1.2.214). Hortensio dresses up. But the deceptions that are practiced lack depth, and belong to the very fast-moving world of amorous intrigue. Everyone receives the appropriate reward, and the two who are married at the end of this plot, Lucentio and Hortensio, have wives who, as G.R. Hibbard says of Bianca, have realized that "deception is a woman's most effective weapon."[4]

Inside this action is the other, that of Katherine and Petruchio. This can also be seen in the primary colours of hunting, acting and a special richness. It is so clearly set inside, like a jewel in a mounting, that the resulting extension of the signficances comes to be unmistakable. By this device, the action is moved on to another plane, as it were: almost on to another dimension. If *The Taming of the Shrew* is seen as a set of Chinese boxes, then the opening of the last one has some magic qualities. Katherine is most firmly inset. Consider: the audience is in a theatre watching a play about a Lord who makes a play for a tinker who watches a play about two young Italians who watch "some show to welcome us to town" (1.1.47) inside which is a play about the surreptitious wooing of an *amorosa* by a love-sick hero and his rivals. Inside that is set another play about, by contrast, the very blatant wooing of her sister. Katherine does not say very much; compared with Rosalind, or even Beatrice, she is positively silent; but she is undoubtedly the heart of the play. She is introduced at five removes, it might be said, from street-level. At each remove the illusion increases. (We might note that Petruchio's very late entry into the action could well be said to make a sixth remove; the play has run for 524 lines at his entry, before which he is not even mentioned.)

On this interior plane, displacements are not of name or clothes, but of two entire personalities, a very different thing altogether. Indeed, Petruchio has announced himself vigorously from his first entry into the action, and he bombards Katherine, in the very first seconds of their first meeting, with her own name—eleven times in seven lines. He forbids his wife the new cap and gown the Tailor has provided, and his change of clothes for the wedding makes a mockery of dressing-up.

Nor are the displacements, like the others, temporary. Katherine, her "lesson" learned, will not revert to being a shrew. Petruchio, having tamed her, will not revert to bullying. Except that I do not believe that Shakespeare's play says anything quite so obvious, or so final. If, rather than dramatic life on a different plane, there were a straight parallel here with the Bianca plot, it would have to be argued that Petruchio was "really" a gentle person who put on roughness only while he was wooing Kate. To say so is to forget that he enters the play knocking his servant about and his servant calls him, twice, quarrelsome and mad (1.2.13–32). It is to argue too that Kate is "really" an emotionally mature young woman ready for marriage thrown temporarily into desperation by her impossible father and sister. But within thirty-five lines of meeting someone who has come to woo her, who announces "Good Kate; I am a gentleman" she is crying "That I'll try" and "*She strikes him*" (2.1.216). Both have strong violent streaks. Katherine says she will not be made a puppet (4.3.103) to be knocked about, or not, for ever after. Rather, as the further inside, the more the increase of illusion, so the illusion now is of a greater "reality," not less. Unlike "Cambio" and "Licio," Katherine and Petruchio are "real" people. *Their* theatrical dimension allows them to do something quite different, and much more interesting. Katherine and Petruchio can be seen to grow to share an ability to use theatrical situations to express new and broadening perspectives in a world as unlimited as art itself.

I want to come at this now from another direction. Brian Morris, in the introduction to his Arden edition, says "There are few points of possible comparison between *Shrew* and the first tetralogy of history plays."[5] I feel that this is not quite true. There may well turn out to be quite a number—certainly more than it is possible to comment on here. In the first place, there are large areas of superficial similarity in the use of verse, where so often the rhythms of the lines of the *Henry VI* plays are clearly from the same mind as made *Shrew*. Equally generally, there are similarities in certain single lines where the reader, meeting the line on its own, would be hard put to it to place the line in the right play. Thus "I see report is fabulous and false" might be from either a history play or *Shrew*. It is *1 Henry VI*, 2.3.18, where, like *Shrew*'s "And now I find report a very liar" it is in a sexually charged two-hander in the first heat of a meeting.

> Thus have I politicly begun my reign,
> And 'tis my hope to end successfully

taken alone, would be put in the first tetralogy; it is of course Petruchio at 4.1.172–173, though it resembles *2 Henry VI*, 3.1.341, and the tenor of the "jolly thriving wooer" at *Richard III* 4.3.36–43. The *2 Henry VI* line, "Well, nobles, well, 'tis politicly done" also comes early in a soliloquy announcing a programme of action to win a personal triumph, and has the only other use of "politicly" in Shakespeare. The game can be continued. I suppose "Cease, cease these jars and rest your minds in peace; / Let's to the altar" might be mistaken for *Shrew* instead of *1 Henry VI*, 1.1.44–45. Stamping a hat under a foot does not just belong to Kate—Gloucester does it to Winchester's hat at *1 Henry VI*, 1.3.49. There are some similarities of situation. The duel of wits between Petruchio and Kate might be said to parallel the duels between Joan la Pucelle and the Dauphin, or Joan and Talbot, in *1 Henry VI*, act 1, scenes 2 and 5, or more plausibly between Richard's outrageous wooing of Anne, and Elizabeth, in *Richard III*, act 1, scene 1, and act 4, scene 4. Eyes dazzled by the sun—in particular relation to a dramatically significant father—are the basis of special wordplay and action in both *Shrew* act 4, scene 5, and *3 Henry VI* act 2, scene 1. The "martial" quality of Joan and the bluff chivalry of Talbot suggests casting the same kind of actors as Katherine and Petruchio. Fancy can multiply parallels and echoes. It is odd that the only early plays of Shakespeare not mentioned by Francis Meres are the three parts of *Henry VI* and *Shrew*. Further analysis of what they might have in common, especially audiences, needs to be done.

Yet it is not entirely fanciful to see that from the moment of Petruchio's Richard-like soliloquy ("Thus have I politicly begun my reign") the Petruchio-Katherine relationship brushes against the world of the history plays, and indeed with their principal source. The other main plots, concerning Lucentio and Bianca, and the Lord and his servants, are Ovidian in tone and reference, as can be easily demonstrated. Katherina, however, suffers in a different key. Her description of herself as "starv'd for meat, giddy for lack of sleep; /

With oaths kept waking, and with brawling fed" (4.3.9–10) belongs more to Shakespeare's world of war than to anything remotely like the Ovid found elsewhere in the play. The "Beggars that come unto my father's door" who "Upon entreaty have a present alms" of the same speech suggest the same world, of displaced soldiery. She feels herself threatened with "deadly sickness or else present death." Her violent reaction to Grumio's tantalizing game with beef and mustard is to beat him, with words which could be from a woman in the later plays of the tetralogy:

> Sorrow on thee and all the pack of you
> That triumph thus upon my misery!

Her experience of noise and violence and hunger and misery belongs to the earlier history plays.

Petruchio's courtship moves through several areas of reference. Just before he met Katherine, he saw his wooing in Petrarchan terms (2.1.169–72). He can flatter her with classical affinities—"Dian," "Grissel," Lucrece; and carry on like any swashbuckler (3.2.229–35). It is only from the end of act 4, scene 1 that he hopes to end his "reign" both "politicly" and "successfully," and the idea of the warlike is never far away after that. Even his violence about the gown is in battlefield terms: "'Tis like a demi-cannon . . . up and down, carv'd . . . snip and nip and cut and slish and slash . . ." (4.3.88–90). Lucentio, indeed, presently thinks he announces the end of a civil war.

> At last, though long, our jarring notes agree;
> And time it is when raging war is done
> To smile at scapes and perils overblown. (5.2.1–3)

Petruchio won his first victory some time before that, in Katherine's apparent submission over the matter of the sun and the moon: "What you will have it nam'd, even that it is" (4.5.21), and at that point Hortensio thinks all is over: "Petruchio, go thy ways, the field is won" (l. 23). Petruchio, however, has not finished. Almost at once, Vincentio enters, and Petruchio greets him as "gentle mistress":

> Tell me, sweet Kate, and tell me truly too,
> Hast thou beheld a fresher gentlewoman?
> Such war of white and red within her cheeks! (ll. 28–30)

For the moment, Kate has agreed no more than to play his game of presence. It has cost her a good deal, no doubt, and it is a real step forward, which he acknowledges. But he himself goes "forward, forward" (l. 24) from the "war of white and red" to something more than one victory, more even than "peace

... and love, and quiet life, / An awful rule, and right supremacy ... what not that's sweet and happy" (5.2.108–110) when she has won his wager for him. He does not know the full measure of his success until she has spoken her last, and famous, speech.

It is hard not to see in that "war of white and red" a hint of the Wars of the Roses, however well-worn the notion of white and red cheeks was for Elizabethans. The probable dates of the writing of the first tetralogy encompass the likely dates for the writing of *The Taming of the Shrew*. Certainly, close to the time of writing the comedy, Shakespeare put on the stage a symbolic scene in which an imaginary origin is given for the name of the wars, an incident in the Temple Garden when English lords and others pluck red and white roses.

> PLANTAGENET. Meantime your cheeks do counterfeit our roses;
>   For pale they look with fear, as witnessing
>   The truth on our side.
> SOMERSET. No, Plantagenet,
>   'Tis not for fear but anger that thy cheeks
>   Blush for pure shame to counterfeit our roses,
>   And yet thy tongue will not confess thy error. (*1 Henry VI*,
>   2.4.62–67)

In Shakespeare, these wars end with a marriage, a union. His principal source, Hall's Chronicle, is properly entitled *The Union of the Two Noble and Illustre Famelies [. . .]*, and Hall's direction is not just visible in his title. His brief preface, setting out the necessity and value of the writing of history, concludes his address to Edward VI with references to the marriage which healed the national split.

> Wherefore . . . I have compiled and gathered (and not made) out of diverse writers, as well forayn as Englishe, this simple treatise whiche I have named the union of the noble houses of Lancaster and Yorke, conjoyned together by the godly mariage of your most noble graundfather, and your verteous grandmother. For as kyng henry the fourthe was the beginnyng and rote of the great discord and devision: so was the godly matrimony, the final ende of all discencions, titles and debates.[6]

These matters would be merely curious were it not for the metaphoric strain of Katherine's last speech, which is either the proper climax to a marriage-play or it is nothing. Here, indeed, she is speaking in terms which could also be lifted from Shakespeare's earlier history plays.

> Fie, fie! unknit that threatening unkind brow,
> And dart not scornful glances from those eyes

To wound thy lord, thy king, thy governor. (5.2.136–38)

She refers to "thy lord, thy life, thy keeper, / Thy head, thy sovereign" (ll. 146–47) who "craves no other tribute at thy hands / But love, fair looks, and true obedience" (ll. 152–53). There is owed "Such duty as the subject owes the prince" (l. 155): if not, the result is "a foul contending rebel / And graceless traitor" (ll. 159–60). She is ashamed that women "offer war where they should kneel for peace; / Or seek for rule, supremacy, and sway" (ll. 162–63).

Why Katherine chooses such language is the heart of the problem of her last speech. Is she really saying that a disobedient woman is a "foul contending rebel and graceless traitor"? Partly she is, because she is specifically addressing two women, Bianca and the Widow, who have been "disobedient" and who have seemed to have got the upper hand by an unpleasant kind of deception. But the dynamic of the play assuredly means that she has to be saying something private to Petruchio as well. Whatever happened between them, they have been together, and not with the others, all through the play, as a rule. They are spectators, merely, of the wild complications of the Pedant-Vincentio scene, act 5, scene 1, in which the rest of the plots of the play are resolved, and their enjoyment has included enjoyment of each other, so much that at the end Katherine can kiss Petruchio, even in public, adding "now pray thee, love, stay" to which her husband replies "Is not this well? Come, my sweet Kate" (ll. 133–34).

H. J. Oliver has noticed how the matter of Katherine and Petruchio keeps becoming too *well-understood* for farce. "It is as if Shakespeare set out to write a farce about taming a shrew but had hardly begun before he asked himself what might make a woman shrewish anyway ... We sympathize with Katherine—and as soon as we do, farce becomes impossible."[7] This is right, but I take it far further than Oliver would have approved. *The Taming of the Shrew* is a play unusually about marriages as well as courtships, and the quality of the marriage of Katherine and Petruchio might be expected to depend, as I said at the beginning of this essay, on more than a wink and a tone of irony, or a well-delivered paper on the necessity of order in the State. I am suggesting that a special quality of mutuality grew between Katherine and Petruchio as the play progressed, something invisible to all the others in the play and sealed for them both by Kate's last speech. It is surely unsatisfactory for Kate simply to flip over from one state into its opposite, or for Petruchio to have "really" been gentle all along. I suggest that they have found, led by Petruchio, a way of being richly together with all their contradictions—and energies—very much alive and kicking. Beatrice and Benedick go into their marriage at the end of *Much Ado About Nothing* as witty and spirited as ever, but together and not apart. I believe that Katherine and Petruchio do the same, and do it through an understanding of the power of acting, of being actors.

That Petruchio sets out to play a part is now commonly understood. Theatricality, however, attaches to him rather more than has been seen. He is an actor—a man who loves acting with a full-spirited craftsmanship far ahead of the Lord's thin-blooded connoisseurship. He has a violent streak, and is impetuous: but he has an actor's power of control, as well as an actor's apparent sudden switch of mood. He arrives quarrelling with his servant and is still smouldering when Hortensio has parted them (1.2.1–45). But presented instantly with Hortensio's offer of a "shrewd ill-favour'd wife" (which is only Hortensio's thirteenth line) Petruchio shows excellent manners, saying like any easy guest "Sure I'll go along with it." More, he says it as if he were Pistol, in high style full of classical tags:

> Be she as foul as was Florentius' love,
> As old as Sibyl, and as curst and shrewd
> As Socrates' Xanthippe or a worse. (ll. 67–69)

We then watch him move, step by step, towards Katherine. He learns that their fathers knew each other, so he is on visiting terms. He discovers that she has a wider reputation as "an irksome brawling scold" (l. 184) but is loud in his claim not to be put off: indeed, he speaks like a mini-Othello:

> Think you a little din can daunt mine ears?
> Have I not in my time heard lions roar?
> Have I not heard the sea, puff'd up with winds,
> Rage like an angry boar chafed with sweat?
> Have I not heard great ordnance in the field,
> And heaven's artillery thunder in the skies?
> Have I not in a pitched battle heard
> Loud 'larums, neighing steeds, and trumpets' clang? (1.2.196–203)

Of course he hasn't: or at least, some of it is unlikely. He has only just left home by his own confession, apparently setting off for the first time (ll. 48–56). He is using one of his voices. We soon hear another one, in the one delicious sentence from the sideline with which he sums up Tranio's posturing (as opposed to acting)—"Hortensio, to what end are all these words?" (l. 246). He visits Baptista to present "Licio" (Hortensio) and sees for himself the peculiarities of the household. He understands the "little wind" with which the father and sister increase Katherine's fire, and offers himself, in another voice, as a "raging fire."

He quickly takes two big steps towards her, first when Hortensio enters *with his head broke* (2.1.140) and then when he hears as it were a tape-recording of her voice in Hortensio's report ("'Frets, call you these?' quoth she 'I'll fume with them'") and finds that she can make a theatrically appropriate strong action while saying a witty line, and that she has a liberated

tongue ("with twenty such vile terms")—in other words, she could well turn
out to have the stuff of actors too. He is eager to see her, and sets up in soliloquy a programme not based on violence ("raging fires") but on his actor's
ability to present her with a new world for her to live in ("I'll tell her plain /
She sings as sweetly . . .").

They meet, and fall in love. Both are taken aback. Petruchio is surprised
to lose some rounds of the wit-contest on points. But he holds to his purpose,
though she has struck him and made him forget the part he is acting ("I swear
I'll cuff you, if you strike again" [2.1.217]).

Thereafter it is possible to watch him acting his way through his relationship with her, and with everyone else. From the moment of meeting, he is
hunting, and in deadly earnest. He uses all his skills to make worlds for her to
try to live in, as he does, as an actor, even in what appears to be bullying.[8] (She
seems, pretty well from the start, to understand him as an actor. "Where did
you study all this goodly speech?" she asks [2.1.255].) In all his dealings with
her, he acts out a character, and a set of situations, which present her with a
mirror of herself, and in particular her high-spirited violence and her sense of
being out in the cold and deprived. She who had tied up her sister's hands—
apparently because she was dressed up (2.1.3–5)—finds her own hands tied,
as it were, in the scene with the Tailor, where she can't actually get her hands
on the finery that was ordered. The speed of all this action in the central
scenes, in the third and fourth acts, helps by presenting not so much development of "character" as a set of projected slides, almost cartoons, of the wedding, the journey, the honeymoon, and so on. Katherine is not alone in finding
it all "unreal": it is part of a play.

But the play has a clear direction. It is always worth asking what Shakespeare does *not* do. Brian Morris points out what can be learned by seeing
what appealed to the young playwright looking for ideas in the old Italian
comedy. Shakespeare's Lucentio is not desperate for money, and has not
seduced Bianca and got her pregnant, as Erostrato, his equivalent in *Supposes*,
has done. Instead, he is seen "to fall instantly, rapturously, romantically in love
with her at first sight . . . It is this potential for romance, for love leading to
marriage, which Shakespeare detected and exploited in Gascoigne's work."[9]
Indeed, no one in *Shrew* is desperate for money. There is no seduction or rape.
The horrifying violence of such folk-tales of shrews tamed as have been sometimes produced as "sources," or even analogues, is removed far away, merci-
fully, as is any tone of cynicism.

The direction of the play, for Katherine and Petruchio, is towards marriage as a rich, shared sanity. That means asserting and sharing *all* the facts
about one's own identity, not suppressing large areas. Sly, floundering in the
Lord's trickery, tried to assert himself like that (Induction 2.17–23). But then
he sinks into illusion and is never undeceived. That is important. He "does *not*
become what others pretend him to be."[10] Nor does Katherine. If she is a true
Shakespearian heroine, in marriage she becomes herself only more so: in her

case, almost as capable of future strong, witty, over-verbalized action as Beatrice. Marriage is addition, not subtraction: it is a sad let-down if the dazzling action of the play produces only a female wimp. But at the end of the play she shows that she shares with Petruchio an understood frame for both their lives. Whatever Petruchio has done, he has given her his full attention in action; she has learned to act too, in both senses. This, with the special ability of acting to embrace and give form to violence, is the mutuality they share.

Her first clear step was when she learned that simple deception worked (something her sister had, infuriatingly, known by instinct). She privately called the sun the moon, and then publicly greeted Vincentio as a "Young budding virgin, fair and fresh and sweet" (4.5.36). Soon after this, she and Petruchio are shown not only married, but tenderly in love (the kiss). Her final step is when she shows to Petruchio that she has understood that they, the two of them, can contain violence and rebellion in their own mutual frame.

> Now civil wounds are stopp'd, peace lives again—
> That she may long live here, God say amen! (*Richard III*, 5.5.40–41)

are the last lines of the Roses tetralogy. The "war of white and red" ends in a true union of strong, almost over-strong, dynasties, and not in the impoverishment of one side. (Sly had suggested such a link in the fourth line of the play—"Look in the chronicles.")

Muriel Bradbrook made clear what a new thing Shakespeare was making. "Katherine is the first shrew to be given a father, the first to be shown as maid and bride. . . ."

> Traditionally the shrew triumphed; hers was the oldest and indeed the only native comic role for women. If overcome, she submitted either to high theological argument or to a taste of the stick . . . Petruchio does not use the stick, and Katherine in her final speech does not console herself with theology.[11]

Instead of the stick, or theology (which is certainly present at that point in *A Shrew*) Shakespeare makes Kate move herself further into, rather than out of, a play-world. Her final deed is to act a big theatrical set-piece, speaking the longest speech in the play, its length totally disrupting the rhythms presented by the other plot. "Women," she says—that is, the conventionally married in front of her—are to be submissive. But she has been hunting with Petruchio as a couple for some time now, and she sends him, inside the speech, a message about themselves, Katherine and Petruchio, in the language of dramatized civil war. The play would founder—which it doesn't—if Katherine had merely surrendered to a generalization about "women," and said nothing intensely personal about herself and Petruchio.[12]

She concludes, and starts the final run of couplets, by admitting that women are weak in such wars, and must accept it, and indeed, with a startling theatrical gesture she demonstrates it ("place your hands below your husband's foot"). She has successfully acted a long speech with interior reference to an imaginary history play, though only Petruchio can appreciate that. Partly she is telling him that the civil war in her is over, and she will not fight her rescuer. Partly she is rejoicing in their new world.

Brian Vickers demonstrates "the speed and fluidity with which Shakespeare can modulate from one medium to the other as his dramatic intention requires." He comments on the last lines of *Shrew* act 5, scene 1 ("kiss me, Kate"). He also analyses the verse and prose of the Sly scenes, making an excellent point about the "new" Sly's blank verse, "a step up to an assumed dignity and style," which is then exploited "by inserting into this new frame fragments of the old Sly that we used to know . . . The incongruity between style and subject-matter is now so marked that it re-creates on the plane of language the visual effect of Sly sitting up in bed, newly washed and nobly attired."[13] I see a much developed and mature incongruity in the violence with which Katherine uses, in a speech about the experience of marriage, the vocabulary and rhythms of a contentious claimant to a throne from a history play. It is right that it is incongruous. The married state of Katherine and Petruchio has, from the end of the play, no connection with the married state of Lucentio and Bianca or Hortensio and his Widow. ("If she and I be pleas'd, what's that to you?" [2.1.295].) For them, as Lucentio fatuously said, the war was over. For Katherine and Petruchio, it has barely started. This is the play which is beginning. *The Taming of the Shrew* has shown us ("So workmanly the blood and tears are drawn" [Induction 2.58]) a conflict of very close relationship—in play terms. Petruchio, having met her, "thought it good" that she should "hear a play" (Induction 2.131). Now she shows that she has understood. They go back to the beginning, as it were, to watch a play that they are creating. That is the true Shakespearian touch, going back at the end of a comedy, in a spiral movement, to the same point only higher. Thus Portia and Bassanio *begin*, at the end of *Merchant*, in a Belmont modified by the play-scene of the trial in Venice. Thus Beatrice and Benedick, at the end of *Much Ado*, start again ("Then you do not love me? . . . No, truly, but in friendly recompense"), but now together and changed by the play-scene at the church.

Together, Katherine and Petruchio have filled in many more areas of the capability of theatre than seemed possible at the beginning. In particular they have, like Beatrice and Benedick after them, created an open world for each other; they are themselves, only more so being now together. Their mutuality is based on the power of acting. Kate's speech is rivalled in length only by those of the Lord in the Induction when he is setting up a play-world. This shared power can encompass continual challenges for sovereignty, and even violence, together. Far from such things splitting their marriage apart, they will bring them into closer union. "We three are married, but you two are sped."

NOTES

Originally published in *Shakespeare Survey* 37 (1984): 23–31. Reprinted with the permission of David Daniell and Cambridge University Press.

1. Brian Morris concludes the introduction to his Arden edition (1981) with a long section "Love and marriage" (London and New York: Methuen), 136–49.
2. G. R. Hibbard, Introduction to *The Taming of the Shrew* (Harmondsworth, Penguin, 1968), 8; Morris, 105; H. J. Oliver, *The Taming of the Shrew* (Oxford, 1982), 57.
3. "His contemporaries found the implied play metaphor of the induction device extremely attractive; Shakespeare himself seems to have preferred the less artificial form of the play within the play." Anne Righter, *Shakespeare and the Idea of the Play* (1962), 104.
4. Hibbard, 35.
5. Morris, 59.
6. Edward Hall, *The Union of the Two Noble and Illustre Famelies ...* (1548), vi, vii.
7. Oliver, 51.
8. John Russell Brown, in *Shakespeare and his Comedies* (1957), 98, comes near to making this point, but then veers off to something else.
9. Morris, 82, 83.
10. Oliver, 38.
11. M. C. Bradbrook, "Dramatic Role as Social Image; a Study of *The Taming of the Shrew*," *Shakespeare-Jahrbuch* 94 (1958): 139, 134–35.
12. The play would go down even faster if she were using the forty-four lines to declaim a thesis about "order," as maintained by G. I. Duthie, *Shakespeare* (1951), 58, and Derek Traversi, *An Approach to Shakespeare 1: Henry VI to Twelfth Night* (1968), 89.
13. Brian Vickers, *The Artistry of Shakespeare's Prose* (London and New York, 1968), 13, 14.

The Ending of *The Shrew*

MARGIE BURNS

The central thematic and formal principle in *The Taming of the Shrew* is its conversion of oppositions into dialectics, so that initially adversarial relationships or hierarchies become vehicles of reciprocal exchange. This is accomplished in the relationship between Kate and Petruchio, in the relationship between the Induction and the main play, and ultimately in the relationship between the ending and the "missing" ending. All of these relationships are subsumed by the ending of the play.

The conclusion of *Shrew* poses two famous problems, the remarkable disappearance of Christopher Sly and the other Induction characters after Act 1, and the ambiguity of Katherina's self-extinguishing speech in Act 5 (2.13–79).[1] At the beginning of the play, Sly disappears, to be replaced by Katherina the shrew; at the end of the play, Katherina the shrew disappears, to be replaced by someone evidently rather . . . sly.[2] As this charming symmetry of beginning and end suggests, I think, the play coheres, without the addition of any supererogatory ending. I shall argue that the two problems mentioned above are connected and that, by virtue of their connection, they can be resolved; the exchange between them—and between beginning and ending—partly indicates the formal complexity of the play, but also evidences the unity of the play. To explain the ending of *Shrew*, one should posit not that half a frame is missing, but that the unity of the play is its frame.[3] Thus Sly's loss can be discussed as the play's gain, because the discontinuation of Sly's story actually helps develop the Kate-Petruchio story. Leaving aside for now the traditional assumptions of *Shrew* criticism, therefore, I shall concentrate at first on purely formal considerations. Rather than hypothesize a missing ending, I shall focus on the manifold connections between the Induction and the final scene in particular, and between the Induction and the main play overall.

84

Modern readers have reawakened to some of the thematic connections between the Sly story and the rest of the play, as sketched by Richard Hosley in his overview of the play: a "threefold structure of induction, main plot, and sub-plot, unified as these elements are by the 'Supposes' theme".[4] Among recent readers, Maynard Mack guides the consensus, emphasizing the charactural parallels between Sly and Kate: "what the Lord [sic] and his servants do in thrusting a temporary identity on Sly is echoed in what Petruchio does for Kate at a deeper level of psychic change."[5] Sidney Homan similarly emphasizes the parallels between Sly and Kate, in his reading of the metadramatic parallels between, respectively, spectator and actor.[6] Alongside the consensus on the links between Sly and Kate, however, other readers have noted analogous links between Sly and Petruchio, following the direction pointed out by the fair-minded Harold Goddard:

> In the Induction to *The Taming of the Shrew*, Christopher Sly the tinker, drunk with ale, is persuaded that he is a great lord who has been the victim of an unfortunate lunacy. Petruchio, in the play which Sly witnesses (when he is not asleep), is likewise persuaded that he is a great lord—over his wife.[7]

Goddard's attractive insight, partly a corrective to a rather sexist and elitist emphasis on Kate and Sly as solely the weaker partners in parallel manipulations, will be pursued farther. First, however, to substantiate any of the larger characural relations between Induction and play, one must observe the detailed relations between scene and scene in the Induction and Act 5.

Both the Induction and the final scene necessitate a "banquet," an atmosphere of communal festivity somewhat self-consciously evoked:

> Sirs, I will practice on this drunken man.
> What think you, if he were convey'd to bed,
> Wrapp'd in sweet clothes, rings put upon his fingers,
> A most delicious banquet by his bed,
> And brave attendants near him when he wakes . . .?   (Ind.1.36–40)

In each scene, the festivity celebrates a marriage and / or the reaffirmation of a marriage; in obvious burlesque of comedy's traditional celebratory ending, the Induction bestows a rejoicing wife on the semi-sentient Christopher Sly, before an onstage audience of the whole comic community. So complete a happy ending, indeed, almost obviates any other ending; in a structural pun, its very completeness jocosely explains the absence of a coda for Sly. In fact, the two "ending" scenes of the Induction and Act 5 jocosely reflect each other: the Induction festivity shows a husband restored to his senses; the final scene shows a wife restored to hers; so far, so good (though I think the ironies in the former pinpoint those of the latter, as Goddard suggested). As one would expect from Renaissance drama, especially Shakespearean, the same process of reflection extends further, throughout the structure of the play: the happy ending of the Induction is picked up in act 5, scene 2, and the unhappy ending of Kate and Petruchio's wedding in act 3 is reflected in Sly's unconsummated marriage in the Induction and in the absence of any consummation at all for him after act 5.

With contradictory open-endedness, the end-stopped Induction belies its own form, partly by setting up further developments, as the players enter and commence arrangements for a play. Furthermore, it also sets up the audience: since anyone first seeing the play would expect Sly to be its protagonist, the swift transmutation of roles at the end of the Induction comes like a practical joke. Like the lord, the playwright has a near-supine creature to practice on, and in both cases the butt of the joke metamorphoses into bemused (and perhaps reluctant) spectator, his mind on other things. Beyond the initial foolery, however, the playwright's joke suggests a more fruitful sense of "practice," and Sly's happy ending also provides a warm-up, a rehearsal, for that of the main play. Parallels between the Induction and the final scene generate what might be called a familial relationship between the Induction and the play. Seen in such perspective, the Induction stands as a sort of little sister to the main play, applying itself to "practice" as a younger sister should:

> BAP. Well, go with me and be not so discomfited:
> Proceed in practice with my younger daughter;
> She's apt to learn and thankful for good turns. (2.1.164–66)

> TRA. Shall sweet Bianca practice how to bride it? (3.2.253)

Incidentally, the suggestions about "practice" for Bianca, while juxtaposing her to Katherina, hint subliminally at her constantly ongoing if quiet rehearsal as understudy in the role of shrew.

Following the overall pattern of familial resemblances (and familial stresses), the main play, which apparently must be finished before Sly's induction can be completed, falls into a kind of Leah-and-Rachel relationship to the induction, like an older sister who must be married off before the younger sister can marry. In *The Taming of the Shrew*, both the main play and the older sister are initially presented—objectified—as things to get rid of:

> 'Tis a very excellent piece of work, madam lady: would 'twere done!
> (1.1.258–59)

> I am agreed; and would I had given him the best horse in Padua to begin his
> wooing that would thoroughly woo her, wed her and bed her and rid the
> house of her! (1.1.147–50)

Happily, the disregarded potential both in Katherina and in her story comes to
fruition, as both become (cf. Kant) ends in themselves. Meanwhile, the Sly
frame, like the sly Bianca, proves other than what it seemed originally, perhaps balks at expanded development, and finally disappears, subsumed within
a larger perspective.

In the overall temper of energized humanism thus sustained by the play,
a humanism based on a rather optimistic concept of the potentials in individualism, one outstanding quality in the play is its openendedness—at times, its
double-endedness. The Induction and the final scene, for example, are
enriched by the open-ended dialectic of literal and figurative language that
connects the two scenes. Centered around parallel occasions, the scenes also
center around parallel conversations about hunting; however, the literal hunting *topos* of the Induction metamorphoses into the figurative *topos* of the final
scene:

> This bird you aim'd at, though you hit her not;
> Therefore a health to all that shot and miss'd.
>
> O, sir, Lucentio slipp'd me like his greyhound,
> Which runs himself, and catches for his master;
>
> 'Tis well, sir, that you hunted for yourself;
> 'Tis thought your deer does hold you at a bay. (V.2.50–56)

In the Induction, the men enter arguing about which of three hunting dogs is
best; in the final scene, the men argue about which of three wives is best—
an infelicitous parallelism which boomerangs on at least two of them, since
only one wife proves a retriever (of her husband's wager, and incidentally of
the other wives). Beneath the jollification (often dubious, in such scenes in
Shakespeare's plays), Lucentio and Hortensio's uneasy banter about escape,
retrieval, and entrapment betrays their underlying unease, the contradictory
sensations of hunters unsure of their prey and of objects of prey themselves.
With the play's brilliant doubleness, the colliding forms of edginess produce, for the two characters, a hint both of their own possible entrapment
and of a possibly slipping grasp on the yet-untamed wives. Briefly stated,
the edginess comes from a tension between denial and fulfillment and is
exploited in the wedding-night wager and exacerbated by the wives, who
first leave the room (shift their "bush," as Bianca says [5.2.46])[8] and then

withhold their appearance. Again, the polite theatrical indication of the wives' future sexual behavior reflects or is reflected by the action of the Induction, when Sly's wife similarly withholds herself.

Drawing the two scenes yet closer together, the two hunt conversations employ not only the same images but even the same numbers. Like the lord, who enters boasting about his hound—"Saw'st thou not, boy, how Silver made it good / At the hedge-corner, in the coldest fault? / I would not lose the dog for twenty pound" (Ind.1.19–21)—Lucentio proposes to wager "twenty crowns" on his wife's obedience (5.2.70) and Petruchio boasts of *his* wife— "twenty crowns! / I'll venture so much of my hawk or my hound, / But twenty times so much upon my wife" (ll. 71–73). In the dreamlike dependency of numbers as in other images, the final scene uses and re-uses the materials of the Induction and transposes them to higher terms—or at least to more expensive terms. Indeed, the earlier hunt may echo in the final scene even through the names of the hunting dogs, which chime interestingly with the wives' characters: "Bellman" suggests Kate's voice and function in the play; "Silver," like "Bianca," suggests light coloring; and "Echo" adequately describes the unnamed widow whose speeches largely just echo Bianca's.[9] Such linguistic echoes reverberate Petruchio's implicit connection of his wife with his other hunting creatures, further widening the uneasy tension between a view of the wives as hawks, hounds, etc., and a view of the wives as "deer" (with the obvious pun). Whether in tandem or in opposition, the Induction and final scene interact to enrich each other; when the playwright pursues contradictions far enough, the progressive complexities involve release as well as tension. Like the progression from literal to figurative "sly" character mentioned before, the progression from literal to figurative hunt draws the beginning and ending of the play closer together and enlarges the play from the literal, confining bounds of its beginning.

The sense of expansion at the ending is amplified by Katherina. Following the men's jokes and the men's wager in a last-but-not-least position, Kate's big speech to the audience seems at first to endorse a downplaying of the woman's role. Its immediate impact in the theater, however, certainly does not downplay *her* role, and like many other readers, I think it proceeds through—and succeeds theatrically by means of—intentional though extemporaneous irony, along the lines of Kate and Petruchio's gamesplaying in act 4, scene 5.[10] Kate's strategic rhetorical position at the end, her eyebrow-lifting overenthusiasm, the vivid language she uses to delineate women's weakness, all support the strongest possible reading of her part at this juncture:

> Fie, fie, unknit that threat'ning unkind brow,
> And dart not scornful glances from those eyes,
> To wound thy lord, thy king, thy governor. (ll. 136–38)

The haphazard order to the lord/King/governor terms, by the way, suggests their rather loose application. To support a political hierarchy, they should form a linguistic hierarchy, as in Portia's incomparably more serious and therefore more elevated use of the same terms:

> Happiest of all is that her gentle spirit
> Commits itself to yours to be directed,
> As from her lord, her governor, her king. (*MV*, 3.2.165–67)

Katherina, in contrast, sites the real power of her speech in women; above, she begins by emphasizing that women should avoid injuring men; continuing, she similarly emphasizes that women should avoid injuring themselves:

> It blots thy beauty, as frosts do bite the meads,
> Confounds thy fame, as whirlwinds shake fair buds. . . . (ll. 139–40)

While Katherina warns women that they could injure themselves or others, the speech never introduces a more sinister dimension of any equivalent threat from men. Like Katherina herself at every point in the play, the speech continuously displays strength and animation. Thus it dwells on the concept of womanhood, and in such a way as to produce images of strong passions and elemental forces—pungently reinforced through Kate's own language and behavior (even in this speech):

> Come, come, you froward and unable worms!
> My mind hath been as big as one of yours,
> My heart as great, my reason haply more,
> To bandy word for word and frown for frown; (ll. 169–72)

With a pre-Freudian and almost Victorian limpidity, she pronounces that "our [women's] lances are but straws" (l.173); but she nonetheless represents women's duty with a particularly "unfeminine" image which, in effect, endows women with "lances":

> Such duty as the subject owes the prince,
> Even such a woman oweth to her husband;
> And when she is froward, peevish, sullen, sour,
> And not obedient to his honest will,

(surely the inclusion of the word "honest" is important here)

> What is she but a foul contending rebel,
> And graceless traitor to her loving lord? (ll. 155–60)

Most appropriately, the multiply-ironic military idiom in this passage produces the reverse battle cry of "Let's lay down our weapons," a genre whose energies carry it from the *Lysistrata* through the Sixties slogan of "make love, not war." Of course, the strategy employed by Katherina at this juncture (as in the *Lysistrata*) is the time-honored one of carrying the battle to favorable terrain.

Throughout her speech, Katherina exhorts women to offer dutiful obedience freely; the speech addresses (ostensibly) not the men in the audience but the women themselves, and it argues not masculine coercion but masculine privation:

> Thy husband is thy lord, thy life, thy keeper,
> Thy head, thy sovereign; one that cares for thee,
> And for thy maintenance; commits his body
> To painful labor, both by sea and land;
> To watch the night in storms, the day in cold. . . . (ll. 146–50)

Indeed, as with the dubious image of the "foul contending rebel" preceding, Kate's evocation of the ways in which men can be distressed becomes almost a reverse cheer. Proclaiming in lavish detail the difficulties which men must face, Kate shows such gusto as to overwhelm any poor-little-woman argument in the speech; the zest which characterizes Kate's language certainly extends to the subject of men's burdens.

Overall, the speech presents the concept of mutual support between the sexes, clearly based on women's freedom as well as men's, to offer or to withhold. Critics of all political persuasions have passed over this salient point. Indeed, little serious analysis has been devoted to the language of the speech itself; most criticism has its *starting point* in the supposed tenor of the speech and then addresses itself to justifying or debunking the supposed message.[11] The language which presumably couches the message has been neglected. Partly diverging from such a pattern, however, Juliet Dusinberre notes the difference between this speech and the analogous one in *A Shrew*, though her conclusion differs from mine.[12] More in line with my own view of the presentation, Margaret L. Ranald refers to the concepts of partnership and mutuality in discussing both the speech and the play;[13] and similarly Anne Barton takes as her emphasis "a Katherina of unbroken spirit and gaiety" at the end of the play, "who has learned the value of self-control and of caring about someone other than herself."[14] In this regard, the speech corresponds fully to the rest of act 5, scene 2: notwithstanding superficial appearances, the entire last scene of *The Taming of the Shrew* cleverly reinforces a fundamental reciprocity and equality (however raucous) between the sexes. Paradoxically, even the men's wager sustains the reciprocity (unbeknownst, probably, to Hortensio and Lucentio); after all, the men bet on their wives' willingness to appear rather than simply compelling their wives' appearance. It is not suggested that they could compel their wives to appear; what they do, instead, is to reciprocate the treatment asked of woman in Kate's speech, in a willing compliance, a submission based (in one case) on trust: they watch and wait for their spouses to return (from the "bush" outside). In other words, they bet on their wives. This reciprocity is sustained throughout the scene, even to the inclusion of slight touches like the final couplet—which comments equally on Petruchio's taming and on Kate's allowing herself to be tamed:

> Hor.   Now go thy ways, thou hast tam'd a curst shrew.
> Luc.   'Tis a wonder, by your leave, she will be tam'd so.

In the previous wedding scene, a similar tag expresses the same exchange:

> Bian.   . . . being mad herself, she's madly mated.
> Gre.   I warrant him, Petruchio is Kated. (3.2.245–46)

Despite the belittlement in such comments, the audience can see that, if Katherina gives herself and her image into Petruchio's protection, Petruchio's stature—as either "tamer" or simply person—rests in Kate's keeping, in the reciprocal estate of marriage.[15]

I have been arguing that the inequalities ostensibly espoused by Katherina's speech are belied by the energizing individualism of her rhetoric—its vividness, strength and ironies combined in a game of seeming ease analogous to and infused with *sprezzatura* (even if the latter is more typically considered the exclusive property of the male courtier of the period). In this respect, the final speech reflects the play as a whole, where the same interaction of superficial inequalities against the more fundamental energies of developing individualism results in much the same outcome: a "taming" which stars Katherina as the pivot of the whole play. In particular, the ostensible or gamesmanlike imbalance of Katherina's speech reflects the fate of the Induction, further tightening the formal connections between Kate's problematic speech and Sly's problematic disappearance. With the unfinished Induction, after all, the play concludes on a seeming imbalance between the beginning and ending fully as audacious as the seeming imbalance between the sexes with which Kate's speech concludes. The imbalance itself thus generates a balance, both between the beginning and ending of the play and between the Induction and the play as a whole. *The Taming of the Shrew* seems to be poised at a moment of relative optimism, which envisions the energies of humanistic individualism reconcilable with the stresses it imposes on family relationships.

In any case, the connections between the Induction and the final scene of the play lead inevitably to the larger connections between the Induction and the play as a whole. At this juncture, however, to argue for those connections becomes a more complex proposition, partly because to point out the parallels or connections between the Induction and the rest of the play often necessitates references from the text of the play to the context imposed by its history in criticism. Historically, criticism of the play shows that the apparent inequalities in Katherina's speech and in Sly's disappearance invite—or almost compel a speculation (as in this essay). Unfortunately, much such criticism, though by no means all, has reacted to these dazzling provocations to thought by hypothesizing a missing ending for Sly and a missing earnestness for Kate, extending both Sly's story and Kate's conversion beyond the text. Since I think that the play has more than sufficient aesthetic unity to justify its nonending or its non-final ending (depending on one's preference for terms), I would hypothesize that the artificial extensions imposed by such readings serve chiefly to get both Sly and Kate home—and to keep them there. This point must, however, await the substantiation offered by the further formal connections between play and Induction.

To justify the ending of *The Taming of the Shrew*, I would term it not a missing ending but a non-final ending, and I would look to the advantages (formal and theatrical) for the playwright implicit in such lack of finality, as well as to the consistency of such lack of finality with the movement of the play as a whole. The metadramatic approach which has proved useful to other readers proves useful again in this context. One recent reader suggests, for example, that the difference between the play's Induction and ending reflects the difference between farce and comedy; thus with Sly's disappearance the farce also disappears, in a metadramatic sloughing-off of old wineskins which nicely signals the author's development into a playwright of genuinely comic stature.[16] Similarly, a student concluded that as the Induction characters get farther and farther into the play, they simply get swallowed up; like the audience watching, they become *lost in the play*, and therefore the lord's joke partly metamorphoses into a joke on himself, as he and his attendants are swept away by the action which they themselves initiate. Reinforcing the metadramatic approach on this point, the traditional *topos* of the biter bit brings the Induction closer (once again) to the main play. For just as Kate has the tables turned on her, seeing her shrewishness reified in another personality, as in the therapeutic technique of commanding the double bind that requires correction, Petruchio also sees his game successfully played back at him by Kate, when she mimics and outdoes his Baroque flipflops (4.4 and 5.2). As Erasmus recommends in the former instance,

> *Malo nodo malus quarendus cuneus.*—To a crabbed knot must be sought a crabbed wedge. A strong disease requyreth a stronge medicine. A shrewed wyfe a shrewed husbande to tame her. A boysteous horse, a boysteous snaffel.[17]

And in the latter, he similarly recommends,

Fallacia alia aliam tradit.—One discept driveth out another, As we see one nail driven out with another nail, so doth many times one craft and guile expel another.[18]

In the play, the energetic series of proverb-salted processes—tormentor tormented, fighting fire with fire, one nail drives out another—returns on itself ("Petruchio is Kated"), as Kate's domineering recoils on herself, Petruchio's supposed lordship on himself, and the lord's joke on himself, all combining in one of the more therapeutic veins of theatrical comedy.

In part, I would contend that the combination succeeds because it is actually a re-combination, resulting from correspondences between Kate, Petruchio, and the other main-play characters and the figures from the Induction who actually offer shadowy equivalences for the main-play characters. The play's reversals, inversions, and reciprocities include an exchange which connects characters in the Induction to characters in the main play. Thus Kate's situation resembles not only Sly's, but—as has already been touched on—other links connect Kate to the lord and Petruchio to Sly. In fact, Kate's character includes, like Petruchio's, elements of both Sly and the lord (and in Kate's case, of the page and the hostess), relationships which derive support from the original doubling of actors' parts. Presumably, for example, the same actor played either Sly and Petruchio or the lord and Petruchio; perhaps the same boy actor played the hostess of the Induction and Kate; or perhaps, more appealingly, the page of the Induction played Kate, while the hostess doubled as either Bianca or the Widow.[19] If the original pairings remain uncertain, their thematic import at least remains correspondingly open to conjectural use.

As one instance of key parallelism, when the page of the Induction becomes a lady, he also becomes, like Kate, a model wife. Consider the course of his instruction in how to personate a wife:

> Tell him from me, as he will win my love,
> He bear himself with honorable action,
> Such as he hath observ'd in noble ladies
> Unto their lords, by them accomplished. . . .
> And say, "What is't your honor will command,
> Wherein your lady, and your humble wife,
> May show her duty and make known her love?"
> And then with kind embracements, tempting kisses,
> And with declining head into his bosom. . . . (Ind.1.109–18)

If the page does play Kate, his practice in receiving instruction ("taming," so to speak) amply fits him to do so; like Kate afterward, he rehearses the role of wife, under the tutelage of his "lord," in order to win that lord's "love" (1.109). Furthermore, the fact that the page's role as wife runs counter to his previous role does not make the theatrical joke any less effective—although it does, of course, prevent any ultimate consummation onstage (the *page's* story does not have an ending, either). Incidentally, the lord's speech indicates that the lord, like Petruchio, seems to have devoted some thought and energy to the course of instruction as a husband.

Where the page resembles Kate, Christopher Sly also resembles Petruchio; where Kate's character seems to contain elements of the page and the hostess, Petruchio's seems to contain elements of the lord and Sly, a transference which proves significant. In his own way, Sly shows a propensity, like Petruchio's, to treat his wife from the start as (as we say) a person:

> SLY.   Where is my wife?
> PAGE.   Here, noble lord, what is thy will with her?
> SLY .   Are you my wife and will not call me husband?
>   My men should call me "lord"; I am your goodman. . . . (Ind.2.102–5)

Fascinatingly, Sly's comic celerity here in assuming a social distance between him and his "men" anticipates the way Petruchio and Kate bond with each other, leaving other members of their respective genders to engage in a sort of post-play battle of the sexes as groups, rather than as individuals. To do so, however, he assumes the same distance between his servants and his wife—a distinction which, the play suggests, would be sloughed off swiftly by a "real" lord. As Petruchio expostulates, dogmatically,

> She is my goods, my chattles; she is my house,
> My household stuff, my field, my barn,
> My horse, my ox, my ass, my anything; (3.2.232–34)

Petruchio's over-emphasis on the legal situation at least brings it out into the open and signals his own uneasiness here. Indeed, I think that the ensuing mock-heroic scene dramatizes Petruchio's genuine underlying desire to remove Kate from the situation enunciated:

> I'll bring mine action on the proudest he
> That stops my way in Padua. Grumio,
> Draw thy weapon, we are beset with thieves;
> Rescue thy mistress, if thou be a man,
> Fear not, sweet wench, they shall not touch thee, Kate:
> I'll buckler thee against a million. (ll. 236–41)

The comedy points up an actual need for individual protection against a community of people like Baptista, a need which Petruchio seems to recognize.

Like Petruchio later, Sly shows his recognition of his wife as a person, by exploring the possibilities of the wife's name (also commencing the instant intimacy which he desires):

> SLY. What must I call her?
> LORD. Madam.
> SLY. Al'ce madam, or Joan Madam?
> LORD. Madam, and nothing else, so lords call ladies.

The last is a telling comment, underlined by the fact that the lord himself has no name, and evidently repudiated by Sly:

> SLY. Madam wife. . . . (ll. 108–12)

Similarly, Petruchio opens with Kate's name:

> You lie, in faith, for you are call'd plain Kate,
> And bonny Kate, and sometimes Kate the curst;
> But Kate, the prettiest Kate in Christendom,
> Kate of Kate-Hall, my super-dainty Kate,
> For dainties are all Kates, and therefore, Kate,
> Take this of me, Kate of my consolation. . . . (2.1.185–90)

Sly and Petruchio attest the wife's identity by emphasizing the wife's name, in an authorial word-play which reflects adversely on the nameless Widow and the colorless Bianca—as well as on the unnamed lord and the namechanging "Supposes" characters, among the men.

From such connections, the roles in Induction and main play recombine, sometimes to produce rather androgynous results (e.g., the treatment of the page, both by his own lord and by Sly). In the doubling-up typical of the play, moreover, the characters also form their thematic bonds in pairs; when Petruchio becomes a lord, like Sly, and Kate becomes a lady, like the page, the two pairs of characters reflect each other's situations, partly in the mutuality of their mock-elevations. In fact, the social elevations are validated chiefly by their mutuality—converted, like so much else in the play, from oppositions to dialectics. As briefly stated at the beginning of this essay, each initial opposition or hierarchy—Kate and Petruchio, Sly and the lord, Induction and play—metamorphoses into a vehicle of dialectical exchange, as does even the opposition of "ending" and non-ending (or missing ending), where the non-ending can serve as an ending, and the ending can serve as an open door.

Here enters much of the thematic point of the ambiguous ending—again, attesting a moment of rather optimistic humanism, even in the form of the play; when the dichotomy between "formal" and "thematic" or contentual also becomes recognizable as dialectic, and the form can be seen as homologous with the relationships among the characters, then the open-end-edness of the play vindicates the open-endedness of the central characters' relationship. If both Sly and Petruchio have jokes played on them, the ending of the play finally gives the jokes some point; Kate's mock-elevation of Petruchio results in a genuine elevation, a release from the limitations of his earlier role (fortune-hunter, bully, etc.), reflecting her release from her role. While the joke on Petruchio takes on a point, however, the joke on Sly—as just a joke—remains pointless, and the play outgrows it. The disappearance of Sly and the other Induction characters partly constitutes the disappearance of a sly joke, and the play proves its enlargement at the end by enlarging the audience from the sly state of mind.

In examining this point, I found that the concept of a developing dialecticism in the form of the play elucidates the minor puzzle of Sly's name. While the significant name "Sly" can hardly be accident, given the way Shakespeare plays with names, the name seems not to fit Sly's egregiously straightforward personality.[20] Perhaps, then, the name conveys less the individual character than the frame of reference which he provides. In such a sly frame of reference, either Kate or Petruchio must be seen as beaten, while the other must be narrowly seen as victor, a reductive view which downgrades the characters to manipulators and bullies (or to shrews and slys). Given the direction of the play, such a view would result in the loss of Kate and Petruchio, and the playwright chooses fittingly to jettison Sly instead. Only characters like Lucentio and Hortensio cling to their sly jokes, and their attitude toward Kate and Petruchio tends if anything to arouse the audience's protectiveness toward the latter. In a neat structural pun, the "Supposes" remain sly—merely sly, like spectators, eavesdroppers, bystanders—at the frame rather than at the center of things, leaving the viewer or reader to identify (as most do) with the central intelligences. Finally, indeed, with Kate's address virtually directly to the audience, the playwright allows the audience itself to "frame" the play from its vantage point as bystanders in a different and larger sense, released—like Kate and Petruchio—from the initial configuration of response.

In other words, the playwright declines to put the lid on, recork the bottle, at the end of *The Taming of the Shrew*; to return to the Sly framework would imply regression, inappropriate to a play whose action celebrates so much progression. The confinement of a single limited role for Sly, whether in a manor or in the gutter, would diminish the playwright's options and those of his characters; and if Sly's story is not over, perhaps Kate and Petruchio's is not over either. Their wedding occurred back in act 3, after all, so the audience knows that a wedding does not necessarily signify closure any more than it necessarily signifies the happy ending; and the end of the play reinforces the point, partly through Bianca and the Widow's weddings and partly through its own lack of closure. For Kate and Petruchio, the open ending is the most persuasive happy ending, because the open threshold promises them room to grow; as Kate and Petruchio make their final exit with the other characters gaping after them, their development suggests a dimension beyond closure into the adult future of the "real world."

Professor Anne Barton, introducing the play in a student text, observes of the traditional joke-on-a-beggar story that "inherent in all versions is the return of the beggar to his original state and his conviction that all the wonders he has seen and enjoyed were only an exceptionally vivid dream."[21] In *The Taming of the Shrew* version, perhaps the author wishes to do more than tell an old joke. Perhaps the Sly framework disappears because any enclosing form would ill-suit an action of release and expansion; like the audience watching and some of the characters within it, the play escapes from limits initially imposed on it, reflecting its own action in the farthest-reaching optimism of Renaissance dramatic mirroring. In such form, the story represents a dream come true, less for the tinker turned lord than for the married couple turned friends and for the audience turned party to its own entertainment in the fictional characters' happiness.[22]

As mentioned, emphasis on the formal unity of the play extant has ramifications beyond the text of the play to the context of previous criticism. In my opinion, the play has traditionally been read with an elitist and antifeminist bias which reifies relationships as hierarchies and then endorses those hierarchies. Where the play itself makes elaborate jokes out of its hierarchies—including the highly sanctioned ones of youth and age ("Young budding virgin, fair and fresh . . ." [4.5.37]), father and son ("Thy father! O villain! He is a sailmaker in Bergamo" [5.1.80–81]), and master and servant ("Knock you here, sir!" [1.2.9]) critics have too often solemnly taken them to be fixed, normative, and ordained. The play itself leaves virtually nothing fixed; rather, its action proceeds and unfolds chiefly through a series of exchanges, including exchanges of role which entail exchanges of status, which leave status mobile and suspended in mobility at the end of the play.

Instead of focusing on the mobility, or suspension, sustained by the text, however, and analyzing the consequences or significance of such mobility, much criticism has concentrated instead on the "missing" ending, proceeding not from the text itself but from the underlying assumption that Sly should return to his "rightful" state. (Analogously, as observed above, Kate's final speech is often approached from the assumption that she, too, is coming to her senses and returning to the ordained subservient status of women.) I wish to examine the assumptions underlying such criticism, despite the inexplicitness of the assumptions. Obviously, the fact that Sly does not have an ending leads to the question, "Why not?" But this valid question, with which I have attempted to deal on formal grounds, differs considerably from its implicit reformulation in much *Shrew* criticism, which asks not, "Why doesn't Sly have an ending?" but rather, "Of course, Sly must have *had* an ending; where did it go?" If the cumbersomeness of this proposition renders it suspect (in chess or in logic, an attempted resolution entailing two steps is called inelegant if only one is needed), its disingenuousness renders it even more suspect. As an ostensible starting point, it not only does not begin with the beginning—namely, with the text that we possess—but also conceals this slippage. I would argue that, in the absence of social or critical presupposition, the logical question would ask why the ending is the way it is, rather than why it is *not* as it is *not*.

I shall return to the presuppositions shortly, but only after dealing with the two most nearly solid grounds on which they rest: The idea that Sly *should* have an ending has two bases: an implicit comparison to the ending of the other extant "shrew" play, *A Shrew*, and an implicit comparison to a more overtly regular dramatic closure. In regard to the first: given the tremendous uncertainty, from the time of initial productions and revivals of *The Taming of the Shrew* to now, about the relationship between *The Shrew* and *A Shrew* which is the source of the other, whether either is the source of the other, whether one or both draw directly or indirectly from yet a third play now lost, and so on[23]—hypotheses about the relationship of any part of the plays must be cautiously advanced. In any case, Shakespeare altered so many sources in so many significant ways that "source" alone, today, would determine almost no textual decisions. In regard to *Shrew*, an instructive caution lies in earlier scholars' eagerness to excise parts of the play from the Shakespearean canon (the parts regarded as too brutal, too farcical, etc.).[24] And in regard to endings, given the augmented dramatic effect accruing to an ending, caution is also behooved; eighteenth-century readers of Shakespeare provided the all-time nadir of negative examples, as in altering the ending of *King Lear* (a trifling change from sad to happy) to resemble that of the sources.

If the norm provided by *A Shrew* is obscure, the norm provided by a sense of closure or by any desire for such sense in regard to this play is invisible. In the first place, one might reasonably ask whether the desire for a more regular ending—whatever regularity entails—prescribes *any* particular ending for Sly, especially if the irregularities of the ending coalesce with the larger irregularities of the play. An *a priori* application of invisible norms of regularity actually begs the question, for Shakespeare manipulates and/or disappoints expectations of satisfactory endings in a multitude of forms throughout the canon. Looking at that segment of the canon into which *The Taming of the Shrew* falls, one notes immediately that *Love's Labor's Lost* ends with no marriages at all but only the commutation of the men's original sentence from three years to one; and *The Two Gentlemen of Verona* ends with the surprising denouement of attempted rape which produces the final reaffirmation of love and friendship. Needless to say, both endings strike numerous readers as in some way unfinished. With a paradoxical symmetry, therefore, the relevant period of the author's career comprises three lopsided or oddly ended comedies in a row, framed by *Comedy of Errors* before and *Midsummer Night's*

Dream after, both of which self-consciously call attention to their links between beginning and ending in play-within-play devices which constitute frames. If I were forced to speculate about this period of the author's career, I would conclude that Shakespeare is metadramatically memorializing his own development in the virtuosity of beginnings and endings, by playing off frame plays against skewed-frame plays.

When neither the norm provided by *A Shrew* nor the norm provided by *a priori* appeals to a sense of closure dictate any particular ending for *The Shrew*, I consider the historically variable and laborious explanations of where Sly's ending "went" to be a social reflex to Sly's change in status, a reflex of some emotionalism. Although this proposition cannot be proven ultimately, one could create a strong supposition to such effect. Thus, it is remarkable that wherever a reading of this play deals with the "missing ending," its thrust deals exclusively with Sly's story. Despite the lord's longer speeches, greater number of lines, greater complexity of character and greater impact on the action—which the lord, after all, initiates—criticism never focuses on the lord's story as unfinished, presumably because he at least remains in the manor house which is his rightful place. Such a consistently limited focus suggests that the truncation of Sly's story jars less our sense of closure than our sense of status. Further corroborating this position, the page's story also lacks completion, leaving the page in a position surely even more anomalous than Sly's, but far less regarded by scholarship than Sly's.

Here I am reluctantly forced to differ with readers who have, with some courage, argued explicitly in favor of the missing ending theory (in contradistinction to those who simply finesse the argument altogether). Both types of readers have applied themselves seriously and responsibly to hypothesizing an ending which fills the perceived gap. One ingeniously constructs an ending designed, in regard to the "ladies of London" in the audience, to be non-sexist: Sly awakens at the end of the play with a hangover, starts home to tame his own wife, and is foreseen (though not shown) to fail signally in the attempt.[25] This surmise, however, relies entirely on the existence of a character unmentioned in the play, a wife for SLY. While such a character could arguably be added by a director interested in the concept, the text itself provides absolutely no support for such an addition. Therefore, it seems implausible: how, in speeches of such detail as Ind.2.18–26 and 85–98, which mention *personae* never heard of again such as "Cicely Hacket," "old John Naps of Greece," and *"twenty* more such names and men as these" (ll. 95, 97; italics mine), could a wife of Sly's fail to be mentioned?

The other reader employs a casting analysis of the last scenes—also purely hypothetical—to argue that a Sly ending was cut from the play because of its excessive demands on the personnel.[26] The problem with this hypothesis, however, is that the idea of insufficient personnel to include Sly still does not establish that an ending for Sly was written and then dropped. Even admitting the problem, which cannot easily be established, given the uncertainties attendant on part-doubling, it could equally have been obviated by never writing an ending at all; could the author not see the end coming? In general, efforts in academe to prove a previously existing ending for Sly do founder on this objection; while *A Shrew* and numerous theatrical productions prove the relative ease of inventing an ending, nothing shows how one came to be lost. There is great difficulty in accounting for a hypothetical ending's being lost or cut, leaving not a wrack behind.

For the alert reader, the Induction of *The Taming of the Shrew* should provide a foretaste of the limitations of supposititious lordship. In a simulacrum of the dialectic that develops in the main play, just as Petruchio becomes a lord when Kate becomes sly, so Christopher Sly becomes a lord when the lord becomes sly; Sly's induction into the aristocracy depends on an induction of the aristocracy into slyness. Both parts of the play translate a hierarchy—less rigid than it seems, even in the Induction—into mobile reciprocity. Nor does the Induction circle back to repress Sly, although the play puts him to sleep before he can tinker (to use the word in its Elizabethan sense) with it further.[27] Rather, Sly's comic-economic mobility commences before the start of the play (1.2.18–22) and continues beyond the end. If the exchange between real and mock lords chiefly indicates that any man can be induced to think himself a lord, the flimsy distinction evaporates completely in the metadramatic reminder that both roles depend on an actor and a few props. The distinctions between the real and the mock lords undermine themselves, as the lord successfully dupes Sly only by demoting himself to Sly's mock-entourage—"O noble lord, bethink thee of thy noble birth" (1.2.32–48)—becoming a "tinker" in order to create Sly a "lord." As with any delusional victim, the ironies of the joke on Sly resemble those of the treatment of Don Quixote, where others must participate in the victim's fantasy (a fantasy, by the way, foisted off on the victim by the "real world" to begin with) to bring him into their world; victimized by the victim, they enter into his order of things as much as or more than he enters theirs (as with Kate and Petruchio). Where the Induction ends, both key characters display "sly"-ness and "lord"-ship in a hierarchical relationship coterminous with their persons and their roles, which disappears when they disappear.

Evidently, the wish to provide an ending to Sly's story proceeds from a wish to "complete" two actions: to return Sly to his original lowly state, and to send Sly home to tame his own wife. What the reader must question, however, is the nature of such completion. One who does not view the dual repression as necessarily desirable will probably not view it as *a priori* more complete than the play extant; such a concept of completion rests on presuppositions about the hierarchies initially presented in the play. But notwithstanding an emphasis on putatively Elizabethan terms of "degree" by readers in the vein of E. M. W. Tillyard,[28] a hierarchy in practical politics is not an essentialist entity, external to and independent of the persons who in their various relationships sustain it. Hierarchies change when the persons, roles, and relations which compose them change. As the action of *The Taming of the Shrew* reflects, the potential of such alteration is the regenerative potential of such social constructs; when the initial oppositions in the play become vehicles of reciprocity, Sly can enliven the lord's house, Kate and Petruchio can enliven and regenerate stale courtship patterns (including those of the theater), and a surprise non-ending can enliven the traditional ending of comedy. Thus the wish for closure can be exchanged for the pleasures of vitality. In the play's structural exchange between ending and non-ending, neither is entirely either, and both have qualities of the other, with a self-reflexiveness which would seem almost vertiginous in modern literature but which is contained within the effortless dialecticism of Renaissance drama. In the similar exchange between main play and frame, incidentally, the crucial thematic shift between "inner" and "outer" within the action of the play is reflected when the apparent play-within-a-play becomes the outer half, at the end, while the apparent frame disappears within the play.[29]

In the same multiplicity of self-reflection, the play's stories also exchange patterns on a broader basis: the public relationship, the hierarchy of status between Sly and the lord's household, becomes a "marriage," while the private relationship, the marriage of Kate and Petruchio, becomes a highly public political division, a battle of the sexes which polarizes the entire comic community. The relationship between Induction and main play—again, one of reciprocal exchange—manifests itself in the movement from division to marriage in the former, from marriage to division in the latter (and back), an ironic series of inversions where each marriage results in an "equality" of sorts—more apparent than real in the Induction, more real than apparent in the main play. Undermining conventional distinctions between the personal and political, the class division between Sly and the lord translates into a tongue-in-cheek familial relationship, and the union of Kate and Petruchio (initially characterized by the language of commerce anyway [2.1.11–31]) creates a politicized struggle for dominance, or, in modern jargon, sexual politics.

The resultant continuum between psychological and political, between private and public and individual and society, provides a healthful perspective for reading the play. With the transformation of Sly and Petruchio into supposed lords, *The Taming of the Shrew* administers to the audience the traditional sugar-coated pill of comedy. Beneath the humor, one salient phenomenon manifests itself through the symmetrical action: predictably, where there is a lord around, the spectator will often be confronted with the choice of beholding a shrew or beholding the sly. If this parallelism is indeed pointed thus, then the audience has a lesson to learn. Christopher Sly has a name but no title; the lord has a title but no name; and when the anonymous lord and the eponymous Sly vanish together, the play suggests a to-be-dreamed-of dimension of life from which both lordship (or repression, or force) and slyness (or resistance, or fraud) can be excluded. Such a dimension is not created entirely by the play, of course; Petruchio and Kate just drive the same terms into a higher plane of material and emotional satisfaction, creating a vital little realm of their own, relatively independent of the pettiness around them. If Sly and the lord are excluded by the world of the play, Kate and Petruchio seem themselves to exclude that world—at least insofar as represented by the other key characters.

Since the play does not assert the completeness (or even the complete possibility) of either alternative, excluding "the world" or being excluded from it, both alternatives leave a sense of unfinished work behind them. Only thus, however, does *Shrew* leave something unfinished: it recognizes that in human relationships, including relationships between the individual and the social structures, much remains to be done and few solutions to be found. To insist that the play is literally, formally unfinished violates its formal expansiveness. In the absence of textual or historical evidence, the idea of a missing ending must be regarded as myth with the usual function of myth, to explain puzzling sensations or puzzling phenomena, such as the impression created at the end of *The Taming of the Shrew* that much does indeed hang in the balance.

NOTES

Originally published in *Shakespeare Studies* 18 (1986): 41–64. Reprinted with permission from Margie Burns.

1. All citations of text refer to *The Complete Works of Shakespeare*, Hardin Craig, ed. (Glenview, Ill.: Scott, Foresman, 1961).

2. Tightening the parallel between the words *shrew* and *sly*, the *OED* gives the latter repeatedly as a noun (thirteenth through fifteenth centuries) to describe a person, a sly. Chaucer's Miller's Tale provides an instance not recorded in the *OED*: "Alwey the nye slye / Maketh the ferre reeve to be looth." (The "nye slye," of course, is "hende Nicholas.")

3. In regard to the concept of "frame," especially the implied necessity of completing a frame, it should be pointed out that modern use of the word *frame* differs from that found in Shakespeare. Of some seventy-seven instances including variants in *The Harvard Concordance to Shakespeare*, Marvin Spevack, ed. (Cambridge: Harvard University Press, 1973), most are verbs. *Shrew* itself uses the word only as a verb (Ind. 2.135; 1.1.232); nor does any other language in the play suggest a finished product or an unfinished product. In Shakespeare's plays overall, *frame* signifies an internal shape, an order of principle, rather than a finite or rigid structure externally imposed (e.g., a picture frame, a cucumber frame). Only Sonnet 24 approaches the latter, but even there the frame is held within, allowing a play on the senses of human form or human body. The complexity of the con-

cept of a frame stems partly from the related word *induction*. While I, too, have found the term useful, it nonetheless remains an addendum, not found in the Folio but inserted later by Pope. According to the *Concordance*, Shakespeare never uses the word in Pope's sense; while *induce* and *inducements*, etc., appear on occasion, *induction* signifies only "plot" (*1H4*, 3.1.11, and *R3*, 4.4.5 and 1.1.32). One wonders what a difference Pope might have made for scholarship, had he applied a term like *proem, prologue;* no reader insists that a play with a prologue requires an epilogue or vice versa.

4. Richard Hosley, "Sources and Analogues of *The Taming of the Shrew*," *Huntington Library Quarterly* 27 (1964): 289–308.

5. Maynard Mack, "Engagement and Detachment in Shakespeare's Plays," in *Essays ... in Honor of Hardin Craig*, Richard Hosley, ed. (Columbia: University of Missouri Press, 1962), 279–80. Among other readers who pursue the same idea, Brian Morris provides a useful history of the problems arising from the segmentation of the play, in the New Arden edition of *Shrew* (New York: Methuen, 1981).

6. Sidney Homan, "Induction to the Theater," unpublished reprint from the 1978 MLA Convention Special Session, "Shakespearean Metadrama."

7. Harold Goddard, "The Taming of the Shrew," in *The Meaning of Shakespeare* (Chicago: University of Chicago Press, 1960): 1: 68–73. For a similar point see Sears Jayne, "The Dreaming of the Shrew," *Shakespeare Quarterly* 17 (1966), 41–56.

8. Wordplay gives *Shrew* much of its liveliness and explains part of its longevity; when Bianca uses the word *bush*, for example, she puns on the senses of bird in the bush and a bush for wine; when students read the line today, current slang adds yet another sense. The play lends itself to wordplay in the classroom, in the following suggestions for alternative titles: "Sly and the Family Minola," "Tinker, Tailor, Soldier, Sly," and of course, "The Turn of the Shrew," used elsewhere.

9. Compare Goddard's analogous discussion of the echoes of the hunt in *MND*, I: 75–78.

10. Perhaps Goddard is the most famous of the older generation of readers to agree with this sense of Kate's speech. More recent readers include Nevill Coghill, Margaret Webster, and Coppélia Kahn, all cited in a useful overview by John C. Bean, in "Comic Structure and the Humanizing of Kate in *The Taming of the Shrew*," in *The Woman's Part: Feminist Criticism of Shakespeare*, Carolyn Lenz, Gayle Green, and Carol T. Neely, eds. (Urbana: University of Illinois Press, 1980), 65–78. While I find Bean's article helpful and intelligent, I disagree with his use of the terms "revisionist" and "anti-revisionist," borrowed from Robert B. Heilman's "The *Taming* Untamed, or, The Return of the Shrew," *Modern Language Quarterly*, 27 (1966): 147–61. If readers who emphasize the ironies in Kate's language and demeanor are to be called "revisionists," I think the usage begs the entire question. Rather than insist, as such readers seem to do, that irony entails a narrow perspective of Kate as sneak and Petruchio as dupe, I would suggest that the effortless dialecticism of Renaissance dramatic verse (especially Shakespeare's) allows some latitude on the point; irony and earnestness, joke and gravity, etc., are related to each other, not merely antitheses.

11. See, for example, Heilman; Marilyn French in *Shakespeare's Division of Experi-ence* (New York: Summit Books, 1981), 82–85; and George Bernard Shaw, *Shaw on Shakespeare*, Edwin Wilson, ed. (New York: Dutton, 1961), among widely var-ied others.

12. In Juliet Dusinberre, *Shakespeare and the Nature of Women* (London: Macmil-lan, 1975), 78–79.

13. Margaret L. Ranald, "The Manning of the Haggard; or *The Taming of the Shrew*," *Essays in Literature* 1 (1974), 149–65.

14. Anne Barton, Introduction to *Shrew* in *The Riverside Shakespeare*, G. Blakemore Evans, et al., eds. (Boston: Houghton Mifflin, 1974).

15. Chaucer's Wife of Bath's Prologue and Tale, which ends with Alison adjured to keep her husband's estate and honor and fully willing to do so—if another hus-band comes along, provides fascinating parallels; some are noted by David M. Bergeron, "The Wife of Bath and Shakespeare's *Shrew*," *University Review* 35 (1969), 279–86. Each work, segmented into an introduction and a marriage story, portrays a power struggle between the sexes, structured with attendant ironies through a series of inversions and dialectical exchanges.

16. Mark Scheid, unpublished discussion, 1978. See also Bean: "Shakespeare's *The Taming of the Shrew* rises from farce to romantic comedy to the exact extent that Kate, in discovering love through the discovery of her own identity, becomes something more than the fabliau stereotype of the shrew turned household drudge" (66). This approach recasts and dynamizes an older distinction between the Kate-plot as farce and the Bianca-plot as comedy; cf. E. M. W. Tillyard, "The Taming of the Shrew" in *Shakespeare's Early Comedies* (London: Chatto and Windus, 1965).

17. Desiderius Erasmus, *Proverbes or Adagies with newe addicions gathered out of the Chiliades of Erasmus*, by Richard Tauerner (London, 1539; repr. Amsterdam, N.Y.: Da Capo Press, 1969), fol. 5v.

18. Ibid., fol. 33r. Erasmus has been cited in other respects as part of the influence behind this play; see Peter Alexander, "The Original Ending of *The Taming of the Shrew*," *Shakespeare Quarterly* 20 (1969), 111–16.

19. Frustratingly little direct evidence exists on the doubling of parts in early pro-ductions of the plays. Furthermore, doubling in the comedies even from the nine-teenth century is "intermittent and hard to trace" (Arthur Colby Sprague, *The Doubling of Parts in Shakespeare's Plays* [London: Society for Theatre Research, 1966], 29), making it difficult to infer an earlier stage tradition from one more recent. However, as a "matter of course" Sly was removed at the end of the first act in nineteenth-century productions (Sprague, *Shakespeare and the Actors* [Cambridge: Harvard University Press, 1945], p. 56). Sly's remaining on stage until the end of the first act does not insuperably bar the actor from doubling the parts of Sly and Petruchio, in any case; modern stagecraft offers the easy solution of concealing Sly in darkness, from which his voice can be heard while Petruchio exits into the same darkness. While the broad daylight of Elizabethan staging offered less concealment, by the same token it also demanded less deference to verisimilitude in physical details—cf. Oberon's "I am invisible" among countless examples.

20. Several influences probably operate here. Since one actor in Shakespeare's own troupe was named Will Sly, the character's name suggests some joke on the casting of the play. Marston subsequently uses the same name, emphasizing its low-life tenor: two characters in the Induction to *The Malcontent* are named Will Sly and Sinklo, suggesting a possible tradition in connection with the name. As Thelma Greenfield suggests, the name may be retained from sources, since *A Shrew* uses the same name (*The Induction in Elizabethan Drama* [Eugene: University of Oregon Press, 1969], 104). For a larger discussion of Shakespearean name-play, see Harry Levin, "Shakespeare's Nomenclature," in *Shakespeare and the Revolution of the Times* (New York: Oxford University Press, 1976), 51–77.

21. Anne Barton, op. cit., 108.

22. For the topic of "dream" in connection with *Shrew*, see Goddard, Jayne, and Marjorie Garber, *Dream in Shakespeare: From Metaphor to Metamorphosis* (New Haven: Yale University Press, 1974). The dynamics of dream energize the play; dream imagery pervades the language, the main play has a dreamlike dependence on the Induction, and the entire play with its open-ended structure serves as an induction to the author's next play, *A Midsummer Night's Dream*. While I disagree with the idea that Sly falls asleep and dreams the Kate-Petruchio story, it certainly has more dignity than the idea that is its deep structure—that Shakespeare fell asleep and neglected to finish the play. Furthermore, the undoubted relevance of dream to the play has the appeal of uniting two different literary influences—the folk tale of the joke on a beggar and the literary genre of dream-*visio* narrative—in a dialectic which contributes to this play among others of Shakespeare's.

23. See, among others, Greenfield, and Hosley, "Sources and Analogues," and "Was There a 'Dramatic Epilogue' to *The Taming of the Shrew?*" *Studies in English Literature* 1 (1961): 17–34; as well as Morris.

24. As mentioned by Tillyard, *Early Comedies*.

25. Peter Alexander, "Original Ending."

26. Karl P. Wentersdorf, "The Original Ending of *The Taming of the Shrew*: A Reconsideration," *Studies in English Literature* 18 (1978), 201–15.

27. In Elizabethan usage, the word *tinker* is generally deprecatory, cf. *OED* ca. 1592: "to work at something clumsily or imperfectly, esp. in the way of attempted repair or improvement," a definition relevant not only to Sly's role in *Shrew* but also to Petruchio's and the lord's (to say nothing of producers who either add an ending or subtract a beginning, as Jonathan Miller did in the BBC production of *Shrew*. Revealingly, I think, Miller's open assertion of *Shrew* as antifeminist resulted in a lifeless production, which robbed both *Shrew* and John Cleese of much of their comic genius).

28. E. M. W. Tillyard, in *The Elizabethan World Picture* (London: Chatto and Windus, 1943). Predictably, Tillyard, in *Shakespeare's Early Comedies*, supports the theory that Sly once had an epilogue (74. But see Ernest P. Kuhl, "Shakspere's Purpose in Dropping Sly," *Modern Language Notes* 36 (1921): 321–29.

29. For related use of the terms *inner* and *outer*, see Rene Wellek and Austin Warren, *Theory of Literature* (New York: Harcourt, Brace, 1956), 140.

"Love Wrought These Miracles"
Marriage and Genre in *The Taming of the Shrew*

MARGARET LAEL MIKESELL

Literary form "is not simply a matter of empty patterns and techniques . . . genres and conventions subtly express value judgments and present methods of ordering and interpreting reality" (9). Shaped by a medley of genres and conventions, *The Taming of the Shrew* aptly illustrates this observation of George E. Rowe. Its Bianca plot derives from the English translation of an Italian descendant of New Comedy; moreover, Petrarchan conventions appear in its language. And the Kate plot relies on oral folk tales and ballads about shrew taming for many of its features.

Yet in his adaptation of his sources, Shakespeare seems to have found many of the "value judgments" and "methods of ordering and interpreting reality" inimical to his own understanding of reality, for his changes systematically undermine the assumptions and effects of both New Comedy and shrew-taming stories.[1] A comparison of both plots of *The Taming of the Shrew* with their sources will demonstrate how systematically Shakespeare's alterations brought his play into conformity with the vision of marriage found in Protestant conduct books of his time.[2] My paper proposes to study Shakespeare's renovations of his sources from this perspective and to consider what kind of new meanings his remodeled plots create.

The domestic tracts, a motley group of books and essays written by Protestant divines of all persuasions, espouse an ideology of marriage that remains largely unchanged throughout the sixteenth and early seventeenth centuries.[3] Key to a study of *Shrew* is their insistence on the power of marriage to insure the "whole health and prosperyty of mankynde, of publique weales, of kyngdomes, and finally of all degrees . . ." (Becon 1560, fol. Dcxvi.v). From this view of the definitive nature of marriage emerges the related concept of husband and wife as the primary social unit—a function which transcends their obvious domestic roles. It is to the couple in the domestic sphere, however, that the tract writers devote most of their attention.

Their concept of marriage and of the reciprocal obligations of each spouse within it are replicated in *The Taming of the Shrew.*

Marriage, or "mutuall love matrimoniall," as the reform minister Heinrich Bullinger (1543) terms it (65r-v), is consistently presented as a union of close and loving intimacy:

> For what thing is sweter, then with her to liue, with whom ye may be most straightly coupled not only in the beneuolence of the minde, but also in the coniunction of the bodye? . . . it is an especiall swetenesse to haue one, with whom ye may communicate the secreat affeccions of your mind with whom ye may speke euen as it wer with your own self. . . . (Becon 1560, Dcxlix.v; also Erasmus [1530], 22)

Love—expressed physically, intellectually, and spiritually—is the linchpin of the companionate marriage described in the domestic tracts.

This love, a mutual "felowship and partakyng of al thynges," with "one harte, wyll and mynde," to return to Bullinger (1543, 67r), was however based upon strict observance of hierarchy within the household. A number of writers stress the closeness in rank between spouses, William Gouge (1622) (after being attacked by his female parishioners for debasing woman's place) arguing that there is only "small inequalitie . . . betwixt the husband and the wife" (271). However, he and all the other tract writers do insist upon the significance of that small difference. As Samuel Hieron (1614), an early seventeenth-century divine, puts it,

> God hath placed her neere, & so indeed she is next to the husband; but yet still he is the head, and her obedience must be his crowne, the grace, the credite, the ornament of his gouernment . . . . (407; cf. also C[leaver] 1598, 226)

Their respective places in the hierarchy determine the differing obligations of husband and wife to one another. For many writers, those duties may be summarized as follows; a man's authority is vested through love, and a woman's love through her obedience.[4] What emerges is a kind of tension between the seemingly incompatible notions of dominance and mutuality, a contradiction that Mary Beth Rose (1988) has discussed at length (31–42, passim; see also Amussen 1985, 201). While this contradiction has caused great difficulty for some critics of *Shrew*,[5] the play quite obliviously insists upon the coexistence of dominance and mutuality, a paradox addressed in both its plots.

Shakespeare's play creates a vision of mutuality within hierarchy by disposing of the threats that assail this balance from both sides: while too much mutuality destroys order, too much hierarchy brings domestic tyranny. Shakespeare's sources each portray one of these excesses. The romantic passion fueling George Gascoigne's *Supposes* (and New Comedy generally) demands the defiance of hierarchy, seen not only in the egalitarian alliance of the lovers but also in their rebellion against their parents. The shrew-taming stories threaten the companionate marriage from the other side; the brutal imposition of hierarchy brings submission without love. Although many of the conventional episodes and devices found in the sources remain in the Kate and Bianca plots, both of these threats to the companionate marriage have been effectively dismantled, and the altered plots are allied in a contrapuntal fashion (Hibbard 1964, 19) to foreground the companionate marriage. The strategies for renovation differ markedly for each plot.

The Bianca plot consistently weakens New Comedy conventions[6] to devalue passionate, romantic love. In New Comedy, the plot is launched by the lovers' rejection of the arranged marriage. This kind of marriage is always presented as morally corrupt because it is motivated by parental greed, an impulse that is excoriated in the tracts. Robert Cleaver (1598) touches on the various issues involved when he censures parents for their "most vnnaturall and cruell part . . . to sell their children for gaine and lucre" into what he terms "bondage" (320).[7] Thus in New Comedy and didactic literature alike, arranged marriages based solely on considerations of wealth, lineage, and status are passionately rejected.

However, the two genres offer radically different views of arranged marriage itself. In New Comedy, the desire for financial aggrandizement invariably lies behind the arranged marriage. This conjunction of parental greed and parental control legitimates the passion and secrecy of the lovers. However, it is a conjunction which does not appear in the tracts.[8] There, while parents are admonished not to match their children for profit, they are urged to retain responsibility for the actual selection of the spouses. Manual writers warn repeatedly of the disasters which befall children who preempt this task, especially if they resort to secret marriages. Many reasons pertaining to decorum and the obligations of hierarchy are offered to justify this prohibition, but the most important one for a study of *Shrew* is the perceived inability of children to make a suitable choice for a successful love marriage. William Whately typically advises,

> Be wise therefore, and be godly, yee children; let judgement rule you, and not passion; neither giue your affections, nor your selues, nor follow your passions in bestowing your selues, but with the priuitie and good allowance of those, from whom you had your selues.[9]

Cleaver [1598] similarly warns that lovers choosing for themselves often change "a short delectation and pleasure, into a continuall sorrow and repentance" (152). This insistence that romantic passion is destructive rather than empowering sets up a disjunction between didactic and dramatic genres that everywhere shapes Shakespeare's adaptations of Gascoigne's *Supposes*, the source for the Bianca plot and a typical New Comedy play in its Elizabethan transform.[10] While *Supposes* celebrates passion, the Bianca plot systematically deflates it, in the establishment of the conflict, the ensuing intrigue, and the comic resolution.[11]

Supposes vindicates love first in its reliance on the traditional alliances between old age and wealth in opposition to youth and love. The hero Erostrato offers a bitter and obscene description of his beloved's father that succinctly positions his role in the play; Damon "hath greater respect to the abundance of goods, than to his owne naturall childe. He beareth well in minde to fill his owne purse, but he litle remembreth that his daughters purse shalbe continually emptie " (2.3, 126). Indeed the rival suitor Cleander, a man Erostrato describes as old enough to be Damon's father-in-law, is attractive solely for his wealth. Thus the conventional conjunction of age and loveless wealth provides the "irrational law" that creates the conflict of *Supposes*.

The formidable alliance between these blocking figures extends for the entire play. Damon never settles on the supposed Erostrato over the aged Cleander. In fact, Erostrato is continually battered by the threat of an imminent settlement on Cleander. Intrigue is, then, necessary to the plot of *Supposes*, and since Erostrato displays the conventional helplessness of the lover ("Alas, alas, I may go hang my selfe" [2.1, p. 122]), the machinations of the tricky servant, prior to the denouement at least, are key to the lovers' success. The supposed father becomes an essential contrivance to break the deadlock between Erostrato and Cleander.

All of these strategies have been altered in Shakespeare's adaptation of *Supposes*. Although the traditional conflict between young lovers and old blocking figures remains, and age and money still dominate over youth and love, these plot devices have been established only to be decentered and defused. The irrational law, for instance, has been shifted from wealth and status to Baptista's announcement that none may wed Bianca until Katherine has been married. This becomes the "bar in law," as Hortensio terms it. "Cruel father," Lucentio calls Baptista. Yet Kate's engagement renders this law inoperative almost as soon as it is invoked. In the subsequent negotiations over Bianca's fate, Baptista does indeed establish criteria for selecting her husband that place him well within the confines of a New Comedy blocking figure like Gascoigne's acquisitive Damon. Although in the main plot he insists that love is "all in all," here he equates love and money: he "That can assure my daughter greatest dower / Shall have my Bianca's love" (2.1.386–87).[12] Yet, while Lucentio suggests to Bianca in the best New Comedy tradition that "we might beguile the old pantaloon" (3.1.40), in fact the necessity for deception has been averted by Baptista's ready agreement to the supposed Lucentio's financial offer.[13] By the end of act 2 the conventional standoff between marriage for love and for money has been transformed into a unanimity of desires between parent and child. The "supposed" Lucentio, negotiating with the father, and the real Lucentio, courting the daughter, both gain Bianca at about the same time—thus disengaging the mutually exclusive desires of father and suitor that conventionally trigger the conflict and move the plot.

The role of Tranio as tricky servant follows exactly the same pattern of disengagement. The diminished intergenerational conflict weakens the urgency of his intrigue, and the conventional subterranean plot with its false father and false dower is played for its humor rather than to rescue hero and heroine. Indeed, the secret wedding that Tranio engineers is propelled by no motive beyond his need to be busy on his master's behalf; it is so patently unnecessary that even Lucentio voices misgivings.[14]

Supposes vindicates passion not only in its arrangement of conflict and intrigue patterns, but also in its depiction of the relationship of the lovers. Initially the play vividly depicts the destructive powers of passion, which overrules wealth, rank, and social law. Both lovers risk reputation, family, and status for their "furious flames of love." Erostrato "cast[s] aside both long gowne and bookes," temporarily forfeiting status and name in order to "apply his study" to Polynesta alone (1.1, 113–14). And Polynesta herself, seemingly the "very maydenly," "holy yong woman" (3.4, 135), in turn relinquishes her virginity to Erostrato—to the anguish of her father, who reduces her price on the marriage market.

It is these same "extreme passions" (1.1, 112), however, which in typical New Comedy fashion are rewarded in the play. Because *Supposes* begins *in medias res* the lovers' passion is validated by its two-year duration. As Erostrato laments, "the more I have, the more I desire" (1.3, 119). And the quality of their affection is demonstrated in the first scene, where Polynesta manifests the loving and casual well-being as Erostrato's lover that marks a mature relationship.

At the end of the play, romantic love triumphs and its destabilizing energies are reabsorbed into conventional society. For their deception and betrayal of their duty, the lovers are rewarded with the blessings of their relieved parents for their "amorous offence" "youthfully and not maliciously" committed (5.10, 157). The benefits of this love match accrue not only to bride and groom but also to the rest of their society; all the other characters profit materially from their marriage. *Supposes* privileges romantic love, which, through the potentially disruptive and illicit intrigue of the powerless children, ultimately produces precisely the financial and social benefits for which the acquisitive parents have been striving. Northrop Frye (1965) says that youth wins over age and love over money *(*87, 118). Actually, the new society promises to be a fair reproduction of the old; New Comedy celebrates this return to the status quo, all through the power of passionate love.

The conventional New Comedy endorsement of romantic passion that is apparent in *Supposes* is undercut in *The Taming of the Shrew*. A seemingly minor change in the time scheme forms the foundation for this deflation: instead of beginning *in medias res*, Shakespeare begins *ab ovo* (Hosley, 1966, 144; 1963–1964, 304), a strategy which places the stress not on the strength but on the absurdity of passion. Love at first sight, conventional in comedy, is inherently both desirable and ridiculous. As Renaissance sonnets admirably demonstrate, the artful use of convention can mitigate the absurdity. Shakespeare structures this meeting of the lovers to achieve precisely the opposite effect. Lucentio, lovestruck, complains that Bianca's "sudden sight hath thralled my wounded eye" (1.1.217).

> Tranio, I burn, I pine, I perish, Tranio,
> If I achieve not this modest young girl,
> Counsel me Tranio, for I know thou canst;
> Assist me Tranio, for I know thou wilt. (1.1.158–61)

Here, artifice—both the Petrarchan and New Comedy lovers may be found in these lines—serves to trivialize Lucentio's passion (Hibbard 1964, 26). This unflattering view of the lover is given further substance in his unseemly competition with Hortensio for Bianca's attention in the schoolroom, a scene that assures his status as comic butt rather than romantic hero. Another consequence of beginning *ab ovo* is that fidelity cannot be invoked to legitimize the relationship. In fact, Erostrato's two years of growing love are replaced by Lucentio's total misapprehension about Bianca, whom he commends in the first scene for her "mild behavior and sobriety": "Sacred and sweet was all I saw in her" (1.1.180). This early reading of her character is called into question in the schoolroom scene and exploded at the banquet, where the conventional New Comic version of love is finally defeated.

Lucentio's portrayal is trivialized by an excess of artifice. Bianca sabotages New Comedy goals by a departure from convention rather than an immersion in it. Although New Comedy heroines are usually mute, and even the spirited and independent Polynesta of *Supposes* speaks no lines after the first scene, Shakespeare has expanded Bianca's role considerably, and his expansions empower her, creating the only rebel to patriarchy in the play.[15] The wooing scene presents her two-layered appropriation of power; at the same time that Lucentio and Hortensio conventionally resort to subterfuge to bypass Baptista's socially sanctioned power to choose his daughter's husband, the daughter herself wrests this privilege from her suitors in a violent departure from the passive role allotted the New Comedy heroine. As George R. Hibbard (1964) points out, her "true disposition" emerges in this scene (25), where she coolly cuts through her suitors' squabbling—"Why, gentlemen, you do me double wrong / To strive for that which resteth in my choice" (3.1.17–18)—and chooses for herself. She subsequently betrays her father in a "clandestine and double-faced elopement" (Coghill 1950, 11). And no

sooner has she passed from father to husband than she disobeys her spouse—
and chides *him* for *her* disobedience. Her defiance not only rebukes the
"punch line" of the wife-taming joke, which conventionally rests upon the
wife's unquestioning obedience, but probes the power of patriarchy from
which that punch line draws its legitimacy.

The play itself does not endorse Bianca's rebellion. The expansions that
Shakespeare has wrought upon her yoke her assertiveness with a personality
that elicits disapproval rather than sympathy from the audience. She is presented as spoiled and deceptive; there is something unprepossessing in the
way her independence lies hidden beneath her "Maid's mild behavior and
sobriety" (1.1.73; Thompson 1984, 15). Alexander Leggatt (1974) observes,
"Her sweet disposition is part of a deeper strategy, as Katherine recognizes"
(48). Bianca is neither the passive, invisible wife of New Comedy nor the pliant wife of the marriage tracts.

The banquet scene occurs in the happily ever after where New Comedy
and its descendants tread at their peril. There, the Bianca plot finally self-
destructs. Lucentio gleefully anticipates the joyful stasis which conventionally closes New Comedy: "happily I have arrived at the last / Unto the wished
haven of my bliss" (5.1.130–31). However, far from exemplifying a loving
energy that may revitalize society, Lucentio and Bianca are last seen bicker-
ing in an ugly jockeying for domestic power which banishes the promises that
passion and romantic love generally offer in New Comedy. Traditionally, the
purpose of the New Comedy plot is to circumvent the arranged marriage for
a more valued and viable love marriage. Yet in *Shrew*, the love marriage
toward which so many unnecessary energies have been directed is shown to
be shallow, its attractions unreliable. The implications of these alterations of
Supposes are spelled out in Leggatt's (1974) discussion of Lucentio: "Both
socially and artistically, he has won a conventional sweetheart in a conventional way; and when the prize turns out to have been a baited trap, not merely
the character but the conventions he has operated under are mocked" (48).

The Bianca plot, to summarize, subverts the typical processes and effects
of New Comedy. Its comic energies are generated by the intrigue alone, as
when the two Vincentios confront each other, rather than by the more common triumph of youth over age and rigidity. What is the significance of this
pattern, and how does it contribute to the intentions of the play as a whole?

The repetitive tract injunctions against romantic love and secret marriage
suggest how antithetical New Comedy passion is to Protestant marriage ideology. Conversely, the plethora of comic plots in narrative and dramatic form
indicate the formidable competition offered that ideology by literature. Shakespeare's adaptation of Gascoigne's conventional New Comedy dismantles that
challenge. Because the love marriage of the Bianca plot is not borne of struggle, and because the intrigues on its behalf are redundant rather than necessary, it is devalued. Moreover, the offenses against hierarchy that romantic

passion dictates spread disorder rather than establishing the "new society" supposed to be engendered by the defiance of the lovers. In short, closure in this new, New Comedy destabilizes rather than integrates the individual, the couple, and the household. This subversion redirects audience sympathies toward the more substantial and less conventional relationship of the Kate plot. The companionate marriage found there is thus foregrounded.

Two general sources for the Kate plot account for virtually all of its action. One encompasses the numerous folk versions of the shrew story, meticulously catalogued by Jan Brunvand. Plot devices found in both folk tales and Shakespeare's play include a wealthy father with good and bad daughters, warnings to the suitor about the shrew, the groom's indecorous attire and rowdy behavior at the wedding, the couple's return to the groom's home before the wedding banquet, some version of the sun-moon episode, and the wager banquet (347, 350–51). The other source is *A Merry Jest of a Shrewd and Curst Wife Lapped in Morel's Skin, for her Good Behaviour* (ca. 1560), a ballad that shares with *Shrew* the "basic situation," character portrayals in rough outline, the development of the action, and some verbal echoes (Hosley, 1963–1964, 297–98).[16]

Although shrew-taming stories coexisted with the domestic tracts, they are antithetical in almost every respect. Both espouse a hierarchical relationship between men and women, but the physical dominance that is a staple of the shrew-taming stories and their misogynistic orientation are both rejected in tract ideology.

Conduct-book writers inveigh against wife-beating with a fervor that suggests how common the practice must have been. Their reasons emphasize their insistence that hierarchy be fully integrated with intimacy. As Gouge explains, "That small disparity . . . betwixt man and wife, permitteth not so high a power in an husband, and so low a seruitude in a wife, as for him to beat her" (390). Froward women present a special problem to tract writers, but their prohibition of beating does not waver. In passages surely pertinent to Shakespeare's play, Gouge counsels that the shrewish wife "be restrained of libertie, denied such things as she most affecteth, be kept vp, as it were, in hold" (392). And Cleaver, copying almost verbatim from Juan Luis Vives's *Office and Duetie of an Husband*, advises that she "bee pleased and mitigated with loue, and ruled with majestie" (173; Vives [1555?], N7v-N8r). Cleaver sums it up in his own argument that the "tyrannie" lying behind wife-beating "may force the bodie, but not the will, in the which all loue and amitie doth consist and stand" (216). Thus the intimacy that is such a crucial component of the ideal married relationship prevents the husband's exploitation of the power allotted him by tract writers. Tyranny and love, mutually antithetical, sum up the distance between shrew stories and marriage manuals.

As with his treatment of New Comedy, Shakespeare's renovations of the shrew story bring it into conformity with Protestant marriage ideology.[17]

Three basic strategies are apparent. Every device in the shrew stories designed to privilege the husband is swiveled in *Shrew* so that it performs the same function for the couple. And simple domination is replaced by the concept of mutuality within hierarchy found in the tracts. Finally, love replaces brute force as the catalyst for change.

Both the folk versions of the shrew tale and *A Merry Jest* locate audience sympathy securely and exclusively with the beleaguered husband. This orientation is particularly apparent in the leisurely narrative of *A Merry Jest*, where it is created through the contrasting portrayals of husband and wife. Richard Hosley (1963–1964) speaks of the "sadistic relish" that characterizes the husband's actions in this ballad (296). However, while physical brutality forms the centerpiece of the narrative, the portrayal of the husband seems designed to disarm easy charges of sadism. He is presented as an ordinary, reasonable fellow who, while definitely drawn to the financial benefits of the marriage, clearly desires a loving relationship as well. His gentleness and forbearance prior to the taming are emphasized; his loving attempts to reason with his wife show that he is not a brute: "What can it auayle you for me to greeue, / That loueth you so well as I doe mine harte?" (*Merry Jest* 1875, 435). And his decision to resort to violence comes after a long meditative ride where hopelessness turns to "vengeaunce."

The temperament and behavior of the wife contrast in every way. She is presented as her mother's offspring both by nature and by nurture, hence irredeemably shrewish; word and deed reveal her impulse "Sometime to be mayster withouten misse" (*Merry Jest* 1875, 423). In her conflict with her husband she is unreasonable, brutal, and preemptive. Moreover, the source of the conflict—her unwillingness to care properly for their hired help—puts her as squarely in the wrong as her husband is in the right. And in the ensuing melee, her language is indeed "frantick" (*Merry Jest* 1875, 440) and her actions violent. This contrast in character between the reasonable, loving husband and the shrewish wife skews the ballad inexorably toward the husband.

In spite of the emphasis upon Petruchio's dominance in *The Taming of the Shrew*, this imbalance is largely righted. The portrayals of both Petruchio and Kate contribute to an egalitarian distribution of audience sympathy between them. From the time that Petruchio appears onstage, a humorousness answering Kate's is emphasized, for example in the knocking episode with the much beleaguered Grumio. And the epithet "mad" is applied to him at least as often as to Katherine. Finally, his outspoken intention to profit hugely by his marriage—"wealth is burden of my wooing dance" (1.2.69)—places him closer to the traditional comic blocking figure than to the lover.[18]

More important are the changes in Katherine. In *A Merry Jest* the alliance between the father and his docile younger daughter is balanced by the connivance of mother and older daughter. In *Shrew* this alignment is abolished by the absence of any kind of mother at all; a significant readjustment takes place as a result. As many critics have noticed,[19] Katherine is presented as the embittered victim of her father's long-standing preference for her younger sister. Consequently, her shrewishness does not appear to be a fixed quality of temperament, as in *A Merry Jest*, but is her response to a familial imbalance. This pattern, subtly apparent throughout the first scenes between father and daughters, becomes explicit when Kate cries,

> Nay, now I see
> She is your treasure, she must have a husband;
> I must dance barefoot on her wedding-day,
> And, for your love to her, lead apes in hell.
> Talk not to me: I will go sit and weep
> Till I can find occasion of revenge. (2.1.35–40)

The connection between her perceived sense of favoritism, spinsterhood, and her hostile behavior could not be clearer. Not only is the etiology of Kate's shrewishness changed, but its manifestation is considerably softened. As she promises, she vents her rage on Bianca and her hapless suitors;[20] in contrast to the source, there is a connection between the causes of her shrewishness and her victims.

The depiction of Kate as a conformist also enhances her stature relative to the wife's in *A Merry Jest*.[21] The wife, as her father, mother, and she herself acknowledge, defies prescriptions for female behavior in her urge to master her husband. Kate's fierce resentment, on the other hand, stems from her exclusion from the normal female life-trajectory within patriarchy; what she wants is marriage. In her violent persecution of Bianca, she speaks only of her sister's suitors. And as the above speech reveals, her fierce unhappiness and frowardness arise not from the independence of rebellion or even of eccentricity, but from deprivation. These hints of conformity coalesce in the banquet scene, where her happy assimilation into marriage, hierarchy, and patriarchy is as clearly proclaimed as Bianca's defiance. And in contrast to the play's lack of support for Bianca the rebel is the manner in which Kate claims audience approval, her frowardness notwithstanding. Shakespeare rewards conformity in *Shrew*; Kate's desire for what every comic heroine takes for granted is one of the many strategies that tips audience sympathy toward her.

Instead of being presented merely as the appropriate object of her husband's righteous brutality, Kate has been elevated to a position dramatically and morally equivalent to Petruchio's. This fundamental shift in perspective in *Shrew* is apparent in Shakespeare's strategies for handling humor and violence. In farce, humor is allied to violence. Whether the violence is actually vented on the wife, as in *A Merry Jest*, or merely directed toward her in a threatening challenge to her shrewishness, as in the folk stories, she is essentially the butt of a prolonged misogynistic joke. As Robert Heilman (1982) has argued, "Genuine feelings [in farce] are excluded by convention" (98); the wife, her portrayal distorted by caricature, is not constituted to elicit audience sympathy.[22]

This pattern is absent in *Shrew*. Two strategies predominate. First, for the most part the humor and violence that the husband traditionally vents on the wife are deflected from Katharine onto subsidiary characters such as Grumio, the sexton, Petruchio's household servants, the tailor.[23] For instance, in 4.3 Kate is the direct victim of the humor primarily in the food episode which prefaces the scene. However, her tormenter there is not Petruchio but Grumio. In the tailor scene that follows, the pattern of frustration that marks the food scene reappears—but with the tailor as Petruchio's victim. "Braved in mine own house with a skein of thread!" is the challenge Petruchio tosses to the tailor—not to Kate, whom he consistently treats with restraint (4.3.119). Thus the torment of wife by husband has been twice redirected. In fact, Petruchio aggressively exemplifies Bullinger's (1543) advice that the husband show "curtesy, kyndnesse, and playnnesse, and gentlenesse" to his spouse (66r). And Kate herself, formally the center of the scene, is essentially mute in the farcical parts. Invariably she is deliberately misunderstood or ignored. Her interjections are not funny but plaintive, wretched. One of her key speeches occurs in this episode when she says, "My tongue will tell the anger of my heart, / Or else my heart, concealing it, will break" (4.3.84–85). Her seriousness in the midst of the humor eddying about her allows her a substance separate from it, largely exempting her from the demeaning role of victim that the wife is forced to play in the sources.

Second, when the humor does concentrate directly on Katherine, it is as part of a shared exchange with Petruchio, where both are creators as well as targets of the wit. Their first scene together demonstrates this balance. While the interchange leaves no uncertainty about Petruchio's will and ability to dominate, the couple are presented as temperamentally and dramatically equal. They exhibit a zany, electric compatibility that appears in the easy reciprocity of their caustic humor;[24] the tension between their disputatiousness and their compatibility gives the scene a power that is shared between them dramatically. The fast thrust and parry of their exchange is apportioned equally between them until Petruchio's firm closing lines. A similar pattern is apparent in the sun-moon episode. These changes in the strategy of humor cause a significant shift in the moral and emotional structures of this shrew-taming story, as compared with its sources: Kate loses her perpetrator status, becoming, if anything, victim of her husband's rugged taming, and the couple rather than the husband alone commands audience approval.

From this foregrounding of the couple emerges the second strategy of revision, the transformation of simple male dominance into that complex tincture of mutuality and hierarchy that defines patriarchal marriage in the tracts. In traditional shrew-taming stories, the husband's physical and then psychological domination of his recalcitrant wife comprises action and closure. This process is invariably accomplished by proxy in the folk versions; as Brunvand (1966) summarizes, "the secret of the successful taming is the husband's trick of administering excessively severe punishment to an animal in order to frighten his bad wife" (347). In *A Merry Jest* physical combat between husband and wife marks the taming, as each struggles for "maystership." The husband's inevitable physical victory assures his wife's obedience in the marriage. After whipping her until she swoons, he wraps her in the salted hide of his faithful old horse, killed especially for the occasion, and threatens to keep her there forever. This straightforward domination produces the wife's capitulation: "your commaundementes I will, both far and neare, / Fulfil alway in euery degree" (*Merry Jest* 1875, 445).

The husband's vow in *A Merry Jest*: "I wyll be mayster, as it is reason, / And make her subiect vnto me" (439): unquestionably applies to Shakespeare's play as well. However, constant—and consistent—tinkerings with the details of the source episodes conspire to enlarge the vision of the marital relationship. From these alterations emerges not simple domination but the same kind of mutuality within hierarchy celebrated in the conduct books as the foundation for a healthy marriage, family, and society.

Consider the pattern: in the sources, the husband uses threats to compel the wife to leave the wedding feast (Brunvand 1966, 358); in *Shrew*, Petruchio pretends that both he and Kate are beset by "thieves," and he "rescues" her by effecting their joint escape. The physical brutality central to the training in the sources becomes in Shakespeare metaphorical—and the analogy is to falcon training, a process which, according to Margaret Loftus Ranald, suggests marriage as a partnership marked not only by obedience but also by mutual respect and love.[25] The husband in the composite version eats a hearty meal while depriving his wife of all sustenance; in *Shrew* neither husband nor wife eats ("for this night we'll fast for company" [4.1.175]) or sleeps ("if she chance to nod I'll rail and brawl / And with the clamor keep her still awake" [193–94]).[26]

The sun-moon episode is similarly transformed from the portrait of simple domination found in its folk sources. There, animals—ravens, storks, wolves, and sheep—are used in a grim reality contest between husband and wife (Bay 1899, 266). The sun and moon found in *Shrew* evoke entirely different associations. According to Jeanne Roberts (1983), they signify a powerful hermaphroditic emblem of partnership in marriage (169). Gouge (1622) refines on the nature of this partnership:

There may be *fellowship* in the very same things wherein is *inferiority* . . . as in *giuing light* the Sunne and Moone haue a fellowship, but . . . the Moone hath not so much light as the Sunne, and that which it hath it hath from the Sunne. . . . Euen so is it betwixt man and wife . . . . (357–58)

This pattern does not eliminate the celebratory nature of the episode. The docile acquiescence of the wives in the source stories becomes in *Shrew* an energetic, sparkling, and finally loving exchange between Petruchio and Katherine; her submission is encased within their collaborative jest with the bewildered Vincentio. As John Bean (1980) comments, the episode is "not a taming but a renewal and rebirth" (73; also Seronsy 1963, 23).

And finally, the banquet scene: in *A Merry Jest*, the newly tamed wife is paraded by her complacent husband before his approving guests, who agree that "he dyd well in euery maner degree" (*Merry Jest*, 1870, 447). Husband and guests, a kind of normative community, are ranged against the wife. In *Shrew* elements of this pattern remain, but from it emerges a different configuration. The banquet begins with unkind shrew jests ("a very mean meaning," as Katherine replies to one of them) which threaten to establish the conventional social alliances from which she would be excluded. The wager, in fact, proceeds out of the unfriendly wit of Tranio, Lucentio, Hortensio, and Baptista. And Petruchio's closing remarks suggest the same windy self-satisfaction that marks the husband's attitude in *A Merry Jest*. Yet the wager also signals the departure of Shakespeare's play from its sources, since both husband and wife win it, a triumph marked by Petruchio's assured conviction of his married happiness and the certainties found in Katherine's final speech (discussed below).

Consistently, then, the emphasis on the husband's dominance in the shrew-taming stories has been adroitly enlarged in *Shrew* to embrace a loving alliance between husband and wife. Marriage becomes a shared fate: as Gouge (1622) argues, "Though the man be as the head, yet is the woman as the heart" (271).

The third significant strategy marking Shakespeare's conversion of the shrew-taming story into conformity with Protestant marriage ideology is his replacement of physical force with love. During the banquet scene in *A Merry Jest* the daughter ushers her unbelieving mother to the cellar to view the instruments of her defeat, the rods and salted horse's hide. In *Shrew* physical brutality, such as it is, is deposited on the patently untamable Grumio. The catalyst for Kate is love. Listing Petruchio's taming tactics, she concludes bitterly, "And that which spites me more than all these wants, / He does it under name of perfect love" (4.3.12–13). Indeed, from their first meeting, Petruchio aims toward her a barrage of loving epithets: "sweet Katherine" (2.1.299, and another ten or so times in varying forms); "sweeting" (4.3.39), "love" (4.3.42), "my honey love" (4.3.57). In 1594 the minister Henry Smith reminded husbands, "[h]er cheekes are made for thy lippes, and not for thy fists" (44).[27]

If the Bianca plot disposes of the dangers to the companionate marriage offered by romantic love, what then is the function of the Kate plot? The easy answer is that it assails the opposite threat to marriage, found in the shrew-taming stories—that is, the tyranny of hierarchy. It does not of course banish hierarchy but essentially makes it palatable by removing the coercion and raw submission accompanying it. And it celebrates a vision of married love, characterized by mutuality within hierarchy, that is articulated in the conduct books. However, a more complex answer emerges from analysis of Kate's banquet speech, a speech that addresses all the significant issues raised by the Kate plot.

The passionate critical debate over this speech concerns the extent or perhaps better the success of Kate's taming, with each side claiming its own interpretation of "success." The controversy is significant, for it aptly sums up the major division in critical opinion about the play, which coalesces in opposed analyses of Katherine's portrayal. Let me review the arguments[28] and then offer a conciliatory proposal.

In the straight reading, Kate, a successfully, happily tamed shrew, celebrates her conversion. As I basically support this kind of interpretation, let me couch it in terms of my argument for the Kate plot. In this speech, Kate illustrates the truth of Alexander Niccholes's (1615) assessment of the benefits of marriage for the individual: by marriage "are thy wilde and vnbrideled affections reduced to humanity and ciuility, to mercy and clemency, and thou thy selfe called backe to looke into thy selfe, and to vnderstand the substance and truth of things" (6; addressed to husbands but pertinent to Kate). Her running concern is to fit a castigation of froward wives into a broader view of marriage. She applies the full range of metaphors found in the speech—from nature, politics, and the military—to shrews, and she freely acknowledges herself to have been one, having used mind and heart "To bandy word for word and frown for frown" (5.2.194). She criticizes frowardness precisely because it is inimical to the reciprocal obligations of the companionate marriage articulated in the tracts. Loving obedience, Kate makes clear, is the wife's part of that reciprocity, and it is that which she offers to Petruchio. Many of her sentiments in this speech may be found in the domestic tracts (Bean 67; Underdown 1985, 117); some, such as the monarch-subject analogue, come close to paraphrase. In fact Kate becomes a kind of mouthpiece for tract ideology, which she joyfully, not ironically, articulates.

In the second reading, Kate delivers the speech ironically, having learned through her taming that the solution to the demands of patriarchy is overt (and "playful," according to some[29]) submission and covert defiance. Taming, then, has taught her how to get along within the system; it has not subdued or essentially changed her. This reading is based upon the troublesome contradiction between her assertive actions in the final scene and her words, which counsel submission.

The two readings each pursue a different part of the contradiction between words and action. The literal one "hears" the words while the ironic one "sees" the actions. (See Wayne 1985, 172.) The ironic view may seem more compatible with late twentieth-century feminism than with fifteenth-century marriage dogma. Clearly, however, both plot and speech allow—indeed invite—such a latitude of interpretation. In fact, the ironic reading releases one of the significant oscillations found in the text itself. By promoting both a happily docile and a covertly liberated Kate, the speech performs one of the larger functions of the Kate plot as a whole. For it, like the marriage tracts that have shaped its transformation, conceals within it a "polemic," or perhaps better an advocacy, of marriage over spinsterhood. The speech participates in that polemic.

Two rather different factors seem to have promulgated a distrust of unmarried women in the English Renaissance, one anti-Catholic in impetus and the other pro-Protestant. The first was clearly the legacy of the break with Roman Catholicism. Prior to the Reformation, the convent provided a viable alternative to marriage for women, particularly rich women. Protestantism of course closed off this possibility of a measure of female autonomy. Yet various kinds of evidence suggest that the celibate life remained a lingering attraction, hence a threat in Protestant England. For instance, reformers failed to provide schooling for girls "partly because all-female institutions were too closely associated in Protestant thought with Catholic nunneries and female celibacy" (Warnicke 1983, 154, 157; also Fitz 1980, 8). Suggestions of similar fears are apparent in some of the conduct books. In Thomas Becon's preface to Bullinger's treatise on marriage, the two kinds of life are polemically opposed, with celibacy leading to whoredom and the decay of society, and marriage ensuring personal virtue and a flourishing state (A2r–A3r). Further removed from mid-sixteenth-century instabilities, Gouge offers a less strident, though perhaps equally condemnatory contrast: "If these two be duly poised, and rightly weyed, we shall finde single life too *light* to be compared with *honest* marriage" (211; emphasis mine).

Many manuals silently amputate the former alternative altogether, offering women a seamless passage from daughter to wife. Their omission suggests that the second factor involved in the distrust of unmarried women is embedded within Protestant marriage ideology itself; the clue, I believe, lies in the nexus between marriage and political stability that is affirmed so frequently in the tracts. William Gouge explicitly makes the analogy, arguing that if "inferiours . . . cannot be subject in a familie; they will hardly be brought to yeeld such subjection as they ought in Church or common-wealth" (18). S. D. Amussen (1985), who discusses this connection in detail, suggests its political significance:

> The analogy between the family and state . . . often supported an authoritarian-absolutist, and usually a divine right, theory of monarchy: political theory allowed no resistance of subjects, any more than household manuals allowed the resistance of wives or children. (198; see also 200)

Single women, at least theoretically free of domestic restraint,[30] would elude one of the two most powerful sources of social control. Thus both in reaction to Catholicism and in support of Protestant ideology, spinsterhood seems to have been the sometimes explicit sometimes silent antagonist to marriage.

Louis Montrose's (1983) comment on one of Hermia's speeches in *A Midsummer Night's Dream* suggests the connection between society and literature: "The self-possession of single blessedness is a form of power against which are opposed the marriage doctrines of Shakespeare's culture and the very form of his comedy" (68). *The Taming of the Shrew* participates in this privileging of marriage over celibacy. As in the tracts, embedded within its celebration of the companionate marriage is a subtext—a dismissal of virginity and spinsterhood, and a simultaneous promise that not they but marriage releases the power of women.

The first of these covert goals, the elimination of the threat of virginity, is couched in Katherine's process—the play would argue progress—from the abject desperation, loneliness, and social expendability of her spinster status to her position as happy, socially necessary, and beloved wife—an evolution that is made didactically clear in her final speech. Northrop Frye (1965) remarks wryly that Kate is the same at the end as at the beginning—a bully— but she "has learned how to do it with social approval on her side" (80). However, a substantial change marks this sameness; all the force of her personality initially absorbed in peevish misery is allowed to blossom in the end—in joyful defense of patriarchal marriage. Thus, the play suggests, it is only the bridle and bit of patriarchy that can liberate women's power. This conjunction of female power with patriarchal marriage is, I believe, the second covert goal of both tracts and play, and it is picked up in the banquet speech. The contradiction that the tracts establish between hierarchy and mutuality is resolved in *Shrew* by allotting to Kate not only the promise of deep fulfillment in her role as submissive wife but also and perhaps especially by offering her the power that is most apparent in her final scene. There she is allowed to be definitive, to prescribe, at the very moment that she proclaims her submission to patriarchy. It is that oxymoronic power that the ironic reading of the speech releases.

Shakespeare has performed an admirable transformation of his sources. From two genres of proven popularity—New Comedy and shrew-taming stories—which are both deeply inimical to contemporaneous marriage ideology, he has created a text which celebrates that idea of marriage. In his adaptation of *Supposes*, the comic machinery is dissociated from the meaning that generally propels it. The impoverishment of comic devices in the Bianca plot weakens the power of romantic love. This is apparent in the inaccuracy of Lucentio's exultant cry at the point of comic cognitio: "Love wrought these miracles" (5.1.112). "Miracles" turns out to be a misnomer for what happens in the Bianca plot, and love did not in any case work them; intrigue did. Rather than fulfilling New Comedy trajectories, the Bianca plot suppresses them, functioning instead as a pointer to the Kate plot, which contains the ideological message of the play. There, Shakespeare employs substitution and enrichment to dismantle the challenge to the companionate marriage of the shrew-taming stories. Simple dominance is replaced by a struggle for a viable, intimate marriage structured by hierarchy. The play privileges this endeavor by letting all the love and miracles happen in the Kate plot. Thus the vision of the companionate marriage shaping the play arises from the deconstruction of its two literary threats.

NOTES

Originally published in *Renaissance Drama* 20 (1989): 141–67. Reprinted by permission of Margaret Lael Mikesell and *Renaissance Drama*. This research was supported in part by grants from the PSC-BHE Research Award Program of the City University of New York.

1. Howard C. Cole (1983) has recently argued that "an uncritical acceptance of their sources' values characterizes Shakespeare's earliest comedies" (409). However, the scholarship in this area has established, on the contrary, that the changing values of his times underlie many of Shakespeare's substantial alterations of his sources. For reflections on the challenges involved in the analysis of Shakespeare's alterations of his sources, see McEachern 1988, especially 169–274. Richard Hosley's (1966) seminal "The Formal Influence of Plautus and Terence" discusses how Elizabethan social customs shaped dramatic adaptations of New Comedy conventions. In the course of larger studies, critics such as Alexander Leggatt (1974), J. Dennis Huston (1981), and Edward Berry (1984) observe how the Bianca plot has inverted New Comedy conventions in one way or another, and they have reflected on the significance of these changes. And Robert Heilman and John C. Bean explore the conversion of the Kate plot from its farcical sources into a story with more "humanized" characterization (Bean 1980, 66, 74), "one based upon a genuine humanity of feeling and intelligence" (Heilman 1982, 102).

2. John Bean (1980) and Marion Perret (1983) are among the few critics to demonstrate how closely Shakespeare shapes the portrayals of Katherine and Petruchio to the ideal husbands and wives found in this didactic literature. On the whole, critics have seen Shakespeare as more progressive than the tract writers, whom Margaret Loftus Ranald (1974) terms "repressive" (149) in her illuminating discussion of falconry and *Shrew*. Ann Thompson (1984) typically argues that the play's "final statement on marriage . . . is quite enlightened when we compare it with analogous literary texts or with theologically sanctioned views of intrinsic feminine inferiority" (30). Such a view is enticing, and it could accurately be applied to Shakespeare's treatment of love and marriage in his more mature comedies. *The Taming of the Shrew*, however, duplicates the orthodox sex role prescriptions articulated in the marriage tracts.

3. "Largely" unchanged represents my cautious assessment of a long-standing controversy about whether changes in marriage and the family in fact took place dur-

ing the English Renaissance, and if so, their nature and extent. The traditional cases for change are represented by the well-known studies of Lawrence Stone (1977) and William and Malleville Haller (1941–1942). Stone writes at length about the changes he has found in family structure (4–7 and chaps. 3–8). The Hallers place the development of the concept of the companionate marriage in the Protestant didactic literature of the sixteenth and seventeenth centuries. For opposing views, see Kathleen Davies (1981) and Linda Fitz (1980), who both argue that little change took place in marriage ideology as a result of the Reformation. Mary Beth Rose (1988), finely tuning both argument and evidence, offers a different view of the changes and discusses their implications for drama (see especially her introduction and chap. 1).

4. Taylor 1883, 227; see also Vives [1555?] CCl.

5. Coppélia Kahn's (1975) article rests in part, I think, on her uneasiness with it. She views the "psychological realities of marriage in Elizabethan England" as a situation "in which the husband's will constantly, silently, and invisibly, through custom and conformity, suppressed the wife's" (94). This process is more apparent in *A Merry Jest* than in *Shrew* and the marriage tracts.

6. My discussion of comic conventions relies throughout on one of Northrop Frye's two comic paradigms: boy meets girl, encounters obstacles (usually in the form of parents, or "blocking figures," who invoke an arbitrary law to rationalize their resistance), overcomes obstacles by resorting to intrigue—with the essential help of a tricky servant—and gets girl (Frye 1949, 166). The cognitio allows the desires of children and blocking figures to coincide, and the marriage heralds a "new society" in which love, not money, is the vital social currency. (See Frye 1949; 1957, 163–71, and 1965, chap. 3.)

7. For similar sentiments, see Vives [1555?], T2v; Whetstone 1582, F1; Becon 1560, cccclxiiv.r.

8. Thus George Hibbard's (1964) claim that both romantic comedy and didactic tracts reject the arranged marriage (18) is not accurate.

9. Whately 1624, 71; see also Stockwood 1589, 11, 44; Whetstone 1582, H1v.

10. As a New Comedy, *Supposes* contains clandestine lovers pitted against aged blocking figures, parasite, tricky servant, and an essentially mute heroine—along with the conventional comic action described in note 6 above. Particularly Elizabethan features that appear in Gascoigne's play include the introduction of chastity and marriage as issues vital to the plot, an initially active heroine, and fathers and aged suitors as blocking agents, to mention a few that also figure in *Shrew* (Hosley, 1966, 137, 144).

11. Brian Morris (1981) would not agree: "Romantic love is allowed full weight in the play. It is not mocked. It is seen as the source of endless ingenuity, invention, and youthful exuberance." He does contrast Lucentio's late adolescent romanticism with Petruchio's more mature and clear-sighted love (143). Alexander Leggatt (1974) has astutely discussed this aspect of *Shrew*. His entire argument is of interest, but see especially 46–47, 61.

12. All quotations have been taken from the Folger edition, edited by Louis B. Wright and Virginia A. LaMar (Shakespeare 1963).

13. Carol F. Heffernan (1985) argues, in contrast, that unlike in *Supposes*, "Shakespeare makes the possibility of marriage to the *amans senex* very real" (8).

14. Hosley (1963–1964), too, terms it "not strictly necessary for the conduct of the plot" (304). For an opposing view, see Heffernan, who presents Lucentio as "quite right" in seeking an elopement. His behavior is part of his general readiness "to evade ordinary bourgeois expectations (9).

15. Kate has usually been regarded as the defiant sister (Hibbard 1964, 23 and Newman 1986, 90, for instance).

16. See also Morris 1981, 70–76 and Oliver 1982, 49–50 for more recent analysis of source material for the Kate plot.

17. As my discussion indicates, Ranald's (1974) otherwise incisive article is incorrect in arguing that in transforming the wife-beating farce, "Shakespeare has skillfully remolded his material to portray an *atypical* attitude towards marriage" (149; emphasis mine). Hosley (1963–1964) demonstrates more cogently that Shakespeare's play relies primarily on the humanist rather than the *fabliau* traditions for its taming techniques (301). See also Bean 1980, 66.

18. When Petruchio and Baptista meet, the former bluntly inquires after Kate's dowry. It is Baptista who must remind him of the necessity of obtaining her love, "for that is all in all." By the standards of the marriage tracts, Petruchio's mercenary designs are unacceptable. "If money or nobilitie coulde perceyue and vnderstande that they were beloued, they would yf they had anye felynge at all of loue, requite it with loue: but when the soule is loued, inasmuch as it may loue, it geueth loue for loue, and loueth agayne" (Vives [1555?] N7v; quoted without attribution in Cleaver 1598, 173). See Heffernan (1985) for a solid discussion of Petruchio's "station in life and financial worth" (4–6). The taming of *him* includes an "attack on certain middle-class values and conventions" (12). For an analysis of Petruchio which leaves him firmly in the tamer role, see Baumlin 1989, especially 239.

19. See Roberts 1983, 163; Coghill 1950, 11; Ranald 1974, 154, 156; Saccio 1984, 36; and Ruth Nevo (1980), who observes that Katherine "has become nothing but an obstacle or a means to her sister's advancement. Even the husband they seek for her is in reality for the sister's sake, not hers" (41).

20. Valerie Wayne (1985) points out that Katherine is mad at nearly everyone except her husband; therefore Petruchio "becomes not an object of wrath but an agent for concord" (170).

21. Acknowledging but rejecting this argument for conformity, Karen Newman (1986) uses D. E. Underdown's (1985) analysis of shrews as a basis for her interpretation of Kate as rebel: the issue is not so much her "lack of a husband, or indeed her desire for a marriage partner, but rather her distaste at those folk customs which make her otherness, her place outside that patriarchal system, a public fact, a spectacle for all to see and mock" (94).

22. The version that I heard as a child from my father went as follows: "A man marries a shrew. On the trip home the horse stumbles. 'That's once,' says the husband. It stumbles again. 'That's twice.' It stumbles a third time. Saying, 'That's three times,' the husband pulls out a gun and shoots the horse. The wife launches an impassioned protest. "That's once," says the husband. And he never has any trouble out of her again." Great guffaws, mine included. Sympathy for the wife never crossed my mind.

    Shakespeare's "humanization" of the farcical elements of the Kate plot—how much and in what way—has generated much critical discussion, most acutely by

Heilman, 1982; Bean 1980; and Saccio 1984. Two factors, in my view, pull the plot away from farce. One is Kate's consistently "realistic" response to the horse-play, and the other is the play's emphasis on the couple; both interrogate the joker-target nexus, which must be accepted unquestioningly for farce to work.

23. See Wayne 1985, 171. Kate McLuskie (1977) would vehemently disagree. She argues that Petruchio is presented as a "triumphant wit" straight through the play. "However, the joke is always at Katherine's expense and the consistency of the play's tone requires that we find Petruchio's systematic destruction of Katherine's will no less funny than his puns" (35).

24. Ranald 1974, 156, 162; see also Nevo 1980, 44 and Baumlin 1989, 242. For an acute analysis of this scene that stresses the incompatible objectives of the two, see Cooper 1981, especially 5–11.

25. Ranald 1974, 153, 158. See also Hibbard 1964, 24. For an opposing view of this passage, see Coppélia Kahn (1975), who argues, "The animal metaphor shocks us and I would suggest was meant to shock Shakespeare's audience, despite their respect of falconry as an art." It shows "the status of woman in marriage as degrading in the extreme" (95–96; cf. also Andresen-Thom 1982, 134 and McLuskie 1977, 37). Brian Morris (1981) views the play as shaped by two tam-ing images, the shrew, which gives way halfway through the play, and the falcon (124–29).

26. Likening this process to falconry, Ranald (1974) comments, "This method of gaining obedience [from falcons], though cruel, is one that lays equal demands on both bird and keeper" (159; see also Henze 1970, 237; Huston 1981, 60). By embedding the training sessions in the necessities of everyday married life, as Marion Perret (1983) astutely points out, Katherine learns *how* to be a wife (228–29 for instance; also Leggatt 1974, 53). And in depriving her of food, clothes, and rest, Petruchio forces upon Kate precisely the everyday physical dependence allocated to the wife in the manuals—and to which Kate approvingly refers in the banquet speech. The training arises from the substance of her oblig-ations as wife, as defined in the conduct books. In their first scene together, Petru-chio accurately promises to bring her from a "wild Kate to a Kate / Conformable as other household Kates" (2.1.279–80).

27. The marginal gloss on this admonition is a bit more astringent: "Husbands must hold their hands and wiues their tongues" (Smith 1593, 44). See Baumlin (1989) for an extended analysis of Petruchio's use of language rather than physical force in his taming (passim, but especially 238–39).

28. See Novy 1984, 58–59, Morris 1981, 144–47, Burns 1986, 45–49, and Daniell 1984, 27–28, for instance, for readings of the speech similar to mine, and Kahn 1975, 98–99, Wayne 1985, 171–73, and McLuskie 1977, 35, 38, for critical read-ings. H.J. Oliver argues that because of the dominance of farce in the play, "it can-not logically be taken seriously, orthodox though the views expressed may be" (57; similarly, Heilman, 1966, 159). Analyzing the articles of Heilman and Kahn, Marilyn Cooper (1981) uses this speech to explore their disagreement and some of the play's central controversies.

29. Wayne 1985, 171–72, Saccio 1984, 39, for instance.

30. See also Wilson 1987, xxvi–xxvii and Fitz 1980, 8, 18. The reality may have been quite different. Although tracts in Reformation England offer almost as a truism

the equation Protestant women = wife, statistical evidence indicates that in fact a "substantial proportion"—and a growing one—of all women never married (Wrightson 1982, 68). Estimates of the percentage of spinsters at the turn of the century run from around ten (Wrightson 1982) to fifteen percent (Stone 1977, 44). The lot of the spinster during this period, distinguished as it was by social and financial marginality, was grim, as Miriam Slater (1984) has shown in her discussion of one landed family (78, 84–89; see also Warnicke 1983, 180). And the cyclical persecution of so-called witches and scolds suggests how threatening (or how convenient as scapegoats) single women were to some communities (see Underdown 1985 passim).

WORKS CITED

Amussen, S. D. 1985. "Gender, Family, and the Social Order, 1560–1725." In *Order and Disorder in Early Modern England*. Edited by Anthony Fletcher and John Stevenson. Cambridge: Cambridge University Press.

Andresen-Thom, Martha. 1982. "Shrew-taming and Other Rituals of Aggression: Baiting and Bonding on the Stage and in the Wild." *Women's Studies* 9: 121–43.

Baumlin, Tita French. 1989. "Petruchio the Sophist and Language as Creation in *The Taming of the Shrew*." *Studies in English Literature, 1500–1900* 29: 237–57.

Bay, J. Christian, ed. 1899. *Danish Fairy and Folk Tales* New York: Harper.

Bean, John C. 1980. "Comic Structure and the Humanizing of Kate in *The Taming of the Shrew*." In *The Woman's Part: Feminist Criticism of Shakespeare*. Edited by Carolyn Ruth Swift Lenz, Gayle Greene, and Carol Thomas Neely. Urbana: University of Illinois Press.

Becon, Thomas. 1984. Preface. *The Christen State of Matrimonye*. By Heinrich Bullinger. Translated by Berry, Edward. 1984. *Shakespeare's Comic Rites*. New York: Cambridge University Press.

———. *The Booke of Matrimony. Worckes*. Vol. 1. London.

Brunvand, Jan Harold. 1966. "The Folktale Origin of *The Taming of the Shrew*." *Shakespeare Quarterly* 17: 345–59.

Bullinger, Heinrich. 1543. *The Christen State of Matrimonye*. Translated by Miles Coverdale. London.

Burns, Margie. 1986. "The Ending of *The Shrew*." *Shakespeare Studies* 18: 41–64.

C[leaver], R[obert]. 1598. *A Godlie Forme of Hovseholde Government*. London.

Coghill, Nevill. 1950. "The Basis of Shakespearian Comedy: A Study in Medieval Affinities." *Essays and Studies* nos. 3: 1–28.

Cole, Howard C. 1983. "Shakespeare's Comedies and Their Sources: Some Biographical and Artistic Inferences." *Shakespeare Quarterly* 34: 405–19.

Cooper, Marilyn M. 1981. "Implicature, Convention, and *The Taming of the Shrew*." *Poetics* 10: 1–14.

Daniell, David. 1984. "The Good Marriage of Katherine and Petruchio." *Shakespeare Survey* 37: 23–31.

Davies, Kathleen M. 1981. "Continuity and Change in Literary Advice on Marriage." In *Marriage and Society: Studies in the Social History of Marriage*. Edited by R.B. Outhwaite. New York: St. Martin's.

Erasmus, Desiderius. [1530]. *A ryght frutefull Epystle . . . in laude and prayse of matry-mony*. Translated by Richard Tavernour. London.

Fitz, Linda T. 1980. "'What Says the Married Woman?': Marriage Theory and Femi-nism in the English Renaissance." *Mosaic* 13, no. 2: 1–22.

Frye, Northrop. 1949. "The Argument of Comedy." *English Institute Essays*. Edited by D. A. Robertson. New York: Columbia University Press. (Reprinted in *Mod-ern Shakespearean Criticism: Essays on Style, Dramaturgy, and the Major Plays*, edited by Alvin B. Kernan [New York: Harcourt, 1970]; and in *Shakespeare: Modern Essays in Criticism*, edited by Leonard F. Dean [New York: Oxford Uni-versity Press, 1961].

———. 1966. *Anatomy of Criticism: Four Essays*. 1957. New York: Atheneum.

———. *A Natural Perspective: The Development of Shakespearean Comedy and Romance*. New York: Harbinger-Harcourt.

Gascoigne, George. 1957. *Supposes: Narrative and Dramatic Sources of Shakespeare*. Edited by Geoffrey Bullough. Vol. I. London: Routledge.

Gouge, William. 1622. *Of Domesticall Duties: Eight Treatises*. London.

Haller, William, and Malleville Haller. 1941–1942. "The Puritan Art of Love." *Hunt-ington Library Quarterly* 5: 235–72.

Heffernan, Carol F. 1985. "*The Taming of the Shrew*: The Bourgeoisie in Love." *Essays in Literature* 12: 3–14.

Heilman, Robert B. 1966. "The *Taming* Untamed, or, The Return of the Shrew." *Mod-ern Language Quarterly* 27: 147–61.

———. "Shakespeare's Variations on Farcical Style." In *Shakespeare's Craft: Eight Lectures*. Edited by Philip H. Highfill, Jr. Carbondale: Southern Illinois Univer-sity Press.

Henze, Richard. 1970. "Role Playing in *The Taming of the Shrew*." *Southern Human-ities Review* 4: 231–40.

Hibbard, George R. 1964. "*The Taming of the Shrew*: A Social Comedy." In *Shake-spearean Essays*. Edited by Alwin Thaler and Norman Sanders. Knoxville: Uni-versity of Tennessee Press.

Hieron, Samuel. 1614. *All the Sermons*. London.

Hosley, Richard. 1963–1964. "Sources and Analogues of *The Taming of the Shrew*." *Huntington Library Quarterly* 27: 289–308.

———. 1966. "The Formal Influence of Plautus and Terence." *Elizabethan Theatre*. Edited by John Russell Brown and Bernard Harris. Stratford-upon-Avon Studies no. 9. London: Arnold.

Huston, J. Dennis. 1981. *Shakespeare's Comedies of Play*. New York: Macmillan.

Kahn, Coppélia. 1975. "*The Taming of the Shrew*: Shakespeare's Mirror of Marriage." *Modern Language Studies* 5: 88–102. (Reprinted in *The Authority of Experience: Essays in Feminist Criticism*. Edited by Arlyn Diamond and Lee R. Edwards. Amherst: University of Massachusetts Press, 1977.)

Leggatt, Alexander. 1974. *Shakespeare's Comedy of Love*. London: Methuen.

McEachern, Claire. 1988. "Fathering Herself: A Source Study of Shakespeare's Fem-inism." *Shakespeare Quarterly* 39: 269–90.

McLuskie, Kate. 1977. "Feminist Deconstruction: The Example of Shakespeare's *Taming of the Shrew*." *Red Letters* 12: 33–40.

A Merry Jest of a Shrewd and Curst Wife Lapped in Morel's Skin for Her Good Behaviour. 1875. In *Shakespeare's Library.* Edited by William Carew Hazlitt. 2d ed. Part I. Vol. 4. London: Reeves and Turner, 1875.

Montrose, Louis Adrian. 1983. "'Shaping Fantasies': Figurations of Gender and Power in Elizabethan Culture." *Representations* 2: 61–94.

Morris, Brian. 1981. Introduction. *The Taming of the Shrew.* The Arden Shakespeare. London: Methuen.

Nevo, Ruth. 1980. *Comic Transformations in Shakespeare.* New York: Methuen.

Newman, Karen. 1986. "Renaissance Family Politics and Shakespeare's *The Taming of the Shrew.*" *English Literary Renaissance* 16: 86–100.

Niccholes, Alexander. 1615. *A Discourse, of Marriage and Wiving.* London.

Novy, Marianne. 1984. *Love's Argument: Gender Relations in Shakespeare.* Chapel Hill: University of North Carolina Press.

Oliver, H. J. Introduction. 1982. *The Taming of the Shrew.* The Oxford Shakespeare. Oxford: Clarendon.

Perret, Marion D. "Petruchio: The Model Wife." *Studies in English Literature, 1500–1900* 23: 223–35.

Ranald, Margaret Loftus. 1974. "The Manning of the Haggard; or *The Taming of the Shrew.*" *Essays in Literature* 1: 149–65. (Reprinted in *Shakespeare and His Social Context: Essays in Osmotic Knowledge and Literary Interpretation.* New York: AMS, 1987.)

Roberts, Jeanne Addison. 1983. "Horses and Hermaphrodites: Metamorphoses in *The Taming of the Shrew.*" *Shakespeare Quarterly* 34: 159–71.

Rose, Mary Beth. 1988. *The Expense of Spirit: Love and Sexuality in English Renaissance Drama.* Ithaca: Cornell University Press.

Rowe, George E., Jr. 1979. *Thomas Middleton and the New Comedy Tradition.* Lincoln: University of Nebraska Press.

Saccio, Peter. 1984. "Shrewd and Kindly Farce." *Shakespeare Survey* 37: 33–40.

Seronsy, Cecil C. 1963. "'Supposes' as the Unifying Theme in *The Taming of the Shrew.*" *Shakespeare Quarterly* 14: 15–30.

Shakespeare, William. 1963. *The Taming of the Shrew.* Edited by Louis B. Wright and Virginia A. LaMar. The Folger Library General Reader's Shakespeare. New York: Washington Square.

Slater, Miriam. 1984. *Family Life in the Seventeenth Century: The Verneys of Claydon House.* London: Routledge.

Smith, Henry. 1593. "A Preparatiue to Mariage." *The Sermons of Maister Henrie Smith.* London.

Stockwood, John. 1589. *A Bartholmew Fairing for Parentes.* London.

Stone, Lawrence. 1977. *The Family, Sex and Marriage in England, 1500–1800.* New York: Harper.

Taylor, Jeremy. 1883. "The Marriage Ring." In *The Whole Works.* Edited by Reginald Heber. Revised edited. Vol. 4. London.

Thompson, Ann. 1984. Introduction. *The Taming of the Shrew.* The New Cambridge Shakespeare. Cambridge: Cambridge University Press.

Underdown, D. E. 1985. "The Taming of the Scold: The Enforcement of Patriarchal Authority in Early Modern England." In *Order and Disorder in Early Modern*

England. Edited by Anthony Fletcher and John Stevenson. Cambridge: Cambridge University Press, 1985.

Vives, Juan Luis. 1983. *The Office and Duetie of an Husband*. Translated by Thomas Paynell. London.

Warnicke, Retha M. 1983. *Women of the English Renaissance and Reformation*. Contributions in Women's Studies no. 38. Westport, Conn.: Greenwood.

Wayne, Valerie. 1985. "Refashioning the Shrew." *Shakespeare Studies* 17: 159–87.

Whately, William. 1624. *A Care-cloth: Or A Treatise of the Cumbers and Trovbles of Marriage*. London.

Whetstone, George. 1582. *An Heptameron of Ciuill Discourses*. London.

Wilson, Katharina M. 1987. Introduction. In *Women Writers of the Renaissance and Reformation*. Edited by Katharina M. Wilson. Athens: University of Georgia Press.

Wrightson, Keith. 1982. *English Society 1580–1680*. New Brunswick, N.J.: Rutgers University Press.

Scolding Brides and Bridling Scolds
Taming the Woman's Unruly Member

LYNDA E. BOOSE

For feminist scholars, the irreplaceable value if not pleasure to be realized by an historicized confrontation with Shakespeare's *The Taming of the Shrew* lies in the unequivocality with which the play locates both women's abjected position in the social order of early modern England and the costs exacted for resistance. For romantic comedy to "work" normatively in *Shrew*'s concluding scene and allow the audience the happy ending it demands, the cost is, simply put, the construction of a woman's speech that must unspeak its own resistance and reconstitute female subjectivity into the self-abnegating rhetoric of Kate's famous disquisition on obedience. The cost is Kate's self-deposition, where—in a performance not unlike Richard II's—she moves centerstage to dramatize her own similarly theatrical rendition of "Mark, how I will undo myself."

Apparently from the play's inception its sexual politics have inspired controversy. Within Shakespeare's own lifetime it elicited John Fletcher's sequel, *The Woman's Prize, or The Tamer Tam'd*, which features Petruchio marrying a second, untamable wife after his household tyranny has sent poor Kate to an early grave. As the title itself announces, Fletcher's play ends with Petruchio a reclaimed and newly lovable husband—"a woman's prize"—and, needless to say, a prize who still has the last words of the drama. Yet Fletcher's response may in itself suggest the kind of discomfort that *Shrew* has characteristically provoked in men and why its many revisions since 1594 have repeatedly contrived ways of softening the edges, especially in the concluding scene, of the play's vision of male supremacy. Ironically enough, if *The Taming of the Shrew* presents a problem to male viewers, the problem lies in its representation of a male authority so successful that it nearly destabilizes the very discourse it so blatantly confirms. Witness George Bernard Shaw's distress:

> No man with any decency of feeling can sit it out in the company of a woman
> without being extremely ashamed of the lord-of-creation moral implied in
> the wager and the speech put into the woman's own mouth.[1]

Yet the anxiety that provokes Shaw's reaction hardly compares with what the
play's conclusion would, by that same logic, produce in women viewers. For
Kate's final *piece de non résistance* is constructed not as the speech of a discrete character speaking her role within the expressly marked-out boundaries
of a play frame; it is a textual moment in which, in Althusserian terms, the
play quite overtly "interpellates," or hails, its women viewers into an imaginary relationship with the ideology of the discourse being played out onstage
by their counterparts.[2] Having "fetched hither" the emblematic pair of offstage
wives who have declined to participate in this game of patriarchal legitima-
tion, Kate shifts into an address targeted at some presumptive Everywoman.
Within that address women viewers suddenly find themselves universal con-
scripts, trapped within the rhetorical co-options of a discourse that dissolves
all difference between the "I" and "you" of Kate and her reluctant sisters. Kate
vacates the space of subjectivity in

> I am ashamed that women are so simple
> To offer war where they should kneel for peace,
> Or seek for rule, supremacy and sway,
> When they are bound to serve, love and obey . . .
> Come, come, you froward and unable worms,
> My mind hath been as big as one of yours,
> My heart as great, my reason haply more,
> To bandy word for word and frown for frown.
> But now I see our lances are but straws,
> Our strength as weak, our weakness past compare,
> That seeming to be most which we indeed least are.
> Then vail your stomachs, for it is no boot,
> And place your hands below your husband's foot. (5.2.161–64, 169–77)[3]

In doing so, she rhetorically pushes everyone marked as "woman" out of that
space along with her. And it is perhaps precisely because women's relationships to this particular comedy are so ineluctably bound up in such a theatri-
calized appropriation of feminine choice that Shakespeare's play ultimately
becomes a kind of primary text within which each woman reader of successive eras must renegotiate a (her) narrative.

Inevitably, it is from the site/sight of the subjected and thoroughly spec-
tacularized woman that virtually all critiques of *The Taming of the Shrew* have
felt compelled to begin. For when Kate literally prostrates herself in her final
lines of the play and thus rearranges the sexual space onstage, she reconfig-

ures the iconography of heterosexual relationship not merely for herself but for all of those "froward and unable worms" inscribed within her interpellating discourse. Not surprisingly, the discomforts of such a position have produced an investment even greater in female than in male viewers in reimagining an ending that will at once liberate Kate from meaning what she says and simultaneously reconstruct the social space into a vision of so-called mutuality—an ending that will satisfy the "illusion of a potentially pleasureable, even subversive space for Kate."[4] Thus, the critical history of *Shrew* reflects a tradition in which such revisionism has become a kind of orthodoxy. For albeit in response to a play which itself depends upon the exaggerations of gender difference, the desires of directors, players, audiences, and literary critics of both sexes have been curiously appeased by a similar representation: whether for reasons of wishing to save Kate from her abjection or Petruchio from the embarrassment of having coerced it, almost everyone, it seems, wants this play to emphasize "Kate's and Petruchio's mutual sexual attraction, affection, and satisfaction [and] deemphasize her coerced submission to him."[5] Ultimately, what is under covert recuperation and imagined as tacitly at stake is the institution of heterosexual marriage.

To insist upon historicizing this play is to insist upon placing realities from the historically literal alongside the reconstructive desires that have been written onto and into the literary text. It is to insist upon invading privileged literary fictions with the realities that defined the lives of sixteenth-century "shrews"—the real village Kates who underwrite Shakespeare's character. Ultimately, it is to insist that a play called "The Taming of the Shrew" must be accountable for the history to which its title alludes. However shrewish it may seem to assert an intertextuality that binds the obscured records of a painful women's history into a comedy that celebrates love and marriage, that history has paid for the right to speak itself, whatever the resultant incongruities.

As dominant onstage as the ameliorative tradition of *Shrew* production has been,[6] the impulse to rewrite the more oppressively patriarchal material in this play serves the very ideologies about gender that it makes less visible by making less offensive. To tamper with the literalness of Kate's physical submission onstage deflects attention away from an equally literal history in which both Kate and the staging of her body are embedded. As it turns out, the play's most (in)famous theatrical moment owes far less to Shakespeare's imagination than it does to a concrete analogue that Kate's prostration seems to be staging. For whatever else may be going on in *The Taming of the Shrew*'s finale, the scene dramatizes a now correctly ordered version of the play's earlier negated, parodic marriage. It represents a ritually corrected replay of both the offstage church ceremony that had been turned into anti-ceremony by Petruchio's irreverent behavior and the bridal feast at which Kate was displaced and re-placed by the seemingly virtuous Bianca, who, at the end of 3.2, was chosen to "bride it" in her wayward sister's stead. Finally, after Kate is allowed to return to Padua for Bianca's wedding, it is Kate who displaces Bianca as the virtuous and honored bride. This displacement converts what was billed as Bianca's bridal feast into the missing communal celebration to honor the earlier marriage that Kate's staged submission here recuperates into communal norms. Neither the feast nor the postponed consummation may take place in this play until the hierarchical features of the marriage rite have thus been restoratively enacted.

The referential context for Kate's bodily prostration in 5.2 is anchored by its placement inside a speech that incorporates verbatim the "serve, love and obey" (1. 164) of a bride's wedding vows. Not only do her words re-present those vows, however; her body reenacts them. For what transpires onstage turns out to be a virtual representation of the ceremony that women were required to perform in most pre-Reformation marriage services throughout Europe. In England this performance was in force as early as the mid-fifteenth century and perhaps earlier; and it may well have continued in local practice even after Archbishop Cranmer had reformed the Book of Common Prayer in 1549 and excised just such ritual excesses.[7] Kate's prostration before her husband and the placing of her hand beneath his foot follow the ceremonial directions that accompany the Sarum (Salisbury) Manual, the York Manual, the Scottish Rathen Manual, and the French Martene (*Ordo IV*) for the response the bride was to produce when she received the wedding ring and her husband's all-important vow of endowment.

According to the Use of Sarum, after the bridegroom had given the vow, "With this rynge I wedde the, and with this golde and siluer I honoure the, and with this gyft I dowe thee," the priest next "asks the dower of the woman." If "land is given her in the dower," the bride "prostrates herself at the feet of the bridegroom." In one manuscript of the Sarum Rite, the bride is directed to "kiss the right foot" of her spouse, which she is to do "whether there is land in the doury or not."[8] The York, Rathen, and Martene manuals, however, direct "this courtesying to take place only when the bride has received land as her dower." As Shakespeare's audience knows, Petruchio has indeed promised Baptista that he will settle on his wife an apparently substantial jointure of land. And while Kate offers to place her hands below her husband's foot rather than kiss it, the stage action seems clearly enough to allude to a ritual that probably had a number of national and local variants. Thus Giles Fletcher, Queen Elizabeth's ambassador to Russia, writes of a Russian wedding:

> the Bride commeth to the Bridegroome (standing at the end of the altar or table) and falleth downe at his feete, knocking her head upon his shooe, in token of her subjection and obedience. And the Bridegroom again casteth the cappe of his gowne or upper garment over the Bride, in token of his duetie to protect and cherish her.[9]

Within the multi-vocal ritual logic of Christian marriage discourse, the moment in which the woman was raised up probably dramatized her rebirth into a new identity, the only one in which she could legally participate in property rights. Yet the representation of such a public performance obviously exceeds the religious and social significances it enacts. Giles Fletcher, for instance, reads the Russian ceremony through its political meanings. In its political iconography the enactment confirms hierarchy and male rule. And yet in its performance both in church and onstage, the woman's prostration—which is dictated by the unvoiced rubrics of the patriarchal script—is staged to seem as if it were an act of spontaneous gratitude arising out of choice.

From the perspective of twentieth-century feminist resistance, it is hardly possible to imagine this scene outside the context of feminine shame. Yet is it necessarily ahistorical to presume the validity of such a reading? Absent any surviving commentaries from sixteenth-century women who performed these rituals, perhaps we can nonetheless indirectly recover something about such women's reactions. In 1903 the Anglican church historian J. Wickham Legg transcribed the French Roman Catholic cleric J. B. Thiers's discussion of the ways that eighteenth-century French women had come to restage this ceremony:

> the bride was accustomed to let the ring fall from her finger as soon as it was
> put on. Necessarily she would stoop to pick up the ring, or make some
> attempt at this, and so a reason would be given for her bending or courtesy-
> ing at her husband's feet, and the appearance of worship paid to him would
> be got rid of.[10]

What seems at work in the women's behavior is the same impulse that motivates certain feminist *Shrew* criticism—the creation of explanatory scenarios that will justify Kate's actions. Confronted by a ritual of self-debasement, the women strive to construct another narrative that will rationalize their stooping.

To locate the staging of *The Taming of the Shrew*'s final scene inside of the pre-Reformation English marriage ceremony may provide the missing historical analogue, but it hardly explains why Shakespeare chose to use it. For the wedding ceremony that Shakespeare's text alludes to, while almost certainly recognizable to an audience of the 1590s, was itself an anachronistic form outlawed by the Act of Uniformity over forty years earlier. Embedding the Kate and Petruchio marriage inside of a performance understood as prohibited inscribes the play's vision of male dominance as anachronism; but the very act of inscription collocates the anachronistic paradigm with the romantically idealized one and thus also recuperates the vision into a golden-age lament for a world gone by—a world signified by a ceremony that publicly confirmed such shows of male dominance. On the other hand, through just that collocation, the play has situated the volatile social issue of the politics of marriage on top of the equally volatile contemporary political schism over the authority of liturgical form. By means of constructing so precarious and controversial a resolution, the play works ever so slightly to unsettle its own ending and mark the return to so extremely patriarchal a marriage as a formula inseparable from a perilously divisive politics.

Thus it seems appropriate to perceive both *Shrew* and the world that produced it as texts in which gender is foregrounded through the model of a layered social fabric, with crisis stacked upon social crisis. According to David Underdown, the sense of impending breakdown in the social order was never "more widespread, or more intense, than in early modern England"; moreover, the breakdown was one that Underdown sees as having developed out of a "period of strained gender relations" that "lay at the heart of the 'crisis of order'."[11] The particular impact of this crisis in gender speaks through records that document a sudden upsurge in witchcraft trials and other court accusations against women, the "gendering" of various available forms of punishment, and the invention in these years of additional punishments specifically designated for women. As the forms of punishment and the assumptions about what officially constituted "crime" became progressively polarized by gender, there emerged a corresponding significant increase in instances of crime defined as exclusively female: "scolding," "witchcraft," and "whoring." But what is striking is that the punishments meted out to women are much more frequently targeted at suppressing women's speech than they are at controlling their sexual transgressions. In terms of available court records that document the lives of the "middling sort" in England's towns and larger villages, the chief social offenses seem to have been "scolding," "brawling," and dominating one's husband. The veritable prototype of the female offender of this era seems to be, in fact, the woman marked out as a "scold" or "shrew."

SIXTEENTH-CENTURY SCOLDS AND NINETEENTH-CENTURY ANTIQUARIANS

Much of what we can recover about the lives of sixteenth- and seventeenth-century English women and men we owe to the English antiquary societies that arose during the nineteenth century. Just past the midpoint of that century, on one side of the Atlantic Ocean one English-speaking nation moved inexorably towards a civil war—over the proprietary ownership of slaves. On the other, more ancient and presumably more civilized, parent side of the ocean, in the calm of an autumn evening in 1858 at the home of a member of the Chester Archaeological Society in the County of Chester, Mr. T. N. Brushfield, Medical Superintendant of the Cheshire Lunatic Asylum, presented a two-part paper, "On Obsolete Punishments, With particular reference to those of Cheshire."[12] His title betrays no sense that his real fascination throughout both parts of the paper is with devices that were used in bodily punishments meted out in sixteenth- and early seventeenth-century English villages and towns to women judged guilty of so egregiously violating the norms of community order and hierarchy as to have been labelled "scolds" or "shrews." What becomes apparent from Brushfield's material is that being labelled a "shrew" or "scold" had very real consequences in the late sixteenth century—consequences much more immediate and extreme than the only one that overtly confronts Shakespeare's Kate, which is to play out the demeaning role of being a single woman in married culture and to have to "dance barefoot on her [younger sister's] wedding day" and "lead apes in hell" (2.1.33–34).

Among the "obsolete punishments" of Brushfield's disquisition lie the real consequences. The instrument to which one part of his presentation is devoted is the "cucking stool," a chair-like apparatus into which the offender was ordered strapped and then, to the jeers of the crowd, was dunked several times in water over her head—water that might be a local river but was equally likely to have been the local horsewash pond. Although Brushfield is unaware of the point, gender-specific punishments for minor offenses only became the rule in English towns and villages by the fifteenth century.[13] The cucking stool, which had apparently originated as a punishment for crimes most often linked with marketplace cheating on weights or measures, had been used until then as a punishment for men as well as women.

The cucking stool—which seems to have originated as a dung cart and in many places retained its association with excrement through such designs as the privy-stool model[14]—went by several different names and existed in a variety of models in several English counties. Often it seems to have been either mounted on a cart or affixed with wheels in order that the occupant could be drawn through the streets and publicly displayed en route to her ducking. Indeed, in the first of the Padua scenes, the very real cultural consequences of being defined as a scold leak through the layers of fictive insulation. What the old pantaloon Gremio proposes—that instead of "courting" Katherina a man should "cart her rather" (1.1.55)—is a fate probably much like that which a Norfolk woman was ordered to undergo: "to ryde on a cart, with a paper in her hand, and [be] tynkled with a bason, and so at one o'clock be led to the cokyng stool and ducked in the water."[15] As folklorist John Webster Spargo makes clear, "Punishing scolds was not . . . the semihumorous hazing which it sometimes seems to be."[16] According to a 1675 legal summary,

> A Scold in a legal sense is a troublesome and angry woman, who by her brawling and wrangling amongst her Neighbours, doth break the publick Peace, and beget, cherish and increase publick Discord. And for this she is to be presented and punished in a Leet, by being put in the Cucking or Ducking-stole, or Tumbrel, an Engine appointed for that purpose, which is in the fashion of a Chair; and herein she is to sit, and to be let down in the water

over head and ears three or four times, so that no part of her be above the
water, diving or ducking down, though against her will, as Ducks do under
the water.[17]

Punishing scolds with the cucking stool and male brawlers with the pillory
was apparently so orthodox a response to disorder that the practices are
affirmed even in the Book of Homilies. In the words of Hugh Latimer in his
homily "Agaynst strife and contention":

> And, because this vice [of contention] is so much hurtful to the society of a
> commonwealth, in all well ordered cities these common brawlers and scold-
> ers be punished, with a notable kind of pain, as to be set on the cucking stool,
> pillory, or such like. . . . If we have forsaken the devil, let us use no more dev-
> ilish tongues.[18]

As to exactly what kinds of brawling, wrangling, breaking of the public
peace and begetting of public discord were considered disruptive enough to
define a woman as a scold, most descriptive evidence from court records simply problematizes the definition further by expanding the term. In the mid-six-
teenth century at Halton, one Margaret Norland was ordered to the cucking
stool for having "made an attack upon Robert Carrington, and struck him with
her hand contrary to the peace"; Alice Lesthwyte, widow, is likewise ordered
cucked "for entertaining other men's servants"; and the wives of three towns-
men are similarly sentenced because they "were common liars and scolds."[19]
Woven into various court records is the information that women called "common chiders amonge their neighbours" or women haled in for the offense of
"Flyten or chiden"[20] might likewise belong to the category of "common scold."
Above all, the scold seems to have been an assumed category of community life.
But since this almost exclusively female category[21] was defined by an exclusively male constabulary, and since the number of charges for verbal disrup-
tion brought against males are by comparison negligible, one can speculate that
a "scold" was, in essence, any woman who verbally resisted or flouted authority publicly and stubbornly enough to challenge the underlying dictum of male
rule. What is ultimately at stake in the determination to gender such criminal
categories as "scold" and "brawler" is the reinforcement of hierarchy through
the production of difference. And when the society's underlying model of "the
publick Peace" is inseparable from and constituted by the reinforcement of gender difference, then behavior that is tolerated—even tacitly encouraged—for
the gander can, for the goose, become perceived of as a serious offense.[22]

   The records of cucking-stool punishments occasionally make a reader
aware of the victim's fear, pain, and jeopardy. Both this instrument and the
scold's bridle, however, were devised primarily as shaming devices; both are
implicated in the long history of women's socialization into shame and its cul-

turally transmitted, narrowed allowances of female selfhood that linger on as omnipresent, internalized commandments long after the historical experiences from which they arose have passed from memory. And in this regard the ritual of female punishment seems fundamentally different from that of punishments devised for men. The cucking of scolds was turned into a carnival experience, one that literally placed the woman's body at the center of a mocking parade. Whenever local practicalities made it possible, her experience seems to have involved being ridden or carted through town, often to the accompaniment of musical instruments of the distinctly "Dionysian" variety,[23] making sounds such as those that imitated flatulence or made some degrading association with her body. By contrast, the male ritual of being pilloried in the town square, while a more protracted and in some respects physically harsher ritual of public exposure, did not spectacularize or carnivalize the male body so as to degrade it to nearly the same extent. Nor for that matter was the body of a male offender subjected to the same disequilibrium of being hoisted and immersed, a movement that spatializes the social categories of high-low/male-female, or to the loss of self-possession that is literalized by depriving the scold of the ability to stand her ground. Furthermore, for a woman to be paraded through town in a cart carried the special disgrace of being made analogous to a capital offender, the only other criminal transported by cart to meet his/her punishment.

The punishments designated for scolds were part of an ideological framework through which a patriarchal culture reinscribed its authority by ritual enactment. Because scolds were seen as threats to male authority, their carnivalesque punishments of mocking enthronement partake of the inverted structure of "world-upside-down" rites.[24] Especially given the restriction of both the crime and its punishment to women, however, such enactments also suggest a blunted form of community sacrifice, a scapegoating mechanism through which the public body expels recognition of its own violence by projecting it onto and inflicting it upon the private body of a marginal member of the community.[25] Thus both the figure of the "scold" and the cucking stool belong to the purview of comedy in ways that the male brawler and his punishment at the pillory do not. The shrew is, according to M. C. Bradbrook, "the oldest and indeed the only native comic role for women."[26] And during this period, the "scold" or "shrew" flourished as the object of mockery in such literary forms as the drama and ballad. In Fletcher's shrew play, *The Woman's Prize, or The Tamer Tam'd*, outraged husbands mock their rebellious wives by imagining them as explorers of a new world who discover not a continent of riches but islands of obedience:

> We'l ship 'em out in Cuck-stooles, there they'l saile
> As brave *Columbus* did, till they discover
> The happy Islands of obedience. (2.1.57–59)[27]

Yet beneath these frequent belittlements of women's authority lurk the anxieties that must have prompted such displacements in the first place. Below, in the lines of a late-sixteenth-century ballad that is representative of the genre, the parodic picture of a female monarch who had "rid in state" and sat "inthroned" suggests the kind of cultural hysteria that Underdown documents between 1560 and 1640.[28]

> She belonged to Billingsgate
> And often times had rid in state,
> And sate i' th bottome of a poole,
> Inthroned in a *cucking-stoole*.[29]

Beyond the obvious patriarchal capital, the creation of the social mechanism of shaming rituals for women is paradoxically even more effectively conservative for the way it sets up an equally powerful counter-site for the containment of men. For the abjection of what is already subordinate or marginal creates a social space where, by mere association, the dominant group may itself be controlled.[30] It is fear of that very association that makes Mr. T. N. Brushfield react with an excessive and inappropriate overflow of sympathy when he reads about a group of thirteenth-century male bakers who cheated their customers at market and who were consequently sent to the cucking stool along with guilty female brewers. When he reads of men being made to endure a punishment he assumes must always have been used exclusively for women, Brushfield rallies his indignation against the "excesses of mayors and others having authority" for having caused the "greater degree of degradation" that the bakers "must have felt . . . by being exposed to the public gaze" in a punishment "reserved for females."[31] Characteristically, he passes over various descriptions of women's punishments unremarked. As a nineteenth-century Englishman, Brushfield simply assumes both the gendering of punishment and the abjection of the feminine and thus erroneously projects that model back onto the social space of thirteenth-century England.

During the sixteenth century, local authorities seem to have recognized how effectively male social behavior could be controlled by kidnapping the popular traditions of gender inversion and using them to shame acts of male rebellion inside the abjected feminine space. As Natalie Davis has demonstrated, gender inversion in European folkloric tradition originates as a means by which the overthrow of social order could be ritually represented.[32] It had thus evolved as a subversion from below. By the late sixteenth century, however, the political symbolism of the crossdressed, unruly woman seems to have been appropriated for new uses, this time from above. In reactions against enclosure that Underdown aptly defines as involving a complex "combination of conservatism and rebelliousness,"[33] peasants from especially the western wood-pasture regions of England dressed as women and, through riot, attempted to return the world to the status quo that enclosure had turned upside down. In Wiltshire the leaders of "skimmington" peasant riots adopted the name of "Lady Skimmington," a folk hero(ine) signifying unruliness, and led "skimmingtons" (demonstrations) against "Skimmington," an authority figure.[34] In another enclosure riot in Datchet, Buckinghamshire, near Windsor, in 1598, the men crossdressed, likewise signifying their rebellion under the sign of the universal figure of disorder. When the Datchet rioters and later the "Lady Skimmington" leaders from Braydon were caught, they were punished by being made to stand pilloried in women's clothing.[35] By signifying male rebellion against hierarchical privilege as a feminized act, the authorities located insurrection within the space where it could be most effectively controlled: in the inferiorized status of a "womanish" male. The women convicted of the Datchet riot were, by contrast, sentenced to their usual punishment at the cucking stool, wearing their usual clothing. The site of shame for both sexes was, it seems, the same: the space of the feminine.

In *The Merry Wives of Windsor* (written perhaps in the same year as the Datchet riot) Falstaff's public humiliation is played out by featuring him crossdressed at a fictional site closely associated with the place where the Datchet rioters were punished. In *The Taming of the Shrew* Kate is the archetypal scold whose crime against society is her refusal to accept the so-called natural order of patriarchal hierarchy. But since Kate cannot be socially controlled by gender inversions that would treat her like a man, she, like her sister scolds of the era and the rebellious women in Datchet, is instead treated to ritual humiliation inside the space of the feminine. In Shakespeare's play the shaming rites begin at the famous wedding. Kaja Silverman's comments on clothing are helpful in understanding this scene. As Silverman rightly notes, it is historically inaccurate to equate spectacular display in the sixteenth century with the subjugation of women to the controlling male gaze. Until the eighteenth century, when "the male subject retreated from the limelight, handing on his mantle to the female subject . . . in so far as clothing was marked by gender, it defined visibility as a male rather than a female attribute."[36] On the day of the bridal— traditionally named for the bride because she is the ritual figure being honored on that day—Petruchio's actions make Kate the object not of honor but of ridicule. Usurping the bride's traditional delayed entry and robbing her by his outlandish attire of the visual centrality that custom invests in brides synecdochically in the bridal gown,[37] Petruchio spectacularizes himself in such a way as to humiliate the bride. Without ever falling into the abjected space of being "womanish" himself, he deprives her of the reverence that she is on this one day due. To her father's distress at "this shame of ours" (3.2.7), Kate rightly insists that Petruchio's delayed arrival—which initiates a behavior that he will later insist is "all ... in reverend care of her" (4.1.175)—is really an instrument by which publicly to shame her:

> No shame but mine ...
> Hiding his bitter jests in blunt behaviour.
> And to be noted for a merry man,
> He'll woo a thousand, 'point the day of marriage,
> Make feast, invite friends, and proclaim the banns,
> Yet never means to wed where he hath wooed.
> Now must the world point at poor Katherine,
> And say, 'Lo, there is mad Petruchio's wife,
> If it would please him come and marry her.' (3.2.8, 13–20)

Having cuffed the priest, quaffed the bridal Communion,[38] sworn in church "by gogs-wouns," thrown the sops in the sexton's face, then grabbed "the bride about the neck / And kissed her lips with such a clamorous smack / That at the parting all the church did echo" (ll. 167–69), Petruchio succeeds in converting the offstage wedding ceremony into such a disgrace that its guests depart the church "for very shame." He then follows up this performance by asserting his first head-of-household decision. In spite of custom, community, and even an unexpected entreaty from Kate herself, this "jolly surly groom" refuses Kate her bridal dinner, defining his wife as his material possession and making the arbitrary, even anti-communal determinations of a husband's authority supreme:

> I will be master of what is mine own.
> She is my goods, my chattels; she is my house,
> My household-stuff, my field, my barn,
> My horse, my ox, my ass, my anything. . . . (ll. 218–21)

Because shame is already a gendered piece of cultural capital, Petruchio can transgress norms of social custom and instigate the production of shame without it ever redounding upon him. He politicly begins his reign, in fact, by doing so. By inverting the wedding rite in such a way that compels its redoing and simultaneously depriving Kate of her renown as the "veriest shrew" in Padua, he seizes unquestioned control of the male space of authority. Of course, all the woman-shaming and overt male dominance here are dramatically arranged so as to make Kate's humiliation seem wildly comic and to festoon Petruchio's domination with an aura of romantic bravado bound up with the mock chivalry with which he "saves" Kate by carrying her away from the guests in a ritual capture, shouting, "Fear not, sweet wench, they shall not touch thee, Kate" (l. 227). But what is being staged so uproariously here is what we might call the benevolent version of the shaming of a scold. Kate is not being encouraged to enjoy even what pleasures may have attended the narrowly constructed space of womanhood. She is being shamed inside it. For, as Petruchio says in 4.1, she must be made, like a tamed falcon, to stoop to her lure—to come to know her keeper's call, and to come with gratitude and loving obedience into the social containment called wifehood. But she will do so only when she realizes that there are no other spaces for her to occupy, which is no doubt why Petruchio feels such urgency to shunt her away from the bridal feast and its space of honor in Padua and lead her off to the isolation defined by "her" new home, the space over which Petruchio has total mastery. Petruchio's politic reign is to construct womanhood for Kate as a site of seeming contradiction, the juncture where she occupies the positions of both shamed object and chivalric ideal. But it is between and inside those contradictions that the dependencies of "wifehood" can be constructed. When Kate realizes that there are no other socially available spaces, and when she furthermore realizes that Petruchio controls access to all sustenance, material possession, personal comfort, and spatial mobility, she will rationally choose to please him and encourage his generosity rather than, as he says, continue ever more crossing him in futile imitation of birds whose wings have been clipped—birds that are already enclosed but nonetheless continue to try to fly free: "these kites"—or kates— "That bate and beat and will not be obedient" (ll. 166–67). Ultimately, in her final speech, Kate does, literally, "stoop" to her lure.

Kate is denied her bridal feast. Nonetheless, the bridal feast that is absent the bride acts as a particularly apt metaphor for the entire play, for the space of the feminine is actually the space under constant avoidance throughout. Even Bianca, who has seemed to occupy the space with relish, bolts out of it in the surprise role reversal at the end of the play. But in a world where gender has been constructed as a binary opposition, someone is going to be pushed into that space. Inside the pressures of such a binary, if the wife refuses or escapes this occupation, the husband loses his manhood. And thus, as Kate is being "gentled" and manipulated to enter the feminine enclosure of the sex-and-gender system, the audience is also being strategically manipulated to applaud her for embracing that fate and to resent Bianca for impelling poor adoring Lucentio into the site of non-manhood. Through Bianca's refusal to compete in the contest of wifely subordination, Lucentio is left positioned as the play's symbolically castrated husband whose purse was cut off by a wife's rebellion. Since someone must occupy the abjected space of a binary—and since doing so is so much more humiliating for men—better (we say) in the interest of protecting the heterosexual bond that women should accept their inferiorization. By dramatizing Kate's resignation as her joyous acceptance of a world to which we recognize no alternatives exist, Shakespeare reinscribes the comfortingly familiar order inside of a dialogue that challenges the social distributions of power but concludes in a formula that invites us to applaud the reinstatement of the status quo.

* * *

In the past fifteen years or so, historical scholarship has shifted away from its perennial concentration on the structures of authority and has begun to view history from the bottom up. What has emerged from approaching historical records in entirely new ways and proposing newly complex intersections of such data[39] is a picture of England that requires us to read the social text in terms of such phenomena as the widespread and quite dramatic rise in the years 1560–1640 in those crimes labelled as ones of "interpersonal dispute," that is, ones involving sexual misconduct, scolding, slander, physical assault, defamation, and marital relations. Keith Wrightson and David Levine offer an instructive explanation of this phenomenon: the statistical increase during these years reflects less a "real" increase in such crimes than a suddenly heightened official determination to regulate social behavior through court prosecution.[40] This itself reflects the wider growth of a "law and order consciousness," the increase of fundamental concern about social order that manifested itself in the growing severity of criminal statutes directed primarily against vagrants and female disorder. In other words, what had sprung into full operation was a social anxiety that came to locate the source of all disorder in society in its marginal and subordinate groups. And in the particular types of malfeasance that this society or any other seeks to proscribe and the specific groups it thereby implicitly seeks to stigmatize, one may read its ideology.[41]

For Tudor-Stuart England, in village and town, an obsessive energy was invested in exerting control over the unruly woman—the woman who was exercising either her sexuality or her tongue under her own control rather than under the rule of a man. As illogical as it may initially seem, the two crimes— being a scold and being a so-called whore—were frequently conflated. Accordingly, it was probably less a matter of local convenience than one of a felt congruity between offenses that made the cucking stool the common instrument of punishment. And whether the term "cucking stool" shares any actual etymological origins with "cuckold" or not, the perceived equation between a scolding woman and a whore or "queen" who cuckolded her husband probably accounts for the periodic use of "coqueen" or "cuckquean" for the cucking stool.[42] This particular collocation of female transgressions constructs women as creatures whose bodily margins and penetrable orifices provide culture with a locus for displaced anxieties about the vulnerability of the social community, the body politic. Thus Ferdinand, in saying that "women like that part, which, like the lamprey, / Hath nev'r a bone in't. / . . . I mean the tongue,"[43] jealously betrays his own desire for rule over what he sees as the penetrable misrule of his Duchess-sister's body/state. In his discussion of the grotesque tropes that connect body and court, Peter Stallybrass comments on the frequency with which "in the Jacobean theater, genital differentiation tended to be subsumed within a problematically gendered orality."[44] Within that subsumption the talkative woman is frequently imagined as synonymous with the sexually available woman, her open mouth the signifier for invited entrance elsewhere. Hence the dictum that associates "silent" with "chaste" and stigmatizes women's public speech as a behavior fraught with cultural signs resonating with a distinctly sexual kind of shame.[45]

Given these connections between body and state, control of women's speech becomes a massively important project. By being imagined as a defense of all the important institutions upon which the community depends, such a project could, in the minds of the magistrates and other local authorities, probably rationalize even such extreme measures as the strange instrument known as the "scold's bridle" or "brank." Tracing the use of the scold's bridle is problematic because, according to Brushfield,

> notwithstanding the existence at Chester of so many Scold's Bridles, no notice of their use is to be found in the Corporation [town or city] books, several of which have been specially examined with that object in view. That they were not unfrequently called into requisition in times past cannot be doubted; but the Magistrates were doubtless fully aware that the punishment was illegal, and hence preferred that no record should remain of their having themselves transgressed the law.[46]

Since the bridle was never legitimate, it does not appear, nor would its use have been likely to be entered, in the various leet court records with the same unselfconscious frequency that is reflected in the codified use of the cucking stool. Because records are so scarce, we have no precise idea of how widespread the use of the bridle really was. What we can know is that during the early modern era this device of containment was first invented—or, more accurately, adapted—as a punishment for the scolding woman. It is a device that today we would call an instrument of torture, despite the fact—as English legal history is proud to boast—that in England torture was never legal. Thus, whereas the instrument openly shows up in the Glasgow court records of 1574 as a punishment meted out to two quarreling women, if the item shows up at all in official English transactions, it is usually through an innocuous entry such as the one in the 1658 Worcester Corporation Records, which show that four shillings were "Paid for mending the bridle for bridleinge of scoulds, and two cords for the same."[47]

In the absence of what historians would rank as reliable documents, very little has been said by twentieth-century historians about the scold's bridle.[48] There are those who attempt by this lack of evidence to footnote it as an isolated phenomenon that originated around 1620, mainly in the north of England and one part of Scotland. I myself have some increasingly documented doubts. And while problems of documentation have made it possible for historians largely to ignore the scold's bridle even within their new "bottom-up" histories of topics such as social crime, I would argue that its use and notori-

ety were widespread enough for it to have been an agent in the historical production of women's silence. As such, the bridle is both a material indicator of
gender relations in the culture that devised it and a signifier crucial for reconstructing the buried narrative of women's history. Records substantiate its use
in at least five English counties as well as in several disparate areas of Scotland; furthermore, likely pictorial allusions turn up, for example, on an eighteenth-century sampler handed down in an Irish family originally from
Belfast,[49] or in the frontispiece of the 1612 edition of Hooker's *Laws of Eccle-
siastical Polity*, where a woman kneels, a skull placed close by, and receives
the Bible in one upstretched hand while in the other she holds a bridle, signifying discipline.[50] As I will argue below, the instrument is probably also signified in a raft of late sixteenth-century "bridling" metaphors that have been
understood previously as merely figurative; the item itself may well have
appeared onstage as a prop in Part II of *Tamburlaine the Great* and *Swetnam
the Woman-hater Arraigned by Women*. Moreover, it almost certainly appears
as the explicit referent in several widely read seventeenth-century Protestant
treatises published in London.

In Mr. T. N. Brushfield's Cheshire County alone he was able to discover
thirteen of these 200–250-year-old artifacts still lying about the county plus
an appallingly large number of references to their use. In fact some eighteen
months after he had presented his initial count in 1858, Mr. Brushfield, with
a dogged empiricism we can now be grateful for, informed the Society that he
had come across three more specimens. There are, furthermore, apparently a
number of extant bridles in various other parts of England, besides those in
Chester County that Brushfield drew and wrote about,[51] and each one very
likely carries with it its own detailed, local history. Nonetheless, so little has
been written about them that had the industrious T. N. Brushfield not set about
to report so exhaustively on scolds' bridles and female torture, we would have
known almost nothing about these instruments except for an improbable-
sounding story or two. As it is, whenever the common metaphor of "bridling
a wife's tongue" turns up in the literature of this era, the evidence should make
us uncomfortably aware of a practice lurking behind that phrase that an original audience could well have heard as literal.

Scolds' bridles are not directly mentioned as a means for taming the scold
of Shakespeare's *Shrew*—and such a practice onstage would have been wholly
antithetical to the play's desired romantic union as well as to the model of
benevolent patriarchy that is insisted on here and elsewhere in Shakespeare.[52]
What Shakespeare seems to have been doing in *Shrew*—in addition to
shrewdly capitalizing on the popularity of the contemporary "*hic mulier*"
debate by giving it romantic life onstage—is conscientiously modelling a
series of humane but effective methods for behavioral modification. The methods employed determinedly exclude the more brutal patriarchal practices that
were circulating within popular jokes, village rituals, and in such ballads as

"A Merry Jest of a Shrewde and Curste Wyfe, Lapped in Morrelles Skin, for Her Good Behavyour," in which the husband tames his wife by first beating her and then wrapping her in the salted skin of the dead horse, "Morel." In 1594 or thereabout Shakespeare effectively pushes these practices off his stage. And in many ways his "shrew" takes over the cultural discourse from this point on, transforming the taming story from scenarios of physical brutality and reshaping the trope of the shrew/scold from an old, usually poor woman or a nagging wife into the newly romanticized vision of a beautiful, rich, and spirited young woman. But the sheer fact that the excluded brutalities lie suppressed in the margins of the shrew material also means that they travel, as unseen partners, inside the more benevolent taming discourse that Shakespeare's play helps to mold. And, as Ann Thompson's synopsis of *Shrew*'s production history clearly demonstrates, such woman-battering, although not part of Shakespeare's script, repeatedly leaks back in from the margins and turns up in subsequent productions and adaptations (including, for instance, the Burton-Taylor film version, to which director Franco Zefferelli added a spanking scene):

> In the late seventeenth century, John Lacey's *Sauny the Scott, or The Taming of the Shrew* (c. 1667), which supplanted Shakespeare's text on stage until it was replaced in 1714 by David Garrick's version called *Catherine and Petruchio*, inserts an additional scene in which the husband pretends to think that his wife's refusal to speak to him is due to toothache and sends for a surgeon to have her teeth drawn. This episode is repeated with relish in the eighteenth century in James Worsdale's adaptation, *A Cure for a Scold* (1735).[53]

What turns up as the means to control rebellious women imagined by the play's seventeenth- and eighteenth-century versions is, essentially, the same form of violence as that suppressed in Shakespeare's playscript but available in the surrounding culture: the maiming/disfiguring of the mouth.

The scold's bridle is a practice tangled up in the cultural discourse about shrews. And while it is not materially present in the narrative of Shakespeare's play, horse references or horse representations—which are, oddly enough, an almost standard component of English folklore about unruly women—pervade the play.[54] The underlying literary "low culture" trope of unruly horse/unruly woman seems likely to have been the connection that led first to a metaphoric idea of bridling women's tongues and eventually to the literal social practice. Inside that connection, even the verbs "reign" and "rein" come together in a fortuitous pun that reinforces male dominance. And there would no doubt have been additional metaphoric reinforcement for bridling from the bawdier use of the horse/rider metaphor and its connotations of male dominance. In this trope, to "mount" and "ride" a woman works both literally and metaphorically to exert control over the imagined disorder presumed to result from the "woman on top." Furthermore, the horse and rider are not only the standard components of the shrew-taming folk stories but are likewise the key feature of "riding skimmington," which, unlike the French charivari customs of which it is a version, was intended to satirize marriages in which the wife was reputed to have beaten her husband (or was, in any case, considered the dominant partner).[55]

In shrew-taming folktale plots in general, the taming of the unruly wife is frequently coincident with the wedding trip home on horseback.[56] The trip, which is itself the traditional final stage to the "bridal," is already the site of an unspoken pun on "bridle" that gets foregrounded in Grumio's horse-heavy description of the journey home and the ruination of Kate's "bridal"—"how her horse fell, and she under her horse; . . . how the horses ran away, how her bridle was burst" (4.1.54, 59–60). By means of the syntactical elision of "horse's," the phrase quite literally puts the bridle on Kate rather than her horse. What this suggests is that the scold's bridal/horse bridle/scold's bridle associations were available for resonant recall through the interaction of linguistic structures with narrative ones. The scold's bridle that Shakespeare did not literally include in his play is ultimately a form of violence that lives in the same location as the many offstage horses that are crowded into its non-representational space. The bridle is an artifact that exists in *Shrew*'s offstage margins—along with the fist-in-the-face that Petruchio does not use and the rape he does not enact in the off-stage bedroom we do not see. Evoked into narrative possibility when Petruchio shares his taming strategy with the audience—

> This is a way to kill a wife with kindness,
> And thus I'll *curb* her mad and headstrong humour.
> He that knows better how to tame a shrew,
> Now let him speak—'tis charity to show (4.1.179–82, my italics)

—the scold's bridle exists in this drama as a choice that has been deliberately excluded.

The antiquarians and few historians who have mentioned this instrument assign its initial appearance to the mid-1620s—a date that marks its first entry in a city record in northern England. There is, however, rather striking literary evidence to suggest that the scold's bridle not only existed some twenty to thirty years earlier but was apparently familiar to the playwrights and playgoers of London. The bridle turns up in Part II of Christopher Marlowe's *Tamburlaine the Great* (ca. 1587) not as a metaphor but explicitly described as an extremely cruel instrument of torture that Tamburlaine devises for Orcanes and the three Egyptian kings who dare to protest when he kills his son, Calyphas, for being too womanish to fight. Demeaning their protest as dogs barking and scolds railing, Tamburlaine determines how he will punish their insolence:

> Well, bark, ye dogs! I'll bridle all your tongues
> And bind them close with bits of burnish'd steel
> Down to the channels of your hateful throats;
> And, with the pains my rigor shall inflict, I'll make ye roar. . . .[57]

The scold's bridle is, furthermore, the key referent to understanding the condign nature of the punishment that the women jurors of the 1620 *Swetnam the Woman-hater Arraigned by Women* devise for the pamphlet writer, Joseph Swetnam, who had publicly declared himself the chief enemy to their sex. The dramatists, most probably women, dared—at a unique moment in English theater history—to produce and have put on the stage at the Red Bull theater a bold, political retaliation against the author of the notoriously misogynist pamphlet, *The Arraignment of Lewde, idle, froward, and unconstant women.* Having brought "Misogynos" to trial, they order him to wear a "Mouzell," be paraded in public, and be shown

> In every Street i' the Citie, and be bound
> In certaine graces to Post or Stake,
> And bayted by all the honest women in the Parish.[58]

The above lines describe the standard humiliations involved in the bridling of a scold. Probably because so little has to date been said about scolds' bridles, Simon Shepherd gives a tentative and parenthetical interpretation that "(presumably 'Mouzell' alludes again to [Rachel] Speght's pamphlet)."[59] Unwittingly, the gloss obscures the key point in the women dramatists' triumph. Onstage, their play seeks poetic parity through condemning Swetnam to endure precisely the kinds of humiliation that women were sentenced to undergo based on nothing more than the kinds of stereotyped accusations Swetnam's pamphlet reproduces.

Another pre-1620 allusion where the literal bridle seems once again the likely referent occurs in the exchange Shakespeare earlier wrote for his first "shrew scene," the argument between Antipholus the Ephesian's angry wife, Adriana, and her unmarried, dutiful, and patriarchally correct sister, Luciana. Luciana's insistence that "a man is master of his liberty" and Adriana's feminist challenge, "Why should their liberty than ours be more?" provokes a dialogue that seems to turn around a veiled warning about scolds' bridles from Luciana and the furious rejection of that possibility from Adriana.

> *Luc.* O, know he is the bridle of your will.
> *Adr.* There's none but asses will be bridled so.
> *Luc.* Why, headstrong liberty is lash'd with woe. . . .
> (*The Comedy of Errors*, 2.1.13–15)

Another likely scold's bridle allusion turns up inside the shrew discourse in *Mundus Alter et Idem*, the strange voyage fantasy purportedly written by the traveler "Mercurius Brittanicus" but actually written by Joseph Hall and published (in Latin) in 1605. The work—which Hall never publicly acknowledged but which went through several printings and was even "Englished" as *The Discovery of a New World* in an unauthorized 1609 translation by John Healy[60]—is accompanied by elaborate textual apparati that include a series of Ortelius's maps, on top of which Hall has remapped his satiric fantasy. In Hall's dystopia the narrator embarks on the ship "Fantasia" and discovers the Antarctic continent, which is geographically the world upside down and therefore contains such travesties of social organization as a land of women. This is named "New Gynia, which others incorrectly call Guinea, [but which] I correctly call Viraginia, located where European geographers depict the Land of Parrots."[61] The geography of Viraginia includes Gynaecopolis, where Brittanicus is enslaved by its domineering women until he reveals "the name of my country (which is justly esteemed throughout the world as the 'Paradise of Women')."[62] In the province of "Amazonia, or Gynandria," the fear of a society based on gender inversion emerges into full-blown nightmare: men wear petticoats and remain at home "strenuously spinning and weaving" while women wear the breeches, attend to military matters and farming, pluck out their husband's beards and sport long beards themselves, imperiously enslave their husbands, beat them daily, and "while the men work, the women . . . quarrel and scold."[63] What constitutes treason in this fantasized space is for any woman to treat her husband gently or with the slightest forbearance. As punishment for such treason, Hall's misogynistic satire adds one more twist to the shame-based model of gendered punishment by invoking a scenario of transvestite disguise similar to that which Shakespeare exploits in the boy-actor/Rosalind/Ganymede complications of *As You Like It*: the guilty wife "must exchange clothes with her husband and dressed like this, head shaved, be brought to the forum to stand there an entire day in the pillory, exposed to the reproach and derisive laughter of all onlookers . . . [until she] finally returns home stained with mud, urine, and all sorts of abuse. . . ."[64] Mercurius Britannicus is able to escape only because, since he is dressed in "man's attire and . . . in the first phase of an adolescent beard,"[65] he is assumed to be female and thus enjoys a woman's freedom of movement.

Hall's Amazon fantasy—in which men may not select their dress, eat their food, conduct any business, go anywhere, speak to anyone, or ever speak up against their wives' opinions—is, of course, only an exaggeration of the lessons Kate is compelled to learn in Petruchio's taming school. The parallels derive from the fact that underlying both Hall's satire and Shakespeare's play is the same compulsive model that underwrites their culture—the male fantasy of female dominance that is signified by the literary figure of the shrew/scold. Long before the Amazon fantasy emerges, the shrew story is implicit even in Mercurius Brittanicus's opening description of Viraginia's topographical features. In the region of Linguadocia (tongue), the society has ingeniously devised a means to control the "enormous river" called "Sialon" (saliva) that flows through the city of "Labriana" (lips). The overflow from Labriana could "scarcely . . . be contained even in such a vast channel, and indeed, . . . the Menturnea Valley [chin]—would be daily threatened by it had not the rather clever inhabitants carefully walled up the banks with bones."[66] In the Healey translation the reference to scolds and the implied model of containing them is even clearer. In Healey almost all provinces and cities are associated with women/excess voicing/mouth through such names as "Tattlingen," "Scoldonna," "Blubberick," "Gigglottangir," "Shrewes-bourg," "Pratlingople," "Gossipingoa," and "Tales-borne." To control the river "Slauer" from bursting out and overflowing "Lypswagg," the "countrimen haue now deuised very strong empires of bones and bend lether, to keepe it from breaking out any more, but when they list to let it out a little now & then for scouring of the channell."[67]

Scolding is a verbal rebellion and controlling it was, in the instrument of the bridle, focused with condign exactitude on controlling a woman's tongue—the site of a nearly fetishized investment that fills the discourse of the era with a true "lingua franca," some newly invented, some reprinted and repopularized in the late sixteenth to mid-seventeenth century. Among this didactic "tongue literature" there is a quite amazing play by Thomas Tomkis that went through five printings from 1607 to 1657 before its popularity expired. In this play, called *Lingua: Or The Combat of the Tongue, And the five Senses For Superiority*, a female allegorical figure—Lingua, dressed in purple and white—is finally brought to order by the figures of the five senses who force her into compelled servitude to "Taste."[68]

If—as I have speculated—the underlying idea for bridling a woman comes initially from a "low-culture" material association between horse/ woman, it was an association being simultaneously coproduced on the "high-culture" side within a religious discourse that helped to legitimate such a literalization. For in addition to a number of repopularized theological treatises in Latin that dedicate whole chapters to the sins of the tongue and emblem book pictures that show models of the good wife pictured as a woman who is literalizing the metaphoric by grasping her tongue between her fingers, the era is stamped by that peculiarly Protestant literature of self-purification in which the allegorical model of achieving interior discipline by a "bridling of the will" appears as an almost incessant refrain. From the Protestant divines came a congeries of impassioned moral treatises that, as they linguistically test out their truths by treading the extreme verge between literal and metaphoric, frequently move close to eliding any boundary between interior and exterior application of self-discipline. Such suggestions occur in works like

The Poysonous Tongue, a 1615 sermon by John Abernethy, Bishop of Cathnes, in which the personified tongue—"one of the least members, most moueable, and least tyred"—is ultimately imagined as an inflamed and poisonous enemy, especially to the other bodily members, and therefore the member most worthy to be severely, graphically punished.[69]

Discourse about the tongue is complexly invested with an ambivalent signification that marks it always as a discourse about gender and power—one in which the implied threat to male possession/male authority perhaps resolves itself only in the era's repeated evocation of the Philomela myth (a narrative that Shakespeare himself draws upon in a major way for three different works)—where a resolution to such gender contestation is achieved by the silencing of the woman, enacted as a cutting out—or castration—of her tongue. It was a male discourse that George Gascoigne had already taken to perhaps the furthest limits of aggression in 1593. Reduced to a court hack by the censorship of his master work, *A Hundreth Sundrie Flowers* (which he had retitled *The Posies* and tried without success to slip past the censors), Gascoigne, in his last moralistic work, *The Steel Glas*, created a poetic persona who has been emasculated—hence depotentiated into the feminine—only to be raped and then have her tongue cut out by "The Rayzor of Restraint."[70]

A discourse that locates the tongue as the body's "unruly member" situates female speech as a symbolic relocation of the male organ, an unlawful appropriation of phallic authority in which the symbolics of male castration are ominously complicit. If the chastity belt was an earlier design to prevent entrance into one aperture of the deceitfully open female body, the scold's bridle, preventing exit from another, might be imagined as a derivative inversion of that same obsession. Moreover, the very impetus to produce an instrument that actually bridled the tongue and bound it down into a woman's mouth suggests an even more complicated obsession about women's bodies/women's authority than does the chastity belt: in the obsession with the woman's tongue, the simple binary between presence and absence breaks down. Here, the obsession must directly acknowledge, even as it attempts to suppress, the presence in woman of the primary signifier of an authority presumed to be masculine. The tongue (at least in the governing assumptions about order) should always already have been possessed only by the male. Needless to say, theologians found ways of tracing these crimes of usurpation by the woman's unruly member back to the Garden, to speech, to Eve's seduction by the serpent, and thence to her seductive appropriation of Adam's rightful authority. Says the author of a sermon called *The Government of the Tongue*:

> Original sin came first out at the mouth by speaking, before it entred in by eating. The first use we find *Eve* to have made of her language, was to enter parly with the temter, and from that to become a temter to her husband. And

immediately upon the fall, guilty *Adam* frames his tongue to a frivolous excuse, which was much less able to cover his sin than the fig-leaves were his nakedness.[71]

Through Eve's open mouth, then, sin and disorder entered the world. Through her verbal and sexual seduction of Adam—through her use of that other open female bodily threshold—sin then became the inescapable curse of humankind. All rebellion is a form of usurpation of one sort or another, and if Eve's sin—her "first use of language" through employment of her tongue— is likewise imagined as the usurpation of the male phallic instrument and the male signifier of language, the images of woman speaking and woman's tongue become freighted with heavy psychic baggage. Perpetually guilty, perpetually disorderly, perpetually seductive, Eve and her descendants become *the* problem that society must control.

In relation to scolds' bridles and the ways that the violent self-discipline urged by these treatises seeks to legitimate a literal practice, Thomas Adams's 1616 sermon, "The Taming of the Tongue," is of particular interest. With a title suggestively close to that of Shakespeare's play, it envisions a future of brimstone and scalding fire for the untamable tongue and warns that the tongue is so intransigent that "Man hath no bridle, no cage of brasse, nor barres of yron to *tame* it."[72] Likewise, in a sermon by Thomas Watson, we are told that

> The Tongue, though it be a little Member, yet it hath a World of Sin in it. The Tongue is an unruly Evil. We put *Bitts* in Horses mouths and rule them; but the Tongue is an unbridled Thing. It is hard to find a Curbing-bitt to rule the Tongue.[73]

Thus, when William Gearing dedicates his ominously titled treatise, *A Bridle for the Tongue: or, A Treatise of ten Sins of the Tongue* to Sir Orlando Bridgman, Chief Justice of the Court of Common Pleas, his use of the bridle goes too far beyond the metaphoric to be construed as such. If anything, it seems prescriptive. In the dedication Gearing points out that the "Tongue hath no Rein by nature, but hangeth loose in the midst of the mouth," and then invokes the Third Psalm to proclaim that the Lord will "strike" those who scold "on the cheekbone (jawbone), and break out their teeth." Speaking here in an already gendered discourse, Gearing appears to invoke scriptural authority as justification for legalizing the iron bridle as an instrument of official punishment.[74] In the process, his scriptural reference graphically suggests what could well have happened to the hapless women who were yanked through town, a lead rope attached to the metal bridle locked firmly around their heads, their tongues depressed by a two-to-three-inch metal piece called a "gag." Besides effecting the involuntary regurgitation that the term suggests, the gag could easily have slammed into their teeth with every pull, smashing their jawbones and breaking out their teeth, until finally the offending shrew would be tied up and made to stand in the town square, an object to be pissed on and further ridiculed at will.

There is one known account written by a woman who was bridled. We may infer from Dorothy Waugh's testimony that she experienced the bridling as a sexual violation. When her narrative reaches the moment of the gag being forced into her mouth, her embarrassment nearly overwhelms description and her words stumble as they confront the impossibility of finding a language for the tongue to repeat its own assault. Repeatedly, she brackets off references to the bridle with phrases like "as they called it," as if to undermine its reality. Physically violated, made to stand bridled in the jail as an object of shame for citizens to pay twopence to view, and released still imprisoned in the bridle to be whipped from town to town in a manner that parallels the expulsion of a convicted whore, Dorothy Waugh several times asserts "they had not any thing to lay to my Charge," as if the assertion of her innocence could frame her experience within the discourse of legality and extricate it from the one of sexual violation that it keeps slipping towards. Waugh's account of her *"cruell usage by the Mayor of* Carlile" occurs as the final piece of seven Quaker testimonies that comprise *The Lambs Defence against Lyes. And A True Testimony given concerning the Sufferings and Death of James Parnell* (1656). Originally haled off to prison after she had been "moved of the Lord to goe into the market of *Carlile*, to speake against all deceit & ungodly practices," Dorothy Waugh's implicit subversions of the local authority and substitution of biblical quotations as a source of self-authorization is clearly what impelled the mayor into so implacable an antagonism. To the mayor's question from whence she came, Waugh responded:

> I said out of *Egypt* where thou lodgest; But after these words, he was so violent & full of passion he scarce asked me any more Questions, but called to one of his followers to bring the bridle as he called it to put upon me, and was to be on three houres, and that which they called so was like a steele cap and my hatt being violently pluckt off which was pinned to my head whereby they tare my Clothes to put on their bridle as they called it, which was a stone weight of Iron by the relation of their own Generation, & three barrs of Iron to come over my face, and a peece of it was put in my mouth, which was so unreasonable big a thing for that place as cannot be well related, which was locked to my head, and so I stood their time with my hands bound behind me with the stone weight of Iron upon my head and the bitt in my mouth to keep me from speaking; And the Mayor said he would make me an Example. . . . Afterwards it was taken off and they kept me in prison for a little season, and after a while the Mayor came up againe and caused it to be put on againe, and sent me out of the Citty with it on, and gave me very vile and unsavoury words, which were not fit to proceed out

of any mans mouth, and charged the Officer to whip me out of the Towne, from Constable to Constable to send me, till I came to my owne home, when as they had not any thing to lay to my Charge.[75]

If we may be thankful about anything connected with the scold's bridle, it is that so many were found in a county whose antiquarian groups were especially diligent in recording and preserving the local heritage. Mr. T. N. Brushfield meticulously preserved all records he uncovered, even to the extent of making detailed drawings of the bridles he found in Cheshire and neighboring areas. But in doing so, he also unwittingly managed to preserve some of the ideas and attitudes that had originally forged these instruments. Thus his own discourse, as he describes these appalling artifacts and instances of their use, stands smugly disjunct from its subject and seems disconcertingly inappropriate in its own investments and responses. As he opens his introduction of the scold's bridle, for instance, he rhetorically establishes a legitimating lineage for his authority by deferring to—without ever considering the implications of the text he invokes—the work of one of England's earliest antiquarians. He thus begins: "In commencing a description of the Brank or Scold's Bridle, I cannot do better than quote a passage from Dr. Plot's *Natural History of Staffordshire*" (1686). He then proceeds, without the slightest dismay or query, to pass along the following description from Dr. Plot:

> Lastly, we come to the *Arts* that respect *Mankind*, amongst which, as elsewhere, the civility of precedence must be allowed to the *women*, and that as well in punishments as favours. For the former whereof, they have such a peculiar *artifice* at *New Castle* (under Lyme) and *Walsall*, for correcting of *Scolds*; which it does, too, so effectually, and so very safely, that I look upon it as much to be preferred to the *Cucking Stoole*, which not only endangers the *health* of the *party*, but also gives the tongue liberty 'twixt every dipp; to neither of which is this at all lyable; it being such a *Bridle* for the *tongue*, as not only quite deprives them of speech, but brings shame for the transgression, and humility thereupon, before 'tis taken off . . . which, being put upon the offender by order of the magistrate, and fastened with a *padlock* behind, she is lead round the towne by an *Officer* to her shame, nor is it taken off, till after the party begins to show all external signes imaginable of humiliation and amendment.[76]

To be released from the instrument that rendered them mute, the silenced shrews of Dr. Plot's narrative were compelled to employ their bodies to plead the required degradation. Yet to imagine just what pantomimes of pain, guilt, obeisance to authority and self-abjection might have been entailed is almost as disturbing an exercise as is imagining the effects of the bridle itself.

Although Brushfield did unearth evidence that the scold's bridle had been used as late as the 1830s, it is clear that the use of such an instrument of torture at any time in England's history had managed to disappear beneath a convenient public amnesia until only a decade prior to his 1858 report. No longer used in public punishments, the bridles had been recycled behind the walls of state institutions; most turned up in places like women's work houses, mental institutions, and other such establishments that, by the nineteenth century, had conveniently removed society's marginal people from public view. In the 1840s the scold's bridle seems to have caught the eye of the antiquarians, and Brushfield is therefore at pains to describe in detail the variety of bridles in the rich trove he has collected in Cheshire. Some, he tells us, are

> contrived with hinged joints, as to admit of being readily adapted to the head of the scold. It was generally supplied with several connecting staples, so as to suit heads of different sizes, and was secured by a padlock. Affixed to the inner portion of the hoop was a piece of metal, which, when the instrument was properly fitted, pressed the tongue down, and effectually branked or bridled it. The length of the mouthpiece or gag varied from 1 1/2 inch to 3 inches,—if more than 1 1/2 inches, the punishment would be much increased,—as, granting that the instrument was fitted moderately tight, it would not only arrest the action of the tongue, but also excite distressing symptoms of sickness, more especially if the wearer became at all unruly. The form of the gag was very diversified, the most simple being a mere flat piece of iron; in some the extremity was turned upwards, in others downwards; on many of the specimens both surfaces were covered with rasp-like elevations. The instrument was generally painted, and sometimes in variegated colours, in which case the gag was frequently red .... A staple usually existed at the back part of the instrument, to which was attached a short chain terminating in an iron ring;—any additional length required was supplied by a rope.
>
> Wearing this effectual curb on her tongue, the silenced scold was sometimes fastened to a post in some conspicuous portion of the town—generally the market-place....[77]

One bridle that was formerly used in Manchester Market "to control the energetic tongues of some of the female stall-keepers," as Brushfield puts it, was found in the mid-nineteenth century still retaining its original coverings of alternating white and red cotton bands; its "gag being large, with rasp-like surfaces; the leading-chain three feet long, and attached to the front part of the horizontal hoop."[78] The spectacular red and white carnival festivity of the Manchester bridle would have no doubt been augmented not only by some appropriately carnivalesque parade and by the bridled woman comically resembling a horse in tournament trappings but likewise by the colorful if painful effects that almost any gag would have been likely to produce. Such effects are vividly illustrated in the account of a witness to a 1653 bridling, who saw

> one Ann Bidlestone, drove through the streets, by an officer of the same cor-
> poration [i.e., the city of Newcastle], holding a rope in his hand, the other
> end fastened to an engine, called the branks, which is like a crown, it being
> of iron which was musled, over the head and face, with a great gap [*sic*], or
> tongue of iron, forced into her mouth, which forced the blood out; and that
> is the punishment which the magistrates do inflict upon chiding, and scould-
> ing women.[79]

The same witness declared that he had "often seen the like done to others."

Brushfield—having described some six or seven variations of the bridle, including one "very handsome specimen" that was "surmounted with a dec-orated cross"[80]—leads up to his tour de force, the "STOCKPORT Brank." This "perfectly unique specimen, ... by far the most remarkable in this county," currently belongs, he tells as, to the corporate authorities of Stock-port, whom he thanks effusively for granting him the honor of being the very first person privileged to sketch it:

> The extraordinary part of the instrument ... is the gag, which commences
> flat at the hoop and terminates in a bulbous extremity, which is covered with
> *iron pins*, nine in number, there being three on the upper surface, three on
> the lower, and three pointing backwards; and it is scarcely possible to affix
> it in its destined position without wounding the tongue. To make matters still
> worse, the chain (which yet remains attached, and ... measures two feet) is
> connected to the hoop at the fore part, as if to *pull* the wearer of the Bridle
> along on her unwilling tour of the streets; for it is very apparent that any
> motion of the gag must have lacerated the mouth very severely. Another
> specimen was formerly in the WORKHOUSE AT STOCKPORT, and was
> sold, a few years ago, as old iron![81]

As he recounts the unauthorized sale of this extraordinary item as scrap iron, Brushfield rises to outrage. He then launches into an indignant description of how this bridle—which was originally and legally the property of Brushfield's own Chester—had been given away some thirty years before by the Chester jailer. Of this abuse of property rights, Brushfield insists that, while "The lib-erality of the donor cannot perhaps be questioned ... the right of transfer, on the part of that official, is altogether another matter!" Therefore, "An inven-tory of these curious relics, taken once or twice a year under the authority of the city magistrates, would," Brushfield exclaims, "effectually curb these 'fits of abstraction.'"[82] And as T. N. Brushfield's disquisition on scolds' bridles devolves to issues of male ownership, legitimate transmission, and proprietary rights, as his language slides into a recommendation for *curbing* dangerous signs of liberality, and as he speaks forth his own authoritative proposals for instituting control over rights to own these brutal instruments that carry with them a silenced women's history, it may well seem to the stultified reader that 1858 is really still 1598 as far as any progress in the complexly burdened history of women's space within culture is concerned. Were we to shift the venue from sex to race, the assumption would be accurate. For while Mr. T. N. Brushfield read his paper on "obsolete punishments" and registered genteel disapproval over his forefathers' use of such a barbaric control on the fair sex of Chester County, on the other side of the Atlantic, England's cultural heirs had carried this model of control one step further. By 1858—as readers of Toni Morrison's *Beloved* will recall—the scold's bridle had been cycled over to the American South and the Caribbean, where in 1858 it was being used to punish unruly slaves.[83]

Among historians, "scolds" or "shrews" are commonly defined as a particular category of offender, almost without exception female. In David Underdown's descriptive scenario, "women who were poor, social outcasts, widows or otherwise lacking in the protection of a family, or newcomers to their communities, were the most common offenders. Such women were likely to vent their frustration against the nearest symbols of authority."[84] And, we might add, such women were also the most likely to have the community's frustration vented against them. But the evidence that T. N. Brushfield has left about the bridle suggests that this definition of scolds—which is derived mainly from various legal records, most of which are, in any case, documents of cucking-stool punishments—may be far too narrow.

From the rich evidence T. N. Brushfield compiled from a variety of archaeological journals, offbeat treatises, collective town memories, and information given him by senior citizens acting as quasi-official transmitters of oral history in towns and cities around Cheshire, we discover that the scold's bridle was apparently a symbol of mayoral office that passed from one city administration to the next, being delivered along with the mace and other recognized signs of officialdom into the keeping of the town jailer. The jailer's services, we learn,

> were not unfrequently called into requisition. In the old-fashioned, half-timbered houses in the Borough, there was generally fixed on one side of the large open fire-places, a hook; so that when a man's wife indulged her scolding propensities, the husband sent for the Town Jailer to bring the Bridle, and had her bridled and chained to the hook until she promised to behave herself better for the future.[85]

One member of Brushfield's antiquary group was a former mayor of the town of Congleton, where hooks on the side of fireplaces still existed.

According to his account, so chilling was the memory of this method of controlling domestic disputes that husbands in nineteenth-century Congleton could still induce instant obedience from their wives just by saying, "If you don't rest with your tongue, I'll send for the Bridle, and hook you up." The local bookseller at Macclesfield reported to Brushfield that he had frequently seen the bridle produced at petty sessions of the court "*in terrorem*, to stay the volubility of a woman's tongue; and that a threat by a magistrate to order its appliance, had always proved sufficient to abate the garrulity of the most determined scold."[86] By 1858, although the signified object had disappeared from social practice, it still existed within the culture as a powerful signifier of what had become a silenced history of women's silencing.

For evidence like the above we probably owe T. N. Brushfield a debt of gratitude. He preserved material that suggests a whole secondary, shadowed subtext to the history of women and the law—a history outside the law and yet one that took place inside England's much touted rule of law; a history that had no juries, no court trials, no official sentences, and that left few telltale records of itself: yet a history that was nonetheless passed down, circulated, and tacitly authorized in town after town, inside county courthouses, city jails, mayoral offices, corporate holdings, and authenticated by an entire set of legitimating signifiers. In the town of Congleton, not only was a husband "thy lord, thy king, thy governor/ . . . thy life, thy keeper,/Thy head, thy sovereign" (*Shrew*, 5.2.138, 146–47), he was also the law, and his tyrannies were supported by the existing legal institutions. And while such a grim history as that which is carried by the iron bridle may seem far indeed from Shakespeare's zesty comedy about the taming of shrews into conformable Kates, I would insist that it is not. For Kate the fictional shrew is but one of those women whose real history can all too easily be hidden behind and thus effectively erased by the romanticized version of her story that Shakespeare's play participates in creating.

*   *   *

Around 1640 the proverbial scold seems virtually to disappear from court documents. As Susan Amussen informs us, the "formal mechanisms of control were rarely used after the Restoration."[87]

> The prosecution of scolds was most common before 1640; while accusations of scolding, abusing neighbours, brawling in church and other forms of quarrelling usually make up between a tenth and a quarter of the offences in sample Act Books of the Archdeacons of Norwich and Norfolk before 1640, they do not appear in the samplebooks after 1660.[88]

Why did "scolds" apparently disappear? Were they always just the projections of an order-obsessed culture, who disappeared when life became more orderly? Or is the difference real and the behavior of women in the early modern era indeed different from the norms of a later one? Did they really brawl, curse, scold, riot, and behave so abusively? Brushfield clearly assumes that they did, and thus is able to rationalize the otherwise disturbing fact that so many of these illegal instruments of torture turned up in good old Cheshire County, his own home space. As he says, "if such a number of tongue-repressing Bridles were required," then they were so because the women must have been so disorderly as to have turned Cheshire into "a riotous County indeed." Benevolently, however, he then continues, forgiving England its disruptive foremothers and invoking the authority of the Bard himself to authorize his beatific vision of silent women:

> Suffice it, however, for us to say,—and I speak altogether on behalf of [all] the gentlemen,—that whatever it may have been in times gone by, yet it is certain that the gentleness and amiability of the ladies of the present generation make more than ample amends for the past; and Shakespeare, when he wrote those beautiful words,
> "Her voice was ever soft,/Gentle and low; an excellent thing in woman,"

unintentionally, of course, yet fully anticipated the attributes of our modern Cheshire ladies.[89]

And it well may be that in his work on scolds' bridles, T. N. Brushfield may unwittingly have described the silent process of how gender is historicized. He may have recorded the social process by which the women of one generation—perhaps as rowdy, brawling, voluble, and outspoken as men have always been authorized to be—were shamed, tamed, and reconstituted by instruments like cucking stools and scolds' bridles, into the meek and amiable, softspoken ladies he so admires in his own time.[90] Perhaps the gentle and pleasing Stepford Wives of mid-nineteenth-century Chester are precisely the products that such a searing socialization into gender would produce—and would continue to reproduce even long after the immediate agony of being bridled or of watching a daughter, mother, or sister being paraded through the streets and forced to endure that experience had passed from personal and recorded memory. The history of silencing is a history of internalizing the literal, of erasing the signifier and interiorizing a signified. The iron bridle is a part of that history. Its appropriate epigraph is a couplet from Andrew Marvell's "Last Instructions to a Painter"[91]—a couplet that could in fact have been written at exactly the moment that some curst and clamorous Kate in some English town was being bridled:

> Prudent Antiquity, that knew by Shame
> Better than Law, Domestic Crimes to tame.

NOTES

Originally published in *Shakespeare Quarterly* 42, no. 2 (Summer 1991): 179–213. Reprinted by permission of Lynda E. Boose and *Shakespeare Quarterly*.

  1. *Saturday Review*, Nov. 6, 1897, as quoted in editor Ann Thompson's introduction to the New Cambridge Shakespeare *The Taming of the Shrew* (Cambridge: Cambridge University Press, 1984), 21. See Thompson's introduction for further instances of this reaction. All *Shrew* citations refer to this edition, and quotations from other Shakespeare plays refer to *The Riverside Shakespeare*, ed. G. Blakemore Evans (Boston: Houghton Mifflin, 1974); all references will appear in text.
  2. Louis Althusser, "Ideology and Ideological State Apparatuses" in *Lenin and Philosophy and Other Essays*, trans. Ben Brewster (London: New Left Books, 1971).
  3. My discussion does not impinge upon the textual controversies surrounding the play. Nonetheless, an essay that has influenced my thinking about the text is Leah S. Marcus's as yet unpublished essay, "The Shakespearean Editor as Shrew Tamer"; see also Marcus's "Levelling Shakespeare: Local Customs and Local Texts," *Shakespeare Quarterly* 42, no. 2 (Summer 1991).
  4. The phrase comes from Barbara Hodgdon's essay, forthcoming in *PMLA*, "Katherine Bound, or Pla(k)ating the Strictures of Everyday Life" [reprinted in this volume], which offers an insightful assessment of the visual pleasures that performance of this play makes available to the female spectator.
  5. Carol Thomas Neely, *Broken Nuptials in Shakespeare's Plays* (New Haven: Yale University Press, 1985), 218. Other essays that specifically address the knotty problem of reading through gender that this play in particular poses include Shirley Nelson Garner, *"The Taming of the Shrew*: Inside or Outside of the Joke?" and Peter Berek, "Text, Gender, and Genre in *The Taming of the Shrew*," both in *"Bad" Shakespeare: Revaluations of the Shakespeare Canon*, ed. Maurice Charney (London and Toronto: Associated University Presses, 1988), 105–19 and 91–104; Joel Fineman, "The Turn of the Shrew," in *Shakespeare and the Question of Theory*, ed. Patricia Parker and Geoffrey Hartman (London: Methuen, 1985), 138–59, esp. 141–44; Marianne L. Novy, "Patriarchy and Play in *The Taming of the Shrew*," *English Literary Renaissance* 9 (1979), 264–80; Kathleen McLuskie, "Feminist Deconstruction: Shakespeare's *Taming of the Shrew*," *Red Letters* 12 (1982): 15–20; Martha Andresen-Thom, "Shrew-Taming and Other Rituals of Aggression: Bating and Bonding on the Stage and in the Wild," *Women's Studies* 9 (1982): 121–43; John Bean, "Comic Structure and the Humanizing of Kate in *The Taming of the Shrew*," in *The Woman's Part: Feminist Criticism of Shakespeare*, ed. Carolyn Ruth Swift Lenz, Gayle Greene, and Carol Thomas Neely (Urbana: University of Illinois Press, 1980), 65–78; Jeanne Addison Roberts, "Horses and Hermaphrodites: Metamorphoses in *The Taming of The Shrew*," *Shakespeare Quarterly*, 34 (1983): 159–71; Coppélia Kahn, *"The Taming of the Shrew*: Shakespeare's Mirror of Marriage," *Modern Language Studies* 5 (1975): 88–102; Robert B. Heilman, "The *Taming* Untamed, or, The Return of the Shrew," *Modern Language Quarterly* 27 (1966): 147–61; and Richard A. Burt, "Charisma. Coercion, and Comic Form in *The Taming of the Shrew*," *Criticism* 26 (1984): 295–311.
  6. For accounts of this production history, see Thompson, New Cambridge edition, 17–24. In his discussion of the inappropriate historicization at work in Jonathan

Miller's attempt to imagine Petruchio as spokesman for the new Puritan ideals of companionate marriage, Graham Holderness demonstrates how the Miller BBC television production provides yet another instance of a theatrical attempt to save this play from its own ending (*The Taming of the Shrew* in the Shakespeare in Performance series [Manchester and New York: Manchester University Press, 1989], 21–25).

7. J. Wickham Legg, *Ecclesiological Essays* (London: de la More Press, 1903), 190.

8. George Elliott Howard, A *History of Matrimonial Institutions*, 2 vols. (London: T. Fisher Unwin, 1904), 1: 306–7. *"Tunc procidat sponsa ante pedes ejus, et deosculetur pedem ejus dextrum; tunc erigat eam sponsus"* (*Surtees Society Publications*, 63, 20 n.). See also Legg, 189–90, and *The Rathen Manual: Catholic Church, Liturgy and Ritual*, ed. Duncan MacGregor (Aberdeen: Aberdeen Ecclesiological Society, 1905), 36. In comments on the wedding-ritual structure that underwrites the scene of Lear, Cordelia, and her suitors, I had earlier suggested the possibility of such a literal, ceremonial basis to the line "I take up what's cast away" (1.1.253) that France speaks to Cordelia ("The Father and the Bride in Shakespeare," *PMLA* 97 [1982]: 325–47, esp. 333–34).

9. Giles Fletcher, *Of the Russe Common Wealth*, chap. 24, fol. 101, as quoted in Legg, 190.

10. Legg, 190. See also J. B. Thiers, *Traité des Superstitions qui regardent les Sacremens*, 4th ed. (Avignon, 1777), book 10, chap. 11, 457. Although the "falling at the feet of the husband" had been banished from the Anglican Rite for some 350 years by the time Legg wrote, his recognition of the women's resistance in the French text prompts him to decry "innovators in their slack teaching on the subject of matrimony" and comment acerbically that "the modern upholders of the rights of women would never endure this ceremony for one moment." As stays against such "modern ideas," he then invokes Augustine and Paul and digresses from his topic (marriage customs) to include Augustine's definition of a "good *materfamilias*" as a woman who "is not ashamed to call herself the servant (*ancilla*) of her husband" (190–91).

11. David Underdown, "The Taming of the Scold: The Enforcement of Patriarchal Authority in Early Modern England," in *Order and Disorder in Early Modern England*, ed. Anthony Fletcher and John Stevenson (Cambridge: Cambridge University Press, 1985), 116–36, esp. 116, 136.

12. T. N. Brushfield, "On Obsolete Punishements, With particular reference to those of Cheshire," *Chester Archaeological and Historic Society Journal*, 3 (1855–1862), 31–48, 203–34.

13. Underdown, 123.

14. In his otherwise quite useful book, *Juridical Folklore in England: Illustrated by the Cucking-stool* (Durham, N.C.: Duke University Press, 1944), John Webster Spargo spends pages trying to deny the cucking stool-privy stool connection and invalidate, one by one, the etymological links in the numerous terms that support that connection. His argument is finally unpersuasive and seems ultimately to depend upon no more than his own determination not to believe that this could have been possible. It seems to me, however, quite logical to believe that cucking-stool punishments would have included the additional humiliation of enthroning a woman on

a privy stool before riding her through town and ducking her. The punishment was primarily a shaming ritual to begin with, and women's shame has a long history of connection to the body "privates."

On matters of the reliability of T. N. Brushfield's research, however, Spargo's comments—together with his widely accepted respectability as a folklorist—prove quite helpful. In Spargo's own work on cucking stools, he relied often upon Brushfield's research, calling his paper on punishment the "best of all" and "most comprehensive" (chap. 1, n. 15, and p. 11).

15. Brushfield, 219. Since the use of "rough music," or noise-making instruments to call people out of house to watch the shaming of the scold is common to this punishment, I assume "bason" refers to such an instrument. The paper that the Norfolk woman carries would most likely have had "scold" written on it for her to display and thus participate in her own humiliation.

16. Spargo, 122.

17. William Sheppard (or Shepherd), *A Grand Abridgment of the Common and Statute Law of England* (London, 1675), s.v. "scold," as quoted in Spargo, 122.

18. Church of England, *Certain Sermons or Homilies* (London: Society for Promoting Christian Knowledge, 1908), 154.

19. Quoted from Brushfield, 217.

20. Ibid. 222.

21. In "Sex Roles and Crime in Late Elizabethan Hertfordshire" (*Journal of Social History* 8 [1975]: 38–60), Carol Z. Wiener notes that she has found two cases of male scolds (one in 1584, another in 1598) in the St. Albans archdeaconry court (59, n. 64).

22. Lewis Coser has even suggested that violence cannot be considered entirely deviant for men, since within certain subcultures it begets respect ("Some Social Functions of Violence," *Annals of the American Academy of Political and Social Science* 364 [1966]: 8–18); and Carol Z. Wiener, citing Coser, suggests that Elizabethan communities may have admired the violent behavior of males, even when it was illegal (59, n.65). Such attitudes would logically produce different ways of seeing verbal disruptions and noisy challenges to authority.

23. L. J. Ross, "Shakespeare's 'Dull Clown' and Symbolic Music." *Shakespeare Quarterly*, 17 (1977): 107–28, discusses the distinction that was made between the use of "Apollonian" and "Dionysian" music for specific occasions. The charivari is, of course, another "rough music" ritual.

24. On inversion, see Natalie Zemon Davis, "Women on Top," *Society and Culture in Early Modern France* (Stanford, Calif.: Stanford University Press, 1975), 124–51; Peter Stallybrass and Allon White, *The Politics and Poetics of Transgression* (Ithaca, N.Y.: Cornell University Press, 1986); Ian Donaldson, *The World Upside-Down: Comedy from Jonson to Fielding* (Oxford: Clarendon Press, 1970); and essays in *Popular Culture in Seventeenth-Century England*, ed. Barry Reay (New York: St. Martin's Press, 1985), including Reay's introduction (1–30), Martin Ingram's "Ridings, Rough Music and Mocking Rhymes in Early Modern England" 166–97, and Peter Burke's "Popular Culture in Seventeenth-Century London" (31–58).

25. See especially René Girard, *Violence and the Sacred*, trans. Patrick Gregory (Baltimore: Johns Hopkins University Press, 1977). But see also Patricia Klindienst

Joplin's perceptive critique of Girard's failure to consider how issues of gender relate to the selection of a scapegoat figure on whom a society's own violence can be both enacted and blamed ("The Voice of the Shuttle is Ours," *Stanford Literature Review* 1 [1984]: 25–53).

26. M. C. Bradbrook, "Dramatic Role as Social Image: A Study of the *Taming of the Shrew*," *Shakespeare-Jahrbuch* 94 (1958): 132–50, esp. 134.

27. *The Dramatic Works in the Beaumont and Fletcher Canon*, ed. Fredson Bowers, 7 vols. (Cambridge: Cambridge University Press, 1979), 4: 43.

28. See "The Taming of the Scold" (cited in n. 11, above).

29. Quoted from Brushfield, 226.

30. The totalizing power of Lady Macbeth's three-word injunction—"Be a Man!"—whether spoken by a woman or another man and whether spoken in 1591 or 1991, is so powerfully controlling only because the threatened category it invokes—woman—has been culturally defined as the space of abjection. Conversely, note how powerless is the injunction to "Be a Woman!"

31. Brushfield, 212.

32. See Davis, "Women on Top."

33. David Underdown, *Revel, Riot, and Rebellion: Popular Politics and Culture in England 1603–1660* (Oxford: Clarendon Press, 1985), 110.

34. See especially 106–12 in *Revel, Riot, and Rebellion* for a detailed discussion of "skimmington" and of the complex political associations that were deployed through gender inversions in the popular politics preceding the Civil War. Also see Buchanan Sharp, *In Contempt of All Authority: Rural Artisans and Riot in the West of England, 1586–1660* (Berkeley: University of California Press, 1980), 100–8, 129.

35. Underdown, 111, n. 20.

36. Kaja Silverman, "Fragments of a Fashionable Discourse," in *Studies in Entertainment: Critical Approaches to Mass Culture*, ed. Tania Modleski (Bloomington: Indiana University Press, 1986), 139–52, esp. 139.

37. The attention paid to Hero's dress in *Much Ado About Nothing*, 3.4, fits into this tradition.

38. As another indicator that *Shrew*'s wedding ceremonies evoke the pre-1549 rite, the offstage act of Communion to which the text alludes is, once again, an anachronism. Prior to the reform, the Sarum, Hereford, Exeter, Westminster, and Evesham books had all included a special bridal Communion of bread and wine. Legg even notes the connection: "Shakespeare, no doubt describing an Elizabethan marriage in . . . *Shrew*, speaks of the drink brought at the end of the ceremony and of the sops in it (196).

39. For an exemplum text on working with multiple documents coming from a variety of sources, including hitherto unused ones, see Alan Macfarlane, with Sarah Harrison, *The Justice and the Mare's Ale: Law and Disorder in Seventeenth-Century England* (New York: Cambridge University Press, 1981).

40. Keith Wrightson and David Levine, *Poverty and Piety in an English Village: Terling, 1525–1700* (New York: Academic Press, 1979). See also J.A. Sharpe, *Crime in Early Modern England 1550–1750* (London: Longman, 1984), 53; and "Crime and Delinquency in an Essex Parish 1600–1640," in *Crime in England 1550-1800*, ed. J. S. Cockburn (London: Methuen, 1977), 90–109.

41. In the twentieth century the social offenders who had four centuries earlier been signified by whoring, witchcraft, scolding, and being masterless men and women have been replaced by those whose identity may be similarly inferred from the fetishized criminality the state currently attaches to abortion, AIDS, street drugs, and, most recently, subway panhandling (read homelessness).

42. Spargo devotes considerable time to examining this and other etymological questions (see esp. 3–75). An exchange in Middleton's *The Family of Love* depends on the equation. In response to her husband's threat, "I say you are a scold, and beware the cucking-stool," Mistress Glister snaps back, "I say you are a ninnihammer, and beware the cuckoo" (*The Works of Thomas Middleton*, ed. A. H. Bullen, 8 vols. [London: Nimmo, 1885], 5.1.25–28). My thanks to Sarah Lyons for this reference.

43. John Webster, *The Duchess of Malfi*, ed. Elizabeth M. Brennan (New York: Norton, 1983), 1.2.255–56, 257.

44. Peter Stallybrass, "Reading the Body: *The Revenger's Tragedy* and the Jacobean Theater of Consumption." *Renaissance Drama* 18 (1987), 121–48, esp. 122. See also Frank Whigham, "Reading Social Conflict in the Alimentary Tract: More on the Body in Renaissance Drama," *English Literary History* 55 (1988), 333–50; and Patricia Parker, *Literary Fat Ladies: Rhetoric, Gender, Property* (London and New York: Methuen, 1987).

45. The stigma that joins these two signs is clearly a durable one, for even in the twentieth century, if a woman is known as "loud mouthed" or is reputed to participate (especially in so-called mixed company) in the oral activities of joking, cursing, laughing, telling boisterous tales, drinking, and even eating—activities that are socially unstigmatized for males—she can still be signified negatively by meanings that derive from an entirely different register.

46. Brushfield 46.

47. Ibid. 35 n.

48. David Underdown's "The Taming of a Scold" is a notable exception. Literary essays that have brought the scold's bridle into focus and have included depictions of it include Joan Hartwig's "Horses and Women in *The Taming of the Shrew*" (*Huntington Library Quarterly* 45 [1982], 285–94); Valerie Wayne's "Refashioning the Shrew" (*Shakespeare Studies* 17 [1985], 159–88); and Patricia Parker, who calls the scold's bridle "a kind of chastity belt for the tongue" (*Literary Fat Ladies*, 27).

49. The sampler is an heirloom in the family of Michael Neill, who provided this information.

50. My knowledge of this bridle comes from Deborah Shuger. In the frontispiece the woman with the bridle is only one figure in a quite complex visualization of interior Protestant virtues, and it is impossible to know whether the bridle she holds intentionally depicts the instrument used on scolds or is purely an allegorical representation of interior discipline. But in a culture where the allegorical is simultaneously the literal and a bridle is being used to produce exterior discipline on unruly women, the problem of signification is such that one representation cannot, it seems to me, remain uncontaminated from association with the other.

51. I am particularly indebted to Susan Warren for her invaluable research in Cheshire County into this issue. Not only was she able to locate the whereabouts of several of these items, but she discovered from an overheard conversation between two

women that the notion of a woman "needing to be bridled" was apparently still alive in the local phrasing.

52. See especially Peter Erickson, *Patriarchal Structures in Shakespeare's Drama* (Berkeley: University of California Press, 1985).

53. Thompson, 18–19.

54. See especially Joan Hartwig (cited in n. 48, above) and Jeanne Addison Roberts (cited in n. 5, above), as well as Linda Woodbridge, *Women and the English Renaissance: Literature and the Nature of Womankind, 1540–1620* (Urbana: University of Illinois Press, 1984).

55. Antiquarian folklorist C. R. B. Barrett notes the first recorded skimmington at Charing Cross in 1562. See Barrett, " 'Riding Skimmington' and 'Riding the Stang,' " *Journal of the British Archaeological Association* 1 (1895): 58–68, esp. 63. Barrett discusses the way that a skimmington usually involved not the presentation of the erring couple themselves but the representation of them acted out by their next-door neighbors, other substitutes, or even effigies. Thomas Lupton's *Too Good to be True* (1580) includes a dialogue that comments acerbically upon the use of neighbors rather than principles.

    As Martin Ingram (cited in n. 24, above) notes, "the characteristic pretext" for such ridings "was when a wife beat her husband or in some other noteworthy way proved that she wore the breeches" (168). The skimmington derisions frequently incorporated the symbolics of cuckoldry—antlers, or animal horned heads, once again collapsing the two most pervasively fetishized signs of female disorder into a collocation by which female dominance means male cuckoldry.

56. See Thompson, 12.

57. Christopher Marlow, *Tamburlaine the Great, Parts I and II,* ed. John D. Jump (Lincoln: University of Nebraska Press, 1967), 4.1.180–84.

58. *Swetnam the Woman-hater: The Controversy and the play*, ed. Coryl Crandall (Purdue: Purdue University Studies, 1969), 5.2.331–33. Given the impetus behind the writing of this play, it seems at least worth speculation that if women ever did dislodge the convention of boy actors during this period and appear onstage in women's roles themselves, this play would seem a prime location for such a possibility.

59. Simon Shepherd, *Amazons and Warrior Women: Varieties of Feminism in Seventeenth-Century Drama* (New York: Harvester Press, 1981), 208.

60. [Joseph Hall], *The Discovery of a New* World, trans. John Healy, ed. Huntington Brown (Cambridge: Harvard University Press, 1937).

61. [Joseph Hall], *Another World and Yet the Same: Bishop Joseph Hall's* Mundus Alter et Idem, trans. and ed. John Millar Wands (New Haven and London: Yale University Press, 1981); see "Book Two: Viraginia, or New Gynia," 57–67, esp. 57.

62. Ibid., 58.

63. Ibid., 64.

64. Ibid., 65.

65. Ibid., 66.

66. Ibid., 57.

67. Brown edition, 64–65.

68. Catherine Belsey also refers to this play; see *The Subject of Tragedy: Identity and Difference in Renaissance Drama* (London and New York: Methuen, 1985), 181.

69. Other tongue treatises include an address by George Webbe, Bishop of Limerick, called *The Arraignement of an unruly Tongue. Wherein the Faults of an euill Tongue are opened, the Danger discouered, the Remedies prescribed, for the Taming of a Bad Tongue, the Right Ordering of the Tongue . . .* (London. 1619); an offering by William Perkins in *A Direction for the Gouernment of the Tongue according to Gods Word* (Cambridge, 1593); a sermon by Thomas Adàms on *The Taming of the Tongue* (London, 1616); a series of "tongue" sermons by Jeremy Taylor (1653); and Edward Reyner's *Rules for the Government of the Tongue* (1656). The latter is accompanied by a prayer that the book shall prove "effectuall to tame that unruly Member thy Tongue, and to make thee a good Linguist in the School of Christ." Spargo provides further data on the publication of all these treatises (11–120).

70. In particular see Richard C. McCoy's essay "Gascoigne's *'Poëmata castrata'*: The Wages of Courtly Success," *Criticism* 27 (1985), 29–55.

71. As quoted in Spargo, pp. 118–19, n. 28; Spargo notes that there has been considerable controversy over authorship.

72. Quoted here from Spargo, 115 n. 21, the sermon was first printed in Adams's *The Sacrifice of Thankfulness* (London, 1616).

73. Thomas Watson, "On the Government of the Tongue" appears in *A Body of Practical Divinity . . .* (London, 1692), 986–94.

74. William Gearing, *A Bridle fot the Tongue: or, A Treatise of Ten Sins of the Tongue* (London, 1663); Spargo concurs with my reading (118, n. 26).

75. Pp. 29–30. My thanks to Ann Blake for alerting me to the existence of this first-person account.

76. Quoted from Brushfield, 33.

77. p. 37.

78. Brushfield, 269. This information was forwarded to the Chester Archaeological Society some eighteen months after Brushfield had read his paper and is included by the secretary in the April 4, (1860?) minutes. In the body of the paper, he had earlier noted that bridles with their leading-chains attached to the nose-piece or front of the horizontal hoop—as is the chain on the Manchester bridle—were those designed to "inflict the greatest lacerations to the wearer's tongue" (37).

79. Brushfield, 37.

80. Ibid., 44.

81. Ibid., 45.

82. Ibid., 45.

83. In Morrison, Paul D. carries with him the memory of having "had a bit in [his] mouth . . . about how offended the tongue is, held down by iron, how the need to spit is so deep you cry for it. [Sethe] already knew about it, had seen it time after time. . . . Men, boys, little girls, women. The wildness that shot up into the eye the moment the lips were yanked back. Days after it was taken out, goose fat was rubbed on the corners of the mouth but nothing to soothe the tongue or take the wildness out of the eye" ([New York: Alfred A. Knopf, 1987], 69, 71).

84. "The Taming of the Scold" (cited in n. 11, above), 120. It was thought unseemly to duck or publicly punish women of higher status, primarily because in that class the status of the husband was invested in the wife, no doubt making officials reluctant to sentence such wives to punishments more harsh than a fine.

85. Brushfield, 42.

86. Ibid., 42.
87. S. D. Amussen, *An Ordered Society: Gender and Class in Early Modern England* (London: Basil Blackwell, 1988), 130.
88. Ibid., 122.
89. Brushfield, 47. The Shakespeare lines Brushfield quotes are, of course, King Lear's words as he bends over the dead—and very silent—Cordelia.
90. Such a progress would complement the transformation Margaret George defines as "From 'Goodwife' to 'Mistress': the transformation of the female in bourgeois culture," *Science and Society* 37 (1973), 152–77.
91. I defer to David Underdown, who earlier used these lines as an epigraph to "The Taming of the Scold."

Figure 5. Henry Woodward in the character of Petruchio. Published for Bell's Edition of Shakespeare, January 5, 1776. Used with the permission of the Folger Shakespeare Library.

The Taming of the Shrew
Women, Acting, and Power

JULIET DUSINBERRE

The opening of *The Taming of the Shrew* is strikingly different from that of the related play *The Taming of a Shrew* in offering the audience in the first ten lines a battle between the sexes. The Beggar, who calls himself Christopher Sly, threatens to "pheeze" the Hostess who throws him out of her inn, not just for drunkenness, but for not paying for broken glasses. Threatening Sly with the stocks, the Hostess exits, determining to send for the constable. In *A Shrew*, the innkeeper is a Tapster, and Slie's offence simply inebriation. Shakespeare's Sly defies the Hostess in a strange little speech: "Ile not budge an inch boy. Let him come, and kindly." He has in the course of eleven lines quoted Kyd's *Spanish Tragedy* and challenged her abuse of him as a rogue: "Y'are a baggage, the Slies are no rogues. Look in the Chronicles, we came in with Richard Conqueror: therefore *paucas pallabris*, let the world slide: Sessa" *(First Folio)*. He sounds momentarily like John Durbeyfield in Hardy's *Tess*, claiming an ancient and declining stock. The little interchange offers a vignette in which a man and woman engage in a power struggle: she, only a woman, but with a trade and a function which give her access to authority over him: he a beggar with illusions of grandeur, ancestral memories of great men, culture, a power he no longer possesses. But why does he call her "boy"?

I want to argue that he calls her boy because she is a boy. The Hostess must, in Shakespeare's theatre, have been played by a boy actor. But if Sly addresses her as a boy, then a new dimension is added to the interchange. In his drunkenness he seems momentarily to refuse to enter the play: to be, not a drunken beggar, but a drunken actor, who forgets that his dialogue is with a Hostess, and thinks that the boy actor is getting above himself. In other words, the theatrical illusion seems to be tested before it is even under way. Is Sly a beggar, or is he an actor who must play a beggar?

In *The Taming of the Shrew*, more than in any other play, Shakespeare uses the relationships between actors as a commentary on the social relation-

168

ships represented in the self-contained world of the play, the drama of *The Shrew* which is performed before the Beggar (persuaded to believe that he is a lord) at the request of the "real" Lord of the Induction who enters from hunting to refresh himself at the inn and is visited by a company of players. The audience in the theatre is required to react to two competing dramas: a stage representation of a traditional courtship and taming drama; and a more covert drama which constantly interrupts and comments on the taming drama, one generated by the actual structures of relationship present in the company which performs the piece. Sly's use of the term "boy" to the boy actor is only one of many oddities which suggest to the audience the presence in the play itself of actors, not just impersonators of characters. I want to demonstrate how this works in a number of interchanges in the play, and to reinterpret Kate's role in the light of its original theatrical provenance: that Kate would have been played, like the Hostess, Bianca, the Widow, and the young Biondello, by a boy. How would this material condition of Shakespeare's theatre have modified audience perception of the power structures represented in the fiction of *The Taming of the Shrew*?[1]

If Kate is played by a boy in the position of apprentice, then the dynamic between Kate and other players on stage, and between Kate and women in the audience, is altered from what it is in the modern theatre. The boys stood in the position of apprentice towards the adult sharers in the company.[2] It was not a guild apprenticeship, but more of a personal arrangement, such as that between Pepys and his boy Tom Edwards in the 1660s, a child whom he employed as his attendant from the Chapel Royal: well-educated and a good singer (Pepys 1971, V [1664], 228, 234 n.1, 255). The boys in Shakespeare's company would each have had a particular master; Burbage was master to Nicholas Tooley, and Augustine Phillips—another boy in the company—spoke in his will of Tooley as his "fellow" in the company (Greg 1931, I: 47). The master-pupil relationship between the apprentices and the adult actors and sharers in the company is a highly significant one in the dynamics of the company and can be seen to be in operation in *The Shrew*. The Lord sends instructions to his page on how to play the lady, as any master might have instructed his apprentice on how to play Kate. Furthermore, the apprentice's role in the company creates for him a special relationship with the women in the theatre audience. He must, when the play is done, return to a position of dependency. But great ladies enjoyed a position of social superiority to that of apprentices (Howard 1989, 31–40). The apprentice has within the world of the play access not only to that momentary social superiority but also access to the stage power of the female heroine. Women in the theatre audience may return to the subservient lives of women in Elizabethan social structures, but they too have been allowed within the theatre the fantasy of different kinds of power which link them in sympathy with the boy himself as he represents women on stage. Sly, as an actor refusing to play his part—there was, after all, an actor in

Shakespeare's company called William Sly—defies his inferior in the company, the boy playing the Hostess. But the play gives the Hostess authority over him: she demands that he pay for the broken glasses and sends for the constable.

The Taming of the Shrew creates for the audience images of power in the male world in the roles of Petruchio, Baptista, Lucentio, but it also undermines them with a different kind of power, generated by the counterpointing of the actor with the role he plays. This special energy enters the play through the ambiguous medium of Sly, but is sustained throughout the drama by the covert juxtaposing in Kate's role of the heroine and the boy apprentice who must act her. Similarly, the actor who plays Tranio with histrionic virtuosity oscillates between the subservience of his social role and the dominance of his acting role as Lucentio.

Curiously, various snippets of information back up a theory that the Induction of *The Shrew* deliberately places before the theatre audience not a fiction, but a group of players whom they may identify as actors, rather than as characters, as a modern audience might identify repertory players or particular actors and actresses in a number of different roles. Two actors who appear in the Induction set this line of enquiry in motion. *The Taming of the Shrew* contains a number of prefixes in the text which refer directly to the names of actors: possibly Sly himself, and certainly Sincklo: named as the Second Player in the Induction. This seems to be more than accident as the play constantly obliges the audience to remember that behind the character in the play is an actor who has his own reality and his own relation to the other figures on the stage, a relation forged in the acting company, not in the Italian society world in which he plays a part.

Shakespeare's Sly may in fact have been played by William Sly, a member of both the Pembroke's men in the early 1590s (McMillin 1972) and subsequently of Shakespeare's company, the Chamberlain's men, later the King's men. His name is on the list of Shakespeare's company at the beginning of the 1623 Folio. In 1604, William Sly appears in the new induction which the playwright John Marston wrote for *The Malcontent*. He is named in the *Dramatis Personae* under a special heading: "*Actors of the King's Men, at the Globe Theatre, who appear in the Induction*: WILLIAM SLY, JOHN SINKLO, RICHARD BURBAGE, HENRY CONDELL, JOHN LOWIN." In this Induction, Sly pretends to be a member of the audience with social pretensions who has come to sit on the stage as if he were a gallant. The Tire-man, realising that he is not a gentleman, tries to shoo him off: "Sir, the gentlemen will be angry if you sit there." Sly calls for the other actors, saying that he has seen the play often and "can give them intelligence for their action." When the actor John Sincklo enters, he greets Sly familiarly: "Save you, coz." They gossip, and call for the players, Burbage, Condell and Lowin. At a certain point, Sly seems to be rambling and one of the actors begs him to leave the stage, this time successfully. The part is a curiosity in its transparent disguising of two actors for audience members, while on the page they remain simply actors.

Odder still, Sincklo appears in *The Shrew*, just seventy lines after Sly has fallen into a drunken sleep. The Players enter and the Lord turns to the second player, named in the Folio prefix, probably on Shakespeare's own authority, Sincklo. Sincklo was distinguished in Shakespeare's company by his appearance: he was extremely thin and cadaverous-looking, and he played parts which suited this physiognomy. He is named in *2 Henry IV* as the Beadle who arrests Mistress Quickly and Doll. He played the forester in *3 Henry VI* who arrests the King. He probably played the emaciated Apothecary who supplies Romeo with poison, and Robert Faulconbridge in *King John*, mocked by the Bastard for his lack of sex appeal (Gaw 1926, 289–303; Wentersdorf 1980; McMillin 1972, 155, 157). The Lord remembers him in a particular part:

> This fellow I remember
> Since once he played a farmer's eldest son—
> 'Twas where you wooed the gentlewoman so well—
> I have forgot your name, but sure that part
> Was aptly fitted and naturally performed.[3]

This passage is always taken straight: Shakespeare made a friendly gesture towards an actor for a good performance. But its jests seem to me to huddle in upon each other. The Lord cannot remember his name, although Shakespeare names him in his text: he is John Sincklo. You were a wonderful lover, remarks the Lord to someone who looks like a jailer or a supplier of poison. It is a theatre company's joke, but it becomes much funnier if the audience has seen the actor in other parts and can share the joke. They would have been able to share the joke if they had just seen *2 Henry IV*; *The Shrew* was certainly performed in these years.

But one must perhaps also ask whether Shakespeare's play was written sometime in 1595–1597, not in the earlier period. Sincklo's presence in the Induction to *The Shrew*, together with the possible references to his other roles, particularly in *2 Henry IV*, might imply a later date for Shakespeare's play than is usually suggested.[4] *The Shrew* would then enter the constellation of plays in which Shakespeare probably used Sincklo: *Romeo and Juliet*, and *King John*. The interchanges between Sly and the Hostess at the beginning of *The Shrew* are rich partly because they recall the interchanges in the two parts of *Henry IV between* Mistress Quickly and Falstaff.

Sincklo's name for the Second Player immediately raises the question of doubling. The Elizabethan custom of theatrical doubling would have made it possible for *The Shrew* to be acted with only thirteen players (nine adults and four boys), excluding hired men.[5] It has been suggested that the absence of a return to the Sly plot at the end, and of the interventions in the play made by Slie in *A Shrew*, result from a theatrical exigency when the Players were touring at the time of theatre closures because of the plague. With his talent for making a virtue out of necessity, Shakespeare seems often to have constructed his plays with doubling written into their artistic conception. Hippolyta may have been doubled with Titania, and often is so on the modern stage; In *Pericles*, it is almost certain that the incestuous Princess at the beginning doubles with Marina, the virtuous and chaste Princess at the end. Many correspondences in structure and language make doubling part of the play's emotional impact. If Shakespeare used an economical touring cast of only thirteen actors, all the players who appear in the Induction to *The Shrew* must originally have played parts in the drama presented to Sly. Did Shakespeare, as was his custom, consider the artistic implications of doubling in relation to the fiction he was creating in the main body of the play, and if so, how did that theatrical necessity affect the construction of the action? Sincklo as Second Player must have acted a part in the main action of *The Shrew*. But which part?

The question can be answered by returning to the peculiar partnership between Sly and Sincklo, in theatrical terms, in both the Induction to *The Shrew*, and later in Marston's *The Malcontent*. The doubling process seems in *The Shrew* to create a special line of communication with the audience particularly evident in the scene in which Lucentio's father Vincentio is brought face to face with the Pedant who pretends to be the father. The scene acquires a special point if Sly doubles with Vincentio. Artistically, Sly makes an ideal Vincentio. The Beggar took little convincing (although much more than in the quarto play) that he was a lord; he is doubled with a wealthy man incapable of entering a world of illusion, whether created by drink or disguise, a man of solid single identity, the antithesis of an actor. Vincentio is a "sober ancient gentleman" who is presented with a tale about his own identity: that he is an imposter.

This is not Vincentio's first encounter with a challenge to his own self-perception. Kate has greeted him on the road to her father's house:

> Young budding virgin, fair and fresh and sweet,
> Whither away, or where is thy abode?
> Happy the parents of so fair a child!
> Happier the man whom favourable stars
> Allots thee for his lovely bedfellow. (4.5.37–40)

Vincentio is gentleman enough to take it all in good part as a merry joke between gentlefolk. But the habits of sobriety which determine his good-humoured acceptance of a joke at his expense threaten to turn the second comic denial of his identity into a scene more tragic than comic. Turning on Tranio, disguised as Lucentio, he cries: "O, he hath murdered his master! Lay hold on him, I charge you in the Duke's name. O my son, my son!" (5.1.67–69). In *The Taming of the Shrew*, where everyone tries his or her hand at playing a part, Vincentio's rugged adherence to a God-given role is both a weakness and a strength. It underlines Vincentio's social reality as a man of wealth and position but heralds in the play itself the end of the play-acting, by defining the limits of theatricality for both actors and audience. Vincentio's distress provides a necessary agent between the brilliant carnivalesque of the sun and moon scene on which he enters, and the sobering domestic closures of the obedience speech. Sly may not re-enter Shakespeare's scene, but the world in which he is a beggar is reasserted in Vincentio, the rich man who refuses even for one moment to play another part.

At the height of Vincentio's alarm about his son, in the anonymous *The Taming of a Shrew*, Slie intervenes: "I say wele have no sending to prison" (Holderness and Loughrey 1992, 80). In Shakespeare's play, the intervention is made by Gremio, the unsuccessful suitor to Bianca, billed in the stage direction as a "pantaloon" (the shrunken old man from the Italian *commedia del'arte*): "Take heed, Signor Baptista, lest you be cony-catched in this business. I dare swear this is the right Vincentio" (5.1.93–95). Gremio has a curious part in *The Shrew* not paralleled by anything in the quarto. He is old and rich and unsuccessful. His suit is the source of an interchange between Katherina and Bianca in 2.1. Kate tries to find out which of the suitors Bianca affects. Bianca denies Hortensio, and the following exchange ensues:

> KAT.   O then, belike, you fancy riches more:
>   You will have Gremio to keep you fair.
> BIA.   Is it for him you do envy me so?
>   Nay then, you jest. (2.1.16–19)

You *must* be joking, remarks Bianca, in the confident tone of a woman who can choose, which infuriates her suitorless sister more than anything. Gremio at the end does not get a wife either to obey him or not. But he has one important moment in the play. He protests against sending Vincentio to prison and declares that he is sure this is the right Vincentio.

That Slie intervenes in *A Shrew* but Gremio intervenes in Shakespeare's version is odd. Shakespeare's Hostess threatened Sly with the constable; in his drunken apprehension of the play this episode could plausibly have reminded him that he might go to prison for not paying for the broken glasses. A possible ending for the play would indeed be the return of the Hostess with the officer, perhaps played by John Sincklo, who played the Beadle who arrested Mistress Quickly in *2 Henry IV*, an inversion of roles which would have its own theatrical irony for audiences who had seen both plays. But the Slie who intervenes and prevents Vincentio's arrest is the *other* Slie, the one in *A Shrew* where there is no Hostess, and no threat of prison (although, confusingly, there may have been the same John Sincklo acting in the play). Why did Shakespeare give the intervention to Gremio when it would have been much more appropriate in the drama he had himself written, to give it—as in the anonymous text—to Sly?

The easy answer is of course that Sly was needed for the part of Vincentio. But another answer based on theatrical realities suggests itself. Gremio, old shrunken and unsuccessful suitor to Bianca, must have been doubled with the Second Player of the Induction, the man called Sincklo, whom the Lord praised for acting the lover so well. Skinny, cadaverous, with a stage history of arresting people, Sincklo, having failed yet again to be a good ladies' man, steps forward to protest against sending people to prison. It is a joke based on the acting company and aimed at a repertory audience. Beneath the role of Gremio is the reality of Sincklo, the actor who looked like a jailor. Beneath Vincentio, a man who resists the denial of his identity, is Sly, willing to apprehend being a Lord. Almost, the two parts coalesce: Sly as Vincentio is momentarily in danger of going to prison after all, and possibly Vincentio's acting should register, however fleetingly, his own double role as rich man and Beggar, until he is returned to singular identity by Sincklo, protesting that in this play he is not a jailor but a man who plays the (albeit unsuccessful) lover. *The Taming of the Shrew* never completely conceals the presence of the actor behind the mask, showing the audience two competing power structures, one social, the other theatrical.

One of the peculiarities of the anonymous *The Taming of a Shrew* is that instead of Slie's rising in status under the influence of the trick, he stays the same, and the Lord descends to his level, the level of good fellows. Slie in this play only recognises his new state through his clothes: "Jesus, what fine apparell I have got" (Holderness and Loughrey 1992, 46). He is easily persuaded, where Shakespeare's beggar resists: he would much rather drink beer than sherry; he doesn't want to wear a doublet, and he accuses his attendants, as Vincentio accuses the Pedant and his accolade, of trying to make him mad. He is ultimately convinced not by clothes but by poetry, and responds—as Sebastian responds to the equally unexpected raptures of Olivia in *Twelfth Night*—by adopting the poetic idiom:

> Am I a lord, and have I such a lady?
> Or do I dream? Or have I dreamed till now?

He is still asking for beer, but he tries to translate it into an aristocratic idiom: "And once again a pot o'th' smallest ale" (Ind. 2.62–71). Shakespeare's Sly unwillingly becomes an actor in an aristocratic show. The Slie of *A Shrew* remains himself, but brings the actors into his orbit. The Lord remains with him all the time, and has become "Sim," a good fellow. But oddly, this name also seems, like Sincklo's name, to link the Lord with a particular player, because at the very beginning of the play-within-a-play the direction reads: "Enter *Simon*, *Alphonsus*, and his three daughters" (Holderness and Loughrey 1992, 48). Simon, the Lord who gulls Slie, is already on stage, however. Possibly the actor who played Alphonsus was one Simon Jewell, a player in the Queen's or Pembroke's Men, who died of the plague in August 1592.[6] But it is also possible that, as in the 1960 John Barton production (Holderness 1989, 31), an actor playing in the play stepped out of it to address Sly, when he intervened, about the prison, and also during the negotiating with Alfonso. Simon, the Lord, never seems, even when he comes from hunting, remotely like a lord. He is much more like an actor, one of the boys.

In Shakespeare's play, the Lord is emphatically never one of the boys: he is an instructor of boys, both those he would call boy because they are his social inferiors, Sly, the player who must not spoil the show by laughing—and those who really are boys—Bartholomew the page who must play Sly's lady; he calls to one of his men:

> Sirrah, go you to Barthol'mew my page
> And see him dressed in all suits like a lady
> That done, conduct him to the drunkard's chamber,
> And call him "madam", do him obeisance.
> Tell him from me—as he will win my love—
> He bear himself with honourable action
> Such as he hath observed in noble ladies
> Unto their lords, by them accomplished.

He not only advises on the idiom, how the boy is to behave and speak, but on practical matters, how he is to produce tears:

> And if the boy have not a woman's gift
> To rain a shower of commanded tears,
> An onion will do well for such a shift,
> Which in a napkin being close conveyed
> Shall in despite enforce a watery eye.

He is confident that all will be satisfactorily performed:

> I know the boy will well usurp the grace,
> Voice, gait and action of a gentlewoman. (Ind. 2.101–28)

In the next scene he instructs Sly: to be a lord requires a mind stocked with poetry and luxury, hawking and hunting, the arts and music, and the ideal. Sly is beguiled by the language of birth, the imaginative world which opens before him: "I smell sweet savours and I feel soft things" (Ind. 2.66). When the Lady enters, she plays her part to perfection:

> My husband and my lord, my lord and husband,
> I am my wife in all obedience.

Does she, one might ask, overplay it a little? Sly announces that he seems to have slept fifteen years, and the Lady responds:

> Ay, and the time seems thirty unto me,
> Being all this time abandoned from your bed.

The effect is instantaneous:

> SLY: 'Tis much. Servants, leave me and her alone.
>   Madam, undress you and come now to bed. (Ind. 2.102–12)

If this is a page acting, one suspects that he willfully overplayed his part to make the onlookers laugh. The moment has the zest of purest amateurism: a naughty boy let loose in a woman's clothes, pushing his luck as far as it will go.

Ben Jonson's play *Cynthia's Revels*, which was acted by a children's company at court, opens with an Induction in which three children in the company quarrel about who is to speak the prologue:

> *2 Child*   I thinke I have most right to it:
>   I am sure I studied it first.
> *3 Child.*   That's all one, if the Author thinke
>   I can speake it better.
> *1 Child.*   I pleade possession of the cloake.

This child appeals, brandishing his costume, to the audience: "Gentles, your suffrages I pray you." A voice [*within*] calls out angrily: "Why, *Children*, are you not asham'd? Come in there" (4.35). Admittedly this is a company of children (of the Chapel Royal); but the apprentices could be as young as ten and most people would feel it is not only children who are capable of such speeches. Bottom is more genial, but he still wants the best part: indeed he wants every part.

The sense of the power invested in the actual part which is played is not confined to the apprentice boy actor in *The Taming of the Shrew*. A parallel can be drawn with the role of Tranio, servant to Lucentio, who gets to play the master. One presumes that the less proficient actor was given what seems on the face of it to be a side-lined part, until one realises that he is in fact required to take over from Lucentio, who thus becomes an onlooker, and a subordinate: the schoolmaster of Bianca, not the acknowledged wealthy lover. Presumably the more skilled actor actually took the part of Tranio. But the servant, Tranio, is almost too convincing in his role of master, Lucentio. It seems to me false to play Tranio as a man who transports into the role of master the common-ness of a servant.[7] He plays Lucentio, as the Page is to play Sly's lady, as one who knows how, if necessary, to imitate a good actor and thus become one; this is an Elizabethan view of education even if not ours. The reason for Tranio's success in the part of Lucentio is his command of a noble language, the language of Petrarch in Petrarch's city, Padua. When Lucentio devises the disguise, Tranio accepts in these terms:

> In a brief, sir, sith it your pleasure is
> And I am tied to be obedient—
> ... I am content to be Lucentio. (1.1.202–7)

The servant must obey the master, but the actor is jumping for joy that he is to play the bigger part, the part of the master, not the servant. His first speech is to his rival suitors to Bianca, defending his right to enter the competition:

> And were his daughter fairer than she is,
> She may more suitors have, and me for one.
> Fair Leda's daughter had a thousand wooers;
> Then well one more may fair Bianca have.
> And so she shall: Lucentio shall make one,
> Though Paris came in hope to speed alone.

Gremio is as startled as we are: "What, this gentleman will out-talk us all!" Lucentio, newly demoted, is sour: "Sir, give him head. I know he'll prove a jade" (1.2.235–42). Access to the language of class which Tranio as actor can command as easily as he can play his previous role of obedient servant, gives him stage power.

By the end of the play, Tranio has also acquired some social power within its structures. When he sits at the wedding feast and sees the brides already squalling, he is locked into a fellowship with Petruchio, Baptista, Lucentio and Hortensio which seems to offer no cognizance of his renewed status as servant. It is as if, from playing the master, he has acquired the manners of a master and now sits in easy fellowship with the real masters. But equally one could say that fellowship is resolved into actors playing a new kind of role, that of audience. As they share the comradeship of actors watching their fellows play a scene, social distinctions in the world of the play are momentarily forgotten in the theatrical climax. Actors, amateur and professional, will recognise the special comradeship between performers in a particular production and how relationships off-stage intertwine with relationships on stage. This is the stuff of *The Taming of the Shrew*, and more so than in the anonymous *A Shrew*, which is a play dominated by class conflict: them and us, or the workers and the toffs, as Holderness puts it in his edition of the play (Holderness and Loughrey 1992, 18–19). In Shakespeare's play, class is a necessary element of the drama.[8] But its centre of vitality is acting and theatre: the relation of the players beneath the masks to the parts they play, and the special power generated from a sense of interweaving relationships within the theatrical world which comment on the relationships impersonated in the social world of the play.

The Shrew may have been written with particular actors in mind for other parts besides those of Sincklo and Sly. This early comedy, oddly enough, though apparently dating from the early 1590s, reminds one of *Hamlet*. The arrival of the company of professional players, their sophistication: no one is going to laugh at the antics of the mad lord watching the play; the respect with which the hunting Lord of the Induction treats them and above all, that Lord himself, all invoke the world of *Hamlet*. The Lord, like Hamlet, fancies himself as a playwright and has already constructed his own little drama of deceiving Sly before the Players arrive, which then becomes more complex when he has more actors, and more professional actors ready to hand. Hamlet instructs the Player to insert a speech of his own writing into *The Murder of Gonzago* and holds forth about acting. The Lord in *The Shrew*, spurred on by the arrival of the Players, still plans his own amateur show in which his page will play the lady. His speech of instruction is not, to my mind, an instruction on marriage but an instruction on how to act an obedient well-born lady, and the incentive given is that the page will win the Lord's love, or one could say, that the apprentice will win the master's love. Hamlet was played by Burbage. Did that remarkable actor, who joined the newly formed Chamberlain's men at the same time as Shakespeare in 1594–1595, perhaps also play Petruchio? Did Shakespeare rewrite the early play in order that it would provide a fit vehicle for this actor? If so, the memorial construction theory must go out of the window, and so must the attendant—and far from convincing—very early date for *The Shrew*. Be that as it may, the possibility that Petruchio and the Lord were played by Burbage seems worth entertaining from the evidence of the play itself.

Burbage was no doubt a fascinating actor to be apprenticed to, and probably very demanding. Shakespeare seems to have written scenes for Burbage which allowed both actor and dramatist to incorporate into the play the rehearsing of how it should be acted. An elegiac tribute to Burbage in Thomas May's *The Heir*, written in 1620, the year after his death (Gurr 1987, 44), recalls that when he acted:

> . . . Ladies in the boxes
> Kept time with sighs, and teares to his sad accents
> As he had truely been the man he seem'd.

Hamlet's advice to the players to hold the mirror up to nature is tailor-made for such an actor. It is not only the Lord's interest in acting in *The Taming of the Shrew* which seems to link him with the roles which Shakespeare created for Burbage in the mid-1590s. Another inhabitant of Shakespeare's stage in the mid-1590s is conjured up by Petruchio's dedication to the wooing of Kate:

> Think you a little din can daunt mine ears?
> . . . Have I not in a pitched battle heard
> Loud 'larums, neighing steeds and trumpets' clang?
> And do you tell me of a woman's tongue,
> That gives not half so great a blow to hear
> As will a chestnut in a farmer's fire?
> Tush, tush, fear boys with bugs! (1.2.193–204)

Petruchio here sounds like Hotspur in *1 Henry IV*, whose troubled dreams of battle alarm another Kate. Both men, Petruchio and Hotspur, share a rhetoric of sport: Hotspur is as much a huntsman on the battlefield as the hawking Petruchio is a warrior in wooing. But they share their love with someone else: the Lord in the Induction, who enters praising his hounds as enthusiastically as Theseus in A *Midsummer Night's Dream*. I want to suggest that the Lord in the Induction was played by the same actor as Petruchio (Burns 1986, 51) and that that actor was Richard Burbage, who joined the Chamberlain's men in 1595, along with Shakespeare himself. Burbage's theatrical career begins, in our records, with a sensational stage brawl (Greg 1931, I:44) not too dissimilar to the first scene between Petruchio and Kate. Hotspur himself, of course, is in Shakespeare's play boisterously matched with Kate (in defiance of history).

Many of Kate's lines carry a Dionysiac charge for most women, of things thought but never said, as when she bursts out to Petruchio, over the business of the cap:

> Why, sir, I trust I may have leave to speak?
> And speak I will. I am no child, no babe.
> Your betters have endured me say my mind,
> And if you cannot, best you stop your ears. (4.3.72–76)

Oddly, these lines have found their way into the first Quarto of *Hamlet* (1603), which precedes the more usually authenticated 1604 Quarto 2. Hamlet says of the Players, about to enter:

> The clowne shall make them laugh
> That are tickled in the lungs, or the blanke verse shall halt for't,
> *And the Lady shall have leave to speake her minde freely.* (my italics)

In both the 1604 text and the Folio, the link with *The Shrew* passage has been obscured by a slight re-wording: "The Clown shall make those laugh whose lungs are tickled o'th' sear, and the Lady shall say her mind freely, or the blank verse shall halt for't" (*Complete Works* 2.2.324–26). The implications are obvious. The line stuck in the theatre audience's mind, and perhaps was the key moment of Burbage's stage performance with his apprentice. Natalie Zemon Davis has written of the unruly woman on top in European culture: Kate is anarchic. She seems to obey not only no social conventions but no theatrical ones either, speaking when she is supposed to be silent, according to everyone else's rules. This includes the ending of the play too, where she is supposed finally, after a play of speaking her mind, not to speak her obedience. Her final rejection of the heroine's giving way gracefully is marked by her wonderful long outburst. If it is about obedience, its provenance is marked by an apprentice's joyful sense not of the social, but of the theatrical arena, in which, like Tranio, he is a free citizen chosen on merit. The play creates within the comic context a charge of anarchic delight comparable in intensity and verve to the tragic energy of Hamlet himself. It is as though the reality of the boy beneath the role speaks to the reality of the women in the audience, allowing them stage power even as he proclaims social submission.[9]

The incentive offered to the apprentice who plays Kate is not just the winning of his master's love—and the satisfaction of an actor like Burbage must have been worth winning—but his own pride of place in the play. Stage power appears here, even if the price of it is a speech on social submission. Furthermore, behind the text of Kate's obedience speech is the powerful evocation of manhood: dangerous, challenging, adventurous, painful (Burns 1986, 46–47). As the apprentice enters the woman's discourse, the dramatist has seen to it that he conjures up a vision of his own entry into the position of master: the one who takes the risks.[10] But this is also mirrored in his stage situation, because the play stands or falls on the apprentice's performance in the last scene, just as Petruchio's wager stands or falls, and as the husbands gather round to witness their wives' performance, so the masters gather round to see whose apprentice will play the big part: the one with the cloak, the one who studied it first, or the one that the author thought would speak it best. One of the reasons why *The Shrew*, with its apparently timebound folk-origin conservative dogmas about women, has not simply died a quiet death like all the other Elizabethan plays in the taming genre, is that it releases into the auditorium an energy created through a dialectic of opposed wills, command versus obedience, and power versus powerlessness, which is polarised in the utterance of the boy actor playing the woman.

In *The Taming of the Shrew*, the apprentice has virtually the last word. As the stage heroine mouths obedience, the apprentice eyes his female audience, both the querulous wives on the stage and the women in the audience. Did the women in the audience register the exhilaration of the apprentice actor seizing his chance to be master, to realise stage power even if the price of it was a recognition of the submission to which he and they would have to return once the play was over? The triumph of *The Shrew* is the triumph of art over life, of making a beggar believe that he is part of the play, or of making a drunken actor enter an illusory world and use its language. Men and women in the theatre audience in Shakespeare's play become the watcher, Sly, and take his place as witnesses of the play, but also become seduced, as the Beggar is, into entering the play world, believing it to be real, as the ladies believed Burbage's acting to be real. In this play, Shakespeare has allowed the apprentice to upstage the master, perhaps originally Burbage himself. No one bothers much about Petruchio's reality because they are so busy talking about Kate's. Her speech steals the show. Beneath an ostensible message of humility it generates the suppressed exhilaration of its stage power: the seizing of mastery by the apprentice even as he proclaims a master's doctrine of subjection.

What did Shakespeare's contemporaries make of it? I maintain that they were not all out ducking their wives in the pond.[11] Sir John Harington, who owned a copy of *The Taming of a Shrew* (given that Shakespeare's contemporaries made no distinction between their title, which *Shrew*?) wrote in 1596 in *The Metamorphosis of Ajax*: "For the shrewd wife, reade the booke of taming of a shrew, which hath made a number of us so perfect, that now every one can rule a shrew in our countrey, save he that hath her. But indeed there are but two good rules. One is, let them never have their willes; the other differs but a letter, let them ever have their willes, the first is the wiser, but the second is more in request, and therefore I make choice of it" (153–55). A year later, in 1597, Harington wrote his wife a poem on their fourteenth wedding anniversary, entitled "To his wife after they had been married 14 yeares":

> Two prentiships with thee I now have been
> Mad times, sad times, glad times, our life hath seen.
> Souls we have wrought four payr, since our first meeting.
> Of which two souls, sweet souls were to to fleeting.
> My workmanship so well doth please thee still
> thou wouldst not graunt me freedom by thy will,
> And Ile confess such usage I have found
> Mine hart yet nere desir'd to bee unbound.
> But though my self am thus thy Prentice vowd,
> My dearest Mall, yet thereof bee not proud,
> Nor claym no rewl thereby, there's no such cause,
> For Plowden who was father of the laws,
> which yet are read and ruld by his indytings,
> doth name himself apprentice in his Writings.
> And I, if you should challenge undew place,
> could learn of him to alter so the case.

> I playn would prove I still kept dew priority,
> and that good wives are still in their minority,
> But far from thee my Deare bee such audacity,
> I doubt more thou dost blame my dull capacity,
> That though I travaile true in my vocation,
> I grow yet worse and worse at th'occupation. (14–15)

In this remarkable poem the husband is the apprentice to his wife and has served two seven-year terms, which have given him such content that he prefers bondage to freedom. In Harington's *Epigrams*, printed after his death, the compositor has either made an error, or failed to understand the significance of the fourteen years: that the apprentice's bonds were up. In this poem Harington, who always claimed that his poems were not fiction, but truth, warns his wife that if she should prove proud, he could prove in law that the situation might be reversed, and she would find that she was the one who was still in her minority, in the apprentice position. However, he is not afraid that that boldness will be taken by her, but rather that he will fail her in his vocation.

The sexual intimacy of this poem within a domestic context makes it most extraordinary, yet the sustained image of the apprentice suggests that it was not only in the theatre that apprentices and women shared a common minority status, but also that the equality which the apprentice boy might gain as heroine, might have its counterpart in the true interchange between apprentice and master which is created in the delight of Petruchio at the end of the play in the boy's performance. Harington, who was fond enough of Shakespeare's plays to possess fifteen of them in quarto, and three duplicates (Furnivall 1890, 283–93), may have felt that for his own wife and for himself, the witty jesting godson of the queen, the play had much to say. But that that message is a humiliating one for women, however much it may be so in a theatre where women actresses play Kate, seems to me in Shakespeare's theatre to be belied by the realities of the theatrical world in which the boy actor earns his momentary supremacy by means of a brilliant performance of a speech proclaiming subjection. If the boy actor winked at Petruchio, he might also have winked at the women watching him in the theatre. Did the women in the audience hear words which send them back to domestic drudgery, or did they share the heady sensation of mastery which the boy actor infuses into one of the longest and most exciting parts he has ever played, in which, in the end, he silences with his eloquence the greatest actor in Shakespeare's company, and surpasses even that actor's wildest expectations of good performance? The boy actor invites women in the audience to participate not in what he says, but in the theatrical power which orchestrates the act of speaking.

NOTES

Originally published in *Studies in the Literary Imagination* 26, no. 1 (Spring 1993): 67–84. Reprinted with the permission of Juliet Dusinberre and *Studies in the Literary Imagination*.

1. The valuable edition of *The Taming of a Shrew* by Graham Holderness and Bryan Loughrey has stimulated a number of questions in this paper, although I disagree with some of the editors' conclusions, and find it surprising that in a cultural materialist edition there should be no specific analysis of the effect on the play of the theatrical condition that Kate would have been played by a boy.
2. Bentley (1984) argues that although there was no player's guild to which boys were officially apprenticed, there is plenty of evidence that boys were attached as apprentices to particular adults in the company. Rastall (1985) finds no evidence that post-pubertal youths played Shakespeare's women.
3. Induction 1.79–83, *The Taming of the Shrew*. All quotations from Shakespeare's *Shrew* are from this edition unless otherwise stated.
4. Leeds Barroll's argument for the bunching of plays in the Jacobean period when Shakespeare could foresee performance in the public theatre, if taken back to the earlier decade, must oblige scholars to rethink the dating of the plays in relation to outbreaks of plague in the 1590s. *The Shrew* on this reckoning might have been written after the 1592–1594 outbreaks which would put it in the same period as the plays discussed in my text, although of course this speculation would force a reconsideration of the memorial reconstruction theory in relation to *A Shrew*.
5. I am indebted to Wentersdorf's (1978) analysis of the ending of *The Shrew* although my conclusions differ from his, as he believes that Shakespeare did provide a "Sly" ending to the play. Wentersdorf remarks that its absence in the Folio may be because the Folio editors "believed the revision to have been carried out with Shakespeare's approval and therefore that the shortened text constituted an authentic if artistically less satisfactory version" (215).
6. Thompson1984, 3. This would put early 1592 as the last possible date for the composition of *A Shrew*.
7. In the 1992 Royal Shakespeare Theatre production at the main house in Stratford-upon-Avon, directed by William Alexander, Tranio almost succeeded in wooing Bianca, and the tension between his performance as Lucentio and the subservient role the real Lucentio was forced to play became a notable part of the drama.
8. The Victorian William Cory (1865) wrote in his journal: "I have formerly thought I should like to see gentlefolks act *Taming of the Shrew*, of course as a mere trifle" (398). His wish might have been fulfilled in the RSC 1992 *Shrew*, which rewrote the Induction in order to emphasize its modern upper-class equivalents and forced these genteel persons then to play the parts of Petruchio's servants.
9. Fineman's argument for the restoration of patriarchal modes at the end of the play ignores this vital dimension of underlying theatrical interchange between audience and player, which creates its own dynamic of difference.
10. My argument is based on a theatrical exigency: the ways in which the playwright has written into the part the realities of the player's own situation in order to facilitate his representation of the woman he plays. The effect in this speech is not to present the woman as a construction of "masculine self-differentiation" (Green-

blatt 1986, 51) but to draw out of the woman's own role an energy implicit in the creation of Kate herself, and related to Zemon Davis's (1978) perception of "unruliness" discussed earlier.

11. This is not to underestimate the importance of Boose's (1991) fascinating research into the treatment of scolds in Elizabethan England, although I do find it more relevant to the world of *The Taming of a Shrew*, with its much more popular frame of reference, than to Shakespeare's (to my mind) very courtly play.

WORKS CITED

Barroll, Leeds. 1991. *Politics, Plague and Shakespeare's Theater: The Stuart Years.* Ithaca: Cornell University Press.

Bentley, Gerald Eades. 1984. *The Profession of Player in Shakespeare's Time 1590–1642.* Princeton: Princeton University Press.

Boose, Lynda. 1991. "Scolding Brides and Bridling Scolds: Taming the Woman's Unruly Member." *Shakespeare Quarterly* 42: 179–213.

Burns, Margie. 1986. "The Ending of *The Shrew.*" *Shakespeare Studies* 18: 41–64.

Cory, William. 1865. *Extracts from the Letters and Journals.* Edited by Francis Warre Cornish. Oxford, n.p.

Duthie, G. I. 1943. "*The Taming of a Shrew* and *The Taming of the Shrew.*" *The Review of English Studies* 19: 337–56.

Fineman, Joel. 1985. "The Turn of the Shrew." *Shakespeare and the Question of Theory.* Edited by Patricia Parker and Geoffrey Hartman. London: Methuen.

Furnivall, F. J. 1890. "Sir John Harington's Shakespeare Quartos." *Notes and Queries,* 7th Series, 9 (May 17): 382–83.

Gaw, Alison. 1926. "John Sincklo as One of Shakespeare's Actors." *Anglia* 49: 289–303.

Greenblatt, Stephen. 1986. "Fiction and Friction." *Reconstructing Individualism.* Ed. Thomas Heller, Morton Sosna, and David E. Wellbery. Stanford: Stanford University Press,1986.

Greg, W. W. 1931. *Dramatic Documents for the Elizabethan Playhouses.* Oxford: Clarendon.

Gurr, Andrew. 1987. *Playgoing in Shakespeare's London.* Cambridge: Cambridge University Press.

Harington, Sir John. 1591. *Epigrams.* Bound into the *Orlando Furioso, in English Heroical Verse.* London: Richard Field.

———. 1962. *Sir John Harington's A New Discourse of a Stale Subject, called The Metamorphosis of Ajax.* Edited by Elizabeth Story Donno. London: Routledge.

Hinman, Charlton, ed. 1968. *The First Folio of Shakespeare: The Norton Facsimile.* London: Hamlyn.

Holderness, Graham. 1989. *The Taming of the Shrew: Shakespeare in Performance.* Manchester: Manchester University Press.

Holderness, Graham, and Bryan Loughrey, eds. 1992. *The Taming of a Shrew.* Memel Hempstead: Harvester Wheatsheaf.

Howard, Jean E. 1989. "Scripts and/versus Playhouses: Ideological Production and the Renaissance Public Stage." *Renaissance Drama* 20 (1989): 31–40.

Jonson, Ben. 1966. *Cynthia's Revels. Ben Jonson*. Edited by C.H. Herford and Percy Simpson. Oxford: Clarendon.

Marston, John. 1967. *The Malcontent*. Edited by Bemard Harris. London: The New Mermaids, Benn.

McLuskie, Kathleen. 1987. "The Act, the Role, and the Actor: Boy Actresses on the Elizabethan Stage." *New Theatre Quarterly* 3: 120–30.

McMillin, Scott. 1972. "Casting for Pembroke's Men: The *Henry VI* Quartos and *The Taming of A Shrew*." *Shakespeare Quarterly* 23: 141–59.

———. 1976. "Simon Jewell and the Queen's Men." *Review of English Studies* 27: 174–77.

Moore, William. 1964. "An Allusion in 1593 to *The Taming of the Shrew?*" *Shakespeare Quarterly* 15: 55–60.

Pepys, Samuel. 1971. *The Diary of Samuel Pepys*. Edited by Robert Latham and William Matthews. London: Bell.

Rastall, Richard. 1985. "Female Roles in All-Male Casts." *Medieval English Theatre* 7: 21–51.

Shakesepeare, William. 1968. *The First Folio of Shakespeare: The Norton Facsimile*. Edited by Charlton Hinman. London: Hamlyn.

———. 1984. *The Taming of the Shrew*. Edited by Ann Thompson. Cambridge: Cambridge University Press.

———. 1986. *The Complete Works*. Edited by Stanley Wells and Gary Taylor. Oxford: Clarendon.

———. 1992. *The Tragicall Historie of Hamlet Prince of Denmarke*. Edited by Graham Holderness and Bryan Loughrey. Hemel Hempstead: Harvester Wheatsheaf.

Taming of a Shrew, The. 1992. Edited by Graham Holderness and Bryan Loughrey. Hemel Hempstead: Harvester Wheatsheaf.

Thompson, Ann. 1982. "Dating Evidence for *The Taming of the Shrew*." *Notes and Queries* 29: 108–9.

———, ed. *The Taming of The Shrew*. Cambridge: Cambridge University Press, 1984.

Trewin, J. C. 1978. *Going to Shakespeare*. London: Allen and Unwin.

Wentersdorf, Karl P. 1978. "The Original Ending of *The Taming of the Shrew*: A Reconsideration." *Studies in English Literature* 18: 201–15.

———. 1980. "Actors' Names in Shakespearean Texts." *Theatre Studies* 23: 18–30.

Zemon Davis, Natalie. 1978. "Women on Top: Symbolic Sexual Inversion and Political Disorder in Early Modern Europe." *The Reversible World*. Edited by Barbara A. Babcock. Ithaca and London: Cornell University Press, 1978.

Mr KEMBLE & MISS DE CAMP as CATHERINE & PETRUCHIO.

Fear not, Sweet Wench, they shall not touch thee Kate.

London, Published as the Act directs by J. Roach, Russel Court Drury Lane, March 4 1802.

Figure 6. Mr. Charles Kemble and Miss Theresa DeCamp as Catherine and Petruchio, 1802. Used with the permission of the Folger Shakespeare Library.

The Performance of Things in *The Taming of the Shrew*

LENA COWEN ORLIN

From the opening complaint of the Hostess that Sly has "burst" glasses for which he refuses to pay, *The Taming of the Shrew* is cluttered with references to and displays of objects, and especially household furnishings.[1] Add to these the text's preoccupations with apparel, with food, and with material wealth, again both described and exhibited, and we are confronted with a play unusually rich in "things."[2] Such things, especially those sufficiently common and flexible to be required with any confidence by an Elizabethan theatrical performance, would seem to have little mystery for us. According to Pierre Bourdieu, however, "cultural consecration" confers not only upon the persons and situations it touches but also upon objects "a sort of ontological promotion akin to a transubstantiation."[3] For the sake of the argument of this essay, I intend to begin by treating the Elizabethan theatre as a discrete culture susceptible of ethnohistorical investigation; to take as a case study in that theatrical culture *The Taming of the Shrew*; to investigate some ways in which *The Shrew* consecrates its objects; to proceed as if their "transubstantiation" entails a form of personalization, an intuition of their motivation and agency; and to look then at the reflexive ontology that objectifies *The Shrew*'s persons.

To the extent that this essay offers a reading of *The Taming of the Shrew*, it engages the three most vexed issues of *Shrew* criticism: the relation of *The Shrew* to *The Taming of a Shrew*, the role of the induction, and the nature of Katherina's last speech. For the first, the exact textual and authorial relationship of *The Taming of the Shrew* and *The Taming of a Shrew*[4] is for me of less interest than is the interpretive significance afforded by their semiotic redundancy; *A Shrew* shares with *The Shrew* the three plots of the peasant tricked into believing he is a lord, the taming of a shrew, and the courtship of her sister(s), and all three plots rely upon things: the goods that convince the peasant of his transformation, the items that are withheld for the purpose of taming the shrew, and the wealth that confirms the successful betrothal. For the second, I take the two opening scenes of the play (to which Pope first gave the name "induction"[5]) just as we have received them, that is, as substantive elements which, very much because they function outside the narrative of the play "proper," require no narrative resolution but which must in consequence be expected to and which from the present theoretical perspective do prove themselves ideologically inextricable from the whole; in fact, they point the theme of "things" and their cultural meaning. Finally, for the third (and this last is the issue with which I am most explicitly concerned), I examine the role of "things" in the accommodation that Katherina reaches; it is an accommodation that, to be read ironically, must be read characterologically,[6] and it is largely in order to pose an alternative to characterologic criticism that I have turned to the performance of things in this text.

My working notion is that things have a cultural project; my methodological hypothesis is that an analysis of the uses, values, trajectories, and imperatives of things may reveal the nature of their project. Before I proceed in this fashion to analyse the things of *The Taming of the Shrew*, however, I must clarify some points of reference. In citing Pierre Bourdieu, I mean to emphasize that the cultural consecration in which I am interested is fundamentally anthropological rather than specifically theatrical; that is, I am not here concerned with the stage symbolism of dramatic properties that has been so persuasively decoded in a series of publications by Alan Dessen, Frances Teague, and others.[7] Rather, my approach is principally informed by the work of Arjun Appadurai, who proposes that things have "a social life"; by Igor Kopytoff, who suggests that they have "a cultural biography"; by Mary Douglas and Baron Isherwood, for whom goods constitute "an information system"; and by Maurice Godelier, who would dissolve the distinction between "the material and the mental," as well as by that of Bourdieu.[8]

The writings of these sociologists and anthropologists offer an important complement to Marcel Mauss's *Essai sur le don*, a work that has become a common tool of literary and social historians, that has been understood to have inaugurated an economic anthropology, and that is occupied with (in the familiar terms of Mauss's translator) "the forms and functions of exchange."[9] Appadurai, for example, assumes his revisionist posture as follows:

> Even if our own approach to things is conditioned necessarily by the view that things have no meanings apart from those that human transactions, attributions, and motivations endow them with, the anthropological problem is that this formal truth does not illuminate the concrete, historical circulation of things. For that we have to follow the things themselves. . . . This methodological fetishism, returning our attention to the things themselves, is in part a corrective to the tendency to excessively sociologize transactions in things, a tendency we owe to Mauss.

Or, as Appadurai also argues, "even though from a *theoretical* point of view human actors encode things with significance, from a *methodological* point of view it is the things-in-motion that illuminate their human and social context."[10]

While I am indebted to Appadurai for his authorization of a methodological fetishism that initiated this essay (and that debt will become fully apparent below), I differ from him and from most anthropologists to the extent that their primary concern continues to be with things when they are "in motion," in circulation or exchange: that is, as active commodities. The distinction may become clearer if I refer to Kopytoff, who, as Appadurai summarizes it, argues that "the commodity phase of the life history of an object does not exhaust its biography. . . . Objects may be moved both into and out of the commodity state." Kopytoff would construct a biography by considering the derivation and genesis of a thing, the possibilities inherent in its status and defined by its culture, the degree to which the thing realizes these possibilities, its recognizable ages or periods, its uses as they change over time, and its fate when it reaches the end of its usefulness, as well as its history of exchange.[11] Without using the term "biography," Patrick Geary also suggests one when he outlines the three stages of creation, evaluation, and circulation for commodities.[12] Because *The Taming of the Shrew* presents us with things at varying points in their own biographies, however, I am interested in objects at whatever phase of their career they enter the text, not just at that stage that makes them eligible for exchange.

This means that I cannot entertain some other common anthropological distinctions, in particular those regarding the forms of circulation. Geary, for example, categorizes those forms as including sale, exchange, gift, and theft (and he further defines theft as variously larceny, plunder, extortion, ransom, and tribute); Appadurai recognizes the three forms of commodity exchange, direct exchange (that is, barter), and gift exchange.[13] But some awareness of these forms is useful to the extent that they are not unrelated to the definition of things, or, rather, to their familiar separation into the categories of commodities, gifts, and currency; or, as Bronislaw Malinowski influentially put it, into those of commodities and valuables;[14] or even, most common of all, to the subdivision of commodities into necessaries and luxuries.

Objects of all definitions enter *The Taming of the Shrew.* To resort to a sixteenth-century legal distinction rather than a twentieth-century anthropological one, they tend most often to be movables or chattels; they include in the first place an assortment of apparel, rich and also shabby, a cap, a gown, a cloak, a hat, boots; various foods and drinks; horns and trumpets; such hunting apparatus as dead rabbits or a bow;[15] a basin, ewer, cups, and trenchers; hand cloths; a rope or scarf; two notes, or one used twice; a lute, some books; a candle or lantern; stools or chairs; a sword; perhaps a thimble; coins or a purse—routine and readily accessible items all.[16] In cataloguing some activities of these things I include not only the properties directly called for and listed above but also those figured for us through narrative, for what the text imagines is at least as suggestive of cultural meaning as what it shows.[17]

Douglas and Isherwood, whose notion that goods are an information system I finally find most useful, also argue persuasively against "the Cartesian dichotomy between physical and psychic experience": "Goods that minister to physical needs—food or drink—are no less carriers of meaning than ballet or poetry. Let us," they exhort, "put an end to the widespread and misleading distinction between goods that sustain life and health and others that service the mind and heart—spiritual goods."[18] Certainly, *The Shrew* invokes the function of goods to supply subsistence needs; it primarily does so through want, when at Petruchio's house Katherina is surrounded by water to quench her thirst, food to satisfy her hunger, and a (reported) bed to ease her rest, but is permitted to make use of none. A basin of water is let fall; meat, trenchers, and cups are refused; pillow, bolster, coverlet, and sheets are flung aside, until she complains that she is "starv'd for meat, giddy for lack of sleep." Meat is brought on stage for a second time only to maintain the edge of her hunger; Petruchio enlists Hortensio to "eat it up all" to prolong her enforced fast (4.3.9, 35 s.d.–50). Petruchio explains in soliloquy that deprivation is his "politic" method to "curb" her mad and headstrong humor" (4.1.209). The text is conscious, in other words, that even this elemental quality of things is susceptible of social and political definitions and uses.

Douglas and Isherwood further advise that "if it is said that the essential function of language is its capacity for poetry, we shall assume that the essential function of consumption is its capacity to make sense. . . . Forget that commodities are good for eating, clothing, and shelter; forget their usefulness and try instead the idea that commodities are good for thinking."[19] What sorts of sense do things make in *The Taming of the Shrew*? Because the sorts that I propose to discuss in this first part of my essay are but one means to, not the end of, my argument, to list them is to appear to give them a greater substantive weight than I intend; but because a list will help to organize that argument, it follows.

1.   They construct an environment.
2.   They fix identity.
3.   They register distinction.
4.   They create a system of value.
5.   They provoke competition.
6.   They arouse expectation.
7.   They substantiate deceit.
8.   They effect social bonds.
9.   They offer compensation.

10.   They resist certain control.
11.   They perform transactions.

This list numbers eleven projects of things in order to emphasize how artificial it is, incomplete, redundant, idiosyncratic, and very much guided by my interest in Douglas and Isherwood's notion that things make "visible and stable the categories of culture."[20]

1. The environment that things construct in *The Taming of the Shrew*, for example, is a specifically human environment, as distinct from the natural world, furbished with what we none the less call "creature" comforts that appeal to the "natural" human senses, but more susceptible than is the wild to social and political control and cultural definition. Petruchio on his arrival at his theatrically imagined house calls for men to remove his boots and bring him slippers (4.1.144, 153), thus marking the transition from a harsh outer world to the humanly determined and humanely hospitable interior; marking, too, the irony of a subverted transition for Katherina. Sly, like Katherina, is surrounded with things that serve to dislocate him, and the objects of the Lord markedly transcend his subsistence needs: the tinker is offered not just sustenance, but a banquet, served with basin, ewer, and diaper; not just water, but "rose-water," in a "silver basin" and "bestrewed with flowers," to "cool," not merely wash, his hands; as well as rings, clothes that are "sweet," and a suit that is "costly" (Induction 1.38–59).[21] Key to the illusion of completeness with which Sly is presented is the Lord's orchestration of objects to activate all the senses: wanton pictures hung for sight; sweet wood burned for smell; musical instruments played for sound; sack and conserves served for taste; clothing and diaper offered for touch. As Sly observes, "I do not sleep: I see, I hear, I speak; / I smell sweet savors, and I feel soft things (Induction 2.70–71).

In the self-contained theatrical space identified as the Lord's "fairest chamber" (Ind. 1.46) and then again in that presented as Petruchio's "house," objects, in other words, expand in significance to create the illusion of a little world, and apparent fullness and wholeness effect their own magical insinuation. For Sly, multiple sensory experiences countervail the arguments of memory and logic; in fact, his "sense of self," precisely because it is less tangible, is vulnerable to the alternative and persuasive testimony offered by the physical senses as they are stimulated by objects. For Katherina, removal from a familiar physical context and from a familial support system and transport to an isolated and fully realized "house" under Petruchio's exclusive control enact the common sixteenth-century notion that the domestic establishment launched by marriage is itself a little world or "petty commonwealth,"[22] with her own subordinate role in Petruchio's household kingship adumbrated by his command of its accoutrements (as well as of its fellows).

2. As Sly's dissociation in particular demonstrates, things fix identity. In fact, as often as the pronoun "my" is coupled with an object—my hounds, my

house, my port, my chamber, my goods, my chattels, my household stuff, my field, my barn—self-definition is asserted through possession. As an external trigger of identification and of role, clothing substantiates Lucentio's scheme to switch places with Tranio; cues Biondello's characterization of the Merchant as "formal in apparel . . . surely like a father" (4.2.64–65); and permits the Merchant's transformation to Lucentio's surrogate father, according to a stage direction "dress'd like Vincentio," "booted and bareheaded" (4.4.s.d.). Even as Tranio takes the part of Lucentio and the Merchant assumes the paternal function of Vincentio, through costume, so, too, Bartholomew adopts the role of Sly's fictive wife. The Lord orders his page to be "dress'd in all suits like a lady" (Ind. 1.106), a ruse that is of course threatened with exposure when Sly orders the page to undress for bed. Sly, who is persuaded by the Lord's goods-rich practice to "forget himself" (Ind. 1.41), in his further susceptibility to Bartholomew demonstrates to us the semiotic capacity of clothing as well as of household objects.

Things are gender signifiers (and thus identifiers) through circles of association as well: the objects to which Katherina has linguistic recourse are domestic ones, reflecting the gender-determined sphere of her knowledge. Thus, she threatens to beat Hortensio with "a three-legg'd stool;" she analogizes blood to cosmetic "paint" (1.1.64–65); she calls Petruchio a "moveable" and "join'd-stool" (2.1.197–98); and she ends Petruchio's quibble over whether light is shed by sun or moon by offering, if he would have it so, to "call it a rush-candle" (4.5.14). Similarly, when Baptista orders Katherina to "go ply thy needle" (2.1.25), he refers to the most common of household objects to "place" and contain her in the context of an occupation socially acceptable for women.

3. Things also register class distinctions. The Lord convinces Sly that he is a lord by suggesting that he will have not only music, but the music of Apollo and of "twenty caged nightingales;" not only a couch, but one "softer and sweeter than the lustful bed / On purpose trimm'd up for Semiramis;" not only horses, but horses with "harness studded all with gold and pearl" (Induction 2.35–42). Goods are presented as status signifiers throughout. When Lucentio remarks to Tranio, "Nor can we be distinguish'd by our faces / For man or master" (1.1.200–201) and then exchanges hat and cloak with him, and when Vincentio fears the consequences as he discovers Tranio wearing clothes more appropriate to master than to man (5.1.65–68), all acknowledge that because class is external to person, clothing is its necessary marker. Similarly, Tranio transforms the Merchant into a Vincentio by arranging "to clothe you as becomes" a man of such position (4.2.121), and Katherina recognizes of another object of apparel that "gentlewomen wear such caps as these" (4.3.70). Objects are necessary, that is, to the construction and perpetuation of status systems. In this activity the customary opposition of necessaries and

luxuries is elided, because, as Douglas and Isherwood observe, luxury, too, "serves a cultural function" that is essential to its culture.[23]

Much of the humour of Sly's transformation derives from his stubborn incapacity to appreciate the objects offered him. Most obviously, he prefers small ale to sack and conserves of beef to conserves of fruit (Ind. 2.1–8).[24] Status preferences are not natural, in other words; they are learned and Sly's vocabulary in the complex language of things is at best rudimentary. Other readers of *The Shrew* have emphasized that the Lord's "wanton pictures" are interpreted for Sly in erotic terms, and Bourdieu relevantly observes that "the capacity to see (*voir*) is a function of the knowledge (*savoir*). . . . A work of art has meaning and interest only for someone who possesses the cultural competence, that is, the code into which it is encoded."[25] It must be remembered, however, that Sly's exposure is at yet one more cultural remove from Bourdieu's schema, for in *The Shrew* the pictures seem only to be described, not displayed, and the unillustrated myths of Cytherea and Adonis, Io and Jove, and Daphne and Apollo are undoubtedly commodities to which Sly again has no informed access and for which the descriptions of the Lord's servants may well be inadequately explicit (Ind. 2.48–60). The Lord finds his pleasure, in the event, in the reassurance that Sly provides him of his own solid superiority of taste. As Bourdieu again remarks, such objects "fulfill a social function of legitimating social differences."[26]

4. Further, things construct a system of value. The registrar of difference to whom we are first introduced is the Lord; the possessions of the Lord that we first encounter are his hounds. There are four frames of reference for his relationship with them: the first, his directions that they be "tendered well" pays tribute to their value; the second, his description of Silver's action in the hunt, establishes that the value of these possessions inheres in their performance to his pleasure; the third, his declaration that he "would not lose [one particular] dog for twenty pound," translates that value into the terms of commodity; and the fourth, his argument concerning their varying performances, with Silver contextualized among Merriman, Clowder, Belman and Echo, establishes that value is qualified by comparison, is not absolute, is subjective, and solicits an investment of the owner in the form of his judgement of them (Ind. 1.16–29). Building upon the thought of Georg Simmel, Colin Renfrew relevantly observes that to "speak of value as if it were inherent within the object or commodity" is to "create a metaphor, or mask a reality"; instead, "value is a property that is assigned to an object in a manner that arises from the social context in question."[27]

As Douglas and Isherwood analyse the values that motivate consumption, they conclude that "if we reject envy . . . we are left with a mild wonder about the irrational human wish for fine carpets and new kitchens, much as one might question why dogs should want jeweled collars as well as food and exercise."[28] But *The Shrew* indicates that envy undergirds possession (or possessiveness) as well as consumption. The Lord's boast that he would not take twenty pounds for Silver suggests that some value resides in the covetousness of others, or, at least, in the owner's happy presumption of others' covetousness of his things.

5. Thus, things provoke competition. The Lord's argument with his First Huntsman over the relative merits of Silver and Belman implies that the accumulation and valuation of possessions incite rivalry. And clearly the contest for Bianca's hand, for example, is impelled in part by the desire of her suitors to demonstrate their ability to compete; clearly, too, they locate their "ability" in their possessions. As has been frequently remarked, Baptista sees the competition in material rather than affective terms: he "that can assure my daughter's greatest dower / Shall have my Bianca's love." His challenge elicits, first, Gremio's sensuous catalogue of his house, plate, gold basins, ewers, hangings, coffers, chests, arras, apparel, tents, canopies, linen, cushions, valens, pewter, brass, cattle, and oxen; next, Tranio's implication that he can multiply all this by three or four and then compound it with an annual rental income of two thousand ducats; third, Gremio's counter of an argosy; again, Tranio's rebuttal that he will inherit three argosies and, moreover, two galliasses and twelve galleys; and, finally, Tranio's preemptive assurance that he can put up "twice as much, what e'er thou off'rest next" (2.1.342–80). It is this last stroke, signalling to us that Tranio's is an exercise in rhetoric rather than of catalogue, that removes competition from its illusion of "objective" basis in reality and reminds of the subjective needs that even "luxury" objects serve.

6. So familiar are the rules of things that their very presence projects certain performances; so faithfully are the rules observed that only failure occasions notice. Katherina's physical torture is intensified because she is given every objective evidence that her hunger will be appeased, as the basin, meat, and dishes are served in. Occupying the "bridal chamber" with its pillow, bolster, coverlet, and sheets, she similarly can expect no "sermon of continency" nor all-night "watches" (4.1.178–202).[29] When the informational codes are disrupted by the intervention of a conflicting agenda, such as Petruchio's, in other words, goods stop making sense.

When expectations of them hold, however, things can carry the force of tradition and can perform as what Douglas and Isherwood call "ritual adjuncts." At one quotidian extreme of social ritual is the household custom of hand-washing before dinner, pointed with the offer of a basin (Ind. 1.55; Ind. 2.76–77; 4.1.149 s.d.). At the other extreme is the life passage of marriage, marked with special apparel, household furnishings, ceremonial objects, and celebratory feasts: Baptista, for example, follows ritual form, directing Bianca to "help to dress your sister's chamber up" for the wedding day (3.1.83), "prepar[ing] great store of wedding cheer" (3.2.186). Douglas and Isherwood assert that the more effective rituals use material things, and the more costly the ritual trappings, the stronger we can assume the intention to fix the meanings to be."[30]

In this context, it is not surprising that things also carry the burden of moral expectation. Bourdieu, for example, associates with "working-class people" the notion that "every image [should] explicitly perform a function, if only that of a sign, and their judgements make reference, often explicitly, to the norms of morality or agreeableness. Whether rejecting or praising, their appreciation always has an ethical basis."[31] In just this manner, Sly holds that the Hostess's bed must be a "cold" one in complement of her behaviour toward him (Ind. 1.10).

7. Their semiotic force is such that things can substantiate deceit. They organize fictions as large as that of the devised world, identity, and life history of Sly; as small as the feigned tears of Sly's pretended wife, for which, according to the Lord, only an onion in a napkin is necessary provocation (Ind. 1.124–28); and as incidental as the inn hostess's practice of serving inadequate measures of ale by concealing them in "stone jugs and no seal'd quarts" (or so Sly would have it [Ind. 2.88]). Clothing, too, cloaks fraud. As apparel effects the disguise of Bartholomew, so also for Lucentio, presenting himself as a master of philosophy; for Tranio, playing the part of his master; for Hortensio, posing as a master of music; and for the Merchant, enlisted as a surrogate father to the substitute Lucentio. In one case, that of Sly, disguise is imposed upon an unknowing wearer, and the disguised is deceived by his own disguise.

8. Social relationships are mediated by objects: by gifts and by the artefacts of hospitality. Douglas and Isherwood write that "sharing goods and being made welcome to the hospitable table and to the marriage bed are the first, closest fields of inclusion," and both table and bed are of the essence in a plot that in its brief course accomplishes the integration of two strangers into a community and into a family.[32] Newly arrived in Padua, Lucentio understands that his first business must be to "take a lodging fit to entertain / Such friends as time in Padua shall beget"; even when his plans are diverted, Tranio will maintain the expected presence: "Keep house and ply his book, welcome his friends, / Visit his countrymen, and banquet them" (1.1.44–45, 196–97). Lucentio's house eventually requites his investment, as it shelters the travelling Merchant who provides assurance for his marriage, hosts marital negotiations with Baptista, and then celebrates the transfer of Bianca from her father's care to her new husband's with continued celebration and desserts after the "great good cheer" of Baptista's wedding feast. In welcoming guests to his banquet, Lucentio prescribes that their purpose is "to chat as well as eat" (5.2.10–11); as Douglas and Isherwood again observe, "eating is always social; even during eating, the meal is subject to community rule, to conversation."[33]

9. For a series of characters in the play, things offer compensation. Bianca, directed in to the protective shelter of her father's house—"mew'd up," as Gremio, among others, would have it (1.1.87, 183)—announces her

resort: "My books and instruments shall be my company, / On them to look and practice by myself" (1.1.82–83). When Gremio's hopes are frustrated, he, too, finds material consolation: "My cake is dough, but I'll in among the rest, / Out of hope of all but my share of the feast" (5.1.140–41). When language is inadequate or requires added emphasis, moreover, things serve as an alternate or compensatory medium of expression. For Katherina, they expand limited resources in expressing emotion, frustration, and anger, as when she breaks the lute over Hortensio's head. For Petruchio, they can be more shocking than words, as when he causes the book containing the marriage service to fall and when he throws sops in the sexton's face. He understands the supralinguistic utility of objects: one of the most immediate ways for him to demonstrate Katherina's docility to others is by commanding her publicly to remove her cap and trample on it.

If there seem limits, though, to what things can do for Gremio and Hortensio (for, for them, even Katherina's dowry is insufficient to counterpoise her "loud alarums" [1.1.124–33]), the theme none the less finds its climax in Petruchio's avowal that wealth will make acceptable even the foulness of Florentius's love, the age of Sibyl, and the shrewishness of Xanthippe. He then, of course, conducts the process of behavioural conversion that simultaneously transforms material compensation into overplus.

10. For Douglas and Isherwood, the consumer cannot be content merely to get information from the system that goods constitute: "There has to be a concern to control it. If he is not in any position of control, other people can tamper with the switchboard, he will miss his cues, and meaning will be swamped by noise. So his objective as a rational consumer also involves an effort to be near the center of transmission and an effort to seal off the boundaries of the system."[34] Goods thus require management, as do the Lord's hounds and as do Vincentio's transactions in Padua, and they demand protection, which is the objective of the various dowry negotiations and the reported terms of inheritance.

The text, however, is rife with anxiety about the effectiveness of such measures of control. Vincentio is notably less concerned with the health of his son, when he sees Tranio dressed in Lucentio's clothes, than with his own goods: "O, I am undone, I am undone! While I play the good husband at home, my son and my servant spend all at the university" (5.1.68–70). And attempts to compel obligation through reward are, throughout, redundant and ineffectual. To the point, Hortensio enlists Gremio and Tranio to support Petruchio in his courtship of Katherina, but his investment does not yield the expected return of Bianca's hand; Gremio purchases Lucentio's agency, but Lucentio, too, serves his own ends rather than Gremio's.[35] Goods, in other words, can have an uncertain trajectory. And their independence can read as a form of treachery. As Simmel usefully remarks, "we call those objects valuable that resist our desire to possess them."[36]

11. Finally, to return to the functions of things with which my anthropological sources began, they of course perform transactions. Tranio, for example, knows to offer gifts (a lute and a packet of books) and knows also (as does Mauss) that Baptista's acceptance of them engenders his obligation to honour Tranio's accompanying request that he "may have welcome 'mongst the rest that woo, / And free access and favor as the rest" (2.1.96–97).[37] The negotiation for which this is a mere intimation of a theme is, of course, the marriage settlement. Petruchio lays on the table the fact that he is his father's only heir; Baptista responds that Katherina will inherit half of his lands and then raises the stakes by pledging immediate transfer of twenty thousand crowns; Petruchio seals the bargain with assurance of provision in the event of Katherina's widowhood (2.1.116–27). In this negotiation and in the satisfaction of their owners' differing objectives and desires, the possessions of Baptista and Petruchio achieve their optimal destinies. For Godelier, notably, "property only really exists when it is rendered effective in and through a process of concrete appropriation."[38]

As I indicated before embarking on this catalogue of the projects of things, the eleven listed are not intended to exhaust the active and provocative roles of objects in the text of *The Taming of the Shrew*. Nor are the items on the list mutually exclusive. Some categories are internally contradictory for, in what is in fact a further tribute to their power, things can both arouse expectation and frustrate it, can both compel control and resist it, and so on. Further, it is not as if *The Shrew* does not acknowledge that things are susceptible of manipulation to individual (human) satisfaction: Petruchio, after all, is a master manipulator (and violator) of things, object-ive expectations, and cultural consecrations. These eleven are merely the performances that strike me as most useful for attacking the cultural project of things in *The Shrew* text.

This is a text, after all, populated with characters for whom displays of wealth have superseded even the illusion of chivalric exploit. To wit, Gremio vows that Bianca is "beloved of me, and that my deeds shall prove," but Grumio provides the gloss for "deeds," "and that his bags shall prove." In the same manner, Baptista declares that "'tis deeds must win the prize" of his daughter's hand but immediately continues that "he of troth / That can assure my daughter greatest dower / Shall have my Bianca's love" (1.2.176–77; 2.1.341–43). *The Shrew* is also a text in which the male lead makes the infamous declaration that Katherina "is my goods, my chattels; she is my house, / My household stuff, my field, my barn, / My horse, my ox, my ass, my any thing" (3.2.230–32), incorporating her into the comprehensive catalogue of domestic objects that constitute his little kingdom. As remarked by one of the play's more instructive readers, Coppélia Kahn, "his role as property owner is the model for his role as husband; Kate, for him, is a thing."[39]

There are in fact many such depersonalizations of the text's characters, not all of them anti-feminine, as the Lord puts Sly through psychically disorienting paces to his own amusement, as the Lord forgets the name but remembers the pleasing performance of a player, as Baptista makes Katherina what Ruth Nevo calls "nothing but an obstacle or a means to her sister's advancement,"[40] as Hortensio and Gremio resolve to "get a husband" for Katherina (1.1.120), as Tranio resolves to "get a man" to serve as Vincentio (3.2.131), as Petruchio takes the tailor and Vincentio as instruments to his practice upon Katherina, as Lucentio "slip[s Tranio] like his greyhound, / Which runs himself, and catches for his master" (5.2.52–53), and as persons are analogized to animals throughout.

The obvious corollary to a methodology that personalizes objects is one that objectifies persons. To put it another way, just as the things that I have charted are the inventions and properties of a dramatic text, so, too, are its "artificial persons" (a term I borrow from Leeds Barroll).[41] And in fact, in *The Taming of the Shrew* the performance of persons intersects with that of things with significant regularity and in markedly similar ways. If I observe, for example, that persons, too, substantiate deceit (number 7), I mean not that Lucentio conceives a scheme to gain a place in Baptista's household, but that Tranio is deployed to facilitate the scheme in much the same way that a thing might be used; not that Tranio bargains with Baptista on Lucentio's behalf, but that in inventing a Vincentio to "assure" Baptista of the marital agreement he manipulates the person of a merchant much as he does "inanimate" apparel.

Similarly, persons arouse expectation (number 6), whether of role, as that Baptista ironically assumes for the false Vincentio, "that like a father you will deal with him" (4.4.44); of status, as that Baptista assumes for Lucentio, because his father is "A mighty man of Pisa" (2.1.104); or of "nature," as that Petruchio enforces for Katherina, that "thus the bowl should run, / And not unluckily against the bias" (4.5.24–25). Persons, too, ground social ritual: "the servingmen in their new fustian" are necessary to the initiation of a new household (4.1.47); guests are essential to the observance of marriage; and the wedding celebration cannot advance without bride and groom—or, in their default, without the surrogates Baptista assigns.[42] As is true for things, the expectations of persons are never more noticeable than in their violation, a fact that Petruchio (rather more even than Katherina) demonstrates. Baptista, for example, calls Petruchio's barbarous appearance on his wedding day a "shame to your estate" ([3.2.100] that is, to his status and descent and the expectations they generate), and Tranio (speaking on behalf of Lucentio) stigmatizes Petruchio's costume as "unlike yourself" (3.2.104), or, at least, unlike the "self" anticipated either from his position or from his previous behaviour.

In related fashion, persons require management (number 10), as do the Lord's servants and Grumio; they demand protection, as do Bianca (the "treasure" stored in Baptista's "keep" [1.2.118]) and Katherina (of whom Petruchio threatens, "touch her whoever dare, / I'll bring mine action" [3.2.234]); and they none the less resist certain control, as demonstrated when the courtship of Bianca proceeds even despite her "mewing up." Social restraints of order and taste are inadequate to contain Petruchio, who argues that a cap that "doth fit the time" is "lewd and filthy" (4.3.65–69); who dismisses a gown that is again made "according to the fashion and the time" as instead "masquing stuff" (4.3.87–95); who avers that "honor peereth in the meanest habit" (4.3.174); and who violates religious sacrament, civic ceremony, and nuptial tradition.[43]

Like things, the text further asserts, persons construct an environment (number 1): Hortensio believes that to be married to Katherina is "to be married to hell" (1.1.125); Petruchio by taming her is able to predict a petty commonwealth of "peace . . . and love, and quiet life, / [Of] awful rule, and right supremacy"; both thus pay tribute to her atmospheric capability (5.2.108–9).[44] Persons fix identity (number 2): as Kahn recognizes, "it is Kate's submission to him that makes Petruchio a man."[45] They also register distinction (number 3): Sly's pretend wife is "the fairest creature in the world"; the list of thirteen names in Petruchio's household gives some notice of his status (Ind. 2.66; 4.1.89–136). They create a system of value (number 4): the two sisters comprise a polar, relative, and reversible scale that begins with Bianca as her father's treasure and ends with Katherina figured as "another" and rarer daughter, "for she is chang'd, as she had never been" (5.2.115).[46] Persons provoke competition (number 5), as Bianca inspires the rivalry of Grumio, Hortensio, and Lucentio. They effect social bonds (number 8): Bianca serves the purpose for those who compete over her, as Tranio observes when he enters the contest, inviting Hortensio and Grumio to "quaff carouses to our mistress' health, / And do as adversaries do in law, | Strive mightily, but eat and drink as friends" (1.2.275–77). They offer compensation (number 9), of the sort the widow affords Hortensio after he loses the marital stakes for Bianca. And finally, persons, like things, perform transactions (number 11): Cambio and Litio are given as "gifts," in deference, to Baptista, and Katherina is "bestowed" during a negotiation in which her father says he "play[s] a merchant's part, / And venture[s] madly on a desperate mart." The high bidder for Bianca, Tranio, professes a similar understanding of her value (significantly employing the impersonal pronoun): " 'Twas a commodity lay fretting by you. / 'Twill bring you gain, or perish on the seas" (2.1.326–29).[47]

For all that the Induction and taming plot are concerned with enforced metamorphosis, the way in which the text manipulates its persons very much as it does its things is in fact nowhere more clear than in the "courtship" plot (and in the last-scene denouement that brings together the courtship and taming plots). To begin with, the text finds two sisters the optimal number to perform its initial function of semiotic distinction (three are muddily redundant, as is demonstrated in *A Shrew*, where the two younger sisters are for all practical purposes indistinguishable as scripted). Contrast between only two can be clearly drawn, with the opposing values of the sisters powerfully conveyed through the surplus of attention to Bianca and the failure of demand for Katherina. But the text also discovers in accomplishing its reversal of this opening assessment that triangulation finally becomes more useful to it than does dichotomy: Katherina's value is appreciably more rare and her triumph emphatically more dramatic if she is unique among several. And so, as contested courtship is succeeded by trial of obedience, the two sisters are succeeded by three wives. The "wealthy widow," Hortensio's eventual wife, is introduced by reference as late as the second scene of the fourth act and finally appears for the first time only during the closing scene, *femina ex machina*.

Again, female characters are not the only such objects of the text's deployments. For romantic purposes, for example, two suitors are entirely sufficient to the courtship of Bianca; instead, there are three. When Lucentio joins Gremio and Hortensio among her suitors, the text in fact acknowledges its unconventional surplus: "She may more suitors have, and me for one. / Fair Leda's daughter had a thousand wooers, / Then well one more may fair Bianca have" (1.2.241–43). In any case, because the contest is pursued on two fronts, the plot in fact requires two different rivals for Lucentio. Disguised as Cambio, he satisfies the conventions of folk romance by gaining Bianca's affections in direct competition with Hortensio. Through its surrogate, Tranio, he simultaneously pursues the more significant competition regarding wealth and dower, in indirect competition with Gremio. Once the betrothal is accomplished, however, the text is careless of the two who have served its plot functions. Hortensio takes offence at Bianca's preference for a "stale" and voids the romantic contest voluntarily. And Gremio acknowledges his defeat and then fades away, in a fashion that has disturbed readers more preoccupied with individual "character" than is the text itself.[48]

Now, it can fairly be objected that in my earlier analysis of *The Taming of the Shrew* I have over-personalized things and that the activities that I have ascribed to them are "merely" the functions of their use and manipulation by "humans." But obviously I wish to argue in turn that others have over-personalized *The Shrew*'s characters, "who" are functions of their use and manipulation by the text. My anthropological superstructure and methodological fetishism were adopted in large part to dissolve the standard dichotomy between persons and properties in a text. Or, more precisely, to recognize a dissolution of the dichotomy that is accomplished by the text itself.

The relevant paradigm that Claude Levi-Strauss has established, to take my argument to its next step, is of three parts rather than two: that is, he characterizes the forms of exchange that constitute social life as not only the exchange of wives and the exchange of goods but also the exchange of words or meaning, in correspondence with the three branches of anthropology: kinship, economics, and mythology.[49] This paradigm finds a parallel in *The Taming of the Shrew*, which in fact projects a sympathy of behaviour in persons, things, and plays through its central, synthetic metaphor of "household stuff."

The term refers first and most obviously to things. Second, in Petruchio's declaration that "she is my goods, my chattels; she is my house, / My household stuff," these things are identified with, as if indistinguishable in function from, a(n artificial) person (a semiotic integration adumbrated in his earlier vow to "bring [her] from a wild Kate to a Kate / Conformable as other household Kates" [2.1.277–78]).[50] But there is, further, a third association. In the Induction, an artificial person who is incidentally and totemically identified as a tinker—that is, a repairer of household objects— and who is practiced upon in a manner that objectifies him to the delight of his multiple audiences, including us as well as the Lord, is presented with a self-reflexive theatrical performance:

> *MESS*: Your honor's players, hearing your amendment, Are come to play a pleasant comedy . . .
> *SLY*: . . . let them play it. Is not a comonty a Christmas gambold, or a tumbling-trick?
> *PAGE*: No, my good lord, it is more pleasing stuff.
> *SLY*: What, household stuff? (Ind. 2.129–40)

In Sly's apparent misunderstanding, the text unites itself, by its nature or genre, with its things and persons. Through the term "household stuff," the performances of things, of persons, and of plays are suggestively analogized.

The analogy holds, for example, in the way that a play text creates a human environment (number 1 again), its little world of rooms and streets and families and citizens, and in the way that it substantiates deceit (number 7), as its actors body forth its brief illusion of "reality." This text, moreover, flatters the discrimination of its audience as the Induction does that of the Lord (number 3), for we, too, feel superior to the Sly who prefers small ale to sack, who requires interpretation of the wanton pictures, and, especially (the cream of the jest), who does not appreciate the play performed for him, who does not know what a comedy is, who "nods" during the first scene, who knows not that more is to follow the first scene, and who sighs, "would 'twere done!" (1.1.249–54).

Of more moment, the text manipulates the members of its audience by arousing their expectations (number 6): all Grumio's scene-setting talk at Petruchio's house—"Where's the cook? Is supper ready, the house trimm'd, rushes strew'd, cobwebs swept" (4.1.45–47)—is spoken to our hearing, not to Katherina's, so that we are as much taken by surprise (for us, to the comic end of our amusement) as is she by the unreadiness that she discovers. The "Induction," too, engenders anticipation, preoccupying scores of readers with the frustration of their aesthetic demand for the closure of what they (but not the text) have categorized as a framing device. So does the very genre of the text, provoking our apparently inexhaustible desire that the play be a romantic comedy. And the text resists certain control (number 10), as evidenced particularly by the many conflicting readings of the purpose of the "Induction" and of the meaning of Katherina's closing speech.[51]

The Levi-Straussian paradigm, cited above, effects distinctions (whether he intended them or not): three forms of exchange, three branches of anthropology. In applying it to *The Taming of the Shrew*, however, I am less interested in the three than in the one, in the significance of a sense of commonality in the performances of persons, objects, and playtexts as "household stuff." One meaning of this synthesis would have to be that the text recognizes its own economic nature. This meaning resonates in its semiotic twin, *The Taming of a Shrew*, where the Lord asks the travelling players "what store of plaies have you" (with the word *store* suggesting the stockpiling of goods for marketing), and the first player responds: "Marrie my lord you maie have a Tragicall / Or a commoditie, or what you will." The second player corrects his Dogberry with "comedie," but the transactive signification lingers.[52] This collapse of playtext into "household stuff" and "commoditie" is of interest primarily as a substantiating variation on my central themes of the cultural power of things and of the textual erasure of difference between persons and things; that is, *The Taming of the Shrew* implicates itself in a material world view.

For a concluding perspective on these themes, one that is inflected by Levi-Strauss's notion that the three categories of exchange are fundamental components of social life, I add to my list one last project of things in the material culture theatrically represented by *The Taming of the Shrew*:

12. They legitimate the social order.

The early modern social order was constituted in hierarchies; that which concerns me here is gender rather than class. The gender issue, as for so many others in *The Taming of the Shrew*, is mooted in the Induction, where the idea of a woman proves itself a universally signifying object as a place-marker against which a man can position himself in the hierarchy. Sly lacks the *savoir* to appreciate the objects with which he is surrounded until he is told "thou hast a lady"; his abilities to see, hear, speak, smell, feel—and believe—are released by this discovery.[53] Certainly the information system conveys implications of status: Bartholomew is directed to bear himself "as he hath observ'd in noble ladies" (Ind. 1.111), and the Lord is confident that his servant will "usurp" the behaviours of a "gentlewoman"; but Sly is persuaded that "I am a lord indeed" even before he has seen the lady, before he has apprehended her gentility, and also before he has marked her beauty: the news of her existence alone converts to belief. One experience that is universal to early modern men of all stations is that of male authority over women; Sly's previous experience of marriage proves his touchstone in this uncertain new world and provides a model for expanded authority; merely at the report of a wife, Sly is empowered to issue his "lordly" commands over two "objects:" "bring our lady hither to our sight, / And once again a pot o' th' smallest ale" (Ind. 2.72–75).[54] Through Sly we get our first glimpse in *The Shrew* of a power relationship that constructs male authority as key to social order.

Katherina's last speech makes explicit the notion that for women "thy husband is thy lord"; more, he is "thy life, thy keeper, / Thy head, thy sovereign." A healthy measure of the speech is occupied with the political role of the wife, who in this world view is compelled to offer "such duty as the subject owes the prince" and who is stigmatized as a "foul contending rebel / And graceless traitor" when "not obedient to his honest will" (5.2.146–60). But of particular interest to this essay is the way in which the husband's political roles of lord, head, and sovereign are grounded economically, in his roles as life and keeper:[55]

> one that cares for thee,
> And for thy maintenance; commits his body
> To painful labor, both by sea and land;
> To watch the night in storms, the day in cold,
> Whilst thou li'st warm at home, secure and safe. (5.2.151–55)

Other readers have pointed out how little this description of the husband's activities corresponds to the (dramatized) facts of Petruchio's behaviour.[56] But the paradigm voiced by Katherina articulates a logic that is independent of the characterologic. This logic organizes a necessary social myth in the culture of the early modern period of which *The Taming of the Shrew* is an artefact.

The material culture of the English Renaissance was, notably, an expansive one. Joan Thirsk, Chandra Mukerji, and Jean-Christophe Agnew are among those who have described the economy of the period in terms, first, of the proliferation of available commodities and, second, of the ongoing reclassification of objects, as once-rare luxuries became increasingly popular and widely available possessions. Mukerji emphasizes that the market economy was an international one, as imported silks, glass, spices, and carpets, for just a few examples, found their way into private homes that ranged some distance on the social scale. Thirsk writes of how noblemen, gentlemen, yeomen, and merchants shared "an almost encyclopedic body of knowledge" about the best market sources for an ever-enlarging inventory of goods.[57] The explosion of objects and choices necessarily effected a material consciousness of the sort that is witnessed in Gremio's catalogue of luxurious household stuff in *The Taming of the Shrew*.

One phenomenon is progenitor to such economic manifestations as Gremio's cushions from Turkey, valances from Venice, and argosy anchored at Marseilles; Mukerji's avidly collected imports; Katherina's mythical husband labouring on sea and land: it is travel. The early modern market was implicated in the move away from a culture of relatively high self-sufficiency and self-containment to one of getting, trading—and travelling—to achieve the new standard of living. And that phenomenon is of some significance to the construction of the gender order. By the end of the sixteenth century, a common formulation of marital roles held that:

> The dutie of the husband, is to get goods: and of the wife, to gather them togeither, and save them. The dutie of the husband is, to travell abroad to seeke living, and the wives dutie is to keepe the house. The dutie of the husband is, to get mony and provision: and of the wives, not vainely to spend it. The dutie of the husband is, to deale with many men: and of the wives, to talke with fewe. The dutie of the husband is, to be entermedling: and of the wife, to bee solitarie and withdrawne. The dutie of the man is, to bee skilfull in talke: and of the wife, to boast of silence. The dutie of the husband is to be a giver: and of the wife, to bee a saver. The dutie of the man is, to apparrell himselfe as he may: and of the woman, as it becometh her. The dutie of the husband is, to bee Lord of all: and of the wife, to give account of all. The dutie of the husband is, to dispatch all things without doore: and of the wife, to oversee and give order for all things within the house. Now where the husband and wife performeth these duties in their house, wee may call it a Colledge of quietnesse: the house wherein these are neglected, we may terme it a hell.[58]

Notice how all manner of political roles and gender assignments proceed from the notion that that responsibility to "get goods" belongs to the husband and that the responsibility entails his travel. Notice, too, how many of these "duties" resonate with the operative order of *The Taming of the Shrew*, beginning with Katherina's mythical husband whose duty is to get goods, ending with Hortensio's notion that marriage to the undutiful Katherina might be termed a hell and with Petruchio's confidence that her taming will afford him a college of quietness.

Notice, finally, in the passage I have quoted from Katherina's last speech, the way in which the fiction that Petruchio must risk his (physical) life to get goods sustains the reciprocal notion that his provision of goods merits in exchange her (political) life. Katherina's set-piece figures her "maintentance" or "keep" as his service to her, accepts that that service is one for which she is indebted beyond the possibility of requital, and finds obedience "too little payment for so great a debt." The fact that Katherina's obedience is thus offered consentually accords with a hegemonic strategy that Godelier has recognized: "For there to be such shared conceptions" as social order requires, "the exercise of power must appear as a *service* rendered by the dominant to the dominated that creates a *debt* of the latter to the former—which can only be discharged by the gift in return of their goods, their labour, their services or even their lives." As Godelier continues, consent, which "involves a certain co-operation in the reproduction of this domination," is more effective in per-petuating hierarchy than is violence, "is the portion of power added by the dominated to that which the dominant directly exercise over them."[59]

The final turn of *The Shrew*, then (to appropriate Joel Fineman's apt wordplay[60]), with respect, that is, to things, is that things purchase the consent that perpetuates the gendered social contract. They enable the prevailing power relationship between men and women by grounding it in contractual terms, by lending it a logic: specifically, by interposing the economic logic of exchange. The dramatic text's erasure of difference between persons and things and its exposure of interest in the performance of things predict this social contract and expose its conceptual underpinnings.

NOTES

Originally published in *The Yearbook of English Studies* 23 (1993): 169–88. Reprinted with the permission of Lena Cowen Orlin and *The Yearbook of English Studies*.

For direct and indirect encouragement in writing this paper, I would like to thank Andrew Gurr and Catherine Belsey. My greatest debt is to Leeds Barroll, who followed, challenged, redirected, and improved my argument through several versions of it.

1. My text is the Riverside Shakespeare *The Taming of the Shrew*, ed. G. Blakemore Evans (Boston: Houghton Mifflin, 1974).
2. Camille Wells Slights also calls the world of the play "a world of objects," although to the different end of characterizing it as "almost too cluttered to move about in freely," with an "oppressive atmosphere" ("The Raw and the Cooked in *The Taming of the Shrew*," *JEGP*, 88 (1989): 172.
3. Pierre Bourdieu, *Distinction: A Social Critique of the Judgement of Taste*, trans. by Richard Nice (1979; Cambridge, Mass.: Harvard University Press, 1984), 6.
4. For bibliography on the textual relationship between *The Shrew* and *A Shrew*, see Riverside Shakespeare, *Taming*, 140.
5. As Ann Thompson notes in her edition for the New Cambridge Shakespeare of *The Taming of the Shrew* (Cambridge: Cambridge University Press, 1984), 46 n; and as David Daniell emphasizes in "The Good Marriage of Katherine and Petru-chio," *Shakespeare Survey* 37 (1984), 24.
6. John Bean has influentially divided *The Shrew* criticism in the "two camps" of "revisionists," who read Kate's last speech ironically, and "anti-revisionists," who read the play as a farce. (See "Comic Structure and the Humanizing of Kate in *The Taming of the Shrew*," in *The Woman's Part: Feminist Criticism of Shake-speare*, ed. Carolyn Ruth Swift Lenz, Gayle Greene, and Carol Thomas Neely [Urbana: University of Illinois Press, 1983], 65.)
7. See for example Alan C. Dessen, "Hamlet's Poisoned Sword: A Study in Dra-matic Imagery," *Shakespeare Studies* 5 (1969: 53–69; *Elizabethan Drama and the Viewer's Eye* (Chapel Hill: University of North Carolina Press, 1977); and *Eliz-abethan Stage Conventions and Modern Interpreters* (Cambridge: Cambridge

University Press, 1984). Just as I completed this essay, Frances Teague's useful *Shakespeare's Speaking Properties* was published (Lewisburg: Bucknell University Press, 1991).

8. Arjun Appadurai, "Introduction: Commodities and the Politics of Value," in *The Social Life of Things: Commodities in Cultural Perspective*, ed. Arjun Appadurai (Cambridge: Cambridge University Press, 1986), 3–63; Igor Kopytoff, "The Cultural Biography of Things: Commoditization as Process," in *The Social Life of Things*, 64–91; Mary Douglas and Baron Isherwood, *The World of Goods* (New York: Basic Books, 1979); Maurice Godelier, *The Mental and the Material: Thought Economy and Society*, trans. Martin Thom (n.p.: Verso, 1986). For related perspectives on the embeddedness of cultural and material meanings, see also Jean Baudrillard, *Le Systeme des Objets* (Paris: Gallimard, 1968), and Marshall Sahlins, *Culture and Practical Reason* (Chicago: University of Chicago Press, 1976).

9. Marcel Mauss, *The Gift: Forms and Functions of Exchange in Archaic Societies*, trans. Ian Cunnison (1925; New York: W. W. Norton, 1967). Mary Douglas identifies *The Gift* as the "brilliant start" of economic anthropology in "The Exclusion of Economics" (1973), collected in *In the Active Voice* (London: Routledge, 1982), 174. .

10. Appadurai, 5.

11. Appadurai, 17; Kopytoff, 66–68.

12. Patrick Geary, "Sacred Commodities: The Circulation of Medieval Relics," in *The Social Life of Things*, 169.

13. Geary, 169, 172; Appadurai, 9.

14. Bronislaw Malinowski, *Argonauts of the Western Pacific* (London: Routledge, 1922).

15. I assume such properties to bear out the stage direction *"Enter a Lord from hunting,"* following the argument on this matter of Dessen, *Elizabethan Stage Conventions*, 32–33.

16. I include items of costume when they function as properties, as do Petruchio's wedding apparel and Katherina's gown and cap. I completed this catalogue before the publication of Frances Teague's *Shakespeare's Speaking Properties*, but her finding list (p. 158) congrues more or less with mine, is more rigorous, and provides helpful citations.

17. For example: the beds of Sly and of Katherina, the Lord's wanton pictures, Gremio's possessions, the book and glass of wine abused by Petruchio during his wedding ceremony, and so on.

18. Douglas and Isherwood, 72.

19. Douglas and Isherwood, 62.

20. Douglas and Isherwood, 59.

21. Other creature comforts (not needs) include the candle or lantern called for when, in the explicit setting of "this chamber," Petruchio gestures to "this light whereby I see thy beauty" (2.1.259, 273). Several references are made to stools or chairs, as Sly directs his "wife" to "sit by my side" (Ind. 2.142–43); as Bianca commands her tutors, "here sit we down" (3.1.21), and as at her wedding banquet Petruchio exclaims that there is "nothing but sit and sit, and eat and eat!" (5.2.12).

22. For just one example, see John Dod and Robert Cleaver, "A Housholde is as it were a little commonwealth," in *A Godly forme of Household Gouernnment* (London: 1598; STC no. 5382), sig. B1 ʳ.

23. Appadurai calls luxuries "goods whose principal use is *rhetorical* and *social*, goods that are simply *incarnated signs*. The necessity to which *they* respond is fundamentally political" (38).

24. Slights in "The Raw and the Cooked" points "a contrast between the cultivated and the brutish," but our readings thereafter diverge. She sees as entirely more benign the Lord's "gracious familiarity" with, "effortless authority" over, and "protective care" for his servants, as well as their "respectful deference" towards him (169).

25. Bourdieu, 2; for earlier recordings of the scene, see especially Marjorie B. Garber ("These Ovidean reminiscences are of course a form of sexual temptation") in *Dream in Shakespeare: From Metaphor to Metamorphosis* (New Haven: Yale University Press, 1974), 31–32.

26. Bourdieu, 7.

27. Colin Renfrew, "Varna and the Emergence of Wealth in Prehistoric Europe," in *The Social Life of Things*, 158. See also Georg Simmel, *The Philosophy of Money*, 2d ed., trans. by Tom Bottomore and David Frisby (1907; London: Routledge, 1978), Chapter 1. I find Renfrew's emphasis upon the formative influence of social context upon value particularly useful.

28. Douglas and Isherwood, 19.

29. A similar understanding informs Vincentio's disappointment when he is denied entry at the place indicated by Petruchio's assurance that "here's the door, this is Lucentio's house." His dismay is compounded by the violation of his paternal entitlement and by the public disgrace of social incapacity that follows upon an invitation he had issued in sanguine expectation: "You shall not choose but drink before you go. / I think I shall command your welcome here; / And by all likelihood some cheer is toward" (5.1.8–13).

30. Douglas and Isherwood, 65.

31. Bourdieu, 5.

32. Douglas and Isherwood, 88. The Lord's welcome to the players is a distantly related form of hospitality that finally has more in common with charity; it is incumbent upon him as a responsibility of privilege.

33. Douglas and Isherwood, 73.

34. Ibid., 95.

35. See 1.2.214–15, 271–72, 275.

36. Simmel, 67.

37. See on this subject Mauss, 10–12.

38. Godelier, 81.

39. Coppélia Kahn, *Man's Estate: Masculine Identity in Shakespeare* (Berkeley: University of California Press, 1981), 110.

40. Ruth Nevo, *Comic Transformations in Shakespeare* (London: Methuen, 1980), 41.

41. J. Leeds Barroll, *Artificial Persons: The Formation of Character in the Tragedies of Shakespeare* (Columbia: University of South Carolina Press, 1974).

42. "Lucentio, you shall supply the bridegroom's place, / And let Bianca take her sister's room" (3.2.249–50). One definition of "room," according to *OED*, is "the particular place assigned or appropriated to a person."
43. Appropriate to Petruchio's sense of license (if not to his precise class) is Bourdieu's remark of "all aristocracies" that "the essence in which they see themselves refuses to be contained in any definition" (24).
44. In another parallel with things, the persons of the text furnish creature comforts: the "low submissive reverence" of the Lord's servants (Ind. 1.53) are as requisite to Sly's transformative pleasure as are the silver basin and the costly apparel.
45. Kahn, 117.
46. Jean E. Howard observes that in the course of the play "the audience reverses its initial assumptions about the relative value of the two women" ("The Difficulties of Closure: An Approach to the Problematic in Shakespearian Comedy," in *Comedy from Shakespeare to Sheridan: Essays in Honor of Eugene M. Waith*, ed. A. R. Braunmuller and J. C. Bulman [Newark: University of Delaware Press, 1986], 115).
47. Appadurai is one of many to observe that "marriage transactions might constitute the context in which women are most intensely, and most appropriately, regarded as exchange values" (15).
48. See on this subject Kristian Smidt, *Unconformities in Shakespeare's Early Comedies* (New York: St. Martin's Press, 1986), 67–69; see also Thompson, in her New Cambridge edition, 163–64 (including her quotation of Gary Taylor).
49. Levi-Strauss develops the paradigm in various texts (and in various formulations), especially in *The Elementary Structures of Kinship*. rev. ed., trans. by James Harle Bell, John Richard von Sturmer, and Rodney Needham (1949; London: Eyre and Spottiswoode, 1969) and *The Savage Mind* (1962; Chicago: University of Chicago Press, 1966). The formulation I present is preferred by Mary Douglas in "Goods as a System of Communication," in *In the Active Voice*, 24; compare Douglas and Isherwood, 87–88. In private conversation, James Boon has pointed out that Levi-Strauss's *femme* has too often been translated, as by Douglas, as "woman," when the more accurate translation is "wife."
50. In private correspondence, Andrew Gurr emphasizes the richness of the construction "household Kate," which refers to an edible cate as well as to property. On this subject see Mary Douglas, "Food as a System of Communication," in *In the Active Voice*, 82–124.
51. For the most recent reviews of the criticism, see Thompson's introduction to the New Cambridge *Taming of the Shrew*.
52. My text is Geoffrey Bullough, *Narrative and Dramatic Sources of Shakespeare* Vol. 1: *Early Comedies, Poems, Romeo and Juliet* (London: Routledge, 1957), 69–108, 70–71.
53. Karen Newman similarly points out that "Sly is only convinced of his lordly identity when he is told of his 'wife'" in "Renaissance Family Politics and Shakespeare's *The Taming of the Shrew*," *English Literary Renaissance* 16 (1986), 88.
54. I am interested in the relationship of "lady" to "pot" as objects to be commanded. But just as women can be commodified through marriage, so men can be commodified through service, as the Lord's men are in this very command.

55. My (economic) reading of the term "keeper" (i.e., as relating to Katherina's "keep") differs from that of Valerie Wayne, who writes that "keeper" suggests that a husband is an agent for imprisoning his wife as one might cage an animal, which Petruchio has nearly done" ("Refashioning the Shrew," *Shakespeare Studies* 17 [1985]: 173). But she continues that " 'life' implies that she is so totally dependent on him for support and nurturance, as Kate sometimes appears to be, that she must have a husband in order to survive"; in this, our interpretations are more in sympathy.

56. Peter Saccio, for example, calls the passage "rich in private irony," but his characterological concern is the "private" rather than the "irony," as he distinguishes the presumed response of Katherina and Petruchio from that of the other characters ("Shrewd and Kindly Farce," *Shakespeare Survey* 37 [1984]: 39).

57. Joan Thirsk, *Economic Policy and Projects* (Oxford: Clarendon Press, 1978); Chandra Mukerji, *From Graven Images: Patterns of Modern Materialism* (New York: Columbia University Press, 1983); Jean-Christophe Agnew, *Worlds Apart: The Market and the Theater in Anglo-American Thought, 1550–1750* (Cambridge: Cambridge University Press, 1986). See especially Thirsk, 119.

58. Dod and Cleaver, sigs. M4^v.–M5^r.

59. Godelier, 12–14.

60. Joel Fineman, "The Turn of the Shrew," in *Shakespeare and the Question of Theory*, ed. Patricia Parker and Geoffrey Hartman (New York: Methuen, 1985), 138–59.

Framing the Taming
Metatheatrical Awareness of Female Impersonation in *The Taming of the Shrew*

MICHAEL SHAPIRO

Kate's speech of submission at the end of *The Taming of the Shrew* raises problems for producers and critics who want to dissociate Shakespeare from normative Elizabethan views about the subordination of married women to their husbands. Some modern directors have devised stage business for subverting Kate's declaration of submissiveness, occasionally using it to grant her subtle or not-so-subtle powers of manipulation and control. Although much of the critical debate over the play has centred on whether the ending subverts or reinforces patriarchal attitudes, Linda Woodbridge concludes a brief survey of feminist efforts to recuperate the play and its ending with the sceptical observation that "I see little evidence that he was ahead of his time in his attitudes toward women."[1] Other critics whose work is no less historically based than Woodbridge's find reason to argue that the play is more problematic than conventional. As Michael Hattaway asserts, "there can be *no* authoritative reading."[2]

Some directors and critics have tried to solve the problem by enclosing the submission of Kate in some kind of frame, thereby hoping to find an ironic perspective which undercuts the wife-taming, or at least qualifies it. In the Folio text, the Induction provides such a perspective, but unfortunately it disappears after the first act. Some directors, following Pope, adopt the ending from *The Taming of A Shrew*, the so-called bad quarto published in 1594. Stanley Wells and Gary Taylor have recently buttressed the authority of this ending by suggesting that it may reflect "Shakespeare's final text . . . more fully than the Folio does" or else may be a "paraphrase or imitation" of an earlier Shakespearian text behind the Folio version.[3]

New historicist criticism provides another kind of frame, the social context. Karen Newman cites an actual case of a skimmington, a traditional practice in which villagers directed mockery and "rough music" at couples suspected of deviance from accepted patriarchal norms of family organization. On such occasions, young men impersonated wives believed guilty of adultery, scolding, and disobeying or beating their husbands, thereby presenting caricatured antitypes of the ideal obedient wife. Perhaps London theatre-goers recalled such ritualized female impersonations of unruly women when attending plays in which young male actors represented similar types of women. Newman suggests that idealized female stereotypes, such as the submissive Kate, might have been deconstructed by audiences' awareness of crossgender casting.[4] But as her reading of the play relies on framing-by-contextualization, she does not pursue the idea.

I propose that the text itself, as originally performed by an all-male cast, generated deconstructive power of its own by creating a metatheatrical frame. Beginning with the Induction, the play flaunted its theatricality, principally by underscoring the use of male actors in female roles, and Shakespeare sustained that effect even after the Induction framework itself disappeared from view. As the female roles taken by these male performers were either idealized married gentlewomen or their unruly antitypes, they appeared not only as theatrical constructions but also as female stereotypes as outlined in conduct books and marriage manuals. Before exploring the play's exposure of its female characters as being both theatrically and culturally constructed, we need to consider the practice and probable effects of crossgender casting more broadly and in some detail.

I

Although casting of male actors in female roles was the accepted practice on the English stage, there is no way to prove if or when or to what extent spectators were aware of the performers representing female characters. Such awareness of the crossgender casting would have come not from the actors' deficiency, for the evidence indicates that the young male actors who specialized in female roles were quite capable of representing women, or of rendering the theatrical codes used to represent women. Although Colley Cibber was later to disparage the "Boys, or young Men of the most effeminate Aspect" who played female parts as "ungain Hoydens," most pre-Restoration accounts suggest that these "boy-actresses," as Granville-Barker termed them, were highly skilled. There was ample time and opportunity to develop whatever talent they had, for they were apprenticed from the age of ten or slightly older for seven or more years to individual members of adult companies, who were responsible for their training and maintenance.[5] Because puberty came several years later than it does now, they could play women well into adolescence, but probably with a seemingly precocious intellectual and emotional maturity proportionate with their chronological ages.[6] Extant casting lists for seven plays acted by the King's Men between 1611 and 1632 indicate that young performers like Richard Robinson, Robert Pallant, and Richard Sharpe changed from female to male roles at about the time their apprenticeships ended. Ezekiel Fenn was evidently nineteen when he played his first adult male role.[7]

It is not exactly clear just when female roles became the exclusive speciality of apprentices and younger actors. Doubling schemes printed on title pages indicate such specialization when all female roles are assigned to one or two actors.[8] Further evidence of such specialization is suggested by a short exchange in *Sir Thomas More* between the title character and the leader of an itinerant troupe consisting of "ffoure men and a boy:"

> MOORE.   But one boy? then I see, ther's but fewe women in the play.
> PLAYER.   Three my Lord: dame Science, Lady vanitie, and wisedome she her selfe.
> MOORE.   And one boy play them all? bir Lady, hees loden.[9]

More assumes correctly that all three female roles will be played by the same boy, whose doubling in these parts adds theatrical point to Witt's mistaking of Lady Vanity for Lady Wisedome.

By the 1590s, when the more successful troupes found more permanent venues in London, apprenticeships for younger actors might have become readily available, more stable, and perhaps more attractive, with a concomitant rise in the quality of female impersonation. There seems no reason to doubt that boys or youths who assumed female roles for Shakespeare's troupe created compelling illusions of femininity. According to one spectator, Henry Jackson, who saw *Othello* at Oxford in 1610, "Desdemona [and not the boy playing the role] moved the spectators with *her* expression" [my emphasis]. Other witnesses reflect spectators' ability to maintain a sense of the male actor playing the female role without any loss of aesthetic pleasure. Lady Mary Wroth uses the female impersonator, or "play-boy," as a metaphor for technical virtuosity.[10] Defending the practice of female impersonation against puritan charges that it violated biblical injunctions against transvestism and so blurred gender boundaries, Thomas Heywood claimed that spectators recognized male actors and understood they were watching a temporary theatrical illusion:

> To see our youths attired in the habit of women, who knowes not what their intents be? who cannot distinguish them by their names, assuredly, knowing they are but to represent such a lady, at such a time apoynted?[11]

Although Heywood assumes a high level of metatheatrical awareness of female impersonators, a dual consciousness of male actor and female character might also have been activated by moments of self-referentiality. The best known, of course, is Cleopatra's fear that a young male actor will "boy" her greatness, but one should also consider references to such strong gender markers as primary or secondary sex characteristics, as when Cleopatra describes herself as suckling an asp. Crossgender disguise is another such gender marker, for as the female character assumed a fictive male identity, the male performer resumed his authentic male identity. But it also seems likely that female characters played by male actors were readily "deconstructed" when seen next to other female characters portrayed in contrasting styles or representing other stereotypes. The dissonance produced by such contrasts alerted the audience to a fact, which, as Samuel Johnson says, spectators "always know": that it was watching theatrical constructions of femininity created by male actors. Such awareness of theatrical artifice would inevitably lead to an awareness that these male performers were offering versions of femininity, versions which might reflect, refract, or refute images of women most readily available to the culture.[12]

Another way pointing up the phenomenon of female impersonation was for a male character deliberately to burlesque or caricature a female character, as *in Jack Juggler* (ca. 1555), where Jenkin Careaway describes a fellow servant by the name of Alison Trip-and-go:

> She simperith, she prankith and getteth without faille
> As a pecocke that hath spred and sheweth hir gaye taylle
> S[h]e mynceth, she bridelethe, she swimmith to and fro
> S[h]e tredith not one here a wrye, she tryppeth like a do
> A brod in the stret going or cumming homward
> She quaverith and warbelith like one in a galiard
> Everie joint in her bodie and everie part
> Oh it is a joylie wenche to myns and devyd a fart.[13]

T.W. Craik comments on the contrasting styles:

> As Alison makes an appearance in the play, there must have been visible points of difference between the acting of the boy playing her and that of the boy playing Jenkin and (in that character) burlesquing her. The former would mimic a woman's walk with little or no extravagance; the latter would lard his mimicry with every imaginable affectation.[14]

The situation is even richer than Craik suggests. Alison makes one very brief appearance and has a single speech (ll. 749–58), which is shorter than Jenkin's description/parody of her. Jenkin's burlesque of Alison is in fact preceded by a similar description/parody of Dame Coy, the other female character in the play. Although the title-page lists Dame Coy as a gentlewoman, Jenkin describes her as "a verie cursed shrew . . . / And a verye divell" (ll. 211–12), who spares neither servants nor her husband corporal punishment and the rough side of her tongue.

What was the precise effect of Jenkin's burlesques? Did they make the female characters, when they appeared, seem more or less natural? Was Jenkin mocking women or was he rather mocking men's stereotyped ideas about women? Or both? On the one hand, the actors playing Alison and Dame Coy clearly offered a more "natural" version of femininity than Jenkin did in his burlesques. On the other hand, his more obviously constructed travesties drove home the fact that both performances were theatrical constructions, especially when the audience was reminded of what it "always knew," that both Dame Coy and Alison were played by male actors. As women, they corresponded to the familiar social constructs of the young flirt and the old shrew, but as female impersonations they seemed to correspond to two opposing theatrical constructions: one illusionistic and the other self-consciously parodic.[15]

Jenkin's burlesques of female characters anticipate the moments in later plays by Shakespeare and others when male characters impersonate women within the world of the play. One such moment occurs in *The Merry Wives of Windsor* when Falstaff appears disguised as the Witch of Brentford alongside Mistress Ford and Mistress Page. The effect produced depended on a clear contrast between Falstaff's farcical, awkward, deliberately unconvincing (to the audience) representation of a grotesque female figure and the apprentices' more realistic portrayal of female characters, as was their speciality. In other words, the play contrasts an adult male actor playing a man pretending to be a "woman" with young male actors playing female characters.[16]

Usually the contrast between "women" and female characters is more subtle. In the "boy bride" plays listed by Victor Freeburg, young male characters are disguised as young "women" in order to deceive other male characters, as in *The Merry Wives* where Slender and Caius each finds his intended bride to be "a great lubberly boy."[17] Such plays presented two levels of female impersonation: actors playing female characters (women), and actors playing boys playing "women." Unless a surprise effect was intended, as in *Epicoene*, one assumes a stylistic differentiation between the two levels—companies presented "real" women more realistically than "boy brides," or else relied on the audience's knowledge of context to create a sense of the difference. Whereas Chapman, Jonson, and Marston usually make the "boy bride" part of a con game or practical joke, Shakespeare often heightens the metatheatricality of such moments, as in *A Midsummer Night's Dream*, where an amateur actor, Francis Flute the bellows-mender, is cast as Thisbe in the first mechanicals' scene, and is shown briefly rehearsing the role before finally performing it in the last act.

The casting scene of *A Midsummer Night's Dream* is in general a mine of reflexive effects, but in particular it uses Flute to promote metatheatrical awareness of female impersonation. Flute hopes to play a "wand'ring knight" (1.2.45), the romantic male lead of the play, and is thus unhappy at being assigned a female role: "Nay, faith; let me not play a woman; I have a beard coming" (1.2.47–48). Although the mechanicals are referred to as men, the name Flute suggests a high voice, while both the touchy masculine pride and the allusions to the incipient beard suggest a boy of roughly the same age as those performing the four female roles in Shakespeare's play. As fifth female impersonator, Flute may not have been as good at it as the other four boys. More likely he was even better, possibly an experienced young actor now old enough to abandon female roles, perhaps like Dick Robinson in Jonson's *The Devil is an Ass*. Some Elizabethan spectators would have recognized Flute/Thisbe as a distorted reflection of what was happening within the larger play, where boy actors pretended to be Hippolyta, Hermia, Helena and Titania.[18]

A similar situation occurs in *Hamlet*, where the female impersonator, like Flute, is first singled out for special attention and then seen performing in an inserted playlet before "real" women. In his greeting to the players Hamlet warmly welcomes them all (the stage direction in the second Quarto mentions "*The Players*," while the Folio specifies "*four or five Players*," although only three actors are required to play the scenes we see of "The Murder of Gonzago"). In greeting the Players, Hamlet takes particular notice of two—a man with a beard and a female impersonator—and notes their gender-marking attributes:

> You are welcome, masters, welcome all. I am glad to see thee well. Welcome, good friends. O, old friend! why, thy face is valenc'd since I saw thee last; com'st thou to beard me in Denmark? What, my young lady and mistress! By'r lady, your ladyship is nearer to heaven than when I saw you last, by the altitude of a chopine. Pray God your voice, like a piece of uncurrent gold, be not crack'd within the ring. Masters, you are all welcome. (2.2.421–29)

The adult male actor has grown a beard since Hamlet last saw him, while the boy has grown taller, by an amount Hamlet compares to an "additional base [attached] to a lady's shoe to increase height."[19] Like Flute, whose name may refer to a voice undergoing adolescent change, the boy's voice too may be "crack'd within the ring," a phrase suggesting both the defectiveness of a damaged coin and the loss of (female) virginity, a playful confusion of real and feigned gender identities.

As in *A Midsummer Night's Dream*, where "Pyramus and Thisbe" is performed before three ladies of the court, "The Murder of Gonzago" is played to an audience which includes Gertrude and Ophelia. It is played twice, once as a dumb-show and once with dialogue. The dumb-show is obviously stylized and the spoken version, like the inserted playlet in *A Midsummer Night's Dream*, is stylized in terms of diction and metre and therefore asks to be presented in a different style as well in order to differentiate this fictive world from the world inhabited by the onstage spectators. Watching and listening to the Player Queen through Hamlet's eyes and ears, the playhouse audience sees the boy they had met previously now playing a noble lady devoted to her husband but wooed and finally won by his murderer. Played in a more formal style, she had seemed an icon of female constancy and so contrasted with the more naturalistically enacted roles of Gertrude and Ophelia, both of whose loyalties Hamlet has come to doubt, but in the end proved as weak and inconstant as they now seem to him, verifying his belief that "frailty thy name is woman," in art no less than in life.

II

In *The Taming of the Shrew*, the two scenes of the Induction provide several opportunities for reflexive contrasts in levels and styles of female impersonation. The first Induction scene opens with the Hostess claiming that Sly owes her money "for the glasses you have burst" (1.7–8) and threatening to "fetch the thirdborough" (1.12), or constable. The Hostess is probably ejecting Sly from her premises by force, for in the following scene one of the Lord's servants tells him that in his recent state of "distraction" he would speak "idle words" such as claiming "ye were beaten out of door" and would then "rail upon the hostess of the house" (2.85–86). In short, the opening lines of the Folio text present a dominating, aggressively violent lower-class woman, played as always by a boy.

Moreover, the presence of the young male actor was not merely a latent metatheatrical fact, but became explicit when Sly's defiant response to the Hostess's threat to call the police includes the line, "I'll not budge an inch, *boy*" (1.14; my emphasis). Like most other editors, Ann Thompson glosses the word as "a contemptuous form of address to a servant or inferior." But the next sentence undermines this suggestion: "This is the only example in Shakespeare of it being applied to a woman, so perhaps it is another drunken error."[20] But surely not Shakespeare's. Assuming the word is not an error by a scribe or compositor, Sly hurls "boy" at the Hostess in order to insult her. In performance, this word may have indicated Sly's drunkenness, confusion, or anger, or simply been given to him to use as a meaningless intensifier, but it may also, like Cleopatra's "boy my greatness," have reminded some if not all spectators of what they "always knew"—that the female character was in fact played by a boy. This exposure of artifice in the play's opening lines reveals the Hostess to be a theatrical construct, just as the scuffle with Sly labels the character as a stereotypical social construct—the familiar scold of Tudor misogynist lore, literature, and legal records.

An even more explicit allusion to the theatrical representation of women by male performers occurs a few lines later, shortly after the players arrive. A stage direction, "*Enter* PLAYERS" (1.78), preceding the Lord's invitation to "bid them come near," indicates that at least two of them appear onstage, and indeed two of them have speeches. The Lord recalls having seen the company before and recognizes the First Player, "Since once he play'd a farmer's eldest son" (1.84). Addressing the actor directly, he remembers the play: " 'Twas where you woo'd the gentlewoman so well" (1.85), thereby accentuating the general practice of crossgender casting if not the presence of the same female impersonator who had played the role of the gentlewoman. As soon as the Players leave, the Lord orders a servant to recruit "Barthol'mew my page, / And see him dress'd in all suits like a lady" (1.105–6).

The exchange between Lord and Players is handled differently in the Quarto, where a stage direction clears up some of the uncertainties of the Folio: "*Enter two of the players with packs at their backs, and a boy.*"[21] They are clearly just in off the road, not yet in costume. The Lord does not recognize any of the Players nor does he refer to any previous roles. He asks the "play-boy," to use Lady Mary Wroth's term, rather than his own servant to take the part of Sly's wife:

> And sirha go you make you ready straight,
> And dresse yourselfe like some lovelie ladie,
> And when I call see that you come to me,
> For I will say to him thou art his wife,
> Dallie with him and hug him in thine armes,
> And if he desire to goe to bed with thee,
> Then faine some scuse and say thou wilt anon.
> Be gone I say, and see thou doost it well. (Ind. 1.71)

The boy departs, promising to "dandell him well enough / And make him thinke I love him mightilie" (Ind. 1.79–80). As promised, the female impersonator returns as Sly's "wife," thereby reminding the audience that all female characters were played by male actors.[22]

In the Folio, the Lord's instructions are far more detailed. On one level, they need to be spelled out because the performer he recruits to play Sly's wife is a household servant and not the experienced professional female impersonator of the Quarto. The Folio Lord is also a connoisseur of acting, and although he may have forgotten the name of the actor who played the farmer's eldest son, he is "sure that part / Was aptly fitted and naturally perform'd" (Ind. 1.86–87). Instead of simply ordering the boy to "do . . . it well," the Folio Lord specifies the features involved in this construction of femininity, as well as suggesting some of the tactics to be employed to create the kind of naturalistic illusion he admired in the play he saw, and seems to relish in paintings as well.

Whereas the Quarto Lord simply envisions a "lovelie ladie," the Folio Lord's instructions sketch a model of upperclass femininity, but its constructedness is readily apparent. As a model presented by an aristocratic male character for his youthful male servant to adopt in representing a "woman," it not only alludes reflexively to the standard theatrical practice of crossgender casting but also conforms to the well-defined social role of a married gentlewoman:

> Tell him from me, as he will win my love,
> He bears himself with honorable action,
> Such as he hath observ'd in noble ladies
> Unto their lords, by them accomplished;
> Such duty to the drunkard let him do,
> With soft low tongue and lowly courtesy,
> And say, "What is't your honor will command,
> Wherein your lady, and your humble wife,
> May show her duty and make known her love?" (Ind. 1.109)

The Lord's idealized image of a married gentlewoman is derived from English and continental conduct books of the period, although Shakespeare emphasizes external features which can be readily represented both by the boy actor and the page. Conduct books regularly enjoin wives to silence, reverence, and obedience, and the ideal wife as constructed by the Lord is soft-spoken, deferential, and not only obedient to her husband's will but tenderly solicitous of his well-being.[23] Whereas the Quarto Lord advises the boy player to establish his role as wife chiefly if not solely through strong sexual advances to Sly, the Folio Lord urges his page to enact the role of noble lady by expressing concern for his welfare and thereby classifying potentially erotic gestures as wifely solicitude and celebration of his recovery:

> And then with kind embracements, tempting kisses,
> And with declining head into his bosom,
> Bid him shed tears, as being overjoyed
> To see her noble lord restor'd to health. (Ind. 1.118)

The dallying and dandling of the Quarto "wife" is discouraged by some conduct books on the grounds that married women should remain modest in connubial sexual behaviour, while even those tracts (mainly Puritan) which encourage sexual relations within marriage counsel moderation. While William Perkins in *Christian Economy* (1609) looks with favour on the "due benevolence" of the marriage bed, he warns that "even in wedlock excess in lusts is no better than plain adultery before God."[24]

In the Folio, Shakespeare points up the artifice involved in the construction of a married gentlewoman by having the Lord instruct his page how to make himself cry real tears by means of a theatrical trick, women evidently having the ability to induce tears at will, if not by nature then by subtler artifices of their own:

> And if the boy have not a woman's gift
> To rain a shower of commanded tears,
> An onion will do well for such a shift,
> Which in a napkin (being close convey'd)
> Shall in despite enforce a watery eye. (Ind. 1.124)

The Lord sends one of his servants off, perhaps remaining alone on stage and so giving additional emphasis to his final eight lines, which might be considered a soliloquy directed at the playhouse audience.

He begins this segment of the speech by reasserting his confidence in Barthol'mew's ability to imitate a real lady:

> I know the boy will well usurp the grace,
> Voice, gait, and action of a gentlewoman. (Ind. 1.131)

In specifying such features as deportment, vocal quality, movement, and gesture, the Lord is again outlining a social construction of a married gentlewoman such as the conduct books of the period describe. Wives should maintain a discreet but not total silence. Richard Braithwaite's advice in *The English Gentlewoman* (1631) is typical: "Bashfull silence is an ornament to their Sexe ... It suites not with *her* honour, for a *young woman* to be prolocutor. But especially, when either men are in presence, or ancient Matrons, to whom shee owes a civill reverence, it will become her to tip her tongue with silence."[25]

Whereas most conduct books concentrate on inward or moral aspects of married life, Braithwaite devotes some attention to such external considerations as carriage, for, as he puts it, "It is no hard thing to gather the *disposition* of our *heart*, by the *dimension* of our *gate*." He thus recommends that "your *Carriage* ... should neither be too precise, nor too loose," and later describes inappropriate kinds of "gates" in scornful detail: "What a circular gesture wee shall observe some use in their pace, as if they were troubled with the *vertigo*! Others make a tinkling with their feet, and make discovery of their light thoughts, by their wanton *gate*. Others with a jetting and strutting *pace*, publish their hauty and selfe-conceited minde." Model women of "preceding times" "had not the art of imitating such huffing and mounting *gates*, as our light-spirited Dames now use."[26]

"Grace" is a more elusive term than "voice," "gait," and "action," but can be glossed by the conduct books as modesty of demeanour, which Ruth Kelso defines as "a kind of timidity, that is, a shrinking from drawing attention to oneself, a desire to be inconspicuous, a fear of adverse comment, or to give it positive force and a more praiseworthy connotation, moderation" (p. 105). He wants his page to represent this version of an idealized married gentlewoman with what he considers verisimilitude ("aptly fitted and naturally performed") rather than exaggerated theatricality. His own presence will prevent excessive mirth from deflecting the page's performance towards broad caricature.

In the second Induction scene a Lady enters, whom the audience has been prepared to recognize as Barthol'mew "dressed in all suits like a lady." However accurate his imitation of a great lady, spectators would have known that this "boy bride," like female characters, was being played by a boy or young man. Although there may have been moments when the Page revealed himself non-verbally to the Lord or to other servants and hence to the audience without Sly's noticing it, the text stipulates no such "breaking" of character, which suggests that the boy remained in his female role throughout the scene, solicitous about Sly's welfare and treating him with appropriate, perhaps ironically exaggerated, deference and humility: "My husband and my lord, my lord and husband, / I am your wife in all obedience" (2.105–7). In declaring her obedience to her husband's authority, Sly's "lady" echoes the central duty of a wife according to manuals of the period. "An Homily of the State of Matrimony" (1563), quoting 1 Peter 3:1, defines that duty quite simply: "*Ye wives, be ye in subjection to obey your own husband.*"[27] Carrying out his master's instructions, Barthol'mew thus provided a doubly theatrical construction of the social construction of a married gentlewoman, the role Kate will adopt by the end of the play.

A crisis in this doubly constructed performance occurs when Sly commands his wife to "undress you, and come now to bed" (Ind. 2.117). Up to that point, the text gives him little opportunity to kiss and embrace Sly. The tinker's sexual appetite has already been whetted, by descriptions first of erotic mythological pictures and then of his wife, "a lady far more beautiful / Than any woman in this waning age . . . the fairest creature in the world," even now her "lovely face" although marred by tears, "inferior to none" (Ind. 2.62–67). His wife enters, full of tender solicitude and obedience, as the Lord has directed Barthol'mew. Once Sly accepts her as his "wife" and is reminded how to address her, his sexual interest is renewed when she laments that she has been "abandoned from your bed," a lament possibly reinforced by kisses and embraces albeit in the manner of "noble ladies" rather than the more forward manner of the Quarto "wife."

In Shakespeare's day, the enactment of some sexual intimacy in the world of the play and the possibility of still more to come may have raised some mild anxieties about the prospect of homoerotic contact between two male characters and two male actors. If so, then the audience was probably relieved when the page extricated himself from the problem of inventing the excuse, "in character," that Sly's doctors have ordered "her" temporarily to "absent me from your bed," lest sexual activity cause a recurrence of "your former malady." But the page concludes with a possible sexual innuendo—"I hope this reason stands for my excuse" (2.122–24)—which Sly seizes upon to acknowledge the difficulty of sexual abstinence once he has been aroused: "Ay, it stands so that I may hardly tarry so long. But I would be loath to fall into my dreams again. I will therefore tarry in despite of the flesh and the blood" (2.125–28).

The Quarto abbreviates and modifies the equivalent passage. It omits the pictures, shortens the description of the wife, leaves out the farcical by-play of Sly's not recognizing her as his wife and not knowing what to call her, and allows her only a single speech, less noteworthy for its tenderness and deference than for its frank erotic appeal:

> Oh that my lovelie Lord would once vouchsafe
> To looke on me, and leave these frantike fits,
> Or were I now but halfe so eloquent,
> To paint in words what ile performe in deeds,
> I know your honour then would pittie me. (Ind. 2.38)

The anticipated "dandling" may have come toward the end or after this speech, the tone of which suggests not the decorous sexual behaviour of the conduct books but coarse sexual farce such as occurs in Italian popular comedy.[28] More of a seductress than is Barthol'mew's noble lady, the Quarto "prettie wench" (Ind. 2.37), as Sly first called her, comes on so strongly that Sly seems to recoil, postponing sexual intimacy by enacting his alehouse version of courtly largesse:

> Harke you mistresse, wil you eat a peece of bread,
> Come sit downe on my knee, *Sim* drinke to hir *Sim*,
> For she and I will go to bed anon. (Ind. 2.43)

His drinking buddy "Sim," i.e., the Lord, announces the readiness of the Players, perhaps, to extricate the boy from an awkward situation. The Quarto "play-boy" had failed to heed the Lord's advice to devise an excuse, unlike Barthol'mew, and now seizes the opportunity to "go bid them begin their plaie" (Ind. 2.54). Sly orders his "wife" to "come againe" (Ind. 2.55), but there is no indication that "she" returns, although the boy may have reappeared in a female role in the play the company is offering for Sly's entertainment.

In the Folio, by contrast, Barthol'mew/Lady evidently remains at Sly's side after the messenger enters to announce the Players and they watch the first part of the play together. Where they watch from is not certain. They, and possibly some servants, may be "aloft," as the initial stage direction of the second Induction scene stipulates, or if they are on the main playing level, as the Quarto suggests, perhaps they withdraw to one side or the rear of the main playing area.[29] In either case, Barthol'mew/Lady, this acknowledged female impersonator, known to the audience and all characters but Sly, remains visible to the audience at least through their one and only subsequent bit of dialogue at the end of 1.1.

Sly and his "wife" are onstage and visible when Baptista and his two daughters enter at 1.1.47. The implied contrast between Barthol'mew/Lady on the one hand and Kate and Bianca on the other raised the same questions as did the contrast between Flute and the other female characters in *A Midsummer Night's Dream*. A male character in the world of the play pretending to be a woman was exactly what several female impersonators were doing in the world of the playhouse. The deconstructive effect was even stronger in *The Taming of the Shrew* because Kate and Bianca may have already been seen as, or were understood to be, members of the troupe of players whom the Lord welcomed, onstage, in Induction 1, whereas Hypolita, Hermia, Helena, and Titania appeared only as women with no explicit allusion to male actors playing the roles in the world of the play.

As characters in a play performed before Sly and his "wife," Kate and Bianca, like Thisbe, might have been played in a style that contrasted with Barthol'mew's Lady. They, after all, are supposedly being played by professional female impersonators, not by reluctant amateurs like Flute or eager but inexperienced amateurs like the Lord's page. In *Hamlet*, the inserted playlet of "The Murder of Gonzago" is written in rhymed couplets and archaic diction, enforcing a stylistic differentiation between the onstage players and the onstage spectators. The Player Queen, who was seen as a boy in 2.2, contrasts with Gertrude and Ophelia, who were played by professional female impersonators in the world of the playhouse. If *Hamlet* is a guide, then Kate and Bianca, as characters in a play-within-a-play would have been played, at least initially, in a more stylized, artificial and theatrically self-conscious mode than the Lady. That possibility may seem unlikely to us, given our knowledge of the centrality of Kate and Bianca, but spectators seeing the play for the first time would not yet possess that knowledge.

Lucentio's opening speech of 1.1 suggests such stylization. It is a stiff, formulaic piece of exposition ostensibly informing his servant, who surely already knows, that they are now in Padua, that it is a famous university town, and that he has come there to study.[30] Petruchio's opening speech of 2.2 is a condensed version of the same formula. The entrance of the Minola family, along with Gremio and Hortensio, is presented as a kind of inserted playlet, "some show to welcome us to town" (1.47), as Tranio puts it. He and Lucentio, who are themselves characters within a play performed before the mock-Lord and his Lady of the Induction, "*stand by*" like spectators to watch the scene.[31] To the naïve spectator, Baptista and his daughters are stock *commedia* figures, deriving from material domesticated decades before Gascoigne, to whose work, *The*

Supposes (1566, published 1579), adapted from Ariosto's *I Suppositi* (1509), Shakespeare's play twice alludes. Nested within two other concentric planes of reality, the world of the playhouse and the world of the Induction, Kate and Bianca might well have been played at the outset in a style consistent with the conventionality of the Italianate material. If so the male actor would have been required to offer a more self-consciously artificial representation of femininity than Barthol'mew's had provided in impersonating a married English gentlewoman along the naturalistic lines suggested by his Lord.

This initial pattern of stylistic differentiation, however, begins to change in the Folio version at some point after Sly and his "wife" disappear following the end of 1.1. The change accelerates as Shakespeare adds disguises and intertwines or crosses different strands of the plot, and as Petruchio's wooing of Kate moves away from Italianate neoclassical comedy and evolves into a more vigorous and original adaptation of native oral tales of "wife-taming."[32] The Quarto, by contrast, sustains the Induction frame throughout and indeed ends the play with Sly's reflections on the "dream" he has just had. But if the curtailment of the frame in the Folio text is deliberate and not the result, say, of faulty printer's copy, then the intended effect may well have been an intricate kind of eversion, whereby the play literally turns itself inside out, as the inner play comes gradually to eclipse the Induction framework, as figure and ground, frame and vision, switch places.[33]

The disappearance of the Induction characters may have stylistically enhanced this process of eversion, for once Sly's "Lady," initially played by the Page in a relatively naturalistic mode disappeared from view, that style became available, so to speak, for the young male actor playing Kate, as did the image of the married gentlewoman, an explicitly theatrical reconstruction of the idealized wife of conduct books and marriage manuals.

Even before Kate's complex transformation into this idealized wife, Shakespeare found other ways to remind the audience of a slight variation on this doubly constructed image of a married young gentlewoman. The first wooing strategy he devises for Petruchio is to sketch this idealized lady in language. Although Petruchio has been told and clearly believes that Kate is "an irksome, brawling scold" (Ind. 1.2.187), he tells Baptista that he has heard of "her beauty and her wit, / Her affability and bashful modesty, / Her wondrous qualities and mild behavior" (Ind. 2.1.48–50) and tries to impose this image on Kate by a kind of verbal magic. First he tests this strategy in soliloquy, using stock similes for female attractiveness:

> Say that she rail, why then I'll tell her plain
> She sings as sweetly as a nightingale;
> Say that she frown, I'll say she looks as clear
> As morning roses newly wash'd with dew. (2.1.166–69)

Abandoning the similes, he determines to create the model wife he seeks by simply superimposing his own version of reality on Kate's actual behaviour, substituting more direct language for the stock images:

> Say she be mute, and will not speak a word,
> Then I'll commend her volubility,
> And say she uttereth piercing eloquence. (2.1.170–72)

After an initial wit-combat with Kate, he tries out his plan:

> I find you passing gentle:
> 'Twas told me you were rough and coy and sullen,
> And now I find report a very liar;
> For thou art pleasant, gamesome, passing courteous,
> But slow in speech, yet sweet as spring-time flowers.
> Thou canst not frown, thou canst not look askaunce,
> Nor bite the lip, as angry wenches will,
> Nor hast thou pleasure to be cross in talk;
> But thou with mildness entertain'st thy wooers,
> With gentle conference, soft, and affable. (2.1.235–44)

One sign of the strain involved in this verbal magic is the simile of the hazel-twig, which leads him to describe her complexion as "as brown in hue / As hazel-nuts" (2.1.254–55), which in fact may not be such a compliment, as fashionable Englishwomen covered their faces to preserve an aristocratic pallor. But Petruchio recovers adroitly, if somewhat menacingly, in finding her "sweeter than the kernels," suggesting that her hard exterior can be cracked to expose the tender meat within.

The implied threat of violence is partly carried out once the play moves to Petruchio's house. Whereas many wife-taming tales involve direct physical assault of various kinds against the shrew, others displace the violence by having the husband kill or maim an animal by way of warning his wife.[34] Petruchio's cuffing or kicking of his household servants in 4.1 (added by eighteenth-century editors) is the theatricalized comedic form of such aggression. But he quickly moves to another phase, borrowed not from oral tales but from techniques used in taming falcons and other hunting birds, the withholding of food and sleep. What links both phases, intimidation by violence and subjugation by deprivation, is the exaggerated solicitude Petruchio claims to be showing toward Kate and the exquisite politeness of his manners. At the verbal level, he is treating her as if she were an ideal gentlewoman, while at the physical level he is trying to terrify her with displays of violence and break her spirit by weakening her body.

Petruchio's tactics up to this point are unsuccessful, as they must be if the play is not to end prematurely. His next phase seems to involve a return to his initial gambit, superimposing the image of gentlewoman upon his ungentle wife, only now done with clothing rather than with words. Although Petruchio several times disparages garments as inconsequential compared with the mind or soul, he tells Kate just after permitting her to eat and wishing "Much good do it unto thy gentle heart!" (4.3.51) that they will return to Padua dressed as befitting their rank—

> And revel it as bravely as the best,
> With silken coats and caps and golden rings,
> With ruffs and cuffs, and fardingales, and things,
> With scarfs and fans, and double change of brav'ry,
> With amber bracelets, beads, and all this knav'ry. (4.3.54)

As the use of loose syntax, bouncy rhythms and rhymed couplets implies, the offer is a ruse, for he will pretend to dislike the cap and the gown that the Haberdasher and tailor have made for her on the grounds that they are excessively ornate. When Kate protests that "gentlewomen wear such caps as these" he retorts that "when you are gentle, you shall have one too / And not till then" (4.3.70–72). As for the gown, in many productions Petruchio all but destroys it as he comments on its various features before ordering Grumio to take it "up," that is, away. From the sartorial details—a loose-bodied gown cut with perforations to reveal another layer of material, demi-cannon or trunk sleeves and a small compassed cape—it seems to be what the Tailor describes as made "according to the fashion and the time" (4.3.95).[35] The image of the gentlewoman is presented this time as clothing, possibly draped over a tailor's dummy, but again Petruchio dismisses garments as merely external, "For 'tis the mind that makes the body rich" (4.3.172), and he withholds them from Kate on the grounds that she cannot lay claim to attire appropriate to her social station until she is gentle in both senses of the word, that is, in behaviour as well as in rank.

In the scene on the way back to Padua, Kate appears to conform to Petruchio's desires, but it is not clear whether her obedience in the "sun-moon" sparring, and in calling Vincentio a young woman represent an inner change on her part, a tactical submission, or a willingness to join her husband in madcap pranks intended to twit their stolidly bourgeois society.

The idealized image of the gentlewoman appears again, not as clothing but rather as a purely verbal construction, as part of the joke on Vincentio. Petruchio conjures "her" into existence by invoking "her" social rank and standard physical attributes, this time with a Petrarchan coloration:

> Good morrow, *gentle* mistress, where away?
> Tell me, sweet Kate, and tell me truly too,

> Hast thou beheld a fresher *gentlewoman*?
> Such war of white and red within her cheeks!
> What stars do spangle heaven with such beauty
> As those two eyes become that heavenly face?
> Fair lovely maid, once more good day to thee.
> Sweet Kate, embrace her for her beauty's sake. (4.5.27–34; my emphases)

Perhaps determined not merely to obey her husband by following his lead in teasing Vincentio, Kate outdoes him by accentuating the "gentlewoman's" sexual status as a pubescent girl and prospective wife:

> Young budding virgin, fair, and fresh, and sweet,
> Whither away, or where is thy abode?
> Happy the parents of so fair a child!
> Happier the man whom favorable stars
> Allots thee for his lovely bedfellow! (4.5.36–40)

When Petruchio relabels Vincentio as "a man" and then begins a new round of teasing by adding increasingly derogatory adjectives ("old, wrinkled, faded, withered"), Kate again trumps her husband's lead with overstated and hence possibly ironic apologies:

> Pardon, old father, my mistaking eyes,
> That have been so bedazzled with the sun,
> That everything I look on seemeth green;
> Now I perceive thou art a reverent father.
> Pardon, I pray thee, for my mad mistaking. (4.5.44–48)

The modest tone of a model gentlewoman is subtly mocked, not only by the exaggerated deference toward Vincentio but by the allusion to Petruchio's previous arbitrariness over the "sun."

The image of the young gentlewoman, which they had both created out of words and images, much to Hortensio's alarm and Vincentio's consternation, they now dissolve. Whereas the image created by clothing was destroyed by Petruchio's tyrannical edict and perhaps even by his violent rending of the gown, the purely verbal image in this scene with Vincentio is created at Petruchio's initiative in the spirit of play, play shared with his wife at the expense of someone else.[36]

Although the text does not specify the motive for Kate's apparent change in this scene or anywhere else, leaving the matter open for performance choice and critical speculation, it does contrast her with several antitypes of the ideal married gentlewomen. One such antitype is her own earlier behaviour as a shrew. Another is her sister, who first appeared as a stereotypically dutiful daughter, later became the object of Lucentio's romantic clichés, and finally emerges as a disobedient wife. The last antitype of upperclass femininity is yet another type of unruly woman, the Widow, that is, a woman who has lived independent of male authority and is therefore a threat or a source of anxiety, as reflected by some (male) authors of conduct books.[37]

In the Quarto, there is no Widow; instead Kate has a second sister who merely replicates Bianca. In the Folio version of the play, the introduction of Hortensio's "wealthy widow," completes the triadic classification of women, in terms of their relationships to men, as maids, wives, and widows. In the Folio text, the introduction of this particular Widow adds a striking deviation from the ideal of the married gentlewoman to the ending of the play. We first hear of her in 4.2, when Hortensio claims that he will marry her "ere three days pass" (4.2.38) and that she has loved him as long as he has been wooing Bianca. Tranio speaks of Hortensio's decision immediately after he leaves the stage almost as if this match will provide another "show" to stand aside and watch: "I'faith, he'll have a lusty widow now / That shall be woo'd and wedded in a day" (4.2.50–51) and jokes with Bianca and Lucentio about whether Hortensio can apply to his bride the lessons he has learned at Petruchio's "taming-school" (4.2.54). Shakespeare makes Hortensio himself repeat this idea three scenes later, when, inspired by Petruchio's success, Hortensio closes the scene with a rhymed couplet:

> Have to my widow! and if she be froward,
> Then hast thou taught Hortensio to be untoward. (4.5.77–78)

But given the difference between Hortensio and Petruchio, the clear implication is that the Widow, now that she has a new husband whose authority she can defy, will become the type of unruly wife commonly labelled as a scold.

Just as the spectators first heard of Barthol'mew and the role he was to play before he entered as Sly's wife, so they hear of the Widow well before her first appearance onstage. Shakespeare implants the idea that she is both froward and lusty, conventional attributes of literary and theatrical widows, and that Hortensio, who is no Petruchio, will fail in his attempt to tame her. Not until the final scene does the audience actually get to see her, at which point she is Hortensio's wife. No sooner do Baptista's guests sit down at the banquet "to chat as well as eat" (5.2.11), than Hortensio complains of his Widow, and Petruchio teases them both, her acerbic retorts lead to a flyting with Kate, and she inspires Bianca to ill-tempered bawdy repartee. From one point of view, the Widow underscores the play's orthodoxy: Kate's shrewishness has been displaced on to this late-arriving figure, a reminder of what Petruchio's wife had once been before becoming (or adopting the role of) a model married gentlewoman. From another point of view, however, the Widow is clearly an antitype of that model, and the two female characters are obviously constructed at both theatrical and social levels. In contrast to Kate's enactment of a gentlewoman—polite, decorous, obedient to Petruchio—the Widow, joined by Bianca, scorns her husband's wishes and mocks Kate's demonstration of wifely obedience.

That demonstration is the play's final embodiment of the model of the married gentlewoman, a model earlier created by the Lord and his page, Barthol'mew, and now re-created by Petruchio and the boy actor playing Kate. Although a wager on the shrew's obedience is included in many of the oral tales cited by Brunvand, Shakespeare dilates and amplifies the motif. Kate comes at Petruchio's bidding, inquires "What is your will, sir, that you send for me?" (5.2.100), and silently agrees to return to the parlour to "fetch" the other wives. Although Petruchio has won the wager, he now proposes to win it

> better yet,
> And show more sign of her obedience,
> Her new built virtue and obedience. (5.2.120–22)

To test her, he orders her to throw her cap "under-foot," perhaps the very cap he had earlier denied her, and then bids her chastise the other wives:

> Katherine, I charge thee tell these headstrong women
> What duty they do owe their lords and husbands. (2.134–35)

Petruchio's language not only invokes the duty of obedience as emphasized in homilies, the marriage service, and the conduct books, but also echoes Sly's "wife" in her deferential declaration to her husband: "My husband and my lord, my lord and husband, / I am your wife in all obedience" (2.105–7).

The climax of Kate's demonstration of obedience is the lecture to the other women, which ends with her own symbolic gesture of submission, placing her hands beneath Petruchio's feet, a gesture which can be staged as anything between humiliating self-abnegation and ironic verbal formula. Whether one takes Kate's lecture as genuine, feigned, or playful, it is the longest speech of the play and requires the performer to display a poise and self-confidence which can seem to belong to the character as well. Whatever intention that performer provides, the attitudes expressed in the speech are conventionally patriarchal. Although the speech makes no reference to God, the Bible, or the sacredness of holy matrimony, it asserts that women "are bound to serve, love, and obey" (l. 64), and thus echoes the minister's question to the bride, found in the *Book of Common Prayer*, "Wilt thou obey him, and serve him, love, honor, and keep him, in sickness and in health?"[38] Whereas the Quarto explicitly invokes the creation myth and the sin of Eve to justify the subordination of women, the Folio relies on the analogy of the prince and the subject, and limited obedience to the "husband's honest will" (5.2.158). Such limitation of a wife's obedience, perhaps more theoretical than actual, was based on the doctrine of Christian conscience and evidently originated with Erasmus in his *Institutio matrimonii christiani* (1526): "If he orders you to do something that is contrary to faith or good manners, gently refuse to obey him; but if he persists in wishing to be obeyed, remember that it is better to obey God than men."[39] In place of the Quarto's scripturally sanctioned denigration of woman, compressed into the familiar pun of "woe is man" (xviii.34), the Folio places conditions on wives' obedience and bases it not on their inherent inferiority but on their sense of obligation and gratitude, and on their desire for domestic harmony, central tenets of many marriage manuals of the period.[40]

There are also possible ironies in the speech, as many directors and critics have noted: its praise of husbands who risk their lives to care for their wives points up the fact that most of the men in the play are landowning gentry or urban upper bourgeoise, the declaration of women's weaker physical traits made by a female impersonator, and the final gesture of submission, the hand beneath the foot, is absurdly hyperbolic. In original performance, even spectators' metatheatrical awareness of female impersonation, a straightforward delivery of the speech would have produced still deeper irony: Kate's transformation into the ideal of wifely obedience is labelled as the fulfillment of a male fantasy, constructed at many levels—by the male performer, by Kate, by Petruchio, by Barthol'mew, by the Lord, and hence by the patriarchal norms of both "Padua" and early modern England.

This deconstruction of Kate as an icon of wifely obedience would have been enhanced by any doubling of male performers in the play's female roles. Some kind of doubling involving the Widow seems quite likely inasmuch as she does not appear until the play is more than half over, while boy actors appearing in the Induction had been available since the Induction framework disappeared, presumably by design, in the first act. If noticed, as I assume it would have been, such doubling would have emphasized the theatrical and social constructedness of the female roles by heightening the audience's metatheatrical awareness of crossgender casting and reminding them of the female roles these same performers had played in the Induction.

All of the doubling possibilities are rich in implications. (1) If the actor playing Barthol'mew/Lady doubled as the Widow, then that original model married gentlewoman now metatheatrically returned, but its constructedness was underscored by the fact that the same performer played both that model and its unruly antitype. This effect would have been heightened if the Hostess and Bianca were doubled by a third boy. (2) If the Hostess and the Widow were doubled, then the unruly antitype of the Induction returned greatly amplified by the repetition. But this male nightmare of rebellious womanhood was metatheatrically deconstructed into a male construct and hence weakened or contained, and also contrasted with its opposite male construct, Kate's embodiment of the role of idealized married gentlewoman. (3) The Widow was "tripled" by the boy who played both the Hostess and Barthol'mew, which is possible as the former disappears early in the first scene of the Induction and the latter does not appear until well into the second scene. That possibility suggests that a skilled female impersonator, such as the boy who played the shrewish and the obedient Kate, could represent both idealized and unruly stereotypes, and had done so in the Induction.

However much such doubling scenes would have enhanced a metatheatrical frame, such an effect was based on the audience's awareness of male performers *per se*, whether or not they reappeared in successive roles. What is repeated at the end of the play is the reinstatement of the ideal married gentlewoman, the deliberate parallel between the reformed Kate, as played by a boy actor, and Sly's lady, as represented by Barthol'mew under his master's direction. Such a reprise of the Induction would have compensated for what many critics of the Folio version have lamented: its failure to complete the framework of the Induction by supplying a dramatic epilogue involving Sly.[41] The Quarto ending does indeed bring Sly back to conclude the frame and does so with acute irony, for he leaves the stage for his final exit as Petruchio's self-proclaimed disciple:

> I know now how to tame a shrew,
> I dreamt upon it all this night till now,
> And thou hast wakt me out of the best dreame
> That ever I had in my life, but Ile to my
> Wife presently and tame her too
> And if she anger me. (xiv. 15)

Sly's swagger, followed by the Tapster's eagerness to accompany him home and "heare the rest that thou has dreamt to night" (Ind. 2.21–22) turns the drunken tinker into a theatrical spectacle to be witnessed offstage or at some future presentation. Sly's swagger also labels him as a henpecked husband in desperate need of a role-model like Petruchio, and makes a similar jibe at male spectators who responded enthusiastically to this wishful fantasy of wife-taming.

The Folio ending is far more subtle. There is no explicit framing of the Petruchio-Kate plot to undercut it with irony. Instead, the text, as originally played with male actors in female roles, provides a metatheatrical frame, a perspective for reading Kate's evident submission as the final incarnation of an elaborately but transparently constructed ideal of upperclass femininity: that is to say, a doubly theatrical replication of a socially generated role. Instead of using Sly to subvert Petruchio as an icon of patriarchal authority, as the Quarto ending does, the Folio playfully contrasts opposing stereotypes of the gentlewoman and the scold and juxtaposes the ideal fantasy with the dreaded nightmare, exploiting the audience's realization that these familiar cultural constructs or roles were theatrical illusions created by male performers.

NOTES

Originally published in *The Yearbook of English Studies* 23 (1993): 143–66. Reprinted with the permission of Michael Shapiro and *The Yearbook of English Studies*.

1. Linda Woodbridge, *Women and the English Renaissance: Literature and the Nature of Womankind, 1540–1620* (Urbana: University of Illinois Press, 1984), 221–22, n. 22.

2. Michael Hattaway, "Drama and society," in *The Cambridge Companion to English Drama*, ed. A. R. Braunmuller and Michael Hattaway (Cambridge: Cambridge University Press, 1990), 101. On the complexity of tone at the end, see also *The Taming of the Shrew*, ed. H. J. Oliver (Oxford: Oxford University Press, 1982), 40–43 and 56–57. The debate between "revisionist" and "anti-revisionist" critics is concisely summarized by John C. Bean, "Comic Structure and the Humanizing of Kate in *The Taming of the Shrew*," in *The Woman's Part: Feminist Criticism of Shakespeare*, ed. Carolyn Ruth Swift Lenz and others (Urbana: University of Illinois Press, 1980), 65–66 and 75–76.

3. Stanley Wells and Gary Taylor, "No Shrew, A Shrew and The Shrew: Internal Revision in *The Taming of the Shrew*," in *Shakespeare: Text, Language, Criticism: Essays in Honor of Martin Spevack*, ed. Bernhard Fabian and Kurt Tetzeli von Rosador (Hildesheim: Olms-Weidmann, 1987), 367–69.

4. Karen Newman, "Renaissance Family Politics and Shakespeare's *The Taming of the Shrew*," *ELR*, 16 (1986): 100. The essay has been reprinted in Newman's book, *Fashioning Femininity and the English Renaissance Drama* (Chicago: University of Chicago Press, 1991), 33–50.

5. Colley Cibber, *An Apology for the Life of Mr. Colley Cibber*, 2 vols. (London: Nimmo, 1889), 1: 90. Harley Granville-Barker, *Prefaces to Shakespeare*, 2 vols. (London: Batsford, 1958), 1: 14. Richard Flecknoe "A Character of a Proud Woman," *Aenigmatical Characters* [London, 1658], sig. Bᵛ.), denigrates the skill of female impersonation at the Red Bull playhouse, when he compares his haughty lady, who "looks high and speaks in a majestic tone," to "one that plaide the *Queens* part at the Bull." On theatrical apprentices, see G. E. Bentley, *The Profession of Player in Shakespeare's Time, 1590–1642* (Princeton: Princeton University Press, 1984), 113–46. Bentley challenges the evidence for the theory that adult male actors played some female roles; see also Richard David, "Shakespeare and the Players," in *Studies in Shakespeare: British Academy Letters*, ed. Peter Alexander (London: Oxford University Press, 1964), 42–45; and J. B. Streett, "The Durability of Boy Actors," *Notes and Queries* 218 (1973): 461–65.

6. Richard Rastall, "Female Roles in All-Male Casts," *Medieval English Theatre* 7 (1985): 25–50.

7. T. J. King, "The Versatility of Shakespeare's Actors," in *Shakespeare and Dramatic Tradition: Essays in Honor of S. F. Johnson*, ed. W. R. Elton and William B. Long (Newark: University of Delaware Press, 1989), 144–50. See also T. J. King, "The King's Men on Stage: Actors and Their Parts, 1611–1632," in *Elizabethan Theatre* 9 (1981), Papers from Ninth International Conference on Elizabethan Theatre, Waterloo, Ontario, 1981, ed. G. R. Hibbard, 32–37. On Ezekiel Fenn, see G. E. Bentley, *The Jacobean and Caroline Stage*, 7 vols. (Oxford: Clarendon Press, 1941–1968), 2: 433–34; Bentley reprints Henry Glapthorne's

poem, "For *Ezekiel Fen* at his first Acting a Mans Part," from his 1639 Quarto, *Poems*.

8. David Bevington (*From "Mankind" to Marlowe* [Cambridge: Harvard University Press, 1964], 79), cautiously observes a gradual but uneven tendency for younger actors to specialize in female roles. Bevington transcribes the doubling schemes on the title pages of plays "offered for acting" (265–73). Specialization in female roles appears to be indicated by the doubling scheme in the manuscript of Merbury's *The Marriage of Wit and Wisdom* (1579) and on the title pages of the printed texts of Pikeryng's *Horestes* (1567), *Trial of Treasure* (1567), Preston's *Cambyses* (1569–1584), Wapull's *Tide Tarrieth No Man* (1576), Garter's *Virtuous and Godly Susanna* (1578), *Mucedorus* (1598), and *The Fair Maid of the Exchange* (1607).

9. *The Book of Sir Thomas More*, ed. W. W. Greg, Malone Society Reprints, no. 24 (Oxford, 1911), ll. 932–35.

10. Michael Shapiro, "Lady Mary Wroth Describes a Boy Actress," *Medieval and Renaissance Drama in England* 4 (1987): 187–94. Jackson is quoted on pp. 189–90.

11. Thomas Heywood, *An Apology for Actors* (London, 1612), C_3^v. Peter Holland ("The Resources of Characterization in Othello," 41 [1989], 128), suggests "divisions between . . . [boys] who play women's parts and those who do not," which seems plausible from the chapter on apprenticeship in G. E. Bentley, *The Profession of Player* (113–46), but I know of no detailed study of the problem. If Holland is right, then some boy actresses, e.g., Dick Robinson and Nicholas Burt, may have been all the more easily recognized, as Heywood claims.

12. Samuel Johnson, "Preface [to Shakespeare], 1765," in *Johnson on Shakespeare*, ed. A. Sherbo, *Works*, 19 vols. (New Haven: Yale University Press, 1958), 7: 77; and S. L. Bethell, *Shakespeare and the Popular Dramatic Tradition* (Durham, N.C.: Duke University Press, 1944), 26 and passim; and "Shakespeare's Actors," *RES*, n.s. 1 (1950): 203. Bethell's position has been restated by P. H. Parry, "The Boyhood of Shakespeare's Heroines," *ShS* 42 (1989): 99–109.

13. *Jack Juggler*, ed. Eunice Lilian Smart, Malone Society Reprints, no. 75 (1933): ll. 229–36. I quote throughout from this text.

14. T. W. Craik, *The Tudor Interlude* (Leicester: Leicester University Press, 1958), 45.

15. According to Susan Savitsky, *Red Pumps, Size 13: Drag Styles at the Pyramid Club* (unpublished master's thesis, New York University, 1987): the New York transvestite theatre uses the terms "comic drag" and "glamour drag," respectively, to refer to caricatured and naturalistic female characters played by men. Savitsky's work is cited in June Schlueter's unpublished paper for the seminar on female impersonation at the World Shakespeare Congress, 1991. I am also indebted to the other participants in the seminar, particularly to Henk Gras, Peter Hyland, Yoscharu Ozaki, Francis Barasch, and Bruce Smith.

16. Crossgender disguise films like *Some Like It Hot* and *Tootsie* create similar effects, as women playing women in a relatively natural style are in constant relationship with men playing women in a much broader manner. English Pantomime regularly contrasts the Panto Dame, played farcically by an adult, male actor (often a comedian of large girth) with other female roles, not to mention the male

lead, or principal boy, who is always played by an actress. See the interesting observations by the comedian Roy Hudd on the two chief contrasting styles of female impersonation included in an edition of *The Birth of Merlin* (Shaftesbury: Element Books, 1989), 58–59.

17. Victor O. Freeburg, *Disguise Plots in Elizabethan Drama* (New York: Columbia University Press, 1915), 101–20. *The Merry Wives of Windsor*, in *Riverside Shakespeare*, ed. G. B. Evans (Boston: Houghton Mifflin, 1974), 5: 5., 184. Unless otherwise noted, subsequent references to Shakespeare are to this edition.

18. William Ringler ("The Number of Actors in Shakespeare's Early Plays," in *The Seventeenth-Century Stage*, ed. Gerald Bentley [Chicago: University of Chicago Press, 1968], 110–34, suggests that four adult actors doubled as Titania's attendants and as Flute and three other mechanicals. But this suggestion seems unlikely given the brevity of fairies' lines and Bottom's condescending attitudes toward them. Richard Fotheringham ("The Doubling of Roles on the Jacobean Stage," *Theatre Review* 10 [1985]: 21), also observes that 3.1 and 4.1, the two scenes in which Titania's fairies appear, "are both effectively directed by the major actors; the first by Titania . . . and the second by Bottom." For fuller discussion of reflexive effects involving female impersonation in *A Midsummer Night's Dream*, see my essay in *Elizabethan Theatre XIII* (forthcoming). On Robinson, see Anne Barton, *Ben Jonson, Dramatist* (Cambridge: Cambridge University Press, 1984), 228.

19. *Hamlet*, ed. Philip Edwards (Cambridge: Cambridge University Press, 1985), 2.2.389 n. In Kosintev's film, the boy dons a blond wig with one long thick braid, which replicates Ophelia's hair style and which Hamlet catches himself caressing.

20. *The Taming of the Shrew*, ed. Ann Thompson (Cambridge: Cambridge University Press, 1984), 470.

21. *The Taming of a Shrew*, 1.57, in *Narrative and Dramatic Sources of Shakespeare*, ed. Geoffrey Bullough, 8 vols. (London: Routledge, 1957–1975), I: 70. Subsequent citations refer to this text. The relationship of *A Shrew* and *The Shrew*, or Quarto and Folio as I shall for greater convenience refer to them, is still unclear. Some scholars believe the Quarto came first, others that it was derived from the Folio text, a third group that both derive from a lost version. The arguments are reviewed by Ann Thompson, 164–74; and H. J. Oliver, 22–34.

22. Scott McMillin ("Casting for Pembroke's Men: The *Henry VI* Quartos and *The Taming of a Shrew*," *Shakespeare Quarterly* 23 [1972]: 152 n), suggests that "the boy actor of the visiting players (Induction) doubled as one of Alfonso's daughters in the rest of the play." McMillin argues that Pembroke's Men regularly employed four female impersonators.

23. Several secondary works survey the manuals and treatises on the duties and responsibilities of married women: Ruth Kelso, *Doctrine for the Lady of the Renaissance* (Urbana: University of Illinois Press, 1956), 78–135; Joan Larsen Klein, "Women and Marriage in Renaissance England: Male Perspectives," in *The Elizabethan Woman, Topic* no. 36 (Washington, PA: Washington and Jefferson College, 1982), 20–37; Suzanne W. Hull, *Chaste, Silent and Obedient* (San Marino: Huntington Library, 1982), 47–56; Ian Maclean, *The Renaissance Notion of Woman* (Cambridge: Cambridge University Press, 1980), 51–59.

24. William Perkins, *Christian Economy* (1609), chapter 10, "Of the Communion of Married Folks, and of Due Benevolence," quoted in *Daughters, Wives, and Widows: Writings by Men about Women and Marriage in England, 1500–1640*, ed. Joan Larsen Klein (Urbana: University of Illinois Press, 1992), 170. I am grateful to Professor Klein for allowing me to examine parts of the book in typescript and for commenting on a draft of this essay. Perkins's warning is amplified by R[obert] C[leaver], *Godly Forme of Householde Government* (1598): "So that marriage is not a mad and dissolute estate, neither are husbands to turne their wives into whores, or wives their husbands into whoremasters, by immoderate, intemperate, or excessive lust" (1600 ed., sig. K7^v). See also sig M4^v and Kelso, 100.

25. Richard Braithwaite, *The English Gentlewoman* (1631), 89 (sig. N). Compare Kelso, 101.

26. Braithwaite, 42, 82–83 (sig. G^v, M^v–M$_2$). Compare Kelso, 106.

27. "An Homily of the State of Matrimony," *The Second Tome of Homilies* (1563), quoted in *Daughters, Wives, and Widows*, 17. The importance of the duty of obedience is stated with equal bluntness in one of the most often reprinted marriage manuals of the period, Juan Luis Vives, *A Very Fruitful and Pleasant Book Called the Instruction of a Christian Woman* (1523), trans. Richard Hyrde (1529), *The Second Book of the Instruction of a Christian Woman*: "Neither I wolde that she should love her husband as one loveth his friend or his brother, that is to say, I will that she shall give him great worship, reverence, great obedience, and service also; being which thing not only the example of the old world teacheth us, but also all laws, both spiritual and temporal, and Nature herself cryeth and commandeth that the woman shall be subject and obedient to the man. And in all kinds of beasts the females obey the males, and waiten upon them, and fawn upon them, and suffer themself to be corrected of them. Which thing Nature sheweth must be and is convenient to be done." (Quoted in *Daughters, Wives, and Widows*, 114). See also Kelso, 94.

28. At various times, *commedia dell'arte* troupes contrasted romantic heroines played by women with comic servants played by men, as Frances Barasch demonstrates in an unpublished paper for the World Shakespeare Conference, 1991.

29. See Ann Thompson, 181–85.

30. H. J. Oliver, 60.

31. G.K. Hunter, *John Lyly: The Humanist as Courtier* (London: Routledge and Kegan Paul, 1962), 309–10, and *Leo Salinger, Shakespeare and the Traditions of Comedy* (Cambridge: Cambridge University Press, 1974), 270–72. For another example of "standing by," see 1.2.142.

32. Jan Brunvand, "The Folktale Origin of *The Taming of the Shrew*," *Shakespeare Quarterly* 17 (1966): 345–59. Brunvand's doctoral dissertation (Indiana University, 1961): from which this article is derived, has been reprinted under the title *"The Taming of the Shrew": A Comparative Study* (New York: Garland, 1991).

33. Barbara Freedman, *Staging the Gaze: Postmodernism, Psychoanalysis, and Shakespearean Comedy* (Ithaca, N.Y.: Cornell University Press, 1991), 126. See also fig. 10, M. C. Escher's *The Print Gallery* (1956), 125, and Freedman's commentary on framed material enclosing its frames.

34. See Brunvand for examples.

35. See Walter Hodges' illustration of the gown and cap in the Cambridge edition (33).
36. Brunvand (354), points out that the "absurd statements" are found in many oral wife-taming tales. For "playful" readings of the play, see J. Dennis Huston, *Shakespeare's Comedies of Play* (New York: Columbia University Press, 1981), 64; Marianne L. Novy, *Love's Argument: Gender Relations in Shakespeare* (Chapel Hill: University of North Carolina Press, 1984), 61; Alexander Legatt, *Shakespeare's Comedy of Love* (London: Methuen, 1974): 41–62. Camille Wells Slights ("The Raw and Cooked in *The Taming of the Shrew*," *JEGP*, 88 [1989]: 187–89, who finds that such "playful" readings overstress the separation of Petruchio and Kate from their community, argues that they, and Shakespeare, ultimately endorse its basic social values but assert active control over them.
37. See the section on widows in Kelso, 121–32.
38. "The Form and Solemnization of Matrimony," from *The Book of Common Prayer* (1559), quoted in *Daughters, Wives, and Widows*, 6.
39. Quoted and trans. by Constance Jordan, *Renaissance Feminism: Literary Texts and Political Models* (Ithaca, NY: Cornell University Press, 1990), 62, who comments as follows:

> The parallel between the family and the state is a rediscovery of humanists, but Erasmus is the first of them to link a wife's obedience to the more general injunction against disobedience to governing authorities which applies to all Christians. Discussing instances in which a wife may disobey her husband, he follows a line of reasoning identical to that of Luther when he argues for the right of Christians to liberty of conscience.

Similar attitudes are expressed in other manuals. See Robert Cleaver's *A Godly Forme*: "Ye must not this obedience so far extend, as that the husband should command any thing contrary to her honour, credit, and salvation, but as it is comely in the Lord" (sig. P_2); compare sig. $P_5{}^v$–P6. For commentary, see Jordan, 217–18.

40. Bean, 67–71.
41. The debate on whether or not the dropping of the Sly framework is deliberate is concisely summarized by Ann Thompson (170–73).

Cultural Control
in *The Taming of the Shrew*

LAURIE E. MAGUIRE

To say that Shakespeare's *The Taming of the Shrew* is a play about taming is
to state the obvious: the "wooing" of Katherine by Petruccio, perhaps more
than any other main plot in Shakespeare, dominates performance and criticism
of the play. But taming can take many forms, and I want to argue that *The Taming of the Shrew* is imbued with three forms of cultural control: the hunt,
music, and marriage. These variations on a theme are linked subtly but crucially by the central image of music, and are introduced through the cynegetic
motif that occupies the play's first two scenes.

I. HUNTING

The Taming of the Shrew opens with Christopher Sly, "old Sly's son of Burton Heath, by birth a pedlar, by education a cardmaker, by transmutation a
bearherd, and now by present profession a tinker" (Ind. 2.17–20). Further
demoted by drink from tinker to "swine," the sleeping Sly is discovered by a
creature from the opposite end of the social hierarchy, a Lord, who is abroad
with his men enjoying that activity of the allegedly civilized classes: the hunt.

The sixteenth-century hunt embodied class and privilege.[1] As Richard
Leppert (1993) explains (123), it was a "ritualized exercise" requiring exercise and control, the choreography of men and hounds.[2] It took place on one's
own land; it was a musical activity; it was predominantly a male sport; and it
demonstrated male power and ownership in its most primitive form: "the right
to kill" (Leppert 1993, 126).

The musical component of Renaissance hunting was tripartite: a
sequence or blend of the twelve-note French horn, the baying of hounds, and
the human voice "sometimes playing separately and according a role to the
individual soloist, sometimes joining in a spontaneous and joyful polyphony,
crowned by a formal and triumphal coda" (Cummins 1988, 160). The French

horn, more complicated and sophisticated than its English counterpart, delivered "calls" to direct the hunt. Sequences and combinations of long and short notes are described (and sometimes transcribed in linear form) in all hunting manuals. Thus, the musical sequence can indicate hounds running, a view of an animal (a different sequence for each kind), water, bay and request for help, death, a call for hounds to assemble, a call for hunters to assemble, a retreat, and so forth. Some of these situations also permitted oral calls, although usually the human voice was restricted to the encouragement or subduing of hounds. The hounds themselves were the most musical part of the hunt, selected more for their cry than for their speed (Theseus's hounds are "slow in pursuit, but matched in mouth like bells": *MND* 4.1.122). Gervase Markham (1615) acknowledges "sweetnesse of cry," *"loudnes of cry,"* and "deepnes of cry" as important factors in selecting a pack of hounds, and advises on breeds for bass, counter-tenor, and treble—beagles, for example, for trebles (1: 7–8). "Of these three sorts of mouthes," he continues, "if your Kennell be (as neer as you can) equally compounded, you shall finde it most perfect and delectable: for though they haue not the thunder and loudnesse of the great *dogges*, which may be compared to the high winde instruments, yet they will haue the tunable sweetnes of the best compounded consorts, & sure a man may finde as much Art and delight in a *Lute*, as in an *Organ*" (1: 10). Whereas the horn's pitch was constant, hounds enriched the musical atmosphere through their variety of pitch. Such variety was not simply for acoustic pleasure. As John Cummins (1988) explains, this canine music was "crucially informative to the hunter skilled in its interpretation and intimately aware of the notes of each individual hound" (169).

Renaissance quarry were many and various, the noblest being the deer, although foxes and hares were frequent targets, particularly toward the end of the seventeenth century when deforestation, combined with the introduction of firearms, reduced the number of deer (Carr 1986, 23–24). Foxhunting had a long history, if only as a form of pest control,[3] and the anthropomorphization of the fox as wily and cunning makes one dwell on the appropriateness of the Lord finding a creature who is literally Sly. Hunting took place very early in the morning: early morning is the ideal time to trap foxes, who feed at night and are slow and lethargic before dawn, their evening meal undigested. (Theseus, enjoying an early-morning hunt in *A Midsummer Night's Dream*, greets the sleeping lovers with the sarcastic surmise that they have risen early to observe the rite of May, and, in the eighteenth century, Sir Walter Bagot reprimanded his sons for their tardiness in arriving at four in the morning [Auden 1905, 3].) Christopher Sly is similarly victimized by his evening in the tavern, his inebriation not yet neutralized by sufficient sleep. Despite a temporary reprieve, in which he is elevated to a Lord and offered, as aesthetic pleasure, images of the chase (Venus and Adonis, Jove and Io, Apollo and Daphne), Sly is killed off by the dramatist in the course of the play.

Of the three pictures of the chase offered to Sly in the induction, two concern women being pursued and/or raped by a god, and show the relevance of the hunt to issues of gender. The characterization of women as the sexual victims of the male hunter has a long tradition. Virgil presents the lovesick Dido as "a doe caught off her guard and pierced by an arrow from some armed shepherd" (*Aeneid*, 99). The poem "The wofull wordes of the Hart to the Hunter" in *The Noble Arte of Venerie* presents the stag at bay in sexually suggestive terms: "Since I in deepest dread, do yelde my selfe to Man, / And stand full still betwene his legs, which earst full wildly ran" (Turbervile 1575, 136). *Titus Andronicus* makes this connection more explicitly when Chiron and Demetrius view the rape of Lavinia as a variant of the more usual hunt:

> My lords, a solemn hunting is in hand . . .
> Single you thither then this dainty doe. (2.1.113, 118)

> Chiron, we hunt not, we, with horse nor hound,
> But hope to pluck a dainty doe to ground. (2.2.25–26)

In *Troilus and Cressida* Pandarus sings a salacious song underpinned by complex metaphors of sex and hunting:

> For O love's bow
> Shoots buck and doe.
> The shaft confounds
> Not that it wounds,
> But tickles still the sore.

> These lovers cry, "O! O!", they die.
> Yet that which seems the wound to kill
> Doth turn "O! O!" to "ha ha he!"
> So dying love lives still. (3.1.112–20)

David Willbern (1978, 164) lists further examples from medieval literature to Shakespeare that show the traditional association of hunting with sexuality.

In general in the Shakespeare canon, images of hunting evince nothing but sympathy of the hunted, who is presented as an innocent victim. Julius Caesar, harmlessly deaf, epileptic, and unfit, is butchered:

> Here wast thou bayed, brave hart;
> Here didst thou fall, and here thy hunters stand
> Signed in thy spoil and crimsoned in thy lethe.
> O world, thou wert the forest to this hart;
> And this indeed, O world, the heart of thee.

> How like a deer strucken by many princes
> Dost thou here lie! (3.1.205–11)

The slaughtered children of Macduff are "murdered deer" (*Macbeth* 4.3.207). Duke Frederick is troubled by conscience when killing venison in the forest of Arden, questioning why the "native burghers" should "in their own confines with forked heads / Have their round haunches gored" (*AYLI* 2.1.23–25). Similar scruples are voiced by the Princess of France in *Love's Labor's Lost* (4.1.7–35).[4] Such sympathetic reactions were atypical in the sixteenth century, the notable other exceptions being Erasmus, More, and Montaigne (Cartmill 1993, 76–78).

Shakespeare's sympathy is of interest in light of the association of both Sly and Katherine with quarry in *The Taming of the Shrew*. These two social subordinates are linked in that both are manipulated and "practised upon" by a Lord. The common denominator of class and gender issues in the cynegetic motif is made clear in act 5, when the subject of the hunt is revisited metaphorically, thereby concluding Sly's apparently incomplete tale analogously in a discussion of marriage. The three husbands in act 5 compare and bet on their wives' performance, as the three huntsmen compare and wager on their dogs in the induction; the induction's wager of twenty pounds becomes the twenty crowns of act 5, a sum rejected by Petruccio in a hunting analogy: "I'll venture so much of my hawk or hound, / But twenty times so much upon my wife" (5.2.75–76).[5] This episode is imbued with the language and attitude of animal sports, from Petruccio's and Hortensio's hortatory cries ("To her, Kate!" / "To her, widow!" / "A hundred marks my Kate does put her down" [5.2.35–37]) through the characterization of Bianca as a bird ("Am I your bird? I mean to shift my bush, / And then pursue me as you draw your bow" [5.2.48–49 and cf. lines 52–53]) to the depiction of Kate as a deer that attacks ("'Tis thought your deer does hold you at a bay" [5.2.58]). Like the tinker Sly, women are reduced to the status of animals. Shakespeare's sympathetic attitude elsewhere to the victims of hunting may suggest that he viewed the predicament of the cornered female in *The Taming of the Shrew* as one to be condemned, rather than the male position of tamer as one to be celebrated. However, before drawing any interpretive conclusions about the presentation of women as deer in act 5 of this play, we must first consider an analogous topic: the depiction of women as musical instruments.

II. PLAYING

There are over one hundred musical allusions in *The Taming of the Shrew* (Waldo and Herbert 1959 and cf. West 1974). From the Apollonian "twenty caged nightingales" whose singing is offered to Christopher Sly, to Petruccio's musical puns on "sol-fa" and "burden" and his snatches of popular songs; from Hortensio's disguise as a music master, with his broken lute in 2.1 and his new gamut in 3.1, to the matrimonial harmony that Lucentio musically anticipates in act 5—"At last, though long, our jarring notes agree"—the play uses the nodal image of music to chart the development of the characters' personal relationships. More important, musical images and actions reveal the personal makeup of Katherine. The figurative association between bad behavior and bad music was a Renaissance commonplace, and, as T. R. Waldo and T. W. Herbert note (1959, 193), "[t]wo strands of meaning, the musical and the belligerent, are united when Kate uses the musical instrument as a weapon." Decisively rejecting musical instruction and the heavenly harmony associated with it, Katherine seems set to steer the play in the direction of "loud alarums."

From Boethius the Renaissance inherited a tripartite understanding of musical relations: *musica mundana* referred to the harmony of the universe; *musica humana* referred to the harmony that resulted when man was tuned by reason; *musica instrumentalis* referred to practical music making (Hollander 1961, 24–25; Ross 1966, 108; Finney 1953, 88–90). The dominant iconographic image linking all three was a stringed instrument, a universal lute-harp-lyre "possessing the ethical and esthetic values of the Greek *kithara*" (Hollander 128). It was logical that, if the heavens were perceived as "a tuned stringed instrument, so man with his cords and fibers, physiologically associated with stringed musical instruments, could be considered to require an analogous harmonious tuning spiritually as well as medically. Hence the idea of Concord very often is represented . . . by a stringed instrument" (Ross 1966, 109).

Presented as (or presenting herself as) a paragon of personal harmony and feminine perfection (at least in public), Bianca expertly manipulates the conventional musical associations:

> Sir, to your pleasure humbly I subscribe.
> My books and instruments shall be my company,
> On them to look and practice by myself. (1.1.81–83)

Lucentio responds appropriately, comparing Bianca with Minerva (not only the Roman goddess of wisdom but the "mythical originator of musical instruments" [Waldo and Herbert 1959, 197]), an equation restated by Hortensio in 3.1.4–5: "this Bianca is, / The patroness of heavenly harmony." In her Cambridge edition of the play Ann Thompson (1984) reprints Holman Hunt's suggestive painting of *Bianca, Patroness of Heavenly Harmony*, in which Bianca's perfectly tuned character is symbolized by the lute in her hands. Throughout *The Taming of the Shrew* Katherine is presented in musical opposition to her sister as a woman who mistakes her frets, a discordant instrument who must be tuned.

This is just another way of saying that she is a volatile animal who must be tamed, as Katherine herself seems to realize when she rejects the lute and the lute lesson. Although, prima facie, the ambience of this episode seems innocuous enough, Katherine's violence may be prompted by the degrading horse-breaking attitude of her father, implicit in his question to Litio, "thou canst not *break her* to the lute?" (2.1.147, emphasis added; cf. Kahn 1981, 108). The vocabulary of breaking in untamed horses, of teaching them "the manage," is plentiful in the play, and resurfaces in a seventeenth-century treatise, Thomas Tryon's *The Way to Health* (1683). This book of medical miscellany and related advice concludes with a chapter that combines astrological and musical wisdom: "*Cyterns* and *Gitterns* are under the *Moon* and *Venus*, in the Sign [of] *Sagitary*; being well managed, they yield pleasant, soft, effeminate Harmonies" (ch. 21).[6] This musical language, in which citterns (wire-strung members of the lute family) and gitterns (an etymological if not musicological cognate of the guitar[7]) are viewed as female instruments ("under the *Moon*") who must be properly handled ("well managed") before making appropriately feminine sound, epitomizes the treatment of Katherine in the play.

Music was, like woman, both divine and dangerous, capable of soothing or exciting, able to lead progressively to an appreciation of higher things (beauty, the good, the spiritual) or to damnation (for music encourages passivity, idleness: like sex it requires a receptive partner who could be physically or aurally "ravished"; Hollander 1961, 200–1). In this respect music is linked to those other artistic skills, rhetoric and face painting, which may embellish a natural attribute (eloquence, beauty) for the glory of God or may conceal and deceive.[8] In addition, the technical vocabulary used for musical playing was unmistakably suggestive. "Touch" denotes both a musical action and a caress: Rolliardo in James Shirley's *The Bird in a Cage* boasts, "I can touch a Wench better then a Lute" (1.1.11–12), and a gentleman in Thomas Nashe's *Anatomie of Absurditie* tells what it is "to *tickle* a Citterne or haue a sweet *stroke* on the lute" (7; emphasis added). It was hardly a large or difficult step for the Renaissance to map attitudes to music onto attitudes to women.[9]

This equation of music with women leads easily to a series of images in which musical instruments, and music in general, are used as an elaborate synecdoche for sexual organs or sexual activity. In 1566, in Lewis Wager's *The Life and Repentance of Mary Magdalene*, we find explicit and extended sexual/musical punning (lines 837–44):

> *INFIDELITIE*:   Mistresse Mary can you not play on the virginals?
> *MARY*:   Yes sweete heart, that I can, also on the regals,
>   There is no instrument but that handle I can,
>   I thynke as well as any gentlewoman.

> *INFIDELITIE*:   If that you can play vpon the recorder,
> I haue as fayre a one as any is in this border,
> Truely you haue not sene a more goodlie pipe,
> It is so bigge that your hand can it not gripe.[10]

Preparing a seduction scene between Doll Common and the Spanish count in Jonson's *The Alchemist*, Face prompts: "Sweet DOL, / You must goe tune your virginall, no loosing / O' the least time" (where "tune" means "play" as well as "tune"; 3.3.67–68). In the same scene Doll is urged to keep a client nocturnally awake with her "drum" (3.3.44).[11] In *Cymbeline* Cloten confesses:

> I am advised to give her music o' mornings; they say it will penetrate. *Enter Musicians* Come on, tune. If you can penetrate her with your fingering, so; we'll try with tongue too. (2.3.11–14)

The clowns in Lyly's *Midas* make sexual jokes on "fiddle" (1.2.8) and "notes" (1.2.84–87), and there is sexual innuendo on "fiddle" in Middleton and Dekker's *The Roaring Girl* (2.2.20–22). Music, musical "parts," and the touching of instruments all provide double entendres in Ford's *'Tis Pity She's a Whore* (2.1.13–14, 68, 78–79). In Heywood's *A Woman Killed with Kindness* the servant Nick returns the lute to the unfaithful Anne with the aside "would that had been the worst instrument you ever played on"; "instrument" also has a bawdy connotation in the anonymous *Wit of a Woman* (1604, ll. 175–79). In *Pericles* the hero compares Antiochus's daughter to a viol, distinguishing between the heavenly music of sex in marriage and the discordant sounds of illicit intercourse:

> You're a fair viol, and your sense the strings
> Who, fingered to make man his lawful music,
> Would draw heav'n down and all the gods to hearken,
> But, being played upon before your time,
> Hell only danceth at so harsh a chime. (1.124–28)

A madman in Dekker and Middleton's *1 Honest Whore* reprimands an imaginary schoolmaster who taught his wife to "play vpon the Virginals, and still his Iackes leapt vp, vp: you prickt her out nothing but bawdy lessons" (Dekker 5.2.270). In *The Wit of a Woman* (1604) a traditional musical refrain becomes slang for the female pudenda: sometimes women who are dancing jump "so high, that you may see their hey nony, nony, nonyno" (434–435).

The most frequent sexual-musical image in the Renaissance concerns stringed instruments, with lutes being the favorite metaphor. The image of the beloved as a lute to be played upon was a frequent Petrarchan conceit. Thus men could be imaged as lutes, as for example, in the ninth sonnet in the 1599 edition of Drayton's *Idea* or Wyatt's poems "My lute, awake" and "Blame not my lute" or Campion's "When to her lute Corinna sings." In Renaissance drama the association between women and stringed instruments is primarily sexual and far from complimentary. In *The Duchess of Malfi* (2.4.33–36) Webster uses the image of a lute to express the Cardinal's salacity. The Cardinal compares his treatment of Julia with Castruchio's:

> Thou hadst only kisses from him, and high feeding,
> But what delight was that? 'Twas just like one
> That hath a little fing'ring on the lute,
> Yet cannot tune it.

When one considers that those Renaissance musicians who did not have lute cases took their lute to bed with them as protection against cold and damp (Hollander 1961, 139), the sexual equation of women with lutes is doubly appropriate.[12] Furthermore, the lute was sometimes associated with seventeenth-century prostitutes: in Middleton's *Your Five Gallants* (1605), Primero's brothel presents itself as a music school.[13] This identifying accessory of prostitutes may perhaps explain the following reference to a gittern that appeared in the Book of Orders of the Merchant Adventurers of Newcastle upon Tyne in 1554 (*Records* 1982, 25). Rules governing the appearance and behavior of apprentices provide a lengthy list of prohibitions; among them, we are told, no merchant is to allow his apprentice "during the tyme of his apprentishood to daunse. dyse. Carde. or mvm. or vse any gytterns." The denial of social pastimes such as dancing and playing at dice or cards suggests that the gittern reference may refer innocuously to musical entertainment, but it is tempting to suspect a sexual implication.[14]

The terms "fiddle" and "fiddler" were not confined to violin playing but applied equally to the fingering on all stringed instruments. In *The Taming of the Shrew* Katherine rejects not just the lute but the lute-master, who explains, "I . . . bowed her hand to teach her fingering" (2.1.149–50). Given the bawdy associations of "fingering" in *Pericles*, *Cymbeline*, and *The Duchess of Malfi*, it is hardly surprising that Katherine should reject Hortensio's very physical lute instruction.[15] The sexual insult is underlined a few lines later in Katherine's terms of abuse: "she did call me rascal, fiddler." "Fiddler" is a common slang term for a violator of chastity, as in Chapman's *Bussy d'Ambois* ("my chastity . . . you shall neither riddle nor fiddle" [3.2.258–59]) or Dekker's *Match Me in London* (1.1.57–61):

> *BILBO*:   and he [the barber] stood fidling with *Tormiella* [daughter of
>   Malevento].

MALEVENTO: Ha?

BILBO: Fidling at least halfe an houre, on a Citterne with a mans broken
head at it, so that I think 'twas a Barber Surgion.

In this quotation the sexual associations of "fidling" are reinforced by the
reference to "Citterne," which, like the musical instruments cited above, could
function rhetorically as a euphemism for the female genitalia (see, for example, King's *The Passenger* [Benvenuto 1612, 7], in which Pipa does not "permit her wanton louer to lay his hand vpon her Citterne"). Thus, musical
instruments in general, and stringed instruments in particular, have strong
associations with the female body.

I have argued elsewhere that the nonsensical sartorial criticism Petruccio
offers in 4.2, when he sees the pinking on the sleeves of Katherine's dress,
requires emendation. Petruccio's complaint reads as follows:

Whats this? a sleeue? 'tis like [a] demi cannon,
What, vp and downe caru'd like an apple Tart?
Heers snip, and nip, and cut, and slish and slash,
Like to a Censor in a barbers shoppe. (TLN 2073–76; 4.3.88–91)

I have suggested that "Censor" should read "cittern." The cittern
(renowned for its grotesquely carved neck) is used metaphorically elsewhere
by Shakespeare and at least ten of his contemporaries in similarly derogatory
contexts. In the drama of the period the association between barbers and citterns is almost a commonplace: the cittern can be amply documented as a
standard item in barbers' shops, where it was provided for the musical enjoyment of waiting customers. In Jonson's *The Staple of News* (1.5.127–30) Pen-
nyboy Junior recounts how his "barber Tom, . . . one Christmas, . . . got into a
masque at Court, by his wit, / And the good means of his cittern, holding up
thus / For one o' the music." In Lyly's *Midas* (1969, 3.2.35), Motto, the barber, reminds his man that he has taught him several skills of the trade, including the "tuning of a cittern" ("tune" has the dual meaning "play" and "put in
tune"; see *OED tune* 3a). Oliver the weaver, in Middleton's *The Mayor of
Queenborough* (3.3.166–67), tells how he helped a poor barber who, it seems,
was forced to pawn his cittern: "I gave that barber a fustian-suit, and twice
redeemed his cittern: he may remember me." In Jonson's *Epicoene* Morose
chooses his deceptively silent bride on the advice of Cutbeard the barber.
When his bride proves talkative, Morose exclaims, "That cursed barber! . . . I
have married his cittern, that's common to all men" (3.5.58, 60). The equation
of silence with chastity and speech with promiscuity was a Renaissance commonplace; Morose's cittern analogy subtly links his wife's noise-making
capacity with her presumed general availability. Dekker and Middleton similarly suggest sexual availability in *2 Honest Whore* when Matheo denounces

Bellafront as a whore, "A Barbers Citterne for euery Seruingman to play vpon" (Dekker 5.2.151).[16]

The ambience of the barber's shop was social (ale was served and games played), medical, tonsorial—and egregiously masculine. When Katherine rejects the lute (an emblem of femininity á la Bianca) in 2.1, and Petruccio rejects the cittern (an emblem of female pliability and passivity from an exclusively masculine environment) in 4.3, we may perhaps discern the couple's kinship: both are expressing hostility to stereotypical gender associations.

III. MARRIAGE

It cannot be denied, however, that Petruccio's behavior in the sun/moon scene looks suspiciously like that of a man intent on playing an instrument to produce the sounds that he wishes to hear. An eighteenth-century riddle (the answer to which is: a lute) is based on this image:

> Her Back is round, her Belly's flat withal,
> Her metamorphos'd Guts are great and small.
> Her Navel's comely, and her Neck is long,
> Bedeck'd with Ornaments, though small, yet strong.
> Being thus compleat, her Master's chief Ambition,
> Is to make known to all her sweet Condition. (Burton 1737, 97)

The explanation of the riddle concludes: "being very well tuned, the Master is ambitious to delight his Auditors with his Sweet Musick . . . and will not conclude till he hath play'd over his Lessons, to the content of the Company" (Burton 1737, 98). A four-line rhyming observation follows, which describes the journey of a "*Well bred Damsel*" from deformity to "*excellent Virtues*": "*She's then for him that loves her, Musick Sweet*" (Burton 1737, 98).

Such a musical partnership may be viewed positively—a lute cannot make music without a player, and a public performance of music making is the natural consequence of private practice. It may equally be perceived negatively—the lute will always be the passive receiver of, and conduit for, the tunes imposed by the dominant player. The most obvious example of the player's dominant control and the instrument's passivity is seen in the myth of Syrinx, the Arcadian nymph who fled from the attentions of Pan; she was metamorphosed into a reed from which Pan subsequently made a flute. Given dramatic life by Lyly, Pan says:

This pipe, my sweet pipe, was once a nymph, a fair nymph, once my lovely mistress, now my heavenly music. Tell me, Apollo, *is there any instrument so sweet to play on as one's mistress*? (*Midas*, 4.1.13; emphasis added)
Bubulcus in Shirley's *Love Tricks* (1833, 2.1, p. 22) says of his beloved that "there is no music without her; she is the best instrument to play upon." From

one angle Petruccio seems to be behaving as Pan, pursuing his mistress, and metamorphosing her into an instrument for music ("For she is changed as she had never been" [5.2.120]). Rosencrantz and Guildenstern attempt to do the same thing with Hamlet:

> HAMLET: Will you play upon this pipe? [the Player's recorder]
> GUILDENSTERN: My lord, I cannot. . . . I have not the skill.
> HAMLET: Why, look you now, how unworthy a thing you make of me!
> You would play upon me, you would seem to know my stops, you
> would pluck out the heart of my mystery, you would sound me from
> my lowest note to the top of my compass; and there is much music,
> excellent voice in this little organ, yet you cannot make it speak.
> 'Sblood, do you think I am easier to be played on than a pipe? Call
> me what instrument you will, though you can fret me, you cannot
> play upon me. (*Hamlet* 3.2.338–40; 350–60)

Hamlet can resist Rosencrantz and Guildenstern's attempts so easily because these would-be players have no musical skill ("I know no touch of it, my lord" [3.2.344]). Petruccio, however, has considerable musical knowledge, as his vocabulary and snatches of song continually testify. What Hamlet can dismiss in one scene Katherine must struggle against for four acts.

For a more positive musical interpretation we must turn to *Othello*; here Shakespeare uses stringed music to represent marital concord. Othello's and Desdemona's kisses are viewed as "the greatest discords . . . / That e'er our hearts shall make!" (2.1.199–200; the frequent association of heart strings with music strings arose from a "false etymological relationship" [Hollander 1961, 210] derived from Latin puns on cor / cordis / chorda). Iago continues the image with the contemptuous "O, you are well tuned now, / But I'll set down the pegs that make this music" (2.1.200–1).[17] Another "well-tuned couple" in a contemporary domestic tragedy have their nuptial bliss portrayed musically. The Frankfords' happiness at the opening of *A Woman Killed with Kindness* is described by Sir Charles: "There's music in this sympathy; it carries / Consort and expectation of much joy" (Heywood 1.69–70). Heywood presents this musical/marital emblem physically with an onstage lute, a gift from Frankford to Anne, which is symbolically broken at the end of the play when Anne, "who used to make sweet music on her lute, has made sour music of her marriage" (Cary 1973–1974, 114).

Katherine's marriage in *The Taming of the Shrew* may move in the opposite direction to that of Desdemona or Anne Frankford. The Katherine who refuses to play on the lute and makes discordant sounds in the early acts responds harmoniously to the commands of her husband in acts 4 and 5. Harmony in marriage, like harmony in lute-playing, depends on sympathetic pairs. Lute strings are strung in double courses and produce cacophonic sounds when they vibrate against each other in a "struggle for independence" (Hollander 1961, 233). So Katherine's independence in rejecting partners is presented as cacophony: she "[b]egan to scold and raise up such a storm / That mortal ears might hardly endure the din" (1.1.170–71). But as Sidney's (1590) *Arcadia* makes clear (262v), and as Katherine herself comes to realize, "one string [cannot] make as good music as a consort." After some initial clashes of sound as Katherine takes the measure of her partner's musico-rhetorical style, Katherine progresses from the ostinato "dumps"[18] of the play's opening to the harmonious playing in partnership with her musical and marital "consort." All levels of music fuse in the play's conclusion, from the rhetorical duet to the nuptial kiss ("the greatest discord that e'er [their] hearts shall make") to the final exit to bed: "the true concord of well-tuned sounds / By unions married" (sonnet 8, lines 5–6).

It is clear that this optimistic conclusion is not the only possible interpretation of the lute/cittern association and the allied references to stringed music in the play. No matter how harmonious the resultant music, the lute remains an object that the male subject uses for pleasure; and as in so many positive images of the married couple—for example, that of the rider and horse working in partnership—the "well-tuned" image conceals the hierarchical inequality of the relationship between player and instrument. For clarification and contextualization of the interpretive ambiguities of the play's musical images we must return to the motif of hunting.

IV. CULTURAL CONTROL AND THE PRICE OF PROGRESS

As a sport, hunting demonstrates power, predominantly masculine power, over wild nature. It has analogies in the wooing in *The Taming of the Shrew*, where Katherine is a wild creature who must be controlled. Petruccio lays his patriarchal cards on the table:

> I am he am born to tame you, Kate,
> And bring you from a wild Kate to a Kate
> Conformable as other household Kates. (2.1.270–72)

This statement comes in act 2, immediately after the episode in which Katherine has rejected both music and music master by breaking the lute over Hortensio's head. Katherine's violent behavior is not as malapropos or uncivilized as it might appear, for musical instruments such as the lute are, like hunting and marital taming, a paradoxical blend of civilized life and violence, demonstrating male power over nature. Trees are felled, wood is split, to create lutes, harpsichords, virginals, viols da gamba, bandoras, citterns. Man the creator is also man the destroyer. These apparent irreconcilables come together in the figure of Apollo, who is both god of hunting and god of stringed instruments, and in *The Tempest* in the tyrannical/beneficent Prospero who releases the ethereal and musical Ariel by splitting the cloven pine in which he is imprisoned. Violent and destructive action is not separate from so-called civilized behavior, and in some cases may even lead to it, as the mottoes engraved on harpsichords, virginals, and spinets explicitly acknowledge (McGeary 1981, #27, 49, 25):

> Io da le piaghe mie forma ricevo.
> [I receive form from the blows (I received).]
> —Virginal, 1527

> Non nisi mota cano.
> [Not unless struck do I sing.]
> —Harpsichord, seventeenth century

> Intactum sileo percute dulce cano.
> [Untouched, I am silent; strike me, I sing sweetly.]
> —Spinet, 1741

Created by blows (inflicted on wood), or made musical by being struck, musical instruments—the epitome of the civilized classes—are symbiotically linked to violence.

The characterization of violence as a creative or harmonious teleology is disquieting to the twentieth-century sensibility, not least because of the Renaissance's explicit gendering of music and musical instruments as feminine. The aestheticization of violence against women in musical mottoes or virginal lids (see below) suggests that such violence is civilized, productive, acceptable.[19] Although Petruccio does not actually strike the instrument to produce the sweet sounds in act 5, his taming is presented in unremittingly musical terms. Wealth is *burden* of his wooing *dance*; Katherine's railing is, to him, the sweet singing of a nightingale (we remember an earlier ominous reference to the caged nightingales who will sing sweetly for Christopher Sly); and the "Friar of Order Grey" of which Petruccio sings a portion is, as P. J. Croft (1981) explains (8), "a bawdy tale of male domination and female submission." Although critics frequently contrast the taming treatment Katherine receives from Petruccio with the more civilized education in music and the humanities that Bianca receives, the two are not as different as one might think. By this argument both Bianca and Katherine are cornered and controlled.

It is surely no coincidence that, from the sixteenth to the eighteenth centuries, one of the most common topoi to be painted on virginal and harpsichords lids (of which women were the primary players) was the hunt. As Richard Leppert explains, "To place a hunting scene on a clavichord effectively linked this power over life to the activity of music, the apparent radical opposite to the hunting scene. . . . [A]rt and power are one and the same. In other words, the distance is collapsed between art, typically theorized as a spiritual and spiritualized realm of human experience, and a man's power to shape the physical world" (Leppert 1993, 126, 133). Thus considerations of music bring us back to the hunt, for, like the hunt, music is associated with class (the music master comes into the home), with power (musical notation provides orders for players to follow), and with violence (from the creation of wooden instruments to the mottoes that advocate domestic violence as a prelude to harmony). The issues come together dramatically, comically, in venery, which the preface to *The Roaring Girl* promises the reader: "*To the Comicke Play-readers, Venery, and Laughter.*" As Jean Howard explains (170), venery can mean both sexual pursuit and hunting with hounds.

In act 5 Katherine is characterized as a deer (5.2.57–58); but, as Margie Burns points out (44), and as the betting language in the scene makes clear, Katherine also functions as a retriever. This slippage between quarry and helpmate illustrates a duality in Renaissance attitudes to marriage, first broached in *The Taming of the Shrew* in the series of references to horses.[20] Renaissance marriage and equestrian manuals frequently link the training of horses with the training of women: both are taught to obey the "manage." The "brank" or scold's bridle worn by shrews was modeled on the horse bridle, a symbol of harness which survives in miniature in the wedding ring (until recently wedding rings were worn only by women); and yet once the horse was trained, rider and mount were viewed as a noble if unequal partnership, as were husband and wife. (This relationship between animal management and marriage is coincidentally encoded in the homonymic bridle/bridal.)

Thus, despite notable ambiguities in interpretation, it is in the end difficult to see how references to women as hunted animals and musical instruments, in this play at least, can be flattering or ennobling. The linked images of hunting, music, and taming suggest in fact that marital relations are but one part of *The Taming of the Shrew*'s larger skeptical analysis of so-called civilized behavior. The play analyzes cultural control in the three areas of life that are considered indices of man's progress: musical entertainment, sporting activity, and Christian marriage. Man's progress in music, sport, and conjugal relations is grounded in manipulation: of nature, animals, and social subordinates. The underlying motif may be play (the gulling of Sly is a "jest," a "pastime passing excellent"; New Criticism sees Petruccio's taming strategies as an invitation to Katherine to enter a playful world of transforming reality; the recreation in music and hunting is obvious), but such play is not without its victims or its dangers. Although the exiled Duke Senior in *As You Like It* learns to appreciate unadorned nature in the forest of Arden, finding "tongues in trees, books in the running brooks," in reality urban "civilized" man uses trees to make musical instruments and books. Women, animals, and the environment suffer for the sake of conjugal convention, sport, and musical leisure. The creation of civilized life is a paradox, involving uncivilized behavior. Progress comes, quite literally, as the musical references in *The Taming of the Shrew* show, with strings attached.

NOTES

Originally published in *Renaissance Drama* 26 (1995): 83–104. Reprinted with the permission of Laurie E. Maguire and *Renaissance Drama*.

I am grateful to Thomas L. Berger, S. P. Cerasano, Frances E. Dolan, Lynn Hulse, and George Walton Williams for commenting on earlier drafts of this essay. I wish also to record my thanks to the Social Sciences and Research Council of Canada for a grant that funded part of this research.

1. For information in this paragraph, and throughout this section, I am indebted to Carr1886; Cartmill 1993; Cummins 1988; Markham 1595 and 1615; Cockaine 1591; Leppert 1993, ch. 6; Turbervile 1575(this is a free translation of Jacques du Fouilloux's La Venerie [ca. 1561]); and Twiti 1527.

2. The medieval and Renaissance hunt was a much slower activity than its modern descendent, and horses were not always used. For the speed of the Renaissance hunt, see Cockaine 1591, who does not mention horses, and cf. Carr 1986, 28.

3. But see Cockaine1591, which puts the fox above all other quarry.

4. For discussion of these examples, see Cartmill 1993, 78–80.

5. For other similarities between the induction and 5.2, see Burns 1986.

6. I quote from the second edition, 1691, 446.

7. For differing views on this subject, see Munrow 1976, 26 and Ward 1979–1981, *passim*.

8. Thomas Peacham compares music to rhetoric; Phillip Stubbes compares music to cosmetics. For these references, and further information on the equation of women with music, see Austern 1989, 1993, and 1994. Cf. also Hollander 1961, 104–22. For a related analysis of Sir Phillip Sidney's *Defence of Poetry* showing how the terminology of the debate about poesy is also the terminology used in debates about face painting, see Dolan 1993.

9. The conflated sexual-musical associations of "play" are still current in a 1995 Museum of London advertisement, which invites the reader to view Lady Hamilton's guitar with the elaborate pun "See what Nelson's mistress was playing when she wasn't playing the strumpet." A pun on (s)trumpet also seems indicated in *Othello* 2.1.181. Iago concludes the speech in which he has been observing Cassio's over-gallant behavior with Desdemona by announcing Othello's arrival; Iago's phrase resonates with unambiguous elision: "The Moor—I know his *trumpet*" (emphasis added).

10. Although published in 1566, the play seems to have been written in the reign of Edward VI; see White xxii-xxiii.

11. For the sexual significance of "drum" in *All's Well that Ends Well*, see Stanton.

12. In *The Vanities of Human Life* (ca. 1645; National Gallery, London) the Dutch painter Harmyn Steenwyck uses the round-bellied lute to symbolize the female

body, and the phallic flute and shawm (a medieval oboe) to symbolize the male body.

13. For the association between prostitutes and lutes, see Dirck Van Baburen's *Procuress* (1622; Boston Museum of Fine Arts) and Franz Huys's *The Lute Maker's Shop* (sixteenth century, reproduced in Moxey). For discussion of these works, see Williams 1994, 2:834–35 (*lute*) and cf. 3: 1481 (*viol*). In Hieronymus Bosch's triptych *The Garden of Earthly Delights* (ca. 1500; Prado, Madrid), the third panel shows the results of lust: damnation. Male bodies are depicted crushed by, or crucified on, two giant musical instruments: a lute and a harp.

14. I am grateful to S. P. Cerasano for drawing my attention to this reference.

15. In *The Taming of a Shrew* this covert innuendo is made more explicit. Kate's threat of violence is prompted by Valeria's lewd "What, doo you bid me kisse your arse?" (a mishearing, deliberate or otherwise, of Kate's vituperative command to "mend it [her lute playing] . . . , thou filthy asse"). See *The Taming of a Shrew* 6.24–30, in Bullough 1957.

16. For further taunts and criticisms based on cittern metaphors, see Shakespeare, *Love's Labor's Lost*, 5.2.602–16; Fletcher 1976, *Love's Cure*, 2.2.108; Ford 1895, *The Fancies*, 1.2, 234; Ford 1985, *The Lover's Melancholy*, 2.1.36–39; Marston 1887, *The Scourge of Villainy*, 301; and Massinger 1813, *The Old Law*, 533–34.

17. See King 1987 for an analysis of the importance of music in *Othello*.

18. A "mournful song or melody"; see Morris 1981, 2.1.277 n.

19. For a more recent example, see Susan Stroman's choreography for the Gershwin musical *Crazy for You* (1992–1995). Adorned with taut strings from head to toe, the female chorus cleverly emulated basses that the male chorus plucked, while the company sang "*Slap* that Bass" (emphasis added).

20. See Roberts 1983, Wayne 1985, and Boose 1991 on this subject. See also Thomas Tryon's (1983) *The Way to Health* (446), which uses the language of horse training to refer to musical control.

WORKS CITED

Auden, J. E. 1905. *A Short History of the Albrighton Hunt*. London: Edward Arnold.

Austern, Linda Phyllis. 1989. "'Sing Againe Syren': The Female Musician and Sexual Enchantment in Elizabethan Life and Literature." *Renaissance Quarterly* 42: 420–48.

———. 1993. "'Alluring the Auditorie to Effeminacie': Music and the Idea of the Feminine in Early Modern England." *Music and Letters* 74 (1993): 343–54.

———. 1994. "Music and the English Renaissance Controversy over Women." In *Cecelia Reclaimed: Feminist Perspectives on Gender and Music*. Edited by Susan C. Cook and Judy S. Tsou. Urbana: University of Illinois Press, 1994. 52–69.

Benvenuto. 1612. *Il Passagiere*. Translated by "Mr. King." London.

Boose, Lynda E. 1991. "Scolding Brides and Bridling Scolds: Taming the Woman's Unruly Member." *Shakespeare Quarterly* 42: 179–213.

Bullough, Geoffrey. 1957. *Narrative and Dramatic Sources of Shakespeare*. Vol. 1. London: Routledge and Kegan Paul.

Burns, Margie. 1986. "The Ending of *The Shrew*." *Shakespeare Studies* 18: 41–64.

Burton, Robert. 1737. *Winter-evening Entertainments*. London.

Carr, Raymond. 1986. *English Fox Hunting: A History*. Rev. ed. London: Weidenfeld and Nicolson.

Cartmill, Matt. 1993. *A View to a Death in the Morning: Hunting and Nature through History*. Cambridge: Harvard University Press.

Cartwright, William. 1951. *The Ordinary*. In *The Plays and Poems of William Cartwright*. Edited by G. Blakemore Evans. Madison: University of Wisconsin Press.

Cary, Cecile W. 1973–1974. "'Go Breake This Lute': Music in Heywood's *A Woman Killed with Kindness*." *Huntington Library Quarterly* 37: 111–22.

Chapman, George. 1964. *Bussy d'Ambois*. Edited by Nicholas Brooke. London: Methuen.

Cockaine, Sir Thomas. 1591. *A Short Treatise on Hunting*. London.

Croft, P. J. 1981. "The 'Friar of Order Gray' and the Nun." *Review of English Studies* 32: 1–16.

Cummins, John. 1988. *The Hound and the Hawk: The Art of Medieval Hunting*. London: Weidenfeld and Nicolson.

Dekker, Thomas. 1964. *1 Honest Whore*. In *The Dramatic Works of Thomas Dekker*. Vol. 2. Edited by Fredson Bowers. Cambridge: Cambridge University Press.

———. 1964a. *2 Honest Whore*. In *The Dramatic Works of Thomas Dekker*. Vol. 2. Edited by Fredson Bowers. Cambridge: Cambridge University Press.

———. 1966. *Match Me in London*. In *The Dramatic Works of Thomas Dekker*. Vol. 3. Edited by Fredson Bowers. Cambridge: Cambridge University Press.

Dolan, Francis E. 1993. "'Taking the Pencil out of God's Hand': Art, Nature, and the Face-Painting Debate in Early Modern England." *PMLA* 108: 224–39.

Finney, Gretchen L. 1953. "A World of Instruments." *ELH* 20: 87–120.

Fletcher, John. 1976. *Love's Cure*. Edited by George Walton Williams. In *The Dramatic Works in the Beaumont and Fletcher Canon*. Vol. 3. Edited by Fredson Bowers. Cambridge: Cambridge University Press.

Ford, John. 1895. *The Fancies. The Works*. Edited by William Gifford, with additions by Alexander Dyce. Vol. 2. London: Lawrence and Bullen.

———. 1975. *'Tis Pity She's a Whore*. Edited by Derek Roper. London: Methuen.

———. 1985. *The Lover's Melancholy*. Edited by R. F. Hill. The Revels Plays. Manchester: Manchester University Press.

Heywood, Thomas. 1985. *A Woman Killed with Kindness*. Edited by Brian W. M. Scobie. London: Black.

Hollander, John. 1961. *The Untuning of the Sky: Ideas of Music in English Poetry, 1500–1700*. Princeton: Princeton University Press.

Howard, Jean. 1992. "Sex and Social Conflict: The Erotics of *The Roaring Girl*." In *Erotic Politics: Desire on the Renaissance Stage*. Edited by Susan Zimmerman. New York: Routledge.

Jonson, Ben. 1937. *The Alchemist*. In *Ben Jonson*. Vol. 5. Edited by C. H. Herford and Percy Simpson. Oxford: Clarendon.

———. 1979. *Epicoene*. Edited by R. V. Holdsworth. London: Benn.

———. 1988. *The Staple of News*. Edited by Anthony Parr. Manchester: Manchester University Press.

Kahn, Coppélia. 1981. *Man's Estate: Masculine Identity in Shakespeare*. Berkeley: University of California Press.

King, Rosalind. 1987. "'Then Murder's out of Tune': The Music and Structure of *Othello*." *Shakespeare Survey* 39: 149–58.

Leppert, Richard. 1993. *The Sight of Sound: Music, Representation, and the History of the Body*. Berkeley: University of California Press.

Lyly, John. 1969. *Gallathea* and *Midas*. Edited by Anne B. Lancashire. Lincoln: University of Nebraska Press.

McGeary, Thomas. 1981. "Harpsichord Mottoes." *Journal of the American Musical Instrument Society* 7: 5–35.

Maguire, Laurie E. n.d. "Petruccio and the Barber's Shop." Unpublished paper.

Markham, Gervase. 1595. *The Gentlemans Academie; or, The Booke of S. Albans*. London.

———. 1615. *Countrey Contentments*. London.

Marston, John. 1887. *The Scourge of Villainy*. In *The Works of Marston*. Vol. 3. Edited by A. H. Bullen. London: John C. Nimmo.

Massinger, Phillip. 1813. *The Old Law*. In *The Plays*. Vol. 4. Edited by W. Gifford. London: G. and W. Nicol.

Middleton, Thomas. 1605. *Your Five Gallants*. London.

———. *The Mayor of Queenborough*. In *The Works of Thomas Middleton*. Vol. 2. Edited by A. H. Bullen. New York: AMS.

Middleton, Thomas, and Thomas Dekker. 1987. *The Roaring Girl*. Edited by Paul A. Mulholland. The Revels Plays. Manchester: Manchester University Press, 1987.

Morris, Brian, ed. 1981. *The Taming of the Shrew*. London: Methuen.

Moxey, Keith. 1989. *Peasants, Warriors, and Wives: Popular Imagery in the Reformation*. Chicago: University of Chicago Press.

Munrow, David. 1976. *Instruments of the Middle Ages and Renaissance*. London: Oxford University Press.

Nashe, Thomas. 1904. *The Anatomie of Absurditie*. In *The Works of Thomas Nashe*. Vol. 1. Edited by R. B. McKerrow. London: A. H. Bullen.

Records of Early English Drama. 1982. *Newcastle upon Tyne*. Edited by J. J. Anderson. Toronto: University of Toronto Press.

Roberts, Jeanne Addison. 1983. "Horses and Hermaphrodites: Metamorphoses in *The Taming of the Shrew*." *Shakespeare Quarterly* 34: 159–71.

Ross, Lawrence J. 1966. "Shakespeare's 'Dull Clown' and Symbolic Music." *Shakespeare Quarterly* 17: 107–28.

Shakespeare, William. 1968. *The Norton Facsimile of the First Folio of Shakespeare*. Edited by Charlton Hinman. New York: Norton, 1968.

———. 1986. *The Complete Works of Shakespeare*. Edited by Stanley Wells and Gary Taylor with John Jowett and William Montgomery. Oxford: Clarendon Press.

Shirley, James. 1833. *Love Tricks*. In *The Dramatic Works and Poems of James Shirley*. Vol. 1. Edited by William Gifford and Alexander Dyce. London: Murray.

———. 1980. *The Bird in a Cage*. Edited by Francis F. Senescu. New York: Garland.

Sidney, Sir Phillip. 1590. *The Countess of Pembroke's Arcadia*. London.

Stanton, Kay. 1992. "All's Well in Love and War." In *Ideological Approaches to Shakespeare: The Practice of Theory*. Edited by Robert P. Merrix and Nicholas Ranson. Lewiston, N.Y.: Mellen.

Thompson, Ann, ed. 1984. *The Taming of the Shrew*. Cambridge: Cambridge University Press.

Tryon, Thomas. 1683. *The Way to Health, Long Life and Happiness*. London.

Turbervile, George. 1575. *The Noble Arte of Venerie or Hunting*. London.

Twiti, William. 1527. *The Art of Hunting*. Edited by Bror Danielsson. Stockholm Studies in English, no. 37; Cynegetica Angelica 1. Stockholm: Almqvist and Wiksell.

Virgil. 1965. *The Aeneid*. Translated by W. F. Jackson Knight. Harmondsworth: Penguin, 1983.

Wager, Lewis. 1992. *The Life and Repentance of Mary Magdalene*. In *Reformation Biblical Drama in England*. Edited by Paul Whitfield White. New York: Garland.

Waldo, T. R., and T. W. Herbert. 1959. "Musical Terms in *The Taming of the Shrew*: Evidence of Single Authorship." *Shakespeare Quarterly* 10: 185–99.

Ward, John M. 1979–1981. "Sprightly and Cheerful Musick: Notes on the Cittern, Gittern, and Guitar in Sixteenth- and Seventeenth-Century England." *Lute Society Journal* 21: passim.

Wayne, Valerie. 1985. "Refashioning the Shrew." *Shakespeare Studies* 17: 159–87.

Webster, John. 1993. *The Duchess of Malfi*. Edited by Elizabeth M. Brennan. 3d ed. London: Benn.

West, Michael. 1974. "The Folk Background of Petruchio's Wooing Dance: Male Supremacy *in The Taming of the Shrew*." *Shakespeare Studies* 7: 65–73.

Wit of a Woman, The. 1604. Edited by. W. W. Greg. London: Oxford Universtiy Press for the Malone Soc., 1914.

Willbern, David. 1978. "Rape and Revenge in *Titus Andronicus*." *English Literary Renaissance* 8: 159–82.

Williams, Gordon. 1994. *A Dictionary of Sexual Language and Imagery in Shakespearean and Stuart Literature*. 3 vols. London: Athlone.

"What's That to You?" or, Facing Facts

Anti-Paternalist Chords and Social Discords in *The Taming of the Shrew*

THOMAS MOISAN

"To know the conditions of a work," Pierre Macherey once argued, "is to define the real process of its constitution, to show how it is composed from a real diversity of elements which give it substance," a diversity exemplified for Macherey (1978) in Verne's *The Mysterious Island*, which "speaks with several voices at once, exhibiting the contrast between them even if it fails to express and account for this contrast" (49–50). At a glance, Macherey's anti-organicist admonition would seem of little relevance to a study of *The Taming of the Shrew*, critical debate over which has, quite naturally, sought generally to wrest a univocal reading from the eponymous struggle of Petruchio and Katherina. Yet as the growing attention paid in recent years to the induction of the play would suggest, there is profit in listening to *The Taming of the Shrew* with an ear for its polyphony, a polyphony created by the dissident sounds produced by the comic collisions that occur, not simply in the thematic foreground, but in what common sense, the exigencies of plot, and interpretative tradition have deemed the margins of the play, collisions which from the very opening lines of the induction, and with percussive insistence and at times concussive force, give dramatic life to contemporary anxieties, not simply about the relations of husband and wife, but about pervasive transgressions of the social hierarchy that would elide prescribed distinctions between commoner and lord, servant and master, and disrupt the proper relations between fathers and sons, and sons-in-law and newly begotten fathers-in-law.[1] It is to the latter, and to the vein of generational discord and anti-paternalist reference in the play, that I will pay especial attention in this essay, less to note its presence and prevalence than to explore the ways in which it competes with and complicates our response to the "main event." By way of preface, however, I would like to offer a sketch of what I take to be the peculiar texture of the complex negotiation the play transacts with the society it represents. And here, of course, we might recall as a well-worn axiom Louis

Montrose's (1980) observation that the "heterodoxy of Shakespearean drama" is but a sign of its mimetic fidelity, "merely the consequence of its success at holding up the mirror to nature" (66; see also 32–39, 122). With particular regard to the distinctions to be drawn between *The Taming of the Shrew* as we have taken it from the First Folio—and which hereafter I will follow the practice of calling *The Shrew*—and its theatrical doppelganger, the Quarto play *The Taming of a Shrew*—hereafter *A Shrew*[2]—and with an ear for how the strains of social dissidence in the margins of the play interact with its center, I would like to explore the possibility that *The Shrew* echoes the contending voices of its society in its own ultimate equivocations, leaving the patriarchalist fantasy it inscribes unaffirmed, and leaving the subversive dissonances it evokes in counterpoint at once unendorsed but unrepudiated.

I

To be sure, to locate sites of social dissidence in *The Shrew* is ineluctably to acknowledge the very traditional character of the play in which that dissidence gets voiced. How "traditional" the play is, how violent the literary and social antecedents of the tradition of which it is the scion, has, of course, been well documented, and in grim detail (Woodbridge 1984, 201 ff.; Boose 1991; see also Wayne 1985, 159–61 and Dolan 1996, 14–24). And, in fact, it could be argued that in the relationship in the play of tradition and dissidence, *The Shrew* stands merely as a parable on the dynamics of social containment, and a reminder that in the care and feeding of patriarchalism both "tradition" and "resistance" can be said to have been assigned essential and synergetic parts, with the former invoked to withstand and invalidate the perceived challenge of the latter, and with the latter conjured and magnified to justify the assertion, and display the potency, of the former. And if, indeed, we adopt for the moment Eric Hobsbawm's (1983) working definition of "invented tradition" as a set of symbolically coded practices "which seek to inculcate certain values and norms of behaviour by repetition, which automatically implies continuity with the past" (1), then especially "traditional" seems the comic "invention" of *The Shrew*, which, beginning with the framing device of the induction, repeatedly calls attention to its central shrew-taming action as a construct, as a prefabricated piece of theatrical comedy—or what Christopher Sly calls "comonty" (Ind. 2.138)—which the players have in their repertoire and resurrect ad hoc and, at least in *A Shrew*, with expressly exemplary pretensions: "Tis a good lesson for us my lord, for us that are married men" (45).[3]

Yet it is precisely its theatrical self-consciousness that makes the relationship of *The Shrew* to the play of tradition and resistance a complex one to map. Karen Newman (1991) has argued that in the degree to which the induction brings "relationships of power and gender" to the foreground as theatrical constructions, *The Shrew* "deconstructs its own mimetic effect" and permits its audience to hold at a playful distance the patriarchalist claims its central action would seem to affirm (38, 49–50). And even if one hedges at investing Shakespeare's contemporary audience with the kind of modern hermeneutical delight in indeterminacy Newman's reading both allows and presupposes, still, it can be maintained that the more closely one juxtaposes the induction with the "main event," the greater the potential for social and even political destabilization becomes: the very elegant formal parallels that permit us to see Petruchio's treatment and commodification of Katherina mirrored in the Lord's treatment of Sly and discussion of his hounds (Kehler 1987, 39–41) also invite us both to focus upon the cultural relativism of "shrewishness," metonymized in the simultaneously objective and subjective genitive that gives the play its title, and to play with the possibility of eliding significant distinctions between lords and actors and men and women.[4]

So too, in a society not without its apprehensions about the moral propriety of the stage, apprehensions amply chronicled in E. K. Chambers's "Documents of Criticism" and "Documents of Control," and exhaustively analyzed by Jonas Barish et alia,[5] the metatheatricality of the induction effectively dares contemporary critics of the stage not to approve of the means and materials employed in taming shrews and sociopaths like Katherina and Sly. Indeed, the dare is especially pointed in the induction to *The Shrew*, where the players—unlike their counterparts in *A Shrew*—make no pretense that the "pleasant comedy" they are to stage will be exemplary or morally corrective (Ind.2.129–36), and in which it is the playacting Lord, and not the professional players, who clearly derives something other than wholesome pleasure in having Sly provocatively surrounded by "all my wanton pictures" (1.47), and who anticipates, as Lynda Boose (1994) has noted (224), with some voyeuristic glee—if not titillation—watching his cross-dressed page "well usurp the grace, / Voice, gait, and action of a gentlewoman" and listening to him/her "call the drunkard husband" (1.131–33). In the Lord's proleptic delight, in fact, we are offered an instance in which theater seems quite exuberantly to allegorize its own unreliability as a source of moral edification and confirm the darkest suspicions its censors voiced over its power to elicit illicit emotions. For obviously and dangerously confused here is whether the source of the Lord's pleasure is the joke to be played on Sly the "drunkard" or the socially, and politically, more subversive power of the Lord's dramaturgy, the power to stage a spectacle eliding and transgressing the boundaries of gender and social status through the boy's ability to "usurp" and assume "the grace, / Voice, gait, and action of a gentlewoman." And, of course, in the degree to which the audience shares in the Lord's pleasure, it becomes implicated in the moral confusions that pleasure comprises.

What I would suggest here, though, is that the confusions the induction perpetrates are integral to a precarious, but I believe ultimately canny, strategy that enables *The Shrew* on the one hand to "stage" its traditional and culturally reassuring wife-taming fable while, on the other, giving voice to contemporary dissonances and challenges to the very cultural hierarchy Petruchio's triumph over Katherina would seemingly affirm. "At last, though long, our jarring notes agree," Lucentio proclaims at the outset of the final scene (5.2.1), a premature pronouncement, we quickly discover, but also lexically symptomatic of the discordant "notes" with which the action of the play is punctuated. To appreciate the play of these discordancies, however, I would propose shifting to a trope in a visual key.

Years ago Cecil C. Seronsy argued that in its adaptation of its most commonly assumed source, George Gascoigne's *Supposes*, *The Shrew* took for its unifying conceit the image of "supposes," meaning "disguises" or "false pretenses," or as Gascoigne himself glossed it, "nothing else but a mystaking or imagination of one thing for an other" (Bullough 1957, 112). Surely we hear this indebtedness italicized when near the end of *The Shrew* Lucentio makes a pointedly redundant reference to the "counterfeit supposes" by means of which he has surreptitiously wooed, won, and wedded Bianca (5.1.117). So, too, we sense Shakespeare's "out-supposing" of *Supposes* not only in the playful proliferation of disguises and confusions that populate the Lucentio-Bianca subplot—where, of course, we would assume we would hear evocations of *Supposes*—but also, as Seronsy (1963) demonstrated (19–25), in the improvisation that marks Petruchio's shrew-taming strategy as well.

Yet, as I have suggested elsewhere (Moison 1995, 108), "supposing" in *The Shrew* is often expressed as "facing," which, in addition to the connotations of disguising, of "putting on a face" that it shares with "supposes," connotations explored several years ago by Stuart E. Baker (1990, 45–59 passim), also bore for Shakespeare's audience the more aggressive, and socially transgressive, force of "facing something down," of maintaining a pretense or lie "in the face" of, and implicitly in defiance of, and denial of, authoritative contradiction. "For a lie faces God," reads an example of the usage by Francis Bacon cited in the *OED*, "and shrinkes from man." Used in this transgressive sense, "facing" is a word and describes a mode of behavior that link the world of *The Shrew* to the literature of "cony-catching" and the Elizabethan underworld,[6] imparting to *The Shrew* an ethos of verbal and physical confrontation in which the enormity of the offense lies in its openness, and in which those offended and "faced down" reflexively conflate impudence and insubordination, finding "villains" all the more "villainous" in the degree to which they can be taxonomized and vilified as "villeins" acting above their station. "Where is that damned villain Tranio, / That fac'd and braved me in this matter so" (5.1.120–21), Lucentio's father, Vincentio, demands, his paternal relief at discovering that his prodigal son had not been murdered after all not enough, it would appear, to mitigate his patriarchal anger at having been publicly denied and twitted by his servant. Hints of this socially inflected "facing" homophonically present themselves in the very opening lines of *The*

Shrew, where Sly, seeking to face down the hostess over the damages he owes her, threatens to "pheeze" her, and—in an adumbration of the metamorphosis he will shortly undergo—wraps himself in a reassuringly faux gentility; class, and a few particles of ersatz foreign diction, being the first refuge of this scoundrel:

> SLY: I'll pheeze you, in faith.
>
> HOSTESS: A pair of stocks, you rogue!
>
> SLY: Y'are a baggage, the Slys are no rogues. Look in the chronicles; we
>   came in with Richard Conqueror. Therefore *paucas pallabris*, let the
>   world slide. Sessa! (Ind. 1.1–6)

Nor, more important, is it only in the margins of the subplot and induction that we encounter this "in-your-face" brand of social relations. Sensing that she is to have very little voice in the matter of her betrothal to Petruchio, Katherina cleaves to a sense of her own social status in reproaching her father, Baptista, for contracting her to a "madcap ruffian and a swearing Jack, / That thinks with oaths to face the matter out" (2.1.287–89). Which, of course, is what Petruchio presently does in proclaiming to Baptista and the assembled gaggle of suitors, quasi-suitors, and pseudo-suitors how unshrewish Katherina really is, and how well he and she have gotten on (290–310).

On the other hand, while *The Shrew* adopts "facing," with all of its attendant social resonance, as a central trope, it does so while wearing the genially diffusive guise of farce, so that it enacts a set of comic confrontations in which various avatars of social respectability,[7] such as fathers, masters, priests, haberdashers and tailors to the fashionable, are "faced" (2.1.289, 405; 4.3.122; 5.1.121) and "braved" (4.3.110; 5.1.121; see also the widespread occurrence of cognates, such as "brave," "bravely," "bravery," and "braves"), but from which the venom of antagonism is dispelled and the potential threat to the existing order muted or marginalized: a quarreling master and his servants are reconciled (1.2.21–46), a priest receives a "cuff," but offstage (3.2.156–64), a tailor, though mocked and cheated hilariously (4.3.61–162), is quietly told he will get paid after all (4.3.163–65), and a deceived father, the figure with whom the main part of this paper concerns itself, is asked for forgiveness (5.1.112–19). To be sure, this attenuation of social asperity may well square with what Linda Woodbridge describes as Shakespeare's "usual policy of expurgating whatever might prove offensive to the middle-class element of his audience" (207). Yet it must be questioned whether Shakespeare's "expurgations" would have appeased those contemporary critics for whom the antics of wayward youth and women onstage were but symptoms of a deeper malaise and pervasive rejection of authority offstage, critics, for example, like Phillip Stubbes, whose several editions of *The Anatomie of Abuses* seem repeatedly infused with a sense of tradition violated anew. "And as your Lordship knoweth, reformation of maners and amendment of lyfe, was never more needfull" (5v), Stubbes tells the Earl of Arundell in the 1583 edition, to which he adds in the 1595 edition the question, "Was there euer seene lesse obedience in Youth of all sortes, both men and women-kinde towardes their superiours, Parents, Masters, and governors?" (A4d).

The contours of the via media *The Shrew* travels in negotiating the dissident energies to which it gives voice become clearer if one compares, even briefly, the orchestration of the implications of class strife in *The Shrew* with what we encounter in corresponding moments in *A Shrew*. I have written elsewhere of the way in which contemporary mystifications and dissonances touching the relations of masters and servants are at once teased to the surface of *The Shrew* and brushed to the side—but not made to vanish, as, for example, in the comic exchange with which Grumio and Petruchio make their entrance in 1.2, where Petruchio's command to Grumio to "knock" at the gate of Hortensio's house (5) does not, to say the least, elicit the response from Grumio that Petruchio had anticipated or desired (Moisan 1991, 278–82). In the comic world occupied by *The Shrew*, *Supposes*, and *A Shrew*, these literally liminal "knock, knock" jokes invariably seem to produce prolonged moments of non-anagnorisis that "work" comically by rejecting the authority and, thus, calling into question the identity and, of course, the social status of the knocker.[8]

In *The Shrew*, the interrogation of class tension commenced by Petruchio and Grumio's exchange is tabled, though not effaced, by the irenic efforts of Hortensio, whose pacificatory strategy is to insist that masters and servants can be masters and servants and friends at the same time (1.2.20–21, 45–47). Whatever challenge we may see here to Petruchio's authority—not to mention his intellect—that challenge entails a far less frontal assault upon social decorum than is evident in the relationship of Ferando and Sandor, the corresponding master-servant pairing in *A Shrew*.[9] Where Grumio, for example, speaks confidently of the rhetorical mastery with which Petruchio will "figure" and "disfigure" Katherina (1.2.111–16), the servant Sandor is highly and openly unflattering in his critique of his master Ferando's "courtship" of his Kate (53–54), and while all of Grumio's action in the play is on behalf of Petruchio's interests, Sandor allows himself to covet above his station, lusting after one of Kate's sisters, Emelia (63), while fantasizing about the possibility of fixing his master up with his own sister (54).

So, too, if *A Shrew* has a servant say and wish for things we do not hear servants say and wish for in *The Shrew*, it is also true that *A Shrew* provides an explicit corrective to wayward or deviant behavior among the lowly born and other transgressors against authority that we do not encounter in *The Shrew*. Oft noted and pondered has been Shakespeare's failure in *The Shrew* to close the frame to his play by bringing the Sly story to a close. Whatever may be said about the effect of this unclosed frame upon the meaning of *The Shrew*,[10] it is interesting to note when and how the frame is closed in *A Shrew*. In the latter, Slie, having been silent since the beginning of the play, intervenes on behalf of those whom the enraged Duke of Cestus is threatening to have sent to prison for their elaborate masquerade. Insisting that "wele have no sending to prison" (80–81), the incorrigible Slie would appear to have his wish become theatrical law, as the play lurches toward its happy, festive—and nonpunitive—close, but not before Slie himself is removed by the producer-actor-director and thoroughly meddlesome Lord, who, returning Slie to his own clothes and identity, reasserts control over his own play (88), even as the Duke of Cestus reestablishes his authority over his servants and son (82–83), and, of course, even as the Petruchio-figure, Ferando, exerts his masterful, bet-winning, and play-ending control over Kate.[11] Thus, even though it may be argued that the voicings of social dissidence are softer in *The Shrew* than in *A Shrew*, it is also true, as I hope to argue more fully later, that the hints of dissidence and resistance we hear are left more unresolved, or, at least, far less forcibly corrected and unframed by explicit exertions of social and theatrical authority.

II

From here, however, and following the lead taken on this issue by Karen Newman and Marianne Novy in particular, I would like to isolate and explore what I take to be the vein of anti-paternalist reference and action in *The Shrew*, a pattern rendered all the more conspicuous and pointed by comparative glances at *Supposes* and *A Shrew*. To do so is to see Petruchio's apparent triumph as very much a binary operation, involving not simply an ascendancy over Katherina but a displacement of her father, Baptista, and to recognize that in the degree to which Shakespeare's play seems to inscribe and affirm the patriarchalist claims of the husband, it does so by abridging to the point of abrogating the patriarchalist prerogatives of the father. At the same time, to underscore the anti-paternalist strains in *The Shrew* is not only to refine one's perspective on what is at stake in Petruchio's "taming" of Katherina, but also to raise the possibility that in shaping a fable in which the husband advances at the expense of the father, *The Shrew* gives theatrical life to developments in familial structure and in the relations of fathers and sons and husbands and wives in the closing years of the Elizabethan era, bringing to the surface and mirroring in its own ultimate irresolution and resistance to closure the dissonances and tensions those developments entailed, and offering in the process a good example of the complex negotiation Shakespearean theater undertakes with the world it represents.

The anti-paternalist inflections of Petruchio's "taming" of Katherina are adumbrated, of course, in what Petruchio chooses to say about himself to Hortensio in his initial appearance in the play. At a time when, as we know, wealthy fathers exercised a great deal of power over their sons by wielding and manipulating the weapon of the patrimony,[12] Petruchio very much puts himself outside the "loop" of paternal and communal control—and distinguishes himself both from Lucentio and from his counterpart, Ferando, in *A Shrew*—when he declares his father, "old Antonio," to be deceased, with any hint of grief or anxiety at the prospect of being forced fatherless to make his way in the "maze" of the world promptly offset by a reference to the inheritance the death of that parent has likely brought: "Crowns in my purse . . . and goods at home" (1.2.49–57), a "consolation" he reiterates with epigrammatic tartness when he declares shortly afterward to Gremio that "[m]y father dead, my fortune lives for me, / And I do hope good days and long to see" (191–92). So, too, at a time when the institution of marriage was often construed as a commercial enterprise, Petruchio is in the comparatively enviable position of possessing, on the one hand, a father's good name with which to pass Baptista's pedigree reference check, while being unburdened, on the other, with a living father to propitiate or deny him access to his venture capital. To mix epithets from Shakespeare and proclamations of state, Petruchio is at once an "extravagant stranger"—though more extravagant than strange, in being known to someone in the community, Hortensio, and having an estate within easy commuting distance without being of the community—and that happiest of "masterless men"—a man answerable to no master, nor in need of any. Unlike that other notable materialist in love, Bassanio, whose quest for Portia entails no little expense, and jeopardy, to his friend and father stand-in Antonio, Petruchio is financially free to travel the world at least as far as Padua, in hopes of "wiv[ing] it wealthily," and if "wealthily, then happily" (1.2.75–76).

Nor does it take long for the implications for Baptista of Petruchio's independence to become clear. Exemplary is the "peremptory" question rehearsed in the title of this essay, "If she and I be pleas'd, what's that to you?" (2.1.303), through which Petruchio legitimates his claim to Katherina and preempts her objections by denying the legitimacy of Baptista and those gathered in the paternal domicile to speak and voice any objections for her, leaving speechless not only Katherina but, by his own admission, Baptista, who is left with nothing to voice but his blessing (318–19). Disrupted, in the process, is the curious exercise in paternal manipulation in which Baptista had been engaging with Katherina and Bianca: wherein Baptista's insistence upon getting the elder daughter married first to get Katherina off his hands and dowries for both daughters is tempered with, to recall a Jamesian phrase, "detachment in his zeal" and a *festina lente* approach (2.1.111–13), and a clear disposition not to lose his power by using it too quickly.[13] Undermined, in turn, are the various socially sanctioned signatures of paternal control: the right to withhold permission to marry, the paternally staged wedding feast, and, at the end of the play, an even more absolute power. To a daughter, Theseus advises Hermia in *A Midsummer Night's Dream*, a "father should be as a god; / One that compos'd your beauties; yea, and one / To whom you are but as a form in wax, / By him imprinted, and within his power, / To leave the figure, or disfigure it" (1.1.46–51). By the end of *The Shrew*, impressed by Katherina's obedience, Baptista has ceded that power to Petruchio, since, he admits, Katherina "is chang'd, as she had never been" (5.2.115), and Baptista's attempt to reclaim at least a share in that power and reconstitute Katherina as a daughter by offering Petruchio another dowry for her produces an interesting deflection and demurring "Nay" (116–18), unlike the far more open-palmed "Thanks sweet father" the same offer elicits from Ferando in *A Shrew* (88). Indeed, though Katherina's "disfigurement" is, as we have noted, precisely what Grumio had predicted Petruchio would bring about through the use of his verbal and rhetorical "rope-tricks" (1.2.110–15), it is interesting that, as both Novy (1979, 272) and Joel Fineman (1985) have observed (154–55), in the latter part of the play this "disfiguring" power of language is turned against yet another father figure, Vincentio, who in addition to the indignities he suffers through the subterfuges of his son Lucentio, is most memorably disfigured, first by being transfigured as a young girl during one of Petruchio and Katherina's obedience training sessions (4.5.27–41), only to be restored by Petruchio in unflatteringly senescent terms that would put him fairly close to the end of Jaques' seven ages of man: "old, wrinkled, faded, withered" (43), a generational put-down only underscored when Katherina punningly seeks pardon of Vincentio for her transgression on the grounds that she had been "bedazzled with the sun" (4.5.46 ff.).

To be sure, it might be objected that to italicize the anti-paternalist elements of the Petruchio plot is, after all, to consider only half the play, and that however subversive of paternal authority the Petruchio-Katherina plot may be, Shakespeare has provided the Lucentio-Bianca subplot for recuperative balance. Indeed, to the extent to which Shakespeare draws upon Gascoigne's *Supposes* and through him Ariosto and, ultimately, the domestic drama of Plautian comedy, he invokes a paradigm of the ways in which a play can "playfully" balance impulses subversive and recuperative, giving comic delight through scenarios in which aristocratic sons pursue their romantic designs by changing places with their servants in order to deceive elder rivals—or, as Lucentio confides to Bianca, to "beguile the old pantaloon" (3.1.36)—and to circumvent the authority of their fathers, only ultimately to resume their rightful places and beg and receive their benevolent fathers' forgiveness and, no less important, their blessings upon and financial support for the prodigals' marital choices. Thoroughly patriarchalist and "classist," the world of these plays selectively personalizes the relations of master and servant to turn servants into children, while making clear that no transgression is unforgivable if it does not violate status and the rightful order. Hence, in *Supposes* the wily slave Dulypo laments the deceit he has practiced against his master Phylogano, who, he recalls, "hath brought me up unto this day, and

nourished me as if I had bene his owne" (Bullough 1957, 146), while Phylogano's son, Erostrato, is forgiven the otherwise capital indiscretion of having physically seduced the young lady of the household, when the lady's
father, Damon, discovering that Erostrato is a noble youth in servant drag and
the son of the noble Phylogano, rejoices at having "gotten so toward a sonne
in lawe to my selfe, and so worthye a father in lawe to my daughter" (Bullough 1957, 157).

Here again, what is noteworthy about Shakespeare's adaptation of the
Supposes source, and what distinguishes the treatment of the Lucentio-Bianca
subplot in *The Shrew* from its counterpart in *A Shrew*, is the degree to which
The Shrew accentuates its anti-paternalist elements while suppressing or muting those details that would ultimately affirm a view of society and human
relations with a father firmly in charge. For example, it is *The Shrew*, as has
often been observed, that gives Bianca a dramatic life and voicing her fore-
bears in Gascoigne, Ariosto, and Roman comedy decidedly lack; indeed, the
first hard evidence that Bianca is more than the blank her name gives her out
to be, and Lucentio and others take her to be, comes in the tutorial scene, in
which, confirming, perhaps, contemporary misogynists' worst convictions
about what happens when a woman studies the classics, Bianca and Lucentio
subvert the intentions of father Baptista—and grandfather clone Gremio—by
turning the parsing of a text, appropriately about the fall of Troy and its patriarch Priam, into an interlinear tryst, a subversion of the patriarch both in, and,
literally, between the lines (3.1). And if in both *Supposes* (Bullough 1957,
157–58) and *A Shrew* (82) much is made of the rapprochement of peccant
prodigal and benevolent father, in *The Shrew* that exchange is left curiously
unresolved, with Lucentio seeking pardon of Vincentio, but with Vincentio's
actual granting of forgiveness occurring—if anywhere—offstage. Uttered by
the aggrieved father Vincentio near the end of the play are the sentiment and
ideal of behavior so esteemed in the conduct books of the age,[14] and so resonant in, as we have seen, *Supposes* and *A Shrew*: " 'Tis a good hearing when
children are toward" (5.2.182), though here the *sententia* dangles ambigu-
ously, divested of its cautionary force by the unresolved state of affairs
between Vincentio and Lucentio and rendered all the more ambiguous by
being coupled with Lucentio's complaining rejoinder, "But a harsh hearing
when women are froward" (183). In fact, to the extent to which Lucentio's
wooing has obtained a wife no less shrewish than Katherina had been, while
Petruchio's methods produce an obedient wife, the audience might well feel
tempted to read Lucentio's plight as the just reward for the filial deceit in
which he has engaged through much of the play. At the same time, the deference Lucentio must display toward his father at the end of the play, coupled
with the deference he is apparently not about to receive from Bianca, only
reminds us of the degree to which Lucentio has not been his "own man" from

the outset—except in the literal sense that he becomes his "own man" by exchanging identities with "his man," Tranio, a descendant of the "wily slave" figure, who does much of Lucentio's thinking for him throughout the play. Through the characterization of Lucentio, then, subordination to a father's will, a wife's whim, and a servant's wit are drawn into a curious and socially disquieting alignment.

In fact, for all of the commendation due Shakespeare for his theatrically clever intertwining in *The Shrew* of its two comic fables, the integration and juxtaposition of the two plots ultimately produce more a disjunction than a "smooth" blending. For even as Petruchio's "taming" strategy has entailed a forcible dissociation of himself and Katherina from the patriarchal household, rites, and demands of Baptista, so in the latter stages of the play, the actions of the two plots, instead of coming together, actually diverge and peer and leer at each other as at two different and even inimical visions of familial structure and domestic relations. Thus, Petruchio turns Katherina's desire "to see the end of this ado" involving Vincentio and the penitent Lucentio into the occasion for an obedience test, demanding a kiss from Katherina while letting the imbroglio resulting from Lucentio's quest for Bianca slip and play itself out offstage, exacting, in the process, undivided attention, not only from Katherina, but from the audience as well (5.1.142–50). Indeed, the *discordia concors* of the two stories, and the underlying difference in their visions of domestic bliss, get epitomized in Petruchio's parting and rather enigmatic taunt to the suddenly "beshrewed" Lucentio and Hortensio that "[w]e three are married, but you two are sped" (5.2.185); for while the latter half of the distich is often glossed ironically to mean "finished" in the sense of "done for," it is also, and more interestingly, an echo of the rhetoric of the quest that permeates the world and dramatic tradition of *Supposes*. Petruchio's barb underscores the theatrical antecedents of the Lucentio-Bianca plot as if to imply that the "success," the speeding, of Lucentio and Hortensio in their quests to marry has little to do with success in marriage, and implicitly relegates to the world of mere theater the vision of the paternally controlled society that plays like *Supposes* may temporarily disrupt only to reaffirm.

Still, what lies behind the anti-paternalist tropics in *The Shrew*, and how do they affect our sense of the workings of Katherina and Petruchio's relationship? To the first question we may respond by deferring, albeit quite sketchily, to the testimony of the times, which, a number of historians have claimed, witnessed among other things two significant and not entirely compatible developments in the structure of familial and social relations: on the one hand, a reiterated assertion of the dignity of the married state with growing attention to its status as a genuinely corporate enterprise binding man and woman in a partnership with mutual, if complementary, responsibilities; on the other hand, a growing reassertion of patriarchal control in such matters as the choice of a spouse and that of a career, a reassertion that in numerous discourses of the age gets translated and mythologized in the terms of generational strife, of youth versus age.[15]

Thus, in the juxtaposition of its plot and subplot *The Shrew* might be said to bring into a fictitious collision two rather complementary arrangements of familial relations: one exemplative of an older, perhaps more aristocratic order, metonymized in the Lucentio-Bianca plot, in which patriarchy is ensured through control of patrimony and perpetuated through dynastic manipulation, and in which both sons and daughters are treated as currency and units of exchange; the other evoking a newer, emergent variation, in which the marital pair has a greater degree of financial autonomy and, thus, personal independence. At the same time, *The Shrew* also calls attention to complementary notions about parental rights in the disposition of children in marriage, simultaneously exposing the strains in the attempts of a number of commentators to reconcile what were deemed to be the sacred rights of the parents and the sacred obligations of children to their parents with the persistent recognition that the rights of the parents were not absolute in this matter—indeed, that they might not even take precedence over those of the state—and that the need of the married pair to be compatible came before the desires of the parents.[16]

Yet if *The Shrew* can be said to reflect the developments and concerns of its age, the mirror it holds up can hardly be said to be transparent, and if, to use Louis Montrose's (1980) term, the play "mediates" the dissonances of the times (63), its mediation would appear to assume the form of a "playful" legislation. In Petruchio's peremptory question and forcible separation of Katherina from the disposition and intercessory controls of Baptista, the play enacts a peculiarly theatrical—if theatrically distanced—intervention in the world it represents, bringing the strains in familial relations into view through a comic confrontation and rupture in which the new order displaces the old. As Novy (1979) has commented, "in dramatizing the relation of youth to age, [*The Shrew*] gives lip service to patriarchy and victory to youth" (279)—though, in the farcical character of its violence the play laughingly stops short of declaring victory for youth, even as, as we have seen, the "lip service" it pays to age is little more than a murmur.[17] At the same time, even as the comic machinery of the play focuses its audience's attention upon the dynamics of the power struggle between Petruchio and Katherina, *The Shrew* at once articulates and allegorizes, and lets stand unchallenged, many of the recurrent assertions about the structure and powers of the marital state: to wit, that it is a little commonwealth (4.1.182 ff., 5.2.155–60), that, like any commonwealth, it functions best when a state of peace obtains among its members (5.2.108), and that to ensure this peace, the marriage, like any commonwealth, must invest in a strong leader, as Petruchio puts it, "an awefull rule, and right supremacy" (5.2.109).[18]

How, then, are we to respond to Petruchio and Katherina's relationship, and are we to read in Katherina's accommodation of Petruchio's demands merely the superseding of one form of patriarchalist tyranny for another?[19] Fineman, Novy, and Newman have all, with differing formulations and emphases, argued that the effects of the presence of the anti-paternalist elements we have examined are to make us more aware of the play as play, more sensitive to the patriarchal ideology it inscribes as a cultural construct, and more receptive, therefore, to the rhetorical playfulness of Katherina's final speech and Petruchio's final declarations of victory.[20] And, indeed, one effect of Petruchio's verbal and physical belligerence toward icons of paternalism is to underscore the opportunism and artificiality of the larger claims he makes for himself as husband; all the more does his success at demystifying the absolutist claims of the father make his own pretensions to obedience from Katherina seem an exercise in ideological mystification, reminding us as well of a tendency in the arguments advanced on behalf of husbands in writings of the period to arrogate to the husband over his wife powers hitherto accorded the father over his children. For that matter, Gremio's report of Petruchio's cuffing the priest at the marriage ceremony (3.2.157–65) recalls only to burlesque what Lawrence Stone has noted as the tendency in a number of households in the era to concentrate religious authority and responsibility for religious education in the person of the husband (154–55).

In fact, it is questionable whether any play can be taken unqualifiably to affirm a patriarchalist view of experience and marital relations that presents Petruchio as the preeminent embodiment of patriarchy. Quite apart from his assault upon the emblems and personages of paternal authority, Petruchio's farcical entrance into the play in his knockabout exchange with Grumio frames him in a travesty of the master-servant relationship and provides a crude but all too revealing adumbration of the dialectic with which Petruchio "tames" Katherina, with Petruchio's efforts to gain mastery verbally having to give way increasingly to threats and applications of physical coercion. And while, as Newman (1991) has noted, Petruchio's dragging Katherina away from the wedding feast on a caricature of a horse certainly does recall the carnivalesque spectacle of the charivari or skimmington often used to tame shrewish women (131–34),[21] it should not be overlooked that such spectacles involved not simply the shaming of the woman, but the humiliation of the aggrieved husband as well, and that integral to the degradation Petruchio orchestrates for Katherina is his self-degradation, a self-degradation emblematized in Petruchio's garb and behavior. And if, in turn, Petruchio's "winning" strategy for taming is to become, as the servingman Curtis says, "more shrew than" Katherina (4.1.85), co-opting her voice and "shrewish" tongue, the strategy also succeeds in exposing the cultural relativism inherent in the very etymology of the word *shrew*, a word which, when applied to a human, is ever an index of deviation, with women deemed "shrewish" in the degree to which they act like men who are "shrewish" in the degree to which they in some unpleasant ways resemble the beast of that name. Hence, even as Petruchio presses his patriarchalist claims upon Katherina, he does so by effacing the essentialist distinctions upon which patriarchal prerogatives and respectability depend, a case, it would seem, of destroying patriarchy in order to save it.

It could—ever so cautiously—be argued, then, that even as Petruchio's demystification of the emblems of paternalism helps to attune us to the rhetoricity of his own patriarchalist arguments, so does it help us to appreciate the subversively forensic character of the patriarchalist sentiments voiced by Katherina in her climactic speech. "As the Eccho answereth but one for many which are spoken her," the Elizabethan divine Henry Smith (1591) declares, echoing the thoughts of many on the subject, "so a maydes answere should be in a word, for she which is full of talke, is not likelie to proove a quyet wife" (30). Katherina's speech, cued as it is by Petruchio and framed by an expectant audience as if it were a recitation in rehearsal, answers to Smith's notion of an "eccho" neither in quantity nor content, and in its magni- and grandiloquence would seem, superficially at least, a rather indirect means of— to borrow the subtitle of Lynda Boose's (1991) compelling essay—"taming the woman's unruly member." Instead, exemplifying the rhetorical tactic of varying through amplification[22]—and unlike the version of the speech in *A Shrew*, with its unitary refrain that wives must compensate for the First Wife's malefaction (87)—it draws upon the extensive commentary on marriage in the period to offer a contractual reading of the institution which, amidst echoes, as critics have shown, of the Wife of Bath,[23] commits the husband to far more responsibility to his spouse than he might deem ideal, and which effectively qualifies without openly contradicting Petruchio's previous, and equally derivative, formulation of wife as chattel (2.2.230 ff.).[24]

Still—and even though the theatrical framing of Katherina's speech as a performance makes it more tempting to hear in it the inflections of parodic distancing—to invoke Katherina's speech as a subversion of Petruchio's triumph may well resemble all too closely those critical "salvage" operations and efforts to make Shakespeare come out on the "right" side that Woodbridge (1984) has so trenchantly derided (221–22). If, after all, Stone (1977) is correct in his contention that "patriarchy for its effective exercise depends not so much on raw power or legal authority as on a recognition by all concerned of its legitimacy, hallowed by ancient tradition, moral theology, and political theory" (151), then one must contend with an uncomfortable paradox: the less one takes the speech as a piece of patriarchalist ventriloquism forcibly imposed upon Katherina, and the more one hears in it the appropriation and workings of Katherina's mind, then all the more does it seem, with its appeals—if not to moral theology, than surely to "hallowed" tradition and "political theory"—a testimony not simply to Petruchio's "raw power," but to the power of ideological indoctrination.

At the same time, if there is a possibility of subversion in Katherina's speech, it arises from the degree to which Petruchio's "triumph" paradoxically depends for its completion upon the possibility of his wife's resistance, upon the degree to which a vision of the marital state acceptable to Petruchio the would-be patriarch must be entertained and articulated dialogically, even as Petruchio strives to bring the question of Katherina's obedience to him to a monologic resolution. To what extent the argumentation of Katherina's discourse on the married state is culled from her notes on Petruchio's lectures is, of course, left significantly unclear. Not fully clear, for that matter, is the precise rhetorical effect of the speech—indeed, we can only speculate that it is more effective than the "sermon of continency" Petruchio had delivered earlier, and offstage, the report of which, we might recall, had produced titters from his servants, for whom it was but one more example of Petruchio's killing the shrew "in her own humor," eliciting from them an unwonted expression of sympathy for Katherina's tribulations (4.1.179–87). In the immediate aftermath of Katherina's speech, attention is drawn from the substance of its argument to the dramatic and rhetorical "spin" put on it by various of the males onstage. As has been his self-styled signature mode throughout the play (see 2.1.131), Petruchio seizes power through the "peremptory" gesture, declaring victory and withdrawing, sealing his victory, very literally, with what tends in Shakespearean comedy to be the weapon of choice for "taming the woman's unruly member," a kiss. And yet, though Petruchio's kiss may silence Katherina, it does not render inaudible those "jarring notes" of social, indeed, familial, discord Lucentio had earlier declared banished; stichomythically vying for the final word, and moral, instead are, as we have seen, both the aggrieved patriarch Vincentio, who, with a self-serving aptitude for homologous reasoning, draws lessons filial from behavior conjugal, and the admonished *filius* himself, Lucentio, who no less self-servingly changes the subject:

> VINCENTIO 'Tis a good hearing when children are toward.
> LUCENTIO But a harsh hearing when women are froward. (5.2.182–83)

With the hint of this dialogism, as in the vein of anti-paternalist reference, *The Shrew* brings to the surface dissonances in the structure of familial relations that it will ultimately leave unresolved. In mirroring and leaving unresolved such dissonances *The Shrew* may be a truer allegory of its times than is at all convenient for a neat, even neatly ironic, reading, and it enforces upon us a sense of its theatricality and theatrical distance from the world to which it holds up a mirror in its ability to bring its action to an end without bringing the debate to which it has called attention to a close. In its final moments *The Shrew* drops hints of this irresolution even as the characters take their conventionally festive leave, the loudest of these hints, perhaps, in the notorious failure of the play, as we have noted above, to close the frame introduced in the induction, omitting in the process the sort of affirmation of the rightful order one encounters in *A Shrew*. And certainly the finality of the victory to which Petruchio lays claim in *The Shrew* is interestingly interrogated and attenuated in the intertextual elaboration the "history" of Petruchio and Katherina receives in John Fletcher's *The Woman's Prize: Or, The Tamer Tamed* (1611), a play which, set some time after Katherina's death, extends the narrative line of *The Shrew* and with it the struggle Petruchio had declared ended. Commencing from the premise that neither Katherina nor Petruchio enjoyed in their marriage the "peace" and "quiet life" Petruchio had thought a wife's obedience would ensure (5.2.108–10), *The Woman's Prize* locates connubial bliss in a mutual subjugation, with Petruchio subjected to a "taming" at the hands of his unsubmissive new wife, Maria, who—with a nod to Lysistrata and the aid of an army of "killer shrews"—gains psychological mastery over Petruchio, only to vow to be her husband's "servant" (see 1.1.31–38, 1.2.141–45, 5.4.44–54). To be sure, Leah Marcus (1992) has cogently dubbed *The Woman's Prize* an "antidote" to the "patriarchal ideology" she sees as unqualifiably ascendant in *The Shrew* (199).[25] And yet, even as it offers its own variation on the relationship of resistance and tradition in the shrew-taming fable, Fletcher's "sequel" to *The Shrew* may also be viewed as rendering more perceptible the dissonances, the polyphony, *The Shrew* embodies; helping to underscore the complex play of resistance and tradition within Shakespeare's play, it enables us to hear with a sharper, if retrospective, appreciation both the incredulity and admiration contemporary audiences may have heard in Lucentio's play-ending remark, " 'Tis a wonder, by your leave, she will be tam'd so" (5.2.189).

NOTES

Originally published in *Renaissance Drama* 26 (1995): 105–27. Reprinted with the permission of Thomas Moisan and *Renaissance Drama*.

1. See Boose 1992; see also the attention paid by Patricia Parker (1992) to the social implications of the "preposterous" in *The Taming of the Shrew* (198–99). For a comic epitome of contemporary concerns about the rightful relations between fathers and sons, we might recall the nonrecognition scene involving Launcelot Gobbo and his father in *The Merchant of Venice* (2.2.33–101), culminating in Launcelot's proverbial inversion, "it is a wise father that knows his own child" (76–77).

2. For an incisive account of the textual complexities—and critical possibilities— of the relationship between *The Shrew* and *A Shrew*, see Leah Marcus 1992. In my own synoptic glances at the two works, I follow Marcus in taking *A Shrew* as a work for which Shakespearean authorship can neither be said to have been definitively established nor dismissed out of hand. And though, as my commentary would suggest, I diverge somewhat from Marcus in the degree to which I see

the marginal voicings of social dissidence in *A Shrew* more forcibly "contained" than they are in *The Shrew*, like Marcus I take *A Shrew* and *The Shrew* as richly illuminating. See also the summary of the discussion of the provenance of *The Taming of the Shrew* and its relationship to the First Folio *Shrew* in Oliver 1982 (13–34).

3. In his gloss on the word, H. J. Oliver speculates that "comonty" may be Sly's mistake for "commodity" (105), a word which one of the players in the Quarto version employs, apparently, to denote an alternative to the "tragical," only to be admonished by one of his fellow players:

> SAN. Marrie my lord you maie have a Tragicall
> Or a comoditie, or what you will.
> THE OTHER   A Comedie thou shoulst say, souns thout shame us all. (45)

All references to Shakespeare's works are contained within the text. References to *The Taming of the Shrew* are taken from the Riverside (Shakespeare 1974) edition. References to the Quarto play, *The Taming of a Shrew*, are taken from the text of the play edited by Holderness and Loughrey (1992). References to *Supposes* are drawn from the text of the play in Bullough 1957.

4. Nor is it only in the induction that the audience is alerted to the theatrical character of what they are witnessing. In making the case for considering the stage directions of the First Folio *Shrew* to be derived from Shakespeare's own directions, Oliver (1982) notes the frequency with which characters throughout the play are denoted not simply by name but by occupation or sociological status or category, as, for example, "drunkard," "Widow," "servingman," "his boy," "his man," with the effect of reminding the audience that the figures before them are representations, and, thus, fictive constructs (7–9). So, too, the introductory speeches by Lucentio (1.1.1–24) and Petruchio (1.2.1–5), which contain successive announcements of where the scene of the play is set, have the effect of italicizing the scene as scene, as a place-name the audience conventionally, and consciously, agrees to accept as "Padua." So, too, see Michael Shapiro's (1993) argument in "Framing the Taming: Metatheatrical Awareness of Female Impersonation in *The Taming of the Shrew*," that *The Shrew* "flaunted its theatricality, principally by underscoring the use of male actors in female roles" (144).

5. Besides Barish (1980), see Bentley 1971, esp. 145–96; Patterson 1989, esp. 13–51; and Howard 1987.

6. Hence, in *A Disputation Betweene a Hee Conny-catcher, and a Shee Conny-catcher* (1592), Robert Greene has Nan, his "shee" cony catcher, demonstrate how a whore "will face [a gull] quite out of his money, and make him walk like a woodcock homeward by weeping cross, and so buy repentance with all the crowns in his purse" (Judges 1930, 213).

7. Among tradesmen, haberdashers in particular seem to have borne associations of wealth and served at times as the objects of social envy. John Stow's (1602) description of "Bridge warde within," for example, observes that "all the Bridge is replenished on both sides with large, fayre and beautifull buildings, inhabitants for the most part rich marchantes, and other wealthy Citizens, Mercers and Haberdashers" (211). Drawn from an earlier (ca. 1519–1535) stage in the Renaissance development of London as an economic center, "A treatise Concerning the Staple

and the Commodities of this Realme" (cited in Tawney and Power 1924, 111), identifies haberdashers as objects of popular economic discontent as interlopers and sellers of foreign wares to the disadvantage of domestic tradesmen: "now every street is full of theym; which sellith all fantasies and trifell, in distroying all handy crafts, whereby many riche men reson upon that distrution of the pore peple." As for evidence that the tailor was fair game for social satire, see Overbury 1890, 78–79.

8. Compare the comically protracted, and socially humiliating, stretch of stichomythia in *Supposes*, 141–42, in which Phylogano attempts to gain access to what he has been led to believe is the dwelling of his son Erostrato, only to be confronted by the "Scenese" who has been posing as Phylogano, and, thus, have his very identity emphatically challenged and denied.

9. In the introduction to their edition of *The Taming of a Shrew*, Graham Holderness and Bryan Loughrey (1992) suggest that the tendency of the play to take liberties with distinctions of status begins at or near the very beginning, when the Lord "changes himself into a servant, adopting a disguise calculated to render him indistinguishable from the lower orders. . . . The other servants thus become his 'fellowes' (coperpetrators of the practical joke), but also 'fellowes' in a more levelling sense, as the Lord appears to embrace a kind of class solidarity with his companions of the servile fraternity" (19).

10. Newman (1991, 49) paraphrases one possible interpretation of the "missing frame" when she observes that "[b]ecause the play has no final framing scene, no return to Sly, it could be argued that its artifice is relaxed, that the final scene is experienced naturalistically. The missing frame allows the audience to forget that Petruchio's taming of Kate is presented as a fiction."

11. Pertinent here is Marcus's (1992) contention that Slie's reappearance onstage after Kate and Ferando and the other "newlyweds" have departed contributes to a dramatic attenuation of Kate's capitulation speech. Followed immediately by her sister Emelia's defiant embrace of her own shrewishness (88) and then by the reappearance of a no more compunctious Slie, "Kate's message of submission is compromised," Marcus maintains, by being "contained within a series of dramatic events, rather like a nest of boxes, that narrows down its applicability and ideological impact to almost nothing" (188). Still, in the degree to which *A Shrew*, like *The Shrew*, permits us to see initial parallels between Kate and Slie as exempla of "shrewish," sociopathic behavior, the "bearing of Slie" at the end of the play "in his / Owne apparrell againe" would seem a forcible assertion of social reality that would rather underscore than undercut the submissive theme of Kate's speech.

12. See especially Louis Adrian Montrose's (1981) discussion of this phenomenon in the context of *As You Like It* in " 'The Place of a Brother' in *As You Like It*: Social Process and Comic Form."

13. Note Boose's (1992) contention (326) that Baptista, like other obstructive fathers in Shakespeare, arrogates to himself privileges contested in contemporary conduct books.

14. It is, for example, a sentiment that informs virtually every line and piece of instruction inscribed in Francis Seager's *The Schoole of Vertue, and booke of good nurture, teaching children and youth their duties* (1557, 1562).

15. See the discussions of these phenomena in Wright 1935 (201–5), Stone 1977 (131–36, 151–239), and Macfarlane 1986 (265–73). An example of the use of generational rivalry to explain economic displacements and tension surfaces in Bacon's essay (1625) "Of Vsurie," where it is asserted that "it is certain, that the Greatest Part of Trade, is driuen by Young Merchants, vpon Borrowing at Interest" (171).

16. So it is, for example, that Henry Smith (1591) argues that "[w]hen Christ saith, that a man should leave Father and Mother, and cleave to his wife, he signifieth how Christ left his father for his spouse, and that man doth not love his wife so much as he should untill he affect her more tha euer he did his father or mother" (51), while Robert Cleaver (1598) maintains that "[s]urely, if a husband (as nature, reason, and the holie Scripture doe witnesse) bee the head over his wife, and God their father: there ought to bee betweene them such societie and fellowship: yea, and greater then is betweene the Father and his sonne, and not such as is betweene the master and the seruant" (217–18).

17. Worth remembering here is Jeanne Addison Roberts's (1979) comment that "rarely does [Shakespeare] treat the rending of filial bands lightly" (122), though, as I hope the body of my reading would suggest, it is not, contrary to what I believe Roberts implies, simply in the Lucentio-Bianca subplot that the play airs generational discords.

18. See Henry Smith 1591, 52–53 and Cleaver 1598, 176–77.

19. Thus, Woodbridge (1984), for one, has concluded her discussion of the play by noting that "[w]hen all is said and done . . . I find it hard to regard this play as much of an improvement over the earlier shrew-taming tradition. Petruchio starves Kate, deprives her of sleep, publicly humiliates her; for this he is celebrated as having done the state some service" (206–7).

20. Employing a deconstructionist strategy, Fineman (1985) contends that "[t]he subversive language of woman with which the play begins, and in resistance to which the movement of the play is predicated, reappears at the end of the play so that its very sounding predicts the future as a repetition of the same old story" (155). Novy (1979), on the other hand, appropriates for her analysis Johan Huizinga's conception of *homo ludens* to paint an image of Katherina and Petruchio's relationship as a playful partnership, the "game element" in which combines "the attractions of the rhetoric of order and the energy of disorder" and enables Katherina ultimately to affirm traditional roles in marriage without internalizing and capitulating to them (278–79). For Newman (1991), lastly, Katherina's participation in such travesties of icons of paternalism as that enacted in the verbal transformation of Vincentio (4.5.27–57) has the effect of italicizing the gender distinctions in language and of calling attention to such distinctions in general as cultural constructs (47–48).

21. See the discussion of the role of the husband of the scold in the charivari and skimmington rites in Underdown 1985 (127–29).

22. For a discussion of the techniques of achieving rhetorical "amplitude," see Marion Trousdale's (1982) *Shakespeare and the Rhetoricians*, esp. 39–64.

23. To be sure, both David Bergeron (1968–1969, 279–86) and Sister Frances Gussenhoven (1983, 69–79) proceed from the premise that the force of Shakespeare's evocation of the Wife of Bath is to establish an analogy between the ulti-

mate submission, and submissiveness, of Katherina and the final transformation
of the Old Hag in the Wife's tale to a loving and faithful wife. What both pieces
let go unnoticed is the degree to which Katherina actually comes to resemble the
Wife, not by any means in submissiveness, but in rhetorical mastery. Like the
Wife, Katherina comes by the end of the play to "hold the floor" and control the
discourse, even though in doing so she is merely complying with Petruchio's
command. And like the Wife, Katherina makes use of her rhetorical control as an
occasion for reciting, not simply the duties a wife owes her husband, but the
responsibilities of a husband to his wife.

24. Consider the not unrepresentative, and relatively benign, pronouncement of
Thomas Overbury (1890), who from the outset of his "character" defines "A Good
Wife" as "a mans best moveable, a scien incorporate with the stocke, bringing
sweet fruit" (72).

25. See also the discussion of Fletcher's reading of *The Taming of the Shrew* in Molly
Smith (1995, 38–60).

WORKS CITED

Bacon, Sir Francis. 1625. *Essays*. London: Oxford University Press, 1966.

Baker, Stuart E. 1990. "Masks and Faces in *The Taming of the Shrew*." *New England
Theatre Conference* 1: 45–59.

Barish, Jonas. 1980. *The Antitheatrical Prejudice*. Berkeley: University of California
Press.

Bentley, Gerald Eades. 1971. *The Profession of Dramatist in Shakespeare's Time,
1590–1642*. Princeton: Princeton University Press.

Bergeron, David. 1968–1969. "The Wife of Bath and Shakespeare's *The Taming of the
Shrew*." *University Review* 35: 279–86.

Boose, Lynda E. 1991. "Scolding Brides and Bridling Scolds: Taming the Woman's
Unruly Member." *Shakespeare Quarterly* 42: 179–213.

———. 1992. "The Father and the Bride in Shakespeare." *PMLA* 97: 325–47.

———. 1994. "*The Taming of the Shrew*, Good Husbandry, and Enclosure." *Shakespeare Reread: The Texts in New Contexts*. Edited by Russ McDonald. Ithaca:
Cornell University Press.

Bullough, Geoffrey. 1957. *Narrative and Dramatic Sources of Shakespeare*. Vol. 1.
London: Routledge and Kegan Paul.

Chambers, E. K. 1923. *The Elizabethan Stage*. 4 vols. Oxford: Oxford University
Press.

Cleaver, Robert. 1598. *A Godlie Forme of Household Government: For the Ordering
of Private Families, according to the directions of Gods word*. London. STC
5383.

Dolan, Frances E., ed. 1996. *William Shakespeare's The Taming of the Shrew: Texts
and Contexts*. Boston: Bedford.

Fineman, Joel. 1985. "The Turn of the Shrew." In *Shakespeare and the Question of
Theory*. Edited by Patricia Parker and Geoffrey Hartman. New York: Methuen.

Fletcher, John. 1966. *The Woman's Prize: Or, The Tamer Tamed*. Edited by George B.
Ferguson. The Hague: Mouton.

Gussenhoven, Sister Frances. 1983. "Shakespeare's *Taming of the Shrew* and Chaucer's Wife of Bath: The Struggle for Marital Mastery." In *Chaucerian Shakespeare: Adaptation and Transformation.* Edited by E. Talbot Donaldson and Judith J. Kollmann. *Medieval and Renaissance Monograph Series* 2, 69–79. Detroit: Published or Michigan Consortium for Medieval and Early Modern Studies.

Hobsbawm, Eric. 1983. "Inventing Traditions." In *The Invention of Tradition.* Edited by Eric Hobsbawm and Terence Ranger. Cambridge: Cambridge University Press.

Holderness, Graham, and Bryan Loughrey, eds. 1992. *A Pleasant Conceited Historie, Called The Taming of a Shrew.* Lanham, Md.: Barnes and Noble.

Howard, Jean E. 1987. "Renaissance Antitheatricality and the Politics of Gender and Rank in *Much Ado about Nothing.*" In *Shakespeare Reproduced: The Text in History and Ideology.* Edited by Jean E. Howard and Marion F. O'Connor. New York: Methuen.

Judges, A.V., ed. 1930. *The Elizabethan Underworld: A Collection of Tudor and early Stuart tracts and ballads telling of the lives and misdoings of vagabonds, thieves, rogues and cozeners, and giving some account of the operation of the criminal law.* London: Routledge.

Kehler, Dorothea. 1987. "Echoes of the Induction in *The Taming of the Shrew.*" *Renaissance Papers 1986*: 31–42.

Macfarlane, Alan. 1986. *Marriage and Love in England: Modes of Reproduction, 1300–1840.* Oxford: Blackwell.

Macherey, Pierre. 1978. *A Theory of Literary Production.* Translated by Geoffrey Wall. London: Routledge and Kegan Paul.

Marcus, Leah. 1992. "The Shakespearean Editor as Shrew-Tamer." *English Literary Renaissance* 22: 177–200.

Moisan, Thomas. 1991. "'Knock me here soundly': Comic Misprision and Class Consciousness in Shakespeare." *Shakespeare Quarterly* 42: 276–90.

———. 1991. "Interlinear Trysting and 'household stuff': The Latin Lesson and the Domestication of Learning in *The Taming of the Shrew.*" *Shakespeare Studies* 23: 100–19.

Montrose, Louis Adrian. 1980. "The Purpose of Playing: Reflections on a Shakespearean Anthropology." *Helios* ns 7, no. 2: 51–74.

———. 1981. "'The Place of a Brother' in *As You Like It*: Social Process and Comic Form." *Shakespeare Quarterly* 32: 28–54.

———. 1996. *The Purpose of Playing: Shakespeare and the Cultural Politics of the Elizabethan Theatre.* Chicago: University of Chicago Press.

Newman, Karen. 1991. "Renaissance Family Politics and Shakespeare's *The Taming of the Shrew.*" In *Fashioning Femininity and English Renaissance Drama.* Chicago: University of Chicago Press, 1991.

Novy, Marianne L. 1979. "Patriarchy and Play in *The Taming of the Shrew.*" *English Literary Renaissance* 9: 264–80.

Oliver, H. J., ed. 1982. *The Taming of the Shrew.* Oxford: Oxford University Press.

Overbury, Sir Thomas. 1890. *The Miscellaneous Works in Prose and Verse of Sir Thomas Overbury.* Edited by Edward F. Rimbault. London: Reeves and Turner.

Parker, Patricia. 1992. "Preposterous Events." *Shakespeare Quarterly* 43: 186–213.

Patterson, Annabel. 1989. *Shakespeare and the Popular Voice*. Cambridge, Mass.: Blackwell.

Roberts, Jeanne Addison. 1979. *Shakespeare's English Comedy:* The Merry Wives of Windsor *in Context*. Lincoln, University of Nebraska Press.

Seager, Francis. 1562. *The Schoole of Vertue, and booke of good nurture, teaching children and youth their duties*. London. STC 22136.

Seronsy, Cecil C. 1963. "'Supposes' as the Unifying Theme in *The Taming of the Shrew*." *Shakespeare Quarterly* 14: 15–30.

Shakespeare,William. 1974. *The Riverside Shakespeare*. Edited by G. Blakemore Evans. Boston: Houghton Mifflin.

Shapiro, Michael. 1993. "Framing the Taming: Metatheatrical Awareness of Female Impersonation in *The Taming of the Shrew*." *Shakespeare Yearbook* 23: 143–66.

Smith, Henry. 1591. *A Preparative of Marriage*. London. STC 22686.

Smith, Molly. 1995. "John Fletcher's Response to the Gender Debate: *The Woman's Prize* and *The Taming of the Shrew*." *Papers on Language and Literature* 31: 38–60.

Stone, Lawrence. 1977. *The Family, Sex, and Marriage in England, 1500–1800*. New York: Harper and Row.

Stow, John. 1603. *A Survey of London*. Introduction by Charles Lethbridge Kingsford. 2 vols. 1908. Reprint London: Oxford University Press, 1971.

Stubbes, Phillip. 1583. *The Anatomie of Abuses*. London. STC 23376.

Tawney, R. H., and Eileen Power, eds. 1924. *Tudor Economic Documents: Being Select Documents Illustrating the Economic and Social History of Tudor England*. 3 vols. London: Longmans, Green.

Trousdale, Marion. 1982. *Shakespeare and the Rhetoricians*. London: Scolar.

Underdown, D. E. 1985. "The Taming of the Scold: The Enforcement of Patriarchal Authority in Early Modern England." In *Order and Disorder in Early Modern England*. Edited by Anthony Fletcher and John Stevenson. Cambridge: Cambridge University Press.

Wayne, Valerie. 1985. "Refashioning the Shrew." *Shakespeare Studies* 17: 159–87.

Woodbridge, Linda. 1984. *Women and the English Renaissance: Literature and the Nature of Womankind, 1540–1620*. Urbana: University of Illinois Press.

Wright, Louis B. 1935. *Middle-Class Culture in Elizabethan England*. Chapel Hill: University of North Carolina Press.

Household Kates
Domesticating Commodities
in *The Taming of the Shrew*

NATASHA KORDA

Commentary on Shakespeare's *The Taming of the Shrew* has frequently noted that the play's novel taming strategy marks a departure from traditional shrew-taming tales. Unlike his predecessors, Petruchio does not use force to tame Kate; he does not simply beat his wife into submission.[1] Little attention has been paid, however, to the historical implications of the play's unorthodox methodology, which is conceived in specifically economic terms: "I am he am born to tame you, Kate," Petruchio summarily declares, "And bring you from a wild Kate to a Kate / Conformable as other household Kates" (2.1.269–71).[2] Petruchio likens Kate's planned domestication to a domestication of the emergent commodity form itself, whose name parallels the naming of the shrew. The *Oxford English Dictionary* defines *cates* as "provisions or victuals bought (as distinguished from, and usually more delicate or dainty than, those of home production)." The term is an aphetic form of *acate*, which derives from the Old French *achat*, meaning "purchase."[3] Cates are thus by definition exchange-values—commodities, properly speaking—as opposed to use-values, or objects of home production.[4] In order to grasp the historical implications of *Shrew*'s unorthodox methodology and of the economic terms Shakespeare employs to shape its taming strategy, I would like first to situate precisely the form of its departure from previous shrew-taming tales. What differentiates *The Taming of the Shrew* from its precursors is not so much a concern with domestic economy—which has always been a central preoccupation of shrew-taming literature—but rather a shift in *modes of production* and thus in the very terms through which domestic economy is conceived. The coordinates of this shift are contained within the term *cates* itself, which, in distinguishing goods that are purchased from those that are produced within and for the home, may be said to map the historical shift from domestic use-value production to production for the market.

Prior to Shakespeare's play, shrews were typically portrayed as reluctant producers within the household economy, high-born wives who refused to engage in the forms of domestic labor expected of them by their humble tradesman husbands. In the ballad "The Wife Wrapped in a Wether's Skin," for example, the shrew refuses to brew, bake, wash, card, or spin on account of her "gentle kin" and delicate complexion:

> There was a wee cooper who lived in Fife,
> Nickety, nackity, noo, noo, noo
> And he has gotten a gentle wife. . . .
> Alane, quo Rushety, roue, roue, roue
>
> She wadna bake, nor she wadna brew,
> For the spoiling o her comely hue.
>
> She wadna card, nor she wadna spin,
> For the shaming o her gentle kin.
>
> She wadna wash, nor she wadna wring,
> For the spoiling o her gouden ring.[5]

The object of the tale was simply to put the shrew to work, to restore her (frequently through some gruesome form of punishment[6]) to her proper productive place within the household economy. When the cooper from Fife, who cannot beat his ungentle wife due to her gentle kin, cleverly wraps her in a wether's skin and tames her by beating the hide instead, the shrew promises: "Oh, I will bake, and I will brew, / And never mair think on my comely hue. / Oh, I will card, and I will, spin, / And never mair think on my gentle kin," and so on.[7] Within the tradition of shrew-taming literature prior to Shakespeare's play, the housewife's domestic responsibilities were broadly defined by a feudal economy based on household production, on the production of use-values for domestic consumption.[8]

With the decline of the family as an economic unit of production, however, the role of the housewife in late-sixteenth-century England was beginning to shift from that of skilled producer to savvy consumer. In this period household production was gradually being replaced by nascent capitalist industry, making it more economical for the housewife to purchase what she had once produced. Brewing and baking, for example, once a routine part of the housewife's activity, had begun to move from the home to the market, becoming the province of skilled (male) professionals.[9] Washing and spinning, while still considered "women's work," were becoming unsuitable activities for middle-class housewives and were increasingly delegated to servants, paid laundresses, or spinsters.[10] The housewife's duties were thus gradually moving away from the production of use-values within and for the home and toward the consumption of market goods, or cates, commodities produced outside the home. The available range of commodities was also greatly increased in the period, so that goods once considered luxuries, available only to the wealthiest elites, were now being found in households at every level of society.[11] Even "inferior artificers and many farmers," as William Harrison notes in his *Description of England*, had "learned . . . to garnish their cupboards with plate, their joint beds with tapestry and silk hangings, and their tables with carpets and fine napery."[12] *The Taming of the Shrew* may be said both to reflect and to participate in this cultural redefinition by portraying Kate not as a reluctant producer but rather as an avid and sophisticated consumer of market goods. When she is shown shopping in 4.3 (a scene I will discuss at greater length below), she displays both her knowledge of and preference for the latest fashions in apparel. Petruchio's taming strategy is accordingly aimed not at his wife's productive capacity—he never asks Kate to brew, bake, wash, card, or spin—but at her consumption. He seeks to educate Kate in her new role as a consumer of household cates.

Before examining in precisely what way Petruchio seeks to tame Kate's consumption of cates, I would like to introduce a further complication into this rather schematic account of the shift from household production to consumption, being careful not to conflate material change with ideological change. The ideological redefinition of the home as a sphere of consumption rather than production in sixteenth-century England did not, of course, correspond to the lived reality of every early modern English housewife. Many women continued to work productively, both within and outside the home.[13] Yet the acceptance of this ideology, as Susan Cahn points out, became the "price of upward social mobility" in the period and, as such, exerted a powerful influence on all social classes.[14] The early modern period marked a crucial change in the *cultural valuation* of housework, a change that is historically linked—as the body of feminist-materialist scholarship which Christine Delphy has termed "housework theory"[15] reminds us—to the rise of capitalism and development of the commodity form.[16]

According to housework theory, domestic work under capitalism is not considered "real" work because "women's productive labor is confined to use-values while men produce for exchange."[17] It is not that housework disappears with the rise of capitalism; rather, it becomes economically devalued. Because the housewife's labor has no exchange-value, it remains unremunerated and thus economically "invisible."[18] Read within this paradigm, *Shrew* seems to participate in the ideological erasure of housework by not representing it on the stage, by rendering it, quite literally, invisible. The weakness of this analysis of the play, however, is that it explains only what Kate does not do onstage and provides no explanation for what she actually does.

In continuing to define the housewife's domestic activity solely within a matrix of use-value production, housework theory—despite its claim to offer an historicized account of women's subjection under capitalism—treats housework as if it were itself, materially speaking, an unchanging, transhistorical entity, which is not, as we have seen, the historical case. For though the market commodity's infiltration of the home did not suddenly and magically absolve the housewife of the duty of housework, it did profoundly alter *both* the material form and the cultural function of such work insofar as it became an activity increasingly centered around the proper order, maintenance, and display of household cates—objects having, by definition, little or no use-value.

Privileging delicacy of form over domestic function, cates threaten to sever completely the bond linking exchange-value to any utilitarian end; they are commodities that unabashedly assert their own superfluousness. It is not simply that cates, as objects of exchange, are to be "distinguished from" objects of home production, however, as the *OED* asserts. Rather their very purpose is to signify this distinction, to signify their own distance from utility and economic necessity. What replaces the utilitarian value of cates is a symbolic or cultural value: cates are, above all, signifiers of social distinction or differentiation.[19] Housework theory cannot explain *Shrew*'s recasting of the traditional shrew-taming narrative because it can find no place in its strictly economic analysis for the housewife's role within a *symbolic* economy based on the circulation, accumulation, and display of status objects, or what Pierre Bourdieu terms "symbolic" (as distinct from "economic") capital.[20] How did the presence of status objects, or cates, within the nonaristocratic household transform, both materially and ideologically, the "domesticall duties" of the housewife? To what degree was her new role as a consumer and caretaker of household cates perceived as threatening? What new mechanisms of ideological defense were invented to assuage such perceived threats? I shall argue that it is precisely the cultural anxiety surrounding the housewife's new managerial role with respect to household cates which prompted Shakespeare to write a new kind of shrew-taming narrative.

To provide the framework for my analysis of Shakespeare's rewriting of the shrew-taming tradition, I would like to turn from housework theory to the theorization of domestic leisure and consumption, beginning with Thorstein Veblen's *Theory of the Leisure Class*. Like the housework theorists, Veblen maintains that the housewife's transformation from "the drudge and chattel of the man, both in fact and in theory,—the producer of goods for him to consume"—into "the ceremonial consumer of goods which he produces" leaves her no less his drudge and chattel (if only "in theory") than her predecessor.[21] For Veblen, however, the housewife's new form of drudgery is defined not by her unremunerated (and thus economically invisible) productivity but rather by her subsidized (and culturally conspicuous) nonproductivity itself. The housewife's obligatory "performance of leisure," Veblen maintains, is itself a form of labor or drudgery: "the leisure of the lady . . . is an occupation of an

ostensibly laborious kind . . . it is leisure only in the sense that little or no productive work is performed."[22] Just as the housewife's leisure renders her no
less a drudge of her husband, according to Veblen, her consumption of commodities likewise renders her no less his commodity, or chattel, insofar as she
consumes for her husband's benefit and not her own.[23] The housewife's "vicarious consumption" positions her as a status object, the value of which
derives precisely from its lack of utility: "She is useless and expensive," as
Veblen puts it, "and she is *consequently* valuable."[24]

When it comes to describing what constitutes the housewife's nonproductive activity, however, Veblen becomes rather vague, remarking only in
passing that it centers on "the maintenance and elaboration of the household
paraphernalia."[25] Jean Baudrillard offers a somewhat more elaborated account
in his *Critique of the Political Economy of the Sign*, a text strongly influenced
by Veblen. With the advent of consumer culture, he asserts, the "cultural status of the [household] object enters into direct contradiction with its practical
status," and "housekeeping has only secondarily a practical objective (keeping objects ready for use)"; rather, "it is a manipulation of another order—
symbolic—that sometimes totally eclipses practical use."[26] Like Veblen,
Baudrillard views the housewife's conspicuous leisure and consumption as
themselves laborious, though for the latter this new form of housework is
more specifically described as the locus of a "*symbolic* labor," defined as the
"active manipulation of signs" or status objects.[27] The value of the housewife's
manipulation of the "cultural status of the object," Baudrillard maintains,
emerges not from an "economic calculus" but from a "symbolic and statutory
calculus" dictated by "relative social class configurations."[28] For both Veblen
and Baudrillard, then, the housewife plays a crucial role in the production of
cultural value in a consumer society.

It is in the early modern period that the housewife first assumes this vital
new role within what I shall term the *symbolic order of things*.[29] The figure of
"Kate" represents a threat to this order, a threat that Petruchio seeks to tame
by educating her for her role as a manipulator of status objects. To say that
Kate poses a threat to the symbolic order of *things*, however, is to signal yet
another departure from the traditional shrew-taming narrative, in which the
shrew is characteristically represented as a threat to the symbolic order of *language*. This linguistic threat is not absent from Shakespeare's version of the
narrative and has received substantial critical commentary. In order to compare this threat with that posed by her relationship to things, I will briefly consider two compelling accounts of the threat posed by Kate's words.

In Shakespeare's rendering of the traditional topos, Joel Fineman points
out, the shrew's linguistic excess becomes a threat not of too many words but
rather of too much meaning. Kate's speech underscores the way in which language always "carries with it a kind of surplus semiotic baggage, an excess of
significance, whose looming, even if unspoken, presence cannot be kept

quiet."[30] The semantic superfluity of Kate's speech leads to a series of " 'fretful' verbal confusions" in which the "rhetoricity of language is made to seem the explanation of [her] ongoing quarrel with the men who are her master."[31] The example Fineman cites is Kate's unhappy lute lesson, recounted by her hapless music master, Hortensio:

> BAP.   Why then, thou canst not break her to the lute?
> HOR.   Why no, for she hath broke the lute to me.
>   I did but tell her she mistook her frets, . . .
>   "Frets, call you these?" quoth she, "I'll fume with them."
>   And with that word she struck me on the head. (2.1.147–53)

Fineman sees Kate's shrewish "fretting" as a direct result of the rhetorical excess of her speech—in this case, her pun on *frets*. Karen Newman adds that Kate's "linguistic protest" is directed against "the role in patriarchal culture to which women are assigned, that of wife and object of exchange in the circulation of male desire."[32] Kate's excessive verbal fretting turns her into an unvendible commodity. Yet while Newman emphasizes Kate's own position as an "object of exchange" between men, she specifically discounts the importance of material objects elsewhere in the play. The role of things in Petruchio's taming lesson is subordinated in Newman's argument to the more "significant" role of words: "Kate is figuratively killed with kindness, by her husband's rule over her not so much in *material* terms—the withholding of food, clothing and sleep—but in the withholding of *linguistic* understanding."[33]

In contrast to Newman, Lena Cowen Orlin, in a recent article on "material culture theatrically represented," foregrounds the play's many "references to and displays of objects, and especially household furnishings." Orlin does not simply insist on the importance of *res* within the play at the expense of *verba*. She maintains that both material and linguistic forms of exchange, far from being opposed within the play, are repeatedly identified. Drawing on Levi-Strauss, Orlin argues that the play "synthesizes" the three "forms of exchange that constitute social life," namely, the exchange of wives, of goods, and of words.[34] While I agree with Orlin's claim that the play draws very explicit connections between its material and symbolic economies—particularly as these economies converge on what I have called the symbolic order of things—I resist the notion that Kate's position with respect to this order is simply that of a passive object of exchange. Kate is not figured as one more cate exchanged between men within the play; rather, it is precisely her *unvendibility* as a commodity on the marriage market that creates the dramatic dilemma to be solved by the taming narrative. The question concerns the relation between Kate's own position as a cate and her role as a consumer of cates. For Kate's unvendibility is specifically attributed within the play to her untamed consumption of cates.

At the start of the play, Kate's consumption is represented as a threat that Petruchio, in his novel way, will seek to tame. Both Newman and Fineman take Petruchio's first encounter with Kate, perhaps the most "fretful" instance of verbal sparring in the play, to demonstrate that the shrew-tamer chooses to fight his battle with the shrew "in verbal kind."[35] "O, how I long to have some chat with her" (2.1.162), he utters, in anticipation of their meeting. The content of Petruchio's punning "chat" with Kate, however, is principally preoccupied with determining her place within the symbolic order of things. The encounter begins with Petruchio stubbornly insisting on calling Katherina "Kate":

> PET.:   Good morrow, Kate, for that's your name, I hear.
> KAT.:   Well have you heard, but something hard of hearing;
>   They call me Katherine that do talk of me.
> PET.:   You lie, in faith, for you are call'd plain Kate,
>   And bonny Kate, and sometimes Kate the curst;
>   But Kate, the prettiest Kate in Christendom,
>   Kate of Kate Hall, my super-dainty Kate,
>   For dainties are all Kates.... (ll. 182–89)

If Petruchio's punning appellation of Kate as a "super-dainty" cate seems an obvious misnomer in one sense—she can hardly be called "delicate"—in another it is quite apt, as his gloss makes clear. The substantive *dainty*, deriving from the Latin *dignitatem* (worthiness, worth, value), designates something that is "estimable, sumptuous, or rare."[36] In describing her as a "dainty," Petruchio appears to be referring to her value as a commodity, or cate, on the marriage market (he has just discovered that her dowry is worth "twenty thousand crowns" [l.122]).

Yet Petruchio's reference to Kate as "super-dainty" refers to her not as a commodity or object of exchange between men but rather as a *consumer* of commodities. According to the *OED*, in its adjectival form the term *dainty* refers to someone who is "nice, fastidious, particular; sometimes, over-nice" as to "the quality of food, comforts, and so on." In describing Kate as "super-dainty," Petruchio implies that she belongs to the latter category; she is "over-nice," not so much discriminating as blindly obedient to the dictates of fashion. Sliding almost imperceptibly from Kate as a consumer of cates to her status as a cate, Petruchio's gloss ("For dainties are all Kates") elides the potential threat posed by the former by subsuming it under the aegis of the latter. His pun on *Kates/cates* dismisses the significance of Kate's role as a consumer (as does Newman's reading) by effectively reducing her to an object of exchange between men.

The pun on *Kates/cates* is repeated at the conclusion of Petruchio's "chat" with Kate (in the pronouncement quoted at the beginning of this essay) and effects a similar reduction: "And therefore, setting all this chat aside, / Thus in plain terms," Petruchio proclaims, summing up his unorthodox marriage proposal, "I am he am born to tame you, Kate, / And bring you from a wild Kate to a Kate / Conformable as other household Kates" (ll. 261–62, 269–71). And yet, in spite of his desire to speak "in plain terms," Petruchio cannot easily restrict or "tame" the signifying potential of his own pun. For once it is articulated, the final pun on *Kates/cates* refuses to remain tied to its modifier, "household," and insists instead upon voicing itself, shrewishly, where it shouldn't (i.e., each time Kate is named). In so doing, it retrospectively raises the possibility that cates themselves may be "wild," that there is something unruly, something that must be made to conform, in the commodity form itself. This possibility in turn discovers an ambiguity in Petruchio's "as," which may mean either "as other household cates are conformable" or "as I have brought other household cates into conformity." The conformity of household cates cannot be taken for granted within the play because cates, unlike use-values, are not proper to or born of the domestic sphere but are produced outside the home by the market. They are by definition extra-domestic or to-be-domesticated. Yet insofar as cates obey the logic of exchange and of the market, they may be said to resist such domestication. Petruchio cannot restrict the movement of cates in his utterance, cannot set all "chat" aside and speak "in plain terms," because commodities, like words, tend to resist all attempts to restrict their circulation and exchange.

The latter assertion finds support—quite literally—in Petruchio's own chat. The term *chat*, as Brian Morris points out in a note to his Arden edition, was itself a variant spelling of *cate* in the early modern period (both forms descend from *achat*). The term *chat* thus instantiates, literally performs, the impossibility of restricting the semantic excess proper to language in general and epitomized by Kate's speech in particular. In so doing, however, it also links linguistic excess—via its etymological link with the signifier *cate*—to the economic excess associated with the commodity form in general and with cates, or luxury goods, in particular. Within the play, the term *chat* may thus be said to name both material and linguistic forms of excess as they converge on the figure of the shrew. It refers at once to Kate's "chattering tongue" (4.2.58) and to her untamed consumption of cates.

Kate's verbal frettings are repeatedly linked within the play to her refusal to assume her proper place within the symbolic order of things: she cannot be broken to the lute but breaks it instead. It is not clear, however, that her place is simply that of passive exchange object. For to be broken to the frets of a lute is to become a skilled and "active manipulator" (to recall Baudrillard's term) of a status object.[37] My argument thus departs from traditional accounts of the commodification of or traffic in women which maintain that women "throughout history" have been passive objects of exchange circulating between men. Such accounts do little to explain the specific historical forms the domination of woman assume with the rise of capitalism and development of the commodity form. They do not, for example, explain the housewife's emerging role as a manipulator of status objects, or household cates.

I would like to question as well the viability, in the present context, of Veblen's assertion that the housewife's "manipulation of the household paraphernalia" does not render her any less a commodity, "chattel," of her husband. The housewife's consumption of cates, which Veblen views as thoroughly domesticated, was in the early modern period thought to be something wild, unruly, and in urgent need of taming.[38] If *Shrew*'s taming narrative positions Kate as a "vicarious consumer" to ensure that her consumption and manipulation of household cates conforms to her husband's economic interests, it nevertheless points to a historical moment when the housewife's management of household property becomes potentially threatening to the symbolic order of things. Before attending to the ways in which the shrew-taming comedy seeks to elide this threat, we should take the threat itself seriously; only then will we be able to chart with any clarity Kate's passage from "chat" (i.e., from the material and linguistic forms of excess characteristic of the shrew) to "chattel."

At the start of the play, as Newman asserts, Kate's fretting is represented as an obstacle to her successful commodification on the marriage market. When Baptista finally arranges Kate's match to the madcap Petruchio, Tranio remarks: " 'Twas a commodity lay fretting by you, / 'Twill bring you gain, or perish on the seas" (2.1.321–22). Baptista's response, "The gain I seek is quiet in the match" (l. 323), underscores the economic dilemma posed by Kate's speech: her linguistic surplus translates into his financial lack and, consequently, her "quiet" into his "gain." Yet Kate's fretting refers not only to what comes out of her mouth (to her excessive verbal fretting) but to what goes into it as well (to her excessive consumption). The verb *to fret*, which derives from the same root as the modern German *fressen*, means "to eat, devour [of animals]; . . . to gnaw, to consume, . . . or wear away by gnawing" or, reflexively, "to waste or wear away; to decay."[39] Kate's untamed, animal-like consumption, Tranio's remark implies, wears away both at her father's resources and at her own value as well. In describing Kate as a "fretting commodity," as a commodity that not only consumes but consumes itself, Tranio emphasizes the tension between her position as a cate, or object of exchange, between men and her role as a consumer of cates.

To grasp the threat posed by the early modern housewife's consumption of cates, as this threat is embodied by Kate, however, we must first consider more closely what Baudrillard terms the "relative social class configurations" at work within the play. For the discourse of objects in *The Taming of the Shrew* becomes intelligible only if read in the context of its "class grammar"—that is to say, as it is inflected by the contradictions inherent in its appropriation by a particular social class or group.[40] In general terms *The Tam-*

ing of the Shrew represents an *embourgeoisement* of the traditional shrew-taming narrative: Petruchio is not a humble tradesman but an upwardly mobile
landowner. Unlike the cooper's wife, Kate is not of "gentle kin"; she is a
wealthy merchant's daughter. The play casts the marriage of Petruchio and
Kate as an alliance between the gentry and mercantile classes and thus
between land and money, status and wealth, or what Bourdieu identifies as
symbolic and economic capital.

Petruchio is straightforward about his mercenary motives for marrying
Kate: "Left solely heir to all his [father's] lands and goods," which he boast-
fully claims to "have better'd rather than decreas'd" (2.1.117–18), Petruchio
ventures into the "maze" of mercantile Padua hoping to "wive it wealthily . . .
/ If wealthily, then happily in Padua" (1.2.74–75). Likening his mission to a
merchant voyage, he claims to have been blown in by "such wind as scatters
young men through the world / To seek their fortunes farther than at home"
(ll. 49–50). Petruchio's fortune-hunting bombast, together with his claim to
have "better'd" his inheritance, marks him as one of the new gentry, who continually sought to improve their estates through commerce, forays into business or overseas trade, or by contracting wealthy marriages.[41] If Petruchio
seeks to obtain from his marriage to Baptista's mercantile household what is
lacking in his own domestic economy, however, the same can be said of Baptista, who seeks to marry off his daughter to a member of the landed gentry.
The nuptial bond between the two families promises a mutually beneficial
exchange of values for the domestic economies of each: Petruchio hopes to
obtain surplus capital (a dowry of "twenty thousand crowns"), and Baptista
the status or symbolic capital that comes with land (the jointure Petruchio
offers in return [2.1.125]).[42]

Kate's commodification as a marriage-market cate thus proves beneficial
to both her father's and her future husband's households. But it is also the case
that her consumption of cates is represented, at least initially, as mutually
detrimental. At the start of the play, as we have seen, Kate's excessive consumption renders her an unvendible commodity. Baptista is unable to "rid the
house" (1.1.145) of Kate and is consequently unwilling to wed his younger
daughter, Bianca, to any of her many suitors. Kate's fretting represents perhaps an even greater threat to Petruchio's household, however, although one
of a different order. To comprehend this difference, one must comprehend the
place occupied by cates within the two domestic economies. Petruchio's par-
simonious attitude toward cates, evidenced by the disrepair of his country
house and the "ragged, old, and beggarly" condition of his servants (4.1.124),
stands in stark contrast to the conspicuous consumption that characterizes
Padua's mercantile class.[43] Gremio, a wealthy Paduan merchant and suitor to
Bianca, for example, describes his "house within the city" as "richly furnished
with plate and gold" (2.1.339–40):

My hangings all of Tyrian tapestry.
In ivory coffers I have stuff'd my crowns,
In cypress chests my arras counterpoints,
Costly apparel, tents, and canopies,
Fine linen, Turkey cushions boss'd with pearl,
Valance of Venice gold in needlework,
Pewter and brass, and all things that belongs
To house or housekeeping. (ll. 342–49)

If housekeeping at Petruchio's country estate involves little more than keeping the "rushes strewed" and the "cobwebs swept" (4.1.41), in Gremio's description of his city dwelling, it is an enterprise that centers on the elaborate arrangement and display of cates. Each of Gremio's "things" bears testimony to his ability to afford superfluous expenditure and to his taste for imported luxuries: his tapestries are from Tyre (famous for its scarlet and purple dyes), his apparel "costly," his linen "fine," his "Turkey cushions boss'd with pearl." His household is invested, literally "stuff'd," with capital.

The marked difference between the two men's respective notions of the "things that belongs / To house or housekeeping" underscores the differing attitudes held by the minor gentry and mercantile classes in the period toward "household cates." For the mercantile classes conspicuous consumption served to compensate for what, borrowing Baudrillard's terminology, we might call a "true social recognition" that otherwise evaded them; the accumulation of status objects served to supplement their "thwarted legitimacy" in the social domain.[44] As Lawrence and Jeanne Fawtier Stone observe, however, for the upwardly mobile gentry "the obligation to spend generously, even lavishly," as part of their newly acquired social status "implied a radical break with the habits of frugality which had played an essential part in the[ir] . . . upward climb."[45] The lesser gentry could make it into the ranks of the elite only by being "cautious, thrifty, canny, and grasping, creeping slowly, generation after generation, up the ladder of social and economic progress, and even at the end only barely indulging in a life-style and housing suitable to their dignity and income."[46] For the mercantile classes conspicuous consumption functioned as a necessary (though not always sufficient) means to elite status; for the lesser gentry it was an unwished-for consequence of it.

Arriving at their wedding in tattered apparel and astride an old, diseased horse, Petruchio proclaims: "To me she's married, not unto my clothes. / Could I repair what she will wear in me / As I can change these poor accoutrements, / 'Twere well for Kate and better for myself" (3.2.115–18). As if to prove his point that Kate's extravagance will leave him a pauper, his selfconsuming costume seems to wear itself out before our eyes: his "old breeches" are "thrice turned" (l. 42); his boots have been used as "candlecases" (l. 43);

his "old rusty sword" has a "broken hilt" (ll. 44–45). As for his horse: it is "begnawn with the bots [parasitical worms or maggots]" (ll. 52–53) and, even more appropriately, "infected"—as, he insinuates, is his future wife—"with the fashions" (l. 50). The term *fashions* (or *farcin*, as it was more commonly spelled), which derives from the Latin *farcire*, meaning "to stuff," denotes a contagious equine disease characterized by a swelling of the jaw. Kate's taste for fashionable cates is likened to this disease of excessive consumption, which threatens to gnaw away at her husband's estate.

Following the wedding ceremony, Kate's excessive consumption seems to result in her swift reduction to the status of "chattel." Petruchio whisks his bride away after announcing to the stunned onlookers:

> I will be master of what is mine own.
> She is my goods, my chattels, she is my house,
> My household stuff, my field, my barn,
> My horse, my ox, my ass, my any thing,
> And here she stands. (ll. 227–31)

Petruchio's blunt assertion of property rights over Kate performs the very act of domestication it declares; reduced to an object of exchange ("goods" and "chattels"), Kate is abruptly yanked out of circulation and sequestered within the home, literally turned into a piece of furniture or "household stuff." The speech follows a domesticating trajectory not unlike that outlined by house-work theory: it circumscribes Kate within a matrix of use-value production. The relationship between household stuff and household cates may be described as that between mere use-values and exchange-values, or commodities, properly speaking. The *OED* defines *stuff* as "the substance or 'material' . . . of which a thing is formed or consists, or out of which a thing may be fashioned."[47] As such, it may be identified with the use-value of the object.[48] Entering into the process of exchange, commodities, "ungilded and unsweetened, retaining their original home-grown shape," are split into the twofold form of use-value and value proper, a process Marx calls "Stoffwechel"—literally, the act of (ex)change (*Wechsel*) that transforms mere stuff (*Stoff*) into values, or cates.[49] In transforming Kate from an object of exchange into the home-grown materiality of mere stuff, into a thing defined by its sheer utility, a beast of burden ("my horse, my ox, my ass"), Petruchio's speech reverses the processes of commodification. Reducing Kate to a series of increasingly homely things, it finally strips her down to a seemingly irreducible substance whose static immobility ("here she stands") puts a stop to the slippage of exchange evoked by his list of goods. Her deictic presence seems to stand as the guarantee of an underlying, enduring use-value.

As a member of the gentry, Petruchio stands for the residual, land-based values of a domestic economy that purports to be "all in all sufficient" (*Oth-*

ello, 4.1.265). The trajectory traced by his index of goods moves not only from exchange-value to use-value but from liquid capital, or "movables,"[50] to the more secure form of landed property ("house . . . field . . . barn"). Yet Petruchio's portrait of an ideally self-sufficient household economy, in which the value of things is taken to be self-evident and not subject to (ex)change, is belied by the straightforwardly mercenary motives he avows for marrying Kate. Paradoxically, in order to maintain his land-based values, Petruchio must embrace those of the marketplace.[51] In seeking to arrest the slippage of exchange, his speech implicates its speaker in an expanding network or maze of equivalent value-forms ("goods . . . any thing") whose slide threatens to destabilize the hierarchy of values he would uphold. If Petruchio succeeds in mastering Kate, his position as master is nevertheless qualified by his own subjection to the exigencies and uncertainties of the new market economy. In his endeavor to domesticate the commodity form, one might say, Petruchio is himself commodified, himself subjected to the logic of commodity exchange. As Gremio so eloquently puts it: in taming Kate, Petruchio is himself "Kated" (3.2.243).

The contradictions inherent in Petruchio's class status make his task as shrew-tamer a complex one: he must restrict his wife's consumption without abolishing it entirely, must ensure that it adequately bears testimony to his own elite status without simultaneously leading him to financial ruin. The urgent requirement to maintain a proper balance between expenditure and thrift in the elite (or would-be elite) household and the perceived danger of delegating this task to the housewife are described in the following mid-seventeenth-century letter of advice, written by the Marquis of Halifax to his daughter:

> The Art of laying out Money wisely, is not attained to without a great deal
> of thought; and it is yet more difficult in the Case of a *Wife*, who is account-
> able to her *Husband* for her mistakes in it: It is not only his *Money*, his *Credit*
> too is at Stake, if what lyeth under the *Wife's* Care is managed, either with
> undecent *Thrift*, or too loose *Profusion*; you are therefore to keep the *Mean*
> between these two *Extreams* . . . when you once break through those bounds,
> you launch into a wide Sea of *Extravagance*.[52]

At stake in the housewife's proper management of money or economic capital, Halifax suggests, is her husband's credit, or symbolic capital. "Symbolic capital," Bourdieu maintains, "is always *credit*, in the widest sense of the word, i.e., a sort of advance which the group alone can grant those who give it the best material and symbolic *guarantees*."[53] It is not simply that economic capital serves to buttress symbolic capital when it is spent on "material and symbolic guarantees" such as status objects. Symbolic capital in turn attracts economic capital: "the exhibition of symbolic capital (which is always very expensive in economic terms) is one of the mechanisms which (no doubt universally) make capital go to capital."[54] Yet symbolic and economic capital are not always mutually reinforcing. Indeed, insofar as "symbolic capital can only be accumulated at the expense of the accumulation of economic capital," the two are often at odds.[55] In the case of the upwardly mobile gentry in early modern England, as the Stones make clear, the effort to balance the two was an ongoing struggle.

In this context the early modern housewife's new role in the symbolic ordering of household cates takes on its full importance. She was made responsible for maintaining the proper balance of economic and symbolic capital within the household economy. The early modern housewife had to learn to spend enough to ensure her husband's status or cultural credit without overspending his income or economic credit. Domestic manuals of the period repeatedly express anxiety over the housewife's ability to strike this balance and are intent on circumscribing her management of household expenditure within the bounds of her husband's authority. For example, in *Of Domesticall Dvties* William Gouge writes,

> Wives cannot alwaies know their husbands ability: for their husbands may be much indebted, and yet to maintaine his credit, whereby he hopeth to raise his estate, may allow liberall maintenance for his house, if thereupon his wife shall gather that he is very rich, and accordingly be very bountifull in her gifts, she may soone goe beyond his ability, and so increase his debt, as he shall neuer be able to recouer himselfe.[56]

Gouge's warning is specifically concerned with the housewife's ability to distinguish symbolic from economic capital. Wives, he warns, are likely to be lured by symbolic capital, to believe that their husbands, because they spend freely on status objects, must be "very rich." The trick of good housewifery in this period, then, is knowing how to manipulate status objects for others and knowing how *not* to be taken in by them. It is precisely this trick, I maintain, that Petruchio teaches Kate. He seeks to unmask the lure of status objects for Kate while teaching her to deploy this lure skillfully for others.

Culminating in the play's final scene, in which Kate obeys Petruchio's command to take off her "dainty" cap and throw it underfoot, Petruchio's strategy aims to tame Kate's consumption of cates. "My falcon now is sharp [i.e., hungry] and passing empty," he explains, "and till she stoop she must not be full-gorg'd, / For then she never looks upon her lure" (4.1.177–79). Far from simply withholding cates from her, however, he continually offers them to her, only to find "some undeserved fault" in their appearance (l. 186), which, he claims, will make them unworthy of her refined tastes. His taming thus succeeds not by destroying the lure of the commodity but rather by exploiting it, by combatting Kate's daintiness with his own super-daintiness.

Arriving at his country estate at the beginning of Act 4, famished from their journey, Kate sits down to sup; but her dinner is sent back to the kitchen by Petruchio, who refuses it as "burnt and dried away" (l. 157). "Better 'twere that both of us did fast," he assures her, than to eat "such over-roasted flesh" (ll. 160–62). By the third scene Kate is ravenous and begs Petruchio's servant for something to eat: "I prithee go and get me some repast, / I care not what, so it be wholesome food" (ll. 15–16). Momentarily forgetting the discriminations of taste, Kate is eager to fill her stomach with any wholesome stuff that will satisfy her appetite. Grumio does not simply ignore her request but perversely teases her with edible cates, offering her a "neat's foot" (l. 17), a "fat tripe finely broil'd" (l. 20), and a "piece of beef and mustard" (l. 23)—"a dish," Kate acknowledges, "that I do love to feed upon" (l. 24).[57] After listing all of the delicacies on the menu, however, Grumio objects to each as being "unwholesome"; like Kate, he gibes, they are "too hot" and "choleric" (ll. 19, 25, 22). Her temper flaring at this, Kate begins to fret and accuses Grumio of feeding her "with the very name of meat" (l. 32). Here Kate hits on the foundation of her husband's strategy: Petruchio's object lesson in consumption centers on the *symbolic* dimension of cates. By feeding her with nothing but the "*name* of meat," with cates in their pure form as signifiers of taste and social distinction, Petruchio aims to bring home to her their lack of substance, or stuff.

Following their abortive supper, Petruchio summons in the haberdasher, commanding him to display his "ruffling treasure" and "ornaments" (ll. 60–61). When the latter produces the cap he has made for Kate, Petruchio ridicules it, comparing it to an edible cate, or "velvet dish" (an analogy that enables him to extend his lesson in consumption from comestibles to other commodities):

> Why, this was moulded on a porringer!
> A velvet dish! Fie, fie! 'Tis lewd and filthy.
> Why, 'tis a cockle or a walnut-shell,
> A knack, a toy, a trick, a baby's cap.
> Away with it! Come, let me have a bigger. (ll. 64–68)

Petruchio objects to the cap on the grounds that it is unwholesome and insubstantial—a cap, one might say, in name only. "I'll have no bigger," Kate responds. "This cloth fit the time, / And gentlewomen wear such caps as these" (ll. 69–70), revealing that she has indeed been seduced by the lure of the status object. Petruchio continues to expand his list of edible trifles, insisting: "It is a paltry cap, / A custard-coffin, a bauble, a silken pie" (ll. 81–82). In likening the commodities that are brought in after supper to banqueting conceits, commonly known as "voids" or "empty dishes," Petruchio again emphasizes the commodity's lack of substance. To consume such cates is to consume a void. It brings not satiety but only renewed want.

Banqueting conceits, Patricia Fumerton maintains, were made not to satisfy the appetite (indeed, they were often made out of nothing but paper) but rather to serve as signifiers of status and superfluous expenditure.[58] This function was quite explicit in the case of certain "conceited dishes" that were actually made in the likeness of expensive but "trifling" luxury commodities, such as "Buttons, Beades, Chaines . . . Slippers . . . [and] Gloues."[59] As if to secure their purely superfluous status, the consumption of these "empty dishes" took the form of conspicuous waste; at the banquet's end they were ceremonially smashed to pieces.[60] Through his taming lesson, Petruchio aims to separate the stuff of the commodity from its value as a cate. Status objects, he teaches, are not so much things as no-things.[61]

Petruchio continues the analogy, comparing the tailor's latest creation to a dainty dessert:

> What's this? A sleeve? 'Tis like a demi-cannon.
> What, up and down, carv'd like an apple-tart?
> Here's snip and nip and cut and slish and slash,
> Like to a censer in a barber's shop.
> Why, what a devil's name, tailor, call'st thou this? (ll. 88–92)

The dress is refused on account of its "curiously cut" sleeves (l. 141), which are likened to the design of a dainty apple-tart, one that is "carv'd" full of holes. When the tailor objects that the dress was designed "according to the fashion and the time" (l. 95) and in accordance with Grumio's orders, the latter responds: "I gave him no order, I gave him the stuff" (l. 119). Grumio follows his master in distinguishing between the "stuff" of the dress in its "ungilded and unsweetened" form and the labor that transforms it into a cate, a thing of value. "I bid thy master cut out the gown," he says, "but I did not bid him cut it to pieces" (ll. 127–28), further differentiating the utilitarian act of "cut[ting] out" from the stylish "cut[ting] . . . to pieces"—the snipping, nipping, slishing, and slashing that creates its cultural value as an object of fashionable taste.

When the tailor reads out the "note of the fashion" to show that it indeed specifies " 'The sleeves curiously cut,' " Grumio replies: "Error I' th' bill, sir, error i' th' bill! I commanded the sleeves should be cut out, and sewed up again" (ll. 129, 141, 143–44). Grumio's remark suggests that, if Petruchio's taming strategy reveals the "cut" that divides the commodity into its twofold form as use-value and status value,[62] it does so only in order to sew it up again, to reduce the status value, make it conform to the use value. In a commodified world, however, to suture the cut of the commodity and thereby create the ruse that its value is inherent in its substance is to turn the commodity into a fetish. Baudrillard's definition of commodity fetishism is particularly apt in this context. For what is fetishized, he maintains, is specifically "the sign object, the object eviscerated of its substance . . . and reduced to the state of marking a difference."[63] Petruchio's taming lesson unmasks both the cut of the commodity, its function as a differentiating signifier of social distinction, and the lure that sutures this cut by dissimulating the lack of substance, or stuff, it conceals. It does so, however, in order to teach Kate both how better to distinguish and how to deploy them.

The success of this lesson is borne out by Kate's final gestures of obedience, the destruction of her dainty cap and her last speech, gestures that are performed as the final, sweet conceits of the play's concluding scene, which is, not coincidentally, set at a banquet. "My banquet is to close our stomachs up," announces Lucentio, its host, to the play's three newlywed couples, "For now we sit to chat as well as eat" (5.2.9, 11). The ensuing chat is an intricate verbal performance in which the bridegrooms argue over whose wife is the "veriest shrew of all" (l. 64). To decide the matter, Petruchio proposes the test of obedience, which Kate wins when she unhesitatingly obeys his command to come. Although Kate's arrival wins the bet, Petruchio insists on "show[ing] more sign" of his wife's "new-built virtue and obedience" (ll. 118–19) by commanding her to destroy her dainty cap. That Kate should appear at the end of the play sporting a fashionable cap, much like (or, depending on the production, identical to) the one taken away when she was less obedient, confirms that Petruchio's taming strategy is aimed not at closing her stomach up, at abolishing her appetite for cates, but rather at harnessing that appetite, at making it conform to his own economic interests.

The destruction of Kate's confectionary cap, like that of a banqueting void, represents not a renunciation of the commodity but rather an affirmation of its power, of its new hold over the early modern household economy. "Economic power," Bourdieu maintains, "is first and foremost a power to keep economic necessity at arm's length. This is why it universally asserts itself by the destruction of riches."[64] It is a gesture of conspicuous yet carefully controlled waste, demonstrating both Petruchio's ability to afford superfluous expenditure and his control over his wife's consumption. Unlike her earlier breaking of the lute, this destruction of riches demonstrates that Kate has been successfully broken to her proper place within the symbolic order of things.

While Kate's final gesture of obedience signals her readiness to assume an active managerial role in domestic affairs, we never in fact *see* her preside over the household economy or its property. This gesture itself, moreover, is peculiarly self-effacing. It seems that Kate can prove her readiness for this role only through a wholly *passive* gesture that displays her subordination to her husband's authority. She can prove herself a worthy caretaker of commodities only by destroying her own most cherished commodity, her fashionable cap.

The self-consuming nature of the gesture reflects the contradictions inherent in the role of the "vicarious consumer": it must appear wholly idle (efface its status as work); be ostensibly unproductive or superfluous (ideally, an act of conspicuous waste); and, most importantly, be executed vicariously (i.e., *for* another). The vicarious consumer consumes not for herself, in her own interest, but for that of her husband.

What distinguishes Kate from the other wives at the end of the play is not that she has learned how *not* to consume but that she has learned how to consume *nothings* (voids, empty dishes, insubstantial cates) for her husband's benefit. Failing to comprehend this novel form of duty, Bianca and the Widow express their abhorrence at the apparently useless waste of such a fine cap. Baptista, however, is won over by the signs of Kate's "new-built" virtue and obedience, so much so that he awards Petruchio another twenty thousand crowns: "Another dowry to another daughter," he announces, "for she is chang'd, as she had never been" (ll. 115–16). By the end of the play, Kate has successfully learned to manipulate status objects and, in so doing, to bolster her husband's credit in a way that "makes capital go to capital."

If, as Baptista's act demonstrates, symbolic capital is but "a transformed and thereby *disguised* form" of economic capital, it nevertheless produces its "proper effect," according to Bourdieu, "only inasmuch, as it conceals the fact that it originates in 'material' forms of capital which are also, in the last analysis, the source of its effects."[65] It becomes the ideological burden of Kate's final speech to conceal the economic underpinnings of her symbolic labor, to render them culturally invisible. The speech accomplishes this task by defining the housewife's (nonproductive) activity as a form of leisure rather than labor:

> Thy husband is thy lord, thy life, thy keeper,
> Thy head, thy sovereign; one that cares for thee,
> And for thy maintenance; commits his body
> To painful labour both by sea and land,
> To watch the night in storms, the day in cold,
> Whilst thou liest warm at home, secure and safe;
> And craves no other tribute at thy hands
> But love, fair looks, and true obedience;
> Too little payment for so great a debt. (ll. 147–55)

Kate's speech inaugurates a new gendered division of labor, according to which husbands "labour both by sea and land" while their wives luxuriate at home, their "soft," "weak" bodies being "unapt to toil and trouble in the world" (ll. 166–67). It is this new division of labor that produces the economic invisibility and unremunerated status of housework described by housework theory. In erasing the status of housework as work, separate-sphere ideology renders the housewife perpetually indebted to her husband insofar as her "love, fair looks, and true obedience" are insufficient "payment" for the material comfort in which she is "kept."

Within the terms of the play, however, the unremunerated status of housework derives not from its circumscription within a matrix of use-value production but from the cultural necessity of concealing the economic origins of the housewife's symbolic labor. If *The Taming of the Shrew* may be said to map the market's infiltration of the household through the commodity form in late-sixteenth-century England, it also marks the emergence of the ideological separation of feminine and masculine spheres of labor (and with it the separation of home/market and housework/work), which masked this infiltration by constructing the household as a refuge *from* the market. Ironically, Kate's final speech renders invisible the housewife's managerial role as a consumer and caretaker of household cates—the very role for which Petruchio's "taming-school" (4.2.54) seeks to prepare her. At the end of the play, she herself appears to stand idle, frozen within the domestic sphere, like a use-less household cate.

As Lena Cowen Orlin points out, "the husband's political roles of lord, head, and sovereign are grounded economically" in Kate's speech in his role as her "keeper."[66] The speech ingeniously deploys the language of economic debt and indebtedness to secure a political analogy in which the household is figured as a microcosm of the state and the husband its sovereign or prince. Its aim is to restore the husband's "rule, supremacy, and sway" (5.2.164) within a domestic hierarchy that has been threatened by the housewife's managerial role in the household economy. The speech, as Orlin notes, shifts back and forth between political and economic forms of obligation; the husband's political sovereignty over his wife is immediately anchored in his role as her keeper. Once the marital relation is defined in economic terms ("one that cares for thee, / And for thy maintenance") and the wife's position within this relation defined as one of lack ("Too little payment for so great a debt"), the speech returns again to the political analogy, to what "the subject owes the prince," as if the housewife's deficit in the former domain (her economic debt) entails her subjection in the latter (her political duty):

> Such duty as the subject owes the prince
> Even such a woman oweth to her husband.
> And when she is froward, peevish, sullen, sour,
> And not obedient to his honest will,
> What is she but a foul contending rebel,
> And graceless traitor to her loving lord?
> I am asham'd that women are so simple

> To offer war where they should kneel for peace,
> Or seek for rule, supremacy, and sway,
> When they are bound to serve, love, and obey. (ll. 156–65)

The erasure of the economic value of the housewife's nonproductive domestic activity in Kate's speech is thus employed to secure a political analogy that disarms the perceived threat posed by this activity.

The political analogy between "the structure of authority in the family and the state" was not, of course, invented by Shakespeare. It was, as Susan Amussen points out, commonplace in both domestic manuals and political treatises of the period.[67] Yet there was, as Amussen also notes, a marked disparity between patriarchal theory and quotidian practice in the early modern household. Though "theoretically, the husband ruled his wife, and she obeyed him in all things," Amussen asserts, in practice the wife "was joined with him in the government of the household."[68] The political analogy restores the husband's sovereignty or mastery over his wife by devaluing her role in the household economy. Moreover, insofar as it succeeds in domesticating the housewife's relation to household cates by subordinating it to her husband's authority, the speech may be said to circumscribe this relation within the safe boundaries of vicarious consumption. Kate's role as a consumer has by the end of the play been successfully adjusted, made to conform, to her position as chattel (perpetually indebted to her husband for the things he provides her with, she may be said to belong to him). As Orlin argues, the role of things in the final "accommodation" that Petruchio and Kate reach is simply to "purchase the consent that perpetuates the gendered social contract"; they serve merely to "legitimate the social order."[69]

In the commodious conclusion of the comedy, all "jarring notes agree" (5.2.1) and the cut of the commodity has been sutured, or sewn up again. What commodity fetishism seeks, according to Baudrillard, is "the closed perfection of a system," a system that appears to know no lack.[70] Comedy is precisely such a system: "suturing all contradictions and divisions," it "gives ideology its power of fascination."[71] The effect that Kate's final signs of obedience produce in her audience is indeed one of fascination: "Here is a wonder, if you talk of a wonder," Lucentio utters. "And so it is," Hortensio responds; "I wonder what it bodes" (ll. 107–8). The "wonder" produced by Kate's symbolic labor, I would argue, is nothing other than a fascination with a "perfect closure effected by signs."[72] Kate's final chat is fetishized as a "labor of appearances and signs," as a symbolic labor that conceals its own economic motivation and erases all traces of the labor necessary to produce it.

I do not mean to suggest (following the play's so-called revisionist readers) that Kate's speech should be read ironically, as evidence of her deceit, any more than (with its antirevisionist readers) as evidence of her "true" submission.[73] Both readings, it seems to me, leave Kate squarely within the framework of the medieval shrew tradition. In the former she remains a duplicitous shrew, while in the latter she becomes "a second Grissel" (2.1.288).[74] I maintain, rather, that *The Taming of the Shrew* recasts this tradition in entirely new terms, terms that map, through the commodity form itself, the market's infiltration and reorganization of the household economy during the early modern period. From this perspective Kate's "labor of signs" is of interest not because it marks her as a deep or complex subject but rather because it demonstrates the ways in which the housewife's subjectivity was constituted through its relation to status objects, or household cates.[75]

In the terms of this reading, it becomes less important to decide whether Petruchio succeeds in taming Kate than to point out, with Grumio, that in so doing, he is himself "Kated." Petruchio, no less than Kate, is subject to the logic of exchange, to the *perpetuum mobile* of commodity circulation. Grumio's insight also accounts for an ambiguity in my title: Are commodities in this play the subject or object of domestication? Slightly adapting Marx, we may answer this question as follows: The movement of subjects within the play takes the form of a movement made by things, and these things, far from being under their control, in fact control them.[76] Or we might choose to let Kate have the last word, recalling her answer to Petruchio's pronouncement that he has been "mov'd" to make her his wife: "Mov'd, in good time! Let him that mov'd you hither / Remove you hence. I knew you at the first / You were a movable" (2.1.195–97).

NOTES

Originally published in *Shakespeare Quarterly* 47, no. 2 (Summer 1996): 109–31. Reprinted by permission of Natasha Korda and *Shakespeare Quarterly*.

I would like to thank Karen Bock, Krystian Czerniecki, John Guillory, Jonathan Gil Harris, and Jean Howard for their valuable comments on earlier drafts of this paper. I would also like to thank Heather Findlay for inviting me to present an abbreviated version of it for her panel, "Shakespeare's Erotic Economies," at the 1994 meeting of the North East Modern Language Association in Pittsburgh, Pennsylvania.

1. See *The Taming of the Shrew*, ed. Brian Morris (London and New York: Methuen, 1981), 1–149, esp. 70; Richard Hosley, "Sources and Analogues of *The Taming of the Shrew*," *Huntington Library Quarterly* 27 (1963–1964): 289–308; and John C. Bean, "Comic Structure and the Humanizing of Kate in *The Taming of the Shrew*" in *The Woman's Part: Feminist Criticism of Shakespeare*, ed. Carolyn Ruth Swift Lenz, Gayle Greene, and Carol Thomas Neely (Urbana, Chicago, and London: University of Illinois Press, 1980), 65–78. See also note 6, below.

2. Quotations from *The Taming of the Shrew* follow the Arden Shakespeare text, edited by Brian Morris (New York and London: Methuen, 1981).

3. *The Oxford English Dictionary*, 2d ed., prepared by J. A. Simpson and E. S. C. Weiner, 20 vols. (Oxford: Clarendon Press, 1987), 2:978 and 1:66; hereafter cited simply as *OED*.

4. "He who satisfies his own need with the product of his own labour admittedly creates use-values, but not commodities. . . . In order to become a commodity, the product must be transferred to the other person . . . through the medium of exchange" (Karl Marx, *Capital: A Critique of Political Economy, Volume One*, trans. Ben Fowkes [New York: Vintage Books, 1977], 131).

5. Muriel Bradbrook cites this ballad as a possible source for *Shrew* in "Dramatic Role as Social Image: a Study of *The Taming of the Shrew*," *Muriel Bradbrook on Shakespeare* (Sussex, Eng.: Harvester Press; Totowa, N.J.: Barnes and Noble Books, 1984), 57–71, esp. 60. Brian Morris discusses the ballad in his introduction to the Arden edition and in Appendix III, where he reprints several versions of it (75 and 310–16).

6. The prescribed method of shrew-taming prior to Shakespeare's play was typically violent. The more severe the punishment inflicted, the more complete the shrew's "recovery" to the world of work seemed to be. In John Heywood's interlude *Johan Johan the Husband* (1533–1534), cited by Bradbrook as an early Tudor source for *Shrew*, the eponymous Johan spends the first one hundred lines of the play elaborating how he will beat his wife. See Heywood, *Johan Johan the Husband*, The Malone Society Reprints (Oxford: University Press, 1972), sig. AI^v; and Bradbrook, 59–61. In the anonymous verse tale "Here begynneth a merry Ieste of a shrewde and curste Wyfe, lapped in Morrelles Skin, for her good behauyour" (1550), the shrew is forced into a cellar by her husband, beaten mercilessly with birch rods until she faints, at which point he wraps her naked, bloody body in a salted hide, threatening to keep her there for the rest of her life. Thereafter she performs his commands humbly and meekly. See Morris, Arden edition, 70.

7. In the Scottish tale titled "The Handsome Lazy Lass," cited as a folktale source for *Shrew*, a farmer likewise tricks his wife, who "will not do a hand's turn, she is so lazy," into offering to do "the hardest and most exhausting work" on the farm; see Morris, Arden edition, 73–74. In Heywood's *Johan Johan the Husband* the protagonist points to his wife's reluctance to do housework as the reason for beating her: "When she offendeth and doth a mys / And kepeth not her house / as her duetie is / Shall I not bete her if she do so / Yes by cokke blood that shall I do" (sig. AI^v).

8. An interesting exception to this norm is the fifteenth-century cycle of mystery plays (in particular, the Towneley version) in which Noah's wife is portrayed as an overly zealous producer. She refuses to put aside her spinning and board the ark even as the flood waters reach her feet: "Full sharp ar thise showers / That renys aboute. / Therefor, wife, haue done; / Com into ship fast," Noah pleads. "In fayth, yit will I spyn; / All in vayn ye carp," replies this industrious shrew (*The Towneley Plays*, ed. Martin Stevens and A. C. Cawley [Oxford: Oxford University Press, 1994], ll. 506–9 and 519–20). Martha C. Howell speculates that Mistress Noah is spinning not solely for her own household but for the market, and that the play stigmatizes the vital role many women played in late-medieval market production (*Women, Production, and Patriarchy in Late Medieval Cities* [Chicago and London: University of Chicago Press, 1986], 182, n. 19). See also note 13, below.

9. See Susan Cahn, *Industry of Devotion: The Transformation of Women's Work in England, 1500–1660* (New York: Columbia University Press, 1987), esp. 42–46. Cf. Alice Clark, *Working Life of Women in the Seventeenth Century* (New York: E. P. Dutton, 1919); and Roberta Hamilton, *The Liberation of Women: A Study of Patriarchy and Capitalism* (London and Boston: George Allen and Unwin, 1978).

10. See Cahn, 53–56.

11. On conspicuous consumption in early modern England, see F. J. Fisher, *London and the English Economy, 1500–1700* (London and Ronceverte: The Hambledon Press, 1990), 105–18; Joan Thirsk, *Economic Policy and Projects: The Development of a Consumer Society in Early Modern England* (Oxford: Clarendon Press, 1978); Chandra Mukerji, *From Graven Images: Patterns of Modern Materialism* (New York: Columbia University Press, 1983); and *Consumption and the World of Goods*, ed. John Brewer and Roy Porter (London and New York: Routledge, 1993).

12. William Harrison, *The Description of England: The Classic Contemporary Account of Tudor Social Life*, ed. Georges Edelen (New York: The Folger Shakespeare Library and Dover Publications, 1994), 200.

13. See Martha C. Howell's rich and complex account of the types of female labor that took place, both within and outside the home, in late medieval and early modern northern European cities. Howell's book resists the nostalgic overvaluation of female production in precapitalist society which has informed much of the earlier work on this subject and, in particular, that of the housework theorists.

14. See Cahn, 7, 156.

15. In an article first published in 1978, Christine Delphy maintained: "We owe to the new feminists . . . the posing, for the first time in history, of the question of housework as a *theoretical* problem." She asserted that no coherent "theory of housework" had thus far been produced and offered her own preliminary attempt at such a systematic theorization ("Housework or domestic work" in *Close to Home: A materialist analysis of women's oppression*, ed. and trans. Diana Leonard [Amherst: University of Massachusetts Press, 1984], 78–92, esp. 78).

16. As Annette Kuhn observes, feminist materialists of the 1970s "seized upon [housework] as the key to an historically concrete understanding of women's oppression, . . . as the central point at which women's specific subordination in capitalism is articulated" (*Feminism and Materialism: Women and Modes of Production*, ed. Annette Kuhn and Ann Marie Wolpe [London and Boston: Routledge and Kegan Paul, 1978], 198).

17. See Karen Sachs, "Engels Revisited" in *Women, Culture, and Society*, ed. Michelle Zimbalist Rosaldo and Louise Lamphere (Stanford: Stanford University Press, 1974), 221–22; and Kuhn, "Structures of Patriarchy and Capital in the Family," in Kuhn and Wolpe, 42–67, esp. 54. Housework theory is not so much a unified theory as a debate. Not all housework theorists view the unremunerated status of housework as resulting from its circumscription within a matrix of use-value production. Another, more radical strain of housework theory argues that the housewife does produce through her housework a commodity that is recognized and exchanged on the market—namely, the labor power of her husband and family—and that this work should therefore be paid or remunerated; see Mariarosa Dalla Costa and Selma James, *The Power of Women and the Subversion of*

the Community (Bristol: Falling Wall Press, 1972). For critiques of this notion, see Delphy, 88–89; and Paul Smith, "Domestic Labor and Marx's Theory of Value" in Kuhn and Wolpe, 198–219, esp. 212.

18. On the economic invisibility of housework, see Delphy, 84.

19. On commodities as signs of distinction, see Pierre Bourdieu, *Distinction: A Social Critique of the Judgement of Taste* (Cambridge, Mass.: Harvard University Press, 1984); and Jean Baudrillard, *For a Critique of the Political Economy of the Sign*, trans. Charles Levin (St. Louis, Mo.: Telos Press, 1981).

20. Bourdieu, "Symbolic capital" in *Outline of a Theory of Practice*, trans. Richard Nice (Cambridge: Cambridge University Press, 1977), 171–83.

21. Thorstein Veblen, *The Theory of the Leisure Class* (1899; repr. New York: Penguin Books 1983), 83.

22. Veblen, 57–58.

23. "She still quite unmistakably remains his chattel in theory; for the habitual rendering of vicarious leisure and consumption is the abiding mark of the unfree servant" (Veblen, 83).

24. Ibid., 149 (my emphasis).

25. Ibid., 57–58.

26. Baudrillard, 45–46.

27. Ibid., 33, 5 (my emphasis).

28. Ibid., 46.

29. While it is conceptually closer to the work of Jean Baudrillard and Pierre Bourdieu, my phrase carries resonances of Jacques Lacan and Michel Foucault; see Lacan, *Ecrits: A Selection*, trans. Alan Sheridan (New York and London: W. W. Norton, 1977), ix, 30–113; and Foucault, *The Order of Things: An Archaeology of the Human Sciences* (New York: Pantheon, 1970).

30. Joel Fineman, "The Turn of the Shrew" in *The Subjectivity Effect in Western Literary Tradition* (Cambridge, Mass.: MIT Press, 1991), 120–42, esp. 128.

31. Fineman, 127.

32. Karen Newman, *Fashioning Femininity and English Renaissance Drama* (Chicago and London: University of Chicago Press, 1991), 39–40.

33. Newman, 44 (my emphasis). In a book so strongly concerned with the relation of women to commodities in the early modern period, it is curious that Newman so emphatically denies the significance of the commodity's conspicuousness in *The Taming of the Shrew*. My reading of Kate's role with respect to household cates is greatly indebted to several chapters in this volume, in particular "Dressing Up: Sartorial Extravagance in Early Modern London" and "City Talk: Femininity and Commodification in Jonson's *Epicoene*" (109–27 and 129–43).

34. Lena Cowen Orlin, "The Performance of Things in *The Taming of the Shrew*," *The Yearbook of English Studies* 23 (1993): 167–188, esp. 167, 183–85.

35. Fineman, 125.

36. *OED*, 4:218.

37. In " 'Sing Againe Syren': The Female Musician and Sexual Enchantment in Elizabethan Life and Literature" *(Renaissance Quarterly* 42 [1989]: 420–48), Linda Phyllis Austern notes that formal musical training was considered "a mark of gentility" in the period insofar as it was both "costly and time-consuming" (430). It thus became "a functional artifice" used by young women "to attract socially

desirable husbands" (431). (Perhaps this is why Baptista seeks to have his daughter learn the lute.) In a contemporary treatise entitled *The Praise of Musicke* (1586), the art of music is specifically compared to other luxury commodities: "so Musicke is as the most delicate meates, and as the finer apparell: not indeede necessary simply, but profitablie necessary for the comlinesse of life. And therefore *Socrates* and *Plato*, and all the *Pythagoreans* instructed their yong men and maydes in the knowledge of Musicke, not to the provocation of wantonnesse, but to the restraining and bridling their affections under the rule and moderation of reason" (quoted in Austern, 428). The threat of "wantonnesse," of excess, posed by the maids' consumption of musical cates is immediately tamed by the author of this treatise, who quickly shifts from a model of superfluous consumption to one of restraint or discipline. The defensive rhetoric of the treatise, as Austern argues, came in response to contemporary attacks on the playing of musical instruments by women as a form of untamed, "Syrenesque" seduction.

38. Domestic manuals of the period manifest anxiety over the limits of a woman's right to dispose of household property. William Gouge's *Of Domesticall Dvties* (London, 1622), for example, devotes some fifteen chapters to defining the precise limits of the housewife's managerial role with respect to household goods. While it is the responsibility of the "godly, wise, faithfull, and industrious woman," he maintains, to "ordereth all the things of the house," he goes on to specify that this power must never exceed the scope of her husband's authority. In the dedicatory epistle of Gouge's treatise, however, we find that his attempt to limit the housewife's governance of household property was not overly popular with his parishioners: "I remember that when these *Domesticall Duties* were first uttered out of the pulpit, much exception was taken against the application of a wiues subiection to the restraining of her from disposing the common goods of the family without, or against her husbands consent." Gouge defends himself as follows:

> But surely they that made those exceptions did not well thinke of the *Cautions* and *Limitations* which were then deliuered, and are now againe expresly noted: which are, that the foresaid restraint be not extended to the *proper goods of a wife*, no nor overstrictly to such *goods as are set apart for the vse of the family*, nor to *extraordinary cases*, nor alwaies to an *expresse consent*, nor to the *consent of such husbands as are impotent, or farre and long absent*. If any other warrantable caution shall be shewed me, I will be as willing to admit it, as any of these. Now that my meaning may not still be peruerted, I pray you, in reading the restraint of wiues power in disposing the goods of the family, euer beare in minde those Cautions.

Gouge proffers so many mitigating exceptions to his own rule that perhaps it was more often honored in the breach than in the observance.

39. *OED* 6: 185.

40. Baudrillard, 37.

41. Carol F. Heffernan, "*The Taming of the Shrew*: The Bourgeoisie in Love," *Essays in Literature* 12 (1985): 3–14, esp. 5. On the gentry's increasing reliance on commerce in the period, see Lawrence Stone and Jeanne C. Fawtier Stone, *An Open Elite? England 1540–1880* (Oxford: Clarendon Press, 1984).

42. On the "economic and cultural symbiosis of land and money" in the period, see Stone and Stone, 26. The Stones conclude that the perceived symbiotic relation between the landed and merchant classes was more a "question of values and attitudes" than of "the facts of social mobility" (211).

43. Compare William Harrison's description of the "great provision of tapestry, Turkey work, pewter, brass, fine linen, and thereto costly cupboards of plate" found in the houses of "gentlemen, merchantmen, and some other wealthy citizens" (200).

44. Baudrillard, 40.

45. Stone and Stone, 185. On taste as a category of social distinction, see Bourdieu, *Distinction*, passim.

46. Stone and Stone, 187.

47. *OED* 16: 983. Note that this definition dates from the beginning of the sixteenth century.

48. According to Marx, it is "the physical body of the commodity which is the use-value or useful thing.

49. Commodities first enter into the process of exchange ungilded and unsweetened, retaining their original home-grown shape. Exchange, however, produces a differentiation of the commodity into two elements, commodity and money, an external opposition which expresses the opposition between use-value and value which is inherent in it" (Marx, 198–99).

50. The term *chattel* derives from the Latin *capitale* and in the sixteenth century meant either "capital, principal," or, more commonly, "a movable-possession; any possession or piece of property other than real estate or a freehold" (*OED* 3: 59).

51. By the late sixteenth century the landed gentry had to a large extent adopted an emergent-market view of land and labor, though their view of their own society was still governed by residual concepts of feudal entitlement; see Stone and Stone, 181–210.

52. [George Savile, Marquis of Halifax], *The Lady's New-years Gift: or, Advice to a Daughter*, 3d ed. (London: M. Gillyflower and J. Partridge, 1688), 86–90.

53. Bourdieu, *Outline*, 181.

54. Ibid., 181.

55. Ibid., 180.

56. Gouge, 297.

57. The early modern break with medieval cookery was marked by a shift from quantitative display to the qualitative refinement of "conceited" dishes. For the first time, as Stephen Mennell notes in *All Manners of Food: Eating and Taste in England and France from the Middle Ages to the Present* (New York: Basil Blackwell, 1985), "knowledgeability and a sense of delicacy in matters of food" had come to function as markers of elite status—there was now "food to be emulated and food to be disdained." Differences in social standing were expressed not so much through the quantity or kind of food consumed by different social classes but "more subtly through styles of cooking and serving" (75). When it came to meat, the elite were no longer distinguished as those who ate game and fowl as opposed to "gross meats" but as those who ate good cuts of meat as opposed to lowgrade cuts. The "cut" of one's meat, as Jean-Louis Flandrin puts it, literally took on a social function, that of "dividing the vulgar from the distinguished"; see

Jean-Louis Flandrin, "Distinction through Taste" in *Passions of the Renaissance*, ed. Roger Chartier, Vol. 3 of *A History of Private Life*, gen. eds. Philippe Aries and Georges Duby, trans. Arthur Goldhammer, 5 vols. (Cambridge, Mass., and London: Harvard University Press, 1987–1991), 265–307, esp. 273. Cf. Fernand Braudel, "Superfluity and Sufficiency: Food and Drink," in *The Structures of Everyday Life*, trans. Siân Reynolds (New York: Harper and Row, 1981). On the refinement of table manners, cf. Norbert Elias, *The History of Manners*, Vol. 1 of *The Civilizing Process*, trans. Edmund Jephcott, 2 vols. (New York: Pantheon Books, 1978).

58. According to Patricia Fumerton, the "essential food value of banqueting stuffs . . . was *nothing* . . . the culinary referent of the void was zero (*Cultural Aesthetics: Renaissance Literature and the Practice of Social Ornament* [Chicago and London: University of Chicago Press, 1991], 133).

59. John Murrell, A *Daily Exercise for Ladies and Gentlewomen* . . . (1617), quoted here from Fumerton, 130.

60. Fumerton, 130–32.

61. In Marx's terms, Petruchio distinguishes a thing's "stiff and starchy existence as a body" from "its sublime objectivity as a value" (144). "Not an atom of matter," Marx writes, "enters into the objectivity of commodities as values; in this it is the direct opposite of the coarsely sensuous objectivity of commodities as physical objects" (138).

62. "Commodities come into the world in the form of use-values or material goods. . . . This is their plain, homely, natural form. However, they are only commodities because they have a dual nature, because they are at the same time objects of utility and bearers of value" (Marx, 138).

63. Baudrillard, 93.

64. Bourdieu, *Distinction*, 55.

65. Bourdieu, *Outline*, 183.

66. Orlin, 185.

67. S. D. Amussen, "Gender, Family and the Social Order, 1560–1725" in *Order and Disorder in Early Modern England*, ed. Anthony Fletcher and John Stevenson (Cambridge: Cambridge University Press, 1985), 196–217, esp. 196.

68. Amussen, 201. Amussen cites the housewife's supervision of children and servants and her role in the household economy as instances of her joint governorship (203).

69. Orlin, 185.

70. Baudrillard, 93.

71. Ibid., 101.

72. Ibid., 96.

73. Robert B. Heilman was the first to speak of "revisionist" readings of *Shrew* in his "The *Taming* Untamed, or, The Return of the Shrew," *Modern Language Quarterly* 27 (1966): 147–61. John C. Bean then divided *Shrew* criticism into both revisionist and antirevisionist camps in his "Comic Structure and the Humanizing of Kate in *The Taming of the Shrew*."

74. The duplicitous shrew was a common topos in medieval literature. In William Dunbar's "Tretis of the tua mariit Wemen and the Wedo," for example, the shrewd widow gets her way with her husband by feigning submission: ". . . I wes a schrew

evir," she confides to her gossips, "Bot I wes schene [bright] in my schrowd [clothing] and schew me innocent; / And thought I dour wes and cane, dispitous and bald, / I wes dissymblit suttelly in a sanctis liknes: / I semyt sober and sueit, and sempill without fraud, / Bot I couth sexty dissaif [deceive] that suttillar wer haldin." The widow offers the following lesson to future shrews: "Be constant in your governance and counterfeit gud maneris, / ... dowis ay in double forme, / ... Be amyable with humble face, as angellis apperand, / ... Be of your luke like innocentis, thoght ye half evill myndis" (William Dunbar, *Poems*, ed. James Kinsley [Oxford: Clarendon Press, 1958], ll. 108–13 and 116–24).

Antirevisionist readings of the play remain equally within the medieval shrew tradition when reading Kate's final speech as evidence of her "true" submission, giving credit to Petruchio's assertion that he will turn Katherina into "a second Grissel." In Chaucer's version of the story, Griselde's humble origins and predilection for hard labor position her as the very antithesis of the high-born, slothful, duplicitous shrew and lead her to suffer gladly her aristocratic husband's cruel tests. In contrast to the shrew's proverbial duplicity, Chaucer stresses Griselde's unfeigned satisfaction with her degree; see Geoffrey Chaucer, *The Canterbury Tales*, ed. N. F. Blake (London: Edward Arnold, 1980).

75. Orlin similarly proposes an alternative to traditional characterologic readings of the play, one that focuses on the "performance of things" (186).

76. Compare Marx's assertion that "[exchangers'] own movement . . . within society has for them the form of a movement made by things, and these things, far from being under their control, in fact control them" (167–68).

PART III.
The Taming of the Shrew on Stage, in Film, and on Televsion

Figure 7. Mrs. Charles Kemble as Catherine, 1806. Used with the permission of the Folger Shakespeare Library.

Figure 8. Charlotte Cushman as Katharina, 1859. Used with the permission of the Folger Shakespeare Library.

"An Unholy Alliance"
William Poel, Martin Harvey, and *The Taming of the Shrew*

JAN MACDONALD

The production of *The Taming of the Shrew* in the spring of 1913 was the occasion of the "alliance" of William Poel and Martin Harvey, and the attempt at reconstruction which follows is based on a set of unpublished letters from Poel to Harvey, dating from August 1912 to May 1913, the promptbook, and sketches of the set, which I was fortunate enough to acquire some years ago.

At first sight, the collaboration seems unlikely. Martin Harvey, the matinée idol, was a product and supporter of the actor-manager system that Poel abhorred for its commercialism, but the correspondence reveals that both men were interested in a change of direction at this stage in their careers.

Martin Harvey wrote in his autobiography, "I sought the co-operation of William Poel, founder of the Elizabethan Stage Society, whose Shakespeare productions upon a platform stage and without scenery are famous. I had watched my own children give scenes from Shakespeare in the drawing-room, and had seen how little scenery was missed. I wanted Poel to advise me as to how he had found his own audience would accept a Shakespeare play without scenery."[1]

There may have been another reason for Harvey's interest. He appeared in 1912 in the title role of Reinhardt's celebrated production of *Oedipus*, with Lillah McCarthy, Granville Barker's wife, as Jocasta. Barker was then preparing the first of three brilliant but outrageous Shakespearean productions, *The Winter's Tale*, performed at the Savoy in November 1912. It is not presuming too much to imagine that during the rehearsal period of *Oedipus*, the two men discussed new approaches to the staging of Shakespeare. We know that Barker must have been in evidence, for his detailed notes to his wife on her playing of Jocasta imply his presence at rehearsals.[2] It is likely that the ambitious Harvey wanted to mount the "new Shakespeare" bandwagon.

He first approached Poel in August 1912 with the idea of a joint production of *Richard III*. Poel, at this time, was disillusioned and tired. A letter to

Harvey, dated November 6, 1912, reveals that he intended to give up directing plays on his own, and meant to act in future as a kind of *mise-en-scéne* consultant. He refers to his forthcoming production of *Troilus and Cressida* for the Elizabethan Stage Society as his last. "The winding up of thirty years' work is of course a busy moment in one's life [. . . . .] I am also so very anxious now to be satisfied with working for others and not for myself."[3] He was currently collaborating with Bridges-Adams on a production of Sybil Amherst's *The Book of Job*, presented November 28, 1912. He was also rather short of funds, and the correspondence with Harvey is peppered with requests for fees and expenses.

In addition it is only fair to say that Poel respected Harvey as an actor. In 1908 he had tried to sell him the production of *Everyman* for £250. "I think you would act the role admirably and your artistic temperament and great popularity with your public would make the play a great success with your management."[4] In fact, Harvey did play Everyman in 1923, but in Von Hoffmannstahl's version of the piece.

Harvey, as the statement from his autobiography implies, was principally interested in getting Poel's advice on decor. It was perhaps typical of Poel that in the event he was prepared to give advice on anything but. In answer to Harvey's request, Poel replied, "Perhaps I ought to point out to you that, in my opinion, the success of a play on Elizabethan lines does not depend as much on the setting, as upon the complete alteration of methods of elocution and stage-management—that is action—methods which might not be popular either with your actors or audiences."[5]

Considering that even the dedicated Granville Barker had found being shut up by Poel for three weeks to "learn the tunes" of *Richard II* somewhat tedious, one is not surprised that Poel had some reservations about inflicting his methods on a regular commercial company. What is interesting about this letter is that it shows that Poel is becoming less antiquarian in methods of staging. It is on the delivery of the verse and on the blocking that he places most emphasis.

He does show, however, that in his new role as consultant, he is prepared to satisfy consumer demand. He asks for details of the size of the apron, whether there have to be any scene changes, and whether Martin Harvey wanted any of the cast to enter through the auditorium, a practice that he himself had used with great success in *Everyman*. "You will easily realize that I must have some definite form of platform in my mind's eye before I can be arranging the movement."[6] He also in the same letter asks for a cheque. His fee was two guineas a day, for six hours' work.

At this point the whole project almost came to grief, because Martin Harvey abandoned the idea of *Richard III*, and proposed instead *The Taming of the Shrew*. Perhaps he felt, as Benjamin Webster had done before him, that this play with its Induction, its setting in the Lord's house and its visiting troupe of actors performing there, lent itself more readily to the Elizabethan method. Poel was disappointed. He put forward a counter-proposal of *Much Ado*, and then suggested *Macbeth*. *The Shrew* Poel felt had been well enough done in the regular commercial theatre in the recent past. There had just been a successful production by Oscar Asche and Lily Brayton. He also thought that Harvey should choose tragedy rather than comedy for his first venture, especially after his great success in Reinhardt's *Oedipus*. He concedes the point, however, with a typically acid comment. "But I suppose the Shrew has the most money in it. English audiences seem to delight in seeing the same thing over and over again. I suppose it might be all right with striking costume effects and quaint music."[7]

Another problem emerged when it became clear that Harvey intended to cut the sub-plot altogether, surprising perhaps, since the actor-manager talks elsewhere of "Garrick's shamelessly dismembered version of Shakespeare's *Taming of the Shrew*."[8] But actor-managers throughout the nineteenth century had the habit of expressing horror at Restoration and eighteenth-century Shakespearean texts, before proceeding to exercise their own butchery on the plays. Poel pointed out that it would only run one and a half hours minus the "underplots," "in which case you will want another strong piece in the bill, and this would be well, because it might justify shortening the play. Otherwise omitting the underplots will run you foul of the critics, because one of the great objects of the Elizabethan Method is to afford more time for getting in more of the text."[9] Since there was a permanent architectural background and continuous action, time was not wasted on elaborate and lengthy scene changes. It is interesting to note, however, that Poel's own production of *Troilus and Cressida*, on which he was working at the same time as "advising" Harvey on *The Shrew*, was cut considerably, and according to some critics, injudiciously. Poel believed that in *Troilus and Cressida* the dialogue held up the action, and so went to work with his blue pencil.

The idea of a double-bill became increasingly attractive to Poel, when it occurred to him that *Jacob and Esau*, a sixteenth-century interlude, which he had produced the previous February would be the ideal companion piece. Martin Harvey would have none of it, however, and *The Shrew* was presented on its own.

Harvey later complained that he had asked Poel to discuss decor but all *he* had done was talk about cuts. The correspondence scarcely deals with these, but they may have been discussed at one of the production meetings (for which Poel charged two guineas plus expenses). The promptbook, however, provides evidence of the final acting version.[10]

Some 668 lines are cut out of a play of just over 2,500. The play was given in two acts, the interval being taken between the end of the wedding scene (3.2), and the arrival of the couple at Petruchio's house. Most of the cuts are accounted for by the fairly extensive excisions in the Pedant/Vincentio sub-plot, although the bones of it remain. Lucentio's description of his father in 1.1, and the whole of 4.4 (i.e. when the Pedant impersonating Vincentio meets Baptista) is omitted. Much of the "low comedy," for example the scene between Curtis and Grumio in 4.1, goes. This may well have been at Poel's suggestion, for he admitted to Harvey that it was primarily the horseplay that made him dislike the play.

The overall effect of the cutting is to focus the attention on the Petruchio/Katharine story, and, perhaps more significantly, to build up the character of Petruchio, and to stress those aspects of it that Harvey wanted to develop. All references to Petruchio's initial intention to marry Katharine for her money are cut, such as Petruchio's line, "Wealth is the burden of my wooing dance," and the one made famous by *Kiss Me Kate*, "I come to wive it wealthily in Padua." So is Grumio's comment,

> Give him gold enough and marry him to a puppet . . .
> Why, nothing comes amiss, so money comes withal.

It might be felt that this removed all Petruchio's motivation for tackling the rich shrew, but according to J. T. Grein, Harvey played the part as "a jovial smiling Italian gentleman who seemed to get immense fun out of an experiment."[11] In addition, while Petruchio is allowed to dress up in a bizarre fashion for the wedding, Tranio's line, "Yet often times he goes but mean apparelled" is omitted, the implication being that Petruchio, when he is not shrew-taming, is immaculate. . . . Harvey said, "As for my conception of Petruchio, I see him as the greatest gentleman Shakespeare ever drew."[12] He disliked the stage tradition of horse-whipping his wife into submission. His was, according to *Lloyd's News* "an intellectual conquest. Martin Harvey's Petruchio hypnotizes Katherina into reasonableness."[13] However, as Grein put it, "Indeed, so amiable, smiling, smooth-tongued and polite was he in the first act that he seemed inconsistent with the Petruchio that Shakespeare drew"—an instance perhaps of the actor-manager wanting to be loved?

Other cuts show that he certainly wanted to be applauded, for on several occasions a scene is stopped immediately after Petruchio's exit, namely, at the end of 3.1 (i.e. Harvey's Act 1), the scene ends with Petruchio's lines,

> Fear not, sweet wench, they shall not touch thee, Kate!
> I'll buckler thee against a million

Petruchio lifts Katharine on his shoulder and exits, omitting the exchange between Baptista, Bianca and the others, and the play ends similarly with the exit of Katharine and Petruchio, cutting the Hortensio/Lucentio exchange.

Minor cuts are made for the usual reasons of prudery, for example, all references to beds, maidenheads and the like are excised, and of obscurity, for example the classical references to Ovid and Aristotle in Lucentio's speech in Act 1, but the really unforgivable and, perhaps, inexplicable cut is the massacring of Kate's last speech, which is cut from 44 lines to 17. Could the actor-manager not bear his leading lady, even if she were his wife, to have such a protracted last word? According to Grein, Nina de Silva played "her final surrender more in the nature of making the best of a bad job than of submission to a superior will. Indeed one felt there was some reluctance in her yielding, and that her rebuke to the Widow and Bianca proceeded rather from pose than from conviction." This interpretation is borne out by Harvey himself, who writes that hers was "the whimsical surrender of one who should say 'let the man have his way, it saves a lot of time and it keeps him happy,' while being in love with him all the while."[14] Katharine's playing the last scene with a smile is certainly a viable reading but why omit

> My mind has been as big as one of yours
> My heart as great, my reason haply more

which would help this interpretation? The disembowelling of this speech, whoever was guilty of it, shows little feeling for either the verse, the message or the comedy of the play.

Originally the co-directors' plan was that Poel would prepare a prompt-book with movements and cuts indicated. But later he writes to Harvey telling the latter how to make one, "buy two 1 /—copies of the full text (Cassell's National Library for preference) then cut out the pages and cut out all Act and scene headings, and paste the leaves into a scrapbook so that they make one continuous movement."[15]

Poel received the promptbook, and a sketch of the set on October 21. This, and Martin Harvey's subsequent comment that he had carried out "my own growing conception of the decor"[16] makes it clear that the final version was the latter's work. However, Poel was pleased with the result. "I like it very much," he wrote. "It is simple yet dignified."[17] He then proceeded to work out the "movements" as he put it, a task he enjoyed, but he withdrew from preparing a detailed scheme of moves on November 6, "because, as the staging is not strictly Elizabethan the movements and the changes of curtain must be a matter more or less of experiment and modifications. And it would help matters not to be too definite"—an indication perhaps that Poel was finding producing a play by proxy rather hard, and that he would prefer to work things out on the set with actors. He suggested a meeting, which was no doubt more sensible in terms of the theatrical end product, but in the absence of a transcript of the discussion, provides no evidence for the theatre historian.

The set basically consisted of five sets of curtains:

1. Tapestry curtains at the first groove position, used as a backing for the inn in the Induction, where Sly is found by the Lord.
2. What are referred to as "nude women curtains," set immediately in front of the tapestry ones, used as a backing for the Lord's bedroom. The idea for these came from the Lord's lines,

   > Carry him gently to my fairest chamber and hang it around with all my wanton pictures. . . .

3. Black and red curtains at the second groove position, used for Bianca's wooing scene.
4. Silver and grey curtains at the third grooves, used for all the other scenes in Baptista's house.
5. Pink curtains at the fourth grooves, used for Petruchio's house.

Curtain backings were used for interiors. The exteriors were done with screens, and door- and windowpieces when required.

The full set, with movable trellises covered with laurel leaves, was used for the first scene of the play proper, a public place in Padua, for the procession from the church, and for the final banquet. The laurel pieces differently set, so as to make "a leafy lane" provided the backing for the journey of Katharine and Petruchio back to Padua.

The very back of the scene showed an unchanging vista of the Lord's garden. The idea was that the whole of the play proper took place in the Lord's summer house. The moving of the screens and laurel pieces and of the furniture and props was done by the "actors," and the curtains were let down as if they were the Lord's hangings. Sly and the Lord sat in the orchestra "in the musical director's place," and Sly made frequent comments on the action from there, which as Harvey said "were not Shakespeare, but were irresistible."[18]

As Poel had pointed out, the setting was hardly Elizabethan. Scene changes were minimal, allowing almost continuous action. There was an embryonic apron, built over part of the orchestra pit, with steps going down to accommodate Sly and the Lord, but when an upper level was needed in the scene in which Vincentio questions the Pedant, who is at a window, a book-flat, steps, a windowpiece and a doorpiece were found ready waiting behind the drapes. The setting is a modification of normal nineteenth-century decor, rather than an imitation of Elizabethan staging. Despite the fact that the production was billed as being done in "The New Way," it is fairly clear that Martin Harvey was using drapes in a much less imaginative fashion than Barker had done some months earlier in *The Winter's Tale* and *Twelfth Night*.

Poel told Martin Harvey on November 13, "I have now visualized the play—the whole of it and hope it will come out as actable for your company and to your liking." Another discussion was arranged for November 26, but Poel was becoming increasingly involved in *Troilus and Cressida*, "hard and anxious work." At the same time he was playing Keegan in a revival of Shaw's *John Bull's Other Island*, so it is unlikely that he would have had a great deal of time for discussion.

The promptbook does not give very detailed moves, and such groupings as are indicated more often than not show the old-fashioned scheme with principals in the centre and the others gathered round them in a semi-circle. One move that Poel did discuss at some length, however, was the possibility of Katharine and Petruchio entering through the audience on their return from Petruchio's house. He is enthusiastic about this idea, but as he says, if they are to enter this way in Act 2, then they must leave through the audience at the end of Act 1. "This with the horse might be difficult, unless the horse could be brought down stage as far as the apron so that the curtain could come down leaving the four of you outside for a moment and then rise again for you to take the call. For myself I like the idea of Katharine never leaving your horse after her return from the church. It suggests that you did not trust her with her friends."[19]

Neither the horse nor the entry through the auditorium found its way into the finished production. At the end of Act 1 Petruchio put Katharine on his shoulder, and carried her off by the R.U.E. to the cheers of a group of 12 children and a fanfare from the musicians. All principals on SR crossed to SL and looked after the couple. The Stage Direction then reads *PICTURE*, a nice nineteenth-century tableau in the midst of all this ersatz Elizabethanism. After the Act call Petruchio came forward and shook hands with Sly. For the return journey through the aforementioned leafy lane, Katharine and Petruchio entered through R.I.E. In fact, if the convention is that the play is taking place in the Lord's summer house, it would break it rather to go rushing off through the auditorium, with or without a horse.

The costumes, designed by George Kruger Gray, were we are told "inspired by the designs of Benozzo Gozzoli for the frescoes in the Ricardi Palace in Florence,"[20] another echo of nineteenth-century antiquarianism. The costumes are certainly Italianate in design, rather than Elizabethan, and one may assume, therefore, that Poel did not have a hand in their design, since he still believed that Shakespeare should be played in Elizabethan dress. *Troilus and Cressida* was all stomachers and ruffs.

Poel came in again in March to advise on music. His regular musician, Dolmetsch, was in Paris, and so he suggested that Martin Harvey engage a young lady, called Rosabel Watson, who could "produce the music of the period with violins and cellos, so that only the real expert could tell the difference. The performers would all be ladies, but they could dress up as young men."[21]

The production opened in Hull and came to the Prince of Wales' in London on May 15. Poel saw it on May 15. He wrote to Martin Harvey, "You have brought out in an admirable way the joyousness and brightness of the comedy, and removed the horseplay which has always been offensive to me. I limit my criticism, therefore, in great part to the movement"—a clear indication that his advice had not been taken nor his suggestions followed. He goes on, "I like the action to tell a story so that if the words were removed the audience would still know what it was all about. But, you are no doubt right in saying that it is a matter of indifference to the audience."

In general, the production was well reviewed,[22] with comments like "The new way is the only way." *The Saturday Review* called it "the summit of good stagecraft," "the liveliest revival of the play seen in our day." One critic commented that Katharine and Petruchio were so far removed from reality that even the suffragettes could not object to her surrender to him.

Harvey was apparently satisfied. From a commercial point of view the production did well in the provinces drawing over £100 in nightly returns, but despite critical acclaim it was not a financial success in London with average nightly box office takings amounting to only £41. It has been suggested that the popular success of Laurence Irving's *Typhoon*, currently at the Haymarket, drew away the crowds.

Martin Harvey reproduced the play as part of his scheme to mount a Shakespeare season in 1916 to promote the idea of a National Theatre, and so he clearly thought it worth repeating. He also invited Granville Barker to remount his three famous productions, but these did not materialize.

Perhaps it is impossible to reconstruct what each director contributed to a joint production, but it seems clear that what ultimately emerged was more Harvey than Poel. Or was it? An editorial note in *The Mask* raises doubts.

> Who will deny that there was sack and canary in the "Taming of the Shrew" as produced by . . . , but here we come to a broken sentence. Who *was* it produced by? Was it produced by Mr. Harvey *and* Mr. Poel, or was it produced by Mr. Poel alone? Never have we seen anything like that from Mr. Poel's hand before and very little of that character from Mr. Harvey's. It seemed to us to be all Barker.[23]

Further enquiries were made, and in the following April appeared the tantalizing comment, "We now know, for one of the gentlemen has told us. But this is amongst the secrets we shall enjoy keeping."[24]

NOTES

This essay was originally published in *Theatre Notebook: A Journal of the History and Technique of the British Theatre* 36, no. 2 (1982): 64–72. Reprinted by permission of *Theatre Notebook*.

1. *The Autobiography of Sir John Martin-Harvey* (1933), 412.
2. C. B. Purdom, *Harley Granville Barker* (1955), 130–31.

3. *Troilus and Cressida* was performed at the King's Hall, Covent Garden on Dec. 10, 15, 18, 1912, and at the Memorial Theatre, Stratford on Avon on May 12, 1913.
4. Manuscript letter from William Poel to Martin Harvey, June 10, 1908.
5. Manuscript letter from William Poel to Martin Harvey, Aug. 24, 1912.
6. Manuscript letter from William Poel to Martin Harvey, Sept. 16, 1912.
7. Manuscript letter from William Poel to Martin Harvey, Sept. 19, 1912.
8. *The Autobiography of Sir John Martin-Harvey* (1933), 120.
9. Manuscript letter from William Poel to Martin Harvey, Sept. 17, 1912.
10. The text of the play to which the promptbook is compared is that in the New Shakespeare Series, edited by Sir Arthur Quiller-Couch and John Dover Wilson (Cambridge University Press, 1962).
11. *The Sunday Times*, May 21, 1916.
12. *Autobiography*, 414.
13. Quoted in *The Book of Martin Harvey* (n.d.), 108.
14. *Autobiography*, 414.
15. Manuscript letter from William Poel to Martin Harvey, Sept. 20, 1912.
16. *Autobiography*, 412.
17. Manuscript letter from William Poel to Martin Harvey, Oct. 21, 1912.
18. *Autobiography*, 413.
19. Manuscript letter from William Poel to Martin Harvey, Nov. 13, 1912.
20. *Autobiography*, 413.
21. Manuscript letter from William Poel to Martin Harvey, March 10, 1913.
22. Quoted in *The Book of Martin Harvey*, 108, and in *Autobiography*, 414–17.
23. *The Mask*, Oct. 6, 2, 1913.
24. *The Mask*, April 6, 4, 1914.

The Taming of the Shrew,

Presented by Three Rivers Shakespeare Festival
at the Stephen Foster Theatre, Pittsburgh, PA,
June 30–July 16, 1994

PATTY S. DERRICK

Playing *The Taming of the Shrew*, especially the taming plot, without winks to the audience to suggest an ironic reading can be a problem today. This *Shrew* has been set in a comic book world whose cartoon features render the action unreal, too exaggerated to be taken seriously.

Baptista's house is a pink gingerbread, not meant to look real because its proportions are markedly askew—much wider at the top than at the bottom. Some characters arrive in cardboard cut-out cars that they hold in front of them. Petruchio, for instance, dressed like a cowboy in jeans and boots, drives a pink Chevy convertible, while Lucentio, the rich kid in prep school short pants, knee socks, and necktie, arrives in a dark sedan with his chauffeur Tranio. Bianca and Kate are immediately characterized by their clothes, Bianca wearing a yellow frock and gloves on her way to play tennis and Kate wearing rolled-up jeans, sleeveless plaid shirt, and loafers. Lucentio in disguise as the tutor becomes a cartoon nerd with glasses, greased-down hair and a pocket protector, while Hortensio, disguised as the music teacher, looks like an odd combination of Keith Richards and Elvis Costello in a velvet and sequined jacket.

Although all of the characters and the setting are whimsical, the attraction of Katherine and Petruchio has a note of realism. Kate is dubious about this wild cowboy who comes to woo her, but she is nevertheless intrigued, even a bit awed by him. To pick up Kate for the wedding, Petruchio enters to everyone's shock and amusement: plaid bermuda shorts with an oriental sash from which dangle garlic, bells, and a trumpet, one red tennis shoe and one combat boot, a leather jacket covered with chains and medals and adorned by the name "KATE" in gold sequins, a sword in one hand and a kazoo in the other. Katherine stands to the side and considers this apparent maniac, seeming to understand his game very early. While everyone else laughs, her curiosity wins out, and she willingly dashes off with him. At his home, a rustic place with animal heads on the walls, she may be tormented and confused by her new husband, but she tiptoes back, despite her hunger and cold to watch him after he falls asleep in a chair. She is mesmerized by this man's wildness.

When she gives in and plays along with his sun-moon game, she seems only slightly worn down by his antics; she genuinely loves him and wants to join forces. He tosses her the car keys and lets her drive the pink Chevy, signaling their partnership and their re-entrance to the pink gingerbread cartoon of Padua. The final scene, with Petruchio's commands and Kate's speech on a wife's duties, is played without irony, but within this comic strip world in which the final banquet becomes a wienie roast, no one takes any of it very seriously.

NOTE

Originally published as part of "Three Rivers Shakespeare Festival," *Shakespeare Bulletin* 12, 4 (Fall 1994): 28–30. Reprinted by permission of Patty S. Derrick and *Shakespeare Bulletin*.

The Performance of Feminism in *The Taming of the Shrew*[1]

MARGARET LOFTUS RANALD

Performance is ideology! This is particularly true of Shakespeare's *The Taming of the Shrew*, one of his two comedies concerning the behaviour of husband and wife after the marriage ceremony—the other being *The Comedy of Errors*. Here he makes use of what may well be the longest-running English female stock character, the recalcitrant wife, who goes back to Mrs. Noah, the disobedient woman of the mediaeval religious cycle plays. But at the same time he adapts the technique of classical farce to observation of human behavior, by taking an impossible premise (that a wife can he tamed) and extending it logically to the utmost limits of absurdity. He also combines the Mrs. Noah figure with the Judy puppet and the clever woman of the Interludes who outwits her husband, but with one distinctive omission: the physical violence commonly assumed essential to shrew-taming. I believe that here Shakespeare has forged a new dramatic mode by humanizing the intellectuality of rhetorically based classical farce and psychologizing the knockabout physicality of its Plautine offshoot.

Most importantly, an examination of the text reveals that at no time does Petruchio raise his hand against Kate—though she most certainly attacks him and he offers violence to other characters. The battle is fought on a psycho-sexual level, and contrary to the belief of some other feminists, it is not merely a matter of male supremacist psychic murder but rather a combat of two fiercely independent, yet sexually attracted persons seeking a *modus vivendi*. Hence, the nineteenth-century tradition of Petruchio entering with his whip is not justified by the script.

That Kate remained substantially untamed was actually a contemporary tradition, enshrined in the 1611–1612 *The Woman's Prize, or the Tamer Tamed*, John Fletcher's parodic/sequel/tribute to the lasting popularity of Shakespeare's work. Incidently, it offers the refrain "*And the woman shall wear the breeches*," whose humour was undoubtedly emphasized by the crossdressed actors. But later adaptations accentuated violence, most notably that by David Garrick, *Catherine and Petruchio*, which drove Shakespeare from the stage from 1756 to 1886.[2] Kate is not shown as a rejected daughter, too intelligent, witty, and nonconformist for her own good. Instead in 4.2 she expresses "self-denigration and capitulation," demurs as unworthy of love when asked to castigate the recalcitrant wives, and humbly gives her lines on matrimonial duty to Petruchio.[3] She is brought to heel by a dominant male and Bianca is the congenitally submissive feminine ideal. Garrick's adaptation poisoned the Shakespearian well and *The Taming of the Shrew* entered the twentieth century as a wife-beating romp.

In the United States *The Taming of the Shrew* arrived on Broadway by way of touring companies and actor managers. In 1887, in Augustin Daly's company, which also toured Europe, Ada Rehan was tamed by John Drew for 121 performances to great acclaim, in London, the Provinces, and at the Stratford-upon-Avon Memorial Theatre benefit in 1888. Though reviving Shakespeare's text, Daly was still under the influence of Garrick and omitted Kate's "speech expressing hurt and dismay at her father's rejection of her,"[4] thus denying sympathy to the character. Ten years later (1897) Rehan repeated the role and in 1904–1905 was still playing it in repertory. Surviving pictures depict a statuesque woman with features more attuned to tragedy than comedy in a production that seems to have been well upholstered in quasi-Elizabethan costumes. An unidentified London reviewer praised her "imperial presence, the impassioned face, the grey eyes flashing with pride or scorn or melting with tenderness, the true freedom of graceful demeanor, the supple beauty of movement, and the exquisite loveliness of voice which make up the investiture that the actress gave to the part."[5] One famous portrait of her in the role depicts an obstinate woman of grim determination with a "grand air" and fine wardrobe— a "splendid and overwhelming presence" with what the *Times* reviewer called "true womanliness of character underlying an intractable exterior."[6]

The 1904–1905 New York season was a banner year for Shakespeare, since his reputation as Broadway box-office poison had not yet been "confirmed." Nonetheless, commercial-theatre skittishness with reference to Shakespeare was beginning. In May *The Taming of the Shrew* achieved a mere four performances at the Broadhurst Theatre and, in November 1905, the longrunning collaboration between E. H. Sothern and Julia Marlowe (husband and wife after 1911) managed only eight well-dressed performances in repertory, though to crowded houses. Marlowe was said to be "vehement and pungent" but the 1905 New York reviewers were so badly split that it is hard to know what to believe. Certainly Marlowe was sufficiently stung to write a newspaper protest, noting the important fact that they were playing the First Folio, not the Augustin Daly/Garrick adaptation.[7]

Photographs show Sothern as a mustachioed Petruchio with feathered hat in vaguely Renaissance style, while Julia Marlowe, complete with whip, seemed, like Ada Rehan, to depend on fine bones and elaborate costumes; her wardrobe for this production is reported to have cost $1,448.60.[8] However, one original and effective piece of business clearly indicated that Marlowe's Katherine was not totally compliant, perhaps even planning to subdue Petruchio. In 4.3 when Petruchio, having apparently won the battle of the time of day, marched offstage, Kate impudently held up two fingers behind his back to signify her independence. The performances were apparently "vigorous" and the *Evening Telegram* reviewer suggested that the taming was "not so much by physical overbearing as by the arousing of her sense of humor and the ridiculous." This was apparently the key to this collaboration which was repeated biennially until 1923.

In 1914 Margaret Anglin revived the play for a few grouchy performances, and in 1921 the play was done twice. *The Taming of the Shrew* did not usually achieve long runs—but then the long Broadway run is a comparatively recent phenomenon. Perhaps the play made the audience uncomfortable and possibly it needed a gimmick.

In 1927 one was found. The director, H. K. Ayliff (working courtesy of Sir Barry Jackson), put his principals, Mary Ellis and Basil Sydney, into modern dress at the Garrick Theatre, New York, for an unprecedented 175 performances. The setting was a country estate in England, where the honking horsepower of a "flivver" replaced horses for the wedding journey, and contemporary references abounded. The wedding portrait shows Katherine in a handkerchief-hem wedding gown and long veil standing in parodic photopose with her hand on the shoulder of her virile, sporting, bridegroom who is seated on an absurdly spindly French chair. His costume is totally incongruous, with football jersey and boot, blue-jean trouser leg and riding boot, topped off with morning coat, boutonniere, and bowler hat. Incongruity and contemporaneity proved to be the right mix for this couple. Percy Hammond (*New York Herald-Tribune*, October 26, 1927) praised Mary Ellis as "a lovely termagant," reminding him, with nostalgia refracted through the prism of sentimental memory, of "Miss Julia Marlowe's Katherine in the days when she was conquered by the tender Sothern," a comment indicating a serious romanticism at the bottom of a contemporaneity that most critics found foolish and distasteful. The public, however, did not mind.

A second frequently used gimmick (from the time of the Bensons, 1902–1916, and repeated by Sothern and Marlowe after 1911) has been casting the principals with actors known to be married to each other, thereby mitigating the apparent cruelty of the play. This approach salvaged the 1935–1936 season for Alfred Lunt and Lynn Fontanne, whose previous engagement in Noël Coward's *Point Valaine* (January 1935, fifty-six performances) had them scurrying for another vehicle. With *The Taming of the Shrew*, produced by the Theatre Guild and directed by Henry Wagstaff Dribble, they achieved "a very palpable hit" which ran for 128 performances and eight more in its 1940 revival. The Lunts' reputation for high comedy and ensemble playing, together with their famously happy union and decision to make their careers as a team, lent titillation to this play of matrimonial strife. The programme and the reviews note that the text was "arranged" by the principals, including parts of *A Shrew* and making the play into something "most exceedingly low" (Brooks Atkinson, *New York Times*, October 1, 1935). Christopher Sly dozed in a box throughout the performance and Sydney Greenstreet scored well as Baptista. Percy Hammond again used Julia Marlowe as a benchmark, noting that Fontanne combined her "lovely fishwife" with Margaret Anglin's 1914 "sullen and rather lady-like grouch." He also noted Fontanne's histrionic range from hellion through pathetic "broken mare" to "lady of poise and breeding" in the submission scene (*New York Herald-Tribune*, October 1, 1935). Though he thought farce was not Fontanne's true metier Burns Mantle noted that she was not tamed "sweetly and softly . . . but with a mental reservation that she still may have something to say about this business of being tamed" (*New York News*, October 1, 1935).

But, as numerous critics noted, not even a knee injury was able to dull her performance. Lunt as Petruchio was praised by Hammond as "assured, authentic burlesque" and a whipcracking adventurer while Atkinson noted his "incomparable bounce and good humor, beaming with mischief." Burns Mantle thought him "a roistering delight" and the production "an inspired romp," saying perceptively that, "This Petruchio has his moments of being a little uncertain as to whether he will be able to master this clawing, spitting Katherine or not." Certainly a production photograph shows a cheery, masterful Fontanne hugging a somewhat bemused Lunt who, complete with whip, is carrying her off piggy-back style. The production was generally conceded to be dominated by Lynn Fontanne.[9]

This real-life matrimonial approach was also employed in the two commercial films made of this play. In 1929 the then-married swashbuckler Douglas Fairbanks and Mary Pickford, "America's [now slightly superannuated] sweetheart," offered a sixty-eight-minute condensed black-and-white film version of the play—with additional dialogue by Sam Taylor.[10] The purpose of this film was to bolster the fading careers of these two longtime film favourites in this, their first talking film together. To be sure there had been whiffs of scandal in their past matrimonial histories, but at this point their romance was one made in Beverly Hills (Pickfair, to be precise) and their reasonably adequate performances were evaluated through that transitional idyllic golden haze. The film was well designed in a Tuscan style, and authentically costumed (except for coiffures). Fairbanks as Petruchio carried the *de rigueur* whip, displaying a large expanse of well-stockinged athletic leg, and Pickford was superbly dressed in flattering gowns. The genteel performances, however, were the well-mannered result of type-casting and the star system, together with some of the exaggerations of the old silent days. The submission speech concluded with a wink. Nonetheless, the film retained sufficient archaeological interest for it to be reprocessed in wide screen format in 1976.

Part of the reason for this disinterest was probably the 1967, 122-minute colour Columbia film directed by Franco Zeffirelli with those terminally quarreling real-life lovers Richard Burton and Elizabeth Taylor as Petruchio and Kate, with heavily rewritten text.[11] As with the 1929 film, the primary reason for the production was exploitation, this time of the tempestuous and often bibulous passions of Burton and Taylor. Audiences cared less about Petruchio and Kate than their real-life embodiments (perhaps like Woody Allen and Mia Farrow today in *Husbands and Wives*). But where Fairbanks and Pickford projected domesticity, on and offstage, Burton and Taylor flaunted their *Anthony and Cleopatra*–induced love affair and its quasi-"Egyptian" unpredictability.

Consequently, this production was a "knock down, drag out" battle of the sexes, in which Taylor slapped Burton who returned the compliment by walloping Taylor on her not inconsiderable rump. After a rooftop battle they fell on to a woolsack in happy sexual reconciliation. Burton's hirsute, virile Petruchio tried to humiliate Kate in physical confrontation and Taylor responded in snarling kind, showing a great deal of cleavage into the bargain. She portrayed Kate as a liberated oversexed woman, independent, freeloving, contemptuous of conventions, with the truth of her overwhelming passion as self-expression and reason for existence. Nothing could have been further from the respectful, ornamental 1929 production of the *beau sabreur* Fairbanks and the quasi-virginal Pickford. Overall, the first portion of the Burton/Taylor film (with Taylor taking a whip to the acquiescent Bianca of Natasha Pyne) was more successful than the later undisciplined bravura horseplay of the principals—who seemed to have reduced even Zeffirelli to directorial inertia as far as their scenes were concerned.

Sociologically the world had changed utterly between 1929 and 1967, and the drums of the women's liberation movement were sounding loudly, the first salvo in the conflict having been fired in 1963 by Betty Friedan in *The Feminine Mystique*. There she announced to an astonished masculine world that intelligent, educated women were not content with the American familial dream of several children, a commuting husband, a house in the suburbs and everlasting domesticity. And in unexpected numbers, white, educated middle-class women responded. They wanted more social, economic and sexual freedom, and that was the sentiment to which the 1967 *Taming of the Shrew* appealed. Where Fairbanks/Pickford were discreet, and Ingrid Bergman had been blacklisted for her involvement with Roberto Rossellini, Taylor/Burton exploited and appealed to this new liberation movement. And from this time on it has been almost impossible to see *The Taming of the Shrew* as the wife-beating farce it was once considered.[12] Consciousness has been raised, and the oppressive patriarchy of Baptista is no longer acceptable in its insistence on that immutable masculine superiority which passed a woman from the possessive dominance of a father into the hands of an equally sovereign and possessive husband.

Thus the shrewish anger of Kate is now reinterpreted as a comprehensible reaction against sexual and economic domination. She refuses to be passed like a commodity to the highest bidder and, shrewdly assessing Bianca's suitors, sees how far feminine conformity will get a woman. Therefore she actively rebels against a system in which the father plays "a merchant's part" in "selling" his younger daughter in a "desperate mart," however unsuitable the new "owner."[13] *The Taming of the Shrew* is now perceived as a rather subversive "play about marriage in Elizabethan England."[14] As Germaine Greer put it, Kate "opts out" of the traditional mode "by becoming unmanageable," manipulating her father and her suitors in a perilous game which could end in her ruin,[15] while Bianca plays the sneaky game of feminine deception. Kate's risky gamble succeeds thanks to Petruchio, who in effect becomes her true champion and saves her from a matrimonial fate that for her would indeed be worse than death.

The subtlety of Shakespeare's treatment is now more widely appreciated, and the clever nature of Kate's taming has been exhaustively treated,[16] but Greer's 1970 comment still remains appropriate: "He tames her as he might a hawk or a high-mettled horse, and she rewards him with strong sexual love and fierce loyalty."[17] Thus Petruchio manages to achieve for himself a spirited wife well worth the witty battle and, she finds a man who is husband, protector and, above all, a merry friend who understands and enjoys her unconventionality as they indicate by their very existence the folly of traditional matrimonial *mores*. "We three are married, but you two are sped," says Petruchio (5.2.186). And I believe he is right.

To some extent this interpretation of the play was prefigured in the last days of 1948 in its adaptation into a highly successful American Musical, *Kiss Me, Kate* (1077 performances). The eminently witty music was by Cole Porter and the hook by Sam and Belle Spewack. The production boasted some voices of operatic calibre, actors of great personal attraction (Patricia Morison, Alfred Drake, Lisa Kirk) with excellent dancing and good low comedy by Jack Diamond and Eddie Sledge. The action was broad, the hook lightweight, but the show succeeded, because theatricality was its watchword. The father/daughter conflict was omitted and the ludic element emphasized by placing the action within a touring company about to perform *The Taming of the Shrew* in Baltimore, Maryland. Ironically, the motto of the State of Maryland is *Fatti Maschii, Parole Femine*, "Deeds Are for Men, Words for Women," something I doubt that either Porter or the Spewacks knew.[18] The central figures were now an arrogant actor and his temperamental ex-wife who had been engaged to play Kate, with Bianca an impudent *ingenue*.

Nonetheless, the original differentiation of character between the two young women persisted.[19] Kate's great number is "*I Hate Men*" in which she pejoratively lists the kind of wooers customarily available to her, but Bianca's refrain indicates that she will take "*Any Tom, Dick or Harry/Any Harry, Dick or Tom*" with a repetition of the middle name that was distinctly risque in 1948 (as reviewers indirectly noted). The music ran the gamut from the raunchiness of the filler "*Brush up Your Shakespeare*" and "*Too Darned Hot*" to the lyrical "*Wunderbar*" and "*Was Thine That Special Face*," with Kate's submission lyric, "*I Am Ashamed that Women Are So Simple*" lifted totally from the master. However, the most enduring legacy of this frequently revived musical has been the skillful use to which Shakespearian tags are put, so much so that almost every post-1948 American review of the play laments the absence of the Cole Porter music. Also, most Petruchios now burst into Porter's notes whenever they reach the lines "*I've Come to Wive It Wealthily in Padua*" and "*Where Is the Life That Late I Led*." Perhaps they stop there because quotations of more than one line require payment of copyright. This musical has forever inserted itself into the play.

Its influence was further strengthened in 1953 when Metro-Goldwyn-Mayer released its 111-minute colour film produced by George Sidney with Kathryn Grayson, Howard Keel, Ann Miller (of the staccato and suggestive tap dance).[20] The piratically attractive baritone Howard Keel and the energetic Ann Miller were the real stars of the show, while Grayson was out of her depth. However, the film drew attention to the fact that Porter's music belongs in the theatre and requires theatre people to perform it. The fragility of the book also became evident, something that has repeatedly been noted in revivals.[21]

Of course the play has always had a gut-level appeal, as the late Joseph Papp recognized in 1956 when he began his outdoor New York Summer Shakespeare Festival with the aim of introducing the playwright to the general populace. Directed by Stuart Vaughan with Colleen Dewhurst and Jack Cannon, *The Taming of the Shrew* opened in the East River Amphitheatre on the Lower East Side of Manhattan. This was true Proletarian Shakespeare, offered free of charge in the open air with aggressive behavior and an overabundance of mugging. Cast members also reflected the ethnic population of the rather rough area. In addition there was a different Spanish-language cast, something that rather concerns this particular feminist because it smacks of pandering to an ethnic *macho* stereotype. Nonetheless, this was a highly successful production in its later tours of *El Barrio* in a mobile unit.

This production also demonstrated Papp's continued commitment to interracial casting in Shakespearian performances. Of course this was not a new concept, since it had been tried as far back as Ira Aldridge (1807–1867), while the versatile, charming, and intelligent Ruby Dee had performed Kate at the American Festival Theatre in Stratford, Connecticut (1965).[22] However, no white producer had heretofore shown such responsibility to the implementation of such a pledge, as witnessed by the later casting of Jane White, Ellen Holly, and James Earl Jones in this play.[23]

In 1978 Joseph Papp again presented a notable interracial *Taming of the Shrew*, this time under the direction of Wilford Leach in quasi-Edwardian costume with Raúl Julia, his homegrown Puerto Rican star, as Petruchio, and the classically trained white actor Meryl Streep (already successful on both film and stage) as Katharina. This promised to be a sparkling performance contrasting the powerful sexuality of Julia with the suave intelligence of Streep. However, the director seemed slightly ill at ease with the sexual chemistry of Julia's masculinity, toning down his performance into "likeability," and misguiding Streep into occasionally shrill bitchiness. In short, what was conveyed was a rather *macho* Petruchio and a spitfire Kate. Further, since it was eminently clear from the first act that the two were irremediably in love, the action had really nowhere to go, except to show Kate as determined to submit only far enough to give and gain concessions to reach a centrist position. One memorable piece of concluding stage business had Streep defiantly exiting right despite Julia's vehement pestering to the left. Finally, with a *Cosi fan tutte* air, he shrugged and followed her.

Again, in 1990 Papp presented the *Shrew* in Central Park, this time directed by A. J. Antoon, who specializes in transplanting plays into other periods and cultures. Now, *pace* Germaine Greer, it was set in the Wild West, against a backdrop of galloping untamed mustangs, with Morgan Freeman playing Petruchio as a lasso-wielding black wrangler to the much younger white cowgirl of the TV comedienne, Tracey Ullman. The concept was original, but the horse-taming aspect went by default, the Western twang became annoying, and the sexual conflict was not well resolved, largely because Ullman proved more comfortable with short TV skits than extended concept of character. The action of this noisy production was extremely broad, with Freeman's mirror image tantrum unfitting for this essentially dignified actor, though physical violence was kept to a minimum. Certainly there was some "Blaxploitation" in the casting since Freeman had just achieved an Academy Award nomination for his role in *Driving Miss Daisy*. But most importantly no one seemed to object to the taming of a white woman by a black man.

Today the basic problem of the play is the submission scene, which has become rather distasteful to many feminists. The traditional approach to have Kate conclude with a broad wink is rather unsubtle, but Bernard Shaw's embarrassment at this moment has not evaporated. In 1963 Stuart Vaughan tried to overcome the difficulty with an oddly subdued Petruchio (Robert Gerringer), a touching, even pathetic Kate (Nan Martin), and no Christopher Sly, but the fun of the play departed. In 1973 Tina Packard directed the play for the Performance Garage as irreverent slapstick, turning the action into an inconsistent acrobatic happening full of *commedia dell'arte* tumbling in which Kate was too sullen and Petruchio too loutish. The principal characters must indeed be attractive for this play to succeed.

In 1974 the Young Vic brought a mixed British-American company to the Brooklyn Academy of Music, directed by the iconoclastic Frank Dunlop who kept the "rumbustious" Sly (played by the American actor Richard Gere), spicing up his role with numerous contemporary references and incongruous accent. Jim Dale's Petruchio was generous and sincere, while Jane Lapotaire proved a mistress of understatement. Here almost all the reviewers fastened on the submission scene, most of them concluding that Dunlop wished to convey the masculine oppression acceptable in Shakespeare's day. There were even hisses from the audience. Others thought it a post–women's liberation approach, with Jack Kroll arguing that Kate did not abase herself: "she is ritually entering into the erotic complicity that is the human race's way of winning transcendent pleasure and domestic peace" (*Newsweek*, March 25, 1974).

The Royal Shakespeare Company in 1987, directed by Jonathan Miller, opted for sociological archaeology, facing up to the play's patriarchal hegemony as if it were a puritan marriage tract and staging it as an Italian domestic history rather than sexual warfare. This worked well also with Miller's own political views as he reached the conclusion that matrimonial and political stability were two sides of the same coin. The induction was omitted and there was very little horseplay. The Kate of Fiona Shaw was a rather gawky Irish girl, the victim of psycho-social oppression, so emotionally disturbed that she needed the stabilizing power and influence of the stocky middle-aged Brian Cox as Petruchio. Then after her serious, dignified, submission they form an intelligent alliance to take on the world.

Emphasis on the hunting and hawking imagery has also been attempted as a means of making Kate's taming more palatable, and in 1978 the Off-Broadway Equity Library Theatre, New York, trumpeted its use of this approach. The action was set in New York in the era of bootleg gin. Eric Booth was the fortune hunter who liked sports, and Stephanie Cotsirilos was a spitfire who was supposed to be tamed like a falcon, or so said the director, John Henry Davis. However, this interpretation did not become clear in the performance.

The application of falconry to *The Taming of the Shrew* is now becoming more popular and it was well employed in the 1986 Teatr Clwyd production which played in repertory at the Royal Theatre, Haymarket in 1986. The principals were the risk-taking Vanessa Redgrave and the eminently handsome Timothy Dalton. Redgrave began the play as a Kat (the pronunciation used throughout the production) crossdressed in breeches, braces, belt, dagger, but wearing a blonde wig similar to that of Bianca.

She was a provincial lad with a North Country accent, "a reflective piratical image of swaggering tomboyishness, a female Petruchio, in fact" (Sheridan Morley, *Punch*, June 25, 1986). Then, when she put on a dress as Kate the case was altered as she moved toward humility in offering her hand beneath the foot. Dalton, however, seized her wrist and threw her hand back to her as he raised her for a kiss. He was an operatic sword-and-dagger man who obviously understood the rules of falcon-taming so that Kate's spirit was not broken. He controlled the play and educated the heroine so that in the radiance of her genuine loving submission thirty-two years of her own chronological age disappeared and she looked eighteen.

In fact her transformation from tomboy to beautiful young woman who has decided to play along with her lover made her the winner, according to Jack Tinker of the *Daily Mail* (June 11, 1986). However, John Barber of the *Daily Telegraph* (June 12, 1986) was "deeply moved that the fair, lovely maid—or any such—should be so exploited by a male." In an even more politically correct dissent, Benedict Nightingale of the *New Statesman* (June 20, 1986) complained that Redgrave did not fully convey the transition between hoyden and humility, as she entered into "the kind of marriage our age may reject but the Elizabethans thought natural and normal."[24]

This production's use of masculine dress instantly raises the whole question of transvestite actors on the Elizabethan stage. This can be one argument for accepting the violent horseplay of *The Taming of the Shrew*—since the original performance had men and boys beating each other in high-spirited combat there is nothing for feminists to worry about. But in fact the situation becomes more piquant because of this very situation. Obviously the play can never be for us what it was in its original social or theatrical milieu, but one does wonder how the play would go if played entirely by women.

In March 1985, at the Theatre Royal, Stratford East, London, this was indeed tried, in a production directed by Ultz, the *avant-garde* male designer, with music by Martin Duncan. However, a curious thing happened. The male chauvinists, though played by women, were clearly superior to the female characters *in propria persona*, perhaps the result of leaden verse speaking. According to Ros Asquith (*Observer*, March 17, 1985) this was a failed attempt to satirize chauvinism and "Susan Cox's whining, petulant Katherine and Shona Morris's timid Bianca are no match for Fiona Victory's jaunty Petruchio or Johanna Kirby's languorous Lucentio."

The casting did make one rethink Shakespeare's chauvinism, particularly in the use of a scold's bridle, though according to Francis King (*Sunday Telegraph*, March 17, 1985) "the women were as lively as if they were attending a seance." Fiona Victory as Petruchio was indeed plausible, and during the taming (s)he read a book on falconry. Suzie Mackenzie found the production humourless, "a bitter satirical feminist tract about the depersonalization of women," directed with too much attention to a thesis (*Time Out*, March 14, 1985). Susan Cox's submission as Katharina was staged as a hysterical diatribe delivered directly to the audience—to the intense "embarrassment" of the other players who bundled her up in a rug or blanket, reminiscent of folktale and that anonymous and brutal taming pamphlet *A Mery Jest of a Shrewde and curste Wyfe lapped in a Morrelles skin* (1580?), or perhaps of Cleopatra, as they hustled her offstage.[25] The reviewers did not catch these references, but Michael Billington confessed to a "realistic frission" at that moment (*Guardian*, March 12, 1985). In addition, the dominant image of the play was that of an inflatable rubber sex-doll passed from hand to hand with Hortensio's widow at one time seeming to be that very doll, while Lucentio licked at his picture of a nude Bianca. Thus women were perceived as exploitable playthings, and, as Carole Woddis remarked, "I am still waiting for the real 'women's version,' directed by a woman" (*City Limits*, March 15, 1985), while Francis King of the *Sunday Telegraph* (17 March 1985) suggested that, "A true women's version of *The Taming of the Shrew* would surely be found to reverse the sexes and show how a woman can break the spirit of a man and subject him to her own will."[26]

In the post-feminist era the jury is still out on *The Taming of the Shrew*. Male chauvinists will delight in its psychic (and even physical) pain, while feminists, like Shaw, remain uncomfortable at that spectacle. Historical recreation of a period may be an answer, but then the performance of this comedy can be lost. For myself, I believe that Katharina's liberated spirit remains unbroken, but that she has learned the value of *realpolitik* not only in marriage, but also in the even wider world of sociopolitics.

NOTES

Originally published in *Theatre Research Journal* 19, no. 3 (Fall 1994): 214–25. Reprinted with permission from Margaret Loftus Ranald and Oxford University Press.

1. This essay is part of a continuing study of non-traditional performance history and *The Taming of the Shrew*. It was delivered in slightly different form at the Professors' Conference of IFTR, Dublin, September 29–October 3, 1992.
2. Dash 1981, 41. The Garrick text still surfaces occasionally in revivals of *The Taming of the Shrew*—as in the 1987 Alabama Shakespeare Festival where it was also conflated with Sheridan's *The Critic*.
3. Dash 1981, 58, 64.
4. Ibid., 41.
5. Winter 1891, 3.
6. Winter 1891, 56–57. The portrait of her gently wearing a laurel wreath, though listed as Katharina, seems rather to be Rehan as Perdita in *The Winter's Tale*. Irene Dash says that Winter is rather unreliable in photographic attributions.
7. Russell 1926, 343–45.
8. Ibid., 332.
9. This is an unusually well-documented production, with some one hundred photographs in the Vandamm Collection of the Billy Rose Theatre Collection.
10. The film company was United Artists, a company formed in 1919 by Fairbanks, Pickford and Charles Chaplin, with the director D. W. Griffith. The announced policy of these expensive stars was to produce and direct their own pictures—and keep the profits for themselves. Fairbanks gradually gained control of the corporation and with the acquisition of Norma and Constance Talmadge, Gloria Swan-

son, John Barrymore, and Buster Keaton in the 1920s, the company did well. Even in the depression-ridden thirties (after Fairbanks had eased out the no-longer profitable Griffiths), the firm made a profit. Pickford managed to keep control of her own film properties so that even today one must obtain permissions from "The Mary Pickford Company" who, by the way, are very cooperative.

11. The text was rewritten by Suso Cecchi d'Amico, Paul Dehn, and Franco Zeffirelli, with original music by Nino Rota. As usual with a Zeffirelli production, this was profoundly visual and supremely busy. Apart from the principals, the cast contained some distinguished names, including Michael York, Michael Hordern, Cyril Cusack, Alfred Lynch, Natasha Pyne, Alan Webb, and Victor Spinetti.

12. See particularly the articles by Peter Berek and Shirley Nelson Garner in Charney 1988.

13. Desiderius Erasmus in 1529 had already inveighed against such practices in his colloquy "Conjugium Impar," or "The Unequal Match." But though many a writer of conduct and courtesy books followed suit, the economically profitable practice continued even in Shakespeare's day.

14. Hibbard 1964, 15–28; See also Kahn 1975.

15. Greer 1970, 205.

16. Ranald 1987, 117–33.

17. Greer 1970, 206.

18. In 1993, responding to feminist attacks on this motto, the State of Maryland resorted to mistranslation as an expedient: "Strong deeds, soft words."

19. Dash 1981, 50.

20. The musical direction was André Previn and Saul Chaplin, with choreography by Hermes Pan, famous for his many Fred Astaire numbers. One curious and unfortunate decision was to shoot the movie in the new (and ultimately unsuccessful) three-dimensional process, a hyped-up approach which was completely counterproductive and necessitated re-engineering. In addition, an opening scene which included Ron Randall playing Cole Porter introduced an irrelevant and ineffective element of distancing.

21. Sennett 1981, 275–76.

22. In 1939 the Seattle Negro Repertory Company (*sic*) sponsored by the Federal Theatre Project had offered a totally African-American cast in a musical adaptation.

23. For an excellent history of this and allied topics, see Hill 1984.

24. See *London Theatre Records* 1986, 637–42.

25. For a folklore-based study of this traditional approach see Brunvand 1991.

26. See *London Theatre Record* 1985.

WORKS CITED

Brunvand, Jan Harold. 1991. *The Taming of the Shrew: A Comparative Study of Oral and Literary Traditions*. The Garland Folklore Library. New York and London: Garland.

Charney, Maurice, ed. 1988. *"Bad" Shakespeare: Reevaluations of the Shakespeare Canon*. Rutherford, Madison, and Teaneck, N.J.: Fairleigh Dickinson University Press, London and Toronto: Associated University Presses.

Dash, Irene G. 1981. *Wooing, Wedding, and Power: Women in Shakespeare's Plays.* New York: Columbia University Press.

Friedan, Betty. 1963. *The Feminine Mystique.* New York: Norton.

Greer, Germaine. 1970. *The Female Eunuch.* New York: McGraw-Hill.

Hibbard, George. 1964. "*The Taming of The Shrew*: A Social Comedy." In *Shakespearean Essays.* Edited by Alwin Thaler and Norman Sanders. Tennessee Studies in Language and Literature, no. 2. Knoxville: University of Tennessee.

Hill, Errol. 1984. *Shakespeare in Sable: A History of Black Shakespearean Actors.* Amherst, Mass.: University of Massachusetts Press.

Kahn, Coppélia. 1975. "*The Taming of The Shrew*: Shakespeare's Mirror of Marriage." *Modern Language Studies* 5: 88–102.

London Theatre Record. 1985. Vol. 5, Issue 55 (Feb. 27–Mar. 13): 226–28; Issue 6 (27 March): 314–15.

London Theatre Record. 1986. 6, Issue 12 (June 4–17, 1986): 637–42.

A Mery Iest of a Shrewde and Curste Wyfe Lapped in a Morrelles Skin. 1580? London STC 14521.

Ranald, Margaret Loftus. 1987. *Shakespeare and His Social Context: Essays in Osmotic Knowledge and Literary Interpretation.* New York: AMS Press.

Russell, Charles Edward. 1926. *Julia Marlowe: Her Life and Art.* New York: D. Appleton.

Sennett, Ted. 1981. *Hollywood Musicals.* New York: Harry N. Abrams.

Winter, William. 1891. *Ada Rehan: A Study.* 2d ed. New York: Printed for Augustin Daly.

Review of Gale Edwards's
Taming of the Shrew,
Royal Shakespeare Company,
Evening Standard, April 24, 1995

NICHOLAS DE JONGH

It's a sign of this fascinating production's pulling-power that you follow its dream-like course in suspense, wondering how the director, Gale Edwards, will resolve the play's sex war. That Shakespeare allows a triumph for male chauvinism poses a problem today.

But Miss Edwards, with her transforming ingenuity, does not disappoint.

This is *The Shrew* with a late twentieth-century touch—a provocative and visually arresting view, not a conventional feminist riposte.

Our difficulty with this comedy of wooing and wedding concerns the sufferings of the supposedly shrewish Katherina (Josie Lawrence looking defiantly headstrong). To starve, humiliate and brain-wash your wife into submission—as Petruchio so gleefully does—seems these days more a matter of nightmare than farce.

And it's just that sense of nightmare which Edwards stealthily evokes in her psychologically astute production.

The director's first and violent image provides the key: Christopher Sly, the drunken tinker of the play's prelude, collapses in an alcoholic stupor after violently quarrelling with his wife.

In this production, the play becomes Sly's dream of revenge against womankind in which the tinker himself impersonates Petruchio—that fortune hunter who masters the wilful Katherina in marriage.

Russell Craig's stage settings and Marie-Jeanne Lecca's spectacularly bizarre costumes locate the production deep in the realms of a modernish dream-land.

Craig fashions this world as a cluster of mobile two-tier towers in heliotrope and purple. From then, the wild mix of fashion styles and a succession of camp surprises characterise the action.

Michael Siberry's swaggeringly narcissistic Petruchio, hand to foot in black leather, arrives for his wedding in a tiny red car, wearing not much more than coloured feathers, flamboyant codpiece and well-ripped jeans.

His accomplice looks straight out of *Priscilla, Queen of the Desert*. Mark Lockyer, dazzlingly two-faced as the servant Tranio who woos Katherina's bland, blond sister Bianca (Tilly Blackwood) for his master, zooms in astride a Vespa and disguises himself like a 70s rock singer in blue velvet and glitter. The jokey costuming—from Elizabethan ruffs to 90s rough, and the exuberant business, help plot and subplot go with a comic swing: Never before can an asthma inhaler have given this play a fresh comic puff.

But it's Katherina's taming which matters most. And Miss Edwards ensures that fantasy drifts inexorably into nightmare.

Miss Lawrence, whose imposing Katherina is the unloved daughter, furious that life has left her on the shelf, bows down in fear and astonishment as the stage comes to resemble a prison.

Siberry's utterly compelling Petruchio, oscillates between shows of sympathy and eruptions of violence.

As if magically compelled by his love and power, Miss Lawrence acknowledges her subservience.

But in an astonishing theatrical denouement the tables turn. Petruchio falls forward, clutching his brow, the sets vanish and the dream of power abruptly ends leaving Christopher Sly kneeling before his wife, humbly begging pardon.

Here is Shakespeare's *Shrew* brilliantly claimed for today.

NOTE

From *The Evening Standard*, April 24, 1995. Reprinted by permission from *The Evening Standard*.

Petruchio's House
in Postwar Suburbia
Reinventing the Domestic Woman (Again)[1]

ANN C. CHRISTENSEN

When Shakespeare's Petruchio brings his wife home after their wedding in Act 4 of *The Taming of the Shrew*, he proceeds with a taming strategy based on physical deprivation and psychological torment exhaustively commented upon by critics.[2]

Notoriously he starves her ("'Tis burnt, and so is all the meat"; "And for this night we'll fast in company" [4.1.148, 164]), forbids her sleep ("Last night she slept not, nor to-night she shall not"; "And here I'll fling the pillow, there the bolster, / This way the coverlet . . ." [4.1.185, 188–89]), and refuses to buy her the clothes he has promised ("When you are gentle you shall have [a cap] too, / And not till then" [4.3.71–72]). In this way, he claims to "kill a wife with kindness" (4.1). In these tactics, critics have variously found evidence of patriarchal brutality, a cave-man sensibility women find irresistible, an agenda for a bourgeois/Puritan companionate marriage, and radical even revolutionary "individualism." Although critics have thus excoriated, justified, celebrated, and/or deconstructed Petruchio's treatment of Katherine, none (to my knowledge) has noted that Katherine is starved for work as well as starved for meat under the controlling hand of Petruchio.[3]

Shakespeare's play tames the wife by forbidding her the satisfaction of domestic management, which here falls under patriarchal purview.[4]

Whereas the prescriptive literature on "domesticall duties," along with personal accounts—diaries, letters, and documents praising (often deceased) wives—cite the domestic industry of English housewives, this stage-wife is forced into idleness.[5]

Her famous utterance closing the play confirms this, as when she inquires "Why are our bodies soft and weak and smooth, / Unapt to toil and trouble in the world[?]" and when she documents the "painful labor" a husband endures "Wilst [a wife] li'st warm at home, secure and safe" (5.2.171–72; 154, 56). Not only does this speech construct wifely duty as non-productive and sepa-

333

rate from "the world, " but we see this position forced upon her in those scenes in act 4 where she first appears in her new household over which she ought to command as Mistress. At Petruchio's house Katherine encounters men who control her and, significantly, also the household appurtenances. She finds a husband who plays the cook, the chamber maid, and the purchaser of clothing; a staff of male domestic servants, which metes out or deprives her of food; a tailor and haberdasher, who look to the master for the purchase of commodities; and her husband's friend, Hortensio, who "[e]at[s] ... up all" the meal ostensibly given to her (4.3.50). In this way, *Shrew* dramatizes the gendered contest over the meaning and use of domestic space and goods.

What happens when Petruchio's house moves from its English Renaissance moorings to modern stages, films, televisions, and, now, video tapes? What does a domestic woman look like when housewifery itself enjoys the status of an "occupation" as it did by the 1950s? Just as post-reformation England witnessed an ideological redefining of household conduct and the gendering of domestic roles, American society after World War II experienced a reshaping of the "homefront" in part through the unprecedented availability of "modern conveniences."[6]

Without forcing a homology between, say, 1590 and 1950, the present study explores the way in which three postwar adaptations of Shakespeare's play enlist ideas of "the domestic woman" which contrast their early modern manifestations: Cole Porter's *Kiss Me, Kate* (*KMK*), which opened on Broadway in 1948 and was adapted for the big screen, directed by George Sidney in 1953; Paul Nickell's 1950 televised Westinghouse Theater One hour-long version, and Franco Zeffirelli's blockbuster. I focus on these three in the interest of pedagogy since each is readily available on videotape.[7]

The representations of Petruchio's house and Katherine's housewifery in three different media spanning three decades of American (and international, in the case of *Kate* and Zeffirelli's film) popular culture demonstrate identifiable moments in the ongoing ideological production of the "domestic woman." The acquisition and care of household goods, whether linens and spits in the 1590s or Singer sewing machines in the 1950s, in part defined domestic identity for women. First I briefly examine twentieth-century definitions of and assumptions about femininity and domesticity in order to contextualize my reading of the adaptations, which I pursue in reverse chronological order, from Zeffirelli to Nickell to Porter/Sidney.

II

Seventeenth-century ideological constructions of the productive domestic Englishwoman put forth in sermons, treatises, and conduct books set against Katherine's experience of enforced idleness at Petruchio's house reveal a strategic upset in the gendered order of household labor in Shakespeare's

Shrew, and invite us to question the commonplace association of women with the provision of domestic comfort. Turning to twentieth-century accounts of women and home, we see both that the gendering of domestic space is historically specific and that within any one historical period, the ideologies and social practices of domestication conflict (See Meyerowitz 1994). The contemporary popular commentator on architecture and lifestyles, Witold Rybczynski (1986), in *Home, A Short History of an Idea*, exemplifies the unexamined conflation of women with "home":

> It was only when my wife and I built our own home that I discovered at first hand the fundamental poverty of modern architectural ideas. I found myself turning again and again to memories of older houses, and older rooms, and trying to understand what had made them feel so right, so comfortable. I also began to suspect, and in this I was not mistaken, *that women understand more about domestic comfort than do men.* (viii, emphasis added)

This common idealization of the domestic woman merits further exposition. Women, it seems, intuitively "understand" home life and comforts, whereas men like Rybczynski are formally educated to technology and trade.[8]

Other gendered binaries implied in his quotation may be stated structurally: on the one side of the slash stand the categories of wife and homemaker, "own home," memories, and comfort; on the other side are husband, author and architect, others' homes, "modern architectural ideas." Men make houses; women make homes. In his Foreword, the author, Meyerson Professor of Urbanism at the University of Pennsylvania, reflects on his professional training (while he was a professor at McGill University) in which "the subject of comfort was mentioned only once, " and then only in the context of heating and air-conditioning (Rybczynski 1986, vii). His book aims to fill that gap in his education by exploring "not so much the reality of the home . . . as the idea of the home" (Rybczynski 1986, viii). These terms, opposing material "reality" and "idea, " social practice and ideology, architecture and homemaking, underpin assumptions about domesticity. While Rybczynski's book removes us from the old world of Shakespeare's play to the new world and the mid-twentieth century, his assumptions of the givenness of a "woman's place" and her special homemaking skills return us to the questions which framed this essay: how does history represent the domestic woman? What cultural messages are encoded in household labor? What does she do all day? What do "love, fair looks and true obedience" look like (5.2.158)?

In the productions I discuss these traits look useful. Figuring the domestic locus of women's power differently from Shakespeare, these adaptations return the wife safely to the private suburban home (except in the case of *KMK*) where she will not be idle, but busy, making a "home." Yet they recuperate the taming myth, restructuring it to suit modern audiences deeply troubled by and indeed hostile toward working wives and mothers and comforted by reassurance that homemaking satisfies the needs of both women and their families (See Tuchman, et al. 1978, 18, 20). During and after World War II many women were employed outside their homes, yet the ideological picture of women and work in this period—propagated in part by the entertainment industry—sharply diverged from this reality. William Chafe in *The American Woman* (1972) noted, "A job for a wife over thirty-five became normal . . . but most Americans continued to subscribe to the belief that women were (and should remain) primarily homemakers" (quoted in Walker 1987, 199).

The social dislocation of mid-twentieth century America resulted in another kind of "great rebuilding": rural interstate highways stretched to new suburbs, demarcating this period of prosperity (for some, mostly white, middle-class families) from the national housing crisis of the 1940s. As the families of four million veterans cashed in on the G.I. bill for mortgages, single-family homes proliferated (Hartmann 1982, 166–67). Family historians describe the "massive effort" on the part of government, social scientists, and the media to channel women's energy, independence, and indeed fears into "one safe harbor: the family." Elaine Tyler May in *Homeward Bound: American Families in the Cold War Era*, analyzes the ideology of "home" in terms of containment: "Within its walls potentially dangerous social forces of the new age might be tamed, where they could contribute to the secure and fulfilling life to which postwar women and men aspired. . . . More than merely a metaphor for the war on the homefront, containment aptly describes the way in which public policy, personal behavior, and even political values were focused on the home" (quoted in Harvey 1993, xiv).[9]

Married women on whose shoulders fell the work of creating, sustaining, and reproducing the new model household received unprecedented attention from Hollywood and advertisers.

Social histories documenting English gentlewomen's shrinking world in the sixteenth century find uncanny echoes in modern analyses of family structure under late capitalism in the United States.[10]

As one sociologist observes, "while for men [Industrialization] enlarged the world outside the home, chiefly by expanding the range of occupations available to them, for women it has meant an involution of the world into the space of the home" (Oakley 1974a, 32). For modern "middle-class" wives, the prohibitive costs of keeping domestic servants, on the one hand, and, on the other, the associations of the household and family with women's consumerism resulted in housewifery as a bona fide occupation (See Lopata 1971). To return to Rybczynski, women *understand*.

Housework, as the postwar ideologies represent it, provides the ideal outlet for women's "*naturally* nurturant and generous . . . cheerfully self-abnegating" psyches, while at the same time keeping housewives socially isolated (Radway 1984, 94, original italics). From studies of and interviews with women who identified themselves as "housewives," two salient features emerge: their feelings of constant busyness yet social isolation and loneliness."[11]

We see this busyness in Janice Radway's (1984) outline of the remarkable range of the modern housewife's duties:

> A good wife and mother, it is assumed, will have no difficulty meeting the challenge of providing all of the labor necessary to maintain a family's physical existence including the cleaning of its quarters, the acquisition and preparation of its food, and the purchase, repair and upkeep of its clothes, even while she masterfully discerns and supplies individual members' psychological needs. (94)

Ann Oakley, whose important scholarship on housework continues its influence twenty years after its initial publication, notes that in some cultural representations (such as TV advertisements and Hollywood films), housework is not work, but a creative, even leisurely pursuit: "the home is a treasure house 'of unsuspected joys ... the delectable smell of her own bread as it emerges crisp and brown from the oven and the satisfaction of stitching up a new print dress on her own sewing machine ... the smell of fresh earth in her own back yard'" (*Sociology* 41). This aesthetically inviting depiction of the homemaker inadvertently exposes its own dangers: the homemaker's potential loneliness in "*her own*" little world, baking *her own* bread, owning *her own* appliances, planting *her own* garden.[12]

Interviews reveal again and again housewives' feelings of alienation and isolation, their desire to be with people more, leading researchers to conclude that "social isolation of the modern [1956, 1962, 1968] housewife is a powerful motive for women to seek employment outside their homes" (Myrdal and Klein 1968, 83).[13]

III

Nickell's early television experiment and Zeffirelli's film version of *Shrew*—roughly contemporary with many of these early studies of housewifery[14]—construe Petruchio's household as either busy or lonely places for Katherine, while also implying her indispensability there. (*KMK* requires separate treatment since the "Katherine"/Lilli is both professional and urban.) That housekeeping underwent an ideological transition after World War II when women were expected to leave the work force and return to their kitchens is recorded in these contemporary productions, which resolve the Renaissance paradoxes by either documenting Katherine's performance of domestic labor or implying her eventual assumption of the role of country wife—neither resolution available to Shakespeare's Katherine.[15]

By inserting visual text of Katherine contributing a sorely needed "woman's touch" to her new household, productions obviate the Shakespearean problem of her work, effectively accommodating the ideological separation of the spheres which ensured that husbands entered the work force and wives became homemakers, and that the public sphere rather than the family be considered the productive unit.[16]

"The economically and rhetorically enforced allocation and division of productive and reproductive roles according to gender reached the peak of its social installation in the United States between the end of World War Two and the beginning of the American Woman's Movement" (Walker 1987, 197). Feminist film theorists observe the medium's use (especially in the so-called 'woman's film') of gender-differentiated societal spaces, which reinforce the aphorism about "a woman's place" by concentrating women within domestic spaces (Doane 1987, 285).

Petruchio's house in filmed *Shrew*s needs cleaning up; this need posits Katherine as the *sine qua non* of domestic order. In the Shakespearean script, Petruchio's house seems to be disordered only if we trust the master('s) narrative. Although his servant Grumio takes pains to ensure that "the house [be] trimmed, rushes strewed, cobwebs swept, the servingmen [dressed] . . . and every officer his wedding garments on," even instructing the staff on the proper way to bow (4.1.40–43), Petruchio tells a different story. Upon his return home in act 4, he complains about the quality of domestic service: "Where be these knaves? What no man at door / To hold my stirrup nor take my horse? . . . What? No attendance? No regard? No duty?" (4.1.107–8, 113). Barking correctives about everything from his slippers to the meat, Petruchio here intentionally mimics Katherine's shrewishness, admitting later that the faults he finds are "undeserved" (4.1.186). Katherine's defense of the servants against Petruchio's criticism (" 'twas a fault unwilling"; "The meat was well, if you were so contented" [4.1.143, 156]), suggests that the household is in fact adequately provided for and this further displays Petruchio's verbal virtuosity (Newman 1986). Still, modern directors adopt Petruchio's unflattering description of his house probably because cinematic "before and after" shots can show the passage of time in shorthand. This messy *mise en scéne* also has an ideological component.

As if to reinforce the need for feminine service, these productions of *Shrew* alike exaggerate the dirt and/or disorder at Petruchio's house. His variously spare or cramped country estate visually contrasts the opulence and order of Baptista's town house and other men's houses described in the text: in Zeffirelli, Petruchio (Richard Burton) inhabits a dusty, cluttered, and dilapidated hell-hole compared to the palatial Paduan showcase of Baptista (Michael Hordern) and Hortensio's (Victor Spinetti) orderly suites attended by velvet-clad serving men.[17] Nickell's Petruchio (Charleton Heston) occupies a rough-and-tumble hunting lodge compared to Baptista's urban(e) balconied luxury flat aloft the Paduan piazza.[18] The implication in both is that the house is not yet the home it will become under Katherine's ministrations.

This hyperbolic contrast visually embodies fantasies of 1950s housewifery in which women happily leave jobs and school to enter into the safety and seclusion of the suburban domicile. The "ideologies of domesticity that reinforced women's household roles" formed in the mid- nineteenth century were reinforced in the postwar 1950s (DeVault 1991, 6) and are duly reflected in Zeffirelli's and Nickell's productions. This ideology constructed the home as a place not of productivity, but of service, and the wife and mother as the sole provider. Studies of the sociology of housework report a heavy emphasis on the service role of wives: "women 'service' the labour force by catering to the physical needs of men (workers) and by raising children (the next generation of workers) so that the men are free *from* child-socialization and free to work outside the home" (Oakley 1974, 179, original italics).

Zeffirelli's version sentimentalizes the "Elizabethan" housewife by dressing her (Elizabeth Taylor) in a humble house-frock and turban as she takes command and wins hearts at home. Hausfrau Taylor projects an especially remarkable fantasy of wifely duty since she simultaneously figures Cinderella and "'the decadence, sexual license and extravagance'" of the Hollywood of the 1950s and 1960s (Hodgdon 1992, 545). Placing her so firmly (if fleshily) at the helm of the home, Zeffirelli invites the audience to read contradiction: after *Who's Afraid of Virginia Woolf?* and a series of films which showed her at her shrewiest, and after her scandalous part in the destruction of Debbie Reynolds' and Eddie Fisher's marriage and alignment with the equally dissolute Burton, Taylor figures simultaneously the domestic ideal and its dissolution, metacinematically suggesting that show business and domesticity don't mix, a key element in *KMK* as I discuss below (Dove 1995).

The morning after their honeymoons in separate rooms, Petruchio awakens—hung over, as usual—to the clanging and clashing of household stuff amidst laughter and a woman's voice chirping from an outer room. Via Zeffirelli's signature "naturalistic and pictorial treatment" (Holderness 1989, 52) Petruchio finds her knowledgeably advising her staff as she bustles gaily from one work station to the next, concentrated appropriately in the dining room and kitchen—the same locales off limits to Shakespeare's Katherine. The scene focuses on the cooperative dusting of a massive chandelier (among the "goods" Petruchio has inherited from his father), lowered from the ceiling and transformed, like Katherine herself, from a dust-catching ornament to an attractive and—above all—a functioning household appliance. Petruchio views her through its spokes and cobwebs which she assaults with a featherduster—a domestic tool and scepterlike sign of her power, as an ironic reprise of the broken lute incident of act 1. Attempting to avoid him Katherine thrusts the feather-duster into Petruchio's hands and stalks away; he looks at it quizzically and hands it off to his sometime man-servant, now the mistress' minion.

The duster changes hands from Katherine to Petruchio to Grumio, marking Petruchio's surrender to the order that Katherine has imposed on his home. The exchange not only rewrites Shakespeare, but also corrects Zeffirelli's own version of the earlier wooing scene in which Katherine and Petruchio romp around amidst Baptista's stores. There Katherine is finally "won" after a spirited chase through barrels of fruit and garlands of peppers and salami as they drop singly then together into large bin of wool. That wool has been reconstituted into the patriarchal bed and Katherine herself is mistress of what is hers. She lays claim to Petruchio's stuff by cleaning it. Furthermore, whereas the 1590s Katherine had been forced to submit to the "insolent retinue" of Petruchio's servants, Taylor's Katherine handily controls them.

From Mary Douglas's (1966) study of *Purity and Danger*, we have come to recognize that the discourses and activities of cleaning transcend the mere need for hygiene to create order. Thus, the housewife who performs these tasks is rather "separating, placing boundaries, making visible statements about the home" which she builds from "a material house" (68). In laying out the semiotics of dirt, Douglas (1966) in effect defines the ideological function of Zeffirelli's white-tornado Katherine:

> As we know it, dirt is essentially disorder. . . . If we shun dirt, it is not because of craven fear, still less dread or holy terror. Nor do our ideas about disease account for the range of our behavior in cleaning or avoiding dirt. Dirt offends against order. Eliminating it is not a negative movement, but a positive effort to organize the environment. (7)[19]

In the face of Katherine's creation of order, Petruchio looks befuddled, yet inwardly pleased. In the next Verona sequence, Zeffirelli shows the results of Katherine's influence: flowers and fruits grace the once dusty table; a warm fire glows on the hearth; Troilus is carefully deflead; the servants are primped up and gaze adoringly on their new mistress. These shots record the shift in emotional life and indeed authority through the visual metaphors of Katherine's housewifery and what film theorists call "expressive objects"—in this case, of household stuff.[20]

Each object, site, and activity formerly associated with Petruchio—from the table he had upturned to the cold hearth, bad servants, and Troilus's fleas (with which he had shocked the effete Hortensio earlier)—are now reclaimed by the married woman.

In the interest of promoting this vision of the happy homemaker (an ideal completed in the final scene by Katherine's maternal ogling of children), Zeffirelli had to alter Shakespeare's text substantially. The scene where Katherine must beg and grovel to Grumio for food (4.3.1–35) has been cut, for this Katherine has bonded with the men and gained control over her environment, leaving Petruchio not herself out of the domestic loop. Furthermore, the interpolated cleaning sequence shows Katherine freely crossing domestic thresholds. This bird may be yet "sharp" or hungry, but she does have access to the kitchen. Also cut is Petruchio's false offer of a meal of his own device (4.3.36–52) because this Petruchio is clearly out of his element within this suddenly feminized home; besides, he couldn't find his way around the kitchen since she has turned the place inside out. The night before, that room was filthy, the kitchen a smoldering, smoky disaster area, and the servants looked like a band of pirates, as ignorant of laying a table as to making the sign of the cross. A competent housewife is necessary to reform the manners and morals of these lost souls, and—on celluloid—she makes great headway overnight! The image of her utility seems to repudiate the ennui of white middle-class housewives suffering in the 1960s from "feminine mystique." Real women, the message seems to be, do housework. The film's representation of house-turned-home rewrites the particulars of the Elizabethan scene at the same time reproducing its power dynamic. In both cases, women serve a patriarchal ideal: Shakespeare's Katherine through idleness, Zeffirelli's through housework.

In Nickell's Theater One television production, sponsored significantly by Westinghouse, the male homestead hankers after the civilizing influence only a woman can provide. As Barbara Hodgdon (1992) astutely observes, the products offered to the audience by the spokeswoman help as much as the program does to domesticate women as the play finds "its ideal venue: the home" (549). Petruchio's house appears less filthy than isolated, but the master and servants are equally in need of reforming. More than Taylor's Katherine, who quickly ranges about her expansive new home, this one played by Lisa Kirk (who also played Bianca/Lois in the Broadway production of *KMK*) seems trapped within an incompetent and uncomfortable suburban household. When she gets frustrated, for example, after the first dinner and when Grumio refuses to feed her, Kirk retreats into the bedroom off-stage. Partly due to the constraints of the medium (Zeffirelli filmed on location in Italy; Nickell's Padua is a studio street cafe), the private household appears physically and psychologically to confine Katherine. Here housework is not idealized on screen, but presented as a necessary route for Katherine to take to selfhood.

The set for Petruchio's house looks borrowed from *Bonanza*: with stone walls and uncovered dark wood floors, a picnic-style table, wooden hutch and deer's head trophies on the wall, his lodge exploits the "country cousin" relationship between the university city of Padua and more homey rustic Verona. Katherine enters Petruchio's house like an unwilling mail-order bride, an image enhanced by Petruchio's checkered and denim 1950s western wear.[21]

His servants (or hired hands) wear clownish, mismatched clothes and inexplicably act as if drunk or mentally deficient; Grumio wears a propeller-topped beanie, others mutter, drool, and blow cigarette smoke around while serving the meal. Petruchio trips one dullard who falls onto the table jumbling the food and plates. A string of wieners—typical '50s television food—provides the referent for Petruchio's "what dogs are these?" Absurdly exaggerated to frighten and hence tame Katherine, these schticks also imply that this house needs a woman. This dramatic transformation of the household is a Hollywood staple for the woman's touch: from *The Sound of Music* to *The Color Purple*, the houses of widowers and bachelors, whether castles or shacks, are remade into "homes" by the introduction of industrious wives.[22]

I turn to *KMK* last because it most clearly exposes (and exploits) the contradictions within postwar constructions of domesticity, and its musical-about-a-musical genre lends a unique metatheatrical complication to the discussion. In contrast to the later versions of the play, which doggedly keep Katherine at home, *KMK* grants its frame "Katherine" a professional life, though it is inextricably tied to her ex-husband, who is also her co-star and director. Lilli Vanessi (Kathryn Grayson) is a housewife by no historical standards, but a glamorous and successful stage performer. Divorced for a year from Fred (Howard Keel), Lilli is apparently on the verge of a second marriage and honeymoon, but accepts the part in "Cole Porter's" Broadway show because she does not want to allow her rival, Lois Lane, to get the lead opposite Fred. Furthermore, Fred assures her, "You'd make a perfect shrew, " luring her into the part through the Petruchian promise of pretty clothes, the costumes for the show. Thus rivalry, vanity, and vindictiveness in part define the shrewish professional woman, if not femininity itself.

Though not a conventional housewife, Lilli does express stereotypical concern for household matters. Arriving to the flat she had shared with Fred, Lilli uses her characteristic ring of the door bell and is received by Paul, the family servant. (In the settlement, she apparently has retained the services of Suzanne, the French maid, while Fred gets the English valet and butler, Paul—raising other issues about the gendering of domestic service beyond the scope of this essay.) Embodying the internal conflicts and contradictions of a working woman, she appears both sentimental (for example, as she looks wistfully at old pictures displayed on the piano of herself with Fred) and shrewd, as she puts her career ahead of her impending second nuptials. Exhibiting the "woman's touch, " she observes the care and maintenance of persons and goods of the household. For example, she cares enough to inquire about Paul's bursitis, and he instinctively calls her "Mrs. Graham" though, as she corrects him, she has resumed her maiden name. Further, Lilli notices and comments on an ink stain on the couch, advising Fred to "have it taken care of." For his part, Fred insists that Lilli "loves the apartment, " predicting to Porter that "she'll be dying to see if I'd changed anything." Thus the old roles of husband, wife, mistress, and servant exert pressure against the new domestic configuration, presenting Lilli as an ingredient necessary for domestic order if not tranquillity.

The larger than life (and larger than Lilli) entrance of Ann Miller as the

competitor, Lois Lane ("Bianca") announces that show business is bad business for traditional married love. Her class-based crudeness and overfamil-
iarity with Fred, Lilli, and "Mr. Porter" mark her as an interloper. A Copa
dance girl desirous of a part in Porter's show, she tromps in, making herself
at home by playing the hostess: "Sweetie, we're out of ginger ale, " she shouts
to an embarrassed Fred. With the accompaniment (and encouragement) of the
"the boys" in the band, she performs her routine, singing "Too Darn Hot" and
using household stuff as part of the "act." She dances on the tables, jumping
from the long coffee table onto an end-table and magazine case, kicking books
and ashtrays off the table, flinging a window open during a quasi-strip-tease,
flanked throughout by household appurtenances—a fireplace and mantle,
dresser, and other furniture (we see a throw on one of a pair of matching
chairs), and portraits of Fred. While the others sit on the couch, Lois occupies
a table-top; she provides an intentional if secondary reference to Porter's
claim that "there's no place to put it, " meaning her audition number. So while
this "Petruchio's house" is decidedly a Manhattan bachelor pad, it, like the
other filmed households we have seen, nonetheless wants its proper mistress—if not to perform household labor (what Paul and Suzanne do), then to
administer care and supervision to the dissolute master.

In Lois' next big dance number, on the roof of the theater with her other
"sweetie, " Bill Calhoun (Tommy Rall), a gambler who "can't behave, "
domestic objects again frame the action, though, as before the new context
defamiliarizes them. The duet, "Why Can't You Behave?" is performed amid
"laundry" hanging on a clothesline with the cityscape furnishing the further
background. But this is show biz laundry: a pair of newly available women's
stockings, a corset, vintage Frederick's of Hollywood chartreuse slip, and a
red tu-tu.

In its metatheatrical frame, *KMK* deconstructs show business to reveal an
industry unfriendly to traditional domesticity. Lois' crass attempt at domestic
hospitality extends only as far as offering to mix drinks; her complaints in
"Too Darn Hot" include the refusal to "sup with my baby tonight, to refill a
cup with my baby tonight" for the eponymous reason. That which in 1950s
t.v. shows like *Leave It To Beaver* would be a family meal cooked by the
mother and served to an appreciative husband and children in *KMK* appears
on a tray offered to a "show girl" by the backstage maid. Even "Tex, " the
emblem of the traditional American west, where men are men, and so on, cannot make it to opening night because of his cattle ranching business. Furthermore, Lois reveals him to be a beef-wielding playboy, whom she had met "at
the Shamrock in Houston." On-stage, both Petruchio and Katherine disparage
traditional "family values": the boredom of staying at home and the tiresome
production of heirs. She sings cynically of a husband's feigned business trips
with his "pretty secretary" and the bother of a traveling salesman spouse:

"While he's away in Mandolay, 'Tis thee who'll have the baby" in "I Hate Men." As she vows here not to "play the hen, " Petruchio laments the loss of his little black book of Italian girlfriends in "Where is the Life?" The most remarkable example of flouting tradition appears in Fred's hilarious send-up of the Texas range—the equivalent of the suburb to which Lilli almost consigns herself in wedding Tex. Fred graphically envisions the isolated, even desolate "home on the range" she has in store for her: using "reverse psychology, " Fred characterizes the east-coast theater life as a "tawdry" succession of parties and performances in contrast to the "peace, quiet, and solitude" of the West. He visualizes Lilli's rough routine there: "up at five, " "a fifty-mile canter" to the branding area, the stench of seared flesh—domestic tranquillity indeed! Tex himself corroborates the story when he drawls, "You could ride for nigh onto two weeks and see nary a soul." This projection contrasts the busy and productive career Lilli would enjoy in New York, which she would surrender for a lone-star marriage. Still, this opposition between career and domesticity turns out to be false for Lilli and Fred.

Although *KMK* blithely dramatizes the marital infidelity and self-promotion common in show business, it does represent a certain kind of domestic happiness available to Fred and Lilli. In the scene framing "Wunderbar, " they talk of old times, interspersing memories of "home life" and marriage with those of their tours and their extraneous work as "starving actors." The "separate spheres" of personal and professional life are here intertwined for both partners. Lilli acknowledges the first anniversary of their divorce through a token gift, the cork from their first bottle of champagne. This rather exotic emblem, though, has a very homey New York context as Fred recalls their wedding toast transpiring in her "one-room . . . over the Armenian bakery." The two also recollect a ham, a gag gift to Fred, which fed them all winter during a season in Virginia. They seem like a typical married couple, for example, when Lilli remembers her mother's visit while Fred exhibits the requisite sour face and eye-rolling. Waltzing in bathrobes—those visual metaphors of domestic comfort and familiarity, here reconstituted as "dressing gowns"— Fred and Lilli relive their roles in the "Viennese operetta," comically upstaging one another and ending in a kiss. The ineluctability of their resumed domesticity is registered in the stage-manager's approving smile as he opens the door to announce the curtain call. The last off-stage encounter between Lilli and Fred is fraught with theatrical metaphors fitting to both Shakespeare and this prime example of metatheater. Fred argues that Lilli belongs in the theater, but she leaves from the stage-door and hops into Tex's steer-mobile. Lilli's unexpected re-entrance on stage on the line, "What is thy will sir?" shows her wifely duty to Fred, as she reminds him, "That's your cue." Her final speech as "Katherine" about being "unapt to toil in the world" is ironic since the film drives toward keeping Lilli on stage. Still, in token ways, she offers a needed woman's touch.

IV

These forays on film reshape the gender/work issues Shakespeare intended when he left his Katherine idle in the "care" of her husband, "Nathaniel, Joseph, Nicholas, Philip, Walter, Sugarsop and the rest" (4.1.79–80), where the audience sees a woman tamed by enforced idleness. This problem is answered by the modern versions' invention of a need for a woman around the house. As a newspaper food writer noted, "the most powerful ingredient in any dish served at home ... [is] a wife and mother's love for her family" (quoted in Laura Shapiro 1995, 154).

By contrasting the ways in which Shakespeare symbolically "rid[s] the house of" Katherine with the ways that the Broadway, film, and television versions of the 1950s and 1960s bring her back, we recognize that productions of *Shrew* have some authority in constructing an ideology of the domestic woman. As the Lord's page says of the play, "it is a kind of history" (2.140); indeed a history of its productions may present an account of the reallocation of domestic authority and the stewardship of goods in the early years of commodity capitalism and the production of domestic comfort after World War II. The success of Katherine's taming in the Elizabethan play is effected in part by the defamiliarization of domestic space and the dislocation of the mistress from her domestical duties (Orlin 1993). Porter/Sidney, Nickell, and Zeffirelli enact the opposite move by relocating the wife firmly within her home, even if that home is on the road, a ranch, or in the tabloids.

NOTES

The author wishes to thank Carol Thomas Neely, Barbara Hodgdon, and Charles Dove for all their good ideas about shaping this essay and also appreciates the intellectual support of the University of Houston's English Department Women's Reading Group (1992). Partial funding for research on the project was supplied from the NEH-Folger Shakespeare Library Institute, "Shakespeare and the Languages of Performance" and the University of Houston Limited-Grants-In-Aid.

Originally published in *Post Script* 17, no. 1 (Fall 1997): 28–42. Reprinted with the permission of Ann C. Christensen and *Post Script* .

1. See Armstrong 1987, esp. Ch. 1, "The Rise of the Domestic Woman." Some of Armstrong's claims for domesticity in the eighteenth century I make for this earlier period.
2. Several studies of the play focusing on gender and power have influenced my reading. See Berek 1988; Boose 1991; Candido 1990; Gay 1994; Hedrick 1993; Hodgdon 1992; Kane 1989; Kehler 1986; Korda 1996; Maguire 1992; Marcus 1992; Mikesell 1989; Newman 1986, 1991; Novy 1979; Orlin 1993, 1994, 1995; Shapiro 1993; and Slights 1989.
3. The range of critical responses is suggested in titles from "The Good Marriage of Katherine and Petruchio" (Daniell 1984) and "Kate and Petruchio: Strength and

Love" (Williams 1991) to Candido's (1990) "The Starving of the Shrew" and Hedricks's (1993) "Commodity Kate."

4. On this point I distinguish between what the text dramatizes (i.e., Katherine's enforced inactivity) and what Korda (1996) projects for Katherine off-stage—the enactment of "the housewife's new managerial roles" (123, 113). Korda does, however, grant that "we never in fact *see* [Katherine] preside over the household economy or its property" (128).

5. I discuss the textual Katherine elsewhere. For Elizabethan and Jacobean attitudes toward housewifery, see Fenner 1588; Gouge 1612; Tusser 1573; and Whately 1617 and the discussion of these and other writers in Powell 1917.

6. Thomas Hine (1987) emphasizes the "never before" aspect of postwar advertising (esp. Ch.2, "The Luckiest Generation," 15–36). See also Shapiro 1995 and Hardyment 1988.

7. The Broadway production of *KMK* was a big hit: it opened in December of 1948, toured London and Vienna throughout the early 1950s, was revived in the New York City Center production in 1956, which toured Iceland (1958), Trieste (1959), Ankara (1964, where it was hailed as "a smash hit"); and Tokyo (1966). See *New York Times Theater Reviews* vol. 5–8. For another view of videotaped *Shrew*s, see Geimer 1988.

8. See Rybczynski's (1986) pointed opposition between technology and "the idea of home": "for domesticity proved to be an idea that had almost nothing to do with technology" (vii).

9. Meyerowitz (1994) challenges many of these assumptions.

10. In her study of the Willoughby family estate from the mid-1550s to the present, Friedman (1989) observes that the Lady and her attendants maneuvered within "a surprisingly narrow range of activities" (47). She continues to contrast the relative mobility and industry of female servants with the commitment and idleness of gentlewomen: "Free access to the courtyards, service buildings, kitchens, and even to the great hall—still the symbolic if not the actual focus of household life was denied them" (50).

11. Classic, though dated, studies of housework include the following: Oakley 1974, 1974a; Lopata 1971; Myrdal and Klein 1968; and Friedan 1963. More recent work includes Hardyment 1988; Strasser 1982; and Davidson 1986.

12. Oakley is quoting Dorothy Hopper, "But We Must Cultivate Our Gardens," in *American Women: The Changing Image*, ed. Beverly Benner Cassara (Boston: Beacon Press, 1962), 25.

13. The inserted dates reflect editions of the book. In her foreword, Myrdal describes the origins of the study: "a suggestion . . . made to [her] shortly after the last war by the International Federation of University Women, to make an international survey of the needs for social reforms if women are to be put into a position to reconcile family and professional life" (xiii).

14. For example, Mirra Komarovsky's *Blue-Collar Marriage* was published in 1967. Lopata's *Occupation: Housewife* came out in 1971.

15. I am not arguing that "the media" is or was a monolithic or a repressive force in the indoctrination of an ideology of domesticity. See also Meyerowitz 1994.

16. A sociology textbook of the late 1960s makes the following logical statement: "'Industrial society is characterized by the existence of specific institutions set

up to perform economic activities. From this it follows that in such societies the family cannot ... be a productive economic unit'" (C. C. Harris, *The Family* [London: Allen and Unwin, 1969; New York: Praeger, 1970]; quoted in Oakley 1974a, 33).

17. Although Zeffirelli cuts the induction, some of Sly accrues to Burton's drunkard Petruchio, including the fact that Hortensio's servants bring to him a basin of water with rose petals—the same ordered by the Lord and mentioned in stage directions.

18. Other productions pursue this opposition; for example, Petruchio's house appears as a dark, foreboding manor in the middle of nowhere in contrast to a bright pilastered mansion (Taylor 1929), and in Jonathan Miller's 1982 production for the BBC it is a bare-boards Puritan garret, while Baptista's pops straight out of a neat Vermeer interior.

19. Zeffirelli provides an interesting autobiographical corollary to this "household Kate" in his account of the preparations for filming *Shrew* in 1965. As secretary/personal assistant he engages the service of "a young English girl called Sheila Pickles, " whose British sense of efficiency provides "the perfect counterbalance to [Zeffirelli's own] free-wheeling, disorganized Latin spirit." While the director relishes in his self-portraits of irresponsibility (e.g., "like a footloose kid"), he admires the woman who "took on the onerous task of bringing order out of chaos" and celebrates her fortunate coupling of efficiency and "fun": "That she did this without behaving like some dour old harridan was the greatest joy of all. She knew how to have fun while carefully prodding me on to the paths of order and action" (Zeffirelli 1986, 213). In her *Enquiry into the Female Ghetto* of secretaries, Benet (1972) observes the unpleasant parallels between housekeeping and secretarial duties: "Both jobs are custodial, concerned with tidying up, putting away, and restoring order rather than with producing anything" (74). Just as Katherine whips Petruchio's house into shape with a combination of a featherduster, gusto, and maternal instincts, so Ms. Pickles brings to Zeffirelli's office order where there had been chaos. What the woman's touch provides is order "that it may do him ease" (*Shrew* 5.2.180).

20. I discovered this term through the dissertation of McHugh (1991).

21. The video jacket from Video Yesteryear Recording (CBS-TV) flaunts the nostalgic appeal of the production: "The words are the iambic pentameter of the Bard, but the look is definitely 1950!. . . The 'modern' dress version [presents] Mr. Heston sauntering onto the set in shades . . . [and] Lisa Kirk appears in yummy tights slacks."

22. On Hollywood's representations of women's relationships with their homes, see Gledhill 1987 and McHugh 1991.

WORKS CITED

Armstrong, Nancy. 1987. *Desire and Domestic Fiction: A Political History of the Novel*. New York: Oxford University Press.

Benet, Mary Kathleen. 1972. *Enquiry into the Female Ghetto*. London: Sidgwick and Jackson.

Berek, Peter. 1988. "Text, Gender, and Genre in *The Taming of the Shrew*." In *"Bad" Shakespeare: Revaluations of the Shakespeare Canon.* Edited by Maurice Charney. Rutherford, NJ: Fairleigh Dickinson University Press.

Boose, Lynda E. 1991. "Scolding Bridles and Bridling Scolds: Taming the Woman's Unruly Member." *Shakespeare Quarterly* 42: 179–213.

Candido, Joseph. 1990. "The Starving of the Shrew." *Colby Quarterly* 26: 96–111.

Christensen, Ann C. 1996. "Of Household Stuff and Homes: The Stage and Social Practice in *The Taming of the Shrew*" *Explorations in Renaissance Culture* 22: 127–46.

Crowther, Bosley. 1953. Review of *Kiss Me, Kate. New York Times Film Reviews.* (Nov. 6): 23.

Daniell, David. 1984. "The Good Marriage of Katherine and Petruchio" *Shakespeare Survey* 37: 23–31.

Davidson, Caroline. 1986. *A Woman's Work is Never Done: A History of Housework in the British Isles 1650–1950.* 2d ed. London: Chatto and Windus.

DeVault, Marjorie L. 1991. "Family Discourse and Everyday Practice, Gender and Class at the Dinner Table" *Syracuse Scholar* 2: 15–16.

Doane, Mary Anne. 1987. "The 'Woman's Film', Possession and Address." In *Home Is Where the Heart is: Studies in Melodrama and the Woman's Film.* Edited by Christine Gledhill. London: British Film Institute.

Douglas, Mary. 1966. *Purity and Danger: An Analysis of Concepts of Pollution and Taboo.* London Routledge and Kegan Paul.

Dove, Charles. 1995. Personal correspondence. February, 1995.

Fenner, Dudley. 1588. "The Order of Householde, Described Methodicallie Out of the Worde of God." *The Artes of Logike and Rethorike.* London.

Friedan, Betty. 1963. *The Feminine Mystique.* New York: Dell, 1974.

Friedman, Alice. 1989. *House and Household in Elizabethan England: Wollaton Hall and the Willoughby Family.* Chicago: University of Chicago Press.

Gay, Penny. 1994. *As She Likes It: Shakespeare's Unruly Women.* London: Routledge.

Geimer, Roger. 1988. "Shakespeare Live—on Videotape." *Shakespeare and the Triple Play: From Study to Stage to Classroom.* Edited by Sidney Homan. Lewisburg: Bucknell University Press.

Gledhill, Christine, ed. 1987. *Home is Where the Heart Is: Studies in Melodrama and the Woman's Film.* London: British Film Institute.

Gouge, William. 1612. *Of Domesticall Duties, Eight Treatises.* London.

Hardyment, Christina. 1988. *From Mangle to Microwave: The Mechanization of Household Work.*Oxford: Polity Press.

Hartmann, Susan M. 1982. *The Home Front and Beyond: American Women in the 1940s.* Boston: Twayne.

Harvey, Brett. 1993. *The Fifties: A Woman's Oral History.* New York: Harper Collins.

Hedrick, Donald. 1993. "Commodity Kate: Shakespeare's Shrew and the Domestication of Money."*Shakespeare Association of America Convention.* Atlanta, Ga. April, 1993.

Hine, Thomas. 1987. *Populuxe.* New York: Alfred Knopf.

Hodgdon, Barbara. 1992. "Katherina Bound; or, Play(K)ating the Strictures of Everyday Life." *PMLA* 107, no. 3: 538–53.

Holderness, Graham. 1989. *The Taming of the Shrew*. Shakespeare in Performance Series. New York: Manchester University Press.

Kane, Carolyn. 1989. "'Householde Government' and *The Taming of the Shrew*." *Publications of the Arkansas Philological Association* 15: 37–47.

Kehler, Dorothea. 1986. "Echoes of the Induction in *The Taming of the Shrew*." *Renaissance Papers*, 31–42.

Korda, Natasha. 1996. "Household Kates: Domesticating Commodities in *The Taming of the Shrew*" *Shakespeare Quarterly* 47, no. 2: 109–31.

Lopata, Helena Znaniecki. 1971. *Occupation: Housewife*. New York: Oxford University Press.

Maguire, Laurie E. 1992. "'Household Kates': Chez Petruchio, Percy and Plantagenet." In *Gloriana's Face: Women, Public and Private, in the English Renaissance*. Edited by S. P. Cerasano and Marion Wynne-Davies. Detroit: Wayne State University Press.

Marcus, Leah. 1992. "The Shakespearean Editor as Shrew-Tamer." *English Literary Renaissance* 22: 177–200.

McHugh, Kathleen. 1991. "Keeping House: The Discourses of Domestic Economy." Ph.D. diss. Indiana University.

Meyerowitz, Joanne. 1994. "Beyond the Feminine Mystique: A Reassessment of Postwar Mass Culture, 1946–1958." *Not June Cleaver: Women and Gender in Postwar America, 1945–1960*. Edited by Joanne Meyerowitz. Philadelphia: Temple University Press.

Mikesell, Margaret L. 1989. "'Love Wrought These Miracles': Marriage and Genre in *The Taming of the Shrew*" *Renaissance Drama* 20: 141–67.

Miller, Jonathan, dir. 1981. *The Taming of the Shrew*. With Sarah Badel and John Cleese. BBC / Time-Life Shakespeare Series. PBS. Jan. 16, 1981.

Myrdal, Alva and Viola Klein. 1968. *Women's Two Roles: Home and Work*. 2d ed. London: Routledge and Kegan Paul.

Newman, Karen. 1986. "Renaissance Family Politics and Shakespeare's *The Taming of the Shrew*." *English Literary Renaissance* 16: 86–100.

———. 1991. *Fashioning Femininity and English Renaissance Drama*. Chicago: University of Chicago Press.

Nickell, Paul, dir. 1950. *The Taming of the Shrew*. With Lisa Kirk and Charlton Heston. Westinghouse Studio One. Video Images, Video Yesteryear Recording. (Folger Shakespeare Library film archives.)

Oakley, Ann. 1974. *Sociology of Housework*. Bath: Pitman Press, 1974.

———. 1974a. *Woman's Work: The Housewife, Past and Present*. New York: Pantheon.

Novy, Marianne. 1979. "Patriarchy and Play in *The Taming of the Shrew*." *English Literary Renaissance* 9: 264–80.

Orlin, Lena Cowen. "The Performance of Things in *The Taming of the Shrew*." *Yearbook of English Studies* 23: 167–88.

———. 1994. *Private Matters and Public Culture in Post-Reformation England*. Ithaca: Cornell University Press.

———. 1995. *Elizabethan Households, An Anthology*. Washington, D. C.: The Folger Shakespeare Library.

Powell, C. L. 1917. *English Domestic Relations 1487–1653: A Study of Matrimony and Family Life in Theory and Practice as Revealed in Literature, Law, and History.* New York: Columbia University Press.

Radway, Janice. 1984. *Reading the Romance: Women, Patriarchy, and Popular Literature.* Chapel Hill: University of North Carolina Press.

Rybczynski, Witold. 1986. *Home: A Short History of an Idea.* New York: Penguin, 1986.

Shakespeare, William. 1969. *The Taming of the Shrew.* Edited by Alfred Harbage. *The Complete Pelican Shakespeare.* New York: Pelican-Viking Press.

Shapiro, Laura. 1995. "Do Women Like to Cook?" *Granta* 52 (Winter): 153–62.

Shapiro, Michael. 1993. "Framing the Taming: Metatheatrical Awareness of Female Impersonation in *The Taming of the Shrew.*" *Yearbook of English Studies* 23: 141–66.

Sidney, George, dir. 1953. *Kiss Me, Kate.* Music and Lyrics by Cole Porter. With Kathryn Grayson and Howard Keel. MGM/UA videotape.

Slights, Camille. 1989. "The Raw and the Cooked in *The Taming of the Shrew.*" *JEGP* 88, no. 2 (1989): 168–89.

Strasser, Susan. 1982. *Never Done: A History of American Housework.* New York: Pantheon.

Taylor, Samuel, dir. 1929. *The Taming of the Shrew.* With Mary Pickford and Douglas Fairbanks. Columbia.

Thirsk, Joan. 1978. *Economic Policy and Projects: The Development of a Consumer Society in Early Modern England.* Oxford: Clarendon Press.

Tuchman, Gaye, Arleen Kaplan Daniels, and James Benet, eds. 1978. *Hearth and Home: Images of Women in the Mass Media.* New York: Oxford University Press.

Tusser, Thomas. 1573. *Five Hundred Points of Good Husbandry.* London: James Tregaskis and Sons, 1931.

Walker, Janet. 1987. "Hollywood, Freud and the Representation of Women: Regulation and Contradiction, 1945-early 60s." In *Home is Where the Heart Is: Studies in Melodrama and the Woman's Film.* Edited by Christine Gledhill. London: British Film Institute.

Whatley, William. 1617. "A Bride-Bush or A Wedding Sermon." *The English Experience.* Norwood, N.J.: Walter J. Johnson, 1975.

Williams, George Walton. 1991. "Kate and Petruchio: Strength and Love." *English Language Notes* 29 (September): 18–24.

Zeffirelli, Franco, dir. 1966. *The Taming of the Shrew.* With Elizabeth Taylor and Richard Burton. Royal Films International.

———. 1986. Zeffirelli, *The Autobiography of Franco Zeffirelli.* New York: Weidenfeld and Nicolson.

Katherina Bound, or Play(K)ating the Strictures of Everyday Life

BARBARA HODGDON

When Kate delineates a wife's duties to "her loving lord" within a hierarchical configuration of marriage, *The Taming of the Shrew* closes on an image of "woman" that the play's male characters use as a means of speaking to each other about themselves. Her speech, which so radically positions subjection as the determining condition for women's subjectivity and teaches how distinctions between male and female bodies are produced, understood, and maintained within the institution of heterosexual marriage, not only has become a site for examining the abrasive relations among feminisms, postfeminisms, and early modern texts but has turned *Shrew* into highly overinvested real estate, a property without boundary markers that attracts discussions about material histories, material texts, and theatrical as well as cinematic reproductions, where the play, re-textualized and re-textured by actors' bodies and voices, appears in its most material form.

Such discussions invariably understand *Shrew* through its ending, where Kate's so-called sermon on obedience, predicated on a fantasy of the submissive female body that grounds larger cultural narratives about woman's place and position in the order of things, emerges as a fixed coordinate for engendering gender. Yet, at the point of consumption or reception, her speech just as invariably sheds its self-evident fixity and becomes reconfigured as something other than what it appeared to be. In part, such reconfigurations attempt to save the play, and its author, from the apparently coercive no-choice politics of its ending. But there is more at stake in such redemptive moves, especially (though not exclusively) for women readers and spectators. Called into an imaginary relationship with the ideology of the discourse being played out onstage by their counterparts, viewers seek to renegotiate the text's address rather than accept the identifications it encourages. Identification, *Shrew* teaches, does not flow seamlessly into imitation, is not necessarily mimesis.[1] How Kate's subjectivity is constructed is always monitored and adjusted by the perceptions and desires of consuming subjects whose complex histories and multiple cultural affiliations exceed those of the textual subject. Constructions, after all, do not allow everyone in: formed in relation to watchful eyes, subjectivity opens up onto perceivers' histories and onto a desire to carve out the illusion of a potentially pleasurable, even subversive space of choice within *Shrew*'s ending. Perhaps the play's most compelling attraction lies less in its ability to determine gender difference absolutely than in the contradictions it engenders between Kate's seemingly circumscribed position and its openness to the phantasmatic scenarios viewers bring to it.

What this tension between textual and social subjects reveals is that the text called *The Taming of the Shrew* is not the same as that produced and activated by its readers and spectators. To rethink how *Shrew* gets caught up and shaped, at particular historical moments, to secure or contest the subjectivities at work in women's lives, I wish to explore the play's continuing cultural renewal as a popular pleasure, first, by unpacking those texts, histories, and narratives that lurk in its margins; then, by considering a number of film and video performances; and, finally, by turning to several recent stagings. By multiplying the readings that adhere to Shakespeare's play and paying special, though not exclusive, attention to the ending, what I propose is akin to Michel de Certeau's "poaching," which Henry Jenkins characterizes as "an impertinent raid on a textual preserve that takes away only those things that seem useful or pleasurable to the reader."[2] Insofar as such plundering violates a (textual) body, it tropes the intersections between text and context, textually and socially produced subjects, pleasure and displeasure, with which I begin.

A CERTAIN TENDENCY OF THE TAMING OF THE SHREW

Observing traces of sadistic violence in *Shrew*'s taming plot, Shirley Nelson Garner sees the play as a spectacle of dominance mapped across a (cross-dressed) female body and concluding with a woman's abjection to male mastery.[3] Performances have persistently reproduced signs of that narrative: Petruchio may carry a whip, wear a boxing glove, spank Kate, gag and tie her with ropes and chains. So materialized, these taming practices can be read as theatrical vestiges of the shaming rituals Lynda Boose has recuperated as part of the play's early modern social context: the cucking stools and scold's bridles used to punish those late sixteenth-century "shrews" who flouted authority, challenged domestic male rule, and disturbed the "Publick peace" with their "scolding" tongues.[4] Premised on muting the female body and mastering its uncontrolled sexuality, such practices not only embed *Shrew* in a cultural narrative of silencing and enclosing women but also align with the image repertory of classic pornography. In the Induction, "wanton pictures," scenarios of hunt-and-chase violence, and erotic Ovidian lures of near-rape (Ind.

1.43; 2.45–56)[5] circulate a series of images within a context of shifting social and sexual identities that incorporate what Linda Williams terms the most distinguishable feature of sadomasochistic fantasy: "the education of one person in the sexual fantasy of another through complex role-playing cued to works of art and imagination."[6] Elsewhere, too, *Shrew* evokes the pornographic repertory. The image of Bianca tied and bound, at the mercy of Kate the torturer (2.1) hints at a mild "sadie-max" lesbian fantasy; and at the "taming school," which editors often locate in a "country house" reminiscent of remote Sadean territories, Petruchio displaces any overt sadism by humiliating his servants and dismembering Kate's dress (4.1; 4.3). However playfully *Shrew* suspends sadomasochistic desires in fantasy, it nonetheless shares affinities with pornographic films in "relentlessly repropos[ing] sexuality as the field of knowledge and power [and] woman as scene, rather than subject, of sexuality."[7] Yet although the phallus articulates meaning and difference symbolically in both, *Shrew* consistently collapses the sexual into the social to keep "verité" sex just beyond representation.

Lashing sexual and social scenarios together, Charles Marowitz's 1974 *The Shrew* alternates selected scenes from Shakespeare with exchanges between a present-day bourgeois young woman and her working-class lover to exploit the possibility of reading the one through the other. Following Kate's acknowledgment that Petruchio's word has the power to turn sun to moon (transforming nature "naturalizes" Kate [4.5]), Marowitz's collage ends with a dream sequence based on *Shrew*'s Induction and finale. In this Grimms' fairy tale of sinister archetypes and hopeless victims, Petruchio embraces Kate, kisses her, and, Sly-like, commands, "Madam, undress you and come now to bed." When Kate gives the excuse Sly's cross-dressed "madam wife" offers—to pardon her yet for a night or two, at a physician's charge—the men's faces turn grim, Baptista exclaims, "O monstrous arrogance!" and

> KATE is backed over to the table and thrown down. While the servants and Baptista hold her wrists, PETRUCHIO looms up behind her and whips up her skirts ready to do buggery. As he inserts, an ear-piercing, electronic whistle rises to crescendo pitch: KATE'S mouth is wild and open, and it appears as if the sound issues from her lungs.

Following a blackout, lights reveal a surreal tribunal, with Petruchio as judge. Baptista ushers in Kate, dressed in a shapeless institutional garment: "her face is white; her hair drawn back, her eyes wide and blank." She delivers her obedience speech hesitantly—Petruchio must prompt her to say "obey"—and as if another speaks for her. At "My mind hath been as big as one of yours, / My heart as great, my reason haply more," the young couple from the present-day plot, dressed in formal wedding attire, enter; as Kate concludes, "My hand is ready, may it do him ease," they frame her figure, "incline their heads to one another and smile out to invisible photographers for a wedding picture" before the final blackout.[8]

By juxtaposing an image of the "hoked-up, endlessly-spoofed Magic Ritual of marriage" to *Shrew*'s uncovered pornographic plot, Marowitz's collage views both gender and class as categories occupied by powerless victims and proposes a connection between sadism and male dominance which, in the late sixteenth century as in the twentieth, masquerades as an acceptable social practice, legitimated by ancient ceremony. Conceived as a "head-on confrontation with the intellectual substructure of the play" and a challenge to its classical status,[9] Marowitz's *Shrew* alters the generic reading rules institutionalized in "romantic comedy" or "knockabout farce," turning the play into a parallel text for Michel Foucault's *Discipline and Punish* that threatens to strip away Shakespeare's cultural status. At best, Marowitz unsettles the value systems authorized by "high art" and so interrupts dominant reading formations; at worst, by emphasizing brainwashing and concentration-camp brutality, his overreading deprives sexual relations of any humanity or intersubjectivity and thus questions, if not erases, their association with pleasure.

WHY CAN'T A WOMAN'S BODY READ MORE LIKE A MAN'S?

Just as "woman," in her mixed functions of activity and passivity, most interests the genre of heterosexual pornography, a similar oscillation between dominance and submission interests *Shrew*'s comedy of remarriage. In its Elizabethan guise, played out on a stage that "takes boys for women,"[10] the play can be imagined as particularly multivalent: "pleasing stuff," says Sly, that "let[s] the world slip" (Ind. 2.134, 138). The Induction not only authorizes such slippage within class as well as gender (at the Lord's will, as a joke on Sly) but teaches that there is no such thing as a discrete sexed or classed identity. Such identifications, *Shrew*'s frame insists, are themselves constructed in fluid relation to fictional "others." In the taming plot, gender codes move with equal ease across the boy actor's androgynous presence and the adult player's male body. On at least three occasions, the space of "shrew" is doubly occupied, doubly gendered: when Petruchio outdresses Kate on her wedding day, turning ceremony to carnival (3.2), and when he assumes a shrewish guise first, on the journey to his house ("By this reckoning he is more shrew than she," remarks Curtis, responding to Grumio's tale [4.1.63]) and then with his servants and with the haberdasher and tailor (4.1; 4.3). According to anti-theatrical Puritan commentators, his grotesque masquerade, not Kate's silent watchfulness, might be cast as the "whorish feminized spectacle" at the play's center.[11] Yet however bizarre his behavior, Petruchio, like the boy actor who plays Kate's role, can move between masculine and feminine positions at the price of not being subjected because his own subjectivity is never at risk. On the one hand, such cross-coding disperses "shrewness" and its attendant social anxieties onto the male body; on the other, it hollows out the category "woman" to suggest that no unified model of female subjectivity exists, while contradictorily affirming shrewness as *the* ground of feminine representation. For by the play's "law," shrewness must be seen and spoken as feminine: only when Kate slips out from under the sign of the shrew and moves toward the sign of the phallus can "she" be admired as a legitimate spectacle ("a wonder," according to Lucentio [5.2.189]) and given a serious hearing.

I want to pause at this spectacle because, like the Induction, it calls particular attention to the boy actor. In each case, claiming to *be* female is equivalent to claiming *from* the female. Part homily, part marriage rite, part confession, this curiously acrobatic speech, authored by a man for a boy to speak in order to sustain the illusion of femininity, recuperates male subjectivity by mapping the prerogatives of "good husbandry" onto the body of a newly obedient wife.[12] Since this is not soliloquy, the boy actor playing Kate is already set off, "her" difference (and that of the other "wives") clearly distinguished by the presence of adult male actors.[13] Why, then, does the speech insistently rehearse women's attributes and include such special pleading— "bodies soft, and weak, and smooth"; "soft conditions and our hearts" (5.2.165, 167)—on behalf of the female body's "truth"? Such excess betrays an intense anxiety to mark the speaker's body as feminine, and to do so, it pulls out all the culture's—and the theatre's—available capital. Toward the end of the speech, however, the illusion of femininity teeters on its head, threatening to tip "woman" into the androgynous identity of the boy actor:

> But now I see our lances are but straws,
> Our strength as weak, our weakness past compare,
> That seeming to be most which we indeed least are. (5.2.173–75)

Throughout, extraordinary syntactic clarity and balance characterize Kate's speech. Why, at this point, introduce a couplet requiring considerable sense-making effort? "That seeming" elides the "we" that seems to be its subject; subject and object risk conflation; "most" transforms to "least"; comparisons fail altogether. Is it just accident that "least are," together with other lines mentioning women's negative attributes, fall outside the iambic pentameter beat and so would be called, in the Elizabethan age and (until fairly recently) in our own, "feminine rhymes"? Spoken by the boy actor, these lines say that he is indeed the thing he is not, and they say it twice. He is the thing without a working phallus as well as the thing with nothing—that is, a woman.

The difficulty of taming these phrases tropes the difficulty central to both play and culture: the improbability of constructing a female subject (even a

Queen) except across a male identification and as a realization of male desire. Certainly in framing its shrew-taming spectacle as a "kind of history" staged, at the Lord's direction, for Christopher Sly's benefit (Ind. 2.136), the play specifically addresses a male subject's "visual pleasure."[14] Although it also conceptualizes, in Kate and in the wives she addresses, a female spectator, Kate is curiously silent and watchful, only occasionally protesting her assigned place in its victimizing economy. But, whether for the figure of "woman" that *Shrew* constructs or for the real women who attended the early modern theatre,[15] pleasure remains a somewhat muted term. For pleasure, *Shrew* teaches, is not owned by "woman" but is arrived at secondhand: it depends on relative differentiations, not on absolute difference. Whether male or female, *Shrew*'s spectators remain conscious not just of power's unavoidable role in sex, gender, and representation but also of how oscillating gender identities may, on occasion, unfix that power.

SPENDING ELIZABETHAN CULTURAL CAPITAL

It is one thing to reconstruct past acts of comprehension with imaginary bodies and theorized spectators; it is quite another when *Shrew* is played out by and on the bodies of real women and observed by historically situated viewers. For twentieth-century readers, the ambivalent syntax that threatens to expose the gender-bent conventions of the early modern stage marks a possible point of subversion. Like the shrew herself, the contention that we seem "to be most strong, which we indeed least are" could turn to accommodate its opposite: we seem "to be most weak, which we indeed least are." However tempting, such momentary resistance seems more thinkable than playable— an attempt to own property in a speech that, although it purports to negotiate woman's position, finally finds that position non-negotiable, fixed rather than fluid. While in the early modern theatre it appears to be an instance of speaking herself in his body, present-day representation reverses those terms, turning her address to froward wives into recipe discourse for a patriarchal dish to be swallowed whole, like a TV dinner: once Kate ventriloquizes the voice of Shakespeare's patriarchal culture and permits it to colonize her body, she never speaks again. Looking for a Kate other than this apparently conformable one is like scanning the "before" and "after" images in ads for weight-loss programs. Both are inescapably *there*: a viewer searches for the one in the other, wonders (like Lucentio) whether they do represent the same person, and attempts to merge the two images into a single, recognizably discrete identity.

Observing the tendency to tame Kate's taming in order to fracture the play's patriarchal panopticism, Carol Neely writes, "feminists cannot . . . fail to rejoice at the spirit, wit and joy with which Kate accommodates herself to her wifely role," neither can they "fail to note the radical asymmetry and inequality of the comic reconciliation and wish for Kate, as for [themselves], that choices were less limited, roles less rigid and unequal, accommodations more mutual and less coerced."[16] Caught between a reconstructive desire for social equality and the conformist demands of comic form, Neely's remarks align with what Elizabeth Fox-Genovese, borrowing W. E. B. DuBois's term, calls a "lived twoness," the dialectic of a sundered identity, the doubled consciousness of individuals who simultaneously identify with the dominant culture and with the marginal community or group to which that culture assigns them.[17] It is from the space of this curious double bind that women experience *Shrew*'s finale—a spectacle (always) already endowed with enough accumulated cultural capital to enable viewers, stranded between incommensurable identities, to buy into its normative gender economy.

By crystallizing images of dominance and submission in marriage, *Shrew*'s logic teaches that a shrew-wife has neither use nor exchange value and traces an especially canny broker's success in rolling over his initial investment. To find pleasure in this ending, a woman viewer must discover that *Shrew* inextricably weaves voyeurism, fantasy, and consumerism together to produce a dazzling constellation of subject positions. If she takes the direct route that the play offers male spectators (through Sly), desiring herself as a fetish, she acknowledges not only the masculinity that conceptualizes her access to activity and agency but the twists and turns in a woman's often circuitous route to pleasure.[18] *Shrew* can also entice a woman viewer to regress imaginatively, responding as many do to *Gone with the Wind* or as a particular community of readers does to Harlequin romances.[19] By either gliding over the signs of the father in Kate's speech (accepting them as "natural") or choosing to assume that Kate is merely performing and does not believe what she says (or both), readers as well as viewers can produce a scene similar to the happy rape, the fully authorized scene for female sexuality—authorized precisely because it is mastered and controlled. In such scenarios, Kate does not so much defeat the power of the phallus as take over its power in drag to play the "good girl" and so get the "bad girl's" pleasure;[20] moreover, since she achieves pleasure as if against her will, she remains a good girl. Theoretically, *Shrew*'s aesthetic sadomasochism turns into a more acceptable social masochism through which one may negotiate pleasure from a position of relative powerlessness. In one way or another, each of these options enacts a self-consuming fantasy: as Lynne Joyrich observes of all present-day representation, perhaps the consumer's viewing role is the only one that remains stable.[21]

In mapping these positions, I do not mean to devalue the strategies viewers use to alter their relation to the text's ideology. Quite the contrary. Such strategies not only challenge the already improbable fiction of the text's stability;[22] they also reframe its displeasures. That *Shrew* provokes a range of negotiated readings confirms the power of its politics and those of the institution it purports to defend, preserves heterosexual marriage as a fixed locus of desire. As though taking their cue from Kate's silence, such readings repeatedly dismantle textual signs with a vocabulary of cultural signs grounded in the desiring look exchanged between Kate and Petruchio, whether at their initial meeting (2.1), in the sun-moon scene (4.5), or before, during, or after Kate's final speech (5.2). Perceived as exceeding ideology, that gaze enables *Shrew* to conduct the culture's business. The trouble is not that, by investing such looks with pleasure, one disavows critique and so becomes not the culture's analyst but its dupe. Instead, the danger is that such ethnographies of reading buy *Shrew* for a shared feminine mystique through which viewers may even further mystify their cultural positioning (or fate) as a trap, however tender. Thus women neutralize, in pleasant dreams or in nightmare fantasies that lie beyond the play's representational limits, whatever legitimate grievances they perceive, not only in *Shrew*'s early modern patriarchy but in late twentieth-century conditions of lived twoness. In 1594, when *Shrew* was first entered in the Stationers' Register, it was called "a pleasant Conceyted historie," and its vigorous performance history, through many alternative guises, suggests that it gives good conceits as well as good pleasure. Like *Othello*, it can also claim to have given the state some service. For in the twentieth century as in the sixteenth, the public spectacle of a woman behaving properly stamps her with the culture's prerogatives, and being looked at, whether by male or female viewers, reconfirms her meaning.

How has *Shrew*'s cultural capital been invested, repackaged, and spent as a twentieth-century cinematic and theatrical commodity? After all, however meticulously academic studies may construct or deconstruct images of women, it is in these more public arenas that *Shrew* continues to enfold women within representation to make and remake cultural myths with which to negotiate her use. Since the models of looking the play presupposes— voyeurism, fantasy, and consumerism—are all metaphors for film and television viewing, I turn to these first. Moreover, both film and video foreground issues of subjectivity, not only because both media accentuate its constructedness but also because their viewing regimes resonate with social and psychic codes of sexual difference. In remarketing the play's social contract, these forms of representation perfectly exhibit how the containing illusions of popular patriarchies are engendered and sustained.

THE SOUND OF SILENCE

If *Shrew*'s pleasures derive in part from selective reading, silent cinema's strategies for reproducing Shakespeare's texts represent one pole of what has become an orthodoxy. By adopting the "key scene, key image, key phrase" approach prevalent in other cultural ephemera associated with Shakespeare (illustrations, trade cards, and recitals), streamlined versions of the plays proliferated during this century's early decades. As material within the public domain accessible to a wide audience, Shakespeare's texts (and his name) served not only to enhance the cultural respectability of the relatively new cinematic medium, especially among a middle-class audience, but to demonstrate the industry's commitment to moral education.[23] As a play premised on successful pedagogy, *Shrew* was almost ideally suited to fulfilling these goals as well as to affirming a somewhat nostalgic status quo: asserting Petruchio's rights of private ownership in Kate, surviving films not only clothe gender attributes in neo-Victorian robes, but, in bringing Kate to what Ada Rehan called "the saving grace of woman," they celebrate wifely acquiescence, the height of the haut-bourgeois ideal in a period that also spawned Freud's concept of normative female masochism.[24] Moreover, since none reconstructs Bianca as a shrew-wife, they rewrite the play's social contract, which deems the category of shrew so essential to constructing the heterosexual economy that if a Kate disavows the title, another must reclaim it. By attributing shrewishness exclusively to Kate and assuming that her conversion resolves a "universal" battle of the sexes, silent *Shrew*s model films of future decades.

According to its own promotional rhetoric, Biograph's 1908 *Taming of the Shrew* was "one of the snappiest, funniest films of the kind ever made . . . only the stirring, interesting portions of the play are depicted; at the same time the story is clearly, though concisely told." In advertising *Shrew* as "an object lesson—'See ourselves as others see us'"[25]—Biograph ties its product to Petruchio's strategies and anticipates the film's central spectacle, featuring a mustachio-twirling braggart who whips his cowering servants to the floor, beating them with cushions and pots and pans. Lashing gender to class as in Shakespeare's *Shrew*, this masterful display horrifies Kate, presenting a dilemma that the next tableau resolves. Presumably to save her from similar abuse, Baptista arrives, but as Kate starts to leave with her father, Petruchio, whip in hand, holds out his arms, and she runs to him, collapses against his shoulder, and is rewarded with a kiss. Affirming a cultural traffic in women between fathers and husbands, the film glances at the potential shame of a wife returning to her father, catching Kate up in double humiliations before erasing both in its final tableau, where, in a conventionally emblematic midshot, Kate sits by a garden wall while Petruchio, standing behind her, places flowers one by one in her veil to frame her as a "corrected" bride for a final kiss. Here, FTD's "Say it with flowers" takes on transhistorical significance: as the *single* shot that centers Kate in the frame, it suggests that only the domesticated woman represents a worthy spectacle.

Two later *Shrew*s, a 1911 Urban-Eclipse film featuring actors from Paris's Odeon Theatre and a 1923 British and Colonial production directed by Edward J. Collins,[26] use intertitles as a kind of visible male voice—the equivalent of voice-over, sound film's most authoritative speaking position[27]—to shore up the acculturating work of the image. In nine of eleven intertitles in the Eclipse *Shrew*, Petruchio is the subject of a sentence: "Petruchio decides to marry Kate," "Petruchio is betrothed to her," "Petruchio comes late," "Petruchio compels Kate to leave," "Petruchio tactfully prevents her from eating," "Petruchio obliges his wife to sleep in a chair all night," "Petruchio wagers that his wife will prove more obedient," and "Petruchio wins the wager." Moreover, several close shots (rare in the film) mark his dominant subjectivity. One shows him writing in a commonplace book, "Slap to be returned to Kate after our wedding"; another, a letter from Baptista ("Dear Petruchio: Bianca will marry Lucentio tomorrow. We expect you. Come alone, if Katherine refuses"), implies that an obedient son-in-law can replace an unruly daughter. For the most part, the film captures Kate's rage, the couple's Punch-and-Judy slapstick wooing, and Petruchio's outrageous self-display in long takes that lock both figures in farce; but two more intimate moments, keyed by closer camera positions, give the pair some semblance of psychological agency. After depriving Kate of supper and ordering her to sleep in a chair, Petruchio opens a window behind her sleeping figure (the light falling across her face softens her image), kneels beside her, and kisses her temple. Later, as the women wait in a separate room during the wager, the camera privileges Kate rising and turning to face the camera as she leaves, obeying Petruchio's command, as well as her deep curtsy to him in the final tableau bringing his private gestures of love into a public space.[28]

Strikingly, even though the Eclipse film insists on Petruchio's story, it is the *only* silent *Shrew* that represents even a trace of Kate's obedience speech or registers, however briefly, her motivation or desire. Eliding this moment, of course, denies any potential power accruing to either Kate's body or her voice except as the scowling harridan who, as the butt of male laughter within the frame, occupies the place Freud assigned to women in the structure of the obscene joke: that of the object caught between several male subjects (who always have the last laugh).[29] Whereas Collins's 1923 *Shrew*, for instance, ridicules Kate's defiance and erases her voice from its sixty-three intertitles, it celebrates Petruchio's similar display of shrewishness in both image track and intertitles, one of which, following Shakespeare (4.1.159–82), reveals his taming strategy. Slinging Kate over his shoulder, he heads for the bridal chamber where, laughing over his shoulder (at the camera), he strips pillows, coverlets and two mattresses from the wedding bed, masking sexual violence with a camp subtext of manliness that momentarily tips *Shrew* toward *Othello*. Following this invasion, another intertitle, "spoken" by an omniscient (male?) narrator, motivates Kate's reversal—"By noon the next day, though famished and weary for want of food and rest, the Shrew, deep in her heart, admired the man whose temper is stronger than her own"[30]—to generate the classic solution of dominance fantasies that masquerade as romance. Once Kate publicly thanks Petruchio for some unattractive soup, the final shot ("They seal the bargain with a loving kiss") shows her smiling, perched on her husband's knee, her arms entwined around his neck in wedded harmony. In representing that bargain, all three silent *Shrew*s assume an order of things in which marriage is the answer, not the question—a strategy affirmed by closing images of one or several romantic couples that naturalize marriage, offering a utopian mask for *Shrew*'s emphatic configuration of sex and gender through master-servant discourse or in terms of property relations. Except for Eclipse's fleeting gesture toward subjective equity, these films let a single closural image gag Kate's voice as well as her body, amplifying the sounds of a woman's silence to document a reexplosion of social history into the body of the shrew.

As a blueprint through which to know and be known, "wife" was not, however, the only image of female subjectivity available to early twentieth-century women viewers. The serial-queen melodramas, such as *The Perils of Pauline* (1914), feature an often cross-dressed heroine who not only defies domesticity but has considerable power to move where she wishes within the public sphere, traditionally the province of the male hero.[31] Like Kate, the serial-queen is, at some point, invariably gagged (and bound), simultaneously silencing her threat to male subjectivity and figuring her plight at the hands of villains from whom she will eventually be rescued. But although *Pauline* and her sister serial-queens may offer women spectators access to psychic and social fantasies of power and agency, they also suggest that misogynistic sadism goes hand in hand with such tropes; indeed, real women who chose to walk the streets unescorted could, according to contemporary news accounts, find themselves at risk, even similarly victimized. Unlike the relentlessly Johnny-one-note silent *Shrew*s, the serial-queens reveal considerable ambiguities in the social construction of "woman"; both, however, use the figure of a woman's muted voice to thematize, though in different contexts, the pleasures of protective paternalism. If, as these films suggest, there is something to be said for being the subject *of* a narrative rather than its *speaking* subject,[32] a decade or so later, when the *Shrew* talks, such atavistic desires get pulled into frameworks that not only renegotiate the meanings attached to property relations but also, through the contradictory lenses of what Richard Dyer calls "the star phenomenon,"[33] afford spectators a doublesided view of *Shrew*'s coupling comedy and of the psychic, emotional, and social forces at work in real women's lives.

DOUBLE YOUR PLEASURE, DOUBLE YOUR FUN

Famous as the first sound film of a Shakespearean play, Columbia Pictures' *Taming of the Shrew* (1929), starring the legendary Mary Pickford and Douglas Fairbanks, is perhaps even more infamous for its credit line, "by William Shakespeare with additional dialogue by Samuel Taylor," the film's director.[34] (A contemporary cartoon shows a bust of Shakespeare at the Library of Congress being replaced by one of Taylor.) Intriguingly, in the distribution of verbal property, Shakespeare's poetry goes to Fairbanks while Taylor's additions—*except* for a version of Kate's author-ized obedience speech—fall to Pickford, who complained that Fairbanks (once a Shakespearean actor) took advantage of her. According to Pickford's autobiography (and to her largely sympathetic biographers), Fairbanks tamed the "shrew" in real life as well as dominated her before the cameras: he not only played jokes, delayed shooting schedules, and failed to learn his lines, wildly increasing production costs, but he relegated his costarring wife (also his coproducer and cofinancer) to a lower place in the production hierarchy. Writes Pickford, "The making of that film was my finish. My confidence was completely shattered, and I was never again at ease before the camera or microphone."[35] Yet the film opens up contradictions in this confessional portrait of a woman at the mercy of both her husband and the camera apparatus. When the performer known for her golden curls and for a whole bag of coy "Pickford tricks"[36] first confronts Fairbanks's Robin Hood–Black Pirate Petruchio, a frieze depicting Herod's slaughter of the innocents frames her figure, perfectly troping her image as a grown woman pretending to be a little girl as well as her self-characterized victimization. But her costume—a black skirted riding habit, boots, and a sweepingly feathered picture hat—draws on an equally familiar published identity, that of the androgynous tomboy *(Rebecca of Sunnybrook Farm* [1917]), according her the power associated with male masquerade; she, not Petruchio, cracks a mean whip.

However much the image of Fairbanks—clad in rags, a jackboot on his head, slouching against a column, and crunching an apple during the wedding—codes Petruchio's bravado, glossing his shrewish display with his already commodified identity, the film also mocks the alien, romantic manliness associated with his previous roles.[37] After escorting Kate to her bridal chamber, Fairbanks's Petruchio returns to the dining table and attacks the food and drink he had previously rejected. Meanwhile, following a dissolve that transforms Pickford's dirtily dressed Kate into a bride wearing a virginal peignoir, she appears on a balcony overlooking the great hall, where she sees Petruchio sharing his taming strategy with a dog that has replaced her at the table; smiling mysteriously, she disappears before Petruchio asks, "Dost thou know better how to tame a shrew?" and the dog barks in reply. Later, on finding Kate asleep, Petruchio slams the bedroom door, trips over a stool, scatters the bedclothes, and bellows at Kate, who applauds his performance; then, after each opens a window, the couple argue over whether they're looking at the moon or the sun and quarrel over who gets the best bed pillow. If this Noel Coward–like bridal night offers audiences a voyeuristic glimpse of what Booton Herndon calls "the most popular couple the world has ever known," its finale also restages the gender codes of Shakespeare's *Shrew*: after bashing Petruchio's head with a stool, Kate coos, "O Petruchio, beloved"; pats his face to revive him; and, cradling him in her arms, throws her whip into the fire and murmurs a soothing "There, there" as he lays his head on her bosom. Gazing up at her with a puzzled look, Petruchio asks, "The sun is shining bright?" and, reassuringly, Pickford's motherly Kate replies, "Aye, the blessed sun."

In the final wedding-banquet sequence, Petruchio, his head bound with a raffish bandage and looking immensely self-satisfied, sits with one leg hooked over his chair while Kate, standing beside him, swears to love, honor, and obey. As she finishes her vow, a cut to mid–close-up isolates her broad wink, which Bianca, in an ensuing mid-shot, acknowledges. Just as Petruchio is a son playacting the role of husband, Kate is a mother who plays a wife. By turning men into braggart boys with knowing mothers, Taylor's *Shrew* gives the Oedipal scenario a curious spin: while the son may get his mother, articulating that resolution from a woman's point of view turns the familiar plot into a variant of the Freudian joke, with women, not men, having the last laugh. Yet, although the wife's seizing the comic advantage and the mythic power of a heavily coded subject position skews the film's final deshrewing, it only momentarily dismantles the call of Shakespeare's patriarchal culture. In playing out what appear to be competing instructions for marital pleasure, Taylor's *Shrew* simply gives the emperor's text new (and newly contradictory) robes, cut from the cloth of a regressive fantasy that depends on occupying— and performing—infantile roles. If Pickford's wink clears any space for women viewers within *Shrew*'s ending, that space, like the entire film, is already traversed with questions of ownership, whether of Fairbanks's exotically masculine image or of Pickford's identity as "America's Sweetheart." Possessing either, however fleetingly, would effectively (and conventionally) mask whatever cultural tensions remained concerning those who, only a short ten years before, had been enfranchised.[38] But any anxiety the film prompts about Kate's momentary "triumph" is allayed when Petruchio pulls Kate across his lap for a final kiss, Baptista begins a song in which all join, and the camera pulls back, revealing the entire wedding party, to conclude on the sight—and sound—of full social harmony.[39]

A rather different doubleness—or, more appropriately, a "lived twoness" within star discourse—informs Franco Zeffirelli's 1966 *Shrew*, a vehicle for the equally legendary couple Elizabeth Taylor and Richard Burton.[40] Like other *Shrews*, Zeffirelli's circulates around the use and exchange value of a shrew-wife. But locating this image of "woman" in Taylor's body—itself a famous site (or text) of sexual spectacle and spectatorly desire—lends particular resonance to this *Shrew*'s hyperactive narrative. As "the most expensive, most beautiful, most married and divorced being in the world," Taylor both stands for the type "star" and calls into question the ontological distinctions separating stars from "ordinary people." Her star category not only ignores how her offscreen experience models the late twentieth-century crisis within heterosexual monogamy but fails to account for either her "commonness" or her frequent successes in "bitch" roles. Nevertheless, the star system, and Taylor within it, figures "the decadence, sexual license and extravagance" that

characterize 1950s and 1960s American culture and anticipate Foucault's des-
ignation of sexuality as the area of human experience where we may learn the
truth about ourselves. As a fathomless icon of femininity, with stories in her
eyes, her body carries meanings that may supersede, or fuse with, stardom's
ability to embody social categories, especially to promote the idea (and ideal)
of individual agency within culture by suggesting that a private self resides
behind the role and that "truth" lies just beyond the image.[41]

Shrew and the Taylor-Burton team are ideally suited to mapping this contradictory web of discourses and its equally contradictory pleasures. Most
intriguingly, Zeffirelli's film grounds its particular negotiation between textual and social subjects, not just in Shakespeare's play but in reverberations
of two other productions starring the couple: *Cleopatra* (1963), whose filming embraced what Burton called *le scandale* that broke up both stars' previous marriages, and *Who's Afraid of Virginia Woolf ?* (1966).[42] Certainly the
teaser for *Virginia Woolf*—"You are cordially invited to George and Martha's
for an evening of fun and games"—applies equally to *Shrew*. For the game in
Zeffirelli's film is to exchange "Hump the Hostess" for "Get the Guests" and,
by treading the edge of the madonna-whore dichotomy, to transform not just
the unruly Kate but Taylor herself from a published "scarlet woman" to a legitimate wife.

Appropriately, the film's first image of "woman" is that of a blowsy
whore, who replaces the figure of Lent in the opening spectacle of Paduan
Carnival, which refigures Shakespeare's Sly Induction and thematizes the
licensed inversions of *Shrew*'s narrative. Aptly characterizing Shakespeare's
Shrew as "a play not for a sober Monday morning but for a drunken Saturday
night," Jack Jorgens calls Zeffirelli's film a version of Saturnalian Revel, with
Burton and Taylor reigning as the Lord and Lady of Misrule. Not only is Burton's smashed-Welsh Petruchio (a parody of Charles Laughton's portrayal of
Henry VIII in Alexander Korda's 1933 film) seldom without a wine goblet in
his hand, but he throws away Shakespeare's lines with a natural panache that
overpowers Taylor's less expert delivery.[43] As with the Pickford-Fairbanks
Shrew, the male star's ownership of Shakespeare's language reifies the text's
linguistic logic; whereas Petruchio owns the words, silence codes his wife's
presence until the play's end, when Kate talks and talks and talks.[44] Here,
however, Taylor's body language overmatches Burton's facility with Shakespeare: the film not only eroticizes her spectacular body but capitalizes on her
attraction for Burton. Following the wooing scene, an extended romp that ends
with the pair falling into a pile of feathers, a close-up sequence not only privileges Kate's point of view but, by including an extreme close-up of one of
Taylor's famous violet eyes, turns her gaze into a spectacle in which viewers
can meet their own voyeurism. Her look keys a high-angle full shot of Burton's Petruchio, bragging to the other men that he has won her; then, drawing
back from the window's "eye," Kate sinks into a thoughtful pose; and a smile

traces across her face as the sound track's soft, romantic music expresses her private pleasure, inviting viewers to share and, perhaps, extend her fantasy.

That fantasy culminates at Bianca's wedding banquet, where, following an exchange of sidelong glances between Kate and Petruchio, Kate's look keys a shot of several children playing; after a cut-in mid-shot of Kate, they reappear, this time with a large dog. She smiles fondly at them, then gazes tenderly at a bored, wine-drinking Petruchio and, with expressively downcast eyes, raises her own cup to her lips. Moments later, she disdainfully leads the women away from the men's locker-room talk about the Widow. In her eyes, marriage should breed increase, not bawdy puns: this Kate would "keep / By children's eyes, her husband's shape in mind" (Shakespeare's Sonnet 9). Indeed, this spectacle of fortunate issue seems to motivate her later obedience speech and so bends *Shrew*'s ending toward familial myth—and this particular *Shrew*'s intertextual connections.

For both Kate's mothering instinct and her refusal to listen to dirty jokes flood outward, encompassing *Virginia Woolf*'s loudmouthed Martha and George and their imaginary child as well as Taylor's own history. After three caesarean sections, Taylor had decided, on the advice of her doctors, not to have another child, and during *Cleopatra*'s early filming, she arranged to adopt a severely crippled infant girl. Then, as her dangerous liaison with Burton became worldwide news, an open letter in the Vatican City weekly *L'osservatore della dominica* (implicitly if not officially speaking with a papal voice) accused her of being "an erotic vagrant and an unfit mother."[45] Three years later, *Shrew*'s ending seemed specifically Taylor-ed to address those slurs and to prove her moral worth. When Taylor's Kate reappears (even before Petruchio's command), tugging Bianca, the Widow, and a train of (presumably) marginal wives, her spectacle of obedience becomes a serious pledge of wifely duty, complete with a cut-in mid-shot of a weeping peasant woman. As Kate kneels before Petruchio, joyful applause breaks out; after Petruchio raises her, the film cuts to a close-up kiss and then to a full shot of the entire assembly, smiling and applauding this conventional romantic-comedy ending. In close-up, Petruchio addresses his final lines to the less fortunate husbands and to the camera, but when he turns, expecting Kate to be at his side, she has disappeared, and he finds himself trapped in a crowd of other wives. Kate/Taylor's desire for Petruchio/Burton, and for children, has apparently transferred to all women; and Burton's newly eroticized body must fight through this unruly mob to make his exit, much as Burton and Taylor were plagued by intrusive Roman paparazzi wherever they went. Finally, Grumio holds up his hands, as though to say "that's all" and to stop the camera as well as the women from invading an imaginary offscreen bedroom. But it is not all, for outtakes from the hectically paced wooing scene provide a coda that not only restores farcical gaiety but shows what the filmed sequence does not: a pair of jolly, thriving wooers, a model star marriage that appropriates Shakespeare to authenticate a beautiful woman's transgressive body as that of a faithful wife and to confirm the jet-setting couple's Italian, if not international, respectability. "All is [indeed] done in reverend care of her" (4.1.175): within this *Shrew*'s doubled carnivalesque, that ideology prevails precisely because it awards pleasure to both textual and spectatorly subjects.

CONSUMING PLEASURES

However much its box-office success capitalized on viewers' voyeuristic fascination with its stars, Zeffirelli's *Shrew* falls within a high-art tradition of filmed Shakespeare. But more popular representations of *Shrew*—by distancing, dispersing, or redirecting Shakespeare's cultural authority—can more easily accommodate the possibility of containment as well as resistance: what Stuart Hall calls the "double movement" of popular culture.[46] Although *Shrew* is (always) already popular culture, George Sidney's 1953 film of Cole Porter's *Kiss Me, Kate* (1948) moves "Shakespeare" even more definitively toward its popular origins.[47] Adapted to show how Lilli and Fred, a divorced star couple, come together (again), this *Shrew* quite literally swings to another tune. Like most musicals about making a musical, this one equates a couple's ability to perform together onstage with their successful offstage sexual performance, a convention well suited to address the decade's preoccupation with sexuality (1953 marked *Playboy*'s inaugural issue and Kinsey's report on American women's sexual behavior) and to tinsel the pleasures and dangers of sex with a discourse of "pure" entertainment.

Ultimately, *Kiss Me, Kate* is less interested in shrewing around than in placating, through song and dance, the cultural tensions of screwing around: wiving it wealthily in Padua takes second place to floating desire, affecting unruly women ("I will take ... any Harry, Tom or Dick," sings Bianca/Lois) and ex-husbands alike (marriage is fine by day, / "But oh what a bore at night," mourns Petruchio/Fred). Although Kate/Lilli's "I Hate Men" deconstructs macho stereotypes—Jack the Ripper; the athlete with "manner bold and brassy, / [Who] may have hair upon his chest but, sister, so has Lassie"; the traveling salesman "who'll have the fun and thee the baby"; the executive whose "bus'ness is with his pretty secretary"[45]—she finally accepts the contradictory "twoness" of lived experience: "from the mind, all womankind should rout 'em, / But, ladies, you must answer too, what would we do without 'em?" Taking any Dick is not for Kate/Lilli, whose love-hate for Petruchio/Fred's philandering phallus makes her seem willingly complicit in repeated humiliations, including a public spanking ("So taunt me and hurt me, / Deceive me, desert me, / I'm yours 'til I die").[49] However playfully Kate extends *Shrew*'s brief to express women's and men's grievances against monogamy's material circumstances, it not only rigorously polices excessive desires but tolerates no ruptures within male dominance. A well-stuffed cod-piece, a whip, and a banana code Petruchio/Fred's high visibility; and the film's original 3-D version heightens his subjectivity (never Kate/Lilli's), as well as his self-reflexive performance, through the emergence effect, which makes him seem about to break from the screen to become one with the view-ers' reality.[50] Whereas Marowitz turns *Shrew*'s discipline-and-punish regime to pornographic excess, *Kate* reworks Shakespeare as sadistic bard through two Sly-surrogate hoodlums, whose advice—"Brush up your Shakespeare, and they'll all kow-tow"—brushes in the tangled links between Shakespeare's titular erotics[51] and mid-twentieth-century misogyny to recirculate *Shrew*'s discourse of phallic potency:

> If she says she won't buy it or tike it,
> Make her tike it, what's more, "As You Like It,"
> If she says your behavior is heinous,
> Kick her right in the "Coriolanus" . . .
> Just recite an occasional sonnet,
> And your lap'll have "Honey" upon it,
> When your baby is pleading for pleasure,
> Let her sample your "Measure for Measure."

Somewhat predictably, Lilli "kow-tows," canceling her proposed elope-ment with the travestied Texan cowboy whose limousine sports giant cattle-horns and using Shakespeare's obedience speech (set to Porter's music) to tell Fred she loves him. When she waves Fred's little black book in his face, he laughs ("A pox on the life that late I led") and, as Lilli tosses away his record of past conquests, segues into the finale's "Kiss Me Kate," further confirming the myth of heterosexual monogamy and cheerfully accepting its strictures as structure. Superimposed over their playground-stage, the figures of Lilli and Fred, once again through the emergence effect, project into the "eternal pre-sent" of both the film's phantom and its live spectators,[52] joining two cultural spaces in a wedded bliss that has been mediated by, but finally suppresses, a dominant-submissive undertext. All are included guests at this celebratory marriage between the playwright Hollywood calls "Billy Big Boy" and the big-hit, stage-to-screen musical.

Perhaps in order to capitalize on Porter's Broadway smash hit, Westing-house's "live performance" Studio One mounted a televised *Shrew*, directed by Paul Nickell, in 1950.[53] Advertised as "a most unusual modern-dress ver-sion with Mr. [Charlton] Heston sauntering onto the set in shades and down-ing a beer with the boys, [while] Lisa Kirk appears in yummy tight slacks with a riding whip," Nickell's *Shrew*, shot in tableaux reminiscent of silent films, also resembles the silents' strategy of puffing up Petruchio with shtick.

Obsessed with the rugged matinee idol looks of Heston's swaggering Petruchio, it marginalizes Kirk's Kate, whose riding whip has disappeared between publicity rhetoric and performance. Whereas *Kate* vents sadomasochistic fantasies in soft-shoe routines to teach that fighting phallic power can be fun, Nickell's *Shrew* suggests that managing monogamy's double-toil-and-trouble standards is strictly women's business. Wearing a fashionably boat-necked, off-the-shoulder Bianca-like dress ("the look is definitely 1950," claims the video's jacket blurb), Kirk's Kate borrows Pickford's wink as she ends her obedience speech—articulated here in close-up, played directly at viewers who have just seen Petruchio turn away. Her behind-the-back gesture ("We women own the real power, but let's keep it secret," says her look) functions both as a compensatory fantasy and as a classically authorized reply to sociology's then current scientific dissection of marriage. Some twenty-five years later, Kate's wink would ground Maribel Morgan's *Total Woman* strategies for covert domination of husbands, aimed at keeping them in their place—that is, in their wives' beds—as well as Phyllis Schlafly's *The Power of the Positive Woman*, which uses the rhetoric of disenfranchisement to mobilize suburban housewives into an effective political force against the perceived onslaught of radical feminism.[54] But however circuitously it represents Kate's route to pleasure, Studio One's attempt to market its high-culture image generates additional pleasure through representing electricity's magical transformative powers in yet another form of commodified discourse that reveals *Shrew* as a limitless text in which no boundary separates Shakespeare's fictional product and its born-to-shop heroine from its sponsor's commercial products.

Attached to *Shrew*'s narrative through television's seamless flow of discourse, the show's commercial spots not only aim Westinghouse's up-market Shakespeare at variously aged and gendered viewers but endeavor to construct a family, with Betty Furness as its arbiter.[55] The first, positioned just after Petruchio takes Kate away from her wedding reception on his bike, hawks a Westinghouse portable three-way radio with an AC/DC long-life battery— "the perfect graduation gift," according to Furness, a "swell-looking job, easy to lift; it comes in the sturdiest plastic carrying case you ever saw, has a long reach and pulls in your favorite music." The second, which follows the scenes at Petruchio's "taming school," begins with Furness saying, "Do you live in a hothouse?" "You don't have to, you know." The solution: a Westinghouse Mobile Air Fan with "deep-pitched Mycarta blades, explosive air rings and an exhaust fan that adjusts to any window." If these address, respectively, the Hit Parade's teenage fans and "good huswifery," the last commercial, placed after Kate's obedience speech and the romantic embrace that follows, obviously assumes a male spectator, his interest piqued by updated Shakespeare. Here, a man watching night baseball on a (Westinghouse) TV introduces scenes in which Westinghouse magic lights an entire world: highways, a filling station, a backyard barbecue—all the (male) amenities of postwar suburban landed leisure, where a man's home may indeed be his castle and where Westing-house products contribute to enclosing his wife within it. Clearly, *Shrew* had found its ideal venue: the home.

Even more strikingly, the first commercial spot for *Moonlighting*'s 1986 radically rewritten *Shrew* displaces the propertied gender relations of Shake-speare's original onto potential consumers, further erasing any barriers between the fictional text and commercial social reality. Primarily, though not exclusively, addressed to women, each of the four segments invites surrogate Kates to create (or recreate) themselves from multiple products and gendered subject positions. The first opens with a male voice-over—"Satisfying your family is what General Foods is all about"—and shows a man teaching a woman that Grape Nuts contains health, "natural" taste, and sex: "That's a big crunch for such a little thing," she concludes, savoring a bite. In the second, an ad for designer coffees, a mother and daughter look at keepsakes, and the daughter asks, "What was my first word?" "Daddy," replies the mother. "Well, my second must have been 'Mom,' then," laughs the daughter; "No," her mother says, "I think it was chocolate." But if this captured moment invites viewers to remember patriarchal primacy (with the absent father's position filled by the product), the third segment, for Kentucky Fried Chicken, tells a more radical story, in which a cartoon hen bops the narrating rooster's head and takes him off, captive to her desires, in a wheelbarrow. The final com-mercial, the teaser for an upcoming show about TV stars and their mothers, concludes, "Mothers always have the last word." Curiously and uncannily, this commodified gender map functions much like foreshadowing (as if some "guide to quality drama") to presage what is to come.

As part of the "merry war" between Maddie Hayes (Cybill Shepherd) and David Addison (Bruce Willis), *Moonlighting*'s *Shrew* recirculates the relations between body and voice, between parodic gender display and subterranean pornographic connections, that characterize Shakespeare's original, weaving them into a late-twentieth-century kaleidoscope of popular gender fantasies.[56] In her first appearance, Shepherd's Kate polishes off Padua's entire male pop-ulation with a long staff, sending five into a fountain and causing a line of oth-ers to fall, like dominoes, simply by puffing at them. Wearing sunglasses, Willis's Petruchio rides a white horse and, like any macho Western hero, inhales a roast pig, guzzles a wine keg, fights two swordsmen, and, finally, eliminates four Kung Fu masters. "If you're a man, you're gonna love the six-teenth century," he tells viewers, just before he breaks down Katherina's door with an axe, pokes his head through the opening, a la Jack Nicholson in Stan-ley Kubrick's *Shining*, and announces with a leer, "Here's Petruchio!" At the wedding ceremony, where a bound and gagged Katherina kneels at the altar, Petruchio rides into church (here, the horse also wears sunglasses), comments, "How well doth she look in bondage," and puts on a spectacular show. Backed up by a rock combo, he sings, "I've got the fever, you've got the cure," complete with a Mick Jagger strut and harmonica solo, before throwing Kate over his shoulder and storming out. Refusing to sleep with him, Kate claims, "I havest a headache"; later, however, after a male voice-over narrates her change from house afire to housewife, she promises, if he "respects her and holds her in high esteem as a wife and partner," to share his bed. Following the conventional PG-13 pan over rumpled sheets and intertwined legs, the pair confess their love. "In spite of your boorishness and bluster," says Kate, "you're a good man, Petruchio"; and he returns the compliment: "In spite of your shrillness and shrewishness, you're a rather remarkable woman."

As in Shakespeare's *Shrew*, *Moonlighting*'s finale, entitled "The Big Finish," documents a crisis in subjectivity, but exactly whose subjectivity is at stake is not altogether clear. Interrupting Petruchio's prenuptial counseling of Lucentio, Baptista mentions hearing a rumor that Kate just pretends to be tamed and claims, "Marriage is fifty-fifty." Looking worried, Petruchio summons Kate, and when she comes, he preaches to her before the assembled company, "Thy husband is thy Lord, thy life, thy keeper," and asks her, by way of a test, to agree that the moon is shining bright. Following an intercut exchange of pregnant looks, Kate crosses past him, gazes at the sky, and says, "You are mistaken, husband; it is the sun that shines so bright." "The sun, you say?" replies Petruchio. "Then I have but one choice—to look again." After admitting, "I was wrong, and I have learned it from a woman," he renounces his "deal" with Baptista and claims as his only reward "thy company, as long as we both shall live. For Kate didn't need to be tamed—just to be loved."[57] At this, Kate responds, "Kiss me, Petruchio," and pulls him into a 1940s' dip as the camera booms up to a high-angle shot of Padua's newly franchised marital community.

Initially, this ending seems willingly responsive to, even productive of, currents of social change. Renegotiating the gendered exchange of visual pleasure in Shakespeare's *Shrew*, it takes Kate and Petruchio's privately agreed-on bedroom contract into public space and so redefines that space, apparently in other than performative terms. By giving up his "deal," Petruchio rejects owning Kate as property, thus according with Joan Kelly's utopian move toward reconstructing gender relations as personal relations among freely associating individuals.[58] But a number of contradictions play through this seductive discourse. While *Moonlighting*'s finale returns the patriarchal text to its foundational male body, acknowledging that source also returns to Petruchio the power to name obedience, secures his dominance, and turns Kate into a smiling spectator, whose downcast eyes show her submissive to his will or, perhaps more accurately, to Will Shakespeare's masquerading in Willis. Although projecting Kate's voice into Petruchio's body means rewriting the marriage vows to her tune, the newly gendered lyric buys into another myth of male subjectivity: that a woman's love is all a man needs and vice versa. More troublingly, these regendered relations between body and voice position Kate where, in Josette Feral's words, "she says Nothing because she has Nothing to say and because there is Nothing to say about whatever she may say, since it means Nothing."[59] If, as Joel Fineman writes, Shakespeare's *Shrew* portrays "woman" as porous, capable of admitting male discourse and speaking it as her own,[60] then what is Shepherd's "Kiss me, Petruchio," with its accompanying sweeping gesture, but a readmission of that? And though *Moonlighting* also veers toward suggesting that only Kate can make Petruchio a man,[61] or, in this case, a "liberated" man, a male narrator has the last words. Retitling the play "Petruchio and Kate," his voice-over reaffirms the primacy of the gendered male subject, erases the contradictions the videotext has produced, and brings voice and image together to mute woman's "unruly member."[62]

Nevertheless, *Moonlighting*'s gestures toward sociosexual equality do clear a space, even though that space cannot be fully occupied without remystifying the terms of the social contract on a woman's body. While this *Shrew* sends up Marowitz's pornographic morphology, it also exploits and eroticizes another border realm where gender roles remain questionable or unstable. *Moonlighting*'s frame, however, reinvents the trope of dominant-submissive relations at *Shrew*'s center and repositions the plot's arbitrary gender politics. That frame begins with a ten-year-old boy's desire to watch "that show about men and women," at which his mother, evoking the familiar binary between classical and popular cultural realms (and between reading and viewing), warns, "Watching TV won't help you on the Shakespeare test; you've got a lot of reading to do." Just as Shakespeare's *Shrew* pretends to address Christopher Sly, *Moonlighting*'s *Shrew* sells itself as the boy's imagined version of "Atomic Shakespeare" (by William "Budd" Shakespeare). Yet it has no explosive effect on the boy; rather, since it substitutes for a "real" (even more desirable?) *Moonlighting* episode, it demonstrates his competency in reading, not Shakespeare, but other *Moonlighting* episodes, where Maddie Hayes invariably "wins." Rushing downstairs after shutting his rewritten *Shrew* text, the boy—whose face, like his mother's, viewers never see—asks, "Is *Moonlighting* still on?" And his mother, ignorant of the reading he has produced, replies, "It's just over." Rising from the couch to turn off the TV, she adds (referring to the absent *Moonlighting* text), "It wasn't very good, anyway."

Somewhat anxiously, and in keeping with television's domestic contract of containment, this frame not only encloses *Moonlighting*'s *Shrew* but offers another representation of "woman" to viewers who may have enjoyed the episode's potentially subversive pleasures. Finally, in an America ruled (at least on TV) by moms in highly authoritative high heels and by absent dads, everything is in place in late twentieth-century structures of cultural authority. As this last riff on bodies and voices suggests, it all depends on whether you like your patriarchy visible or, as in this case, invisible—spoken by a froward mom, not a former shrew. At its close, *Moonlighting*'s *Shrew* teaches just how thoroughly Shakespeare's *Shrew* ties Kate up. Whether in its early modern guise as a tale of good husbandry or in this recent thrust at histori-cized counter-discourse, the play always represents Katherina bound—even in a (mis)reading that seems to invite its viewers, of whatever gender, to reap-propriate another screen idol's most famous line, "Here's looking at you, kid."

FRAME-WORKS

In most of these film and video *Shrew*s, no frame distances textual from social subjects: if discernible at all, that device has been displaced or radically rewritten, as in the brief Punch and Judy show that introduces the Pickford-Fairbanks film, Zeffirelli's carnivalesque prologue, or *Kiss Me Kate*'s twinned plots. *Moonlighting* offers the most overt frame-up of *Shrew*'s taming sce-nario, one already overdetermined by the narrative histories of the television sitcom's principal characters and further mediated by the boy's imaginative encounter with Shakespeare, which replaces *Shrew* within the intimate view-ing space of everyday domestic dreaming. Read back through Shakespeare's text, the boy and his mother figure Sly and the tavern's Tapster (or Hostess), televisual surrogates for the return of the (long repressed) *A Shrew* end-frame that, as Leah Marcus observes, is fast becoming Shakespearean, largely as a result of being historically situated as Shakespeare-in-performance.[63]

   In part, that trend also marks a desired return to long repressed pleasures that coincides with the recent metadramatic move to redeem *Shrew* from George Bernard Shaw's famous judgment that "no man with any decency of feeling can sit it out in the company of a woman without being extremely ashamed of the lord-of-creation moral implied in the wager and the speech put into the woman's own mouth."[64] Framing the taming potentially destabilizes the relations of both textual and social subjects to ideology, dissolving the play's gender politics into a ludic space where social roles sl(y)de into the-atrical ones. Configuring "play" as a utopian realm empowers Kate's ability to find a witty way round the rules of this particular game, turns *Shrew* into a user-friendly play, and excuses it from the place of shame it has accrued.[65] In such readings, freedom is the name of the frame: as an escape route from *Shrew*'s tie-me-up, tie-me-down binds, it permits viewers to locate the taming scenario in a world elsewhere, resituating it according to the Induction's claim that it offers "a kind of historic," one that can be conveniently attributed to the early modern past. Recent theatrical practice, however, punctures this theatri-calized equivalent of bubble wrap. There, the frame is not just an occasion for acting up but for showing up the consequences of misidentifying *theatre*, with all its insistent materiality, as *theatricality*, its more reassuring, more abstract double. Over the past several decades, *Shrew*'s frame has come into focus as the key to re-viewing as well as re-staging the scene of taming and as a site for its critique.

Two Royal Shakespeare Company (RSC) productions illustrate the selective raiding of *The Shrew*'s and *A Shrew*'s frames that has marked the play's recent cultural destinies. Michael Bogdanov's notorious 1978 staging, which turned the Induction into a complex theatrical signifier of *The Shrew*'s sexual politics, raises most provocatively the question of when the play begins and how it ends.[66] Starting the action in the audience with an exchange between a drunk male theatre-goer and a woman usher, his *Shrew* produced Sly directly out of a real-life context of everyday dominant-submissive behavior and continued to unwrap and double up its subjects when the drunk reappeared as Sly and then as Petruchio and the usher as Kate.[67] Premised on the notion that Shakespeare could be turned into a feminist author bent on exposing the social strictures of his era, Bogdanov's production was set in a thoroughly modern mercantile milieu where, as images from the souvenir program suggested, women's bodies were treated as property: objects of the male gaze, prisoners of their images, matter for tabloid discourse, perhaps the most commodified site for reproducing strands of romanticized victimization. Insofar as appropriating the Induction configured *Shrew* as an especially ugly masculinist wish-fulfillment fantasy, edged only slightly by the irony of Kate's final speech (delivered to cigar-smoking, port-drinking men around a baize-covered gaming table) and by Petruchio's somewhat ambiguous rejection of his own cruel logic, Bogdanov's staging offered an organizing, historicizing moment for *Shrew*'s theatrical culture that engaged with a high moment of feminist and psychoanalytic work. Not only did it challenge the farcical strategies for managing *Shrew* as a consumer product, but, by violating textual boundaries to write contemporary idiom over canonical text, it blurred the powerful cultural dissonances between "high" and "low" to reframe the play as *popular* culture.

Conveniently sidestepping the play's political difficulties for post-feminist 1992 viewers, Bill Alexander, taking his cue from Sly, turned the lens from gender to class by inventing a secondary cast of characters called "Lord Simon's party," a group of "Hooray Henries and Henriettas" who, together with a Sly they have cruelly duped into lordship, watch a sumptuously costumed period piece of sometimes parodic taming commissioned for their Valentine's Day entertainment.[68] In Alexander's staging, actors not only doubled their patrons' class and gender games but, at one point, pulled the watchers into the fiction and cast them as Kate and as Petruchio's servants (4.1). Crossing the frame, they found themselves physically as well as verbally disempowered—so many Sly-like Kates, victimized by the (unalterable) scripts they held in their hands and confronted by an absolute authoritarian whose every word (if not the kick in the stomach one received) had bardic accountability. Although this elaborate friction between frame and fiction did not disrupt the familiar pleasures of Kate and Petruchio's inset play, it did repackage *Shrew*'s desired romantic climax and reposition it away from the close:

wrapped in the role-play of the sun-moon exchange (4.5) and tied with the shared kiss in the street (5.1), Kate's dinnertime homily turned into mere public proof of Petruchio's winning ways. But at the playlet's close, their happy-ever-after marital bliss did not rub off on their surrogates: rejecting Lord Simon's embrace, his Lady went off on her own. And as the players briefly confronted a reawakened Sly, the look that passed between them provided a sense of ending not dissimilar to that of *Thelma and Louise* (1991), in which the convertible carrying the pair soars off the cliff edge, escaping the massed pursuers' guns to be freeze-framed forever in space—a sign that the issues the representation engendered—or, in *Shrew*'s case, class-ified—could not, as yet, be resolved within the larger cultural debate.

Gale Edwards's 1995 Royal Shakespeare Company (RSC) staging addresses and incorporates features of these previous productions, opening up a conversation with past *Shrew*s that also intersects with *Moonlighting*'s *Shrew*.[69] Not only does it knowingly appropriate *Moonlighting*'s double-up framing (here, Sly with Petruchio, Sly's wife with Kate), as well as its refiguration of the play as a boy's dream, but it deconstructs that dream from within. By rethinking the rules of this particular theatrical game, Edwards's performative interventions drive *Shrew* further along the road already taken, one that puts Shakespeare's play on a collision course with a late twentieth-century cultural logic of pre-and post-feminisms. Because processes of selective reading assert a frame at least as powerful as that offered by *The Shrew*, *A Shrew*, or, as in Edwards's staging, some combination of the two, I want to take a cue from this doubles act and set my viewing in relation to that of London's review community, framing their affective and interpretive experiences with my own.[70]

Frames within frames. After quarreling violently with his "married to hell" wife, Sly collapses into a drunken stupor, from which he is roused by six Lords in hunting gear, who set *Shrew*'s theatrical machine in motion by summoning up a replica of the red-velvet-draped main stage and ushering the redressed tinker into it. Tipping their hats to the audience, the Lords gesture aloft, and the red velvet wrapping the stage lifts away to reveal a Crayola world of primary colors, a cartoon-like farcical environment that raids mass culture entertainments (film, TV, music video) to collapse mainstream Shakespeare into something resembling *Moonlighting*'s manic postmodern collage. If these opening moves condense a long history of crossovers that have reframed *Shrew* as popular culture, they also allude to the RSC's institutional history: except for Di Trevis's 1985 *Shrew*, which toured together with Brecht's *Happy End*, the play has been consistently controlled by male directors.[71] But even without access to such insider knowledge, a viewer can hardly avoid noticing, even applauding, how, by whom, and for whose apparent benefit the representational apparatus is being constructed: engendered by the Lords, its upper-class puppet-masters, this *Shrew* reconfirms the play's address to masculine viewing pleasure. Managing the stage space and often calling attention to their work, the Lords' panoptical oversight not only positions them as sorcerer-producers but licenses a range of antic macho posturings, from Tranio's imitation of the rock star formerly known as Prince to Petruchio's outrageous wedding gear: wearing torn black leathers with skateboarders' knee pads, a boxing glove, a feather cloak, and a hawk-beaked, plumed headdress parodying those worn at Elizabeth I's Accession Day Tilts, he appears (together with Grumio, in a pink tutu and Doc Martens) to spirit Kate away in a flame-decorated red mini.

Shortly after the interval, however, a second *Shrew*, the one that cannot be spoken, exposes the relentlessly aggressive male discourse that Edwards's staging so blatantly connects to farce. At once the most regulatory and contradictory form of theatre, farce is premised on body mechanics; yet because it does not (cannot) stop to interrogate its motion, it also overlooks the very bodies it inscribes. Disrupting that motion raises questions, and it is precisely by fracturing *Shrew*'s kaleidoscopic male energies that Edwards demonstrates how the twists and turns of farce efface the subject.[72] As Petruchio completes his wife-taming speech, Kate appears behind him seated on a chair, her face averted from Bianca and Lucentio's downstage larking, and the set's heliotrope and purple walls close in, imprisoning her within a cell-like, windowed space where she is watched by the Lords, now become jailer-voyeurs, and, later, teased and tormented by Grumio, Petruchio, and Hortensio. In a variant of Brecht's "not … but" in which "(s)he who is being shown shows (her)self," Kate's notorious silence becomes part of the performer's subject, exposing her body as the scene of farcical cultural inscription.[73] Proposing sight as a means of making Kate's silence readable as a counter-narrative, Edwards's staging calls attention to the bridling of a script that, by calling attention to the bridling of her voice, constructs Kate as a partial subject. The payoff of this view from elsewhere comes after Petruchio has ripped both sleeves and the bodice from the tailor's new gown, producing two images of stripped women: Kate in an underdress, the dressmaker's dummy nude to the waist. Watching the scene unfold across an image of her own dismembered body, Kate's is an interrupting "third eye": acknowledged within the scene and implicated on the body of the seen itself, the "seen" takes on an agency of her own to wield the "unnerving potential of a subversive reciprocity of vision, an explicit complicity, or mutual recognition between seer and seen, subject and subject, in the scene of viewing."[74] For as the men (at right stage) banter over "tak[ing] up my mistress' gown to his master's use," Kate crosses to the dummy (downstage left) and sinks down beside it, caressing the discarded pieces. Fracturing the stage space, her gest decisively marks off the men's locker-room jokes from a feminine narrative of loss and desire that rivets the gaze.

Rivets *my* gaze, I should say, for members of London's (almost exclusively male) review community were looking through an optic of nostalgia.

According to Michael Billington, seeing events from Katherina's point of view (which he attributed to Edwards's "natural feminist perspective") tainted the masculine logic of framing *Shrew* as Sly's revenge fantasy on women.[75] How the review discourse activated that fantasy once again demonstrates the mobility and fluidity of viewers' relations to performance and clarifies how sociologies of taste and value and contextual protocols for reading reframe materially inscribed theatrical data. One strand of commentary offered to speak for Shakespeare, either by attributing any gender troubles to the play or by defending his subjectivity from the staging and its director, whose "impatient feminism," together with her penchant for pop culture, were held responsible for tampering with the taming scenario. Consistently, reviewers tended to erase distinctions between textual and social subjects in order to reinstall cultural prerogatives, often based on a Sly-like social imaginary of "woman." In a move that registers the critic's desire to maintain his own (gendered) subjectivity while permitting him to monitor how other gendered subjects are constructed, one strategy singled out Michael Siberry's flamboyant, all-conquering Petruchio and turned him into a fantasy: a collection of attitudes, behaviors (lightly flavored with sadism), vocal tics, and mannerisms. Somehow, the actor who puffs up Petruchio in high style need not bother with the dreary business of being a "person"; although reviewers occasionally deplored his tactics, most (silently) upheld his motivations: marrying for money, taming a tempestuous, unruly woman. By contrast, Katherina is required to *have* "character" and to *show* a psychologically coherent "real" denied her by Shakespeare's script.[76] Although many admired her *looks*, most critics faulted Josie Lawrence's fiery, defiantly statuesque Kate for not embodying shrewness.[77] One hinted that Edwards and Lawrence (often paired in the discourse) apparently found it difficult to imagine that such a thing as a "shrew" could actually exist; another aligned Lawrence's Kate with the "picturesque" heroines of romantic period fiction (Daphne du Maurier's *Frenchman's Creek* or Hugh Walpole's *Judith Paris*); yet another judged her most "poignant" in her "scenes of suffering," most "touching" when she decides to "go along with Petruchio's game and realises that she loves him."[78] By refiguring Lawrence as an eager-to-be-mastered heroine and by fixing on the canonical metadramatic pleasures of role-play, critics not only reperformed her Kate but circumscribed her within their own dreams as Everyman's ideal, that most conformable of household Kates.

From my own viewing position, this Kate was anything but a household "thing." For by *performing* Kate's humiliation and hurt feelings, Lawrence had turned to-be-looked-at-ness[79]—especially in the tailor scene—into a powerful piece of politics. Wresting pleasure from displeasure in this way, of course, describes one strand of the feminist project. Several cinematic looks drift into view. Pickford watching Fairbanks lecture the dog and retreating with a superior smile; Taylor observing Burton through the eroticized ocular of her own sight. Or, at the close, Pickford's knowing wink, borrowed by Lisa Kirk, and Taylor's erotically charged gaze at Burton, speaking her desire for family matters. All assume a gaze constructed by and for male viewers but also let women in. While cinema may appropriate a woman's look for the other's desire, arguably Pickford's wink comes closest to offering a view from elsewhere, one that sits on the edge of the cultural reproduction, tipping it toward the histories of women viewers. What is the difference, then, between being allowed to share (already gendered) sightlines and Edwards's or, more accurately, Lawrence's strategy of double exposure? As it turned out, the look was precisely the thing that could catch—or deconstruct—the conscience of the king.

But it came at a different point in the action. Obeying Petruchio's command to bring the other wives, Kate bows toward him, notices the pile of banknotes on the floor—and pauses. By the time she returns, Petruchio has gathered up the money, along with Baptista's fat check, written out on the spot, and she seems perfectly composed, perfectly willing to perform. And her speech, the highlight of this *Shrew*'s doubles act, is a performance, for Lawrence seems to stand beside Kate, observing her rather than necessarily being psychologically enmeshed "in" her "character." Although it is immediately obvious that Lawrence is treating the speech as a performative aria, her initial address to the Widow as well as the sermon on political obedience (targeted at Bianca) are enclosed within the space of representation. Increasingly, however, Lawrence marks out a "space off" that allows viewers to meditate on the actions she has chosen to share with them.[80] Petruchio, of course, is one of these viewers, and the first sign of that widening sphere comes from him: as Lawrence/Kate directs "I am ashamed that women are so simple" to him, he steps back, off the lip of the platform, a move that enhances the performer's already central control over stage space. As she speaks of the fragility of women's bodies, her voice softens and her hands slip down her body, eroticizing its sexual difference; for a moment, it looks as though she will pointedly identify "soft conditions" with her crotch, but she stops just short of that. Although her language denotes a submissive body, her gesture, performed *in public* for the eyes of women as well as men, asserts her control of her own body, coopts any desiring looks for herself.[81] And for other women? Potentially, yes. Turning out to the audience in direct, confrontational address, her "Come, come, you froward and unable worms" is less an inclusionary appeal than a challenge, provoking theatregoers, like Petruchio, to take an unexpected step back. Despite what she says ("Then vail your stomachs, for it is no boot") and what her gesture indicates ("And place your hands below your husband's foot"), this "Kate" is no more the viewer's plaything than Petruchio's, for as she sinks down to the floor, her hand stretched out, he stumbles slowly onto the stage and kneels beside her: one hand drops the money, the other he brings to his forehead, bowing his head as though accepting the space of shame she has so redefined as his own.

Mimicking readers' selective vision, which tends to erase anything that occurs after Petruchio's "Come on and kiss me, Kate" and to forget the other misaligned couples so as to travel offstage with Kate and Petruchio into their own fantasies of wedded sexual bliss, Edwards's staging denies the crucial line. Instead, she substitutes for it an echo of the earlier kiss in the street where, accompanied by throbbing violins and swelling chords borrowed from the sound tracks of romantic comedy, the cyc displays a gorgeously pinked-up sunset toward which the couple walk, arms around each other. Now Kate and Petruchio remain kneeling, and as windows open in the set pieces, a Lord watching from each one, that music reprises Edwards's bow to and send-up of Big Romantic Endings. In the upstage mists, the little theatre ascends, and all the other players exit into it, Tranio and Bianca last. Rising, Kate turns away from Petruchio without a second glance and walks upstage into the little theatre, leaving him stretched out, one hand reaching toward her, as the Lords return to re-dress him as Sly. The theater slowly sinks, and Kate appears in its place as Sly's wife, a long gray coat covering her scarlet dress and a shawl draping her head—a vision that tropes the larger transformation which has displaced *Shrew*'s theatre of submission, together with all its boy's (re)production games, by means of Lawrence's performance. As Sly's wife comes forward, Sly kneels before her: startled at first, she hesitates; then, in the fading light, one hand reaches out to touch his head, another his shoulder. Where *Moonlighting*'s illusionary, intimate viewing space, shot through with doubled parodic conventions, can afford Willis/Petruchio's verbal apology ("I was wrong, . . . and I have learned it from a woman"), this *Shrew*, in bridling Petruchio/Sly, plays its final trick, eliciting a sense of ending that wipes away his dream of power.

But if Petruchio/Sly's double apology embodied a critical attitude that dislodged Shakespeare, taking him down from the top,[82] review discourse reframed it as a risky piece of business that exposed the ideological parameters at stake in upsetting viewers' historical competencies. While a few critics wrote that Edwards had indeed reclaimed *Shrew* for today, calling Petruchio/Sly to account and repositioning him in Kate's place of shame prompted most to slip back into Sly's skin, desperately seeking to reconstruct themselves as the textually inscribed "ideal spectator" who (having slept throughout the action) awakens maintaining he has had "the best dream of [his] life." Viewing *Shrew* as a play devoted to producing and reproducing male (dream) vision and visibility as parts of its labor, John Peter observed, "This is not a Shakespearean ending at all, not because Shakespeare is a male chauvinist or a cheery optimist but because this ending is like a sermon, a sermon saying what? bully your wife nicely? marry somebody more pliant?"[83] Invoking *Shrew*s that had given their imaginary selves canonical free reign, others took the occasion to preach their own sermons on textual obedience. Benedict Nightingale, for one, took Edwards to task for omitting "kiss me, Kate" and the couple's "happy exit bedwards" as well as inventing Sly's wife and adding materials "that don't even have the excuse of coming from *A Shrew*." As for the revisionary program synopsis ("Petruchio slowly realizes what he has been attempting to do to Katherina in the name of love. By the end of the speech, his dream has become a nightmare"), Nightingale remarked, "What tripe! He has Gone Too Far, and both know they should really be at a consciousness-raising workshop at Brent."[84] Although sermonizing and marital therapy of a sort are feature attractions of Shakespeare's *Shrew*, they apparently have value only insofar as they rehearse and preserve male privilege. If asserting that critics saw Edwards's *Shrew* as Petruchio's tragedy risks overreading, hints of that nonetheless appear as they dreamed its central performers into tragic roles, imagining Siberry as Richard III, Antony, or Oberon; Lawrence as Cleopatra or Lady Macbeth—all figures with troubled marital histories.[85] One way to defuse this particular Freudian (or Lacanian) undertext is to recall Oscar Wilde's *The Importance of Being Earnest*, where Algernon observes, "All women become like their mothers. That is their tragedy. No man does. That is his."

Hailed into unfamiliar, discomforting positions, reviewers found in Edwards's *Shrew* no mirror for the seeing eye/I: *it was not about them*. What does a man want from *Shrew*? Apparently, to see "woman" as a construct of a male imaginary that does not look at *women*, and to read her body through the desire to mark it as his own. Above all, to maintain a stable subject position in which no one looks back at him, in which the *gaze at* is never, ever disrupted, interfered with, taken away. Edwards had structured a different viewing economy, one where Kate, when asked to take her place, refigured that taking place so as to challenge, and re-historicize, traditional sightlines.[86] But what does a woman want? Freud famously answered his question by claiming she wanted a phallus, but the reply, as in this case, need not come from the phallus. Rephrasing Freud, "What does a woman want from *Shrew*," Edwards's staging and Lawrence's performance suggest that an apology from the Petruchio/Slys of this world might go some way toward fulfilling her desires. Yet much as I admired how this *Shrew* turned out to address women's histories and so troubled engrained sightlines, Petruchio/Sly's repentance also has a darker history that coincides with the classic narrative of spousal abuse, in which apology is all too symptomatic. Calling up that specter, however, may be less to the point than to say that, like *Moonlighting*, Edwards's staging also suggests that every boy needs a mommy, one who can sort things out in the end, make it all better. Has (m)other come to represent the ideological signifier of 1990s cultural stability? If so, that her figure is the one called upon to destabilize *Shrew* triggers a curious paradox. If the mother's look can indeed displace or upstage Big Daddy as the privileged representational site/sight,[87] it is also the case that, like *Moonlighting*'s mom, Sly's wife—the replacement figure for the Lords of theatrical magic and, in a sense, for Shakespeare—does not (quite) return the look. Nor does she willingly want or accept that role. She is not quite sure what to do. What is the performance now? In the end, Edwards's epilogue is no frame at all. Spilling out from *Shrew*, beyond its textual and representational boundaries, it performs an excess that cannot be framed. Or tamed?

Where do these sites and sightings, this reauthoring of a role by means of performing bodies, lead? Although Lawrence's Kate may displace Shakespeare's authority with that of the performer, her presence does not participate in anything that could be called the "Death of the Character."[88] Instead, what emerges is the sense that something like a new characterology is in process, taking place through and being shaped by the bodies of performers—men as well as women—who insist on their own unruliness, trouble their textually gendered markings, refuse to stay in place. There are lots of them about in the mid-nineties: one thinks of Fiona Shaw's recent Richard II, or, in Baz Luhrmann's *Romeo + Juliet*, a Mercutio in drag and the angelic, feminine Romeo of Leonardo DiCaprio. It is tempting to say that such reauthorized appearances and reembodiments resemble circumstances scholars imagine existing in the early modern theatre, before the Birth of the Author. But if that is indeed the case, it is equally likely that these unruly bodies result from asking a much simpler question: What does this play, this performance, make me that I no longer want to be?

NOTES

From *The Shakespeare Trade: Performances and Appropriations* by Barbara Hodgdon. Copyright © 1998 University of Pennsylvania Press. Reprinted by permission of the publisher.

1. See Louis Althusser, "Ideology and Ideological State Apparatuses," in *Lenin and Philosophy and Other Essays*, trans. Ben Brewster (London: New Left Books, 1971), 127–86; and Sharon Willis, "Hardware and Hardbodies,What Do Women Want? A Reading of *Thelma and Louise*," in *Film Theory Goes to the Movies*, ed. Jim Collins, Hilary Radner, and Ava Preacher Collins (New York and London: Routledge, 1993), 121–24.

2. See Henry Jenkins, *Textual Poachers: Television Fans and Participatory Culture* (New York and London: Routledge, 1992), 24; and Michel de Certeau, *Heterologies: Discourse on the Other*, trans. Brian Massumi (University of Minnesota Press, 1986). Cf. Roland Barthes: "We read a text (of pleasure) the way a fly buzzes around a room: with sudden, deceptively decisive turns, fervent and futile." See *The Pleasure of the Text*, trans. Richard Miller (New York: Hill and Wang, 1975), 31.

3. See Shirley Nelson Garner, "*The Taming of the Shrew*: Inside or Outside of the Joke?" in *"Bad" Shakespeare: Revaluations of the Shakespeare Canon*, ed. Maurice Charney (London and Toronto: Associated University Presses, 1988), 107–8.

4. See Lynda E. Boose, "Scolding Brides and Bridling Scolds," *Shakespeare Quarterly*, 42, no. 2 (Summer 1991): 179–213.

5. All references are to Ann Thompson, ed., *The Taming of the Shrew*. New Cambridge edition (Cambridge University Press, 1984).

6. Linda Williams, *Hard Core: Power, Pleasure, and the "Frenzy of the Visible"* (University of California Press, 1989), 224.

7. Teresa de Lauretis, "Through the Looking Glass," in *The Cinematic Apparatus*, ed. Teresa de Lauretis and Stephen Heath (New York: St. Martin's Press, 1980), 193–94.

8. Charles Marowitz, *The Shrew*, in *Marowitz Shakespeare* (New York: Drama Book Specialists, 1978); quotes are from 177–80.

9. Marowitz, *Marowitz Shakespeare*, 24. See also Graham Holderness, *The Taming of the Shrew*, [*Shakespeare in Performance* series] (Manchester University Press, 1989), 94.

10. See Stephen Orgel, "Nobody's Perfect, Or Why Did the English Stage Take Boys for Women?" *South Atlantic Quarterly*, 88, no. 1 (Winter 1989): 7–30.

11. Katherine Eisaman Maus, "Horns of Dilemma: Jealousy, Gender, and Spectatorship in English Renaissance Drama," *English Literary Renaissance* 54, no. 3 (Summer 1987): 561–83. On masquerade, see Joan Riviere, "Womanliness as a Masquerade" (1929). Reprinted in *Formations of Fantasy*, ed. Victor Burgin, James Donald, and Cora Kaplan (New York: Methuen, 1986), 35–44. See also Stephen Heath, "Joan Riviere and the Masquerade," in *Formations of Fantasy*, 45–61. Pointing to contradictions within gendered masquerade, Judith Williamson observes that present-day fashion images show women with "boyish" figures. See "It's Different for Girls," in *Consuming Passions* (London: Marion Boyars, 1986), 47–55. See also Judith Butler, *Gender Trouble: Feminism and the Subversion of Identity* (New York and London: Routledge, 1990), 46–54.

12. See Lynda E. Boose, "*The Taming of the Shrew*, Good Husbandry, and Enclosure," in *Shakespeare Reread: The Text in New Contexts*, ed. Russ McDonald (Ithaca and London: Cornell University Press, 1994), 193–225.

13. On early modern theatrical strategies for constructing sexual difference, see Lorraine Helms, "Playing The Woman's Part: Feminist Criticism and Shakespearean Performance," in *Performing Feminisms: Feminist Critical Theory and Theatre*, ed. Sue-Ellen Case (Baltimore: Johns Hopkins University Press, 1990), 196–206.

14. For Laura Mulvey's famous term, see "Visual Pleasure and Narrative Cinema" (1975), reprinted in *Feminism and Film Theory*, ed. Constance Penley (New York: Routledge, 1988), 57–68. Mulvey's formulation of gendered spectatorship has been critiqued and rethought, largely on the grounds that it fails to acknowledge the potential range of cross-gendered and marginalized spectator positions. *The Spectatrix*, a special issue of *camera obscura*, is devoted to this continuing debate.

15. On early modern women spectators, see Jean Howard, *The Stage and Social Struggle in Early Modern England* (New York and London: Routledge, 1994), 76–77, 90–92. See also Andrew Gurr, *Playgoing in Shakespeare's London* (Cambridge University Press, 1987), 57–58.

16. See Carol Neely, *Broken Nuptials in Shakespeare's Plays* (New Haven: Yale University Press, 1985), 218–19. See also Peter Berek "Text, Gender, and Genre in *The Taming of the Shrew*," in *"Bad" Shakespeare: Revaluations of the Shakespearean Canon*, ed. Maurice Charney (London and Toronto: Associated University Presses, 1988), 91–104; Marianne L. Novy, "Patriarchy and Play in *The*

Taming of the Shrew," *English Literary Renaissance* 9 (1979): 264–80; Kathleen McLuskie, "Feminist Deconstruction: Shakespeare's *Taming of the Shrew,*" *Red Letters* 12 (1982): 15–22; Martha Andresen-Thom, "Shrew-Taming and Other Rituals of Aggression: Bating and Bonding on the Stage and in the Wild," *Women's Studies* 9 (1982): 121–43; Richard A. Burt, "Charisma, Coercion, and Comic Form in *The Taming of the Shrew,*" *Criticism* 26 (1984): 295–311; Karen Newman, *Fashioning Femininity and English Renaissance Drama* (Chicago: University of Chicago Press, 1991), 33–50; and Maureen Quilligan, "Staging Gender: William Shakespeare and Elizabeth Cary," in *Sexuality and Gender in Early Modern Europe: Institutions, Texts, Images,* ed. James Grantham Turner (Cambridge and New York: Cambridge University Press, 1993), 208–32.

17. Elizabeth Fox-Genovese, *Feminism Without Illusions* (Chapel Hill: University of North Carolina Press, 1991), 139–41.

18. See Jacqueline Rose, "The Cinematic Apparatus: Problems in Current Theory," in *The Cinematic Apparatus,* ed. Teresa de Lauretis and Steven Heath (New York: St. Martin's Press, 1980), 172–86.

19. See Janice A. Radway, *Reading the Romance: The Politics of Popular Fiction* (London: Routledge and Kegan Paul, 1986).

20. For pertinent connections to slasher films, see Carol Clover, *Men, Women, and Chain Saws* (Princeton University Press, 1992), 21–65. Williams critiques Clover in *Hard Core,* 206–08. See also Gilles Deleuze, *Masochism: An Interpretation of Coldness and Cruelty* (New York: George Braziller, 1971); and Gaylyn Studlar, *In the Realm of Pleasure: Von Sternberg, Dietrich, and the Masochistic Aesthetic* (University of Illinois Press, 1988).

21. See *Spectatrix,* 193.

22. On *Shrew*'s textual controversies, see Leah Marcus, "The Shakespearean Editor as Shrew-Tamer," *English Literary Renaissance,* 22, no. 2 (Spring 1992): 177–200.

23. See Richard Abel, *The Ciné Goes to Town: French Cinema 1896–1914* (Berkeley: University of California Press, 1994), 264; and Roberta Pearson and William Uricchio, "'How Many Times Shall Caesar Bleed in Sport': Shakespeare and the Cultural Debate about Moving Pictures," *Screen* 31 (Autumn 1990): 243–61. On silent Shakespeare films, see also Robert Hamilton Ball, *Shakespeare on Silent Film* (London: George Allen and Unwin, 1968); and John Collick, *Shakespeare, Cinema and Society* (Manchester University Press, 1989), 33–57.

24. Ada Rehan quoted in Tori Haring-Smith, *From Farce to Metadrama: A Stage History of "The Taming of the Shrew," 1594–1983* (Westport: Greenwood Press, 1985), 45; and Marcus, "Editor," 192.

25. Quoted in Eileen Bowser, ed., *Biograph Bulletins, 1908–1912* (Octagon Books, 1973), 35. Library of Congress (LOC) print. For further documentation, see Ball, *Silent Film,* 315.

26. Directed by Henri Desfontaines, the Eclipse film runs, according to a Kleine press sheet, about 1,020 feet. A print is in the LOC. See also Ball, *Silent Film,* 129–30; 336. The LOC print of Collins's film runs approximately 2,056 feet. See also Ball, *Silent Film,* 285–86, 377.

27. See Kaja Silverman, *The Acoustic Mirror: The Female Voice in Psychoanalysis and Cinema* (Indiana University Press, 1988), 48–54.

28. See Abel, *Cine' Goes to Town*, 267.

29. See, for instance, Tania Modleski, "Some Functions of Feminist Criticism, or The Scandal of the Mute Body," *October* 49 (1989): 3–24.

30. In the 1594 *A Shrew*, Kate's motivation occurs much earlier, in the wooing scene: "*She turnes aside and speakes.* But yet I will consent and marrie him, / For I methinkes have livde too long a maid, / And match him too, or else his manhoods good" (Scene 5, 40–42). Reprinted in Geoffrey Bullough, ed., *Narrative and Dramatic Sources of Shakespeare* (London: Routledge and Kegan Paul, 1957), 1:77.

31. See Ben Singer, "Female Power in the Serial-Queen Melodrama: The Etiology of an Anomaly," *Camera Obscura* (1990): 91–129.

32. Although no reviewers link *Shrew* films to the controversy over women's voting rights, Ball mentions a 1912 Knickerbocker spin-off, *Taming of the Shrewd*, in which a woman who neglects housework to attend suffragette meetings returns to her proper place in the home after her husband arouses her jealousy by taking another woman to one of the meetings. See *Silent Film*, 149. A mid-1930s British reviewer explains the theatrical popularity of *Shrew* just prior to World War I as due to "the activities of the vote-hungry viragoes who from 1910 to the eve of the War were breaking windows, setting fire to churches, chaining themselves to railings, and generally demonstrating their fitness to be endowed with Parliamentary responsibility. Kate's 'purple patch' concerning the duty of women . . . was a smashing rejoinder to the militant Furies who were making fools of themselves in the ways indicated." Quoted in Thompson's edition, 21–22. See also Susan Carlson, "The Suffrage Shrew: The Shakespeare Festival, 'A Man's Play,' and New Women," paper presented at the Sixth World Shakespeare Congress, Los Angeles, April 1996.

33. Richard Dyer, *Stars* (London: BFI, 1982), 6.

34. This credit appears on the LOC print. Thomas A. Pendleton reports that the credit on the Museum of Modern Art print (donated by Fairbanks) reads, "Adapted and Directed by Sam Taylor." See Robert Windeler, *Sweetheart: The Story of Mary Pickford* (New York: Praeger Publishers, 1974), 160–161. See also Roger Manvell, *Shakespeare and the Film* (New York: Praeger Publishers, 1971), 24–25.

35. Mary Pickford, *Sunshine and Shadow* (Garden City: Doubleday, 1955), 312. See also Windeler, *Sweetheart*, 160–63; and Booton Herndon, *Mary Pickford and Douglas Fairbanks: The Most Popular Couple the World Has Ever Known* (New York: W. W. Norton, 1977), 270–71. According to Herndon, Pickford was the sole source of information for all accounts of the filming.

36. Constance Collier, quoted in Pickford, *Sunshine and Shadow*, 311.

37. Especially in *The Mark of Zorro* (1920), *The Three Musketeers* (1921), *Robin Hood* (1922), *The Thief of Baghdad* (1924), and *The Black Pirate* (1926).

38. On the relations between *Shrew* (in the theatre) and suffrage in Britain, see Carlson, "Suffrage Shrew."

39. The BBC-TV *Shrew*, directed by Jonathan Miller, closes with an image of ideal Puritan companionate marriage: part books appear and all sing Psalm 128, which connects fear of the Lord with a peaceful family life. For the social contexts of song production, see Bruce Horner, "Negotiating Traditions of English Song: Performance, Text, History," *Mosaic*, 27, no. 3 (September 1994): 19–44. Screened in Britain in June 1980 and in the United States on January 21, 1981, Miller's

Shrew aligns uncannily with Thatcher-Reagan conservative agendas. On Miller's BBC-TV and later stage productions, see Holderness, *Taming*, 95–120. On the BBC series as a cultural product, see Collick, *Shakespeare*, 52–57. See also J. C. Bulman and H. R. Coursen, eds., *Shakespeare on Television: An Anthology of Essays and Reviews* (Hanover: University Press of New England, 1988), esp. 80–81; 188–89; and 266–68.

40. Royal Films International, F.A.I., United States and Italy: Technicolor; wide-screen. For representative reviews, see Jack Jorgens, *Shakespeare on Film* (Indiana University Press, 1977), 317–18.

41. Richard Dyer, *Stars*, 49–50, and Dyer, *Heavenly Bodies: Film Stars and Society* (London: Macmillan, 1987), 11; 18. See also Violette Morin, "Les Olympiens," *Communications*, 2 (1963): 105–21.

42. See Dick Sheppard, *Elizabeth: The Life and Career of Elizabeth Taylor* (Garden City: Doubleday and Company, 1975), 299.

43. Jorgens, *Shakespeare on Film*, 67, 73, 78. See also Holderness, *Taming*, 65.

44. Several recent Royal Shakespeare Company Kates discuss "Interpreting the Silence" in Carol Rutter, *Clamorous Voices: Shakespeare's Women Today*, ed. Faith Evans (London: Women's Press, Ltd., 1988), 1–26.

45. Sheppard, *Elizabeth*, 299–300, 309–10. For Zeffirelli's personal investment in maternal figures, and his effort to reconstitute his own fragmented family in his films, see Peter S. Donaldson, *Shakespearean Films/Shakespearean Directors* (Boston: Unwin Hyman, 1990), 146–48.

46. Stuart Hall, "Notes on Deconstructing 'The Popular,'" in *People's History and Socialist Theory*, ed. Raphael Samuel (London: Routledge and Kegan Paul, 1981), 227–40.

47. MGM/UA Home Video; 110 minutes. Kathryn Grayson (Lilli Vanessi/Katherine); Howard Keel (Fred Graham/Petruchio); Ann Miller (Lois Lane/Bianca).

48. The film bowdlerizes Porter's original lyrics, "His bus'ness is the bus'ness he gives his secretary."

49. On *Kate*'s sadism, see Jean Peterson, "Boys Will Be Boys: Sadism, Subtext and *The Taming of the Shrew*." Seminar Paper, Shakespeare Association of America, 1991.

50. Somewhat ironically, 3-D technology developed from an interlock mechanism devised for military missile tracking systems. See David Bordwell, Janet Staiger, and Kristin Thompson, *The Classical Hollywood Cinema: Film Style and Mode of Production to 1960* (New York: Columbia University Press, 1985), 245, 251, 359–60, and 474–75.

51. Memorialized in the perennial joke: wet (*A Midsummer Night's Dream*); dry (*Twelfth Night*); miscarriage (*Love's Labour's Lost*); 3 inches (*Much Ado About Nothing*); 6 inches (*As You Like It*); 12 inches (*The Taming of the Shrew*).

52. See Jane Feuer, *The Hollywood Musical* (Indiana University Press, 1982), 81, 84–85. In "Space, Gender, Performance: The Three Dimensions of Kiss Me, Kate" (paper presented at the 1990 Society for Cinema Studies Conference, Washington, D.C.), William Paul compares the emergence effect to Robert Weimann's designations of *locus* and *platea* stage positions. See Weimann, *Shakespeare and the Popular Tradition in the Theater* (Baltimore: Johns Hopkins University Press, 1978), 73–85; 215–46.

53. Video Images, Video Yesteryear recording. A print is in the Folger Shakespeare Library Film Collection.

54. See Maribel Morgan, *Total Woman* (New York: Revell, 1973); and Phyllis Schlafly, *The Power of the Positive Woman* (New York: Jove, 1977). See also Laura Kipnis, "Feminism: The Political Conscience of Postmodernism?" in *Universal Abandon? The Politics of Postmodernism*, ed. Andrew Ross (University of Minnesota Press, 1988), 149–66.

55. On commercials, see Judith Williamson, *Decoding Advertising: Ideology and Meaning in Advertising* (London: Marion Boyers, 1978). On 1950s marketing strategies, see Mary Beth Haralovich, "Sitcoms and Suburbs: Positioning the 1950s Homemaker," *Quarterly Review of Film and Video* 11, no. 1 (1989): 61–83.

56. First aired on November 25, 1986 and often rerun. See Jack Oruch, "Shakespeare for the Millions: Kiss Me, Petruchio," *Shakespeare on Film Newsletter* 11, no. 2 (April 1987): 7; and Lynne Joyrich, "Tube Tied: Reproductive Politics and *Moonlighting*," in *Modernity and Mass Culture*, ed. James Naremore and Patrick Brantlinger (Indiana University Press, 1991), 176–202.

57. *Moonlighting*'s flip-flop reversal resembles that of John Fletcher's *The Woman's Prize, or The Tamer Tam'd* (ca. 1625), which generates Petruchio as a "new man" and loveable husband. See also David Garrick's 1754 *Catherine and Petruchio*, where, after Catherine speaks the first nineteen lines of Shakespeare's obedience speech Petruchio makes his "submission": "Kiss me, my Kate; and since thou art become / So prudent, kind, and dutiful a Wife, / *Petruchio* here shall doff the lordly Husband; / An honest Mask, which I throw off with Pleasure. / Far hence all Rudeness, Wilfulness, and Noise, / And be our future Lives one gentle Stream / Of mutual Love, Compliance and Regard." (Quoted in Thompson's edition, 20.) Kenneth Bangs's parodic nineteenth-century *Shrew* also gives Kate control: "Shakespeare or Bacon, or whoever wrote the play . . . studied deeply the shrews of his day . . . the modern shrew isn't built that way," to which Petruchio agrees, "Sweet Katherine, of your remarks I recognize the force: / Don't strive to tame a woman as you would a horse." (Cited in Lawrence W. Levine, *Highbrow/Lowbrow: The Emergence of Cultural Hierarchy in America* [Harvard University Press, 1988], 15).

58. Joan Gadol Kelly, *Women, History, and Theory* (University of Chicago Press, 1984), 15.

59. Josette Féral, "Writing and Displacement: Women in Theatre," *Modern Drama* 27 (1984): 549–63.

60. See Joel Fineman, "The Turn of the Shrew," in *Shakespeare and the Question of Theory*, ed. Patricia Parker and Geoffrey Hartman (London: Methuen, 1985), 138–59.

61. Coppélia Kahn, *Man's Estate: Masculine Identity in Shakespeare* (Berkeley: University of California Press, 1981), 117–18.

62. See Boose, "Scolding Brides."

63. Marcus, "Editor," 183–84.

64. *Saturday Review*, Nov. 6, 1897, quoted in Thompson's edition, 21.

65. See, for instance, Richard Henze, "Role-Playing in *The Taming of the Shrew*," *Southern Humanities Review* 4 (1970): 231–40; J. Dennis Huston, *Shakespeare's Comedies of Play* (Columbia University Press, 1981); and Novy, "Patriarchy and

Play," an argument she extends in *Love's Argument: Gender Relations in Shakespeare* (Chapel Hill: University of North Carolina Press, 1984). See also Michael Shapiro, "Framing the Taming: Metatheatrical Awareness of Female Impersonation in *The Taming of the Shrew*," *Yearbook of English Studies*, 23 (1993): 143–66. On how filmed *Shrews* attempt to loosen Kate's bonds as well as those of viewers, see Diana E. Henderson, "A Shrew for the Times," in *Shakespeare, The Movie*, ed. Lynda E. Boose and Richard A. Burt (London and New York: Routledge, 1997), 148–68.

66. See Barbara Freedman, *Staging the Gaze: Postmodernism, Psychoanalysis, and Shakespearean Comedy* (Ithaca: Cornell University Press, 1991), 121.

67. See Holderness, *Taming*, 73–94; see also Christopher J. McCullough, "Michael Bogdanov," in *The Shakespeare Myth*, ed. Graham Holderness (Manchester University Press, 1988), 89–95; and Penny Gay, *As She Likes It: Shakespeare's Unruly Women* (London and New York: Routledge, 1994), 86–119.

68. In an England deep in recession, it was certainly easier to hate a group of overprivileged, shallow yuppies than to engage consciously with issues of women's complicity in their own subjugation. As Boose observes, the particular lens a reading or production chooses depends on whatever category is currently under stress: "the trajectory of displacement that occurs at any given time among [gender, class, and race] will be dictated by the exigencies of the historical moment." See *"Taming of the Shrew,"* 213 n. On Alexander's production, see Carol Rutter, "Kate, Bianca, Ruth and Sarah: Playing the Woman's Part in Shakespeare's *The Taming of the Shrew*," in *Shakespeare's Sweet Thunder*, ed. Michael J. Collins (Newark: University of Delaware Press, 1997), 176–215.

69. It also initiates a conversation with recent Australian *Shrews* and, more particularly, speaks from a postcolonial position. See Penny Gay, "Recent Australian *Shrews*: The 'Larrikin Element,' " paper presented at the Sixth World Shakespeare Congress, Los Angeles, April 1996.

70. On reception study, see Janet Staiger, *Interpreting Films: Studies in the Historical Reception of American Cinema* (Princeton University Press, 1992), esp. 1–98.

71. In an interview with Kate Alderson, Gale Edwards remarked, "People don't think, gee, a man is going to direct *King Lear*, this'll be really good because a man is directing. . . . It's part of what [*Shrew*] is about, isn't it? How strange it is to be a strong woman." See "Interview with Gale Edwards," *Times*, April 21, 1995.

72. For a psychoanalytic reading of farce, see Freedman, *Staging*, 105–8.

73. See Michel Foucault, "the body is the inscribed surface of events." "Nietzsche, Genealogy, History," 148, quoted in Judith Butler, *Gender Trouble: Feminism and the Subversion of Identity* (New York and London: Routledge, 1990), 129. See also Jill Dolan, *The Feminist Spectator as Critic* (Ann Arbor: University of Michigan Press, 1991), 114–15.

74. See Rebecca Schneider, "After Us the Savage Goddess: Feminist Performance Art of the Explicit Body Staged, Uneasily, Across Modernist Dreamscapes," in *Performance and Cultural Politics*, ed. Elin Diamond (London and New York: Routledge, 1996), 157–78.

75. Michael Billington, *Guardian*, April 24, 1995. This and other reviews are reprinted in *Theatre Record* 5, 25, no. 8 (April 9–22, 1995). Curiously enough,

Billington had recoiled from Bogdanov's 1978 *Shrew*: condemning that same logic, he argued for removing the play from the stage altogether.

76. Such responses to Katherina and Petruchio are by no means unique and are also apparent in the review discourse for Bogdanov's and Alexander's stagings. On characters as "simulated personages apparently possessing adequately continuous or developing subjectivities," see Alan Sinfield, *Faultlines: Cultural Materialism and the Politics of Dissident Reading* (Berkeley: University of California Press, 1992), 52–79. See also W. B. Worthen, "Shakespeare's Body: Acting and the Designs of Authority," chapter 3 of *Shakespeare and the Authority of Performance.*

77. Lawrence has her own television series, *Josie*, and is a regular on a popular British television improvisational revue, *Whose Line Is It, Anyway*?

78. John Gross, *Sunday Telegraph*, April 30, 1995; Alastair Macaulay, *Financial Times*, April 28, 1995; Charles Spencer, *Daily Telegraph*, April 24, 1995.

79. Mulvey's term. See "Visual Pleasure."

80. See Dolan, *Feminist Spectator*, 114–16. On "the body in historicization," see also Elin Diamond, "Brechtian Theory/Feminist Theory: Toward a Gestic Feminist Criticism," *Drama Review* 32 (1988): 82–94.

81. In "Visual Pleasure in Shakespeare's Playhouse" (unpublished essay), Paul Yachnin argues that Kate's description of the body's erotic pleasures (gained through Petruchio) falls into the sphere of knowing (which joins sisters under the skin).

82. See Dolan, *Feminist Spectator*, 115.

83. John Peter, *Sunday Times*, April 30, 1995.

84. Benedict Nightingale, *Times*, April 24, 1995.

85. See reviews by Macaulay; Billington.

86. See Phelan, *Unmarked: The Politics of Performance* (London: Routledge, 1993), 10–15; and Freedman, *Staging*, 146–53.

87. Freedman, *Staging*, 150–51; I borrow "upstage Big Daddy" from Ellen Donkin and Susan Clement, eds., *Upstaging Big Daddy: Directing Theater as if Gender and Race Matter* (Ann Arbor: University of Michigan Press, 1993).

88. For perspectives on this issue, see Elinor Fuchs, *The Death of Character: Perspectives on Theater After Modernism* (Indiana University Press, 1996).

Figure 9. Photograph of painting of Miss Ada Rehan as Katharina. Painting by Hillary Bell. Used with the permission of the Folger Shakespeare Library.